Rick Steves

SWITZERLAND

CONTENTS

Welcome to Rick Steves' Europe

Travel is intensified living—maximum thrills per minute and one of the last great sources of legal adventure. Travel is freedom. It's recess, and we need it.

I discovered a passion for European travel as a teen and have been sharing it ever since—through my bus tours, public television and radio shows, and travel guidebooks. Over the years, I've taught millions of travelers how to best enjoy Europe's blockbuster sights—and experience "Back Door" discoveries that most tourists miss.

This book offers a balanced mix of Swiss cities and villages, mountaintop hikes and lake cruises, thought-provoking museums and sky-high gondola rides. It's selective: Rather than listing dozens of mountain getaways, I recommend only the best ones. And it's in-depth: My self-guided scenic rail tours and  city/town walks give insight into Switzerland's fascinating history and today's living, breathing culture.

I advocate traveling simply and smartly. Take advantage of my money- and time-saving tips on sight-seeing, transportation, and more. Try local, characteristic alternatives to expensive hotels and restaurants. In many ways, spending more money only builds a thicker wall between you and what you traveled so far to see.

We visit Switzerland to experience it—to become temporary locals. Thoughtful travel engages us with the world, as we learn to appreciate other cultures and new ways to measure quality of life.

Judging by the positive feedback I receive from readers, this book will help you enjoy a fun, affordable, and rewarding vacation—whether it's your first trip or your tenth.

Gute Reise! Happy travels!

Rick Steves

SWITZERLAND

Little, mountainous, efficient Switzerland is one of Europe's most appealing—and most expensive—destinations. It's an enjoyable mix of bucolic peace and daring adventure: Around every alpine turn, you feel you could get a glimpse of Heidi milking a cow or James Bond schussing past on skis.

Wedged neatly between Germany, Austria, France, and Italy, Switzerland melds the best of all those worlds—and adds a healthy dose of chocolate, cowbells, and cable cars.

While landlocked, Switzerland has more than its share of clear rivers and big, beautiful lakes with a striking mountain backdrop. Nearly half of Switzerland consists of uninhabitable rocks and rugged Alps, with its flat land (and many hills) cultivated into tidy farms.

Despite the country's small size, its geography has historically kept people apart, helping regions maintain their distinct cultures and languages—German, French, Italian, and Romansh. Even with its substantial regional differences, though, the entire country is unmistakably Swiss, dedicated to order and organization. Like the Boy Scouts, the Swiss count cleanliness, neatness, punctuality, tolerance, independence, thrift, and hard work as

virtues...and they love pocketknives. If you find the people to be a little buttoned-up, remember that the payoff is a beautiful country where the trains run on time, the streets are clean, and every flower petal seems perfectly in place.

While it's one of Europe's most progressive "big-government" countries—with high taxation, ample social services, and liberal drug policies—Switzerland also has a conservative streak. Traditional mindsets persist in the remote mountain hamlets—for example, women weren't guaranteed the right to vote in federal elections until 1971 (and were still barred from local elections in one region until 1990).

Switzerland is one of Europe's oldest democracies. Born when three states (cantons) united in 1291, over time the Swiss Confederation grew to the 26 cantons of today. With the exception of the Protestant Reformation and an almost bloodless civil war in 1847, Swiss history has been pretty quiet. The Swiss are happy watching from above the fray as the tides of history swirl around them.

Stubbornly independent, or maybe just smart, Switzerland stayed out of both world wars. But it's far from lax when it comes to national defense: The Swiss are legendary for their military readiness, with a vast reserve army and a countryside embedded with hidden fortresses. Through the tumult of the

A winter's supply of neatly stacked firewood; Lauterbrunnen Valley, at the base of sheer cliffs

Western Europe's Linguistic Crossroads

You'd be forgiven for thinking of Switzerland as a "German" country. The heart of Switzerland, with about three-fifths of the population and most of the famous cities and sights, is linguistically (as well as culturally) Germanic. But even here, Germans and Austrians don't feel quite at home. As if keeping alive an archaic code for insiders, the Swiss speak to each other in the lilting, fun-to-listen-to Swiss German, a.k.a. *Schwyzer-dütsch*, then switch seamlessly to standard German (or English) when interacting with outsiders.

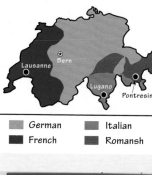

German   Italian
French   Romansh

Surrounding the German-speaking core is a more colorful Romance language-speaking fringe—French (to the west), Italian (to the south), and Romansh (tucked in the southeastern mountains). Switzerland's biggest canton, officially trilingual, is its linguistic melting pot: the southeastern region called Graubünden (in German), Grigioni (in Italian), and Grischun (in Romansh).

Durchgang verboten
Passaggio proibito
Passage interdit
Passage prohibited

Subtle differences in cuisine, climate, and landscape seem to match the linguistic boundaries. German-speaking Switzerland enjoys a vigorous efficiency reminiscent of Germany's. The pace in genteel French-speaking Switzerland is a bit mellower, and the cuisine and lifestyle are more refined, resembling France's. And the relatively balmy Italian-speaking canton of Ticino comes with a touch of chaos and lust for life that's not far removed from Italy proper (which surrounds it on three sides). You can spend a week in Switzerland and feel almost as if you've traveled from Paris to Munich to Rome...without ever crossing a border. ◼

Compact and charming Bern; mountain-encircled Lake Luzern; convivial and delicious cheese fondue; a parade of cows in Appenzell

20th century, no foreign invaders dared to try cracking this alpine nut.

Though not a European Union member—in part because its agricultural lobby doesn't want competition from more efficiently produced EU products—Switzerland still conforms to EU standards to be able to conduct business easily. Major Swiss moneymakers include banking, insurance, watches, chemicals and pharmaceuticals, tourism, precision instruments, and chocolate (Nestlé is the biggest producer).

Switzerland's cosmopolitan cities offer an enticing, I-could-live-here glimpse of the Swiss urban quality of life: efficient trams and buses gliding around town, manicured pedestrian zones teeming with locals enjoying their cities, scenic boats cruising crystal-clear rivers and lakes, eclectic restaurants offering a tasty range of both Swiss and international cuisine, and low-key but thoughtful museums telling compelling stories.

But let's face it: Travelers don't flock to Switzerland for its cities. Spend most of your time getting high in the Alps. You can climb onto a train in one of Switzerland's most bustling stations and, within an hour or two, step off into an idyllic time-warp world where traditional culture still thrives. Alpine villages (such as Gimmelwald) and towns (such as Appenzell) give you a taste of rural Switzerland, and are the perfect base for pastoral countryside hikes or riding lifts to dramatic cut-glass alpine panoramas.

If you're in the countryside on a Sunday, you'll most likely enjoy traditional music, clothing, and culture. At the end of a day of hiking, you can retreat to a village enclave preserving a colorful, rustic, rural way of life. In spring and fall, you might be lucky enough to see a parade of cows on their way up to or back down from the high-mountain pastures.

Cows have also had a big impact on Swiss cuisine—especially cheese. Two of the most revered Swiss cheeses are the smooth Gruyère (from the town of Gruyères) and the stinky Appenzeller (from the region of Appenzell). Shops sell a fragrant festival of mold, perfect for picnicking or for making two famous Swiss culinary specialties: fondue (a pot of cheese melted into wine) or raclette (cheese melted over potatoes and other vegetables).

Switzerland's best attraction might just be traveling

Gondolas in Mürren and Gimmelwald offer views along with transportation.

through its flat-out spectacular scenery. The country is criss-crossed with fine autobahns and arguably Europe's most efficient rail system. Buses fill in the gaps, while boats ply the many tranquil lakes. Try the variety of fun cogwheel trains, funiculars, and cable cars that deliver you—no matter the season—from sunny valleys up to dizzying heights and snowy vistas.

The Swiss railway system markets several scenic journeys, many with special panoramic trains designed to maximize views (for details, see the Scenic Rail Journeys chapter). But don't let the tourist hype give you tunnel vision: A sunny day spent on a train just about anywhere in Switzerland can rank as a memorable trip-capper.

Enjoy Switzerland's famous efficiency and unique mingling of the modern and the traditional. Join cheesemakers in a high valley, call the shepherds on an alphorn, and hike through some of the world's most stunning mountain scenery. Just thinking about a Switzerland trip makes me want to yodel.

Switzerland's Top Destinations

It's a small country, but there's a lot to see in Switzerland. This overview categorizes the country's top destinations into must-see places (to help first-time travelers plan their trip) and worth-it places (for those with extra time or special interests). I've also suggested a minimum number of days to allow per destination.

FRANCE

GERMANY

ZÜRICH

APPENZELL

LIECHTEN-
STEIN

BERN

AUSTRIA

MURTEN

LUZERN &
CENTRAL SWITZ.

BERNER
OBERLAND

LAKE GENEVA
& FRENCH
SWITZ.

❶

❹

UPPER
ENGADINE

❷

ZERMATT
& THE
MATTERHORN

❸

FRANCE

LUGANO

ITALY

SCENIC RAIL JOURNEYS

❶ Golden Pass
❷ Gotthard Panorama Express
❸ Bernina Express
❹ Glacier Express

50 Kilometers

50 Miles

N

**PLACES COVERED
IN THIS BOOK**

▲▲▲ Must See
▲▲ Try Hard to See
▲ Worthwhile

Mediterranean
Sea

MUST-SEE DESTINATIONS

Switzerland's capital Bern is its most charming and fun city, with one of Europe's finest surviving, fun-to-stroll medieval cores. Bern makes a convenient stop on the way to or from the stunningly scenic Berner Oberland and to other parts of the country. On a short trip, I'd prioritize these two areas.

▲▲▲Bern (allow 1 day)

The cozy capital, tucked in a sharp river bend, is my favorite Swiss city. It's urban but easygoing, with arcaded shopping promenades, medieval clock towers, colorful statue-topped fountains, and museums devoted to Albert Einstein and artist Paul Klee. In summer, join the locals at the Marzilibad (an outdoor bathing complex) and see a carefree side to the serious Swiss.

▲▲▲Berner Oberland (3 days)

This mountainous region, highlighted by the Jungfrau and Schilthorn peaks, is worth taking time to savor. It's popular for its traditional alpine villages (such as rustic Gimmelwald and the resort town of Mürren, both on the Schilthorn cable-car line). Scenic hikes, lifts, and train rides ring the valley hub of Lauterbrunnen. Easy trails and pleasant walks on the valley floor, plus the nearby Trümmelbach Falls, are ideal for a cloudy day, as is the nearby Swiss Open-Air Museum at Ballenberg. Touristy Interlaken is the gateway to this area.

Medieval mechanics in Bern's clock tower (opposite); Bern's Aare River; rustic Gimmelwald; hiking in the Berner Oberland; exploring Trümmelbach Falls

*Urban-but-quaint Zürich;
wooden bridge in Luzern;
Luzern's Swiss Transport
Museum; Zermatt and its
Matterhorn view*

WORTH-IT DESTINATIONS

You can weave any of these destinations—rated ▲ or ▲▲—into your itinerary. It's easy to add some destinations based on proximity (if you're going to Bern, Murten is next door), but other out-of-the-way places can merit the journey, depending on your time and interests. I've included scenic rail trips on this list: In this land of dramatic mountains and picture-perfect farms, the journey is the destination.

▲▲Zürich (1 day)
Bustling cosmopolitan Zürich is a transportation center and Switzerland's largest city by far. Along with upscale shops and a charming riverside old-town quarter full of pointy church spires and pealing bells, it's home to the insightful National Museum Zürich, art-packed churches, and the country's top fine-art collection at Kunsthaus Zürich.

▲▲Luzern and Central Switzerland (1-2 days)
Touristy yet lovely Luzern is famous for its historic wood-en bridges, picturesque streets, and vintage steamships that ply Lake Luzern. Ringed by mountains with stunning vistas accessible by high-altitude lifts, Luzern's sights include the Swiss Transport Museum, an impressive Picasso exhibit at the Rosengart Collection, and the underground bunker at nearby Fortress Fürigen. And it's a handy hub for easy excursions to nearby Mount Pilatus and Mount Rigi.

▲▲Murten and Avenches (1/2 day)
Quaint, small, walled Murten—an easy half-hour trip from Bern—sits next to the German/French linguistic fault line, with nearby Roman ruins and museum in Avenches.

▲▲Zermatt and the Matterhorn (2 days)

Zermatt, a glitzy ski resort with old-fashioned touches surrounded by an array of mountain lifts, is a gateway to fine hikes and views—which get even better when that iconic pointy peak of the Matterhorn emerges from the clouds.

▲▲Appenzell (1 day)

The very traditional Swiss region around Appenzell is known for pastoral green hills and carved chalets, cozy small towns (including Appenzell town), cows, folk museums, and, just a cable-car ride away, a rustic cliffside retreat at Ebenalp.

▲▲Lake Geneva and French Switzerland (1 day)

Elegant Lake Geneva is lined with vineyards and resort towns. The region boasts Switzerland's best castle experience at Château de Chillon; the sophisticated, multilevel city of Lausanne, with its engaging Olympic and Art Brut museums; the cute and cheesy medieval town of Gruyères; and a pleasantly scenic countryside.

▲▲Scenic Rail Journeys

Enjoy panoramic views while crisscrossing the country on one of four famous train rides. The Golden Pass route connects Luzern with Lake Geneva; the Gotthard Panorama Express runs from Luzern to Lugano (half by boat and half by train); the Bernina Express connects Lugano with eastern Switzerland (by bus via Italy's Lake Como, plus a train through the mountains); and the Glacier Express travels between Zermatt and eastern Switzerland's resort towns (St. Moritz/Davos).

▲Lugano (1 day)

A hub for two scenic train rides, Lugano is the leading city of Italian-speaking Switzerland, with a tidy urban core, scenic boat trips on its lake, relaxing strolls, and mountain lifts to lakeside peaks.

▲Upper Engadine (1-2 days)

This Romansh-speaking mountain resort region nestles in Switzerland's southeast, with high-altitude viewpoints, tempting hikes, and a rugged landscape. It's anchored by three towns: likeable Pontresina, sleepy Samedan, and swanky St. Moritz. The region makes an easy stopover for travelers on the Bernina Express or Glacier Express scenic train rides.

Planning Your Trip

To plan your trip, you'll need to design your itinerary—choosing where and when to go, how you'll travel, and how many days to spend at each destination. For my best general advice on sightseeing, accommodations, restaurants, and more, see the Practicalities chapter.

DESIGNING AN ITINERARY

As you read this book and learn your options...

Choose your top destinations.
My recommended itinerary (see the sidebar on page 20) gives you an idea of how much you can reasonably see in two weeks, but you can adapt it to fit your own interests and time frame.

Decide when to go.
The summer "tourist season" runs roughly from May through September, though in mountainous areas, it doesn't start until sometime in June.

High summer (July-Aug) has its advantages: the best weather, snow-free alpine trails, very long days (light until after 21:00), and the busiest schedule of tourist fun. But prices and crowds are at their peak.

June and especially September are, for many visitors, the "sweet spot": less crowded but (if you're fortunate) still decent weather. If you're coming to hike, fall is better than spring (when higher trails can still be snow-covered, and some lifts may not yet be running).

In late May and early October, travelers enjoy even fewer crowds, mild but riskier weather, and the ability to grab a room almost whenever and wherever they like. In fact, small mountain towns may feel downright deserted.

During the *Zwischenzeit* ("between time"—that is, between summer and ski seasons, roughly April, early May, late Oct, and Nov), Swiss cities are pleasantly uncrowded, but mountain resort towns such as Zermatt and Mürren are completely dead (most hotels and restaurants are closed, and the weather is iffy).

During ski season (Dec-March), mountain resorts are crowded and expensive, while cities are quieter (some accommodations and sights are either closed or run on a limited schedule). The weather can be cold and dreary, and nighttime will draw the shades on your sightseeing before dinner.

No matter when you go, pack warm clothing for the Alps—the weather can change suddenly. For weather specifics, see the climate chart in the appendix.

Connect the dots.

Link your destinations into a logical route. Determine which cities you'll fly into and out of. Begin your search for transatlantic flights at Kayak.com.

Decide if you'll travel by public transportation, car, or a combination. Switzerland's public transportation system is

*Cliffside dining at Ebenalp (opposite);
Château de Chillon on Lake Geneva;
strolling along Lake Lugano*

tops, whether you want to go across the country or straight up into the mountains, and its breathtakingly scenic rail journeys are an experience in themselves. PostBuses (operated by the post office) pick you up in the rare cases where trains let you down. You can even go *through* the mountains, thanks to long tunnels (but you'll miss the views). A car can be helpful for exploring the French Swiss countryside and the Appenzell area.

To determine approximate travel times between destinations, study the driving map in the Practicalities chapter or check Google Maps; visit Rail.ch for train schedules. Compare the cost of any long train ride in Europe with a budget flight; check Skyscanner.com for intra-European flights.

Write out a day-by-day itinerary.

Figure out how many destinations you can comfortably fit in your time frame. Don't overdo it—few travelers wish they'd hurried more. Allow enough days per stop (see estimates in "Switzerland's Top Destinations," earlier). Minimize one-night stands. It can be worth taking a late-afternoon train ride or drive to settle into a town for two consecutive nights—and gain a full uninterrupted day for sightseeing. Include sufficient time for transportation; many Swiss cities are just a quick hop apart, but reaching the high-mountain areas can take longer.

Staying in a home base (like Gimmelwald in the Berner

Switzerland's Best Two-Week Trip by Train

Day	Plan	Sleep
1	Arrive Zürich Airport, head to Appenzell	Appenzell or Ebenalp
2	All day in Appenzell and Ebenalp	Appenzell or Ebenalp
3	Leave early for Luzern	Luzern
4	Luzern	Luzern
5	Boat, then train to Lugano along Gotthard Panorama Express route	Lugano
6	Bernina Express to Upper Engadine	Pontresina
7	Upper Engadine (Pontresina, St. Moritz, and Samedan)	Pontresina
8	Take Glacier Express; if weather's good, head for Zermatt; if weather's bad, consider going straight to Lausanne (see Day 10)	Zermatt
9	Zermatt and hikes, Matterhorn-view lifts	Zermatt
10	If weather's good, spend more time in Zermatt and go late to Lausanne; if weather's bad, leave early for Lausanne (to visit its fine museums and nearby Château de Chillon)	Lausanne
11	Take the Golden Pass to the Berner Oberland. If weather's good, go early; if weather's bad, linger in Lausanne/Lake Geneva area and leave late	Gimmelwald or Mürren
12	All day for lifts and hikes in the Berner Oberland	Gimmelwald or Mürren
13	More time in the Berner Oberland	Gimmelwald or Mürren
14	On to Bern	Bern
15	Morning in Bern, then train to Zürich Airport to fly home	

Alternative: Zermatt isn't worth the trip in bad weather. If your reservations are flexible, consider skipping that leg and going straight to Lausanne (take the Glacier Express only to Brig, then change for Lausanne).

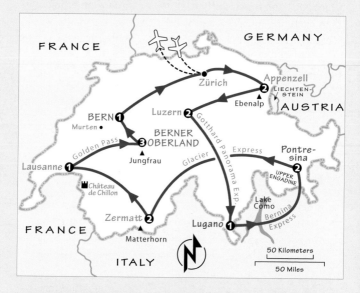

With More Time: In order of priority, spend extra time in: Murten and Bern, Zürich (add a day at the beginning or end of your trip), Lausanne and the Lake Geneva area, Lugano (relaxing), or the Luzern area (day trips).

With Less Time: For a trip of a week or so, focus on the Berner Oberland, Bern, and Luzern.

Rail Pass: A Swiss Travel Pass for 15 consecutive days is typically best for this itinerary; see page 485 for details and confirm the latest prices at RickSteves.com/rail.

By Car: This itinerary works by car with a few modifications. From Appenzell, drive straight to the Upper Engadine, then continue through Tirano and on to Lugano (via Lake Como in Italy). From Lugano, drive to Zermatt (crossing again through Italy) and resume the above itinerary, visiting Luzern at the end before returning to Zürich. The French Swiss countryside and the area around Murten merit more time if you have a car.

Beyond Switzerland: Switzerland splices neatly into a multicountry trip by car or train. For instance, the Appenzell region is a likely gateway to Germany's Bavaria or Austria's Tirol. Italy's Lake Como is a stone's throw from Lugano (the Bernina Express bus drives right alongside it)—and Milan is not much farther. If you're in Lausanne, you're literally looking at France (across Lake Geneva), and a handy train ride whisks you to Lyon or Chamonix. And big Swiss cities are efficiently connected by fast trains to destinations in all these countries and beyond.

Oberland) and making day trips can be more time-efficient than changing locations and hotels. Connect destinations, such as Bern and the Lake Geneva area, with a scenic rail trip, even if it adds an hour or two of transit time: In Switzerland, the views along the journey are a highlight.

Take sight closures and weather into account. It's not worth visiting some places if visibility will be low or hiking will be unpleasant.

While Switzerland lacks a world-class metropolis, the cities I recommend are engaging—especially if bad weather keeps you from heading for the hills. Check if any holidays or festivals fall during your trip—these attract crowds and can close sights (for the latest, visit Switzerland's tourist website, www.myswitzerland.com). Consider whether to buy a Swiss Travel Pass or reserve a scenic train ride in advance.

Give yourself some slack. Every trip, and every traveler, needs downtime for doing laundry, picnic shopping, people-watching, and so on. Pace yourself. Assume you will return.

Swiss thrills: cheese plate; winery near Lake Geneva; via ferrata *cliffside trail in Mürren*

Trip Costs Per Person

Run a reality check on your dream trip. You'll have major transportation costs in addition to daily expenses.

Flight: A round-trip flight from the US to Zürich costs about $900-1,500, depending on where you fly from and when.

Public Transportation: Allow $750 per person. This covers a second-class, 15-day consecutive Swiss Travel Pass, plus high-mountain trains and lifts, and reservation fees for scenic trains. You can purchase a Swiss Travel Pass before you leave home or wait until you arrive in Switzerland—they're also sold at local train stations.

Car Rental: Allow roughly $350-500 per week (booked well in advance), not including tolls, gas, parking, and insurance.

AVERAGE DAILY EXPENSES PER PERSON

$265
Applies to cities, figure on less for towns

Lodging
Based on two people splitting the cost of a $220 double room (includes breakfast)
★★★★★
🛏 **$110**

Meals
$30 for lunch, $45 for dinner, and $5 for chocolate
✗ **$80**

City Transit
Buses, Métro, or taxis/Uber
🚊 **$15**

Sights and Entertainment
This daily average works for most people.
👓 **$60**

Budget Tips

To cut your daily expenses, take advantage of the deals you'll find throughout Switzerland and mentioned in this book.

The Swiss Travel Pass is a swinging deal for most travelers. It offers consecutive-day or flexipass coverage of Switzerland's trains, boats, and buses, and a 50 percent discount off most lifts, including the cable car to the Schilthorn from Mürren (about $430 for 15-day consecutive pass in second class).

The Swiss Travel Pass also doubles as a Swiss Museum Pass (which otherwise costs ▶▶▶

▶▶▶ about $180), covering admission to 500 museums or so on the days your pass is valid. To get the most out of a flexipass, use it to visit a museum, ride a lake boat, or take a lift either on the same day you arrive at that destination or on the day you depart. For a list of sights in this book covered by the Swiss Travel Pass and the Swiss Museum Pass, see the Practicalities chapter (also noted in individual listings).

Avid sightseers without the Swiss Travel Pass can buy local passes that cover multiple museums. If a town doesn't offer deals, visit only the sights you most want to see, and seek out free sights and experiences (people-watching counts).

Many expensive alpine lifts offer discounted "early bird" tickets for the first (and sometimes last) trip of the day. Train trips get cheaper when you choose the right rail pass (for help, see page 485).

Some businesses—especially hotels and walking-tour companies—offer discounts to my readers (look for the RS% symbol in the listings in this book).

Reserve your rooms directly with the hotel. Some hotels offer a discount if you pay in cash and/or stay three or more nights (check online or ask).

Rooms can cost less in spring and fall (May, June, Sept, and Oct). And even seniors can sleep cheaply in hostels (most have private rooms) for under $100 per person. Keep your eyes peeled for *Matratzenlagers* (mattress dorms). Or check Airbnb-type sites for deals.

It's no hardship to eat inexpensively in Switzerland. You can get tasty, affordable meals at buffets or self-service cafeterias (often attached to department or grocery stores). Cultivate the art of picnicking in atmospheric settings.

When you splurge, choose an experience you'll always remember, such as a scenic train journey or a mountain lift. Minimize souvenir shopping; focus instead on collecting wonderful memories. ▮

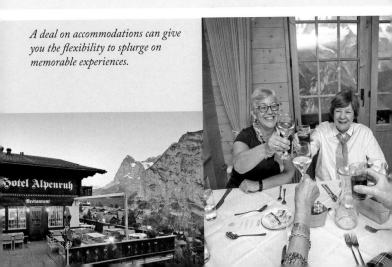

A deal on accommodations can give you the flexibility to splurge on memorable experiences.

BEFORE YOU GO

You'll have a smoother trip if you tackle a few things ahead of time. For more details on these topics, see the Practicalities chapter and RickSteves.com, which has helpful travel-tip articles and videos.

Make sure your travel documents are valid. If your passport is due to expire within six months of your ticketed date of return, you need to renew it. Allow six weeks or more to renew or get a passport (www.travel.state.gov). Check for current Covid entry requirements, such as proof of vaccination or a negative Covid-19 test result.

Arrange your transportation. Book your international flights. Overall, Kayak.com is the best place to start searching for flights. It's worth thinking about buying essential train tickets online in advance, getting a rail pass, renting a car, or booking cheap European flights. (You can wing it once you're there, but it may cost more.)

Book rooms well in advance, especially if your trip falls during peak season or any major holidays or festivals.

Reserve or buy tickets in advance for scenic trains and mountain lifts. In summer, book ahead for the Jungfraubahn train ride described in the Berner Oberland chapter and the rail trips detailed in the Scenic Rail Journeys chapter.

Consider travel insurance. Compare the cost of insurance to the cost of your potential loss. Check whether your existing insurance (health, homeowners, or renters) covers you and your possessions overseas.

Call your bank. Alert your bank that you'll be using your debit and credit cards in Europe. Ask about transaction fees, and, if you don't already have one, get a "contactless" credit card (request your card PIN too). You don't need to bring Swiss francs for your trip; you can withdraw currency from cash machines in Europe.

Use your smartphone smartly. Sign up for an international service plan to reduce your costs, or rely on Wi-Fi in Europe instead. Download any apps you'll want on the road, such as maps, translators, transit schedules, and Rick Steves Audio Europe (see sidebar).

Pack light. You'll walk with your luggage more than you think. I travel for weeks with a single carry-on bag and a day pack. Use the packing checklist in the appendix as a guide.

Rick's Free Video Clips and Audio Tours

Travel smarter with these free, fun resources:

Rick Steves Classroom Europe, a powerful tool for teachers, is also useful for travelers. This video library contains about 500 short clips excerpted from my public television series. Enjoy these videos as you sort through options for your trip and to better understand what you'll see in Europe. Check it out at Classroom.RickSteves.com (just enter a topic to find everything I've filmed on a subject).

The **Rick Steves Audio Europe** app makes it easy to download audio content to enhance your trip. Use the app to listen to audio tours of Europe's top sights, plus interviews (organized by country) from my public radio show with experts from Europe and around the globe. Find it in your app store or at RickSteves.com/AudioEurope.

Travel Smart

If you have a positive attitude, equip yourself with good information (this book), and expect to travel smart, you will.

Read—and reread—this book. To have an "A" trip, be an "A" student. Note opening hours, closed days, crowd-beating tips, and whether reservations are required or advisable. Check the latest at RickSteves.com/update.

Be your own tour guide. As you travel, get up-to-date info on sights, reserve tickets and tours, reconfirm hotels and travel arrangements, and check transit connections. Visit local tourist information offices (TIs). Upon arrival in a new town, lay the groundwork for a smooth departure; confirm the train, bus, or road you'll take when you leave.

Outsmart thieves. Pickpockets abound in crowded places where tourists congregate. Treat commotions as smokescreens for theft. Keep your cash, credit cards, and passport secure in a money belt tucked under your clothes; carry only a day's spending money in your front pocket or wallet. Don't set valuable items down on counters or café tabletops, where they can be quickly stolen or easily forgotten.

Minimize potential loss. Keep expensive gear to a minimum. Bring copies or take photos of important documents (passport and cards) to aid in replacement if they're lost or stolen. Back up photos and files frequently.

Guard your time and energy. Taking a taxi can be a good value if it saves you a long wait for a cheap bus or an exhausting walk across town. To avoid long lines, follow my crowd-beating tips, such as making advance reservations, or sightseeing early or late.

Be flexible. Even if you have a well-planned itinerary, expect changes, strikes, closures, sore feet, bad weather, and so on. Your Plan B could turn out to be even better.

Attempt the language. Most Swiss people—especially in the tourist trade and in cities—speak English, but if you learn just a few pleasantries in the local language, you'll get more smiles and make more friends. Apps such as Google Translate work for on-the-go translation help, but you can get a head start by practicing the survival phrases near the end of this book.

Connect with the culture. Interacting with locals carbonates your experience. Enjoy the friendliness of the Swiss people. Ask questions; most locals are happy to point you in their idea of the right direction. Set up your own quest for the richest hot chocolate, cheeriest window box, or tastiest mountain cheese. When an opportunity pops up, make it a habit to say "yes." And, of course, more cowbell.

Switzerland...here you come!

ZÜRICH

Zürich is one of those cities that tourists tend to skip right over. Since it's a transportation hub, people fly in or change trains here, but don't give stopping a serious thought. The local graffiti jokes: *Zürich = zu reich, zu ruhig* ("too rich, too quiet"). But even though you won't find a hint of Swiss Miss in Switzerland's leading city, Zürich is rewarding and worth getting to know.

In prehistoric times, people lived on pilings near the shores of Lake Zürich. Later, the Romans founded a city here as a customs post. Roman Turicum eventually became Zürich. It gained city status in the 10th century, flourished thanks to the hard work of its many powerful guilds, and was a center of the Swiss Reformation. By the 19th century it was a leading European financial and economic center. Today, thanks largely to Switzerland's long-term economic and political stability, Zürich is a major hub of international banking. Assuming you've got the money to enjoy it, Zürich is by many measures the world's most livable city.

For the traveler, Zürich is a city of contrasts. It's diverse and cosmopolitan, but also quiet and quaint. Fragrant fondue restaurants sit next door to cheap Thai takeout joints and designer boutiques that put Milan to shame. One-third of its residents come from countries other than Switzerland (169 nationalities, at last count), and one-third of its territory is nature ("if you count the river and lake," locals explain).

While not the capital, Zürich is far and away Switzerland's biggest city—a hub for both business and transportation (with the country's dominant train station and airport). Perhaps Zürich's hard-to-pin-down character is rooted in its role as home to Switzerland's Reformation: The city retains a no-fuss, no-muss, nose-to-the-grindstone Protestant work ethic that leaves little time for colorful flourishes. Locals pride themselves on being private, discreet, and no-drama.

Zürich is the only place in Switzerland where I've seen men in ties running in the streets. And it's the only place I've seen a shop clerk dispose of a cigarette by slipping it into the finger hole of a manhole cover, rather than just tossing it on the ground.

PLANNING YOUR TIME

While Luzern and Bern provide more charming and compact urban experiences, Zürich is worth a look. With two weeks in Switzerland, I'd spend a day here. Begin by visiting the impressive National Museum Zürich (a.k.a. Landesmuseum), then wander along the river, using my self-guided walk, and take a river/lake cruise. With less time, do only the walk. With more time, check out the excellent art museum, visit the up-and-coming Zürich West area, or head to the countryside (zoo or Uetliberg viewpoint). While there are more charismatic places to overnight, you won't regret sleeping in Zürich—the city offers plenty to keep visitors engaged.

Orientation to Zürich

Zürich—with about 430,000 people (1.4 million in greater Zürich)—is draped around the northern tip of the long, skinny Lake Zürich (Zürichsee). The grand Bahnhofstrasse cuts through the city's glitzy shopping center, connecting the train station with the lakefront (a 15-minute walk). Across the Limmat River is the Niederdorf neighborhood—a vibrant, cobbled, Old World zone of colorful little shops, cafés, and restaurants. West of the train station is the emerging Zürich West dining and nightlife zone.

TOURIST INFORMATION

The helpful TI is off the great hall of the train station, near the giant blue angel hanging from the ceiling (Mon-Sat 8:00-20:30, Sun 8:30-18:30, shorter hours off-season, +41 44 215 4000, www.zuerich.com).

For a whirlwind visit, consider the TI's **Zürich Card,** which covers public transit (including trips to the airport and up to the Uetliberg viewpoint); river boats and short and mini lake cruises; admission to most of the city's museums and discounts on others; half off the TI's city walking tour; and freebies in many restaurants (27 CHF/24 hours, 53 CHF/72 hours, sold at TI). The one-day card pays for itself if you do the walking tour and one museum.

ARRIVAL IN ZÜRICH

By Train: The slick train station is at the north end of downtown. Many platforms are underground; to orient yourself, follow signs for tracks 3-17, which dead-end at the great hall of the station.

In the hall (with your back to the tracks), the ticket office is to your left (daily 6:00-21:00), with the TI just beyond it. Exiting through the front doors—straight ahead—brings you to the river (cross it to reach most recommended hotels). Lockers are down one flight below the big blue angel, and a pricey WC (with showers) is down two flights. A long-hours Migros supermarket is in the maze-like shopping mall one level down. The right-hand doors of the hall lead to tram stops and Bahnhofstrasse, while the left-hand doors lead toward the National Museum Zürich.

By Plane: If arriving at Zürich Airport, see the end of the chapter.

GETTING AROUND ZÜRICH

Much of Zürich is walkable, but it's big enough that trams, buses, and boats can make things easier. Handy trams run south from the station to the lake on either side of the river: #4 along Limmatquai and #11 along Bahnhofstrasse. The riverboats and short lake cruise are part of the system, but longer lake cruises are not.

The Swiss Travel Pass, Eurail Global Pass, and **Zürich Card** cover all city transit. Otherwise, individual tickets cost 2.70 CHF for a "short stretch" ticket of a few stops *(Kurtzstrecke)*, or 4.40 CHF for one hour *(Einzelbillett)*. A 24-hour pass *(Tageskarte)* for 8.80 CHF is a good investment for a full day in Zürich (13.60 CHF for three-zone version that includes airport and other outlying sights). For transit information, visit www.zvv.ch.

HELPFUL HINTS

Medical Help: The **Permanence** drop-in clinic on the main floor of the train station offers on-the-spot medical aid (daily 7:00-22:00, Bahnhofplatz 15, +41 44 215 4444, www.permanence.ch). The **Bahnhof Apotheke** is a convenient pharmacy next door (daily 7:00-24:00). A dentist is on the lower level.

Laundry: A short ride north from downtown, **Expresswäscherei Selfservice** is next to the Kinkelstrasse tram stop for trams #9 and #10 (daily 7:00-22:00, Wintherthurstrasse 62, +41 76 577 4164 or +41 76 305 1111).

Parking: Parking a car in Zürich will cost you. Downtown garages run about 45 CHF/24 hours; park-and-ride lots on the city outskirts are about 30 CHF/24 hours. For a list of lots, see www.pls-zh.ch.

Shopping on Sunday: Though most stores are closed on Sunday, the vast mall under the train station is wide open.

Tours in Zürich

Walking Tours

Group Tours: The TI's two-hour **guided walk** is similar to the self-guided walk in this chapter (25 CHF, half-price with Zürich Card; leaves from TI Mon, Wed-Thu, and Sun at 11:00, Sat at 13:00; Nov-March tours run Wed and Sat-Sun only; confirm times and book at www.zuerich.com). Unfortunately, the tour is usually given in both German and English (sometimes heavily favoring German—depending on who signs up). The TI website also links to a range of specialized group tours run by private companies.

Private Tours: The TI can arrange private walking tours (280 CHF/2-3 hours). On the TI website (www.zuerich.com) choose "Tours and Excursions" under "Things to Do," then look for the private version request option. Alternatively, write to info@zuerich.com. You can request energetic and informative **Nicole Berger.**

Bus Tours

If you'd rather ride than walk, consider a bus tour. Two companies offer similar two-hour tours several times a day for 34 CHF, leaving from the bus lot behind the train station. It's easiest to book through the TI website (www.zuerich.com).

Zürich Walk

If you're blitzing Zürich from the train station, this self-guided walk is a great way to connect the city center's main sights. It criss-crosses the river en route to the boat dock for a lazy lake-cruise finale (or a quick tram ride back to the station). Allow about 1.5 hours. Add 30 minutes to enter the two major churches (Grossmünster and Fraumünster).

❶ Train Station

We'll start on the ground level of the train station, in the cav-ernous main hall (follow signs for tracks 3-17, and you'll see the hall at the end of the platforms). This major European hub handles 2,000 trains a day, including InterCity expresses to many major capitals. To keep up with Europe's ever-faster transportation ex-pectations, some of the station's tracks have been tunneled two stories underground so trains can zip through the city rather than dead-ending at the station.

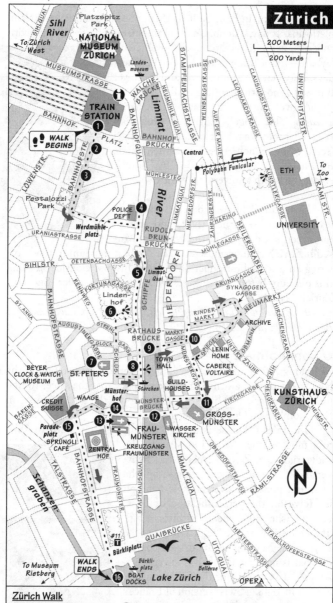

Zürich Walk

1. Train Station
2. Bahnhofplatz
3. Bahnhofstrasse to Pestalozzi Park
4. Police Department
5. Schipfe
6. Lindenhof
7. St. Peter's Church
8. Weinplatz & Roman Bath
9. Rathausbrücke
10. Niederdorf
11. Grossmünster
12. River View
13. Fraumünster
14. Münsterhof
15. Paradeplatz
16. Lake Zürich

ZÜRICH

The vast main hall, built in 1870, once housed six tracks and platforms. Today, it doubles as a community-events venue busy with concerts, exhibitions, and even "beach" volleyball—and a farmers market on Wednesdays. Between the ground level and the lower tracks is a modern shopping mall.

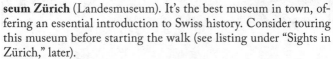

Above you in the main hall hangs a *zäftig* blue angel, Zürich's **"Guardian Angel,"** protecting all travelers. The angel (sculpted by French-American artist Niki de St. Phalle) was placed here in 1997 to celebrate the 150th anniversary of the Swiss rail system.

If the angel hopped down, walked toward the tracks, turned right, and crossed the street, she'd arrive at the **National Museum Zürich** (Landesmuseum). It's the best museum in town, offering an essential introduction to Swiss history. Consider touring this museum before starting the walk (see listing under "Sights in Zürich," later).

• *Exit the station hall to the angel's left, following a passage leading to Bahnhofplatz (also well-signed).*

❷ Bahnhofplatz

Mile-long Bahnhofstrasse, stretching from the train station to the lake, is lined with all the big-name shops. Cross the street (watch for silent trams), but before heading down the street, pause on Bahnhofplatz and look back at the station.

The station facade is a huge triumphal **arch,** built in 1871 to symbolize the rise of industry. In the Industrial Age, Zürich emerged as Switzerland's leading city. Sitting atop the arch and presiding over all this triumph is **Helvetia,** the personification of Switzerland (she sits beneath a Swiss flag). The Helvetii were the Celtic tribe that the Romans defeated in 58 BC to gain control of what is now Switzerland. Helvetia was adopted as a symbol of the Swiss confederation in 1848 (a Swiss version of France's Marianne), when the diverse cantons that banded together to create Switzerland needed some symbol of unity to transcend

all their linguistic and regional differences. The same word was put to use in the Latin name for the new federal state *(Confoederatio Helvetica).* Today, this neutral name is used when there's a need to avoid favoring any of the country's four languages—thus the "CH" on Swiss license plates, in web addresses, and in the abbreviation for the country's currency (CHF).

Helvetia is flanked by allegories of river travel (the goddess sitting on the boat) and rail travel (another goddess sitting on a locomotive), reminding us that Zürich has long been a transportation hub. Zürich's river, the Limmat, starts from the lake and eventually flows into the Rhine (reaching the Atlantic at Rotterdam).

The statue in the foreground honors **Alfred Escher,** the Zürich-born politician who, in the mid-19th century, spearheaded the creation of the infrastructure—railways, universities, and banks—that allowed Switzerland to function efficiently within its mountains and connected this country with the rest of Europe. It was his idea, for example, to link the flat, urban north of Switzerland to Italy with the nearly 10-mile Gotthard Tunnel (completed in 1882). He was also instrumental in founding Credit Suisse bank and Swiss Life insurance company. Without Escher, it's quite possible Switzerland would never have become such an economic powerhouse. Infrastructure!

• *Start strolling down Bahnhofstrasse.*

❸ Bahnhofstrasse to Pestalozzi Park

Bahnhofstrasse was built in the 1860s, when the newfangled train station needed a suitable approach road. Long before there was a train station, this would have been the moat lining the town's 13th-century fortifications. Today, you can stroll the entire boulevard from here to the lakefront. As a center of the banking and insurance industries, there's a lot of wealth in Zürich, as evidenced by the department stores, elegant shops, and banks you pass along the way—and their well-dressed clientele. Locals say that prices go up and shops get fancier as you get closer to the lake.

Among the Swiss, Zürichers have a reputation for being hardworking, impatient, and a bit snobby. Notice how the traffic lights flip from green to yellow to red at an unforgiving pace—nobody has time to waste.

Near the end of the first block are three chocolate shops: Lindt and Bachmann on the right, and Läderach on the left.

• *In two blocks (on the right), you'll see a park.*

The only park along this pedestrian- and tram-only boulevard is dedicated to a famous Swiss educational reformer, **Johann Hein-**

rich **Pestalozzi** (1746-1827). He promoted the then-radical notions that good education should focus on the whole child (not just on specific skills) and should be available to everyone (not only the sons of rich families). He's standing in front of the Globus building, which used to be a school. Parks like this are rare in central Zürich because of sky-high property values—Swiss real estate is among the most expensive in the world.

In the park's far corner gurgles a green, Parisian-style **fountain.** More than 1,200 fun and fresh fountains are sprinkled around town, spouting water that's as good as bottled mineral water (the city regularly checks its quality). This is a blessing in a town where restaurants charge for a glass of tap water. Tourist brochures brag that Zürich is Europe's most "fountainous" city.

• *From the green fountain, turn left across the street and head two blocks down Werdmühlestrasse. Then follow white* Stadtpolizei *signs up and around to the river side of the grand building facing the water. This is the...*

❹ Police Department (Stadtpolizei)

Enter the big police building at Bahnhofquai 3 for a peek at a fine example of Swiss Art Nouveau, called *Jugendstil* in German (free, open daily 9:00-11:00 & 14:00-16:00). The Swiss artist Augusto Giacometti (1877-1947) painted the arched vaults of the building's entry hall in the 1920s. Awash in vibrant orange and red, with flowery motifs, the "Hall of Flowers" reflects the relief and joy the artist felt when World War I ended. (Augusto's nephew, Alberto, is the more famous Giacometti, well known for his tall, skinny statues.) Before the police moved into the building in the early 20th century, it was the city orphanage and prison, and in earlier centuries there was a Dominican cloister on the site.

• *From the door of the police building, head to the right, upstream along the river. (Notice the towering old observatory off to your right.) Ahead of you, the inviting **Schweizer Heimatwerk** shop shows off Swiss folk crafts. It originated long ago as a place for farmers and mountain folk to showcase and retail the handiwork that the boredom of their long winters inspired.*

From there, go down the stairs and continue walking upstream. You'll pass curious and arty little shops and come to a delightful riverside square. (High above you on the right is a viewpoint on a bluff. That's Lindenhof, where we're heading.)

Switzerland's Clear-Headed Drug Policy

Switzerland has a progressive drug policy that aims to reduce the overall harm to its society, rather than focus on punishing users. Even by European stan-

dards, the country's approaches to soft and hard drugs are unusually pragmatic.

Switzerland's policy has swung harder and softer in recent years. When polls showed that more than 30 percent of Swiss people had used marijuana, the parliament decided to decriminalize the drug. But the laws, which vary between cantons, remain ambiguous: The Swiss can possess and use pot, but they can't sell it. Each spring, there's a push for stricter control. Word gets out that Switzerland is no haven for pot, and then things ease up. Now medical marijuana shops can legally sell very weak strains of marijuana that contain less than 1 percent THC. Smoking this gets you relaxed but not high.

Unlike marijuana, hard drugs remain illegal. Still, Swiss laws treat addicts as people needing medical help, rather than as criminals. Zürich was ground zero for junkies in the 1980s and early 1990s. Beginning in 1987, heroin use was tolerated in the park called Platzspitz, along the river just behind the National Museum Zürich. Dubbed "Needle Park," the space became a magnet for thousands of users, a hotbed of crime, and one big public health hazard. In a confrontation that looms large in local history, local police reclaimed Platzspitz in 1992.

That year, Zürich pivoted to a harm-reduction, addiction-maintenance model by providing the heroin replacement drug methadone (or actual heroin) to addicts who couldn't get clean. The city funds needle exchanges and counselor-staffed safe houses where addicts unable to recover can proceed, without endangering themselves or others. If you know where to look, you can see evidence of this policy. For instance, across the river from the station, on the far side of the Walchebrücke bridge, there's a big, nondescript vending machine selling safe, government-subsidized syringes.

The policy shift worked. Nationally, the opioid-related death rate has dropped by two-thirds, and heroin use among young people has dwindled to historic lows. Crime also decreased, and you see very few street addicts in Zürich. A similar approach was quickly embraced nationwide, later confirmed by 70 percent of Swiss voters in a national referendum in 2008. As the US grapples with its own opioid crisis, perhaps we can take inspiration from the pragmatic, compassionate, and highly successful Swiss approach.

❺ Schipfe

Back when the city's trade depended on river traffic, this small street was Zürich's harbor. Today it retains its old river-merchant ambience. This area has several businesses that are subsidized by the city government to support down-on-their-luck locals and worthy causes. On the left at #24, the **Marktlücke** shop aids single mothers; they sell interesting gifts, including items made from recycled materials. At the far end of the little square is a fun waterfront eatery—the recommended **Restaurant Schipfe 16**—that operates as a charity, employing people who are trying to get back on their feet.

Continue past the restaurant, admiring the antiques in the windows of the Vock shop (which painstakingly restores classic pieces). Bear left at the fork, and soon you'll reach an arcade that runs along the river. Head through it, passing an interesting strip of little artisan workshops and boutiques (also subsidized by the local government, to enliven this central area with traditional crafts).

• *Emerging at the far end of the arcade, near a fine fountain, turn right (away from the river) and head up the stairs. Bear right at the fork (with the* Old Crow *sign), then left at Wohllebgasse. Climbing up from the river, watch on the right for Pfalzgasse, which leads steeply to a park with fine views.*

❻ Lindenhof

Important forts and strategic buildings stood on this bluff from Roman times through the ninth-century Carolingian era. The statue commemorates the **local women** who cleverly defended the town in 1292. Their men were engaged in another battle when the Habsburgs encircled the city. The women put on armor and made like a big, rowdy army, tricking the Habsburgs into thinking the whole city was prepared to attack.

In the early 13th century, Zürich became a free city of the Holy Roman Empire, meaning it was relatively autonomous and self-ruling. The townspeople destroyed the fort here and established a law forbidding any new construction. The citizens realized that whoever lived on this hill would control the city—and they didn't want any more such rulers. Today, this is a people's square, where locals relax under linden trees (for which the square is named) and enjoy the commanding city view.

Look out and survey the city. **Zürich University** (behind the skinny green spire) is the largest in Switzerland, with 25,000 students (and was the first German-speaking university to allow women students, in 1847). Left of that is Zürich's renowned **technical college,** the ETH (Eidgenössische Technische Hochschule—the Federal Institute of Technology), with 15,000 students. The ETH has graduated more than 20 Nobel Prize winners, including Albert Einstein and Wilhelm Röntgen (who discovered

X-rays). The ETH terrace offers a great city viewpoint (which you can visit later by riding the little Polybahn funicular). Below these storied institutions, lining the opposite side of the river, the **Niederdorf** is a lively district of restaurants, cafés, and bars. We'll walk through there soon. On a clear day, you can see the Alps beyond the twin domes of the Grossmünster.

• *Descend the stairs at the back corner of the park, just beyond where you entered (near the giant chessboard), to a little square with a fountain. The fountain's armpit points you down Glockengasse. Heading that way, you'll reach a big golden bell (at the Haus zur Glocke); take the narrow lane around its left side (Robert-Walser-Gasse). You'll pass a characteristic eatery,* **Restaurant Kaiser's Reblaube,** *made famous by visits from Goethe in 1779. He'd meet here for long, wine-fueled discussions with the minister of...*

❼ St. Peter's Church (St. Peterskirche)

Founded in the seventh century, this church—Zürich's oldest—has one of Europe's largest clock faces (28 feet in diameter). The town

watchman used to live above the clock. If he spotted a fire, he would ring the alarm and hang a flag out of the window facing the blaze. This system seems to have worked— Zürich never suffered a devastating fire.

• *Continue past the church on Schlüsselgasse and take the first left, down the narrow Thermengasse (Bath Lane). Here we meet a bit of Roman Zürich. Glass cases in the wall contain artifacts, and under your feet are the excavations of a* **Roman bath,** *discovered by accident in 1984. You're standing over studs that elevated the floor, which was heated from below.*

The lane empties out on...

❽ Weinplatz

This pleasant spot was a wine market in centuries past (look for the happy grape picker on the fine little fountain). Zürich never had a centralized market hall, and this is just the first of many such market-themed squares that ran through town; I'll mention several of them in the next few blocks. (Notice the dock here for the riverboat-bus—described later, under "Sights in Zürich.")

• *Now cross the wide...*

❾ Rathausbrücke

Built on the site of the town's first bridge, this is, quite possibly, the ugliest bridge in Switzerland. You'll see a fancy Neoclassical police station (on the left).

At the far end of the bridge, the big building on the right is the 17th-century, Renaissance-style **Town Hall.** Below the second-story windows, find the fruits and vegetables carved into the stonework—a subtle reminder that this bridge was once the Gemüsebrücke, where produce *(Gemüse)* was sold. The bridge still hosts a farmers market on Saturdays in summer (and locals still call it by that old nickname). Above the ground-floor windows, you'll see busts of Greek, Roman, and Swiss heroes, including (at the far end just before the street) William Tell and his crossbow. Before crossing the tram tracks, look back, along the street-facing side of the Town Hall. Instead of veggies, this side is decorated with fish—indicating the historic location of a fish market.

• *At the end of the bridge, cross the street and walk a block straight uphill along Marktgasse. Pause where the street hits a T-intersection. You're standing in the heart of the bustling neighborhood called...*

❿ Niederdorf

"Niederdorf" means "nether town"—across the river from the historic core of Zürich. Today Niederdorf is a district of colorful streets, fun shopping, restaurants, and nightlife. This is a great spot for dinner (scope out menus as we explore, and see my dining suggestions later, under "Eating in Zürich").

Let's take a little loop through Niederdorf to see some facets of this neighborhood that many visitors miss. Turn left to continue along narrow Marktgasse, which was the leading commercial street before the old city wall was torn down to create Bahnhofstrasse. After two short blocks, turn right up **Rindermarkt** ("Cattle Market")—yet another street named for its onetime commerce. Follow this broad street one long block, past high-end shops, art boutiques, furniture shops, and some tempting restaurants. This atmospheric street is still lit with gas lamps.

Just after the Travel Book Shop (on your right), turn left on Froschaugasse. Then, just a few doors down, squeeze through the green doors on the right (just before #8), entering **Synagogengasse** (Lane of the Synagogues). Follow this narrow passage, which is where the city's Jews once lived, mixed in among their non-Jewish neighbors, until the pogrom of 1249. The alley bends right before popping out at Neumarkt, where historically household goods were sold.

Head directly across wide Neumarkt—passing inviting café tables huddled around a fountain—and find the door at #4, with the stone plaque that says *Zvm Vntern Rech.* This is the **City Ar-**

chive (free, closed Sun). If it's open, go in and head straight back to a big room with a wonderfully detailed city model of Zürich around the year 1800 (based on the two maps you see hanging on the wall). Notice the moat—which is now Bahnhofstrasse—and the outer, star-shaped fortifications that beefed up the city in the 17th century. (You can still see echoes of this in a city map.)

Exiting the archive, immediately turn left to head up the narrow lane called Spiegelgasse—watching on the left for a cute little interior garden (at #22). Locals brag about how green their city is; there are many such private, hidden gardens even in the dense medieval center.

Find #16, on the left. Now a clothing store, this was once a butcher. Notice the cleaver motif in the ornate window frames, and peek inside to see how old meat hooks still hang from a meat-themed ceiling fresco.

Next door, at #14, look up to see a plaque identifying where Vladimir Lenin lived in exile from February 1916 until April 1917. When he left here, he traveled north to Helsinki, boarded a train, and was greeted as a conquering hero upon arriving in St. Petersburg, where he took leadership of the revolution that would topple the monarchy and introduce communism to Russia.

Cresting the hill and passing a fountain, continue straight downhill along Spiegelgasse. On the right is the Cabaret Voltaire, where a different type of revolution was taking place. In 1916, the "anti-art" Dada movement was started here by a group of rebellious young artists and writers. Although the Dada movement picked up steam, the cabaret itself lasted only until 1917…complaints about excessive nightly noise forced its closure.

You've made a loop, and you're back near where we started our tour of Niederdorf. Turn left on Münstergasse. A couple of doors down on the right at #19, pop into Schwarzenbach, a delightful specialty grocery store that's been operating here for more than 100 years. They still sell things the old-fashioned way (in loose bags, by weight). Inhale. Pick up 100 grams of dried bananas from Togo or whatever appeals (closed Sun). They also roast coffee beans next door on Tuesday and Thursday mornings, making this whole street smell like coffee.

Across the street and up three steps is Café 1842, a venerable chocolate shop that feels like a time warp, with a fine perch from which to enjoy a cup of coffee or hot chocolate. Across the lane to the left is a Swiss schnapps shop.

• Farther along, Münstergasse runs into the…

⓫ Grossmünster

Literally the "big cathedral," this is where Huldrych Zwingli— whose angry religious fervor made Martin Luther seem mellow—

sparked the Reformation in German-speaking Switzerland. The domes of its towers (early examples of Neo-Gothic) are symbols of Zürich. They were rebuilt following a 1781 fire, and after much civic discussion were left a plain stone color.

Cost and Hours: Church—free, Mon-Sat 10:00-18:00, Sun from 12:30, off-season until 17:00; tower climb—5 CHF, closes 30 minutes earlier than church; cloister—free, Mon-Fri 10:00-17:00, closed Sat-Sun; www.grossmuenster.ch.

Visiting the Church: Step inside and sit down. Let the strength and purity of the 12th-century Romanesque architecture have its way with you. The simple round arches seem strong, and the pulpit—surrounded by none of the old Catholic ornamentation—gave you almost no alternative other than to be riveted by Zwingli's fiery sermons. Zwingli's reforms led to a clean sweep of Catholic decor in 1519. (For the story of the Swiss Reformation, pick up the church's English-language leaflet.)

Behind the altar in the apse are three **choir windows** by Augusto Giacometti (c. 1933). Mary and the Baby Jesus (at her feet) meet two of the three kings bearing their gifts, while angels hover above with offerings of flowers. You can walk to just below the windows for a closer look. While there, check out the 1531 Zürich Bible. (Like Luther, Zwingli was a fan of having the Bible available in the people's language—which is what got them in hot water with the Church.)

In the dank **crypt** (stairs below altar), you'll see an original 15th-century statue of Charlemagne (a copy now fills its niche on the river side of the church exterior).

For a sweeping city view, climb the 187 steps to the top of the **Karlsturm,** one of the church's twin towers.

Leaving the church, go right and into the corner, where a door leads to a fine Romanesque **cloister** ringed with fanciful 12th-century carvings. Upon entering, take 10 steps to the left and meet the sculptor (self-portrait on the highest arch).

Before moving on, circle around to the river side of the church. Up eight steps, find the **bronze door** depicting scenes from the life of Zwingli.

• *Head down to the bridge and walk halfway across the river. Pause in the middle of the bridge for a...*

⑫ River View

This spot—flanked by Zürich's two most important churches—is one of the most scenic places in town.

Look back toward the Grossmünster. The building sticking out into the river on your right is the **Wasserkirche** (Water

Church). According to the city's foundational legend, two early Christians (Felix and Regula) were beheaded by Roman authorities on this spot in the third century. Miraculously, they picked up their heads, walked 40 paces up the hill, and lay back down again on the site of today's Grossmünster. (Later, they were joined by a third headless body—so you'll see the "three headless bodies" motif around the city.) Flash forward 600 years: It's said that Charlemagne was out hunting when he discovered the bodies, and decided that this would be the optimal site of the city's main church. The only statue that adorns the church—high up on the side of the steeple facing this bridge—shows Charlemagne, with his golden crown.

Looking left along the river, you see stately old houses. Many of these are **guildhouses** *(Zunfthaus)*. Merchant towns like Zürich were dominated by guilds—groups of like-minded, wealthy burghers, often of the same profession, who combined to have serious clout. In fact, guilds dominated the city's civic life; the city is sometimes called *Bürgertum* (town of burghers) or *Zunftstadt* (guild city). As we stand between two giant churches, notice that both are called Münster—not "cathedral." Zürich didn't want a cathedral—or the bishop who'd come along with it and constantly boss around the burghers.

Guilds have loomed so large in the story of Zürich, in fact, that they still survive today, as modern-day social institutions (similar to a Rotary or Elks club). There are about a dozen historical guilds, and about a dozen modern ones—but none of them admit women. Each *Zunft* (guild) meets in its own *Zunfthaus*, which have both meeting rooms and restaurants or reception halls that are open to the public. You can see three guildhouses along the water: Below and to the left of the Grossmünster (with the red turret) is the Zunfthaus zur Zimmerleuten (for carpenters); next door is the Haus zum Rüden ("House of the Hound," for an association of noblemen); and across the river is the big, pink fishermen's guild (now the swanky Hotel Storchen).

• *Continue the rest of the way over the river to the tall-steepled church with "1732" on the tower.*

⓭ Fraumünster

This ▲▲ church was founded along with a convent in 853, when Zürich was little more than a village. The current building, which

sits on the same footprint as its predecessor, dates from 1250. With the Reformation of Zwingli, the church was taken by the Zürich town council in 1524 and—you know the drill—gutted to fit Zwingli's taste. Today, the Fraumünster's claim to fame is a collection of 30-foot-tall stained-glass windows by Marc Chagall (1887-1985), the Russian-born French artist. The included audioguide also explains the rest of the church—including the historic crypt with fine and well-described artifacts (stairs from near the altar).

Cost and Hours: 5 CHF, includes excellent audioguide or a brochure; Mon-Sat 10:00-18:00, Sun from 12:00, Nov-Feb until 17:00; occasional evening concerts, www.fraumuenster.ch.

Background: In 1967, Zürich's art museum hosted a Chagall retrospective. It so impressed the Fraumünster's pastor that he offered the world-famous artist a commission. To his surprise, the 80-year-old Chagall accepted. He designed the windows to stand in the church's spacious choir zone behind the altar—a space where he intuitively felt his unique mix of religious themes could flourish.

For the next three years, Chagall threw his heart and soul into the project, making the sketches at his home on the French Riviera, then working in close collaboration with a glassmaking factory in Reims, France. After the colored panes were made, he outlined the figures in black, which were then baked into the glass. Chagall spent weeks in Zürich overseeing the installation, completed in 1970.

Chagall's inimitable painting style—deep colors, simple figures, and shard-like Cubism—is perfectly suited to the medium of stained glass. Blending Jewish and Christian traditions, he created a work that can make people of many faiths comfortable.

Visiting the Church: Grab a seat in the front of the church with the five Chagall windows towering above you and enjoy the entire audioguide description (or follow this explanation).

The five windows depict Bible scenes, culminating in the central image of the crucified Christ. From left to right, they are:

The Prophets (red): The prophet Elisha (bottom) looks up to watch a horse-drawn chariot carry his mentor Elijah off to heaven. Farther up, Jeremiah (blue in color and mood) puts his hand to his head and ponders the destruction of wicked Jerusalem. Up in heaven (top), a multicolored, multifaceted God spins out his creation, sending fiery beams down to inspire his prophets on earth. This window is artificially lit, as it's built into an interior wall.

Jacob (blue—Chagall's favorite color): Jacob (bottom, riding a skateboard amid the deep blue) dreams of a ladder that snakes up to heaven, with red-tinged angels ascending and descending, symbolizing the connection between God above and Jacob's descendants (the Children of Israel) below.

Christ (green): The middle, and biggest, window depicts the central figure in God's plan of salvation—Jesus Christ, who, as the Messiah, fulfills the promises of the Old Testament prophets. Mother Mary suckles Baby Jesus (bottom) amid the leafy family tree of Jesus' Old Testament roots. The central area is an indistinct jumble of events from Christ's life, leading up to his Crucifixion. The life-size ascendant Christ is crucified in a traditional medieval pose, but he's surrounded by a circle that seems to be bearing him, resurrected, to heaven. Chagall signed and dated the work (1970).

Zion (yellow): King David (bottom right) strums his harp and sings a psalm, while behind him stands his mistress Bathsheba, who gave birth to Solomon, the builder of Jerusalem's temple. At the end of history, an angel (top) blows a ram's horn, announcing the establishment of a glorious New Jerusalem, which descends (center), featuring rust-colored, yellow, and green walls, domes, and towers.

The Law (blue): At the very top, Moses—with horns of light and the Ten Commandments—looks sternly down on law-breaking warriors on horseback wreaking havoc. At the bottom, an angel (in red) embraces the prophet Isaiah (very bottom) and inspires him to foretell the coming of the Messiah (in red, above the angel).

Everyone comes away with a different interpretation of this complex work, which combines images from throughout the Bible. Some feel that the tall, skinny windows seem to emphasize the vertical connection between heaven above and earth below, both bathed in the same colored light. Some think Chagall used colors symbolically: Blue and green represent the earth; red and yellow, heavenly radiance. But all recognize that the jumble of images—evoking the complexity of God's universe—reaches its Point Omega in the central window, celebrating the idea of salvation through Christ's Crucifixion.

• *Head into the square alongside the church. This is the...*

⓮ Münsterhof

This original courtyard of a fortified convent was made into a traf-

Switzerland's Zwingli Reformation

Today's Evangelical Reformed Church of Switzerland was founded by Huldrych Zwingli (1484-1531), who preached in Zürich from 1519 through 1531. A follower of the humanist philosopher Erasmus of Rotterdam, Zwingli believed that the Holy Scriptures should be preached freely—in the people's language, rather than in Latin. In 1522, most of German-speaking Switzerland embraced Zwingli's ideas...and that required leaving the Roman Catholic Church.

In 1517, when Zwingli was 33, German church reformer Martin Luther posted his revolutionary *95 Theses* (which questioned the practice of selling forgiveness, salvation, church offices, and so on). Within two years, sellers of indulgences were refused entry to Zürich. As the Reformation swept Switzerland, things heated up. In 1523, rioters were storming churches, and authorities called for an orderly removal of all images in Zürich houses of worship (except stained-glass windows, which were destroyed).

The new, reformed Swiss church let priests marry. (Zwingli, like Luther, promptly took advantage of this freedom.) Fancy Masses were replaced by simple services. At Zürich's main church, the Grossmünster, preachers studied Latin, Greek, and Hebrew in order to translate the Bible into the people's German. In 1531, the Zwingli Bible, a complete translation into Swiss German, was published. It's still used today (like the King James Bible is in English); you can see one here in the National Museum Zürich.

Zwingli gave the Swiss church an unusual austerity: no altar, no pictures, and for a while, not even any music. Church services focused on preaching. Holy Communion was celebrated only on holidays. This puritanical simplicity permeated Swiss society in general. Zwingli was no fan of the "separation of church and state." Pushing for a theocracy, he established an ironclad city

fic-free public space in 2016. Each spring, on the Monday after the equinox, people gather here to celebrate Sächsilüüte—the end of winter. In the middle of the square stands a six-story-tall pyre topped with a giant snowman figure (called the Böögg). The pyre is lit with great ceremony and burns its way up to the snowman, whose head is loaded with fireworks. The bigger the explosion, the better the spring will be.

This square is also home to more of Zürich's surviving **guilds.** At the bottom (river end) of the square is the elegant Zunfthaus zur Meisen, historically the guild for innkeepers, painters, and saddle

law: The government's duty was to oversee public worship, and only preaching that was true to the Bible was to be tolerated.

But Zwingli's reforms were by no means universally supported. The Reformation was a messy process. The Protestant movement split over the proper role of baptism. Luther and Zwingli split over the Eucharist (is Christ's body literally *in* the bread, or there only in a spiritual sense?). And, as old-school Catholics predicted, putting the Bible into the hands of regular people brought chaos—enabling every Tom, Dick, and Hans to "carve his own path to hell." Switzerland became embroiled in a religious civil war, as Protestant cantons fought Catholic ones. In 1531, while fighting as a "citizen soldier," Zwingli was killed in battle. His friend and partner Heinrich Bullinger succeeded him as the leader of German-speaking Swiss Protestantism.

Bullinger collaborated with John Calvin as Swiss Protestantism matured. The Protestant focus on preaching promoted the translation and interpretation of the Bible. Everyone was reading the Bible directly, which promoted literacy. The Reformation provided a basis for the autonomous community spirit, strong work ethic, and high literacy of a prosperous Switzerland for the future. The Swiss church became a place where equals would meet and worship God. As in other Protestant countries, Zwingli's heritage included transferring the notion of social charity from a church phenomenon to the responsibility of any self-respecting modern state. The foundations of Swiss democracy and its present social policies are rooted in Zwingli's teaching. And these Swiss reformers planted the seeds of what became the Presbyterian Church in the United States.

makers. Near the top of the square, behind the fountain, is the Zunfthaus zur Waag—once the wool and linen weavers' guild.

Before moving on, consider a little detour to see some hidden illustrations of Zürich's legendary past: Circle around to face the "front door" of the Fraumünster, then duck through the gate on its right side, into the **Kreuzgang Fraumünster** (free, closed Sun). This passage, once a nunnery, is now part of the city administration building. The inside is painted with vivid, dreamy depictions of important local legends. In one, a magical, glowing deer shows two nuns the place where they should build what is today the Fraumünster. In the other, you can see those early Christian martyrs who, after being beheaded by Romans, picked up their heads and carried them to what's now the Grossmünster (in this version, they are guided by angels carrying doves).

• *Back out on Münsterhof, follow the small lane on the left side of Zunfthaus zur Waag, passing (or walking through) the recommended*

Zeughauskeller restaurant (500 years ago the city armory, it has a weapons theme for its decoration today—including what they call an "authentic replica" of William Tell's crossbow). As you round the corner, you'll hit busy...

⑮ Paradeplatz

Survey the scene, a triumph of urban planning and people-friendly vision: The train station is a 10-minute walk to your right up Bahnhofstrasse, and the lake is a few minutes to your left, down the classiest stretch of Bahnhofstrasse. On the left is **$$$ Sprüngli,** Zürich's top café for the past century. Its "Luxemburgerli" *macarons*— little cream-filled, one-inch *macaron*-meringue treats—are a local favorite (you can buy just a couple; if you buy 100 grams, you'll get a selection of 12). Sprüngli also sells elegant sandwich lunches, either in its café (upstairs/outside) or to go (perfect for a lakeside snack; open Mon-Fri until 18:30, Sat until 17:30, closed Sun).

Across the square is Credit Suisse, with a luxurious ground floor full of fancy shops. If you like, detour a block back up Bahnhofstrasse to #31 and visit the fine little **Beyer Clock and Watch Museum,** in the basement of the elegant Beyer watch shop (10 CHF, Zürich Card valid but not Swiss Travel Pass; Mon-Fri 14:00-18:00, closed Sat-Sun; www.beyer-ch.com).

• *From here, you've seen the heart of Zürich; if time is short, simply hop a tram back to the station.*

But if time allows and you'd like a peek at the city's lake—and the chance to go on a lake cruise—you can head several minutes farther down Bahnhofstrasse. From where you entered the square, turn left and follow Bahnhofstrasse past a few more elegant shops and mighty banks to the boats and riverside terrace at Bürkliplatz. We'll finish this walk at...

⑯ Lake Zürich (Zürichsee)

Lake Zürich is 17 miles long, 2.5 miles wide, and—because it's relatively shallow—warm enough for swimming in the summer. From here, you can enjoy the lakeside promenade (a fine strolling path stretching 3

miles in either direction; left is sunnier and more interesting) or a short cruise. To go back to the station, catch tram #11 (from the inland side, across the street) or the Limmat riverboat. Both cruise and riverboat options are described later, under "Cruises on Limmat River and Lake Zürich."

Sights in Zürich

▲▲National Museum Zürich (Landesmuseum)

By the late 19th century, it was clear that the world was changing, and the Swiss wanted to protect their unique heritage. A national competition was held, Zürich won, and it created the country's national museum. Located in a Neo-Gothic castle dating from 1898—with a striking modern wing added in 2016—this massive museum provides an engaging, in-depth exploration of Swiss history and identity.

If Zürich is your first stop in Switzerland, visiting here for a primer on all things Swiss can help put the rest of your trip in context. Even if you're not staying the night in Zürich, the museum (just across the street from the train station) can be a worthwhile rainy-day excursion from other cities (especially if you have a train pass) or a quick stop while passing through. A stairway from the train station's underground hall leads conveniently up to the museum (look for *Landesmuseum* signs).

Cost and Hours: 10 CHF, covered by Swiss Travel Pass and Zürich Card; Tue-Sun 10:00-17:00, Thu until 19:00, closed Mon; audioguide-5 CHF (or download the free app), guided tours in English available—check website for schedule, mandatory bag check, quality café; Museumstrasse 2, +41 44 218 6511, www.landesmuseum.ch.

Visiting the Museum: The museum is well designed and well described in English. Be prepared to walk up and down stairs, and down long hallways, to traverse the sprawling, mazelike layout. Ask for and review the floor plan before you get going. I've described the permanent exhibits below, but there are good temporary exhibits, too. With limited time, prioritize the History of Switzerland exhibit: To reach it, follow signs left from the ticket desk—you'll go upstairs, then back down.

History of Switzerland: The main exhibit tells the story of this unique land, using ample artifacts to illustrate each theme. The story begins in the **14th century,** as the cantons that would eventually become Switzerland started to unify. This is the time of William Tell and the Rütli Oath, in which the three founding cantons threw off the shackles of the aristocracy to assert self-rule. The bristling column of pikes and halberds symbolizes this militaristic age.

The exhibit proceeds through the **16th century,** when the Reformation split Switzerland—spiritually and ideologically—right down the middle. See Zwingli's Bible translation into German (from 1531, designed to put the Word of God into the hands of the people), and study the giant triptych painting of saints with old Zürich as a backdrop—completed in 1502, removed from display by Reformation iconoclasts in 1524.

Meanwhile, Switzerland became famous for exporting its men as mercenaries in foreign wars (a tradition that continues with today's Swiss Guard at the Vatican). Find the tapestry of Swiss officials renewing their alliance with Louis XIV (inside Notre-Dame) to provide mercenaries. Compare the simply dressed, unpretentious Swiss on the left with the lavish court of the Sun King on the right. Cities also flourished during this age; see the huge cabinet from 1657, displaying the many guilds of Zürich (which survive today).

The **18th century** brought the Enlightenment, including the scientific study of the Alps, the development of alpine infrastructure, and a Romantic appreciation of the beauty of nature, as preached by French-Swiss philosopher Jean-Jacques Rousseau, who presented an idealized image of Switzerland.

In the **19th century,** the federal state of Switzerland was born (1848) with Bern as its seat of government (see model of the parliament). The 1829 painting of 135 Swiss founding fathers includes politicians, scholars, scientists, and Reformers (all identified by the touchscreen). Nationhood came with a single currency (see some of the 800 different coins, issued by 79 authorities, that were phased out in 1850). It also came with neutrality, which both defines Swiss identity and remains one of this country's most controversial features.

This age also saw the rise of tourism, including the first cogwheel train to Rigi (1871—it still runs today) and the Gotthard Tunnel connecting Swiss cities to Italy (1882). See the vintage travel posters and the official rail map from that era. But the mid-1800s were also difficult times for the poor, with many emigrating to find a better life in the New World. The painting *Pain of Parting* shows grief-stricken parents collapsing on the train platform after saying goodbye to their adult children forever.

The **20th century** was a tough time to be neutral, but Switzerland doubled down on not taking sides. See the machine gun and cannon that defended the Gotthard Pass from potential invasion (had it happened, Swiss leadership planned to abandon its cities and hole up in the rugged alpine interior, creating a fortified "Swiss National Redoubt"). To preserve its neutrality, Switzerland turned each of its citizens into a soldier, with standard-issue gear to protect against "NBC" (nuclear, biological, and chemical weapons). Meanwhile, to differentiate themselves from the Nazis ideologically, the

Swiss created the Pro Helvetia movement (for "spiritual national defense"). At the Landi national exhibition on Lake Zürich in 1939, 10 million Swiss celebrated their folk culture and dialects; look for the flags from that event.

Switzerland did take in refugees, though critics say hardly enough: 26,000 in World War I, and 51,000—including 21,000 Jews—in World War II. The exhibit examines this issue with candor; contrast the postcard of Lady Switzerland comforting war refugees with illustrations of desperate refugees waiting at the border. The bullet-holed sign from the Swiss embassy in Budapest recalls how the Swiss diplomat Carl Lutz heroically saved some 62,000 Jews there—while others, including Switzerland's ambassador to Germany, ignored the crisis (find the tattered Swiss flag from the Berlin embassy).

The **postwar era** kicked off with an economic boom, but it also saw Switzerland grapple with social challenges, including workers' rights; the global student movement of 1968; and—in 1971—the vote that finally guaranteed Swiss women the right to vote, which passed by a two-thirds majority. The exhibit ends with a look at the rise of consumer culture and 21st-century challenges, including climate change, migration, and sovereignty in the age of the EU.

While that's the most essential exhibit for the foreign visitor, there are other permanent exhibits worth checking out:

Simply Zürich: This second-floor exhibit displays objects that tell stories about Switzerland's largest city (each one explained by touchscreens), plus a giant sculpture by the local art collective Mickry 3.

Ideas of Switzerland: This small but thought-provoking exhibit explores what it means to be Swiss (enter from the opposite side of the ticket desk, near the café). Virtual "books" introduce you to four prominent Swiss figures: theologian John Calvin, historian Petermann Etterlin, philosopher Jean-Jacques Rousseau, and humanitarian Henry Dunant, who co-founded the Red Cross. Touchscreens next to a giant granite relief map of the Swiss Alps offer an enhanced-reality view of the country's highlands. On the wall is a beautiful 19th-century map of Switzerland; aim the provided binoculars at it to superimpose important statistics.

Archaeology in Switzerland: Here you'll see items found in prehistoric graves, a stela (carved pillar) showing a man from about 3000-2500 BC, an exquisite golden dish made as a gift for the gods (from around 1100 BC), and tools made from stone, bronze, and iron. Meet the Celts (Helvetii—see their large golden rings from around 390 BC, thought to help protect travelers), who were Romanized beginning around the second century BC. Most of the objects are in large cases on the wall; move the giant sliding screen into position over each item to learn more.

The Collection: This large wing shows off over 7,000 pieces of Swiss art and crafts spanning centuries.

Exhibition for Families: This is a partially hands-on kids' zone, optimistically designed to keep small children occupied.

Shop: Before leaving, check out the shop near the ticket desk, which has one of the city's best selections of quality Swiss souvenirs that go beyond the clichés (and, also, some clichés).

▲Kunsthaus Zürich

It's worth the tram/bus ride (or 10-minute stroll up from the heart of Niederdorf) to see Switzerland's top collection of fine art. The museum features a combination of quality works by European masters, mixed in with fine examples by Swiss artists (whom I've highlighted here). For art lovers, it's worth ▲▲. The curator embraces change, so the collection gets shuffled around frequently—and there are often high-quality special exhibits, too. Pick up a map as you enter and go with the flow.

Cost and Hours: 16 CHF, more for special exhibits, includes audioguide, free on Wed, not covered by Swiss Travel Pass; open Tue-Sun 10:00-18:00, Wed-Thu until 20:00, closed Mon; mandatory bag check, café; at Heimplatz 1—take tram #3, #5, #8, or #9, or bus #31 to Kunsthaus stop; +41 44 253 8484, www.kunsthaus.ch.

Visiting the Museum: The collection runs the gamut, from Old Masters (Guardi, Tiepolo, Rembrandt, Brueghel, Hals) to present-day greats.

In the 18th-and-19th-century section, look for works by three Swiss painters. **Johann Heinrich Füssli**—a.k.a. Henry Fuseli (1741-1825)—was born in Zürich but spent most of his career in London. Füssli's works exhibit a marked *chiaroscuro* technique (with a strong contrast between light and dark); the supernatural was a favorite theme of his. **Arnold Böcklin** (1827-1901), from Basel, was a Symbolist who painted fantastical landscapes and evocative creatures. *The War* (1896) began as four horsemen of the apocalypse—but then Böcklin went in a different direction, winding up with three grotesque horseback figures. **Ferdinand Hodler** (1853-1918) was also quite mystical, working with bright, cheery colors, symbolic figures, and shimmering landscapes. *The Day* (1904-1906) depicts five young women in a semicircle, who embody the way that light changes over the course of a day.

The excellent 20th-century collection includes works by Picasso, Kokoschka, Ernst, Beckmann, Corinth, Magritte, Miró, Degas, Renoir, Monet, and Chagall (whose stained-glass windows adorn the Fraumünster). The museum owns the best collection of **Edvard Munch** works outside of Norway; these typically share a room with works by **Giovanni Segantini** (1858-1899). While

Italian-born and trained in Milan, Segantini later moved to the Graubünden and Engadine regions of Switzerland, where he did his best work. His gorgeous, grand-scale *Alpine Pasture* (1893-1894) shows off Segantini's mastery of his late-Impressionist style, where collages of dots and streaks form a vivid, beautiful scene of pastoral Swiss countryside.

There's usually a large exhibition of hauntingly stretched-out sculptures by **Alberto Giacometti** (1901-1966)—one of Switzerland's best-known artists beyond his homeland. Giacometti built on the foundation of Rodin but took things in a Surrealist direction, abstracting and elongating human figures until they were barely recognizable. Over time, Giacometti's style evolved—going through phases with sculptures just a few inches tall to figures several feet tall. Elsewhere, you'll also see paintings by Alberto's father, **Giovanni Giacometti** (1868-1933). Giovanni was the cousin of Augusto Giacometti, whose work we've already seen on the town walk, in the entrance hall of the police station and in the *Grossmünster*. And, of course, you'll see a few works by the great Swiss painter **Paul Klee** (1879-1940), with his exuberant, colorful, abstract, almost childlike compositions. The collection carries through to the present day, with pieces by Warhol, Lichtenstein, Rothko, Merz, Twombly, Beuys, Bacon, and Baselitz.

Cruises on Limmat River and Lake Zürich

A boat ride down the Limmat River or on Lake Zürich can be a nice, lazy contrast to your busy, urban visit. Small riverboat-buses take commuters and joy-riding visitors up and down the river and to points nearby on the lake. Big, romantic ships take tourists on longer rides around Lake Zürich. All boats are run by ZSG and do not include commentary (+41 44 487 1333, www.zsg.ch). The first two options are fully covered by the Swiss Travel Pass, Zürich Card, or 24-hour transit pass (also covered by the Global Pass, but uses a flexi day—so do it the day you arrive or depart).

Riverboat-Buses: These low-to-the-water boats (designed to squeeze under bridges) start where the National Museum Zürich and Platzspitz Park meet on the banks of the Limmat River. The boats do a 55-minute loop, making several stops along the river en route to Bürkliplatz (pier #6, where lake cruises begin), and then a quick circle around the lake before returning to their starting point. You can either do the full circuit, or hop on and off as you like. These boats can be handy for connecting the museum and the lake (4.40 CHF/ride—up to the entire loop, departs from museum 2/hour daily May-Sept 10:50-19:50, April and Oct until 17:20, no boats in winter).

Big Lake-Only Excursion Boats: These start at Bürkliplatz and go farther down the lake. The basic 1.5-hour "short lake cruise" goes as far as Erlenbach, a quarter of the way down the lake (8.80 CHF; 2/hour daily May-Sept 10:00-20:00, April and Oct until 19:00, fewer off-season; buy tickets near pier #3, boats depart from piers #1-6). They also offer longer trips and jazz and dinner cruises (not covered by the Zürich Card or transit passes). With plenty of time, you could even ride the boat all the way to Rapperswil (at the far end of Lake Zürich), enjoy that town for lunch, and then catch the train back to Zürich.

Zürich West (Züri Wescht)

This trendy, up-and-coming former industrial zone is just a few minutes' tram ride behind the train station. Though not as funky or interesting as similar zones in other European cities, it's worth a wander if you're curious to see a contemporary side of this otherwise staid city. Note that many shops here are closed Sundays.

From the train station area, ride tram #4, #13, or #17 to the Löwenbräu stop. Here the arches of two old railway viaducts have been creatively converted into commercial space. The first few arches house **Markthalle Viadukt,** a covered market with cheesemongers, greengrocers, microbrew and wine vendors, and a few eateries, including bakeries with sandwiches and the good **$$ Restaurant Markthalle,** which serves an international menu (check out the selection of vendors at www.im-viadukt.ch). Exit the market hall at the far end, and follow the **viaduct** past the smokestack, exploring as you go the many shops tucked under the 52 arches (selling clothing, housewares, home decor, and more food). At arch #1 (the viaduct's end), turn right and head toward the city's only skyscraper.

Your next stop is the big tower of stacked shipping containers—the flagship store for **Freitag,** which started in Zürich manufacturing bags from recycled materials. Just beyond is **Frau Gerolds Garten,** a mixture of small shops up front and a decidedly alternative beer garden in back. The place has a funky, mismatched-furniture-under-twinkle-lights vibe, but it's also modern and sophisticated—as chic as it is shabby (Mon-Sat 11:00-24:00, Sun 12:00-22:00, shorter hours in winter, Geroldstrasse 23, www.fraugerold.ch).

From Frau Gerolds Garten, continue a few steps toward the skyscraper, then head up the ramp to the overpass, where tram #8 or bus #37 will take you two stops to **Escher-Wyss-Platz.** On the way, you'll pass the Schiffbau theater, occupying a former shipbuilding factory (which is what its name means). At Escher-Wyss-Platz, descend to ground level and look for the stop for trams #4, #13, and #17, which bring you back to the train station along Limmatstrasse.

Museum Rietberg

Filling historic villas set in a beautiful park west of the lake, this museum houses art from Asia, Africa, the Americas, and the South Pacific.

Cost and Hours: 18 CHF, covered by Swiss Travel Pass, discount with Zürich Card; Tue-Sun 10:00-17:00, Wed until 20:00, closed Mon; tram #7 from station (direction: Wollishofen) to Museum Rietberg stop, Gablerstrasse 15, +41 44 415 3131, www.rietberg.ch.

Zürich Zoo

With 360 species, an impressive Madagascar rainforest hall, and a huge indoor exhibit, the city's zoo is a fun place to see locals at play. It's located within a large green space to the east of the center.

Cost and Hours: 29 CHF, slightly cheaper online; daily 9:00-18:00, Nov-Feb until 17:00; tram #6 from Bahnhofstrasse in front of the station (direction: Zoo), ride to last stop, Zürichbergstrasse 221, +41 44 254 2500, www.zoo.ch.

Nearby: James Joyce fans can find the grave of the Irish author (adorned with a life-size statue) in the parklike Friedhof Fluntern cemetery, next to the zoo.

Lindt Home of Chocolate

This museum in the upscale suburb of Kilchberg pays for itself if you think of the visit as a 15-CHF chocolate feast. The sampling stations are the highlight: At the first you taste liquified dark, milk, and white chocolate; at the second, dispensers drop pieces of flavored chocolate into your outstretched hand and invite you to guess the ingredients; at the third, you're welcome to as many Lindor filled chocolate spheres as you can eat. In between, the museum provides an education in chocolate. Exhibits cover cocoa bean harvesting and the history of chocolate-making in Switzerland; there's a model chocolate production line, as well as an array of

games and activities and a room downstairs showing promotional films. A 30-foot-high chocolate fountain towers over visitors in the main hall.

The Lindt & Sprüngli factory surrounds the museum. The Sprüngli family started producing chocolate in Zürich in the 1830s, and in 1899 they bought out the Lindt company (which started in Bern).

Cost and Hours: 15 CHF, Swiss Travel Pass not valid; chocolate-making classes from 28 CHF, reservations essential for classes and recommended for regular entry; daily 10:00-18:00; café, mandatory bag check; Schokoladenplatz 1 in Kilchberg, +41 44 716 2000, www.lindt-home-of-chocolate.ch.

Getting There: Kilchberg is set along the southwest lakeshore, a 10-minute trip from downtown on the S8 or S24 suburban train (4/hour, 13.60 CHF three-zone *Tageskarte* covers round-trip and 24 hours of free transport in Zürich); from Kilchberg station, it's a flat 10-minute walk to the museum (follow *Lindt Home of Chocolate* signs).

Uetliberg

For an interesting 1.5-hour excursion high above the city and lake, take the small red/orange S10 excursion train that climbs from the main train station to this little mountain peak (17.60 CHF four-zone *Tageskarte* covers your round-trip plus 24 hours of free transport around town, also covered by Zürich Card; 2-3/hour, runs 6:30-24:00, 25 minutes, www.zvv.ch). From the Uetliberg station, it's a moderately steep, 10-minute climb up a paved pedestrian road to a hotel and a tall observation tower overlooking the city. The view is particularly striking at sunset.

Sleeping in Zürich

High season in Zürich is May, June, September, and October. In this business-oriented city, rooms tend to be cheaper on weekends and pricier during festivals and conventions (September can be particularly busy). Some hotels let you save a little on the rate by skipping breakfast—ask.

Most of my listings are across the river from the train station (about a 10- to 15-minute walk)—ideal for those passing through or leaving on an early-morning train or plane. To avoid nighttime noise, ask for a room on a high floor.

ACROSS FROM THE TRAIN STATION

With this efficient neighborhood as your home base, you're a quick stroll away from the train station, National Museum Zürich, riverboat-bus dock, a huge underground mall of services and shops (under the station), and the Niederdorf restaurant and nightlife zone. From the station, exit through the front doors of the great hall and cross the river.

$$$ Hotel Bristol, well-run by Martin Hämmerli and his staff, has 56 rooms that are handy to the train station. Though not fancy, it's very comfortable. Martin loves my readers and gives a 12 percent discount when you book direct by email (RS%, family rooms, air-con, elevator, pay laundry, Stampfenbachstrasse 34, +41 44 258 4444, www.hotelbristol.ch, info@hotelbristol.ch).

$$ Hotel Arlette is stuck in a time warp, with 28 no-frills rooms. The central location and affordable rates help make up for the often gruff reception staff (air-con, elevator, Stampfenbachstrasse 26, +41 44 252 0032, www.hotelarlette.ch, hotel@hotelarlette.ch, Schlotter family).

NIEDERDORF DISTRICT

The atmospheric, cobblestoned old town of Zürich is just a few minutes farther from the station than the previous listings. During the day, it's busy with shoppers and workers on lunch breaks; at night, restaurants and clubs keep the pedestrian streets vibrant (and, in some places, noisy). From the train station, cross the Bahnhofbrücke bridge (to your right as you leave the main hall), go through the square called Central, and head to the right along Niederdorfstrasse (or, with wheeled luggage, stay along the river to avoid cobblestones). You can also take tram #4 two stops to Rudolf-Brun-Brücke.

$$$$ Marktgasse Hotel impresses well-heeled urbanites. Located at the quiet end of Niederdorf, its 39 rooms feel sophisticated, with hip, minimalist decor. The first-floor lounge/reception area, with free coffee and big windows, is a tempting place to hang out (breakfast extra, air-con, elevator, Marktgasse 17, +41 44 266 1010, www.marktgassehotel.ch, info@marktgassehotel.ch).

$$$ Hotel Adler, nestled in the heart of the Niederdorf, is the place to stay if you don't want to risk forgetting that you're in Switzerland. It has a popular Swiss restaurant on the ground floor, a cow peeking out over the balcony, and 52 pleasantly cheesy rooms with woody, half-timbered accents (family rooms, air-con, elevator, Rosengasse 10—at Hirschenplatz, +41 44 266 9696, www.hotel-adler.ch, info@marktgassehotel.ch).

$$$ Hotel Alexander is a 41-room business-class hotel in a busy central location. It's right at the edge of a somewhat seedier side of Niederdorf, but it feels solid, well-designed, and well-run, and the serious windows help keep out street noise—though if quiet is a priority, ask for a back room (RS%, family rooms, air-con, elevator, free mobile Wi-Fi boxes, Niederdorfstrasse 40, +41 44 251 8203, www.hotel-alexander.ch, info@hotel-alexander.ch). They also run the **$$ Alexander Guest House,** a block away at Zähringerstrasse 16, housing 20 twin-bedded rooms with modern bathrooms and cheaper prices (breakfast extra, fans, elevator, check in at Hotel Alexander, www.alexander-guesthouse.ch).

$$$ Swiss Chocolate Hotel Zürich occupies a renovated trapezoid-shaped building around the corner from Central square, beneath the Polybahn funicular. The 57 rooms are dark but com-

ZÜRICH

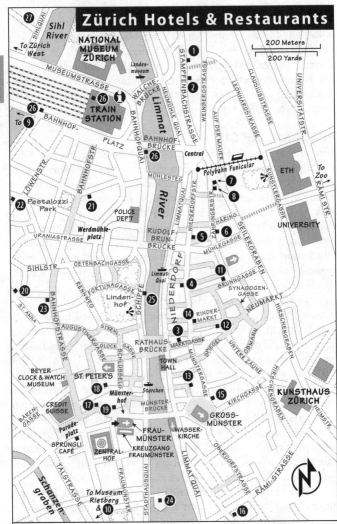

Zürich Hotels & Restaurants

Accommodations
1. Hotel Bristol
2. Hotel Arlette
3. Marktgasse Hotel
4. Hotel Adler
5. Hotel Alexander
6. Alexander Guest House & Raclette Stube
7. Swiss Chocolate Hotel Zürich
8. Hotel Marta
9. To EasyHotel Zürich City Centre
10. To Youth Hostel

Eateries & Other
11. Café Zähringer
12. Bauernschänke
13. Restaurant Mère Catherine
14. Raclette Factory
15. Hasta Ice Cream
16. Sternen Grill
17. Zeughauskeller
18. Restaurant zum Kropf
19. Restaurant Zunfthaus zur Waag
20. Hiltl Vegetarian Rest.
21. Hiltl Dachterrasse
22. Migros Restaurant
23. Co-op Restaurant
24. Rest. Bauschänzli
25. Rest. Schipfe 16
26. Supermarket (3)
27. Bus Tours

fortable, with triple-paned windows that keep out most of the street noise (air-con, elevator, Zähringerstrasse 46, +41 44 267 2670, www.byfassbind.com, scz@byf.ch).

$$ Hotel Marta, on a side street near Central square, is run by a nonprofit foundation that assists women with disabilities in finding employment. The 39 spare yet modern rooms vary in size and quietness (street-facing rooms can be noisy). The hotel's website describes them with unusual honesty and lets you choose (family room, fans, elevator, Zähringerstrasse 36, +41 44 269 9595, www. hotelmarta.ch, info@hotelmarta.ch).

FARTHER FROM THE CENTER

You can sleep a little more cheaply if you're willing to compromise a bit on rooms and location.

$ EasyHotel Zürich City Centre is a decent value in this pricey town, with 33 small, modern rooms located away from all the sights, a 10-minute walk from the station in an area known for its bar scene. It has four floors but no elevator (except for a luggage dumbwaiter); no common space aside from the basement computer room; most bathrooms are teeny, modular installations with opaque glass; and rooms are only cleaned after four nights (no breakfast, Zwinglistrasse 14, +41 43 322 0551, www.easyhotel. com). From the station: Walk or take bus #31 (direction: Schlieren Zentrum) to Kanonengasse stop, walk a block down Kanonengasse with back to train station, then right on Zwinglistrasse to #14.

¢ Zürich Youth Hostel is big, modern, and well-equipped with lots of services in a pleasant neighborhood near the lake that's easy to reach from the station. Its rooms with private bath compete favorably with hotels (fair-trade breakfast, lunch, dinner, and packed lunches available, elevator, no curfew, pay parking, Mutschellenstrasse 114, +41 43 399 7800, www.youthhostel.ch/ zuerich, zuerich@youthhostel.ch). From the station, take tram #7 (direction: Wollishofen) to Morgental, then walk back 5 minutes along Mutschellenstrasse.

Eating in Zürich

While famously expensive and formal, Zürich has a good variety of places to eat memorably. My recommendations include romantic Swiss places (both traditional and modern), cheesy raclette bars, beer gardens, and quality vegetarian choices. If you're up for a splurge, some of Zürich's venerable guildhouses are now convivial traditional restaurants. At finer places, reservations are wise.

Zürich's most typical dish is *Kalbsgeschnetzeltes* (or *Zürcher Geschnetzeltes*)—diced veal with mushrooms in cream sauce, often served with *Rösti*. *Zürcher Eintopf* is a stew of pork, vegetables, and white wine that's satisfying in the winter. You'll also see quite a few traditional country Swiss restaurants featuring raclette and fondue. These are designed entirely for tourists; when the Swiss want these foods, they have them at home. Also, much as the Swiss love their cheese, they're almost comically sensitive about it stinking up their clothing (they don't like the smell unless they're actually eating it). It seems that restaurants either do cheese or don't do cheese.

NIEDERDORF DISTRICT

Niederdorf is Zürich's dining district, and the traffic-free Niederdorfstrasse is its restaurant row. The countless eateries lining this main drag don't offer the best values, though the people-watching is hard to beat. Just a block or two away, you'll feel like you're far from the tourist crush and rubbing elbows with a smarter clientele.

$$ Café Zähringer is an artsy, bohemian co-op serving reasonably priced, healthy food. Linger in the stay-awhile interior, or enjoy the leafy seating with the older hippies out on the square (daily special served all day, always good veggie and vegan plates, breakfasts, organic produce, salads, also meat dishes and good coffee; open Tue-Sat 10:00-24:00, Sun until 22:00, closed Mon; food served 11:30-14:00 & 17:30-22:00; facing the tall steeple at Zähringerplatz 11, +41 44 252 0500, www.zaehringer.ch).

$$$ Bauernschänke (Farmer's Tavern), facing Rindermarkt, is a favorite of upscale local foodies. While the setting is traditional, with inviting wooden tables and paneling, the menu has a modern sensibility. Chef Nenad Mlinarevic won "Swiss Chef of the Year" in 2016 and owns two Michelin stars at another location. When I last stopped by, his menu included a Swiss bento box lunch and spelt risotto with chanterelle mushrooms. Reservations are smart (Mon-Fri 11:30-14:30 & 18:00-24:00, Sat 18:00-24:00, closed Sun, Rindermarkt 24, +41 44 262 4130, www.bauernschaenke.ch).

$$$ Restaurant Mère Catherine is a little oasis of Provençal elegance tucked away in the old town, popular for its south-of-France menu and good wines by the glass. Both the interior and its secluded courtyard are delightful and cozy (Mon-Sat 11:30-15:00 & 17:30-23:00, closed Sun, Nägelihof 3, +41 44 250 5940).

Cheesy Swiss Clichés, Old and New: While having traditional Swiss food in Zürich is like having Southern comfort food in New York City, there are plenty of touristy options to choose from. These two are a good value for getting your melted cheese fix. **$$$ Raclette Stube** is the traditional choice, and the place to go if you want your clothes to smell like good Swiss cheese for days to come. In a bright, modern mountain chalet interior they do only the cheese specialties: all-you-can-eat raclette or fondue (nightly from 18:00, Zähringerstrasse 16, +41 44 251 4130). **$$ Raclette Factory,** the IHOP of melted Swiss cheese, serves your choice on a variety of potatoes with the traditional onion and pickle. You can even do a raclette tasting, combining a selection of different types. Big, open windows ventilate the place, making it less cheesy inside. It's a fun perch overlooking the action in the heart of the Nieder-dorf district (daily 11:30-22:00, Rindermarkt 1, +41 44 261 0410).

Ice Cream: Tucked behind the Grossmünster, **Hasta** is a quality shop with lots of creative flavors (Mon-Sat 12:30-18:30, Sun from 14:00, Zwingliplatz 3).

Popular Sausage Stand: Locally beloved since 1963, **$ Sternen Grill,** about a five-minute walk south of the Grossmünster (at the Bellevue transit hub, by the lake) is Zürich's favorite place to grab a cheap, good-quality sausage (about 10 CHF). They have a few indoor tables and lots of outdoor ones, or you can get your sausage to go and eat along the water. Locals from every walk of life line up here—from scruffy artists to well-dressed theatergoers to formal businesspeople (daily 10:30-23:00, Theaterstrasse 22, +41 43 268 2080).

ON OR JUST OFF BAHNHOFSTRASSE

$$$ Zeughauskeller is a massively popular tourist trap filling an atmospheric 500-year-old armory with medieval battle gear (including a "William Tell crossbow") and the lively energy of happy eaters enjoying typical German-Swiss cuisine. Their fun, accessible menu—designed to stuff out-of-towners—offers big (split-table) portions, traditional dishes (their *Kalbsgeschnetzeltes* is the house special), and lots of soft meats. While it has a few outdoor tables, the interior has all the character and stays cool even when it's hot. On busy evenings, there are lines out the door; you may find yourself sharing a table. Weekday lunch specials go for around 24 CHF (daily 11:30-23:00, plenty of beer and wine, kid-friendly, near Paradeplatz at Bahnhofstrasse 28, +41 44 220 1515, www.zeughauskeller.ch).

$$$ Restaurant zum Kropf serves traditional Zürich cuisine in a grand and dressy beer hall with a sophisticated yet cozy atmosphere (27-CHF weekday lunch specials; Mon-Sat 11:30-14:00 & 18:00-23:00, closed summer weekends and first half of Aug; +41 44 221 1805, next to Zeughauskeller at In Gassen 16, www.zumkropf.ch).

$$$$ Restaurant Zunfthaus zur Waag is your chance to dine inside one of Zürich's historic guildhouses (from 1315), overlooking Münsterhof and the Fraumünster. It's dressy and expensive—a memorable place to enjoy a special occasion (75-CHF fixed-price dinners, Mon-Sat 11:30-14:00 & 18:00-22:00, closed Sun, Münsterhof 8, +41 44 216 9966, www.zunfthaus-zur-waag.ch).

$$ Hiltl Vegetarian Restaurant is a popular treat for vegetarians. In 1898, Ambrosius Hiltl was fighting rheumatoid arthritis.

His doctor said, "No more meat," so Ambrosius established what may have been Europe's first vegetarian restaurant. Over a century later, it's still in the family and a Zürich institution (claiming to be the oldest vegetarian restaurant in the world). The vast and appetizing buffet is the main attraction, with food sold by weight (the tab can add up quickly). There are two seating zones: regular self-service (plain tables) and fancier table service (where you can still visit the buffet, but it costs 20 percent more). The à la carte menu comes with delightful salads, curries, and fancy fruit juices. Hiltl's food is legendary for its freshness and lack of preservatives (Mon-Thu 7:00-22:00, Fri 7:00-23:00, Sat 8:00-23:00, Sun 10:00-22:00, 2 blocks off Bahnhofstrasse where it kinks, Sihlstrasse 30, +41 44 227 7000, www.hiltl.ch).

$$ Hiltl Dachterrasse, closer to Bahnhofstrasse and a bit hipper, is on the third floor of an upscale women's clothing store. The glassy, convivial space, which feels like a chirpy birdhouse, is jammed with locals taking a break from shopping to meet up with friends. It's like the other Hiltl, but all self-service—line up at the counter and pay by weight (Mon-Sat 9:00-23:00, Sun 10:00-22:00, inside the PKZ store at Bahnhofstrasse 88, ride elevator to third floor).

Department Store Cafeterias: As in other Swiss cities, Zürich's Migros and Co-op department stores have top-floor eateries offering solid food at family-friendly prices, plus free tap water. Main dishes are cooked to order, while everything else is served buffet-style, and you can eat well for 20 CHF. The **Migros Restaurant** is a long block from Pestalozzi Park, beyond the Globus building (tap water near the cashiers, Löwenstrasse 31, 4th floor, Mon-Sat 9:00-20:00, closed Sun). The **Co-op Restaurant** is right along Bahnhofstrasse at #57 (tap water by the door, same hours).

Supermarkets and Prepared Foods near the Train Station: A convenient, midsized, long-hours Migros supermarket is in the underground mall at the train station, near the National Museum Zürich entrance/exit (Mon-Fri 6:30-22:00, Sat-Sun from 8:00). Around the corner (also under the station) is the **Migros Takeaway,** which sells big portions of main dishes, packaged to go for about 10 CHF (similar hours). A much larger **Co-op** supermarket is kitty-corner from the station by the Bahnhofbrücke bridge (Mon-Sat 6:00-22:00, closed Sun).

ALONG THE WEST BANK OF THE RIVER

$$ Restaurant Bauschänzli is a leisurely beer garden with a huge buffet line, lots of picnic-table seating, and a fine riverside setting. A block inland from the boat docks at Bürkliplatz, it fills a small island on the river. Its fun-loving and popular self-serve restaurant offers a great beer-garden experience—like a Munich *Biergarten* without the kraut—and it's reasonably priced. Help yourself to the salad bar and the beer and wine from big casks (grab the glass or carafe of your choice). A little vocabulary is helpful: *Bürl* is a roll; *Beilage* is a side dish; *Penache* is a Radler (beer with lemonade). It's open from mid-April through mid-September in good weather only (daily 11:30-23:00, Stadthausquai 2, +41 44 212 4919, www. bauschaenzli.com). Live music sometimes has people up and dancing, giving the place a polka-party feel. For a little peace, grab a table at the quieter tip of the island.

$$ **Restaurant Schipfe 16,** gorgeously and peacefully situated on the river with an old-town view, is part of a city-run organization providing work for hard-to-employ people. It was originally a soup kitchen, but the location was just too charming to stay that way, so it was turned into a restaurant open to everyone. Don't expect polished service; instead, feel good that you're contributing to a worthy cause and enjoying healthy and decent food at a great price. The menu is small—always with a fish, meat, and veggie dish—with lighter dishes available after 14:00. The best seats are right along the river (two-course weekday lunch specials; Mon-Sat 10:00-22:00, closed Sun; Schipfe 16, +41 44 211 2122, www.stadt-zuerich.ch/schipfe, reservations smart).

Zürich Connections

BY TRAIN
From Zürich by Train to: Luzern (2/hour, 40-50 minutes), **Interlaken** (2/hour, 2 hours, transfer in Bern and sometimes Spiez), **Bern** (2/hour, 1 hour), **Murten** (2/hour, 2 hours, change in Bern and sometimes Kerzers), **Appenzell** (2/hour, 2 hours, change in Gossau), **Lausanne** (2/hour, 2 hours, some change in Bern), **Zermatt** (1-2/hour, 3.5 hours, change in Visp and sometimes Bern), **Chur** (2/hour, 1.5 hours), **St. Moritz** (2/hour, 3-3.5 hours, change in Chur or Landquart), **Lugano** (1-2/hour, 2 hours, some change in Arth-Goldau), **Munich** (6/day direct, 3.5 hours—or go by bus from Sihlqual bus terminal), **Frankfurt** (hourly, 4 hours, some change in Basel), **Berlin** (9 hours, 1 change; 1 direct overnight option, 12 hours), **Vienna** (5/day direct, 8 hours; 1 night train, 11 hours), **Paris** (5/day direct, 4 hours, more with transfers). **Train info:** www.rail.ch.

BY PLANE
User-friendly **Zürich Airport** (code: ZRH, www.zürich-airport. com) has three levels and is an eye-opening introduction to Swiss efficiency. On the lower level you'll find a train station (with ticket desk). The main level has a top-end food court, Migros and Co-op supermarkets, fancy souvenir shops, a post office, mobile-phone

shops, banks, ATMs, and lockers. The upper level has departures, TI, lockers, rental car desks, and an observation deck. Check-in areas (numbered 1 through 3) are scattered around the complex; use the screens to identify your zone, then follow signs.

Getting Between the Airport and Downtown: From the station underneath the airport, trains whisk you to **downtown Zürich** in about 10 minutes (6.80 CHF for three-zone single ticket, 13.60 CHF for three-zone 24-hour pass, leaves every 10 minutes 5:00-24:00). You can also ride tram #10 into town (takes much longer—35 minutes; same price as the train). Your ticket into Zürich is also good for one hour on all city public transportation. Either option is much cheaper than the 60-CHF taxi ride.

Sleeping at the Airport: Since most of my recommended accommodations are near the station, and the train connection to the airport is so fast and frequent, there's little reason to sleep at the airport. But if you really want to stay close to the airport, choose a hotel within a few miles that has a free shuttle service, such as the **Ibis Zürich Messe Airport** or the **Mövenpick Hotel** in Glattbrugg.

Zürich Airport Connections: From the airport you can take the train to **Luzern** (2/hour, 70 minutes), **Interlaken** (about 2/hour, 2.5 hours, change in Bern), **Bern** (2/hour, 75 minutes), **Murten** (2/hour, 2 hours, change in Bern and sometimes Kerzers), **Appenzell** (2/hour, 1.5 hours, change in Gossau), **Lausanne** (hourly, 2.5 hours), **Zermatt** (hourly, 3.5 hours, change in Visp), **Chur** (hourly, 1.5 hours, change at Zürich main station), **Lugano** (2/hour, 2.25 hours, change at Zürich main station and sometimes Arth-Goldau), **Munich** (6/day direct, 3.5 hours).

LUZERN & CENTRAL SWITZERLAND

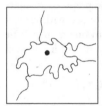

Luzern has long been Switzerland's tourism capital. Situated on the edge of its namesake lake, with a striking alpine panorama as a backdrop, Luzern was a regular stop on the Grand Tour route of Europe during the Romantic era, entertaining visitors such as Mark Twain, Goethe, and Queen Victoria. And with a charming old town, a pair of picture-perfect wooden bridges, a gaggle of fine museums, and a famous weeping lion, there's enough in Luzern to earn it a place on any Swiss itinerary. Beyond the town itself, several spots in the surrounding region (known as Central Switzerland or Zentralschweiz) make for great day trips.

PLANNING YOUR TIME

Luzern is worth at least a full day and two nights. To get the most from a full day in Luzern, begin with the TI's two-hour walking tour, or follow the self-guided walk in this chapter. Then hit the museums that interest you most. In the early evening, take a peaceful boat trip on Lake Luzern, then wander the town's scenic bridges at sunset.

With more time, consider the many fun and well-coordinated excursions within easy reach: boating on Lake Luzern; riding cog railways to mountain summits—the world's steepest (up Mount Pilatus) and Europe's oldest (up Mount Rigi); and exploring Swiss military history at Fortress Fürigen.

Luzern

Luzern (loot-SAIRN, "Lucerne" in English) is Switzerland's touristic darling—an urban hub for visitors seeking easy access to the Alps. Famous for its historic wooden bridges, the city grew up around a monastery. According to legend, it was founded here because an angel shone a heavenly spotlight on the site (the name "Luzern" resembles *lucerna*, Latin for "lamp," but the actual derivation isn't clear).

Today Luzern is a compact, charming, well-organized destination. It boasts an atmospheric old town of vividly decorated buildings, more than its share of watch and pocketknife shops, and a variety of exceptional museums: Art buffs flock to the Rosengart Collection for its Picasso exhibit, historians enjoy the History Museum, and gearheads have a ball at the Swiss Transport Museum. All in all, Luzern is a delightful place. Just be prepared to share it—the city and its nearby mountaintops are jammed with visitors from every corner of the globe. Make a point to find a quiet little corner of Luzern all to yourself...in this fine city, it's not hard to do.

Orientation to Luzern

Midsize Luzern has about 80,000 residents (and a metropolitan area sprawling to more than 200,000). It sits where the Reuss (pronounced "royce") River flows out of Lake Luzern (a.k.a. the Vierwaldstättersee). South of the river is the train station and the bustling new town (Neustadt), and north of the river is the quaint, traffic-free old town (Altstadt). Pedestrian bridges span the river, including two classic wooden ones: the Chapel Bridge, with its famous stone Water Tower, and the Mill Bridge. The riverfront is lively, with restaurants, hotels, and museums lining both sides of the Reuss.

TOURIST INFORMATION

Luzern's helpful, modern TI is inside the train station (Mon-Fri 8:30-17:00, Sat from 9:00, Sun 9:00-14:00, shorter hours off-season, Zentralstrasse 5, +41 41 227 1717, www.luzern.com). Pick up or download the free, informative *City Guide*. The TI sells the Swiss Travel Pass, public transport tickets, and tickets to activities around town, including boat trips.

Sightseeing Passes: The **Swiss Travel Pass** covers most of Luzern's attractions. Without it, consider the **Lucerne Museum Card,** sold through the TI, which covers entry to all Luzern museums over a two-day period (36 CHF); it pays for itself if you visit the Swiss Transport Museum and at least one other museum.

Luzern and Central Switzerland at a Glance

▲▲**Luzern** Pretty, pristine lakeside city boasting excellent museums, painted bridges, and a handful of historic sights. See page 66.

▲▲**Lake Luzern** Irregularly shaped lake at the very heart of Switzerland, traversed by vintage steamships and surrounded by steep hillsides, gravity-defying villages, and snowy peaks. See page 86.

▲▲**Mount Pilatus** Craggy peak hunkering south of Luzern, with sublime views, luge ride, ropes course, and a range of hiking options. See page 95.

▲**Mount Rigi** Mountain mass across the lake and east of Luzern, famous for its sunrise vistas and Europe's first cogwheel train. See page 105.

▲**Fortress Fürigen** Underground bunker southeast of Luzern giving you a peek at Switzerland's hidden defense system. See page 101.

LUZERN

When you check into your hotel, get your free **Visitor Card,** which covers all in-city transit, gives you access to city-run Wi-Fi, and provides 10-20 percent discounts at most Luzern sights and activities (including some lake boats and mountain lifts). Some Airbnbs also provide Visitor Cards. (The "card" is actually a sheet of paper with an ID number and a QR code.)

ARRIVAL IN LUZERN

Luzern's waterfront **train station** is user-friendly, with three levels. The tracks are on the middle (street) level; the TI is along track 3, as are pay lockers. Upstairs you'll find the SBB ticket counters—take the escalator by track 10 (Mon-Fri 7:00-21:00, Sat-Sun until 20:00; international-travel windows close two hours earlier); a serene Tibits vegetarian cafeteria overlooks the tracks. Most other important services are downstairs in the underground Rail-City shopping mall. There you'll find pricey WCs (with showers), ATMs, and shops and eateries (including a Co-op grocery store)—particularly convenient on Sundays, when many shops are closed.

From the bustling plaza directly out front (with the historic arch), buses fan out in every direction; Luzern's lake-boat dock is at the far end of this area.

For a quick exit on foot to the old town and Chapel Bridge,

with the tracks to your back, go downstairs and head to the far end of the underground shopping zone, then escalate up—you'll pop out close to the river and main Seebrücke bridge.

HELPFUL HINTS

Medical Help: The welcoming **Permanence MedCenter** drop-in clinic is located downstairs in the train station (daily 7:00-23:00, +41 41 211 1444, www.medcenter.ch).

Festivals: Central Switzerland's biggest Mardi Gras celebration, **Luzerner Fasnacht,** begins on the Thursday before Ash Wednesday (exact date depends on Easter, https://luzerner-fasnacht.ch). The biggest parades are that day (called Dirty Thursday), but things stay noisy and busy well into the morning of Ash Wednesday. Book accommodations well in advance for this time.

The **Lucerne Festival** draws classical musicians and fans each year from early August to mid-September (www.lucernefestival.ch).

Markets: On Tuesdays and Saturdays, a farmers market borders both sides of the river near the main Seebrücke bridge (6:00-12:00). On Saturdays from May through October, a flea market fills the Vögeligärtli, a park near the train station (7:00-14:00), and on the first Saturday of the month from April to December, craft stalls set up on Weinmarkt in the old town.

Laundry: A 10-minute walk from the train station, **Jet Wasch** can pick up or deliver to your hotel for an extra fee (full service only; Mon-Fri 8:00-12:00 & 14:00-18:00, closed Sat-Sun, Bruchstrasse 28, +41 41 240 0151, www.jetwasch-luzern.ch). For location, see the "Luzern Hotels & Restaurants" map, later.

Bike Rental: Luzern has delightful lakeside cycling paths. The train station participates in the Swiss rail system's bike rental system (see page 491).

Parking: The best downtown parking garage is **Parkhaus Kesselturm** at Burgerstrasse 20 (25 CHF/day if you prepay, go to payment machines after entry and follow instructions, +41 41 410 3117, www.parking-luzern.ch). Avoid the train-station garages, which are much more expensive (unless your hotel can get you a deal).

Water Fountains: Luzern is proud of its clean drinking water and its more than 200 public fountains—each with a fun design—that spout potable water. Take full advantage of these fountains to refill water bottles.

GETTING AROUND LUZERN

Except for the Swiss Transport Museum, Luzern's main attractions are within an easy walk of the station. However, buses can be handy time-savers.

All public transit is included in a Swiss Travel Pass. If you're staying at a Luzern hotel, you'll get a Visitor Card that covers transit in the city center (zone 10—this includes everything in this chapter except the train to Alpnachstad, with the Pilatus cogwheel train). Otherwise, you'll need either a short-stretch ticket (*Kurzstrecke,* 2.50 CHF, good for up to 6 stops), a single ticket (*Einzelbillett,* 4.10 CHF, good for one hour), or a day pass (8.20 CHF). Buy tickets from machines at stops or at the TI. Transit info: www.vbl.ch.

Tell-Pass: If you're home-basing in Luzern for several days without a rail pass, consider the Tell-Pass. It covers up to 10 consecutive days of free rides on lifts, boats, and several area train lines (190 CHF/2 days, 220 CHF/3 days, more for longer durations, cheaper Nov-March when schedules are sparser; buy online or at TIs, train stations, and boat docks, www.tellpass.ch).

Tours in Luzern

For info on boat tours, see page 87.

Walking Tour

The TI offers a two-hour English-only tour several mornings each week in peak season. It covers the same route as my "Reuss River Stroll" below, but with more stories (20 CHF, discount with Visitor Card, May-Oct generally Tue, Thu, and Sat at 10:15, departs from train station TI, confirm days at www.luzern.com).

Tourist Train

This tacky little train does a 40-minute circuit of the city's sights, departing from Hotel Schweizerhof (15 CHF, runs daily April-Oct, hourly 11:00-19:00 in summer, less frequent in spring and fall, www.citytrain.ch).

Reuss River Stroll

This self-guided orientation walk, worth ▲▲, gives you a brief overview of the town. You'll walk up along the Reuss River, see both of Luzern's famous wooden bridges, and wander through the

LUZERN

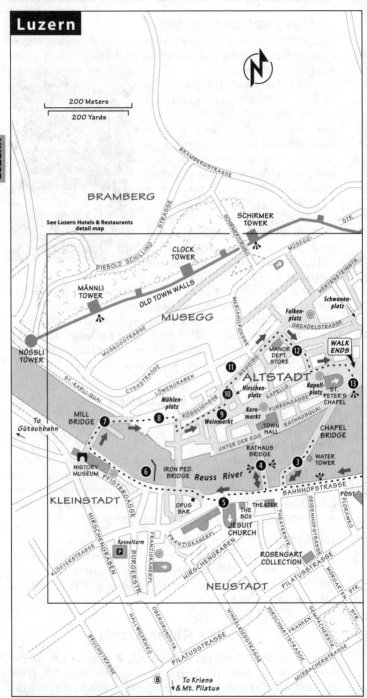

LUZERN

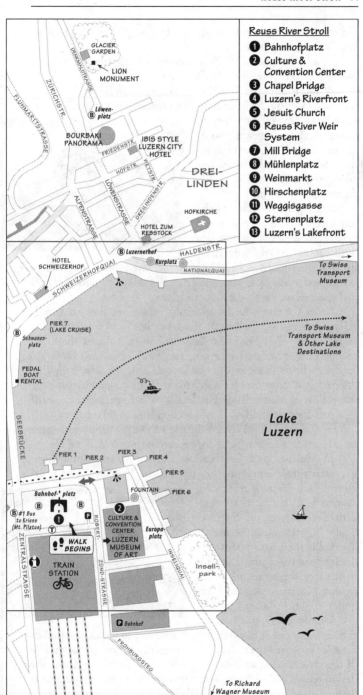

<u>Reuss River Stroll</u>

1. Bahnhofplatz
2. Culture & Convention Center
3. Chapel Bridge
4. Luzern's Riverfront
5. Jesuit Church
6. Reuss River Weir System
7. Mill Bridge
8. Mühlenplatz
9. Weinmarkt
10. Hirschenplatz
11. Weggisgasse
12. Sternenplatz
13. Luzern's Lakefront

old town with its colorfully painted buildings. It takes about an hour at a leisurely pace.

• *Begin at Bahnhofplatz, the busy zone between the lake and the train station. Stand in front of the big stone arch.*

❶ Bahnhofplatz: This is the transportation hub of Luzern—and all of Central Switzerland. From the area in front of the station, buses zip you anywhere in town. And underneath you is the extensive RailCity shopping mall, honeycombed with pedestrian passageways leading to different parts of town.

The big stone **arch** was the entrance of the venerable old train station—built in the late 19th century when Switzerland became a top tourist spot, thanks to the advent of steam-powered trains (and a stay by Queen Victoria). But it burned down in 1971 and was replaced with the modern station.

Cross the street to the lakefront, where you'll reach **Pier 1.** (German-speaking Swiss call the lake the Vierwaldstättersee—"Lake of the Four Forest Settlements," since it lies at the intersection of Switzerland's four original "forest" cantons.) Here you can catch boats to various points around Lake Luzern, including Alpnachstad (cogwheel train to Mount Pilatus) and Vitznau (cogwheel train to Mount Rigi). For details on these excursions, see the "Central Switzerland Day Trips" section later in this chapter.

• *Turn right, and—with the lake on your left—stroll a few steps toward the huge modern building with the big overhanging roof. This is the...*

❷ Culture and Convention Center (Kultur- und Kongresszentrum): This building, finished in 1998 by Parisian architect Jean Nouvel, features a concert hall that hosts the Luzern Festival, one of Switzerland's biggest music events. It also holds the **Luzern Museum of Art** (Kunstmuseum Luzern), which is of interest mainly to serious art lovers (described later, under "Sights in Luzern").

Lake water is pumped up, through, and out of this building; if you were to wander around its far side, you'd see open channels that go right through the middle of the structure, as well as a big pond. The architect claims the design recalls earlier times, when this area was swampland...but it more likely recalls his own original plans. Nouvel wanted to put the building out in the middle of the lake. When he was voted down by the people of Luzern, he decided to surround it with water anyway. The plaza under the roof (which reflects the lake and weather, further incorporating the building into the surrounding environment) is a busy community space popular for open-air concerts. Heaters keep the big, flat roof clear of snow.

• *Now turn 180 degrees and follow the lakeshore away from the conference center. Carry on straight across the busy street and keep following the waterline. Soon you'll have magnificent views of Luzern's most famous landmark, the wooden...*

❸ **Chapel Bridge** (Kapellbrücke): Luzern began as a fishing village. By the 13th century, with traffic between northern and southern Europe streaming through nearby Gotthard Pass, Luzern became a bustling trading center. In the first half of the 14th century, this covered bridge was angled across the river as part of the town's medieval fortifications. Originally this

wooden gallery stretched from the Jesuit Church and St. Peter's Chapel all the way to the pointy twin steeples of the Hofkirche, far to the right. The octagonal stone **Water Tower** (Wasserturm, pictured here), built around 1300, also housed a prison—in the below-water-level cellar.

In the 17th century, the bridge was decorated with paintings depicting the development of the town, starring its two patron saints—St. Leodegar and St. Mauritius. In 1993, a leisure boat moored under the bridge caught fire, and before long, Luzern's wooden landmark was in flames. (A plaque before the start of the bridge tells the story.) The bridge was painstakingly rebuilt—when you venture onto it, you'll notice the lighter colored, newer wood in the middle. But many of its famous paintings were

lost. Those remaining under the wooden roof at the ends of the bridge are restorations of the 17th-century originals; those in the middle were in storage at the time of the fire and therefore spared. Some burnt and charred paintings are still in their original spots.

Boats are no longer allowed under the bridge, it's now strictly non-smoking, and tiny security cameras are everywhere.

• *Wander out onto the bridge.*

Study the colorful **paintings** overhead. Coats of arms on the paintings tell you which aristocratic families sponsored them. Painting #1—immediately above the stairs as you enter—features a legendary and formidable giant, an icon of Luzern. This big boy (sometimes called the Wild Man) dates back to the Middle Ages, when mammoth bones discovered locally were mistakenly identified as the remains of a 15-foot-tall human giant.

Painting #2 shows an angel shining a divine light on the place where the town would be born, and where, in the eighth century, a monastery was founded. Painting #3 shows Luzern circa 1400—see how the bridge was already part of the city fortifications. Painting #6 shows a bigger city, as it looked in 1630. Paintings #9 and #10 remain charred black—a reminder of the bridge fire. In the middle of the bridge (just after the shop), painting #48 features St. Mauritius (a plaque nearby explains why he matters to Luzern).

As you stroll, notice that the "window" openings facing the lake are smaller than those on the inland side. As part of the city defensive system, this design gave defenders more cover from lakeside attacks.

• *Head back over the bridge the way you came, and turn right along the water. Very soon you'll reach another bridge (with great views of the Chapel Bridge). Step out onto this bridge and take a look around at...*

❹ **Luzern's Riverfront:** You're surrounded by Luzern's colorful town center, its beautiful river, and the grand hotels that line its banks. The stately stone building at the end of this bridge is Luzern's historic Town Hall (Rathaus), dating from the early 1600s.

Look out to the Chapel Bridge, with the mountains just beyond. You'll see how Luzern is supremely well-placed as a launch pad for alpine adventures: It sits where the flat, easy-to-traverse central plateau of Switzerland meets the wild and woolly Alps.

But it wasn't until a very famous tourist came here that Luzern really took off. Turn 180 degrees—with your back to the Chapel Bridge—and look up to the fanciful castle-like building, Château Gütsch, on the ridge above. Just to the right is a much lower-profile gray building. This was where a grief-stricken Queen Victoria holed up for a month in 1868. She was still mourning her beloved Prince Albert—who had died seven years before—and came here partly to honor his memory (he had climbed Mount Rigi, the peak across the lake, in 1837, and one of Victoria's treasured keepsakes was a pressed rose he had collected there). Victoria and her ensemble determinedly reached nearby mountain summits by riding donkeys and ponies.

Victoria's subjects were inspired by their intrepid monarch, and English aristocrats began to plan their own trips to Luzern.

Mark Twain followed (in 1878 and 1897). As Luzern became a magnet for international visitors, the lakefront promenade filled in and fancy resort hotels went up.

• *Return to the train-station end of the bridge, turn right, and continue along the river. Pause at the big, white church.*

❺ **Jesuit Church** (Jesuitenkirche): This was the first major Baroque church in Switzerland, built around 1670 and similar to others in Catholic parts of Central Europe (free, Tue-Sun 6:30-18:30 except Mon and Thu from 9:30, www.jesuitenkirche-luzern.ch). It's dedicated to the great missionary Francis Xavier, a co-founder of the Jesuit order, who's shown in a niche on the **facade** blessing a convert. Although surrounded by Protestant strongholds like Bern and Zürich, Luzern withstood the Reformation and remains predominantly Catholic. (I once heard a local put it like this: "North of Luzern, everyone is Protestant all the way to Norway. South of Luzern, everyone

is Catholic all the way to Rome.") Luzern's music school uses the church's pipe organ for practice—if you're lucky, you may catch an impromptu concert.

Step inside the church. The **interior** once dripped with Baroque decoration, but it was later redone in a lighter Rococo style (c. 1750). Rich as it looks, there's no real marble here—what you see on the altar, pulpit, and side-chapel altars is stucco marble made from ground-up stone laid smoothly and economically over wood.

The decorations on the **ceiling** celebrate the life (and afterlife) of Xavier. In the biggest, central panel, you see the missionary traveling heavenward, in an exuberant setting that depicts both this church and Luzern's landmark Chapel Bridge. The pope's representative and townsfolk gather to wish Xavier Godspeed. His cart is pulled by an elephant, leopard, and camel, recalling his mission trips to the exotic Far East.

In the second **side chapel** on the right, you can meet the patron saint of Switzerland: Brother Klaus, a 15th-century hermit who lived in the nearby mountains after leaving his wife (with her consent) and 10 children to pursue a spiritual calling. He was a great peacemaker between the cantons and is considered the original Swiss isolationist. Since Klaus' time, Switzerland has avoided entanglement in foreign squabbles (an ethic that continues today—see the "Swiss Military Readiness" sidebar, at the end of this chapter). The statue wears Klaus' original robe. His walking stick is in a case just beneath.

Back **outside,** you'll likely see a huge, wooden structure to the side of the church. Called simply "The Box," this is a performance venue (and sometimes a café) for the local Luzern Theater (to see what's on, check www.luzernertheater.ch).

• *Continue strolling downriver toward Luzern's other wooden bridge, the Mill Bridge. You'll pass the recommended Opus wine bar/restaurant and an iron pedestrian bridge (at the narrowest crossing spot, marking the location of Luzern's first bridge in the 12th century). Carrying on about 50 more yards, stop at the spiky fence partially damming the river.*

⑥ Reuss River Weir System: This big river flowing out of the lake may seem wild, but it's been tamed. Lake Luzern's main source of water is snowmelt, which trickles in from streams coming off the surrounding mountains. The water drains from the lake here on its way to the Rhine. To prevent the flooding of lakeside villages, in the mid-19th century the city devised and built a simple yet ingenious dam (*Nadelwehr,* "spiked weir") to control

the flow of water and the lake level. When the water is highest (in the spring), spikes are removed to open the flow; as the summer wears on and the water level drops, spikes are gradually added to keep the flow steady. In winter, the dam is closed entirely to keep the lake level high enough for boats. It's a dangerous process as workers, tethered by safety cables, hoist the spikes into position.

• *Continuing down the river, you'll pass the History Museum on your left (described later, under "Sights in Luzern") before coming to the wooden...*

⑦ Mill Bridge (Spreuerbrücke): Unlike the rebuilt Chapel Bridge, this 16th-century bridge is original—and the city is determined to keep it that way. Before you cross the bridge, pause to appreciate the first of its fine 17th-century paintings, which shows Luzern's favorite giant again, with the blue-and-white city and cantonal banners under the double eagle of the Holy Roman Empire (of which the Swiss lands were a part during

the Middle Ages). The flip side shows Judgment Day, with some going to heaven and others to hell.

As you cross the bridge, notice that each painting includes a

Grim Reaper-like skeleton lurking near people in every walk of life. Townsfolk crossed the bridge daily, and these scenes, painted during a time of war and plague, and based on the medieval allegory called the *danse macabre*—or dance of death—provided vivid reminders that, regardless of social standing or status, we must all face death.

Part way across is a little 16th-century chapel, built to ensure divine protection against destruction by flood. While you're paused here, notice the serious woodwork of the bridge construction. Like the Chapel Bridge, this one was part of the city fortifications; its downstream defensive wall is higher.

The far end of the bridge was designed to accommodate wagons delivering grain or whatever else was to be milled. Once upon a time, three mills churned here—this was the medieval industrial center of Luzern. The *"Spreu"* in the bridge's name means "chaff" (the sheath surrounding the wheat), which was separated from the wheat at the mill. You can see sketches of the mills as you leave the bridge (on the red wall on the left). A big turbine that generated power in 1889 sits here quietly now, but the tradition of harnessing water power continues. Beneath you, underwater, a modern hydro-electric plant creates enough power for 1,000 households.

• *After crossing the bridge, turn right to find yourself in...*

❽ **Mühlenplatz:** This traffic-free square marks the entrance to the old town. Riverside benches make a good place for a picnic

lunch or snack. On the left side of the square, at #11 (the Fischer-Stube—look above the first row of windows), a mural shows the city back when the water mills were hard at work.

• *At the top of the square (under the Swiss Marilyn Monroe), head right on Kramgasse, then take the first left onto Weinmarktgasse, which leads to...*

❾ **Weinmarkt:** As the name implies, in medieval Luzern, this square served as a marketplace for wine. The soldiers on the fine 15th-century fountain (which flies the blue-and-white flag of the Luzern canton) remind visitors that this town is tough and strong. Enjoy the fine painted facades all around—a typical feature of Luzern's medieval and Renaissance architecture. Off the bottom right of the square (near where you entered) is the ornate facade of the Hotel Waage/Hôtel des Balances. This was once the court of justice (hence the "scales" theme); the condemned were hanged from a linden tree just in front (about where a contemporary replacement tree is today).

Head higher up in the square, past the fountain. At first glance, the big mural on the green building at the top of the square seems to depict the Last Supper, but it's actually the Wedding Feast at Cana, where Jesus turned water into wine. The wine theme continues on the left side of the square, where a secret message hides in the strange zigzags on the modern shutters of a building. Start at the top left and read: W-E-I-N-M-A-R-K-T.

• *Leave the square on the far left side, which brings you straight into...*

❿ **Hirschenplatz:** History lingers long after things change—especially on this square. Its namesake, the Hirschen ("Deer") Hotel, is gone but its elaborate golden sign will always hang here. Across from that, guess who used to have a shop in the big green building? Yep—the jeweler. (See all the rings?) Notice the until-death-do-us-part ring at far left, and that high above, Cupid has shot his arrow.

To the right of the jeweler, a painted inscription on the corner building declares *"Goethe logierte hier 1779."* Goethe—the "German Shakespeare"—visited Luzern and stayed in a hotel on this corner. It was the city's top hotel at the time...I bet it was named the Golden Eagle. To the left of the jeweler, the grand facade on the Dornach House, from 1899, celebrates the 400th anniversary of the last battle against the Habsburgs. Switzerland has enjoyed a durable understanding that it can have disagreements—but no wars—with its historically aggressive and militaristic neighbors.

Just down the little lane to the right of the golden deer, on the left side, notice the Rent-a-Box shop. A clever variation on a consignment store, the shop invites people to rent display boxes to try to sell old watches and jewelry.

Continue out of the square (diagonally opposite from where you entered) onto the busy ⓫ **Weggisgasse.** As you stroll, you'll pass many international chain stores. However, every building in the old town—whether new or rebuilt—is required to offer residential apartments to prevent this historic zone from becoming only office space and touristy shops. This street is a real community.

• *After two blocks, you'll come to the Manor department store, with the recommended, tasty, and convenient Manora self-service cafeteria on the top floor (with great, free city views from its rooftop terrace). Turn right after Manor and walk one block, then hook left around the corner to...*

⓬ **Sternenplatz:** This tiny square is dominated by the colorful facade of the Restaurant Fritschi. The paintings feature characters and symbols from Luzern's annual Mardi Gras (Fasnacht) celebration—the city's biggest event. Pictured near the top of the building are Mr. and Mrs. Fritschi—the festival cheerleaders, celebrating Fasnacht by wearing masks and throwing oranges. Flanking them are their trusty servants, a nanny and a jester. Below is the story of Fasnacht: The cock calls at 5:00 in the morning the Thursday before Ash Wednesday (on the left), and the people get up to frighten winter away. Mr. and Mrs. Fritschi arrive on their wagon to kick off the festivities (on the right). Flying around the scene

are oranges—traditionally tossed by the Fritschis to their adoring fans. Once rare here in winter, oranges are special to the festivities, as they mark the beginning of spring.

• *Continue down the street at the bottom of the square (Hans-Holbein-Gasse), and you'll come upon a colorful fountain with more Fasnacht fun. Notice the colorful masks...and the oranges. This is where the locals gather, often more than 10,000 strong, at five in the morning to kick off the biggest party of the year—six days long. Continue to the riverfront, walking around St. Peter's Chapel, traditionally the church for Luzern's poor.*

⓭ Luzern's Lakefront: You're back at the wooden Chapel Bridge, having made the full circle. Enjoy the classic Luzern view: the Chapel Bridge and Water Tower, with Mount Pilatus hovering in the background. From here, cross over to the lakeside and stroll to the left.

Any swans out? Residents say they originated as a gift from French King Louis XIV in appreciation for the protection he got from his Swiss Guards. Today, local children (and tourists) make sure the swans get their daily bread.

• *Your town walk is finished. From here you have several options: You can catch a lake cruise (described later under "On Lake Luzern"). You can cross the street and peruse ritzy Swiss watches at the flagship Bucherer store (selling envy since 1888). You can walk along the lake to the Swiss Transport Museum. Or you can cut inland to the Lion Monument. Everything is described in the next section.*

Sights in Luzern

If you'll be doing a lot of sightseeing here, first review your options for saving money on admissions (see "Tourist Information—Sightseeing Passes," earlier).

MUSEUMS IN THE CENTER

Luzern is charming enough that simply strolling its streets and bridges and cruising the lake is enough for a happy day of sightseeing. But the city also offers some fine museums, all within walking distance.

▲Rosengart Collection (Sammlung Rosengart)

In the 1930s and 1940s, wealthy resident and art dealer Siegfried Rosengart palled around with all-star modern artists, financing and collecting their works. At an early age his daughter Angela took an interest in her father's work and eventually became his business partner. This museum displays the fruits of their labor. Angela, now over 90, still visits the museum daily. Worth ▲▲▲ for art lovers, this may be Switzerland's most user-friendly collection of modern art.

Cost and Hours: 18 CHF, covered by Swiss Travel Pass, daily 10:00-18:00, Nov-March 11:00-17:00, mandatory bag check; at the ticket desk, either buy the well-written little English booklet, get the sheet of QR codes to scan with your phone, or borrow the excellent English printouts that describe the collection; a few blocks from the train station in the new town up Pilatusstrasse at #10, +41 41 220 1660, www.rosengart.ch.

Visiting the Museum: The building's three floors boast works from the big names of the late 19th and early 20th centuries, with an emphasis on the art of Pablo Picasso and Paul Klee. The ground and first floors feature an extensive **Picasso** collection focusing on his later works, including 32 paintings and some 100 drawings, watercolors, and graphic and sculptural works. Rosengart was Picasso's leading Swiss art dealer and helped place a number of works in national and international museums.

On the upper floor are black-and-white candid photographs of Picasso (from a rotating collection of 200) by American **David Douglas Duncan.** Documenting the last 17 years of Picasso's life, Duncan's intimate photos of the artist and his family capture the very human personality of this larger-than-life genius, while providing insight into his artistic process and lifestyle. The first floor also has some Impressionist and Modernist works by Braque, Monet, Renoir, Miró, Chagall, Cézanne, Matisse, Modigliani, and Pissarro.

Don't miss the basement, which displays 125 small works by **Paul Klee,** displayed chronologically so you can follow the evolution of his career. Watch as Klee discovers colors and blossoms from a doodler and, at times, watercolor artist into a mature painter.

▲History Museum (Historisches Museum)

This cluttered old museum is a repository for the accumulated bric-a-brac of Luzern's past. It's housed in one of the town's oldest surviving buildings, which was long used to store military weapons and uniforms. The exhaustive collection is displayed on three crowded floors, in an approach reminiscent of a 21st-century cabinet of curiosities. You'll wander through shelves of old weapons, stained-glass windows, church paintings and sculptures, costumes from Baroque times up to the present, folk art, and old-fashioned tourism posters. Each shelf (sometimes each item) has a barcode—scan it with an iPad you'll borrow at the entry to learn more. Don't miss the chilling guillotine on the ground floor—last used in 1940.

Cost and Hours: 10 CHF, covered by Swiss Travel Pass, Tue-Sun 10:00-17:00, closed Mon, Pfistergasse 24, +41 41 228 5424, www.historischesmuseum.lu.ch.

Luzern Museum of Art (Kunstmuseum Luzern)

Located in the lakefront cultural center by the train station, this museum features ambitious special exhibits of contemporary art as well as displays drawn from its permanent collection, which focuses on historical and contemporary works by Central Swiss artists.

Cost and Hours: 15 CHF, covered by Swiss Travel Pass, Tue-Sun 10:00-17:00, closed Mon, Europaplatz 1, +41 41 226 7800, www.kunstmuseumluzern.ch.

LÖWENPLATZ

North of the old town, Löwenplatz was a big deal back in the Romantic Age of tourism, when its three main sights (the lion sculpture, Bourbaki Panorama, and Glacier Garden) made it a destination. It remains a bucket-list stop for large groups but has the tired air of a tourist trap. Drop by for a peek at old-time tourism; behind the tacky souvenir shops, the sights do retain some of their Victorian-era charm.

Getting There: It's a 10-minute walk from the old town or a short bus ride across the river from the station (take bus #1 or #19 three stops north from the train station to the Löwenplatz stop). By the bus stop is the round Bourbaki Panorama (as well as the

Löwencenter mall, with eateries and a Co-op supermarket). The lion and the Glacier Garden are one long block farther up the hill.

▲Lion Monument (Löwendenkmal)

This free, famous monument remains an essential stop if you're visiting Luzern—if only because when you get back home, everyone will ask you, "Did you see the lion?" Open from sunrise to dusk, the huge sculpture (33 feet long by 20 feet tall) is carved right into a cliff face, over a reflecting pool in a peaceful park—the site of a sandstone quarry when it was carved in 1821. Though it's often overrun with tour groups, a tranquil mo-

ment here is genuinely moving: The mighty lion rests his paws on a shield, with his head cocked to one side, tears streaming down his cheeks. In his side is the broken-off end of a spear, which is slowly killing the noble beast. (Note the angle of the spear, which matches the striations of the rock face, subtly suggesting more spears raining down on the lion.)

The lion memorializes a 1792 episode from the French Revolution, during which more than 600 Swiss Guards—hired to protect the French king—were killed or massacred when revolutionaries stormed the Tuileries Palace (the king managed to escape...for a while). The inscription reads, *Helvetiorum fidei ac virtuti*—"To the loyalty and bravery of the Swiss." While a local artist carved it (in 14 months), it was designed by the great Danish Neoclassical sculptor Bertel Thorvaldsen.

Bourbaki Panorama

Here's your chance to get right in the middle of a great painting—literally. In the 19th century, before the dawn of cinema, people were hungry for visual entertainment. Panorama theaters like this were built all over Europe and hosted various gigantic paintings, which were rolled up and taken on road trips.

This 360-degree painting (a 33-foot-tall wraparound canvas with a circumference of 360 feet) tells the story of one of the culminating events of the 1870-1871 Franco-Prussian War, when French forces—routed by the Prussians—withdrew over the Swiss border. Though this was a minor episode in European history, the museum describes it so movingly that it makes for a satisfying sight.

Cost and Hours: 12 CHF, covered by Swiss Travel Pass; daily 9:00-18:00, Nov-March 10:00-17:00; Löwenplatz 11, +41 41 412 3030, www.bourbakipanorama.ch.

Background: After Prussia prevailed, some French soldiers were determined to surrender to the neutral Swiss rather than the enemy. For three days in February 1871, a hungry, weary 87,000-man army led by the panorama's namesake, General Charles-Denis Bourbaki, trudged through the snow and across the Swiss border, near Neuchâtel. Once in Switzerland, they gave up their weapons and surrendered to the Swiss—who, as the story goes, took excellent care of them, nursing them back to health before sending them home with a hefty bill for their stay. Edouard Castres, who painted the panorama, actually witnessed the retreat as a Red Cross volunteer.

Visiting the Panorama: At the ticket office, you'll get a free accordion-style booklet that fills you in on the history and makes for a good souvenir. Ask to borrow the iPad guide (which helps you zoom in and identify details); you'll also want to request the English version of the 10-minute historical soundtrack. Then head up to the second-floor viewing platform to savor all 360 degrees of drama.

After you've viewed the panorama, visit an additional exhibit one floor down. The building also houses the Luzern city library, including a café and other cultural facilities.

Glacier Garden (Gletschergarten)

This complex is a strange sort of miniature theme park with an eclectic hodgepodge of exhibits, most loosely relating to alpine geology. The regular cost is expensive for what you get, but if you have a pass that includes admission here, it's worth a quick look.

Cost and Hours: 22 CHF, covered by Swiss Travel Pass, daily 10:00-18:00, Nov-March until 17:00, Denkmalstrasse 4, +41 41 410 4340, www.gletschergarten.ch. You could buy the inexpensive guidebooklet or install an app that lets you download a free audioguide, but neither is essential.

Visiting the Garden: First you'll walk through the **glacier-grinded grounds** that give the garden its name. While geologists might get a thrill out of this, it was just a bunch of holes to me. Then you can visit the **museum,** in a classic old chalet where the family that founded the garden once lived. Exhibits (labeled in German only) describe glacial processes. There are huge 3-D reliefs of late-18th-century Luzern, the Alps, and the lakes of Central Switzerland, plus bits of local and military history.

Behind the museum is the **Sandstein Pavilion,** showing a

LUZERN

20-minute movie about the Alps. Next to the museum, a *Felsen-welt* sign leads you into a maze of cool, dark, damp tunnels, ending in a stairway (or elevator) up to a **clifftop observation area** where you can look around at the neighborhood and distant peaks. From there, outdoor stairs lead back down to the museum past several more exhibits.

You'll finish with the **Hall of Mirrors** (enter by the *Labyrinth* sign). Made in 1896 for a national exhibition in Geneva, it's a de-lightfully low-tech fun house. You'll grope your way through twisting corridors—with mirrors on all sides—decorated like a Disneyfied Alhambra. It's confusing, dizzying, and claustrophobic, but goofy fun. As you run into yourself (literally) again and again, you'll lament the poor sap who has to clean the smudge

marks off all those mirrors. As you leave, giggling and nauseated, you may find yourself wondering, "So, what exactly did that have to do with glaciers?"

FARTHER FROM THE CENTER
▲Swiss Transport Museum (Verkehrshaus)
This "Swiss Smithsonian," across the lake from the train station, includes hundreds of hands-on, kid-friendly exhibits in an enormous complex covering virtually all modes of transportation. It's pricey and a little overwhelming, but it's an amazing display of Swiss ingenuity and craftsmanship. If you're in Luzern for only one day, skip this and enjoy the museums and ambience in the old town. But with a second day or younger kids in tow, or if

you're obsessed with trains, planes, and automobiles, this museum is worth ▲▲▲—and hours of entertainment.

Cost and Hours: 32 CHF, 14 CHF for kids 6-15, free under 6, half-price with Swiss Travel Pass; more for planetarium, IMAX cinema, and chocolate exhibit; daily 10:00-18:00, Nov-March until 17:00, café, Lidostrasse 5, +41 41 375 7575, www.verkehrshaus.ch.

Getting There: From downtown, it's a 30-minute **walk** to the museum, most of it along a beautiful promenade. To make a bee-line to the museum, take **bus** #6, #8, or #24 from the station and get off at the Verkehrshaus stop. For a more scenic approach in summer, catch a **boat** in front of the train station to Verkehrshaus-Lido (1-2/hour, 10 minutes, 6.40 CHF, www.lakelucerne.ch).

Visiting the Museum: The museum's five main halls are arranged in a circle around a huge central plaza, with full-size airplanes and other attractions. Pick up a map and use the white line on the floor to navigate the full clockwise loop through the complex. Most exhibits are at least partly translated into English. As you enter, check the schedule of demonstrations (ranging from car-crash tests to airport X-ray machines; usually in English on request).

The first building is a long shed packed with train engines and tram cars. You'll learn that hydropower generates 90 percent of the electricity for Swiss trains, and you'll appreciate the evolution of Swiss trains and tunnels over the last century.

The second hall is a car enthusiast's dream, with two floors devoted to road transport. One wall is stacked floor to ceiling with 80 vehicles dating from 1860 to 2005, mostly cars and motorcycles. Interactive screens let you zoom in on any vehicle for insights into its design and history.

The third building covers boats and submarines on the lower two floors and shows off some Swiss cable cars. Be sure to seek out (on the top floor) the  "**Livemap Switzerland**"—an enormous (more than 2,000 square feet), up-to-date aerial photograph of Switzerland. Spread out on the floor like laminated linoleum, this photo map is detailed enough to show virtually every single building within the country's borders. Slide on the Swiss-flag slippers, borrow a map and magnifying glass, and glide across Switzerland, looking for the places you've visited so far.

The next hall is the Hans Erni Museum, showcasing works of a well-known local 20th-century painter and illustrator (they have nothing to do with transport, but are worth a quick peek).

The fifth and final building covers flight (airplanes below, space travel above). The helicopter and airplane simulations are included in your entry price (expect lines). There's also a relaxing parasailing simulator, where you can lie on a smoothly gliding platform and peer down at the countryside below.

Two vintage Swissair planes are parked in the central courtyard (a DC-3 and a Convair 990). You'll also find a miniature train that little kids can ride (small fee), and a high-tech swing set. Simulators, games, giant slides, and interactive exhibits can easily keep children busy all day.

More Sights: Three other attractions share the same grounds and hours as the Transport Museum: a planetarium, the Swiss Chocolate Adventure, and the IMAX Filmtheater. Each costs 16 CHF to enter (or get the 56-CHF ticket that covers everything; see website for showtimes). The Swiss Chocolate Adventure, a chocolate museum structured as a 20-minute amusement-park ride, is entertaining for chocoholics.

Gütschbahn

On a nice day, ride the Gütschbahn funicular up to Chateau Gütsch, the hotel perched in fairy-tale style up the mountain slope west

of downtown. At the top is a free panoramic viewpoint with a red heart statue visible from downtown, as well as a picnic-perfect park with trails and a water fountain.

Note that the pricey restaurant at Chateau Gütsch is owned by a Russian oligarch. The unstaffed funicular runs on demand, like an elevator; it's covered by a regular Luzern public transport ticket.

Getting There: You can walk from the Luzern train station to the base of the funicular in less than 20 minutes, but it's easier to take frequent bus #2 from the station five stops to Gütsch, then cross the street and walk back 50 yards through the underpass.

Richard Wagner Museum

This museum is about a 30-minute walk along the lakefront, south of the train station and housed in a building where the 19th-century German composer once lived. It's worth a visit only for enthusiasts.

Cost and Hours: 10 CHF, covered by Swiss Travel Pass, Tue-Sun 11:00-17:00, closed Mon and Dec-March, café, Richard-Wagner-Weg 27, +41 41 360 2370, www.richard-wagner-museum.ch.

ON LAKE LUZERN

Encircled by mountains, the almost fjord-like Lake Luzern is the most touristed in Switzerland, with great scenic variety. With many boat routes and destinations (35 stops in all), you can take a spin around the lake any time of the year.

Lake Cruises

Round-trip cruises from Luzern range from a one-hour zip across the lake (to Bürgenstock and back) to a full-blown, 5.5-hour exploration (to Flüelen, at the far end of the lake, and back). A few round-trip dinner or sightseeing cruises are available, but most boats have scheduled stops and are designed for you to get out, explore, and then take the next boat back. Romantics will want  to hitch a ride on one of the old-fashioned paddleboat steamers.

Most boats are operated by the Lake Lucerne Navigation Company (+41 41 367 6767, www.lakelucerne.ch). Buy tickets from the dockside offices (Piers 1 and 7), ticket machines, the TI, or online. Ask for advice on which trip best fits your schedule and current weather conditions. Tickets can be purchased onboard as well.

Regular departures are free with a Swiss Travel Pass and half-price with a Eurail Global Pass (it can be smart to do the lake cruise on the day you arrive or depart—when you're already using a flexi-day for your train transportation). Skip a lake cruise if you're planning to take the Gotthard Panorama Express to Lugano (see page 400): You'll be boating the entire length of the lake, so there's little point in doing another lake excursion.

Round-trip cruise options vary by season and day of the week. Visit LakeLucerne.ch, select English, then "Round Trip," then enter "Lucerne" and the date you'll be sailing for a list of suggestions. Or pick up the boat company's *Roundtrips from Lucerne* brochure, which describes all the different routes. A one-hour circuit runs about 20-40 CHF per person; the longest cruise, to Flüelen and back, costs 77 CHF. You can create your own cruise by sailing out on a regular departure and then back the same way.

Consider mixing boat and train: For example, sail one-way to Flüelen, then catch the hourly train back. Or sail to Vitznau, ride the cogwheel train to the Rigi summit, and return via Weggis or Arth-Goldau (see the "Mount Rigi" section, at the end of this chapter).

Pedal Boats

Pricey pedal boats can be rented at Schwanenplatz, just across the bridge from the Luzern train station (20 CHF/30 minutes, 30 CHF/hour; 5 CHF more on weekends, +41 41 368 0808, www. sng.ch).

Sleeping in Luzern

Luzern is busiest—and most expensive—in summer. Spring and fall bring lower prices, and winter has rock-bottom rates. Air-conditioning is rare; to sleep with the window open but avoid nighttime street noise, ask for a room high up.

IN THE CENTER

$$$$ **Hotel Wilden Mann,** a local institution near the river on the new town side, fills a characteristic old house with 48 colorful rooms, each one different. While the prices are high, guests come here for the warm welcome and the history rather than cookie-cutter comfort (air-con in some rooms, elevator, Bahnhofstrasse 30, +41 41 210 1666, www.wilden-mann.ch, mail@wilden-mann.ch).

$$$$ **Hotel des Alpes** is a good bet if you want to sleep right on the river in the old town, next door to Luzern's iconic Chapel Bridge and Water Tower. The 45 classic rooms are bright and well equipped; pricier riverfront rooms, some with balconies, come with beautiful views. The reception entrance is on the back of the building, or you can enter through the contemporary restaurant on the promenade and ride up the elevator, which also accesses the guest rooms (fans, discounts at train station parking garage, Furrengasse 3, +41 41 417 2060, www.desalpes-luzern.ch, info@desalpes-luzern.ch).

$$$$ **Hotel Continental Park,** facing a park alongside the train station, feels fresh and stylish, with prices to match. Its 88 rooms sit over an appealing contemporary lobby and a restaurant featuring Ticinese cuisine—from the Italian-speaking part of Switzerland (family rooms, air-con, elevator, pay parking, Murbacherstrasse 4, +41 41 228 9050, www.continental.ch, hotel@continental.ch).

$$$ **Hotel Waldstätterhof** fills a fine 19th-century building across the street from the train station. Its 96 bright, spacious, and modern rooms have all the amenities, and its rates are reasonable for the level of comfort (can be noisy—ask for a quieter courtyard room, family rooms, elevator, pay parking—reserve ahead, Zentralstrasse 4, +41 41 227 1271, www.hotel-waldstaetterhof.ch, info@hotel-waldstaetterhof.ch).

$$$ **Hotel Zum Rebstock,** a bit simpler, sits a bit farther from the river—on the way to Löwenplatz, across the lake from the train station, at the base of the steps to the twin-spired Hofkirche. Its 32 idiosyncratic rooms come with artistic flourishes (elevator, St. Leodegarstrasse 3, +41 41 417 1819, www.rebstock-luzern.ch, hotel@rebstock-luzern.ch).

$$$ **Schlüssel Hotel,** well run by Marija, offers 10 tastefully decorated rooms with personal touches that make you feel

at home. This recently renovated building, first opened as a hotel in 1545, takes pride in its long history. It's well located on a small square near the river and houses several restaurants (cheaper if you skip breakfast, a few rooms have balconies, elevator, Franziskanerplatz 12, +41 41 210 1061, www.schluessel-luzern.ch, welcome@schluessel-luzern.ch).

$$ Stern Luzern, located in the old shell of a building over a popular restaurant, is a solid value, offering 15 small and basic rooms. They also have eight newer, pricier rooms in an annex closer to the river (family rooms, tiny elevator, check-in at restaurant entrance at Franziskanerplatz 4, +41 41 227 5060, www.sternluzern.ch, info@sternluzern.ch).

OUTSIDE THE CENTER

$$ Ibis Styles Luzern City has 115 modern rooms with colorful accents. It's near the action, but away from much of the noise (breakfast extra, air-con, family rooms, elevator, Friedenstrasse 8, +41 41 418 4848, www.ibis.com, h8549@accor.com). It's a 15-minute walk from the train station, or take bus #1—direction: Maihof, get off at Löwenplatz and walk down Friedenstrasse; the hotel faces the Bourbaki Panorama.

$ Hotel Alpha, once a convent-run boarding house for village girls, is now a respectable hotel for value-minded travelers who don't mind being away from the center. It offers 47 big, bright, dorm-style rooms, most with the toilet down the hall, though some have private baths. It's located in a nice residential area but has some street noise from the nearby school and playing field (many doubles are twins, family rooms, elevator, fans available, comfy lounges and TV room, pay parking—reserve ahead, Zähringerstrasse 24, at intersection with Pilatusstrasse, +41 41 240 4280, www.hotelalpha.ch, info@hotelalpha.ch). It's a 10-minute walk or an easy two-stop bus ride from the train station: Take bus #1, #2, or #12, get off at Pilatusplatz, and continue down Pilatusstrasse.

$ The Bed and Breakfast, lovingly run by Isabelle in her grandmother's former home, offers 13 bright, spacious rooms. Three rooms have private bathrooms, while the other 10 share eight bathrooms. This is a perfect spot for those looking for a more personal experience and who don't mind being a bit away from the center. The kind staff and cozy garden will make you wish you were staying longer (closed Nov-Feb, family rooms, pay parking, Taubenhausstrasse 34, +41 41 310 1514, www.thebandb.ch, info@thebandb.ch). It's a 15-minute walk from the train station, or take bus #1—direction: Kriens-Obernau, get off at Eichhof and walk 100 yards down Taubenhausstrasse.

$ Ibis Budget Luzern City's 128 tight, cookie-cutter rooms are worth considering if you're on a budget and don't mind a soul-

LUZERN

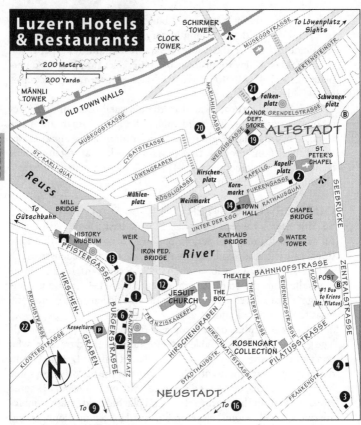

Luzern Hotels & Restaurants

less neighborhood near the train tracks. You get a narrow double bed, sometimes with a bunk bed above it, plus an opaque shower cabinet that opens straight into the room (air-con, breakfast extra, pay parking, Kellerstrasse 6, +41 41 367 8000, www.ibis.com, h6782@accor.com). It's a 10- to 15-minute walk from the train station, or take bus #4 three stops to Brünigstrasse.

¢ **Backpackers Lucerne** is calm and well run, sharing a modern, blocky building with student dorms *(Studentenheim)* in a peaceful residential area a 15-minute walk south of the train station. The place has 39 rooms (each with a balcony), shared toilets and showers, two guest kitchens, a welcoming lounge, and no curfew. The walk to the center is mostly along the lake, through pretty parks and next to a fine beach (no breakfast, elevator, full-service pay laundry, reception open 8:30-14:00 & 17:00-21:00, Alpenquai 42, +41 41 511 8241, www.backpackerslucerne.ch, info@backpackerslucerne.ch). By bus, take #6, #7, or #8 from the station four stops to Weinbergli, then walk left five minutes to the hostel.

LUZERN

Accommodations

1. Hotel/Restaurant Wilden Mann
2. Hotel des Alpes
3. Hotel Continental Park
4. Hotel Waldstätterhof
5. Hotel Zum Rebstock
6. Schlüssel Hotel
7. Stern Luzern
8. To Ibis Styles Luzern City
9. To Hotel Alpha & The Bed and Breakfast
10. To Ibis Budget Luzern City & Restaurant Zur Werkstatt
11. To Backpackers Lucerne

Eateries & Other

12. Opus Wine Bar & Restaurant
13. Nix in der Laterne
14. Restaurant Rathaus Brauerei
15. Restaurant Taube
16. Restaurant Anker
17. RailCity Eateries, Supermarket & Bike Rental
18. Luz Seebistro
19. Manora Cafeteria
20. Tandoori Diner & Mirch Masala
21. Heini Bakery/Café
22. Laundry

Eating in Luzern

Eateries along the river are pricey and a bit touristy, but that's where you'll make the best memories. Reservations are smart. A good

way to eat well but affordably here is to visit a high-end restaurant for lunch, when you can get a filling multicourse meal for around 20-25 CHF (typically weekdays only). For a memorable evening on a budget, consider catching a late one-hour sightseeing boat on the lake (around 19:00) and enjoying a picnic dinner while you cruise.

NEAR THE RIVER

$$$ Opus, next to the big Jesuit Church, is both a trendy wine bar and a good restaurant. Pair your wine with meat, fish, pastas, and vegetarian dishes with Italian and international flair; the lush and varied "antipasti buffet"; or your choice of dried meats and cheeses (sold by weight). They always have a couple dozen bottles of wine open and available by the glass. Sit in the upscale, colorful interior; in the extremely romantic wine cellar with candlelight reflecting in the bottle-lined walls; or out front, under the church and next to the river (long hours daily, Bahnhofstrasse 16, +41 41 226 4141, www.restaurant-opus.ch).

$$$ Nix in der Laterne has a romantic, dressy interior and great outside seats right on the fast-rushing river. Nikki is Swiss-Austrian, and so is his cuisine. Daily options are listed on a chalkboard; their budget option is *tarte flambée*—a savory tart with mix-and-match toppings. Their nice variety of 22-CHF weekday lunches attracts a sophisticated local business crowd. This is a fine spot in a central location that thrives even without tourists (daily 11:30-24:00, Reusssteg 9, +41 41 240 2543, www.nixinderlaterne.ch).

$$$ Wilden Mann, the recommended hotel in a historic building just off the river, has two very different restaurants, each serving well-regarded food in atmospheric surroundings. The very traditional, wood-clad **Burgerstube** offers traditional Swiss cooking, while **Sauvage,** filling a nondescript dining room and a delightful winter garden, is a more French/Mediterranean experience. The menus overlap—review both before choosing (daily 11:30-14:00 & 18:00-22:00, Bahnhofstrasse 30, +41 41 210 1666, www.wilden-mann.ch).

$$ Restaurant Rathaus Brauerei is a lively microbrewery on the river under the Town Hall. While the beer hall is plain, there are plenty of outdoor seats—both under arches and on the river. It's a local favorite for its unfiltered, cloudy Seidel Rathausbier, which you can only get here. Special seasonal brews are on the menu, along with salads, "gourmet" pretzel sandwiches (a light and affordable option), and Germanic main dishes (long hours daily, Unter der Egg 2, +41 41 410 6111, www.rathausbrauerei.ch).

$$$ Restaurant Taube, popular for serving "grandma's cooking," is known for its ham-and-cheese *Rösti*. The food is fine, and the interior is a simple, cozy cellar, but I'd eat here mostly to take advantage of their amazing riverside seating (24-CHF two-course weekday lunches, daily 11:30-23:00, Burgerstrasse 3, +41 41 210 0747, www.taube-luzern.ch).

NEW TOWN

These places are in a more workaday district, closer to the train station than the river and away from the tourist zone. Each is patronized by a smart local clientele.

$$$$ Restaurant Zur Werkstatt has a fun, inventive approach to eating. The seating is semi-communal (big tables), and you choose one of two three-course fixed-price meals, which change each week: the 59-CHF meat option or the 48-CHF vegetarian option. The open kitchen allows you to watch the action and take in the enticing aromas. It's a suitable splurge for the adventurous eater (26-CHF lunch specials, Mon-Sat 11:30-13:30 & 17:00-24:00, closed Sun, Waldstätterstrasse 18, +41 41 979 0303, www.zurwerkstatt-lu.ch).

$$$ Restaurant Anker fills an old ballroom of the once-venerable Hotel Anker with an eclectic blend of old and new—mixing crystal glassware with exposed concrete, hip music, and low lighting. It's a fun and youthful place with an open kitchen and a diverse menu focused on fresh, local ingredients, tasty grilled meats, and pastas (25-CHF two-course weekday lunch specials, daily 11:30-22:00, Pilatusstrasse 36, +41 41 220 8800, www.hotel-restaurant-anker.ch).

FAST AND AFFORDABLE

Train Station's "RailCity": As in every big Swiss city, Luzern's train station comes with a mall bursting with bright, efficient chain eateries. The following are all open long hours daily. Near the TI, a **Migros Daily** serves prepared food. Just down the escalator you'll find a string of creative **fast-food places** with small standup tables (kebabs, salads, burgers, and currywurst) and a big **Co-op supermarket.** Upstairs is **$$ Tibits,** with a self-serve, pay-by-weight salad bar nestled in a modern, peaceful spot overlooking the tracks.

On the Lakefront: Tucked between boat docks directly in front of the train station, **$ Luz Seebistro** has glassed-in indoor seating, a big deck out on the lake, and a takeout window. It's appealingly unpretentious and rough around the edges—a refreshing change in ostentatious Luzern. They serve drinks and a simple menu of burgers, sandwiches, sausages, and salads (long hours daily, Schifflandungsbrücke 1).

Self-Service Cafeteria: For a tasty, efficient lunch, head to **$ Manora,** a cafeteria on the fifth floor of the Manor department store in the old town. In good weather, climb the stairs to the outdoor terrace, with great views over the rooftops of Luzern to the lake and Mount Pilatus. This place can get crowded during peak times—eat early or late, and send your travel partner up top to claim an outdoor table while you buy the food (Mon-Sat 9:00-17:00, closed Sun, Weggisgasse 5).

Indian Food: In the old town, **$ Tandoori Diner** sells budget Indian meals (meat or vegetarian). Choose one of eight combos, and they'll dish it up immediately (cash only, Mon-Sat 11:30-21:30, closed Sun, Löwengraben 4, +41 41 340 5296). **$$ Mirch Masala,** two doors away and run by the same folks, is a bit more elegant (17-CHF lunch buffet, pricier à la carte dinners, Mon-Sat 11:30-14:00 & 17:30-22:00, Sun 16:30-23:00, Löwengraben 8, +41 41 410 6308).

Bakery: Popular with the local lunch crowd, **$ Heini Bakery/ Café,** on Falkenplatz a half-block down from the Manor department store, has a weekday salad bar, sandwiches, quiches, and delectable pastries. There are two sprawling indoor seating areas, plus outdoor tables in good weather (air-con, Mon-Fri 8:00-18:30, Sat until 17:00, closed Sun, Hertensteinstrasse 66, +41 41 412 2020).

Luzern Connections

Luzern is well situated, with convenient connections to anywhere in the country. Note that Luzern is on both the Golden Pass and the Gotthard Panorama Express scenic rail routes (see the Scenic Rail Journeys chapter). **Train info:** Rail.ch.

From Luzern by Train to: Zürich (2/hour direct, 40-50 minutes), **Zürich Airport** (2/hour direct, 70 minutes), **Bern** (hourly, 1 hour), **Interlaken** (hourly, 2 hours, trains run to Interlaken Ost, change there for Interlaken West), **Lausanne** (hourly, 2 hours), **Appenzell** (2/hour, 3 hours, change in Herisau or Gossau), **Lugano** (every 2 hours direct, 1 hour 40 minutes, more with transfer in Arth-Goldau, scenic route via the old Gotthard Tunnel and Airolo takes 3 hours with change in Bellinzona), **St. Moritz** (1-2/hour, 4.5 hours, at least 2 changes; or go by Glacier Express route, 7.5 hours with changes in Göschenen and Andermatt), **Zermatt** (hourly, 3 hours, changes in Bern and Visp).

Central Switzerland Day Trips

Perched on the edge of its scenic lake and ringed by family-friendly mountain peaks, Luzern is a perfect springboard for alpine excursions. Three side trips are especially popular and worthwhile: two famous and accessible mountains—Mount Pilatus and Mount Rigi—and the hidden military fortress of Fürigen. All three can be reached by boat and mountain lifts from Luzern.

Planning Your Time

Mount Pilatus is a jagged pinnacle with a "top of the world" feeling that makes for a fun, relaxed day (especially in good weather). Mount Rigi is lusher and lower, with a range of scenic trails. For either peak, allow the better part of a day for a round-trip.

Note that Fortress Fürigen is open only on weekends from April through October. It's possible to combine Mount Pilatus and the fortress into one jam-packed day trip, although it requires a bit of backtracking (or a taxi)—get an early start to fit it all in.

For any of these side trips, you can go out and back by train, or travel one way by boat. The boat is slower (and more expensive), but adds a scenic, romantic component to your day.

The connections outlined below are well coordinated but don't always leave lots of time between legs; confirm all schedules and logistics locally before embarking.

MOUNT PILATUS

Looming behind Luzern, Pilatus (7,000 feet), worth ▲▲, is a dramatic backdrop to the city and an enjoyable destination. While legend dictates that it's named for Pontius Pilate—whose body is supposedly in one of its lakes, kicking up a fuss if disturbed—it more likely comes from a Latin word meaning "cloudy." It's also said to be infested with dragons (which local marketing relies on heav-

ily—you'll see red dragons everywhere). Pack a picnic before leaving town and spend a glorious day here with the marmots and ibex for company.

Ascending Mount Pilatus

There are two approaches from the base of the mountain to the summit, called Pilatus Kulm. A cogwheel train runs up to the top from the town of Alpnachstad, on the south side of the peak. The other ascent—by gondola and then cable car—runs from Kriens up the north side, with a chance to stop for a luge ride or the ropes course at Fräkmüntegg.

For maximum views, go up one way, down the other—in good weather, the view's spectacular on both sides in both directions. I'd take the cogwheel train up (the uphill ride is a bit more dramatic), and the gondola ride down (to catch more afternoon light).

However you travel, figure at least 4-5 hours for the total round-trip from Luzern (more for serious hikers)—though when it's busy, you may lose some time waiting for the various connections. Leave extra time if you want to do the luge at Fräkmüntegg on the way down.

Cost: 72 CHF round-trip, whether by cogwheel train or gondola/cable car (does not include transportation between Luzern and the mountain). Swiss Travel Pass and Eurail Global pass holders get a 50 percent discount. Keep track of your ticket, as you'll need to scan it several times, up and down, until you exit at the last station.

LUZERN

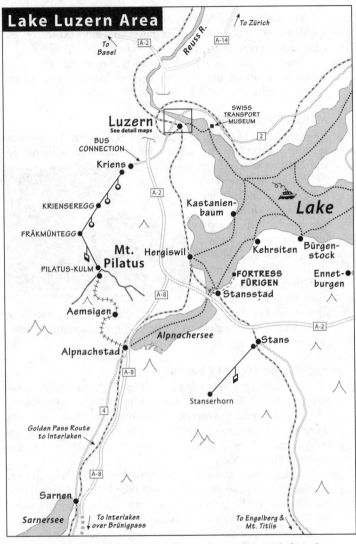

Two **combo-tickets** cover all transportation, including between Luzern and the mountain: the Golden Round Trip (using a boat for the first leg) and the Silver Round Trip (using a train). These tickets don't save money, but they do simplify your journey with just one ticket.

Crowd-Beating Tips: The top of Mount Pilatus is popular and very crowded in summer and on sunny spring and fall weekends. You may have to wait to go up (between 9:00-12:00) and to get back down (15:00-closing time). Reservations are not available.

Information: www.pilatus.ch.

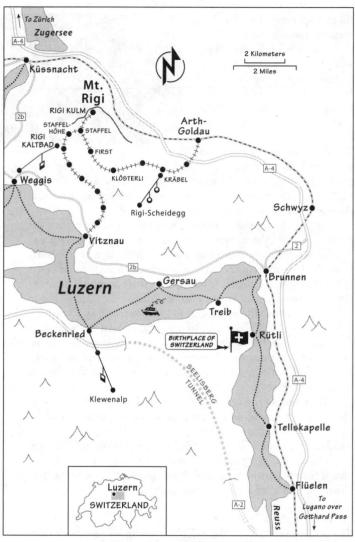

By Cogwheel Train from Alpnachstad: The cogwheel train, with old wooden cabins and red-velvet seats, leaves from the lakeside town of Alpnachstad. To reach Alpnachstad from Luzern, take either the **S5 train** (2/hour, 17 minutes, 8.60 CHF one-way, part of this journey not covered by the Visitors Card—before boarding, buy a 5.80-CHF ticket to cover the stretch from Hergiswil to Alpnachstad) or the **boat,** which leaves from opposite the train station (6/day, 1-1.5 hours, 28 CHF one-way). The cogwheel train runs late May-mid-Nov only (daily, 30 minutes up, 40 minutes down; first train up at 8:10; last train up at 17:10, last train down at 17:45;

shorter operating times in Nov, does not run off-season).

The ride up is dizzying—you'll be keenly aware that this is the steepest cog railway in the world (the grade, marked by signs, maxes out at 48 percent). For the best views, take a downhill-facing seat with your left shoulder against the window. You'll slowly trundle up through thick forest on a skinny stone track, with peek-a-boo views of the lakes below, occasionally passing through chunky-walled tunnels. The train stops halfway up at Ämsigen to let other trains pass—stay on board.

By Gondola/Cable Car from Kriens: The gondola/cable car combination to Pilatus starts from Kriens, a suburb of Luzern.

To reach Kriens, catch city bus #1, which departs frequently from the Luzern train station; the stop is on the other side of the street from where most of the bus platforms are located (15-minute ride, direction: Kriens, stop: Zentrum Pilatus). Exiting the bus in Kriens, cross the busy street and follow *Pilatus* signs 10 minutes uphill to the gondola station. (To return to Luzern from the gondola station, carefully follow blue-and-white signs for *Luzern bus Nr. 1* downhill for several minutes through a pleasant residential area to find bus #1; you don't want the bus stop in front of the gondola terminal.)

The **gondola** runs continuously from Kriens to Fräkmüntegg (30-minute trip; stay on the gondola at the Krienseregg midstation). At Fräkmüntegg, leave the gondola and line up for the **cable car** to the summit (7 minutes, 4/hour). The gondola and cable car run year-round, except for two weeks' maintenance in fall (first ascent from Kriens at 8:30, mid-April-mid-Oct last descent from Pilatus at 17:30, off-season last descent at 16:30).

At the Pilatus Summit

The centerpiece of the Pilatus-Kulm summit—where both cable cars and cogwheel trains arrive—is a vast, underground visi-

tors center. Here you'll find a good information office, souvenir shop, snack bars, and, at busy times, long lines of people waiting to head back down the mountain.

Get oriented by heading out to the big **panoramic terrace,** filling the area between the round, modern Hotel Bellevue and the old-school Hotel Pilatus-Kulm. (The visitors center is beneath your feet.)

Head over to the north (Luzern) side, overlooking the cable car. You're looking at Switzerland's vast central plateau, where more than two-thirds of the Swiss people live (many in the cities of Luzern, Zürich, Bern, and Basel). Immediately below, you can see the city of Luzern clustered around its little corner of the meandering, multifingered Lake Luzern (Vierwaldstättersee). For an even better view over the lake, go to the little gap between the boxy cable-car station and Hotel Bellevue. (The trail up to Esel—described later—begins right here.) Notice how Pilatus forms the first high, jagged peak of the mountains that fan out to the south.

Cross the terrace to the cogwheel-train side and survey the cut-glass peaks of the Swiss Alps—which stretch from this point all the way to Italy. Looking out over this impenetrable wall of granite, it's easy to understand how Switzerland planned to essentially seal off its mountainous interior in case of invasion during World War II. Pilatus and the nearby peaks mark the boundary of the high-altitude fortress system called the Swiss National Redoubt. Exploring the Pilatus area, you'll see signs of hidden Swiss military installations, and the tourable stronghold of Fortress Fürigen is nearby (described later in this chapter).

Sleeping and Eating at the Summit

Sleeping: Two **$$$$** hotels at the summit offer a total of 50 rooms; the information office in the visitors center serves as the reception desk for both. The hotels book as "half-board," meaning room rates include breakfast and dinner. **Hotel Pilatus-Kulm** is in a historic building from 1900; the modern **Hotel Bellevue** is clean and bright, with Nordic-style furniture. The hotels share contact information: +41 41 329 1212, www.pilatus.ch, hotels@pilatus.ch.

Eating: Inside the visitors center is a basic **$ self-service cafeteria;** outside you'll find the cheaper **$ Panorama Grill.** The table-service **$$ restaurant** at the Hotel Pilatus-Kulm has both indoor and outdoor dining areas.

Hiking on Mount Pilatus

Many hiking opportunities—from easy to challenging—lead from the summit to great viewpoints. Review your choices below, and stop by the information office to pick up a map. For a representative sample, I'd ascend Esel, then head up to Oberhaupt and down around the other side.

Easy Hikes: From the outdoor terrace, the peak called **Oberhaupt** (marked with a cross) looms above you and is just a five-minute climb. From there, you can continue on a 15-minute loop that goes along the ridge above Hotel Pilatus-Kulm (toward the

Luge Lesson

Taking a wild ride on a summer luge is a quintessential alpine experience. In German, it's called a *Sommerrodelbahn* ("summer toboggan run"). To try one of Europe's great accessible thrills, take the lift up to the top of a mountain, grab a wheeled sled-like go-cart, and scream back down the mountainside on a banked course. Then take the lift back up and start all over again.

Luge courses are highly weather-dependent and can close at the slightest hint of rain. If the weather's questionable, call ahead to confirm that your preferred luge is open. Stainless-steel courses are more likely than concrete ones to stay open in drizzly weather.

Operating the sled is simple: Push the stick forward to go faster, pull back to apply brakes. Even a novice can go very, very fast. Most are cautious on their first run, speed demons on their second...and bruised and bloody on their third. A woman once showed me her travel journal illustrated with her husband's dried five-inch-long luge scab. He had disobeyed the only essential rule of luging: Keep both hands on your stick. To avoid a bumper-to-bumper traffic jam, let the person in front of you get as far ahead as possible before you start. You'll emerge from the course with a wind-blown hairdo and a smile-creased face.

Key Luge Terms

Lenkstange	lever
drücken / schneller fahren	push / go faster
ziehen / bremsen	pull / brake
Schürfwunde	scrape
Schorf	scab

biggest radar station in Switzerland, housed in an off-limits military zone), down some steep stairs, and around to the other side of the mountain. From here, you'll follow the "Dragonpath"—carved through tunnels and viewpoints in the rock—and eventually return to the visitors center. On the way, you'll look out over a tiny church (and its graveyard) clinging to the sharp crest of a ridge—this is the Klimsenkapelle, built in 1861.

On the other side of the platform, a steep 10-minute hike above Hotel Bellevue takes you up to **Esel** ("Donkey," commemorating the days before cable cars, when Queen Victoria came up to Pilatus on the back of a donkey). From up here, savor 360-degree views over the entire area. Below Esel hides an impressive part of Switzerland's anti-aircraft defense system. Patches of imitation rock in the mountainside hide modern missiles that point to the skies.

Harder Hikes: Hiking to **Tomlishorn** (35 minutes one-way), you'll spot more camouflaged military installations. Stop at the yellow *Echo* sign and shout your message out to the world. Somebody out there keeps yelling it back.

A 1.5-hour hike leads to the 6,700-foot cross-capped summit of **Matthorn** (not Matterhorn). This hike is moderately strenuous—generally uphill, with lots of ups and downs. A visitors' book invites you to sign and leave your impressions on this breathtaking spot.

LUZERN

Activities at Fräkmüntegg

This spot, on the north slope of Pilatus, is a summer-fun zone. If the weather's good, stop here to zip down the nearly mile-long Fräkigaudi, Switzerland's longest **luge ride** (9 CHF/ride, daily mid-April-Oct 10:00-17:00, closed if rainy, mandatory bag check, expect lines on sunny weekends, a 5-minute walk below the cable-car station, +41 41 630 3321, www.rodelbahn.ch).

At the fun **Suspension Rope Park** (Seilpark), you can test your agility on 10 ropes courses with varying degrees of difficulty (28 CHF includes instruction and three hours on the courses, family discounts—separate course for kids under age 8; late April-late Oct daily 10:00-17:00, until 17:30 in July-Aug; next to the cable-car station, www.pilatus.ch).

FORTRESS FÜRIGEN

Fortress Fürigen (Festung Fürigen), built during World War II when Hitler threatened Switzerland, shows you another face of the country. Part of the reason Switzerland has been able to remain peaceful and neutral is its elaborate and secret system of defensive bunkers and fortresses. This fascinating exhibit, worth ▲ (or ▲▲▲ for military history buffs) is

Swiss Military Readiness

Strolling through the charming pastoral greenery of a peaceful Swiss village, my friend walked with me to the door of a nondescript barn. He said, "Stand here," and slid open the door to reveal a solitary, mighty gun—pointing right at me. Crossing a field, kicking a stray soccer ball back to a group of happy grade-schoolers, we came to another barn. This time I noticed the "wooden" door was actually metal, with a clever paint job. Inside was a military canteen, now selling snacks to civilians, and a steel ladder leading down

into a military-gray world that felt like a vast submarine. A network of passages, just big enough for heavily armed soldiers to race down single file, led to a series of gun barns and subterranean command rooms.

Switzerland may be famous for its neutrality, but it's anything but lax defensively. Travelers marvel at how Swiss engineers have conquered the Alps with the world's most-expensive-per-mile road system. But no one designs a Swiss bridge or tunnel without also designing its destruction. Each comes with built-in explosives, so, in the event of an invasion, the entire country can be blasted into a mountain fortress.

Even today, you can't get a building permit without an expensive first-class bomb shelter worked into the plan. Old tank barriers (nicknamed "Toblerones" for their shape) stand ready to be dragged across the roads to slow any invasion. Sprawling hospitals are dug into mountains, still ventilated to be kept dry and ready for use. And halfway up alpine cliffs, Batcave-type doors slide open to allow fighter jets to zoom into action from hidden airstrips cut out of solid rock.

The end of the Cold War in 1989 brought changes even to neutral Switzerland. With deep cuts in its defense budget, Switzerland closed many of its 15,000 hidden fortresses. Some of the forts, such as Fürigen, are now tourist attractions that are no more formidable than medieval castles.

open only on weekends April through October. Visitors explore the facility with the help of audioguides, interactive displays, and short films. It's even possible to fiddle with—and even aim—heavy guns, knowing the ammo is now imaginary.

Cost and Hours: 7 CHF, cash only, covered by Swiss Travel Pass, April-Oct Sat-Sun 11:00-17:00, closed Mon-Fri and Nov-

March, +41 41 618 7340, www.nidwaldner-museum.ch (click on "Festung Fürigen").

Getting There: Fortress Fürigen is just outside the lakefront town of Stansstad, not far from Luzern. It's an easy trip from Luzern on the S4 **train** (8.60 CHF, 2/hour, 16 minutes). From the train station in Stansstad, walk 15-20 minutes, following brown signs to *Festungsmuseum* or yellow hiking signs to *Kehrsiten* (down Bahnhofstrasse to Stanserstrasse, cross and follow signs, turn right on Achereggstrasse—where you'll pass a grocery and bakery that are handy for lunch—and then go left on Kehrsitenstrasse). You'll wind up walking along the lakefront, passing through a nice little park with free WCs and a beach, then cutting inland to circle behind the Aiola restaurant and a marina. Finally, you'll wind along the lake, on the shoulder of a narrow road, under cliffs for a few hundred yards. Watch for the low-profile shed burrowed into the cliff on your right: That's the entrance.

You can also get to Stansstad from Luzern by **boat** (21 CHF, 4/day, 40-80 minutes). From Stansstad's boat dock, walk 10 minutes up to the main street (Achereggstrasse) and keep left, following the brown signs for *Festungsmuseum*.

Drivers arriving in Stansstad should follow white signs to *Kehrsiten* and the lakeside parking lot. From here it's a 5-minute walk along the lake (behind the marina and along the cliffs) to the museum entrance.

Combining the Fortress with Mount Pilatus: The fortress is in the same direction from Luzern as Mount Pilatus, making it possible to combine both sights in one well-organized day. Stansstad (where you'll walk to the fortress) and Alpnachstad (where you'll take the cogwheel train to Pilatus) are on different rail lines, which fork at Hergiswil, so you'll have to backtrack there to change trains. Or consider taking a 10-minute taxi between the fortress and Alpnachstad for about 30 CHF (call ABC Taxi Nidwalden, based near the fortress, +41 41 620 0303, www.abc-taxi-nidwalden.ch).

Background

Fortress Fürigen was built in 1941, at a time when Switzerland found itself surrounded by hostile enemies: Nazi Germany, Nazi-controlled France, and Mussolini's Italy. The Swiss saw themselves as hedgehogs—if threatened, they were ready to curl up into a ball, spines out. In case of an invasion, the Swiss government would retreat to a secret bunker near Brünig in the Berner Oberland, and Swiss troops would abandon the central plateau (and the cities of Luzern, Zürich, Basel, and Bern) and fall back around the alpine stronghold known as the Swiss National Redoubt. The fortress at Fürigen, located at the boundary of that fortified zone (and one of nine such fortresses that ringed Lake Luzern), was meant to protect roads and rail lines that led from Luzern and Zürich along the lake into the mountains. This fortress came equipped with two cannons that could hurl huge artillery shells in the direction of Mount Pilatus. Fürigen (the name comes from a village and former grand hotel on top of the cliff) was one of the smaller fortresses of its type.

After World War II, these fortresses were retooled with a new focus: the threat of the Soviet Union and nuclear war. Fürigen could house and feed 100 people for three weeks. But in 1990, with the end of the Cold War, the practical Swiss decommissioned the fortress, refit it with vintage WWII and early Cold War gear, and opened it to the curious public. It's now administered by the local historical museum.

Visiting the Fortress

The fortress consists of an underground bunker that's invisible from the outside. Enter through an innocent-looking wooden shed. At

the entrance, ask for the brochure (with map) and included English audioguide (which tells the story well). The bunker is always chilly (about 55 degrees Fahrenheit), but no worries: Visitors without jackets are loaned original Swiss Army coats. Allow an hour to visit the various parts of the bunker.

Just inside the entrance, you'll pass a machine-gun emplacement—aimed right at the front door. Then make your way down the 200-yard-long main tunnel. You'll pass the radio room—located near the entrance to assure clear reception—and reach a second machine-gun emplacement, guarding the inner door. Soon after, a detour leads to one of the two heavy artillery emplacements. The giant cannons, each operated by a half-dozen troops, could launch shells more than six miles. You can grab the wheels to aim the massive gun.

Continue deeper down the main tunnel, through heavily

fortified doors, to the fresh-air tunnel, which provided exactly that—creating a buffer in case of atomic attack (you can see the "atom filter" installed in 1960). Beyond that is the second big artillery emplacement. The main tunnel ends at the engine room, which provided electricity and ventilation for those stationed inside, even when shut off from the outside world.

On your way back out the main tunnel, two more worthwhile detours are on the left. First are the living quarters for the troops stationed here. Step into the WC (to see the one shower shared by all 100 men), then into the dining hall, kitchen, and storage rooms. Nearby is the hospital and a rack of guns, all lined up and ready to grab. Upstairs is the big bunk room for the enlisted men (their standard-issue gear is displayed in the cabinets), and the more private officers' quarters and offices.

Farther along—on the way out—step into the former munition magazine, which now houses a well-presented small museum. You'll see one of those huge shells that the big cannons could fire, and watch an informative video about the Swiss plan to use their National Redoubt in case of invasion. Nearby, a cheery cartoon implores homemakers to stockpile food—since they could never be sure when it might be cut off.

MOUNT RIGI

This long, shelf-like mountain, across the lake from Luzern, provides sweeping views of Central Switzerland (and, on a clear day,

Germany and France, too). Even though it's at a lower altitude (5,900 feet) than Pilatus, this so-called Queen of the Mountains boasts the oldest cog railway in Europe (from 1870) and claims to offer the best vistas in the area. Like Pilatus, the top can be busy between 10:00 and 15:00—especially in summer and on good-weather weekends.

Ascending Mount Rigi

You can reach the top of Rigi, called Rigi Kulm, from either its "front" (west, lake-facing) or "back" (east) side. Hourly cogwheel trains chug up to the summit from base stations on both sides (hikers can hop off partway up or down). The west side also has a cable-car option to the lakefront.

The schedules and prices listed here are for April through mid-October (boats and the Vitznau-Rigi Kulm train run less frequently in winter). Trains run hourly, so a missed connection can be a big waste of time; check schedules locally before you go.

Cost: 121 CHF round-trip—that's 49 CHF for the boat ride from Luzern to Vitznau and back from Weggis to Luzern, and 72

CHF for a day pass on the cogwheel train and cable car. With a Swiss Travel Pass, the entire trip is free; with a Eurail Global pass, it's half-price (but you'll have to use one of your flexi-days). To simplify things, buy your Rigi Kulm ticket at the boat dock.

Information: www.rigi.ch.

From the West: From Luzern, coming up the west side makes the most sense, as it gives you an excuse to take a scenic boat ride to the base of the mountain. My recommended round-trip from Luzern: boat to Vitznau; cogwheel train to Rigi Kulm; mountaintop fun up top; cable car back down to Weggis; boat back to Luzern. You could do it the other way around—cable car up, cogwheel train back—but the train is more impressive on

the way up, and doing it this way lets you walk downhill from the cable car to the boat. Figure 5-6 hours for the total round-trip from Luzern.

From Pier 1 in front of Luzern's train station, hourly **boats** leave for Weggis (45 minutes), then continue to the cogwheel train station at Vitznau (one hour). From Vitznau, the **cogwheel train** chugs to Rigi Kulm, the mountain's summit (hourly, 30 minutes up, 40 minutes down, daily 8:15-16:15, later in summer). The train departs from right in front of the boat dock. For the best views up, sit on the side closest to the station, ideally facing downhill. The train makes several stops on the way up, including Rigi Kaltbad (with the cable-car station to Weggis). Stay on the train until it reaches the top, **Rigi Kulm.** There you'll find a small information office, souvenir shop, snack bar, and WCs.

Have fun up top! Enjoy the views, maybe go for a hike (options described later). Eventually, you'll want to wind up at the **Rigi Kaltbad** station (a 15-minute train ride or one-hour downhill hike from Rigi Kulm).

At Rigi Kaltbad, find the **cable car** (Seilbahn), just toward the lake from the train station. It carries you down in 10 minutes to Weggis on the lakefront (2/hour, Mon-Fri 6:30-19:25, Sat-Sun from 8:10). From here you'll walk about 10 minutes downhill to the **boat dock** (follow *Schiffstation* signs) for your cruise back to Luzern (hourly, 45 minutes). In summer, the last boat departs at 20:57 (earlier off-season); if you miss it, you can get back to Luzern by taking the bus to Küssnacht, then the train to Luzern from there.

From the East: If you're visiting Rigi from Zürich, Lugano, or other points to the north, east, and south, it makes sense to ascend the "back" side of the mountain from the Arth-Goldau station, on Switzerland's main north-south rail line. From Arth-Goldau, a cogwheel train takes you up to the summit (about hourly, first train at 7:55, last train at 17:23, runs later in summer, 45-minute ride).

Sleeping and Eating at the Summit

Stay overnight and watch the sun rise, accompanied only by the sounds of the wind and the ringing of a few cow bells.

$$$ Rigi Kulm Hotel is set just below the summit, with 33 rooms, stunning views, and a basic **$ cafeteria** and pricier restaurant (+41 41 880 1888, www.rigikulm.ch, hotel@rigikulm.ch, Käppeli family).

$$$ Rigi Kaltbad Mineral Bath & Spa, at the point where the cable car from Weggis meets the Vitznau-Rigi Kulm train line, has 50 rooms and is a nice place to rejuvenate with its indoor and outdoor pools and bathing areas (+41 41 399 8181, www. hotelrigikaltbad.ch, info@hotelrigikaltbad.ch).

Hiking on Mount Rigi

The mountain is laced with more than 60 miles of hiking trails and other attractions to while away an afternoon. All are well described

in the *Rigi Explorer Guide,* available at Luzern's TI, at lift and cogwheel train stations, and on the Rigi website.

Easy Summit Hike: The obvious choice is the easy, uphill hike to the **summit at Rigi Kulm** (5,899 feet), at the base of a giant Swisscom communications tower. It's directly above the Rigi Kulm station, about 10 minutes if you huff up the steep path, or 20 minutes if you loop around on the more scenic, gentler path (both paved). Up top, you have sweeping views in every direction. The big lake below you is the Zugersee, with the town of Zug on its right side (behind the hill). In the opposite direction the snow-covered peaks of the Swiss Alps recede and overlap all the way to Italy.

Classic Rigi Kulm to Rigi Kaltbad Hike: The lovely downhill ramble from the summit at Rigi Kulm to the cable-car station at **Rigi Kaltbad** takes about one hour. You can also go partway, to the scenic Staffel train station (about 20 minutes), and take the train from there.

If you opt for the whole hike, carry on past Staffel, following the blue *Staffelhöheweg* signs along the train tracks—enjoying a slow-motion look at the same grand views you saw from the train. At the fork, stay right for the 30-minute route to Rigi Kaltbad (the left fork takes 50 minutes). When you reach the next little station, at Staffelhöhe, keep along the trackside trail another 15 minutes to Rigi Kaltbad.

Chänzeli Detour: This detour from the station at Staffelhöhe adds 10 minutes to your Rigi Kaltbad travel time but is well worth it: From the station, veer off to the right, hiking out along one last ridge—flanked by fingers of Lake Luzern and with vistas in all directions. After passing a hilltop crucifix, you'll twist down on switchbacks to the concrete Chänzeli viewpoint (4,800 feet), with excellent views over Pilatus and Luzern. From here it's an easy and level 10-minute walk to Rigi Kaltbad's cable-car station.

Alpkäserei Chäserenholz Route: With a little more time, consider the fun Alpkäserei Chäserenholz (alpine dairy) route from Rigi Kulm down to Rigi Kaltbad (about 1.5 hours), which offers a chance to sample some mountain cheese at a working farm. From the Rigi Kulm train station, walk in the opposite direction from the restaurant—alongside the long barn-like structure at the head of the tracks. From here, follow the unpaved road steeply downhill about 15 minutes, following *Alpkäserei Chäserenholz* signs.

You'll reach a fork in the road, pointing right to the Staffel train station, or left down to the cheese hut. The alpine dairy has a simple menu of drinks and cheese specialties—which taste that much better a mile high, where they're made (cash only, usually open daily in season 9:00-18:00—off-season, confirm it's open before hiking down; also has a few rooms; +41 41 855 0206, chaeserenholz@bluewin.ch). After visiting the hut, hike a steep 5-10 minutes back up to the crossroads and turn left, following *Staffel* signs another 20 minutes to Staffel—on a gravel road, passing through bucolic farmland with mountain views. At the big white tents, fork off to the right to head up to the Staffel station. From here, you can either hop on the train, or walk the rest of the way to Rigi Kaltbad and the cable-car station (follow directions above, under **"Classic Rigi Kulm to Rigi Kaltbad Hike"**). If you're ambitious, add in the Chänzeli detour from Staffel on your way back to the cable car.

Alpkäserei Chäserenholz Extension: For a longer hike from the alpine dairy, continue down Rigi's "back" ridge to the alpine hut **Obere Schwändihütte,** then across the mountain to the Klösterli stop, where you can visit the cute Chapel of Maria-of-the-Snow before hopping on the cogwheel train (1.5 hours from the summit to Klösterli stop). You can also hike along sections of the Mark Twain trail, which traces his route up the mountain (as described in *A Tramp Abroad*), with excerpts from his account signposted along the way.

BERN & MURTEN

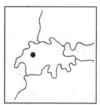

Enjoy urban Switzerland in the charming, compact capital of Bern, with a location that's easily spliced into many Swiss itineraries. This is where Albert Einstein uncovered his genius and where artist Paul Klee set a playful, creative tone that lives on in this likable town. Bern's neighbors are appealing, too: Ramble the ramparts of Murten, Switzerland's best-preserved medieval town, and resurrect the ruins of an ancient Roman capital in nearby Avenches.

PLANNING YOUR TIME

On a quick trip, big Bern and little Murten—about a half-hour apart by train or car—are each worth a half-day. Either makes a fine day trip or overnight stop. Murten, while easy by train, is even better by car.

Bern is a convenient stop between other Swiss destinations (such as going from the Berner Oberland to Murten, Luzern, or Zürich). But a short taste of Bern may leave you wanting more. Consider spending a night (or two) to linger, explore, and savor its livability.

If you're day-tripping, stick your bag in a locker at the Bern station, spend a few hours taking my self-guided "Heart of Bern" walk and visiting some museums, then catch a late-afternoon train to

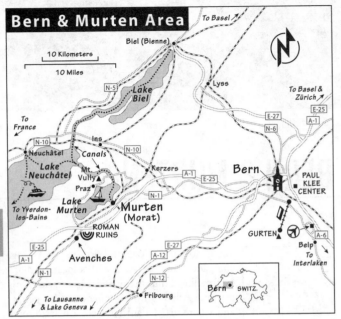

BERN & MURTEN

your next stop. You could combine the destinations in this chapter by ending your busy Bern day in Murten, where you can spend the evening wandering the walls and savoring a lakeview dinner. In the morning, linger in Murten or move on to your next destination.

Bern

Stately but human, classy but fun, Switzerland's de facto capital is the most rewarding place to experience Swiss urbanity. Window-shop along streets lined with cozy, covered arcades, people-watch in the lively market square, and sip from your choice of colorful, historic fountains. Enjoy Bern's excellent museums, quaint-for-a-capital ambience, and delightful river scene. In this city (and canton), look for flags "bear-ing" the symbol of the local mascot: a roaring bear.

The city, founded in 1191, managed to avoid war damage and hasn't burned down since a great fire swept through in 1405. After the fire, wooden buildings were no longer allowed, and Bern took on its gray-green sandstone complexion (using stone quarried nearby). During its 12th- and 13th-century growth spurt, the town grew through two walls. Looking at the map of the city—contained within a bend of the Aare River—you can see how Bern started with a castle at the tip of the peninsula and expanded with a series of walls, each defending an ever-bigger city from its one land-accessible side. The clock tower marks the first wall (1218). A generation later, another wall was built (in 1256, at today's prison tower). The final wall—where today's train station sits—was built in 1344.

In 1353, the surrounding canton (also called Bern) became the eighth to join the Swiss Federation. Today, Canton Bern is Switzerland's second-largest, both in area (after Graubünden) and population (after Zürich). Since 1848, the city of Bern has been Switzerland's seat of government. It's small for a capital (140,000 people, or 400,000 with the suburbs—two-thirds Protestant and one-third Catholic). Though firmly German-speaking, it's strategically located near French-speaking regions, and you'll also hear French around town.

Bern's pointy towers, sandstone buildings, colorful fountains, and riverside setting make it one of Europe's finest surviving medieval towns. Einstein, Klee, and a trio of real, live mascot bears are among the famous Bernese who've contributed to the inviting character of this wonderfully livable small city. And more than 18,000 students help keep Bern young and frisky, despite all the government ministries and bureaucrats.

Orientation to Bern

User-friendly Bern is packed into a peninsula bounded by the Aare River. The train station is located where the peninsula connects to the mainland. From there, a handy main drag leads gradually downhill, straight through the middle of town past most of the major sights, to the tip of the peninsula (then across a bridge and finally to the Bear Park and a hilltop rose garden). Allow a leisurely 30 minutes to walk from the station to the Bear Park following my self-guided walk, later in this chapter.

Tourist Information: The main TI is on the ground floor inside the train station (Mon-Fri 9:00-18:00, Sat-Sun until 17:00, +41 31 328 1212, www.bern.com). If you don't have a Swiss Museum Pass and plan to do some serious sightseeing, ask about the Museum Card, which covers the main sights in town (28 CHF/24 hours, 35 CHF/48 hours).

ARRIVAL IN BERN

By Train: Bern's bustling train station is a thriving three-story mall. The trains almost get lost. The lower level—where the trains arrive—has pay WCs (with showers), a Co-op grocery store, a big Migros takeaway deli, and lots of other long-hours, takeout eateries. The ground floor has the TI, train ticket office (Mon-Fri 7:00-21:00, Sat-Sun until 20:00), and lockers (down a corridor behind the TI). And on the upper level, you'll find another Migros grocery store and a pharmacy (long hours daily).

On arrival, follow signs to exit to *Bahnhofplatz*. Trams and buses fan out from under the glass canopy on this square (use the electronic board and posted maps to find the correct lettered platform—or *Kante*—for your bus or tram). While most of my recommended sights and accommodations are within walking distance, hopping a bus or tram can be smart (and, with the Bern Ticket provided by your hotel, it's free; your lodging confirmation serves as your transit ticket until you get the card at check-in).

By Car: The old town is essentially car-free (only service vehicles and public transit allowed). The most convenient place to park near the old town is the underground Casino Bern garage at Kochergasse 1, very close to the Zytglogge clock tower (3.60 CHF/hour, 28 CHF/24 hours, www.parking-bern.ch). For cheaper parking (especially if staying longer), consider the park-and-ride at the Neufeld exit (2 CHF/hour, 18 CHF/day, includes bus ride downtown to the train station). If you're staying overnight, ask your hotel if they have a discount deal. Another affordable option—if you're day-tripping to Bern and want to visit the Paul Klee Center—is to park there all day (until midnight) for 7 CHF, then hop on bus #12 into the town center.

HELPFUL HINTS

Blue Monday: Most of Bern's museums are closed on Mondays. But you can still follow my self-guided walk, tour the cathedral (and climb its tower), tour the Zytglogge-Turm, watch the parliament in action (generally possible Mon afternoons), ogle the beasts at Bear Park, and go for a stroll along the river.

Market: An outdoor market with clothes, gifts, and other merchandise fills Waisenhausplatz at the north end of Bärenplatz several times per week (Tue 9:00-18:00 and Sat until 17:00, plus April-Oct Thu 9:00-18:00, does not run in Dec, www.marktbern.ch).

Bookstore: A block from the train station, **Stauffacher** is huge, with an entire floor of English books, including a fine selection of writing on Switzerland, and a café (Mon-Fri 9:00-19:00, Thu until 20:00, Sat until 17:00, closed Sun, Neuengasse 37—for location see the "Bern Hotels & Restaurants" map, later, +41 31 313 6363, www.stauffacher.ch).

Laundry: The self-service **Jet Wash** launderette is a three-stop bus ride from the train station (Mon-Sat 7:00-21:00, Sun 9:00-18:00, take bus #20 from platform E in front of station to the Lorraine stop, then find Dammweg 43 on the left, +41 77 417 9502, www.jetwash.ch). For location, see the "Bern Hotels & Restaurants" map, later.

GETTING AROUND BERN

The city is walkable, though its buses and trams can be handy. For short rides of up to five stops—such as between the train station and Bear Park—buy a *Kurzstreckebillet* (short-stretch ticket, 2.60 CHF). For longer journeys—such as going all the way out to the Paul Klee Center—you'll need an *Einzelbillett* (standard single ticket, 4.60 CHF). A day pass is 9.20 CHF (buy tickets from touch-screen machines at stops, credit cards accepted, info at +41 31 321 8844, www.bernmobil.ch). All public transit in Bern is also covered by the Swiss Travel Pass. And if you're overnighting here, your hotel or hostel will give you a Bern Ticket that covers local transit. Be sure to ask for it at check-in (using it may require installing an app on your mobile phone, but after that, the ticket works without an Internet connection).

Tours in Bern

Walking Tours

These leave from mid-April through October from the train-station TI (Wed and Sun at 13:00; Mon, Fri, and Sat at 11:00; off-season Sat at 11:00 only, 1.5 hours, 25 CHF, online booking encouraged, call TI the day before to confirm schedule and ensure the guide speaks English, www.bern.com). This tour can be combined with the TI's tour of the Zytglogge clock (see its description on my "Heart of Bern Walk," next).

Local Guide

Marie-Therese Lauper is a charming and hardworking independent guide who offers special rates for individuals and small groups (+41 079 700 0880, amthlauper@bluewin.ch).

Heart of Bern Walk

Follow this self-guided walk to explore central Bern. You'll start at the train station and finish at the Bear Park at the far end of town, where you can catch a bus back to the station. Along the way, visit a bakery or supermarket to put together a picnic, which you can eat at a terrace behind the cathedral or near Bear Park. (I'll point out a good cheese shop, too.)

❶ Train Station

The station is essentially a bright and airy shopping mall, with a TI and all the

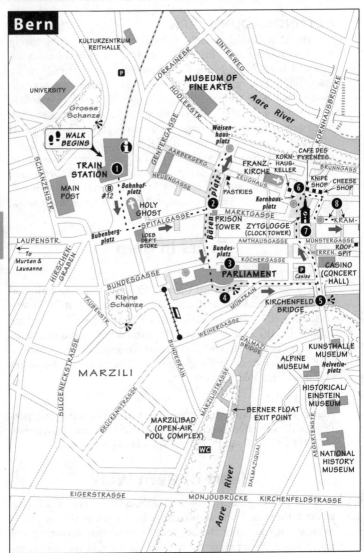

shops you could need. For a grand perch, ride the escalator to the top floor. The huge board listing departures illustrates why so many Swiss urbanites choose not to own a car.

With your back to the big departures board, step outside onto the big square called Bahnhofplatz. The old town was sealed off here with a fortified wall, which was replaced in the 19th century by the train station.

Cross the street to the transit hub under the big glass canopy. Bern's vision is to create a carless city. The striking glass top, de-

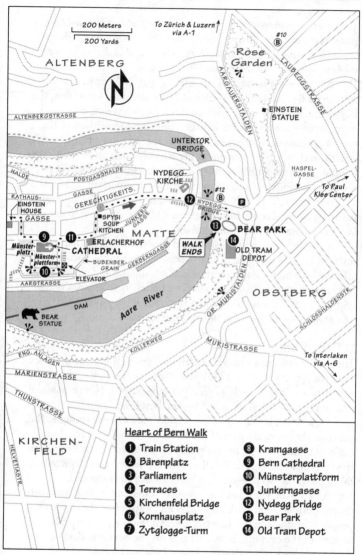

Heart of Bern Walk

1. Train Station
2. Bärenplatz
3. Parliament
4. Terraces
5. Kirchenfeld Bridge
6. Kornhausplatz
7. Zytglogge-Turm
8. Kramgasse
9. Bern Cathedral
10. Münsterplattform
11. Junkerngasse
12. Nydegg Bridge
13. Bear Park
14. Old Tram Depot

signed by renowned Spanish architect Santiago Calatrava, makes riding the bus or tram a bit more elegant.

On the left of the square stands the **Holy Ghost Church** (Heiliggeistkirche). Notice the gray-green Bernese sandstone, used for the church and surrounding buildings. Because this stone is porous and easily eroded by water, Bern's buildings are designed with characteristic oversize eaves. To maintain architectural harmony, even newer buildings (like these) are required to be built with the same local stone (though generally just a thin veneer).

• *Turn left onto the street that runs in front of the church, called Spital-*
gasse. This marks the start of one long street (with four names). The spine
of both the peninsula and our walk, this street rambles downhill through
the heart of town to the bridge and Bear Park.

As you walk under the arcades, about 100 yards down the
street, you'll reach the first of Bern's 11 Renaissance **fountains,** the
Bagpiper. These colorful 16th-century fountains—mostly by the
same artist—are Bern's trademark. The city commissioned them
for many reasons: to brighten the cityscape, to show off the town's
wealth, and to remind citizens of great local heroes and events. The
fountains also gave 16th-century artists something to work on after
the Reformation deprived them of their most important patron, the
Catholic Church. Evenly spaced throughout town, the fountains
naturally became community gathering places—the spot to get the
latest neighborhood news and gossip.

Shopping opportunities abound under the more than three
miles of arcades that line Bern's streets. Stores run the gamut from
affordable to high-end (typically open late on Thu and closed Sun).
In German, the slang for the corridor under these arcades is *Rohr*
(pipe). To stroll through the town is to *rohren* (go piping).

• *Continue* rohren *down Spitalgasse until you reach...*

❷ Bärenplatz

The tram tracks run under the **Prison Tower** (Käfigturm)—once
a part of the city wall (c. 1256). Renovated in the 1640s, the tower
served as a prison until 1897 (*Käfig* means "cage"). Notice how the
hand on the clock really is a hand—and how it was built in a slower-
paced era, when just an hour hand told time precisely enough. The
bears on the tower are part of Bern's coat of arms (with the double-
eagle reminder that Bern was part of the Holy Roman Empire in
the early Middle Ages). You'll see many, many bears depicted all
throughout this walk—and live bears await you at the end.

As each of the town's successive walls and moats was torn
down, Bern was left with an elongated swath of land that's now a
people-friendly "square" like this one. **Bärenplatz** is a top place to
be seen in the evening. It was named for the bear pits that filled a
ditch here, back when this was beyond the town center.

Head to the left 50 yards to find the **Dutch Tower** (Hollän-
derturm). Swiss soldiers were famous mercenaries—guns for hire
who fought all over Europe. Returning from a battle in the Netherlands, the soldiers brought back the habit of smoking. But in the
18th century, smoking tobacco was forbidden within the city walls
of Bern, so they hid in this tower to smoke discreetly. Locals joke
that now that a modern-day smoking ban has come to Bern, this
tower may regain its historic function.

Farther along, about 100 yards down at the far end of the square (here called Waisenhaus-platz), find the modern, mossy **fountain** by the Swiss surrealist Meret Oppenheim. Made in 1983, it symbolizes growth and life and is supposed to demonstrate communication between an object of art and the beholder. It worked

well...too well, in fact, as most citizens immediately communicated their dislike and wanted it destroyed. But Bern's politicians proved braver than expected, and the fountain survived. Time has transformed Oppenheim's gray concrete column into a multicolored pillar topped with moss, grass, and flowers. Residents do like it in the winter, when it's covered with ice. The grand building beyond the fountain—once the city orphanage—is the police station.

Art lovers can detour just a couple of blocks to the left (as you face the fountain) to reach Bern's concise **Museum of Fine Arts,** with one or two quality paintings by virtually all of the great European masters...plus some Swiss artists mixed in (described later, under "More Sights in Bern").

• *With your back to the modern fountain, stroll a few blocks back down toward the south end of Bärenplatz.*

On the nearby corner (with Zeughausgasse), look for the **Glatz** pastry shop; they invented their own local cookie, the *Berner Mandelbärli* ("Bern Almond Bear"). Most mornings except Sunday, this area thrives with market stalls selling local produce, bread, flowers, sausages, cheeses, and other goodies. Farther down, closer to another fountain, are some tempting food carts. Brick-and-mortar restaurants also line the square (see "Eating in Bern," later). Old-timers play giant chess under the trees, and a massive underground parking lot hides under your feet.

• *Just past the end of Bärenplatz looms a giant building. This is the...*

❸ Parliament (Bundeshaus)

You may brush elbows with some high-powered legislators, but you wouldn't know it—everything looks very casual for a national capital. Like so much else in Bern, the parliament building is made of that distinctive green-gray sandstone. When Switzerland became a modern nation in

BERN & MURTEN

1848, Bern became the seat of government for two main reasons: It straddles the German and French parts of the country, and the city offered to build all the necessary buildings. Look right. Look left. This entire chunk of Bern's hilltop is federally owned—including the super-swanky, five-star Bellevue Palace Hotel just up the street to the left, where visiting dignitaries stay. (Legally, Switzerland does not have a "capital"—Bern is simply the seat of government, and the de facto "Federal City," or *Bundesstadt*. But that's a whole other story...)

Check out the building's **statuary:** The woman on the top of the building represents political independence, the one on the left (under the *1291*—when the first three cantons bound together to found the nucleus of Switzerland) stands for freedom, and the one on the right (under *1848*—when the people got their constitution assuring democracy) symbolizes peace.

Switzerland's bicameral system was inspired by the US Constitution, with one big difference: Executive power is shared by a committee of seven, with a rotating ceremonial president and a passion for consensus. This is partly a mechanism to avoid power grabs by any single individual...a safeguard that the Swiss love (and enjoy bragging about lately).

Bundesplatz, the fine granite plaza in front of the parliament (built in 2004 to replace a parking lot), is a favorite spot for demonstrations and markets. On Tuesday and Saturday mornings, it hosts a higher-end market than the one we just saw on Bärenplatz; the choosiest chefs come here to source their ingredients. Hidden in the pavement is a 26-squirt fountain (one for each canton)—a real kid-pleaser and fun photo spot on a hot summer day. On the left is the Swiss National Bank—this country's Fort Knox, with half the Swiss gold stock buried under the square (the rest is in Zürich).

Touring the Parliament: When parliament is in session, the **galleries** are open to the public so you can watch the action (free; generally Mon afternoon, Tue and Thu mornings, and all day Wed; leave ID at entrance, lines can be long, no photos). When parliament is not in session (for example, from mid-July to mid-Aug), you can take a free, guided, hour-long **tour** of the building (English tours typically Wed, Thu, and Sat at 14:00, less frequent outside summer; reserve up to 3 days ahead at www.parlament.ch—click "Services" then "Visiting the Parliament Building," +41 58 322 9022). The visitors entrance is around the back of the building.

• *Walk through the archway to the right of the parliament. You'll pop out overlooking Bern's outskirts from a series of...*

❹ Terraces

From here, you have a commanding view over the outskirts of Bern. Below you flows the Aare River—fed by glaciers, which give it its bright-blue sheen. On a hot day, the river is speckled with locals doing the "Bern float" (described on page 134). On the right side of the river, look for Bern's biggest swimming pool, the **Marzilibad.** Just this side of the pool complex, notice the canal that

cuts away from the river. This was dug recently to allow a safer exit for swimmers floating down the river (before, they had to grab for a pole along the riverbank as they floated past).

Just above the river is Bern's own little "mountain," the **Gurten** (with the view tower poking up above its forested summit). The Gurten is the city's favorite recreation spot, offering a luge ride and music festivals in summer and modest skiing opportunities for children in winter. To frolic with the Bernese, you can either hike up or ride a little funicular to the summit (take tram #9 to Wabern/Gurtenbahn, then ride the funicular from there).

Pan to the left, where, on a clear day, you can see the mirage-like outlines of the **Eiger, Mönch, and Jungfrau**—the highest peaks in the Berner Oberland. The prickly, chalet-style building in front of these peaks holds Bern's Albert Einstein Museum and its Historical Museum, described later and easily reached on the opposite side of the bridge we're about to visit.

Before moving on, look back at the rounded end of the Parliament building; up high, see the colorful seals of the 26 cantons of Switzerland.

• *Turn left and stroll along the terrace walls a few hundred yards to...*

❺ Kirchenfeld Bridge

Walk out to the center of the bridge for great views back on Bern's cathedral and town center—lined up along its promontory and hemmed in by the Aare River. Directly below, notice the security nets. The bridge used to be the favorite place for suicides—to the terror of people living below. Bern has many high bridges, and you'll see this safety netting on all of them.

Look down at the **dam** that runs across the river below you. (Wait—is that a bear out on the dam?) The waterfall here was natural, but a system of modern sluices better controls the flow. Even so, Bern was deluged with dangerous floods until 2005, when a new canal was built upriver—allowing high waters to be diverted harmlessly. Just this side of the dam is the recommended **Schwellenmätteli Restaurant lounge,** where a trendy local crowd enjoys cocktails over the rushing river on nice days. By the way, the Aare begins in the mountains and flows through Interlaken; after leaving Bern, it continues north and joins the Rhine in Basel.

If you continued along this bridge to its far end, you'd reach the sprawling complex of museums (described later, under "More Sights in Bern"); if you're planning to visit any of them, you might do it now.

Otherwise, turn around, and head back to the base of the bridge, then cross the street. The fine building marked *Casino* isn't for gamblers—it's the home of Bern's Symphony Orchestra, and it also hosts graduation ceremonies and wedding receptions. Step into the lobby, then bear right to ogle the vast, opulent café that fills a restored Neoclassical gallery. The outdoor terrace here serves coffee for not much more than other local cafés.

• *Leaving the bridge and the river behind you, follow the tram tracks around the left side of the handsome sandstone house (with the man-and-Swiss-flag mural). You'll reach another swath of land created by the removal of a city wall—first called Theaterplatz, and then...*

⑥ Kornhausplatz

This square is ornamented by the colorful fountain of an **Ogre** (*Chindlifresser,* "child-eater"). Two legends try to explain this gruesome sight. It's either a folkloric representation of the Greek god Chronos, or a figure that was intended to scare children off the former city walls.

Kornhausplatz is a major hub for **tram** traffic, which ground to a halt in the summer of 2019 when record-high temperatures actually warped the tracks. Living in a mountain nation of reced-

ing glaciers, rockslides, and avalanches, the Swiss feel the tangible, everyday effects of climate change. Climate issues are huge in Swiss politics. The country has several environmental parties, and they combined to win an unprecedented 20 percent of available parliament seats a few months after the 2019 heat wave. Meanwhile, Switzerland's far-right, nativist movement has faltered because they've been caught flat-footed on climate issues.

(Apparently, even Swiss racists have a soft spot for the environment.)

The building behind the Ogre, on the left, used to be the granary and now houses the modern public library and the huge recommended **Kornhauskeller** restaurant. If the restaurant is open, wander down the stairs and head inside—even if you're not eating here, you must take a peek at this magnificent subterranean place. Once the vast city wine cellar, this space was built in high Baroque style (1718) and renovated with paintings inspired by the Pre-Raphaelites in 1897. The 12 columns (in the upper level) show traditional costumes of Bernese women. Across the street from the Kornhauskeller, notice the **Café des Pyrénées.** This was a hotspot for Bern's avant-garde in the 1960s; the gray-ponytail crowd still hangs out here today.

Head up the little street next to the café, Rathausgasse, to reach two quality shops selling classic Swiss items (both on the left). First up, at #84, **Klötzli Messerschmiede** sells a wide range of top-quality **knives**—from touristy Swiss Army models, to heirloom-quality pocketknives, to professional chef's knives. Tucked behind the cash register is a special room with a suit of armor and real swords.

Next door at #82, **Zur Chäshütte** (the Cheese Hut) is a little shop with a classic **cheese counter.** Step inside, take a big whiff of the funky aroma, and peruse the well-stocked display case. With more than 150 types of cheese, you may want to buy a few slabs for your picnic. *Rezent* means strong, pungent, and well-aged, while *mitte* is a bit milder. Consider buying a combination: a hard, aged cheese (their "house cheese"—*Hauskäse*—is aged in the cellar below your feet); a more typical, semi-mild Swiss cheese (such as Gruyère, Emmentaler, or the more intense Appenzeller); a goat-milk cheese (Geiss); or perhaps a softer, French-style, brie-like cheese. They also sell yogurt, honey, and jam.

• *Just past the cheese shop, turn right one short block down Zibelegässli. You'll run right into Bern's main landmark...*

❼ Zytglogge-Turm

Bern's famous clock tower was part of the original wall marking the first gate to the city (c. 1250). The clock, which dates back to 1530, performs four minutes before each hour: The happy jester comes to life, Father Time turns his hourglass, the rooster crows (in German, that's "kee-kee-ree-kee" rather than "cock-a-doodle-doo"), and the golden man on top hammers the bells. Apparently, this little spectacle was considered quite entertaining five centuries ago. The word *Zytglogge* is local dialect. The Standard German equivalent, which doesn't actually exist, would be *Zeitglocke* (literally "time bell").

To pass the time waiting for the action, study the clockworks and try to figure out how they work. On the lower disc, does the golden hour hand look like it's running slow? If it does, that's probably because it's showing solar time, and in summer, because of the modern innovation of Daylight Saving Time. You can determine the zodiac, today's date, and the phase of the moon—look at the black-and-gold orb.

Inside the archway under the clock are the old regional measurements (Swiss foot, the bigger Bernese foot, and the *Elle*, or "elbow," which was the distance from the elbow to the fingertip) and the official meter and double meter. It took a strong leader like Napoleon to bring consistency to measurements in Europe; he replaced the many goofy feet and elbows of medieval Europe with the metric system used today (c. 1800).

Touring the Tower: Enthusiasts can tour the medieval internal mechanics—early Swiss engineering at its best—and see the bellows that enable the old rooster to crow (20 CHF, one-hour tour; April-Oct Mon, Fri, and Sat at 14:15, Wed and Sun at 15:15; off-season Sat at 14:15 only; reserve in advance through www.bern. com).

• *With the clock at your back, continue your stroll down the main drag. At this point, you enter the oldest part of town, where bigger department stores are replaced by quainter shops and galleries on...*

❽ Kramgasse

Bern's **arcades,** common in Alpine towns, shelter pedestrians from both sun and snow. Though the arcades are privately owned, own-

ers must keep them clean and allow public access. Then as now, the main activity here is shopping—*kramen* means, roughly, to shop for an assortment of items ("rummage" would be the closest translation). Pop-up stores are popular in Bern—up-and-coming vendors can lease a space for six months to test the market.

Most shops are underneath the arcades, but don't miss the ones in the **cellars** that you can access only from the main road. The cellars, marked by old-time hatches, were (among other things) used for storing wine. The wine was produced around Lausanne on

Lake Geneva, which was then controlled by Bern—so they sent ample amounts of wine here as tribute. People said "merry Bern" was floating on wine, just as Venice was floating on water. The merry times ended in 1798, when Napoleon's army moved in (and drank all the wine). After that, the wine cellars were empty and the city got a new nickname: "sad Bern." Napoleon's soldiers also looted Bern's tremendous treasury, and Napoleon used money from Bern to finance his Egyptian crusade.

In the middle of the street is the **Zähringen Fountain.** It's named for the German duke, Berthold V, the Duke of Zähringen, who founded Bern in 1191. Legend says he couldn't decide on the name, so he went hunting, proclaiming that he'd name the city for the first animal he killed. It was, of course, a *Bär* (bear)—and Bern had its name. Notice the armor-clad bear is holding a flag not of a bear, but of a lion—the family crest of the Zähringers.

Directly in front of and behind the fountain, a **grate** reveals a bit of the canal that used to flow open down the middle of the peninsula, providing people with a handy disposal system, place to wash, and the medieval equivalent of a fire hose. Today, the water that pours from the fountains' spouts is perfectly potable—locals love to brag about the quality of their water. Fill up your bottle and save a few francs.

By the way, although this feels like a pedestrian zone, buses and occasional cars do tend to sneak up on distracted tourists—stay alert. The bus that uses this street—#12—is practically made for visitors, connecting the train station to the Paul Klee Center by way of the main drag...handy to hop on and off at will.

• *Now head down Kramgasse. On the right at #73, chocolate lovers will want to peek into Confiserie Tschirren—the top-end chocolatier and pastry shop in Bern. Keep going. About 200 yards down, on the right at #49, is the home of a very smart man.*

The apartment that Albert Einstein called home between 1903 and 1905—the years when he formulated his special theory of relativity while working in obscurity at the Patent Office—is now the **Einstein House** museum (6 CHF; daily 10:00-17:00, closed late Dec-Jan; +41 31 312 0091, www.einstein-bern.ch). Einstein and his wife Mileva welcomed their first child in this one-bedroom apartment and shared a kitchen and bathroom with the neighbors. Inside, you can see period furniture, including Einstein's Patent Office desk, and a few photos and manuscripts. Another apartment one floor up has been turned into an informative—if dry—exhibit on Einstein's life. This quick, inexpensive visit (well-described in English with a few historic artifacts and a 20-minute video—request English) is just about the right amount of Einstein for most visitors. I actually didn't find it that exciting, but I guess everything's relative.

BERN & MURTEN

Albert Einstein in Bern

The man who changed how we see our universe made his greatest discoveries during the eight years he lived in Bern (1901-1909).

Raised in Germany, Albert Einstein (1879-1955) went to college in Zürich, hoping to land a job teaching math and physics. But the young grad's GPA and résumé were mediocre, so instead he took a job in Bern's Patent Office, inspecting and registering inventions.

Twenty-three-year-old Albert and his new bride Mileva (his brainy college sweetheart) rented an apartment at Kramgasse 49 (today's Einstein House), where Mileva soon gave birth to their first son, little Hans Albert. Einstein punched the clock at the Patent Office and spent his spare time reading, hiking the Bernese countryside, and thinking. At night, he'd join with his mates—the self-named "Olympia Academy"—to smoke, drink beer, and talk math and philosophy. Outwardly, he led an ordinary life, but his thoughts were always on science's Big Questions. At home, in pubs, or at work he'd scribble down equations and ideas, filing them in his self-described "Department of Theoretical Physics"—a desk drawer in his office.

Then, one warm spring day, as Einstein walked on the outskirts of Bern, it all started coming together. So began his annus mirabilis—the miracle year of 1905—in which the 26-year-old amateur physicist wrote five papers that would shock and perplex the world. Published in a major physics journal, they touched on subjects such as how molecules move and how light can appear as either a wave of energy or as a beam of tiny particles.

The most famous paper, his theory of special relativity, described a world in motion. A person on a moving train and someone who's stationary see the world from different perspectives—that's the classic principle of relativity described by Galileo and Newton. But Einstein said there's an exception to the rule—light, which has a speed that remains constant whether it's on a moving train or on the ground. So, a person on a moving train and one at rest won't agree on what they see...yet they're both right.

If this little exhibit piques your interest, consider visiting the Einstein Museum's far more extensive exhibit (triple the price but free with Swiss Travel Pass), located within Bern's Historical Museum (see "More Sights in Bern," later in this chapter).

A bit farther down, you reach the **Samson fountain.** In the statue on top, notice the donkey's jawbone tucked into Samson's waistband. This is the symbol of the butcher's guild, which was

The discrepancies only become obvious as the train travels close to the speed of light. Then, while the person on the train thinks everything is normal, the one on the ground sees the train shrink, train clocks slow down, and the person on the train stops aging!

Einstein's papers initially drew little interest and a measure of skepticism. But over time, other physicists grasped the significance of Einstein's work, seeing how he took earlier findings, wove them together, and did the math that explained it all. Subsequent experiments proved that even Einstein's most bizarre assertions were correct. Time on a fast-moving jet really does slow down (hence, those interminable intercontinental flights).

Einstein was invited to lecture at the local university, though he was still working nine-to-five at the Patent Office. In his spare time, he worked on his next project, general relativity. He theorized that gravity is not a force that attracts things but a curving of space—like a bowling ball on a soft mattress—that affects the motion of nearby objects. In 1909, Einstein's growing reputation won him a job offer to teach in Zürich, and he quit the Patent Office and left Bern for good.

Einstein would never again approach the creative level of his days in Bern. (In 1922, he won the Nobel Prize for his work done during the 1905 annus mirabilis.) Albert and Mileva split, and he married a cousin. When Hitler took power in Germany (1933), Einstein—a pacifist and a Jew—left Europe for America. His curly black hair had turned white, and his aging face later became a pop-culture icon of genius—complete with pipe, moustache, basset-hound eyes, and halo of frizzy white hair (which he backcombed in order to look sufficiently unkempt).

In 1939, Einstein wrote a letter to President Franklin Delano Roosevelt warning that scientists (including some in Germany) could soon discover a way to release an enormous amount of energy. The research was based on a principle he'd outlined back in 1905—that energy is equivalent to mass times the speed of light squared (a very big number). And so, $E = mc^2$ became the principle behind the atomic bomb—a very big bang from an idea hatched in the pubs and arcaded streets of Bern.

To learn more, visit the Einstein House in the town center and the Einstein Museum just across the river (both described in this chapter).

located just to the left, in what is today the music conservatory. Notice how close this fountain is to the previous one. It's believed that the butchers financed this fountain specifically to have one next to their slaughterhouse.

Near the fountain on the right, in the cellar of #37, is **Hanftheke Bern** (*hanf* means hemp), a marijuana shop. In Switzerland, marijuana with less than 1 percent THC (the psychoactive component of cannabis) is legal. This strain is high in cannabidiols, which make you very relaxed...but you can't get high on it. The person behind the counter is happy to explain the local approach to pot.

• *Twenty yards below the Samson fountain, at #29, turn right through the narrow tunnel-lane, Münstergässchen, to the...*

❾ Bern Cathedral (Berner Münster)

Bern's 15th-century Catholic-turned-Protestant cathedral is capped with a 330-foot-tall tower, the highest in Switzerland (finished in 1893). The late-Gothic church was dedicated to St. Vincent of Zaragoza.

Before heading into the church, if it's Tuesday or Saturday, head up the street to your right (Münstergasse) to find a thriving market—this one specializing in meat. At #41 (on the left), look way up high to see a rusted-metal sculpture sticking out from the roofline. This is called **Roofspit,** and it shoots a spurt of water down onto the street below a few times each minute (it's turned off during the market). Notice the 5-CHF coins permanently stuck in the pavement where the water splashes, luring suckers to bend over to grab a coin—and get wet. Who says the Swiss don't have a sense of humor?

Return to the cathedral, and get up close to the **main portal,** with its striking gold-leaf highlights. This seems pretty un-Protestant; it probably survived because its theme, the Last Judgment, showed that no matter how rich you are or what rank you have in Church hierarchy, anyone can end up in hell (an idea Protestants dug). Condemned people are popping in the flames like lottery balls. Notice the humorous details in the commotion of people heading to hell (especially what the little green devil is doing to the sinful monk). Just below on the left are statues of the virtuous virgins (dressed like Bern burghers), while on the right are the foolish virgins who squandered their oil (dressed like the city's historic rivals, the Burgundians).

Cost and Hours: Free to enter cathedral; Mon-Sat 10:00-17:00, Sun from 11:30, shorter hours off-season; audioguide-5 CHF, +41 31 312 0462, www.bernermuenster.ch.

Visiting the Church: Step inside and grab a pew in the nave. The plain interior was once adorned with 26 separate little chapels and altars dedicated to Mary and various saints. An ornate screen separated the priests from the worshippers. But when the Reformation came to town in 1528, all this was swept away. The iconoclasts believed that images distracted worshippers from focusing on God, so they destroyed the distasteful decoration. The new center of attention was the pulpit, where Protestant preachers shared the word of God—not in Latin, but in the people's language.

Those Protestant iconoclasts didn't manage to trash the church's precious painted keystones. Look up to the ceiling, where you can see giant, colorful coats of arms. These don't honor saints, but prestigious Bernese families. Notice that this church isn't a "Cathedral" (that's in Lausanne), but a *Münster.* The local burghers actively discouraged having their church be named a cathedral, because then they'd have a bishop in town, bossing them around. The Bernese burghers remained independent; this church was sometimes called the people's church *(Leutkirche).*

For another bit of decoration that the iconoclasts missed, head to the third glassed-in chapel on the right. High on the far wall (to the left of the window), you can see a bit of an angel's halo; just to the left of this, you can very faintly see an image of Mary kneeling. This was likely a scene of the Annunciation. Historians are using modern technology to uncover pre-iconoclasm art like this.

Continue to the end of the right aisle, and look right for a beautiful, colorful, highly entertaining stained-glass window (from the 1760s) illustrating the "dance of death"—the idea that no matter who you are, no matter how powerful or wealthy, death will still come for you. Spend some time appreciating each of the scenes of a macabre skeleton harassing a Bernese person.

Now head to the giant, black-marble altar under the transept. Look toward the apse; the three stained-glass panels on the left are original, from 1441. Now look up to the ceiling over the choir, where you'll see another 78 colorful keystone decorations, featuring saints and other Christian VIPs.

Climbing the Tower: You can pay 5 CHF to huff up the spiral staircase (more than 300 steps) to a viewpoint at the base of the lacy see-through steeple (same hours as cathedral). From this 210-foot-high vantage point, you enjoy a behind-the-scenes look at the varied courtyards and rooftop gardens hidden behind the conformist building facades. Don't forget to turn around to appreciate an up-close look at the tower's carved figures. On the way down, peek at the cathedral's **bells**—  including the largest bell in Switzerland, a 10.5-ton beauty cast in 1611 and called Susanne (named by a bellringer after his sizeable girlfriend). This bell was so heavy that it took eight men to swing her. If you're up here when the Prayer Bell rings, you may feel the tower sway.

• *Head behind the cathedral to a terrace overlooking the river, the...*

⑩ Münsterplattform

Starting in the 14th century, this terrace was built from all kinds of "recycled" stones from older buildings. Archaeologists have even unearthed some heads of statues that were victims of Reformation iconoclasts.

Look out over the edge of the terrace for another view of the dam in the Aare below you. The base of the terrace, once overgrown, has recently been reclaimed and spiffed up to host many sweet little community gardens.

Twin 18th-century **pavilions** grace the square. On the right is a tiny branch of the city library (providing park-goers with books, *boules,* and table tennis). And in the far left is a café offering a scenic spot under a chestnut tree for a bite or a drink on a sunny day. Behind the café, the elevator (a "vertical tram") has been carrying passengers up and down since 1896 (1.50 CHF).

• *With your back to the river, exit on the right. Walking past the end of the cathedral, turn right and walk down...*

⑪ Junkerngasse

Still the most expensive street to live on in Bern, this sleepy lane was lined with the mansions of the wealthy burghers of Bern—

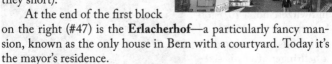

mostly on the right, facing out over the river. But you'd never know it since these mansions blend in with the simple townhouses nearby. The Bernese value thrift and hard work, and pride themselves in not showing off wealth ("That's for Zürich!" they snort).

At the end of the first block on the right (#47) is the **Erlacherhof**—a particularly fancy mansion, known as the only house in Bern with a courtyard. Today it's the mayor's residence.

Just past the building, on the right, notice the **stairs** leading through the wall and down to the river (marked *Bubenbergrain*). Historically, the lower-lying, riverside part of Bern was home to tradespeople: fishermen, tanners, and traders. But they needed to bring their wares up to market in the town, so several of these staircases were built.

A few steps past the Erlacherhof (and the fountain nearby), watch on the left for the tiny lane marked *Ob. Gerechtigkeitsgasse,* with a big sign for *Spysi.* Head down this little lane and look for a door halfway down on the right. This is **Spysi,** a sort of soup kitchen that was established during the Industrial Revolution. Many of the tradespeople who used the steps we just saw were replaced by modern factory jobs, leaving them poor and destitute. Spysi (from *speisen,* "to eat") offered them a very cheap meal. To this day, from November through April, down-on-their-luck Bernese people can get a big bowl of soup and a hunk of bread here for a few coins. Just past Spysi, notice the pissoir—a discrete public urinal for men.

At the end of the little lane is Bern's main drag again—now called Gerechtigkeitsgasse. You're greeted by the **Fountain of Justice,** a blindfolded figure who triumphs over the mayor, pope, sultan, and Holy Roman Emperor. (Notice that Bern's mayor is depicted as being of equal status with these European powers.)

Turn right and walk down the main drag, seeing that—as the terrain changes—the houses get narrower, and the cellar doors are vertical rather than horizontal. Remember that as you walk, you're going back in time, getting closer to the original (and oldest) core of town. The cellars along this stretch are a little less big-corporate and more funky and colorful, from the "Cave of Tango" to the "Seamen's Club."

Near the end of the street on the left, look for the Café Restaurant Treff. Find the three **gutter openings** in the middle of the street out front (sometimes they're covered—if so skip ahead). They're just like the channels we've passed all through town. Except...do you notice anything strange about the middle one? The water is running backward—uphill. This is an elaborate (but very subtle) prank: The water in the middle opening comes from a different source, so it looks like it flows backward, just to, y'know, mess with people. (Swiss humor strikes again!)

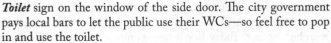

Across the street, find the Junkere Café-Bar at #1. Look for the red *nette Toilet* sign on the window of the side door. The city government pays local bars to let the public use their WCs—so feel free to pop in and use the toilet.

• *From here, you reach...*

BERN & MURTEN

⓲ Nydegg Bridge

Head partway out onto the bridge and look left, where a church sits on the site of the original town castle. Notice the curve of the streets in this part of town: The outer curve follows the path of the original city wall, while the inner curve traces the wall that surrounded the castle. The small bridge below is the oldest in Bern (and, until 1844, was the only bridge crossing the Aare here). High on the ridge, just above the tollbooth's pointy

spire, is the Rosengarten—a delightful garden with a grand view over Bern and a recommended restaurant (described later).

Before you cross the bridge, look upstream. On the side of the tall white building, you can (barely) pick out the words *Fabrique de Chocolat W. Lindt*—the original Lindt chocolate factory, evoking an age when this stretch of river was lined with mills powering the industrial zone of Bern—tanneries, shipyards, lumber mills, and so on. As you look upstream, notice the peaceful path along the left bank, a nice place for a walk.

• *Continue across the bridge, bear right, and look over the railings into...*

⓳ Bear Park (BärenPark)

The symbol of Bern is the bear, and some lively ones frolic along this terraced hillside, to the delight of locals and tourists who crowd along the rails. From 1857 to 2009, Bern housed its mascot bears in two big, barren, concrete pits *(Bärengraben)*. But thanks to the agitation of bear rights' activists, the city government was forced to replace the pits with posher digs. The last of the pit bears died in 2009, and later that year, three-year-old brown bears Finn (a male from

Finland) and Björk (a female from Denmark) moved to the big enclosure between the old pits and the river. Soon they welcomed their female cubs, Ursina and Berna. This ursine family enjoys much better conditions than their fore-bears, including a private fishing channel next to the river. In 2013, the surly teenager Berna was sent to a preserve in Bulgaria due to irreconcilable differences with her mother. Today Bern's bear family is happy, and Berna is shacked up with a new boyfriend in Bulgaria.

The two historic pits are still there. The first one is used from time to time to hold the bears while their enclosure is cleaned. You can visit the second one—find the concrete stairs leading down to the Bären Bistro, a bear-themed bar (for more info, see www.tierpark-bern.ch).

• *Above Bear Park is the...*

⓴ Old Tram Depot (Altes Tramdepot)

This used to be the garage for trams that ran across the bridge from the old town. Now the depot hosts a brewery restaurant/café with a lively beer garden and terrace, a nice public WC, and Eiswerkstatt, a popular ice cream shop.

To continue this walk, you could take a seven-minute hike up the moderately steep, cobbled pathway to the left (with your back to the river).

This takes you to the city's delightful **rose garden** (Rosengarten)—a manicured, picnic-perfect park with inviting benches, a fun kids' play area, the recommended **Restaurant Rosengarten,** and the best viewpoint in town for watching the sunset. A statue of Albert Einstein reposes on one of the benches, inviting humorous selfies.

Alternatively, you could turn right and walk along the river, then return to the center via either Kirchenfeld or Dalmazi bridge.

Or, to return directly to the **train station,** jump on bus #12 (every 6 minutes, get ticket from machine, covered by Swiss Travel Pass or hotel-issued Bern Ticket). For that matter, you could take bus #12 in the opposite direction to head out to the **Paul Klee Center**—just a few minutes' ride.

Wherever you wander in Bern, be sure to get off into the quieter side lanes, which have a fascinating and entertaining array of shops and little eateries.

More Sights in Bern

Some of Bern's top sights are described on my "Heart of Bern Walk," above. With more time, consider visiting some of the city's other sights.

▲Museum of Fine Arts (Kunstmuseum Bern)

Featuring 800 years of art, this three-story museum shows off quality European and Swiss art, plus temporary exhibits. While the specific canvases can change, you'll typically find old masters from the 13th to 19th century (including Fra Angelico and Filippo Lippi); 19th-century Impressionist and Post-Impressionist art by Manet, Monet, Cézanne, Van Gogh, and Toulouse-Lautrec; and 20th-century works by Dalí, Picasso, and Miró. Each artist is represented by one or two fine pieces.

But the stars of the show are the lesser-known Swiss artists, who are mixed in among the big names as if to assert their worthiness on the global stage. Be sure to tune into some of these names: You'll find Paul Klee (1879-1940), of course, with his vivid, almost childlike works. But you'll also discover Adolf Wölfli (1864-1930), who did intricate collages with pencil on paper; Alberto Giacometti (1901-1966), who sculpted rough-textured figures; Ernst Ludwig Kirchner (1880-1938), whose big, colorful, sloppy canvases are reminiscent of Cézanne; Ferdinand Hodler (1853-1918), whose serene landscapes evoke Van Gogh, with bold lines and soothing colors; Pierre Bonnard (1867-1947), an Impressionist with a love of color and a Renoir-like flair; and Johannes Itten (1888-1967), who was influential in the Bauhaus movement and made huge strides in exploring the harmonious use of colors.

Cost and Hours: 10 CHF, extra for some temporary exhibits, covered by Swiss Travel Pass; Tue 10:00-21:00, Wed-Sun until 17:00, closed Mon; no English descriptions—rent the worthwhile English audioguide (6 CHF), café, a block off the north end of Bärenplatz at Hodlerstrasse 8, +41 31 328 0944, www.kunstmuseumbern.ch.

▲▲Paul Klee Center (Zentrum Paul Klee)

Paul Klee wasn't just a great painter—he was an interdisciplinary explosion of creative energy. The center, which fosters music and theater as well as the visual arts, has a mission: to bring art to the people. For example, a huge zone is devoted to a children's creative workshop that includes painting and a shadow theater. The building itself, designed by Italian architect Renzo Piano, is notable: With a wavy design mirroring the wavy landscape of

the Bern countryside, it celebrates the creative spirit of the Swiss-born artist.

Cost and Hours: 20 CHF, covered by Swiss Travel Pass, Tue-Sun 10:00-17:00, closed Mon, audioguide-6 CHF, pick up free English-language booklet for each exhibit, mandatory lockers, café, Monument im Fruchtland 3, +41 31 359 0101, www.zpk.org.

Getting There: From the train station (or other downtown stops), ride frequent bus #12 for 15 minutes to its last stop, Zentrum Paul Klee, then walk 200 yards up the path.

Parking: Museumgoers can park all day (until midnight) for 7 CHF—a great deal if you combine the museum visit with a trip into town afterward. Buy the ticket inside, at the ticket desk.

Children's Workshops: 15 CHF for one-hour workshop (age 4 and up, Tue-Sun at 14:00 and 16:00, Sat-Sun also at 12:00, reservations recommended at +41 31 359 0161).

Visiting the Center: While it owns about 4,000 Klee works, the center has no permanent exhibit; rather, it curates engaging temporary exhibits that pull from its Klee collection—sometimes heavily, sometimes tangentially. (But the curators always make sure there are at least a few Klee pieces on display.) It's the best place in the world to experience and learn about this modernist painter of lively, almost childlike art. Artistically, you can't put Klee in a box. His paintings—mostly from the 1920s and 1930s—are playful yet enigmatic. His art is full of symbolism...or maybe we just think so. Kids love Klee, and they always teach the art snobs a thing or two with their interpretations.

The center fills three connected buildings. As you walk from the bus stop, the first building (no entry fee) has a café, WCs, lockers, and the children's workshop. The second building houses the main exhibition space (with two large halls) and the ticket desk. The third building is mostly administrative, except for a space at the front where visitors can hang out on a giant bench built out of colorful boxes. The grounds surrounding the center, though not that interesting, are open to all. The fancy Restaurant Schöngrün is between the bus stop and the center.

▲Einstein Museum (at Bern Historical Museum)

Fans of the genius will want to visit this museum devoted to Einstein and his times. For those with a keen interest in Einstein or his theories, it's worth ▲▲. This museum is far more engaging than the Einstein House downtown and has many more artifacts from Einstein's life. But it's also much more expensive—so unless you're a serious Einstein fan, or have a Swiss Travel Pass, it may not be worth the money. The Einstein exhibit fills the second floor of Bern's Historical Museum, and the rest of the museum is included in your ticket whether you want it or not—but it's an afterthought to the Einstein section (and skippable).

Cost and Hours: 18 CHF, covered by Swiss Travel Pass, Tue-Sun 10:00-17:00, closed Mon, free downloadable audioguide, +41 31 350 7711, www.einsteinmuseum.ch.

Getting There: It's in the big, prickly, chateau-style building across the Kirchenfeld Bridge from parliament at Helvetiaplatz 5—take tram #6, #7, or #8, or bus #19, or walk a scenic 10 minutes.

Visiting the Museum: Buy your ticket and head up to the second floor. The final ascent—through a mirrored stairway—prepares your brain to expand your ideas about space and time. The exhibit uses photos, displays, and artifacts to thoughtfully trace Einstein's entire life—from his birth in Germany, to his education in Zürich and early working years in Bern, to his professional success in Berlin, to his exile at Princeton after the rise of the Nazis.

The museum explains Einstein's accomplishments and complicated personal life, details his travels after leaving Bern, and places him in historical context, with special emphasis on his Jewish identity (which for Einstein was more cultural than religious). Einstein's concepts are nicely illustrated by video presentations, and everything is well-explained in English (the audioguide is not necessary). You'll learn fascinating details, like the fact that Einstein's second wife was his cousin, and that he was offered the presidency of Israel in 1952 but turned it down.

Other Bern Museums

The Historical Museum and its Einstein exhibit are part of a larger ensemble that includes Alpine, Communication, Natural History, Rifle, and Kunsthalle (contemporary art) museums. All appeal mainly to visitors with specific interests. The Natural History Museum is fun for kids. The TI has a helpful pamphlet describing the museums (all covered by Swiss Travel Pass except Rifle Museum, most open Tue-Sun 10:00-17:00, closed Mon; see "Getting There" for Einstein Museum, above; www.museen-bern.ch).

▲Marzilibad Pool Complex

Within sight of the Swiss parliament building, the riverside Marzilibad is a well-equipped public swimming pool and park with picnic spots, restaurant, lockers, wading pools, games, and more. There are multiple pools for swimmers of different ages and abilities. You can also laze on a wide, green lawn. A Bern institution since the 1780s, it's one of the city's main social hubs.

Cost and Hours: Free, mid-May-mid-Sept daily 9:00-19:00, opens earlier and closes later in midsummer, closed off-season, Marzilistrasse 29, +41 31 311 0046, www.sportamt-bern.ch.

Getting There: The Marzilibahn funicular gets you partway down to the complex from the old town for 1.50 CHF (runs until 21:00, www.marzilibahn.ch), but you can also walk down or take bus #30.

The Bern Float: The Bernese, proud of their very clean river and their basic ruddiness, have a tradition—sort of a wet, urban *paseo*. On summer days, they hike upstream 5 to 30 minutes, then float

back down the river to the Marzilibad. The water—which comes from the high mountains—is clean, vivid blue, and very cold (it maxes out at about 65 degrees Fahrenheit, even in summer).

The TI warns that this activity is only for strong, experienced swimmers (some tourists have drowned in the river after overestimating their abilities). If you think you'd like to join in, first search online for the city of Bern's cleverly named "Aare you safe?" web page and read the Aare River safety rules and tips. Consult with experienced locals, and don't go alone. The river can be hazardous, conditions can change, and there are weirs and dams downstream.

If you choose to try it, hike up the paved riverside sidewalk as far as you like, then take the steps leading into the water whenever you want to "put in." As you approach Marzilibad, be ready to paddle your way over to the canal just beyond it—designed to catch floaters completing their trip. You can also try to grab one of the several poles placed to help people exit the river. The locals make it look easy, but it's not—the current is swift. If you miss the last pole, you're history.

Bern's Edgy Alternative Zone
To see a funky side of staid Switzerland, head to the counterculture art settlement called the Kulturzentrum Reithalle (named for the former "Riding Hall" that's part of the complex, sometimes also called the Reitschule). You'll find graffiti, wood-pallet furniture, stacked containers, skate ramps, drug deals, and other facets of real-life Swiss society that many visitors miss entirely. (Heidi and cowbells it ain't.) The complex, at Neubrückstrasse 8, is tucked along the train tracks a five-minute walk north of the station, near the river—you'll see it as you come in on the train from Interlaken or Zürich (www.reitschule.ch).

Sleeping in Bern

As Switzerland's capital, Bern hosts not only tourists but also waves of businesspeople and politicians, keeping room rates rather high throughout the year. In general, prices rise during the week and drop on weekends; however, frequent conventions and other events can drive demand and prices radically higher. Sleeping within walking distance of the train station is convenient and puts

BERN & MURTEN

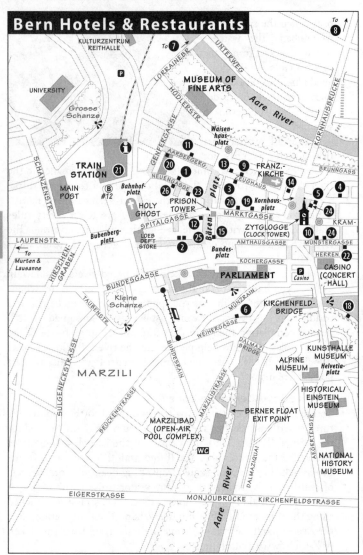

Bern Hotels & Restaurants

you in the endearing heart of the city, but can be pricier and often comes with street noise, especially on weekends when revelers flock downtown. If you don't mind a short tram ride, you can find cheaper, quieter lodgings in the neighborhood across the river to the north. Make sure you get your free Bern Ticket city transport pass code at check-in. You have to install an app on your mobile phone to use the code, but it's a quick, simple process.

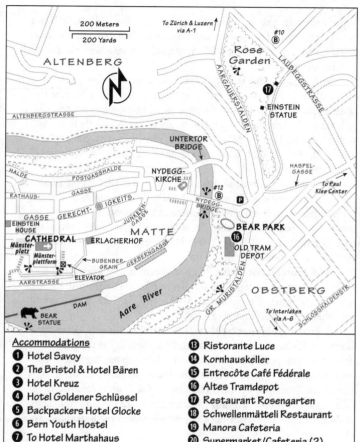

BERN & MURTEN

DOWNTOWN BERN, NEAR THE STATION

These places are within a 5- to 10-minute walk from the train station. The hotels listed here have rates that can skyrocket during conventions, then drop to tempting lows on weekends and at slower times, making a high-end splurge suddenly affordable—check around to find the best rates for your dates. Especially on weekends, light sleepers should request a quiet back-facing room.

$$$ Hotel Savoy is a formal, business-class place located super centrally, just off the main drag near the station. It has a sterile lobby and 64 solid rooms (family rooms, air-con, elevator, Neuengasse 26, +41 31 328 6666, www.hotelsavoybern.ch, info@hotelsavoybern.ch).

$$$ The Bristol is well-located on a quieter side street near the station. It feels young and playful, and aims at a Monty Python-esque sense of humor (with a plaid color scheme and oddball art in the lobby). The 100 rooms are modern, solidly built, and well-equipped (family rooms, air-con, elevator, gym, Schauplatzgasse 10, +41 31 311 0101, www.thebristol-bern.ch, welcome@thebristol-bern.ch).

$$$ Hotel Bären, almost next door to the Bristol, is also modern and convenient, with 69 slightly simpler rooms and more minimalist decor (family rooms, some rooms with air-con, includes breakfast if you book direct, elevator, small gym, self-serve laundry, Schauplatzgasse 4; +41 31 311 3367, www.baerenbern.ch, reception@baerenbern.ch).

$$$ Hotel Kreuz rents 97 good rooms filling a beautiful historic building a few steps off the lively Bärenplatz (family rooms, air-con, elevator, Zeughausgasse 41, +41 31 329 9595, www.kreuzbern.ch, info@kreuzbern.ch).

$ Hotel Goldener Schlüssel is the oldest inn in downtown Bern, but it's been nicely renovated. Its 34 small, Euro-style rooms are fitted with prefab bathroom pods. The quieter, high-ceilinged back rooms are worth reserving in warm weather, as the rooms facing Rathausgasse get café and disco noise from across the street (RS%, family rooms, elevator, Rathausgasse 72, +41 31 311 0216, www.goldener-schluessel-bern.ch, info@goldener-schluessel-bern.ch).

¢ Backpackers Hotel Glocke rents the cheapest beds in the old town. It's a mixture of small dorms (maximum 6 beds) and basic but adequate **$** double rooms, some with private bathrooms. The pubs and cafés along the street keep things noisy until about 23:00, and while the reception desk provides free earplugs, light sleepers may be happier elsewhere. The pleasant common room has a nice view over the bustling city-center streets below (family rooms, no breakfast, elevator, laundry facilities, no curfew, reception open 8:00-12:00 & 15:00-21:00, 10-minute walk from station or take tram #9 to Zytglogge stop, Rathausgasse 75, +41 31 311 3771, www.bernbackpackers.ch, info@bernbackpackers.ch).

¢ Bern Youth Hostel, below the parliament building near the river, is big (188 beds), well-run, and welcoming even to people who don't often stay in youth hostels. In addition to dorm beds, they have doubles and quads with private baths, making this an affordable alternative to expensive downtown hotels (elevator, affordable dinners, pay parking—reserve, Weihergasse 4, +41 31 326

1111, www.youthhostel.ch/bern, bern@youthhostel.ch). To reach the hostel, walk three blocks south from the train station and take the Marzilibahn funicular down to Weihergasse (1.50 CHF, free with hostel confirmation or Bern Ticket, runs until 21:00, after that use bus #30, www.marzilibahn.ch).

NORTH OF THE RIVER

These listings are an easy bus or tram ride from the center.

$$ Hotel Marthahaus is a better value than downtown hotels. Located two bus stops from the train station (walkable without luggage) in a quiet, elegant residential neighborhood north of the river, it's run as a fundraiser by a charitable organization that helps young people and seniors. Half of the 40 bright, simple rooms have shared bathrooms (family rooms, elevator, guest kitchen, pay parking—reserve; take bus #20 from platform G at station to the Gewerbeschule stop, walk up the street to Wyttenbachstrasse and follow the yellow signs two short blocks to Wyttenbachstrasse 22a, +41 31 332 4135, www.marthahaus.ch, info@marthahaus.ch).

$$ Hotel Jardin Bern, with 24 rooms slightly farther out, is tasteful, modern, and family-run by identical twin brothers Andreas and Daniel Balz (family rooms, fans, elevator, laundry service, limited free parking; take tram #9 to the Parkstrasse stop, then walk one block; +41 31 333 0117, www.hotel-jardin.ch, info@hotel-jardin.ch).

Two impersonal but inexpensive **$ Ibis** chain hotels share a big metallic building at the Bern Convention Center (both with air-con, elevator, and pay parking): **Ibis Bern Expo** (+41 31 335 1200) and **Ibis Budget Bern Expo** (+41 31 335 1212, www.ibis.com). From the station, take tram #9 for 10 minutes to the Guisanplatz Expo (direction: Wankdorf Bahnhof, hotels are at Am Guisanplatz 2).

Eating in Bern

OLD TOWN

$$ Restaurant Lötschberg, a local favorite with a fun and youthful vibe, serves old-style Swiss cuisine in a modern space. One long wall is lined with a large variety of Swiss wines. They also have a less-expensive **takeaway counter** at the front of the restaurant, with affordable salads and sandwiches to go (open daily until 23:00, Zeughausgasse 16, +41 31 311 3455).

$$ Restaurant Harmonie, just off Kornmarkt, is a cozy classic. The interior has hard-backed wooden tables filled mostly by locals, and there's a small outdoor terrace draped in ivy. The menu is traditional Swiss with some international flourishes—including a variety of burgers (Mon-Fri 11:00-23:00, closed Sat-Sun, Hotel-gasse 3, +41 31 313 1141).

$$ Gourmanderie Moléson feels refined, high-end, and posh. It's a long, skinny, classy bistro serving healthy and classic dishes with a French flair, including fondue and *tartes flambées* (like pizza without tomato sauce—known as *Flammkuchen* in German). It has a dressy and very Swiss interior with tables that tumble out onto the street (Mon-Fri 11:30-14:30 & 18:00-23:30, dinner only on Sat, closed Sun, Aarbergergasse 24, +41 31 311 4463, www.moleson-bern.ch).

$$ Mishio is a mod pan-Asian place worth considering. The interior has an open kitchen, noisy acoustics, and plain furnishings. The trick here is to get an outside table on the terrace, which overlooks the lively Bärenplatz (Mon-Sat 11:30-22:00, closed Sun, Bärenplatz 2, +41 31 313 1121).

$$ Ristorante Luce brings the cooking of Italy's Emilia Romagna region (with lots of pastas and pizzas) to Bern. Choose between a venerable dining hall and great seating out on lively Bärenplatz (daily 11:30-23:00, limited menu from 14:00 to 18:00, reservations smart, Zeughausgasse 28, +41 31 310 9999, www.ristoranteluce.ch).

$$$ Kornhauskeller, in the palatial cellar of the old granary originally built to house the state's wine cellar, has vaulted archways decorated with colorful murals. This dressy, pricey Mediterranean (Swiss, French, Italian) place offers a fine antipasto bar: Make a meal out of the 25-CHF or 32-CHF plate, telling the person behind the buffet exactly what you'd like (Tue-Sat 11:30-14:30 & 17:30-24:00, closed Sun-Mon, Kornhausplatz 18, +41 31 327 7272).

$$$ Entrecôte Café Fédérale is a dressy and traditional bistro with a reputation for great steak. It sits at the bottom of Bärenplatz, with tables under trees facing the parliament building. Very old-school urban Swiss, it's a quiet place with more local politicians than tourists (daily 11:00-23:00, Bärenplatz 31, +41 31 311 1624, www.entrecote.ch).

ACROSS THE RIVER, WITH VIEWS

$$ Altes Tramdepot, in the Old Tram Depot above Bear Park, offers seating in its big, boisterous microbrewery (which was once the tram shed), or on a leafy Biergarten terrace with a postcard view of the old town's skyline. It's popular, serving good-time Swiss food: meat, fish, burgers, *Rösti*, wurst plates, and *Flammkuchen*. They do 25-CHF weekday lunches and have beer flights for those who want to sample five of their brews (daily 11:00-24:00, reserve in evening for outdoor view seating, bus #12 to Bärengraben stop, +41 31 368 1415, www.altestramdepot.ch).

$$$ Restaurant Rosengarten, perched at the edge of the city's rose garden atop the hill above Bear Park, enjoys commanding city views—especially at sunset (when you should reserve ahead). During the day, come for lunch, or for tea and cake amidst grannies (24-CHF weekday lunch specials). At night, you'll dine with couples enjoying the fresh seasonal menu. The outdoor section, with a big playground next door, feels like an upscale Biergarten (daily 9:00-23:30, Alter Aargauerstalden 31b, a moderately steep walk up from the Bear Park—or take bus #10 from the old town, +41 31 331 3206, www.rosengarten.be).

$$ Schwellenmätteli Restaurant is a chance to join trendy locals for a meal or drink while sitting directly over the river, next to the roar of water racing over the dam. The inside section is peaceful and open all year. The outside, open only in good weather, is loud—not good for conversation—but fun: At the tip of the platform is a lounge complete with sofas, mattresses, and a glass floor that lets you see the river racing underneath. This mod restaurant/lounge has a Swiss-Mediterranean menu (burgers, *Flammkuchen*, veggie dishes, and weekday lunch specials)—but you're here for the setting, not the food (daily until 23:30, reservations smart for dinner, Dalmaziquai 11, cross Kirchenfeld Bridge from downtown and take path downhill to your left, or a pleasant 15-minute riverside stroll from Bear Park, +41 31 350 5001, www.schwellenmaetteli.ch).

CHEAP EATS

Bern offers lots of budget alternatives to formal restaurant dining. Note that many eateries and takeout joints close just before dinner time; if you're planning a picnic dinner, aim to shop in the afternoon. Unless noted, the places below are all **$**.

Self-Service Restaurants: For solid food at budget prices, the **cafeterias** at all three of Bern's major downtown retailers set out a tempting spread, including main dishes for well under 20 CHF, a salad bar, desserts, and much more. The **Manora** restaurant at the Manor department store has fine views from the rooftop (Mon-Sat 9:00-17:00, closed Sun, Marktgasse 10). At the **Co-op** (Aarbergergasse 53), the cafeteria has a nice glassed-in terrace and a roof garden. **Migros** (Marktgasse 46) has free tap water (hidden next to the tray-return conveyor belt). Both the Co-op and Migros restaurants have kids' play zones and are open the same hours as the supermarkets in the same building (see the end of this section). **$$ Tibits,** a busy buffet chain on the ground floor of the train station, offers a huge variety of vegetarian-only salads and sandwiches, plus two different hot dishes. Help yourself to a plate and pile it on. You'll pay by weight: An average helping will cost you about 20 CHF (free water, daily until 22:30, Bahnhofplatz 10, +41 31 312 9111).

Global Food: Some good-value international places hide deep under the arcades in the old town. Popular **$$ Tab-Tim** serves Thai lunches on weekdays for 13-15 CHF—it's a bit more expensive on evenings and weekends. Its outdoor tables spill across the street (Mon-Sat 10:00-22:00, Sun 12:00-17:30, Münstergasse 57, +41 31 311 5936). Shiny, well-kept **Meet Point,** a Middle Eastern takeout counter with a couple of tables under the arcades, sells *döner kebabs* for 12.50 CHF—still a bargain here (Mon-Fri 9:30-21:00, Sat until 20:00, closed Sun, Neuengasse 17).

Bakeries: Small bakeries are all around town. One of many options is **Bread à Porter,** which offers fresh sandwiches, quiches, and salads, with a few casual dine-in tables (Mon-Fri 6:30-19:00, Sat 7:00-17:00, closed Sun, two locations at Kornhausplatz 11 and Münstergasse 74).

Bärenplatz Food Carts: For lunch, drop by the food carts that cluster around the parliament end of Bärenplatz (Mon-Sat mornings). The assortment often includes an organic sausage-and-falafel wagon, tacos, Asian fast food, and more. Grab what looks good and enjoy it on the bench under the Prison Tower. Near the north end of Bärenplatz, consider the takeout counter inside the recommended Lötschberg restaurant (described earlier).

Prepared Meals: You'll get a solid value on takeout food from the two **Migros Takeaway** delis. One is in the bottom level of the train station (long hours daily) and another is at Marktgasse 40 (same hours as the adjacent Migros supermarket; see next). The staff will pack you a hot lunch or dinner to take away for 10-15 CHF. Portions are big—often enough for two—and there are always several options on offer (such as lasagna with side salad or bratwurst with potatoes and veggies), as well as pizzas, quiches, and salads. **Co-op** runs an impressively large, very popular prepared-food court at Marktgasse 24 (Mon-Wed 7:00-19:00, Thu until 21:00, Fri until 20:00, Sat until 17:00, closed Sun).

Supermarkets: Two large supermarkets are in the center— **Co-op** (Aarbergergasse 53, in the basement) and **Migros** (Marktgasse 46, ground floor). Both are open similar hours (roughly Mon-Wed 8:00-19:00, Thu until 21:00, Fri until 20:00, Sat until 17:00, closed Sun). Early, late, or on Sunday, visit one of the midsize supermarkets in the **train station** (Migros on the upper level, Co-op on the lower level).

Bern Connections

From Bern by Train to: Murten (hourly direct, 35 minutes, more with change in Kerzers), **Avenches** (every 3 hours direct, 40 minutes, or hourly with change in Kerzers, 55 minutes), **Lausanne** (2/hour, 1 hour), **Interlaken** (2/hour, 1 hour, a few change in Spiez),

Luzern (hourly direct, 1 hour; scenic route via Interlaken takes 3 hours), **Zürich** (2/hour, 1 hour), **Zürich Airport** (2/hour, 70-80 minutes), **Zermatt** (1-2/hour, 2 hours, transfer in Visp), **Montreux** (2/hour, 1.5 hours, transfer in Lausanne), **Lugano** (hourly, 3 hours, change in Zürich or Luzern), **Appenzell** (easiest with 1 change in Gossau, hourly, 3 hours), **Frankfurt** (hourly, 4 hours, 4/day direct, others change in Basel). **Train info:** www.rail.ch.

Murten

The finest medieval ramparts in Switzerland surround the old town of Murten (pop. 9,000, pronounced MOOR-ten; if you say MURR-ten, you get a quizzical look). You're on the linguistic cusp of Switzerland: 25 percent of Murten speaks French; a few miles to the southwest, nearly everyone does (French-speakers call the town Morat).

Murten's old center is endearing. Its lively streets include a nicely arcaded main drag with breezy outdoor cafés and elegant shops (many closed Mon). Its castle is romantic, overlooking Lake Murten and the rolling vineyards of gentle Mont Vully in the distance. Spend a night here and have a local Vully wine (white, red, or rosé) with dinner. Murten is touristed, but mostly by locals, and never to the point of feeling overrun.

Make time for nearby Avenches (see end of chapter). Though sleepy today, the town was once a powerful Roman capital—as its ruins attest.

Orientation to Murten

TOURIST INFORMATION
Murten's TI is smack in the center of the old town, along the main street (Mon-Fri 9:00-12:00 & 13:00-18:00, Sat-Sun 10:00-12:00 & 13:00-17:00; Oct-March shorter hours and closed Sat-Sun; Hauptgasse 27, +41 26 670 5112, www.regionmurtensee.ch).

ARRIVAL IN MURTEN
By Train: The train station is a five-minute walk from the center, and has a ticket office, free WC, and small pay lockers—the ticket

BERN & MURTEN

office can store bigger bags (Mon-Fri 6:50-18:30, Sat 7:50-18:00, Sun 7:50-12:00 & 13:00-17:00). To reach the town from the station, exit to the right, take the first left, and walk uphill on Bahnhofstrasse, then turn right through the town gate. Murten's old center is tiny, and a delight on foot.

By Car: If you're overnighting here, get parking advice from your hotelier. During the day, don't park inside the town walls; metered prices are steep and there's a strict time limit. Instead, park in the lots outside the walls at either end of town: one next to the Co-op supermarket, the other near the clock tower (2 CHF/hour, pay at machine).

BERN & MURTEN

HELPFUL HINTS

Local Guide: American **Mary Brunisholz,** who married into this part of Switzerland, is an excellent guide with a car (300 CHF/half-day, +41 78 601 7040, mary.brunisholz@vtxnet. ch). The TI has a list of other guides.

Events: The town's **Youth Festival** commemorates the anniversary of the Battle of Murten each June 22. The **Murten Classics** music festival takes place in August and September, and the **Light Festival** lights up the town and the lake in mid-late January.

Murten Walk

This self-guided introductory walk will give you the lay of the land and a lesson on the historic 15th-century Battle of Murten.

• *Start your walk just outside the town's main gate, in front of the public school, where you see a statue of the feisty town hero...*

Adrian von Bubenberg

Burgundy was the aggressive power of the day, and this Murten native stopped a 15th-century Burgundian power grab by beating Charles the Bold. Adrian von Bubenberg (sent by Bern to hold the line against the expansionist Burgundians) stands here, looking across the lake at the distant peaks of the Jura Mountains—the historic border between the Swiss and the French (more on the battle a little later).

The earliest Swiss clockmakers were from those Jura Mountains. Look at the **clock tower—**

where's the minute hand? As part of its lease, the restaurant below takes responsibility for hand-winding the clock each day, as it has since 1712. That's the Bern gate—so called because it opens up onto the road to Bern.

• *Rather than enter the gate, go right instead (hugging the outside of the wall, not downhill). Head around the first turret, and look up at the cannonballs, left in the wall from the 1476 Battle of Murten to remind townsfolk of their incredible victory over the*

Burgundians—*like an Alamo with a happy ending. Turn the corner onto the...*

BERN & MURTEN

Lakeview Terrace

Across the way is Mont Vully (mohn voo-YEE)—one big vineyard and a mecca for lovers of Swiss wines. The lowlands to the right—

a rich former lakebed—are the heart of the fertile Three Lakes Region (Lakes Biel, Neuchâtel, and Murten). The lush farmland is called the "vegetable garden of Switzerland" for its soil, which yields more than 60 varieties of produce.

The ancient Celtic Helvetii tribe settled here and took advantage of the fertility of this land. The Romans located their capital nearby (at Avenches) when they took over the region and established their colony of Helvetia (named after the Celtic tribe—the same word is the Latin origin of Switzerland's official name, Confoederatio Helvetica).

• *Behind you, check out the small...*

French Church

Foreseeing a showdown with Burgundy, Adrian von Bubenberg had the town walls strengthened. As three-quarters of the townspeople were German-speaking, they took a vote and decided to tear down the French church to get more stones. (This little church was rebuilt for the French-speaking community six years after its big one was demolished.)

• *Circle round the church, and if it's open, go inside.*

BERN & MURTEN

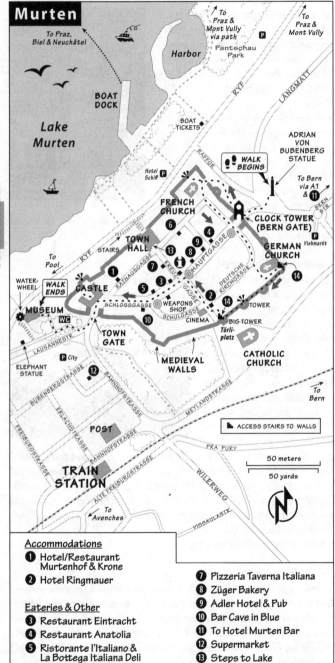

Murten

To Praz & Mont Vully via path

To Praz & Mont Vully

Harbor

Pantschau Park

RYF

LÄNGMATT

To Praz, Biel & Neuchâtel

BOAT DOCK

Lake Murten

BOAT TICKETS

Hotel Schiff

RAFFOR

ADRIAN VON BUBENBERG STATUE

WALK BEGINS

To Bern via A1 & 11

BERN STR.

FRENCH CHURCH

CLOCK TOWER (BERN GATE)

GERMAN CHURCH

Viehmarkt

RYF STAIRS

TOWN HALL

6 • 4 • 13 • 9 • 8 • 7 • i • HAUPTGASSE

DEUTSCHE KIRCHGASSE

To Pool

RATHAUSGASSE

1 •

KREUZGASSE

5 • 3 • 2 •

14

WATER-WHEEL

WALK ENDS

CASTLE

SCHLOSSGASSE

WEAPONS SHOP

10 •

SCHULGASSE

CINEMA

TOWER

BIG TOWER

Törli-platz

14

MUSEUM

WC

LAUSANNESTR.

TOWN GATE

MEDIEVAL WALLS

CATHOLIC CHURCH

To Bern

ELEPHANT STATUE

P City

12 •

BUBENBERGSTRASSE

BAHNHOFSTRASSE

ERLACHSTRASSE

FREIBURGSTRASSE

MEYLANDSTRASSE

⬕ ACCESS STAIRS TO WALLS

POST

PRA PURY

50 meters

50 yards

BAHNHOFSTRASSE

TRAIN STATION

ALTE FREIBURGSTRASSE

WILERWEG

VISSAULASTR.

To Avenches

N

Accommodations

1 Hotel/Restaurant Murtenhof & Krone

2 Hotel Ringmauer

Eateries & Other

3 Restaurant Eintracht

4 Restaurant Anatolia

5 Ristorante l'Italiano & La Bottega Italiana Deli

6 Chesery

7 Pizzeria Taverna Italiana

8 Züger Bakery

9 Adler Hotel & Pub

10 Bar Cave in Blue

11 To Hotel Murten Bar

12 Supermarket

13 Steps to Lake

14 Access to Ramparts (2)

As the Calvinist Reformation swept through Catholic Switzerland in the early 16th century, churches like this were stripped of their rich paintings, sculptures, and stained glass. Elaborate altars were replaced with simple, Bible-topped tables, and pulpits became the focus. The emphasis was teaching the word of God. In this church, about the only exceptions to the "no distractions" rule are

the tiny stained-glass coats of arms—heraldry of the wealthy families who helped fund its construction. The church, still Protestant and serving its French community, is open sporadically.

• *From here, leave the church and head straight toward the pointy spire of the German church across town. Walk along Französischer Kirchgasse past the clock tower and go up the lane to #26 (on left). This is one of few Murten buildings that survived a 15th-century fire that destroyed the then-wooden town. Stand in the doorway and remember that people during the Middle Ages were much shorter. Before the fire, most houses looked like this one. After the fire, building was limited to the characteristic yellow Jura stone (like the former library, across the street, at #31). Continue straight ahead to the...*

German Church

Murten's German church is also post-Reformation Protestant simple. Inside, in the center of the ceiling, notice the big stucco relief with two seals: the bear for Bern and the three castles for Fribourg. As the town is on the border between two cantons (Bern and Fribourg), for 400 years its rule was shared: Every five years, it would flip between cantons. Around 1800, when Switzerland was reorganized under Napoleonic rule, Murten became firmly a part of Fribourg.

The Protestant passion for Bible study is also evident in this church. Explore the choir (two rows of seats on each side for big shots) behind the altar. Find Adrian von Bubenberg's seat. (Hint: The window above shows the war hero in red, with his victorious local yokels in their alpine red-knit hats... underdogs whupping the Burgundians.) The old pulpit was carved in 1460 from a single oak tree. Notice the two prime seats on either side of the altar; the one to the preacher's right was for the leader of

BERN & MURTEN

Bern or Fribourg—depending on who happened to be ruling that year. The front window (crucifixion) dates from 1926.

• *Leaving the church, hook left around the back. Finger the limestone and sandstone tombstones, quarried from Mont Vully for noble families. Then climb the two flights of creaky stairs and start walking along the...*

Ramparts

Strolling Murten's ramparts is a must (free, open daily until dusk). Survey the town and note the uniformity of its architecture. Paint your place the wrong color, and you may be instructed to redo the job—at your own expense. Scanning the countless chimneys and beavertail ceramic roof tiles, think of the enforced conformity that comes with living in a small town (and look to see if there are any oddballs). Telephone and electricity wires are all underground, as in Europe generally. Look back at the roof of the German church. The six-sided "star of David" isn't a Jewish symbol in this case; it recalls the star that guided the wise men to Bethlehem on the first Christmas.

• *Continue 50 yards to the **tower** with the steep staircase. Climb the steps for a commanding town and lake view.*

Enjoy perhaps the ultimate view. The Jura Mountains in the distance (at the border with France) peek above vine-laden Mont Vully. On the right is the German church, Bern Tower, and French church. And to the far left is the castle tower—flying the black-and-white flag of Fribourg Canton—where this walk finishes.

With your back to the lake, look inland and imagine the action on June 22, 1476. Mighty Charles the Bold, with his 20,000 well-armed Burgundians, was camped on the hill (the one with the divided forest) for 10 days, laying siege to the town of 2,000. Runners were sent out from the town to gather help. A makeshift army of about 10,000 villagers gathered on the hills to the left. Just as George Washington attacked when the Redcoats were celebrating Christmas, the Swiss swooped in as the Burgundians were still hungover from a big Midsummer Night's Eve bash. The Battle of Murten was fought in pouring rain—a muddy, bloody mess. More than 10,000 Burgundians were slaughtered—many driven into the lake with their armor to drown (try swimming in a coat of mail). For centuries, French bones would wash ashore. Charles the (no-longer-so-) Bold barely got away on a very fast horse.

This victory demonstrated to the Swiss the advantages of *E Pluribus Unum,* and the gradual unification of the many still-

BERN & MURTEN

fiercely independent Swiss cantons into the Helvetic Confederation snowballed. In this sweet little corner, an influential battle in European history had been fought. Burgundian power ebbed, and Europe got to know a new nation...Switzerland.

• *Walk a bit farther along the wall and descend at the next tower (across from Hotel-Restaurant Ringmauer).*

At the bottom of the stairs, study the fine old **clock** mechanism from 1816. It once powered the big clock in the City Hall tower. Later, it spent decades in a to-be-assembled pile, gathering dust in an attic. Finally, in 1991, a town resident—recognizing a good challenge—reassembled it into perfect working order. Notice how the gearbox powers three clock faces (as the tower had), and how the old hand crank raises the stones that power the clock, which rings on the quarter-hour. The white face displays the clock's time.

• *Step outside the wall, where you'll see the Catholic church (1886), private gardens along the wall, and evidence of how the wall was constructed in several distinct stages.*

The first phase was built with large river stones, some arranged in a neat fishbone pattern. Later, the town ran out of money, and the next stage shows pebbles and rubble mixed with a rough concrete. And finally, when the town prospered again, they finished the wall with finely cut sandstone. The former dry moat is now individual private gardens.

• *Walk back into town, stopping on the first corner at the fire station-turned-community-cinema.*

Contributors are thanked with their names on the **cinema** door. Notice what's playing tonight (in Switzerland, movies are subtitled, not dubbed, to accommodate a two-language audience). At this corner, spin slowly, admiring the town's fine shutters.

• *Then, continue a block (noticing again that most buildings were stone—built after a fire) to the...*

Main Street (Hauptgasse)

In the 19th century, Murten's townsfolk got their water from the three fountains on this street. Turn left along the street and enjoy the colorful store signs—they still hang out their shingles in the traditional fashion. Bakery and *pâtisserie* competition on this street is fierce. Drop into one for regional specialties: *Nidlechueche*, a sweet, doughy cream tart; and *Seeländer Zwetschgen*, a chocolate-covered prune with liqueur.

Near the top of the main street, **Simonet Weapons** sells all the latest products from Victorinox, originator of the Swiss Army knife (closed all day Sun-Mon and Wed afternoon). At the top of the street (#16), Murten's oldest house has fine paintings under its eaves.

• Farther to the right, at the top of town, step into the courtyard of...

Murten Castle (Schloss Murten)

The town castle, which houses the police station in its former prison (tower open to the public), shows off an impressive cannon from 1882. Back outside and just downhill, below the tower, find the overlook where a plaque helps you identify the villages on the other side of the Murtensee.

• If it's open, continue down (passing a free WC) to visit the...

Town Museum (Museum Murten)

The town museum, farther down the hill, earnestly shows off Murten's history in five floors of modern displays, artifacts, and tempo-

rary exhibitions. It fills an old mill that's been nicely renovated (6 CHF, Tue-Sat 14:00-17:00, Sun from 10:00, closed Mon and in winter, described in German and French only—borrow English booklet, +41 26 670 3100, www.museummurten.ch). Out-

side is a functioning water mill, a lane leading down to the lake, and a wooden elephant.

An elephant? Yes, in 1866 an elephant escaped from a traveling American circus. It rampaged through Murten and was killed. To this day, one lane is nicknamed Elephant Alley.

Our walk ends here, but you can backtrack to the Town Hall (past the Hotel Murtenhof & Krone) and descend the steps nearby for some more fine lake views.

Activities in Murten

Lake Activities

To get to Murten's lazy lakefront, you can take the steps by the Town Hall. Or go out the main town gate and take a left down the hill. You'll see the boat dock first. Just beyond the grassy breakwater and the small-boat harbor is a big park flanked by handy eateries. There's mini golf, windsurfing/paddle boarding gear rental and instruction, a snack bar, and a fine lakeside promenade with benches made for sunset views.

Lake Murten Cruises

Boats do a 1.25-hour **loop cruise** at 12:00, 14:15, and 15:40. Consider stopping in a small town (Praz or Môtier) on the French-speaking shore. From there you could hike through vineyards up Mont Vully—where a pretty lake and Alp views await—and return on the lake with your same ticket. Or you can walk back to Murten, clockwise around the lake (about 1.5 hours from Praz) or meet the train at Sugiez in Bas-

Vully. Ask the TI for the Vully Les Vignerons map to help you make a plan and for information on wine tastings in the area.

Another option is the **Three Lakes cruise,** which covers the region's trio of lakes—connected by canals—and stops at several medieval villages on the way to the town of Biel (Bienne in French). The boat leaves Murten at 9:50, arrives in Biel at 14:05, then turns around and heads back along the same route, leaving Biel at 14:45 and arriving in Murten at 18:55. You can condense this full-day trip by taking the boat to Biel and a train back to Murten (1 hour).

Cost and Hours: 1.25-hour loop cruise—22 CHF; boat from Murten to Praz or Môtier—12 CHF; half-day Three Lakes cruise—61 CHF one-way, 69 CHF round-trip; all covered by Swiss Travel Pass and discounted 50 percent with Eurail Global Pass, ask TI about boat-trip discount vouchers; buy tickets on board or at the kiosk at pier 1; boats run daily mid-May-late Sept, Fri-Sun only in off-season, no boats in winter but see website for special Licht Festival trips; +41 32 729 9600, www.lnm.ch.

Swimming Pool

The Olympic-size public swimming pool is outside of town next to the lake, just past the castle (8 CHF; indoor pool open Tue-Fri 9:30-21:00, Sat-Sun until 18:00, Mon 14:00-21:00; outdoor pool daily in summer; Lausannestrasse 2, +41 26 672 3636, www.schwimmbad-murten.ch).

Biking

The Three Lakes region has 100 miles of signposted bike paths. Pick up a free map at the TI. The best easy ride circles the lake and Mont Vully (through vineyards and, if you like, to the summit for a good view). The Murten train station participates in the Swiss rail system's bike rental program (online reservations required; for rates and specifics, see page 491).

Nightlife in Murten

Movies

Murten's cute little community theater plays movies nightly (16 CHF, Schulgasse 18, www.kino-murten.ch). Movies are shown in their original language (capital letter indicates the soundtrack language, small letters indicate subtitles—for example, "E/fd" means English with French and German *(Deutsch)* subtitles).

From early July to early August, Murten hosts an open-air film festival (outside wall, past main gate, details at www.openairkino-murten.ch).

Pubs

There are a few options for nightlife. The **Adler Hotel & Pub** sells drinks and tasty *Flammkuchen* in a fun and welcoming interior or lively exterior along Murten's main drag (daily 11:00-late, Hauptgasse 45, +41 26 672 1920). **Bar Cave in Blue** on the main street is popular with the late-night crowd (daily from 21:30, Schlossgasse 4, +41 26 670 1901). The **Hotel Murten** bar just outside the clock tower is another good place for drinks (daily 15:00-late, at Bernstrasse 7, +41 26 678 8181; don't confuse this with the Hotel Murtenhof & Krone within the walls).

Sleeping in Murten

This adorable town is no secret. The peak time is May through mid-September (especially on weekends)—make a reservation and expect maximum prices. The nearest youth hostel is in Avenches (see the end of this chapter).

$$ Hotel Murtenhof & Krone offers elegance at fair-for-Switzerland prices in 57 nicely appointed rooms—each a stylish mix of old and new. There's a wide range of sleeping accommodations, so email them your needs in terms of size, view, and price (RS%, more expensive rooms with air-con, family rooms, private spa bookable, elevator, pay parking, next to castle at Rathausgasse 3, +41 26 672 9030, www.murtenhof.ch, info@murtenhof.ch, well-run by brothers Marc and Ariste Joachim). They have the best lakeview restaurant in town (described next, under "Eating in Murten"). They can also take you wakesurfing on the lake.

$$ Hotel Ringmauer (Ramparts) sits just under the wall in the quiet corner of town farthest from the lake. It rents 10 small, simple rooms (family rooms, attached restaurant, Deutsche Kirchgasse 2, +41 26 670 1101, www.restaurantringmauer.ch, restaurantringmauer@bluewin.ch, Padmakumara Nawarathna and family).

Eating in Murten

Eating in Murten is a joy. I'd stroll the main drag up one side and down the other to survey the action before making a choice. For elegance and a lake view, you can't beat the restaurant at Hotel Murtenhof & Krone. There are also several good options right on the lake a 10-minute walk down from the town center. Budget eaters can assemble a picnic at the Co-op grocery. Bakeries make good sandwiches, but they close by about 18:00.

RESTAURANTS

Anything called *Seeländer* or mentioning "three lakes" is typical of this Three Lakes region. Traditional restaurants serve *Egli-Filets,* the very popular perch "from the lake" (these days caught in the Bodensee—Lake Constance in English—up by the German border). As this area is Switzerland's vegetable garden, restaurants pride themselves on offering good produce. There's a French accent to the cuisine here, and restaurants offer sophisticated fixed-price meals that tempt gourmet tastes. You'll want a glass of smooth and refreshing Vully (voo-YEE) wine with your meal (about 5 CHF/ glass).

$$$ Hotel Murtenhof & Krone's classy restaurant is perched high above the lake in the old town—reserve ahead for a view table. Its covered terrace keeps diners comfortable regardless of the weather. Sipping a glass of local wine with the right travel partner, while gazing across the lake at hillside vineyards as the sun sets, is one of Europe's fine moments. Order à la carte or get the five-course tasting menu for 89 CHF (Tue-Sun 11:00-14:30 & 17:30-22:00, closed Mon; open Wed-Sat only in winter; +41 26 672 9030, www.murtenhof.ch).

$$ Restaurant Eintracht serves good-value, local cuisine from a fun and unpretentious menu, including old-time chef specials (20-CHF lunch specials include soup and main course, half-portions and healthy specials available, generally Thu-Tue 8:00-23:30 except Sun until 18:00, closed Wed, streetside seating under arcades, Hauptgasse 19, +41 26 670 2240).

$$$ Restaurant Anatolia is an ambitious, upscale Turkish restaurant that's the pride of its welcoming owner, Mehmet. The eggplant stuffed with vegetables and tomato sauce is a winner, as is the three-course, 55-CHF fixed-price fish meal. Dine indoors under a fine mural of Istanbul or watch the main-drag action from an outside table (daily 10:00-23:00, shorter hours and closed Wed evenings off-season, Hauptgasse 45, +41 26 670 2868, www. anatolia.ch).

$$ Ristorante l'Italiano is the town choice for authentic Italian cuisine. As its menu makes quite clear, they don't serve pizza—

just a full range of pastas and Italian meat and fish dishes (Tue-Sat 10:00-14:00 & 17:30-22:30, closed Sun-Mon; outdoor seating, Hauptgasse 11, +41 26 672 2212, Prozzillo family). **La Bottega Italiana,** a deli next door, is owned by the same family.

$$ Chesery is a café (with regional cheese plates, quiches, and other light meals), wine bar, and elegant secondhand store. There's nice outdoor seating and a slightly frou-frou interior. This quirky spot is worth a peek even if you're not eating (Mon and Thu-Sat 11:00-22:00, Sun until 18:00, closed Tue-Wed, Rathausgasse 28, +41 26 670 6577).

$$ Pizzeria Taverna Italiana serves wood-fired pizzas for around 20 CHF, and also has a full Italian menu including risotto, mussels, and other seafood. Its outdoor tables fill a traffic-free side street (daily 10:30-15:00 & 17:00-22:00, Kreuzgasse 4, +41 26 670 2122).

CHEAP EATS

The main street has several **bakeries,** all with ample charm. **Züger** has indoor and outdoor seating, an inviting pastry and confectionary counter, and delicate open-face sandwiches typical of the region. This is the perfect place to try the local *Nidlechueche,* a tart with multiple layers of sweet cream glaze (11.60-CHF breakfast combo—coffee, croissant, and roll; generally Wed-Mon 7:30-18:30, closed Tue, Hauptgasse 33, +41 26 670 2253).

The Co-op **supermarket** towers between the train station and city center (Mon-Fri until 20:00, Sat-Sun until 18:00).

Murten Connections

From Murten by Train to: Avenches (1-2/hour, 7 minutes, direction: Lausanne), **Bern** (hourly direct, 35 minutes, more with change in Kerzers), **Lausanne** (hourly direct, 1.5 hours), **Zürich** (via Bern, 1 hour 40 minutes). **Train info:** www.rail.ch.

ROUTE TIPS FOR DRIVERS

Murten to Lake Geneva (50 miles): The autobahn from Bern to Lausanne/Lake Geneva makes everything speedy (see the Lake Geneva & French Switzerland chapter). Murten and Avenches are 10 minutes off the autobahn; Broc, Bulle, and Gruyères are within sight of each other and the autobahn. It takes about an hour to drive from Murten to Montreux. The autobahn (direction: Simplon) takes you high above Montreux (pull off at great viewpoint rest stop) and Château de Chillon. For the castle, take the first exit east of the castle (Villeneuve); signs direct you along the lake back to the castle.

Near Murten: Avenches

Avenches, four miles south of Murten, was once Aventicum, the Roman capital of Helvetia. Today, it's a quaint little French-speaking town with an ancient amphitheater taking a bite out of it. Below the town spreads a vast field of sparse Roman ruins.

With a pleasant, small-town French ambience, Avenches (ah-VAHNSH) is much quieter than Murten, and its old walls are mostly gone. Just a few minutes away by train, it makes an easy half-day trip. From the unstaffed Avenches train station, it's a seven-minute, somewhat steep walk to the town, amphitheater, and Roman museum. Exploring more of the ruins requires some outdoor walking. The **TI** is on the town's main square (closed Sun, Place de l'Eglise 3, +41 26 676 9922, www.avenches.ch).

Drivers park for free at Parking du Faubourg (along Route du Faubourg), a two-minute walk downhill from the amphitheater. Parking up in the old town has a fee and a three-hour limit.

Sights in Avenches

Roman Avenches

Aventicum was a Roman capital, with a population of 20,000. The Romans appreciated its strategic crossroads location, fertile land, and comfortable climate (in modern times, Avenches has found favor with retirees for its livability). While the population of to-day's Avenches could barely fill the well-worn ruins of their Roman amphitheater, Aventicum was once one of the larger cities of the Roman Empire. Everything sits on Roman ruins, which were quarried nearly to oblivion over several centuries; the scant remains were finally spared in the 19th century, and today, things are carefully preserved. Metal detectors must be registered here. Parents, knowing that turning up anything ancient will bring on the archaeologists, yell at their kids, "Don't dig!" Even the benches on the main street are bits of a 2,000-year-old temple cornice.

The town has five Roman sights: the amphitheater, a museum (next to the amphitheater), a lone tower (viewable in the distance), plus a sanctuary and a theater in a field outside of town. See below for museum cost and hours; the ruins are free and always viewable.

Amphitheater

The **amphitheater,** or arena, which once seated 18,000, is the largest Roman ruin in Switzerland. There's no more gladiator action, but it's still in use—normally busy with an annual opera festival and other musical events. However, during a major renovation to turn it into an even better concert venue (through 2028), you'll still be able to see the amphitheater from above, but not go in.

Walk along the rim of the amphitheater to just past the museum entrance and scan the surrounding countryside. The Roman town filled the low area in front of you (now partly farmland; Avenches' medieval residents retreated to the more easily defensible hilltop). The **tower** on the ridge (on the left)—the only one remaining of the original 73 towers—marks where the wall once stood. In the middle, past the lone standing column of the **sanctuary,** you can see the small **theater** ruins.

Roman Museum

Next to the amphitheater, the museum fills a medieval tower with three floors of Roman artifacts—such as gravestones, mosaics, glass, fishing spears, and many domestic goods. It's not only free, but superbly designed, with touch screens and English booklets that make the exhibits accessible and give you just enough detail. On the second floor, don't miss the "gold" bust of Marcus Aurelius (AD 80) found in an old Roman sewer in 1939. It's actually a plastic copy; the original is in a bank in Lausanne.

Cost and Hours: Free, except for some temporary exhibits; Tue-Sun 10:00-17:00, closed Mon except in June, shorter hours off-season and closed Tue Nov-Jan; +41 26 557 3300, www.aventicum.org.

Theater and Sanctuary

Perhaps the best Aventicum experience is to spend some quiet time

at sunset pondering the evocative **Roman theater** (Théâtre Romaine) and **sanctuary** in the fields, a half-mile walk out of town (tiny free car park at the site). The single column marks "Du Cigognier"—nicknamed the "stork sanctuary" (c. 1700) for the stork nest it supported. The site was a quarry until the 19th century, so almost nothing remains.

Sleeping in Avenches

Sleeping in the Avenches youth hostel is the Murten area's best option for travelers on a tight budget. Coming here works best by car. It's not impossible by train, though hauling your bags uphill from the train station is a chore.

$$ Hotel de la Couronne is an Old World, three-star place with a modern interior. Centrally set on the main square, it's unpretentious, with 20 bright, spacious rooms (family rooms, next to TI at Rue Centrale 20, +41 26 675 5414, www.swisshotel-lacouronne.ch, info@swisshotel-lacouronne.ch).

¢ The Avenches **IYHF hostel** fills a traditional building in a quiet setting on the far side of town. It's a 15-minute walk from the train station—those with wheeled bags can avoid stairs and cobbles by taking the path that circles right around the old town walls. The 85-bed hostel has a homey TV room and a big backyard with a ping-pong table (private rooms available, dinner available if you reserve ahead, no curfew, reception open 7:00-10:00 & 17:00-21:00, pay parking, closed late Oct-March, Rue du Lavoir 5, +41 26 675 2666, www.youthhostel.ch/avenches, avenches@youthhostel.ch).

BERN & MURTEN

BERNER OBERLAND

Interlaken • Schilthorn • Jungfrau

Rather than tackle a checklist of famous Swiss mountains and resorts, choose one region to savor: the Berner Oberland. Here you can frolic and hike high above the stress and clouds of the real world. Take a vacation from your busy vacation. Recharge your touristic batteries high in the Alps, where distant avalanches, cowbells, the whistle of marmots, and the crunchy footsteps of happy hikers are the dominant sounds. If the weather's good (and your budget's healthy), ride a cable car from your home-base village to a hearty breakfast at the revolving Piz Gloria restaurant on top of the 9,748-foot Schilthorn peak. Linger among alpine whitecaps before riding down to the towns of Mürren, Gimmelwald, or Lauterbrunnen. Tunnel through the Eiger mountain on a train ride to the "top of Europe" at 11,333 feet—Jungfraujoch, the saddle between the Jungfrau and Mönch peaks—for exhilarating panoramas, glacier views, and fun snow activities.

Your gateway to the rugged Berner Oberland—the mountainous part of the canton of Bern—is the old resort town of Interlaken. Near Interlaken is Switzerland's open-air folk museum, Ballenberg, where you can climb through traditional houses gathered from every corner of this diverse country.

Ah, but the weather's fine and the Alps beckon. Head deep into the heart of the Alps and ride a lift to a stop just this side of heaven. For me, that stop is the village of Gimmelwald.

By the way, you'll note that I hardly mention the resort town of Grindelwald in this chapter. That's because this famed and highly developed resort is designed for mass tourism and big buses, and lacks the charm I enjoy elsewhere.

PLANNING YOUR TIME

Prime time in this region is about late May until early October (though weather can be iffy on the fringes). Spring is not a good time to visit if you plan on dramatic hikes, as many trails are still snow-covered. And many hotels, restaurants, and shops are closed between the skiing and hiking seasons: from late April until late May, and again from mid-October to mid-December.

Interlaken is the region's administrative headquarters, transportation hub, and tackiest tourist town. Use it for business—banking, laundry, shopping—and as a springboard for alpine thrills... but ideally, not for spending the night.

If the weather's decent, explore the two areas that tower above either side of the Lauterbrunnen Valley, south of Interlaken: On one side is the summit of Jungfrau (and beneath it, the tiny junction of Kleine Scheidegg), and on the other is Schilthorn (overlooking the villages of Gimmelwald and Mürren).

Ideally, spend three nights in the region, with a day exploring each side of the valley. For accommodations without the expense and headache of mountain lifts—and equally handy to both sides of the valley—consider the valley-floor village of Lauterbrunnen. But for the best overnight options, I'd stay on the scenic ridge high above the valley, in the rustic hamlet of Gimmelwald or the resort town of Mürren. I've also listed a few options in other nearby mountain villages.

If you like to hike, it's easy to fill a week of unforgettable days based in the region (either from a home base, hiking from high-mountain hotel to high-mountain village, or doing a mix).

If your time is very limited, spend at least one night: Consider a stay in Gimmelwald, breakfast at the Schilthorn, an afternoon doing the Männlichen-Kleine Scheidegg hike, and an evening train out. A nature lover not spending the night high in the Alps? Alpus interruptus.

The highest-altitude lifts are very expensive, and it only makes sense to splurge if you have a good chance of seeing an alpine panorama instead of fog or clouds. Let your plans flex with the weather. If it's good—go! Webcams showing live video from the peaks are at Jungfrau.ch, Schilthorn.ch, and on video monitors at lift stations. For general weather reports, visit Meteoswiss.Admin.ch (enter the town name under "Local forecasts") or Meteo.Search.ch.

For a summary of the wildly scenic activities this region has

BERNER OBERLAND

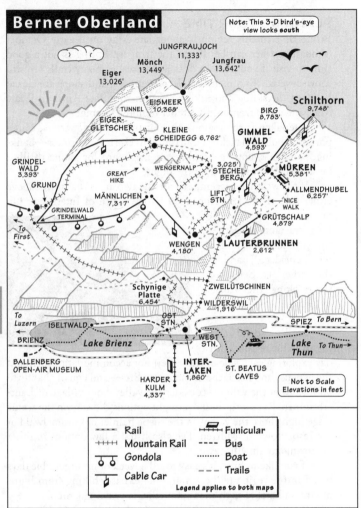

to offer (from panoramic train rides and lifts to spectacular hikes and mountain biking), see "Activities in the Berner Oberland" on page 211.

GETTING AROUND THE BERNER OBERLAND

For more than a century, this region has been the target of nature-worshipping pilgrims. And Swiss engineers and visionaries have made the most exciting alpine perches accessible.

By Lift and Train

Part of the fun here—and most of the expense—is riding the many mountain trains and lifts (gondolas, cable cars, and funiculars).

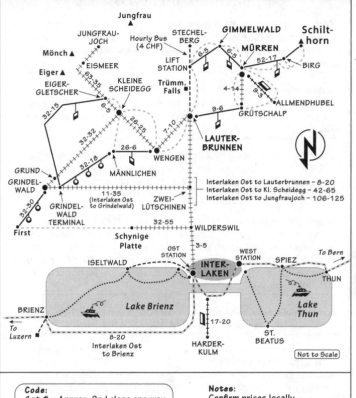

Berner Oberland Transport Time/Cost

Jungfrau ▲

JUNGFRAU-JOCH

Mönch ▲

Eiger ▲ EISMEER

EIGER-GLETSCHER

KLEINE SCHEIDEGG

Hourly Bus (4 CHF)

STECHEL-BERG

GIMMELWALD

Schilt-horn ▲

MÜRREN

52-17

BIRG

63-35

6-5

32-15

26-25

32-32

32-18

26-6

MÄNNLICHEN

11-35
(Interlaken Ost
to Grindelwald)

7-10

LIFT STATION

Trümm. Falls

4-14

9-3

9-6

GRÜTSCHALP

ALLMENDHUBEL

LAUTER-BRUNNEN

WENGEN

ZWEI-LÜTSCHINEN

GRUND
GRINDEL-WALD

32-30

GRINDEL-WALD TERMINAL

First

32-55

WILDERSWIL

Schynige Platte

3-5

OST STATION

ISELTWALD

BRIENZ

To Luzern ■

8-20
Interlaken Ost
to Brienz

Lake Brienz

INTER-LAKEN

WEST STATION

SPIEZ

To Bern →

THUN

Lake Thun

ST. BEATUS

17-20

HARDER-KULM

Not to Scale

Interlaken Ost to Lauterbrunnen – 8-20
Interlaken Ost to Kl. Scheidegg – 42-65
Interlaken Ost to Jungfraujoch – 106-125

N

Code:
1st # = Approx. 2nd class one-way
cost in Swiss francs (CHF)
2nd # = Duration of trip in minutes

Notes:
Confirm prices locally.
Round-trip fares can be cheaper.
Most lifts run twice hourly.

Swiss Passes cover travel to Wengen and Mürren; Eurail/other int'l passes
cover travel only to Interlaken. (Passes offer discounts beyond these points.)

Trains connect Interlaken to Wilderswil, Lauterbrunnen, Wengen, Kleine Scheidegg, the Jungfraujoch, and Grindelwald. Lifts connect Wengen to Männlichen and Grund (near Grindelwald); Grindelwald to First, Männlichen, and Eigergletscher; Lauterbrunnen to Grütschalp (where a train connects to Mürren); and the cable-car station near Stechelberg to Gimmelwald, Mürren, and the Schilthorn.

For an overview of your many options, study the "Berner Oberland Transport Time/Cost" map (above) and the "Berner Oberland at a Glance" sidebar on the next page. Lifts generally go at least twice hourly, and the nationwide timetable at Rail.ch in-

Berner Oberland at a Glance

Towns, Villages, and Resorts

▲▲▲Gimmelwald Wonderfully rustic time-warp village—and a good home-base option—overlooking the Lauterbrunnen Valley. See page 192.

▲▲Mürren Pleasant resort town near Gimmelwald, midway up the Schilthorn cable-car line; a good high-mountain home base for those who find Gimmelwald too small and rustic. See page 202.

▲▲Kleine Scheidegg Small resort area with breathtaking views of Eiger, Mönch, and Jungfrau peaks; hotels and restaurants (see page 239); and train station for ride to the high-altitude Jungfraujoch (see page 215).

▲Lauterbrunnen Small town in the middle of the Lauterbrunnen Valley. From here, a cable car goes up to Grütschalp (with connections to Mürren and Gimmelwald), a train runs up to Wengen (with connections to Kleine Scheidegg and the Jungfraujoch), and the PostBus goes to Stechelberg (near the Schilthornbahn lift). See page 184.

▲Interlaken Big town between Lake Brienz and Lake Thun, at the "entrance" to the Berner Oberland. See page 167.

Top Lifts and Trains

▲▲▲Schilthornbahn Cable car soaring from Stechelberg in the Lauterbrunnen Valley to the 9,748-foot Schilthorn peak, with Piz Gloria revolving restaurant, James Bond exhibit, and stupendous views. Stops at Gimmelwald, Mürren, and Birg along the way. See page 211.

▲▲▲Jungfraubahn Train running from Kleine Scheidegg station and through tunnel inside Eiger and Mönch mountains to 11,333-foot Jungfraujoch saddle, with observation deck, shops, tip-top views, and snow activities. See page 215.

Walks and Hikes

▲▲▲North Face Trail Relatively easy, view-filled hike from top of Allmendhubel funicular to villages of Mürren and/or Gimmelwald, passing farms with food service, Sprutz waterfall, mountain huts, and meadows. See page 222.

▲▲▲Männlichen-Kleine Scheidegg Easy, mostly downhill ridge hike from cable-car station at Männlichen to Kleine Scheidegg, with spectacular views of Eiger and more. See page 229.

▲▲▲**Panorama Way Loop Trail** A breathtaking two-hour loop ridge hike from the top of the Schynige Platte train line. See page 233.

▲▲**Cloudy-Day Lauterbrunnen Valley Walk** Easy trails and pleasant walk (or bike ride) along valley floor, plus short trail to Staubbach Falls at upper end of town. See page 220.

▲▲**Schynige Platte to First** Demanding, all-day ridge walk from Schynige Platte train station to gondola station at First. Fabulous views of Jungfrau-area peaks and Lake Brienz. See page 232.

▲▲**Birg to Gimmelwald via Bryndli** High, scenic, difficult hike from Birg cable-car station below Schilthorn summit to Gimmelwald. Trail winds past knobby summit of Bryndli, with nonstop views. See page 235.

▲**Sefinen Valley to Kilchbalm** Easy trail from village of Gimmelwald up Sefinen Valley to dramatic Kilchbalm, a glacier-carved bowl with streams, waterfalls, and meadows. See page 221.

▲**Allmendhubel to Grütschalp** Fairly easy walk from Allmendhubel down to Grütschalp, with views of the Jungfrau. See page 225.

▲**Grütschalp to Mürren** Super-easy, family-friendly stroll along the ridge with grand views of the Eiger, Mönch, and Jungfrau. See page 226.

▲**Mürren to Gimmelwald** Super-easy, paved, entirely downhill 30-minute stroll. See page 227.

▲**Gimmelwald-Tanzbödeli-Obersteinberg-Stechelberg/Gimmelwald** Difficult yet highly rewarding all-day hike offering spectacular views and relative solitude (aside from goats, cows, chamois, and a cheesemaker). See page 234.

More Sightseeing Options

▲▲**Swiss Open-Air Museum at Ballenberg** Fine collection of traditional buildings near Interlaken, on Lake Brienz. See page 175.

▲**Trümmelbach Falls** Lauterbrunnen Valley's most powerful falls, accessed via elevator ride up into the mountain and dramatic walk through several wet caves. See page 187.

▲**Harder Kulm** Easy funicular ride from Interlaken up to a historic restaurant with a grand view. See page 177.

cludes their schedules. Lift schedules sometimes flex with demand, adding extra departures in between the scheduled ones.

Train Station Ticket Offices: Ticket offices typically close at 19:00 or 19:30. You'll find ticket machines on the platforms, but if you need to talk to a real person, don't wait too late in the day.

Passes and Deals: Trains and lifts can get expensive here—consider money-saving passes. If you have a **Eurail Global Pass,** trains and lifts beyond Interlaken are 25 percent off (doesn't require a flexi-day); with the **Swiss Travel Pass,** they're covered up to Wengen (above Wengen, pass holders get 25-50 percent off) and up to Mürren (ascending from there to the Schilthorn is 50 percent off). While those two passes are the best option for most Swiss trips using public transportation (both described starting on page 485), there are a few others to consider: The **Berner Oberland Regional Pass** covers most trains, buses, and lifts in this area (and all the way to Bern, Luzern, Gstaad, and Birg) but costs about the same as the more versatile Swiss Travel Pass (www.berneseoberlandpass.ch). The **Jungfrau Travel Pass** is more limited in scope, covering transportation on the east side of the valley, plus from Lauterbrunnen to Mürren via Grütschalp; it's worth considering only if you're focusing exclusively on the Wengen-Kleine Scheidegg-Jungfraujoch area (3-8 day versions available, from 190 CHF, www.jungfrau.ch). And the **Junior Travelcard,** valid across Switzerland for families traveling with children, lets kids ages 5-16 travel free with at least one parent (children under age 5 already travel free; 30 CHF/one child, 60 CHF/two or more children, buy at Swiss train stations).

Individual lifts offer a changing assortment of discounts—ask about deals for early-morning and late-afternoon trips, youths, seniors, families, groups (assemble a party of 10 and you'll save about 25 percent), and special promotions. Generally, round-trips are double the one-way cost, though some high-up trains and lifts are 10-20 percent cheaper when you buy a round-trip. It's possible to buy a package covering all of your planned lifts at once, but you'll lose the flexibility to change with the weather.

By Car

Interlaken, Lauterbrunnen, and Stechelberg are accessible by car. You can't drive to Gimmelwald, Mürren, Wengen, or Kleine Scheidegg, but don't let that stop you from *staying* up in the mountains: Park your car and zip up on a lift. For the lift to Gimmelwald, Mürren, and the Schilthorn, use the pay parking lot at the cable-car station near Stechelberg (this is the cheapest long-term parking in the valley, and almost never fills up). For the train to Wengen or Kleine Scheidegg, use the pay parking garage behind the train station in Lauterbrunnen.

By Bus

The handy PostBus #141 connects points along the upper part of the valley, making a 20-minute run from Lauterbrunnen to Trümmelbach Falls to the Schilthornbahn cable-car station to the village of Stechelberg (2/hour, Lauterbrunnen-Schilthornbahn costs 4.40 CHF, pay driver, covered by many transit passes, www.postauto.ch).

HELPFUL HINTS IN THE BERNER OBERLAND

Public Transit Schedules: Use the nationwide timetable at Rail.ch (it includes trains, buses, and lifts). Scheduled departures for each stop are posted there, but general printed schedules are hard to find. Most timings are regular and easy to memorize (for example, departures at 10 and 40 minutes past every hour). Trains and buses are smartly synced to minimize waits between connections. Upon arrival at any connection, you can count on seeing the connecting departure time posted.

Closed Days: On Sundays and holidays (including lesser-known religious holidays), small-town Switzerland is quiet. Lifts and trains run, but many stores are closed.

Visitor Cards *(Gästekarten):* Hotels issue free Visitor Cards (paid for by your room tax) that include small discounts on some sights, as well as other perks that vary by town, such as free bus service in Interlaken.

Money: Interlaken, Lauterbrunnen, and Wengen have plenty of banks and ATMs, but there is no bank or ATM in Gimmelwald nor Mürren. Some high-country hotels and restaurants accept only cash. Plan accordingly.

Rainy-Day Options: When it rains here, locals joke that they're washing the mountains. If clouds roll in, don't despair. They can roll out just as quickly. With good rain gear, proper shoes, and the right choice of trail, you can thoroughly enjoy a hike in the rain, with surprise views popping out all around you as the clouds break. Some good bad-weather options are the North Face trail (but avoid the steep-and-slippery detour to Sprutz waterfall), the easy downhill amble from Mürren to Gimmelwald, the walk from Allmendhubel to Grütschalp or Grütschalp to Mürren, the Sefinen Valley hike to Kilchbalm, and the Lauterbrunnen Valley walk. Also consider a visit to Trümmelbach Falls, the Swiss Open-Air Museum at Ballenberg, or the Lauterbrunnen Valley Folk Museum. Don't stress needlessly about depressing weather forecasts—the icons on your weather app can be deceptive. Many "rainy days" are mostly dry and sunny.

Local Guidebook: For in-depth information on the area's history, folk life, native plants and animals, and hiking options, consider Don Chmura's *Exploring the Lauterbrunnen Valley* (sold at Lauterbrunnen TI).

Local Hiking Guide: Licensed private hiking guide **Doris Schmied** knows local flora, fauna, and culture (contact her for rates, +41 79 689 9816, www.doris-hike.ch).

Skiing and Snowboarding: This is a great winter-sports destination, with good snow on higher runs, nice variety, relatively reasonable prices, and a sense of character that's missing in swankier resort areas. You can even swish with the Swiss down the world's longest sledding run (9 miles long, out of Grindelwald, open only when snow's good). Three ski areas cluster around the Lauterbrunnen Valley: Mürren-Schilthorn (best for experts), Kleine Scheidegg-Männlichen (busiest, best variety of runs), and Grindelwald-First (best for beginners/intermediates, but lower elevation can make for iffier snowpack). For info, see Jungfrau.ch/winter. For more tips, see the Switzerland in Winter chapter.

Hiking Tips: Trails are clearly marked with a signpost at each intersection. Yellow means an easy walk; harder ones are in red and white, and for those, I borrow hiking poles. Your hotel or B&B can likely loan you a set. Poles make my hike much easier, safer, and more relaxed. While helicopters are generally busy making deliveries to high-altitude guesthouses and eateries, they are also standing by for emergency rescues. (Calling 1414 is SOS here in the Alps; from a US phone dial +41 333 333 333.) For more tips, see the "Hiking in the Berner Oberlander" sidebar, later.

Picnic Lunches: My favorite alpine lunches are high-altitude picnics. Co-op and Migros grocery stores (in most villages and near most train stations) seem to be stocked with hikers in mind. A fine picnic for two (fresh bread, local meat and cheese, fruit, vegetables, coffee, and a chocolate treat) is fast, healthy, and can be had for 20 CHF.

Interlaken

When the 19th-century Romantics redefined mountains as something more than cold and troublesome obstacles, Interlaken became the original alpine resort. Ever since, tourists have flocked to the Alps "because they're there." Interlaken's glory days are long gone, its elegant old hotels eclipsed by newer, swankier alpine resorts. Today the town center has been re-envisioned for the needs of mass tourism. It's an alpine gateway town whose shops are filled with chocolate bars and Swiss Army knives. Tour guides squeeze their groups into trains and gondolas, and sunburned backpackers nurse adrenaline hangovers.

Efficient Interlaken (pop. 5,500) is, above all, a good administrative and shopping center. Its streets are a strange combination of faded grand hotels, adventure-travel companies, and curry houses. While handy, it's too bustling and touristy to provide a real mountain experience. Take care of business, give the town a quick look, view the webcam coverage (at the TI) of the weather higher up... then head into the mountains.

Orientation to Interlaken

Interlaken straddles the Aare River, which connects two alpine lakes: Lake Brienz and Lake Thun. The older part of town (called Unterseen) is on the west side of the Aare and has pockets of charm and a cute village square. The newer section (Interlaken proper), with most services and both train stations, is on the river's east side.

TOURIST INFORMATION

A small TI operates at the Interlaken Ost train station in summer and is convenient if you're arriving there (daily 10:00-16:00, though hours may vary; closed Oct-May). Otherwise, visit the main TI, located by the post office at Marktgasse 1 (Mon-Fri 8:00-18:00,

BERNER OBERLAND

Interlaken's Latest Tourism Boom

While the Swiss Alps are now passé for European jet-setters, Interlaken is cashing in on huge group-travel interest from Asia and the Arab world. It's a tourism trend across Switzerland.

Tourists from India come to this region to escape their monsoon season—especially in April and May—and to visit romantic places they've seen in Bollywood movies. (The Alps often stand in for mountainous but politically troubled Kashmir, which is less accessible to film crews.) There's even a restaurant called Bollywood atop the Jungfraujoch. Interlaken is also popular with tour groups from China; the Schilthornbahn marketing department has an office in Shanghai. And tourists from the hot and arid Arabian Peninsula—who grew up visiting cafés adorned with faded wallpaper depicting dreamy alpine scenes—visit to photograph their children frolicking in chilly mist and fog. (Some vacation packages even offer a refund if all they get is sunshine.) Every expectation is that Asian tourism will continue to grow, and this corner of the Swiss Alps will become ever more international—and crowded.

If you prefer to avoid the congestion caused by mass-tourism crowds, sleep in the high country (instead of Interlaken), hike away from the towns, and be active early and late.

Sat-Sun 10:00-16:00; shorter hours and closed Sun Oct-May; +41 33 826 5300, www.interlaken.ch). Pick up the hiking guide published by the Jungfraubahn mountain railway (with a good map of the area). The TI sells tickets for the various mountain trains and lifts, and for adventure sports.

ARRIVAL IN INTERLAKEN

Interlaken has two train stations: Ost (East) and West. Major trains generally stop at both stations, but for ease and economy, confirm which station you want when buying your ticket.

Interlaken Ost is the transfer point for narrow-gauge trains to the high mountains (to Lauterbrunnen, Gimmelwald, Jung-

fraujoch, etc.) and to Luzern. Use this station if you're headed to those destinations or staying at the recommended Interlaken Hostel (next door). Interlaken Ost has free WCs, lockers, ticket counters, and a summer-only branch TI.

Interlaken West is closer to most of my listed hotels and downtown shopping and services. All trains from western Switzerland—Bern, the Golden Pass, Basel—stop at Interlaken West, and then continue to Interlaken Ost. Interlaken West has pay WCs, lockers (by track 1), ticket counters, and bike rental.

From Interlaken Ost to Interlaken West: It's a pleasant 30-minute walk between the West and Ost train stations. Otherwise, it's an easy four-minute trip by train (3/hour, 4.60 CHF), or a 10-minute trip on any of several local buses (#21, #102, #103, or #104; pay 3.60 CHF to the driver, free with Visitor Card). Stops are marked with yellow-and-white PostAuto signs.

Parking: Daytime parking is metered, but you can park free overnight at several spots. Expect to pay about 14 CHF/24 hours.

HELPFUL HINTS

Bike Rental: The **Interlaken West** train station houses a branch of the Swiss rail system's bike-rental program (see page 491). For about the same price, **Flying Wheels,** a short walk from the Ost train station, is a hip, well-organized, family-friendly outfit that specializes in electric bikes and guided bike tours. Its English-speaking staff give tips on where to go and can help you pick the right bike (bikes—35 CHF/half-day, 39 CHF/day; electric bikes—49 CHF/half-day, 59 CHF/day; includes helmet, daily May-Sept 9:00-19:00 in good weather, shorter hours off-season, across street from northeast corner of Höhematte Park at Höheweg 133, +41 76 453 1464—WhatsApp messages answered, www.flyingwheels.ch). For info on their tours, see "Adventure Sports," later.

Eiger Sport, a short walk from the West train station, is another bike rental option (bikes—20 CHF/half-day, 30 CHF/day; electric bikes—65 CHF/day; helmets extra, Mon-Fri 8:45-12:15 & 13:30-18:30, Sat 8:45-16:00, closed Sun; from the West train station, cross the river—it's on the left at Bahnhofstrasse 2, +41 33 823 2043, www.eiger-sport.ch).

"Free" Walking Tours: "Free" tours are actually "pay what you think it's worth" tours—you'll be hit up for a tip at the end. Though light on sights and history, they offer a fun city overview and a chance to join a smart local student on a stroll through their hometown (likely Mon, Wed, and Sat at 18:00 from Arab Service Interlaken at Höheweg 95, www.interlaken-walkingtours.ch).

Interlaken Walk

Most visitors use Interlaken as a springboard for high-altitude thrills (and rightly so). But the town does have some history and scenic charm and is worth a short walk. This 45-minute stroll circles from the West train station, down the main drag to the big

Interlaken

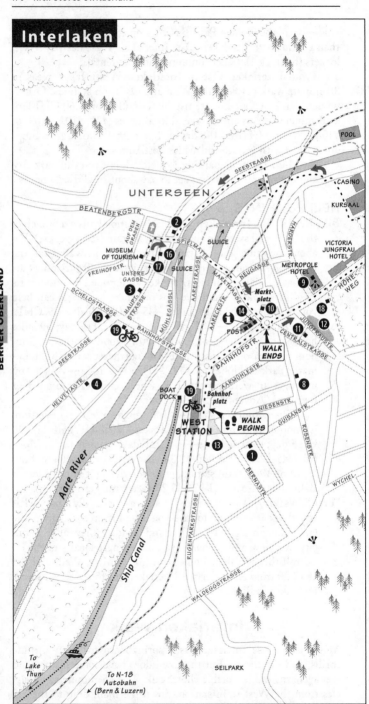

BERNER OBERLAND

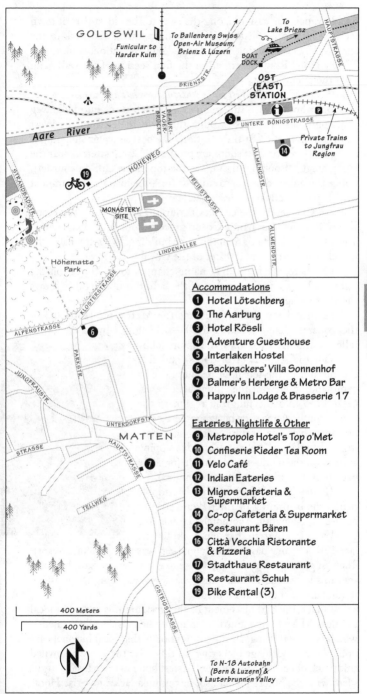

GOLDSWIL

Funicular to Harder Kulm

To Ballenberg Swiss Open-Air Museum, Brienz & Luzern

To Lake Brienz

BOAT DOCK

OST (EAST) STATION

Private Trains to Jungfrau Region

BRIENZSTR.

BEAURI-VAGERI-BRÜCKE

HAUPTSTRASSE

Aare River

UNTERE BÖNIGSTRASSE

ALLMENDSTR.

HÖHEWEG

FREIESTRASSE

MONASTERY SITE

LINDENALLEE

ALLMENDSTR.

STRANDBADSTR.

Höhematte Park

KLOSTERSTRASSE

ALPENSTRASSE

PARKSTR.

JUNGFRAUSTR.

UNTERDORFSTR.

MATTEN

STRASSE

HAUPTSTRASSE

TELLWEG

OSTEIGSTRASSE

Accommodations
1. Hotel Lötschberg
2. The Aarburg
3. Hotel Rössli
4. Adventure Guesthouse
5. Interlaken Hostel
6. Backpackers' Villa Sonnenhof
7. Balmer's Herberge & Metro Bar
8. Happy Inn Lodge & Brasserie 17

Eateries, Nightlife & Other
9. Metropole Hotel's Top o'Met
10. Confiserie Rieder Tea Room
11. Velo Café
12. Indian Eateries
13. Migros Cafeteria & Supermarket
14. Co-op Cafeteria & Supermarket
15. Restaurant Bären
16. Città Vecchia Ristorante & Pizzeria
17. Stadthaus Restaurant
18. Restaurant Schuh
19. Bike Rental (3)

400 Meters
400 Yards

To N-18 Autobahn (Bern & Luzern) & Lauterbrunnen Valley

BERNER OBERLAND

meadow, past the casino, along the river to the oldest part of town (called Unterseen—historically a separate town), and back to the station. If you're coming from Interlaken Ost station, walk to the "Fancy Hotel Row" described in the first section of the walk, and start the circuit there.

• *With your back to the West train station, turn left and walk along...*

Bahnhofstrasse: This main drag, which turns into Höheweg as it continues east, cuts through the town center from the West train station to the Ost train station. The best souvenir shopping is along this stretch (finer shops are on the Höheweg stretch, near the fancy hotels). Looking high up to the top of the cliff on your left, notice the pointy dome of Harder Kulm—the historic restaurant at the "Top of Interlaken" (described later).

On your left at the corner of Marktgasse, just past the Hotel Krebs, is a small but handy Co-op grocery store (long hours daily). The TI and post office are in the same building. WCs are inside the round brown structure in front of the Co-op.

Past here, the main drag name changes to Höheweg; on the right at #2, a TV in the window of the Schilthornbahn office shows the weather up top.

Farther down the street looms the **Metropole Hotel** (a.k.a. the "concrete shame of Interlaken")—at 18 stories, by far the town's

tallest building. Step into the main lobby (through the second set of doors) and ride the elevator to the top-floor restaurant for a commanding view of the "inter-laken" area. Gaze deep into the Jungfrau region to the scenic south. A meal or beverage here costs no more than one back on earth (see "Eating in Interlaken," below). Consider sipping a drink on the outdoor view terrace (or come back tonight—it's open late most nights).

"Fancy Hotel Row": The Metropole marks the beginning of Interlaken's strip of high-end, Romantic Age hotels. Hotels like the Victoria-Jungfrau harken back to the late-19th-century days when Interlaken was *the* top alpine resort. The first grand hotels were built here to enjoy the views of the Jungfrau in the distance. Today, the *junge Frauen* getting the most attention are next door at Hooters.

In fact, the odd placement of that restaurant is rooted in local politics. Most of the tourism industry here is locally owned—which is a good thing. But the downside is that local big shots are not above petty village bickering. In this case, the guy who owned this patch of land in front of the classiest hotel in town lost an argument with the hotel's owner...so, he put up a tacky, low-rise Hooters chain restaurant. That'll teach him. Meanwhile, the CEOs of the two dominant mountain lifts (the Jungfraubahn and Schilthornbahn) don't play well together. There's little coordination, and the map for one system treats the other's lifts like they don't exist.

• *Now turn your attention to the big field across from those hotels.*

Höhematte Park: This "high meadow"—or *höhe Matte* (but generally referred to simply as "the park")—originated as farm-land belonging to the monastery that predated the town (marked today by the steeples of both the Catholic and Protestant churches, just beyond the far end of the park—neither are of sightseeing interest). The actual **monastery site** is now home

to the courthouse and county administration building. With the Reformation in 1528, the monastery was shut down, and its land taken by the state. Later, as developers started to eye the parkland, the town's leading hotels and business families bought it and protected it from commercial use (a very early example of smart town planning). Today, this is a fine place to stroll, hang out on the park benches or at Restaurant Schuh, and watch the paragliders gracefully land.

• *But for now, we'll take a detour toward the river. After the Victoria-Jungfrau Hotel, follow the passage on your left (through a shopping arcade) into the grounds of the...*

Casino Kursaal: The venerable old Kursaal, originally a kind of 19th-century weight-loss retreat, is now a convention center and casino (passport but no tie required to enter). In the garden, at the top of each hour, dwarves ring the toadstools on the flower clock. And, all day long visitors from India pose at the bronze-colored statue of Yash Chopra—the Steven Spielberg of India, who shot many romantic scenes for his Bollywood films here.

• *Circle around the left side of the Kursaal to the river (note the huge public swimming pool across the river—an inviting complex that also has a water slide). Turn left and walk downstream along the riverside path for a few minutes, passing under the train bridge, and cross the pedestrian bridge, stopping in the middle to enjoy the view.*

Aare River: This short stretch of Switzerland's longest river connects Lake Brienz and Lake Thun (with an 18-foot altitude difference that's controlled by sluices—notice it has quite a flow). From Lake Thun, it heads for Bern and ultimately into the Rhine. In the distance (looking downstream), a church bell tower marks a different parish and the technically separate town of Unterseen, across the river—we're headed there next. Behind the spire is the pointy summit of the Niesen (like so many Swiss peaks, capped with a restaurant and accessible by a lift).

• *Cross the rest of the way over the bridge, turn left, and stroll downstream along the far side of the river, toward the church spire. As you walk, watch on your left for one of those old wooden sluices that help control the river flow. The delightful, tree-lined riverside walk is fronted by fine residences. Notice that your Jungfrau view now includes the Jungfraujoch observation deck (the little brown bump in the ridge just left of the peak).*

At the next bridge, turn right and walk a half-block up into the old town square, lined with 17th-century houses on one side and a modern strip on the other.

Unterseen: This was a town when Interlaken was only a monastery, and today it preserves a little of its medieval layout and streetscape. Two recommended restaurants face this square.

In the upper part of the square (behind the big building), the big *Tourismuseum* sign marks the worthwhile—but generally empty—**Museum of Tourism** (grandly named, but really a local history museum). It shows off three floors of classic posters, fascinating photos of the construction of the Jungfraujoch, and exhibits on folk life, crafts, and winter sports (8 CHF, covered by Swiss Travel Pass; Wed-Sun 14:00-17:00, closed Mon-Tue and Nov; Dec-April open only Wed and Sun; Obere Gasse 28, +41 33 826 6464, www.touristikmuseum.ch).

• *From the little square, retrace your steps and continue straight across the big bridge, carrying on straight on Spielmatte. From the bridge, watch on your right for another one of those antique sluices.*

Soon you'll reach a second bridge. On the left is yet another old sluice. If you look closely, you'll notice two heraldic emblems, each featuring an ibex, a wild mountain goat: a yellow one on the left, and a silver one on the right. This marks the border between the two towns/parishes. You're leaving Unterseen and returning to Interlaken.

Back to the Train Station: You're just a five-minute walk from the main drag and a 10-minute walk from the West station where we began. Carry on straight past the second bridge, crossing the train tracks. After about three blocks, a little restaurant-lined square called Marktplatz opens up on your left. The river originally ran through here, and the settlement on this side of the river was called "Aarmühle," named for a mill that was here. But in the 19th century, town fathers mindful of the English tourists flocking here made a key marketing decision: They ditched the difficult-to-pronounce "Aarmühle" and changed the town's name to the romantic "Interlaken" (between the lakes). Judging from the throngs of tourists on the main drag, that was a smart decision.

• *Continuing straight ahead, you'll run into Bahnhofstrasse/Höheweg again. Turn right to head back to the West station—or turn left to go back toward Höhematte Park and, beyond it, the Harder Kulm funicular and the Ost station.*

Sights and Activities near Interlaken

For hikes and walks in the Berner Oberland, see page 220.

EASYGOING EXCURSIONS

▲▲Swiss Open-Air Museum at Ballenberg

At the far end of Lake Brienz from Interlaken, the Ballenberg open-air museum is a rich collection of more than 100 traditional and historic buildings brought here from every region of the country. All the houses are carefully furnished, and many feature traditional craftspeople at work. The sprawling 50-acre park, laid out roughly as a huge Swiss map (Italian Swiss in the south, Appenzell in the east, and so on), is a natural preserve providing a wonderful setting for this culture-on-a-lazy-Susan look at Switzerland.

Cost and Hours: 28 CHF, covered by Swiss Travel Pass, houses open daily 10:00-17:00, grounds and restaurants 9:00-18:00, entire complex closed Nov-March, +41 33 952 1030, www.ballenberg.ch.

Eating: Along with several eateries, picnic tables and grills with free firewood are scattered throughout the park.

Getting There: The trip from Interlaken to Ballenberg takes about 20 minutes by car (pay parking at either entrance), 50 minutes by train and bus, or 2 hours by boat and bus. By public transport, first go to Brienz by train or boat, then from Brienz to Ballenberg by local bus. **Trains** for Brienz leave from Interlaken Ost (8 CHF, 2/hour, 15-20 minutes). **Boats** to Brienz leave from a dock just behind the Ost train station (32 CHF, every 1-2 hours, 1.25 hours, +41 58 327 4811, www.bls.ch).

From the Brienz station or boat dock, catch local bus #151, which stops first at the Ballenberg West museum entrance, then at Ballenberg Ost (1-2/hour, 20 minutes). Use the timetables at Rail.ch to plan your trip, and check bus return times carefully—after 17:15, buses back to Brienz leave only from the park's west entrance. Without a rail pass, ask for the Ballenberg combo-ticket when buying your train or boat tickets: This covers the complete round-trip from Interlaken (or beyond), and saves about 10 percent off your fare and park entry.

BERNER OBERLAND

Visiting Ballenberg: Ballenberg has entrances at either end (east and west, about a mile apart). If you start in the east and go west, it's a generally downhill stroll. Pick up a daily craft-demonstration schedule at the entry, and the free map/guide. There are daily events and demonstrations, hundreds of traditional farm animals (check out the very furry-legged roosters, near the merry-go-round in the center), and a chocolate shop (under the restaurant, just outside the park, on the east side).

There are more historic buildings than you can see in a single visit. Survey your map, note where the demonstrations are happening, and make a plan. Buildings I particularly enjoy are: #1361 (cheese upstairs, cow bells you can ring downstairs); #911 (a big Appenzell house); #611 (barbershop museum upstairs); #321 (sausages hang from the ceiling); and #221 (a house and farm designed for hands-on fun).

Boat Trips

"Interlaken" is literally "between the lakes" of Thun and Brienz, and you can explore these lakes on a lazy boat trip. While more relaxing than exciting—I'd rather spend a sunny day on a high-mountain lift—a lake-boat cruise can be a scenic way to slow your pulse (covered by Swiss Travel Pass or Eurail Global Pass but uses a flexi-day, 5/day July-Aug, 2-4/day spring and fall, +41 58 327 4811, www.bls.ch). You can pay extra for the "first class" top deck, but most people crowd the lower decks; the front deck is smaller but quieter and comes with a nice breeze. The ride begins by heading up a long, boring canal—but then, when the boat reaches the lake, the scenery opens up. From there, boats slowly hopscotch their way up the lake, stopping at middle-of-nowhere docks and offering pleasant views of little shoreline communities and cottages. Returning by train is a good plan, as the boats are slow and run only a few times a day.

Lake Thun: Departing from just behind the West train station (follow signs for *Pier One*), boats on Lake Thun make stops including the St. Beatus caves (Beatushöhlen, 30 minutes from Interlaken, 16.60 CHF, described next) and two visit-worthy towns: Spiez (80 minutes, 29 CHF) and Thun (2.25 hours, 45 CHF). Consider riding as far as one of these two towns, then zipping back on the train. Note: If disembarking in Spiez, the train station is a dull uphill hike away, but a bus stop is near the boat dock. Buses meet some boats and zip passengers right up to the train station (confirm with boat crew that your boat is coordinated with the bus).

The **St. Beatus caves,** named after a legendary medieval monk, take about 45 minutes to visit on a self-guided route (19 CHF, daily 9:00-18:00, closed Nov-March, +41 33 841 1643, www.beatushoehlen.swiss). To avoid the hike up to the caves from the lakeshore, follow this plan: Catch bus #21 from either Inter-laken station (5.20 CHF, about 2/hour, 15-25 minutes, direction: Thun), get off at the Beatushöhlen stop; tour the caves; take the short, steep hike down to the lake; and return to Interlaken by boat.

Lake Brienz: Departing from behind the Ost train station, boats on Lake Brienz are a fun way to get to the town of Brienz (get off here for the Ballenberg open-air museum; see "Getting There" info under Ballenberg listing, earlier); there's also a stop at the super-cute village of Iseltwald on the way.

▲Harder Kulm (Harderbahn)

Standing like a pointy little crown on a forested bluff high above Interlaken is a Romantic Age view restaurant that has rewarded a century of visitors with commanding views of Interlaken, the lakes, and the Berner Oberland peaks. While some make the steep climb up from town on foot, most just catch the Harder Kulm fu-nicular—marketed as the "Top of Interlaken"—which leaves from just over the river from Interlaken Ost train station. It's easy and very scenic, but it's still a "Berner Oberland Lite" experience, with cut-glass peaks farther away than they are from the many grand lifts near the Lauterbrunnen Valley. I'd go up Harder Kulm only if you're a mountain-lift completist, or if you're quickly passing through Interlaken without time to delve deeper. On a nice day, be prepared for lines going up—and going down.

Cost and Hours: 40 CHF round-trip, half-price with Swiss Travel Pass, 25 percent off with Eurail or Interlaken Visitor Card, at least 2/hour, 10 minutes, daily mid-April-late Oct 9:10-21:40, late Oct-late Nov until 17:10, +41 33 828 7233, www.jungfrau.ch (see "Harder Kulm" on the "Experience & Discover" menu).

Visiting the Mountaintop: You'll ride up in a glass-roofed fu-nicular. From the top station, you'll walk about five minutes along a ledge to reach the restau-rant and nearby viewpoint (at 4,337 feet)—cantile-vered to jut out toward the mountain vistas, with Interlaken at your feet. Visitors crowd around on the platform to pose with props: a Swiss flag and a life-size plastic cow.

For a slightly more relaxed experience, hike up the little trail just before the restaurant (marked *pavilion*). Just a few steps takes you above the hubbub, to similar views but without the crowds (and with a few benches for lingering).

The **$$ restaurant** itself has indoor and outdoor seating—all with grand views—and a predictable menu of Swiss and international standards. Some tables are for the little self-service **$ snack bar.** In peak season, there's frequently live folk music out on the terrace.

ADVENTURE SPORTS
High-Adrenaline Trips
Interlaken is a great place for thrill-seekers with money. Choose among rafting, canyoning (rappelling down watery gorges), jet boats, bungee jumping, and paragliding. Costs range from roughly 150 CHF to 200 CHF—more for skydiving and hot-air balloon rides. The dominant operator is **Outdoor** (+41 33 224 0704, www.outdoor.ch), which offers many of these activities itself and acts as a booking agent for others. Their main office is in Matten, near Balmer's hostel (Hauptstrasse 15), but they also have a sales point in Interlaken at Höheweg 95, by Höhematte Park. For an overview of additional options, study the racks of brochures at most TIs and hotels.

Rope Courses
Outdoor's Seilpark offers nine rope courses of varying difficulty and height, giving you a treetop forest adventure through a maze of rope bridges and zip lines—allow two or three hours. Some of the courses are suitable for kids (with supervision).

Cost and Hours: 42 CHF, family deals, no charge for spectators, maximum weight 265 pounds; June daily 10:00-18:00, July-Aug until 20:00, shorter hours off-season, closed Nov-March; last entry two hours before closing time; from Interlaken's West train station, it's a 15-minute walk—head right up Rugenparkstrasse and into the park, then look for signs; +41 33 826 7719, www.outdoor.ch (search for "Ropes Park").

Bike Tours
Flying Wheels offers a guided e-bike tour almost every morning—some days it's a three-hour tour around Interlaken, touching the shores of both lakes (119 CHF), and other days a six-hour tour of the Lauterbrunnen Valley (219 CHF, includes picnic and Trümmelbach Falls visit). For contact info, see "Helpful Hints," earlier.

CASTLES
Three impressively well-kept and welcoming old castles in or near the town of Thun are worth considering for day trips (30 minutes from Interlaken by train or car, or about two hours by scenic boat ride).

Thun Castle (Schloss Thun)

Built between 1180 and 1190 by the Dukes of Zähringen, this castle in the center of Thun houses a five-floor historical museum offering insights into the cultural development of the region over some 4,000 years. From the corner turrets of the castle, you're rewarded with sweeping views of the city of Thun, the lake, and the Alps.

Cost and Hours: 10 CHF, daily 10:00-17:00, shorter hours off-season, Nov-Jan Sun only, +41 33 223 2001, www.schlossthun.ch.

Hünegg Castle (Schloss Hünegg)

Located in Hilterfingen (on the outskirts of Thun), this castle-museum exhibits furnished rooms from the second half of the 19th century. The castle is situated in a beautiful wooded park by the lake, not far from the Hilterfingen boat dock and the #21 bus from Interlaken or Thun.

Cost and Hours: 10 CHF, Tue-Sat 14:00-17:00, Sun from 11:00, closed Mon and mid-Oct-mid-May, +41 33 243 1982, www.schlosshuenegg.ch.

Oberhofen Castle (Schloss Oberhofen)

A 20-minute walk along the lake from Hünegg Castle, this castle is set in a beautifully landscaped park with exotic trees. The castle's museum explores domestic life in the 16th to 19th centuries, including a Turkish smoking room and a medieval chapel.

Cost and Hours: Gardens—free, daily 9:00-dusk; museum—12 CHF, Tue-Sun 11:00-17:00, closed Mon; both closed off-season, by Oberhofen am Thunersee boat dock, or take bus #21 to Oberhofen Dorf stop, +41 33 243 1235, www.schlossoberhofen.ch.

Nightlife in Interlaken

Lively Nightlife: A young frat-party dance scene rages at the **Metro Bar** bomb-shelter disco, with cheap drinks and a friendly if loud atmosphere (at Balmer's hostel, Hauptstrasse 23 in Matten; see lister under "Sleeping in Interlaken"). **Brasserie 17** is a more local scene with craft beers on tap and a down-and-dirty pub/sports bar ambience. Thursday evenings often feature live music (also serves food—see listing under "Eating in Interlaken," in the Happy Inn Lodge hostel at Rosenstrasse 17, +41 33 822 3225).

Mellow Nightlife: To nurse a drink with a park view, the outdoor tables at **Restaurant Schuh** (on the edge of Höhematte Park) are convenient—if you don't mind the schlocky music. The **Top o'Met** restaurant in the Metropole Hotel skyscraper has great indoor and outdoor view seating with reasonable prices, 18 floors above everything else in town (see "Eating in Interlaken," later).

BERNER OBERLAND

While the interior is lit like a grocery store, the outdoor seating is particularly nice on a warm evening.

Sleeping in Interlaken

Interlaken is not the Alps. I'd sleep in Gimmelwald, Mürren, or at least Lauterbrunnen (20 minutes away by train or car). In ski season, however, prices go down in Interlaken while they shoot up at most mountain hotels. Price ratings given here are for summer; they drop a bit in spring and fall and plunge from November to March.

Hotels and Guest Houses

$$ Hotel Lötschberg has a sun terrace and 18 rooms just a three-minute walk from the West train station, but it's still residential and quiet. They have a lounge with microwave, fridge, and free tea and coffee (pay parking, laundry facilities, closed Jan-mid-April; General-Guisan-Strasse 31, +41 33 822 2545, www.lotschberg.ch, hotel@lotschberg.ch).

$$ The Aarburg offers nine plain, peaceful rooms over a restaurant in a traditional, beautifully located building just steps from the charming main square of Unterseen, a 10-minute walk from the West train station. Rooms are small, but guests can enjoy the shared lounge (family rooms, limited free parking, Beatenberg-strasse 1, +41 33 820 4460, www.theaarburg.ch, well-run by British Tim and Kat).

$$ Hotel Rössli, in Unterseen, is nicely located, if a bit dated. Their 32 rooms range across comfort levels, including "economy" rooms with a private bath down the hall and "budget" rooms with shared facilities (closed Dec-mid-Jan, elevator, pay parking—reserve, coin laundry, comfy lounge, Hauptstrasse 10, +41 33 822 7816, www.roessli-interlaken.ch, info@roessli-interlaken.ch).

$ Adventure Guesthouse is a cheery, family-friendly, nine-room place with both hostel beds and rooms with private bath, in a quiet residential neighborhood (family rooms, patio, limited free parking, Helvetiastrasse 29, +41 77 456 2338, www.adventure-guesthouse.ch, info@adventure-guesthouse.ch).

Hostels

Interlaken is a prime destination for hostels—with something for every taste, from efficient and institutional to family-friendly and hotelesque to more party-oriented.

¢ Interlaken Hostel is very convenient—right next to the Ost train station in a big, sterile 220-bed modern building, full of daylight and with plenty of amenities (private rooms available, bike rental, pay parking, coin laundry, check-in 15:00-23:00, Untere

Bönigstrasse 3, +41 33 826 1090, www.youthhostel.ch/interlaken, interlaken@youthhostel.ch). Their modern, welcoming, self-service **restaurant** is open to the public and popular with locals for its good value.

¢ **Backpackers' Villa Sonnenhof** is a creative, prizewinning guesthouse affiliated with the Methodist church. Wholesome without being restrictive, it's fun, colorful, and great for families and travelers of all ages (private rooms, family rooms, view rooms have balcony and WC but shared shower, half-board dinner at nearby restaurant, kitchen, elevator, garden, movies, small game room, free entry to public swimming pool and tennis courts, pay parking, laundry; across park from the main drag at Alpenstrasse 16—a level 15-minute walk from either train station, or take bus #102 to Sonnenhof stop; +41 33 826 7171, www.villa.ch, mail@villa.ch).

¢ **Balmer's Herberge** is high-energy, youthful, and very social. This 200-bed Interlaken institution is many people's idea of backpacker heaven, with movies, table tennis, bar, restaurant, kitchen, hot tub, swapping library, excursions, and friendly, hardworking staff. Within a few doors are a laundromat, Co-op grocery store, outdoor adventure booking agency, and pizza and Asian eateries. It can feel like a frat party, especially on summer weekends (reserve far in advance for private rooms; 20-minute walk from either train station, or take bus #104 or #105 to the Hotel Sonne stop; at Hauptstrasse 23 in the suburb of Matten, +41 33 822 1961, www.balmers.com, mail@balmers.com).

¢ **Happy Inn Lodge,** above the lively, noisy Brasserie 17 pub, has 16 cheap, conveniently located backpacker rooms (3-6 beds/room, bath down the hall), plus two basic doubles with private baths. It's a decent option for the young and scrappy (five-minute walk from West train station at Rosenstrasse 17, +41 33 822 3225, www.happyinn.com, info@brasserie17.ch).

Eating in Interlaken

In the Heart of Interlaken

$$$ **Metropole Hotel's Top o'Met** café/restaurant, capping Interlaken's 18-story aesthetic nightmare, serves good traditional and modern food at down-to-earth prices, with no gouging on drinks. For 5 CHF, you can enjoy a glass of Swiss wine and awesome views from an indoor or outdoor table. The eclectic menu features Swiss, Italian, and Indian dishes (Mon-Sat 10:00-22:00, Sun until 17:00; hot food served 11:30-14:00 & 18:00-21:30, Höheweg 37, +41 33 828 6666, Marco).

$ **Confiserie Rieder Tea Room**—on the charming Marktplatz square just off the main drag—is a sweet bit of local elegance tucked away among all the modern tourism. Along with home-made pastries (their specialty is a chocolatey truffle cake) and pralines, they serve light meals of quiche, toast, and salads (Tue-Sat 8:30-18:00, Sun from 11:00, closed Mon, Marktgasse 2, +41 33 822 3673).

$ Brasserie 17 serves a big menu of inexpensive pub food (burgers, salads, ribs, and wings) from behind a long, dark bar where local craft beers are on tap (food served daily 11:30-13:30 & 18:00-21:30, open until at least 23:00, at the Happy Inn Lodge at Rosenstrasse 17, +41 33 822 3225).

Quality Coffee Shop: Interlaken's hipster coffee joint, **$ Velo Café** has a tucked-away location, a variety of coffee drinks, and healthy light meals, including breakfast. Choose between the stay-awhile interior, or the streetside terrace (daily 9:00-18:00, Unionsgasse 10, +41 79 902 1626).

$ Global Cuisine: An abundance of restaurants caters to Interlaken's many international tourists. **Jungfraustrasse,** a pedestrian street in the center, has a selection of Indian eateries and one lonely Mexican place.

$ Cafeterias: Interlaken's two large supermarkets have handy cafeterias that are a great bet for a fast, inexpensive, self-service meal amidst a local crowd. Ask them to dish up whatever hot dishes look good or choose a quiche or salad; as they strive to sell out, choices dwindle toward closing. **Migros** is in a modern mall across the street from the West train station (hours similar to those of the Migros supermarket—see below; free tap water, Rugenparkstrasse 1). The **Co-op** restaurant is across the square from the Ost train station, upstairs (Mon-Fri 8:00-18:30, Sat until 17:00, Sun 9:00-17:00, Untere Bönigstrasse 10).

Supermarkets: For picnic supplies, the best selection and prices are at the two large supermarkets: **Migros** near the West train station (Mon-Thu 8:00-20:00, Fri until 21:00, Sat until 18:00, closed Sun), and the **Co-op** near the Ost train station (Mon-Thu 8:00-19:00, Fri until 20:00, Sat until 18:00, closed Sun). Later in the evening and on Sundays, head to the smaller long-hours Co-op at the corner of Marktgasse and Bahnhofstrasse (daily 7:30-21:00) or the little grocery stores in each train station.

In Unterseen

This sleepy neighborhood, with a charming village feel around its old-world main square, is a fine place for a good meal. Unterseen is just a short walk from the tourist chaos and a 10-minute stroll from the West train station.

$$ Restaurant Bären fills a classic low-ceilinged gingerbread house with cozy indoor and fine outdoor seating. Lovingly run by Hans-Peter and his family, this is my choice for a traditional dinner. It's a solid value for *Rösti*, fondue, raclette, fish, traditional sausage, and salads (Wed-Fri 16:30-23:30, Sat-Sun from 10:00, closed Mon-Tue, Seestrasse 2, reserve in advance at +41 33 822 7526).

$$$ Città Vecchia Ristorante and Pizzeria serves good Italian meals in a classy indoor space or outdoors on Unterseen's leafy main square. It's top end for an Italian joint so a bit pricey (Thu-Mon 11:30-13:45 & 18:00-22:00, Wed open only at dinner, closed Tue, Untere Gasse 5, +41 33 822 1754).

$$$ Stadthaus, a big, high-energy eatery just across the square, is owned by Wilderswil-born celebrity chef René Schudel. The concept here is quality Swiss food presented without pretense, plus some international dishes. There's a big, inviting, covered terrace and an interior space that feels like an upscale beer hall (daily 11:00-23:00, Untere Gasse 2, +41 33 822 8689).

Interlaken Connections

Interlaken is connected to Montreux (on Lake Geneva) and Luzern via the Golden Pass scenic rail route (see the Scenic Rail Journeys chapter). Interlaken, Bern, Basel, and Frankfurt are linked by an express train, but for most other destinations you'll change in Bern. **Train info:** Rail.ch.

From Interlaken Ost by Train to: Bern (2/hour, 1 hour), **Zürich** (2/hour, 2 hours, usually with one change in Bern), **Zürich Airport** (2/hour, 2.5 hours, usually with one change in Bern), **Luzern** (hourly, 2 hours), **Lugano** (hourly, 4 hours, change in Luzern and sometimes Arth-Goldau), **Zermatt** (hourly, 2.25 hours, change in Spiez and Visp), **Lausanne** (2/hour, 2.25 hours, usually with one change in Bern; longer scenic route via Golden Pass—see the Scenic Rail Journeys chapter).

From Interlaken to the Lauterbrunnen Valley: Note that trains to Lauterbrunnen are covered by the Swiss Travel Pass (or discounted 25 percent with a Eurail Global Pass). **Trains** to **Lauterbrunnen** depart from Interlaken Ost (1-2/hour, 20 minutes, 7.60 CHF). You can **drive** to Lauterbrunnen (20 minutes) or Stechelberg. You can't drive to Gimmelwald (park at the cable-car station near Stechelberg and ride up on the Schilthornbahn lift) or to Mürren, Wengen, or Kleine Scheidegg (park at Lauterbrunnen train station and take the cable car to Mürren or the train to Wengen or Kleine Scheidegg). For details, see "Lauterbrunnen Valley Connections" on page 191.

By Car: For a scenic drive from Interlaken to Montreux, Chamonix, or Zermatt, see my recommended driving route on page 337.

Lauterbrunnen

Lauterbrunnen is the valley's commercial center and transportation hub. Sitting under sheer cliffs in its namesake valley, with its signature waterfall spurting mightily out from the cliff (floodlit at night), Lauterbrunnen is a fine springboard for Jungfrau and Schilthorn adventures. It can get congested—even chaotic—during peak season, especially around the train station. For that reason, I prefer overnighting in Gimmelwald or Mürren, perched on the ledge above the valley.

Orientation to Lauterbrunnen

In addition to its train station and cable car, the town is just big enough to have all the essential services (grocery, bank, bike rental, launderette, and so on)—plus several hotels and hostels. It's idyllic despite the busy road that slices it in two.

Tourist Information: Stop by the friendly TI to check the weather forecast, find out about guided walks and events, and buy hiking maps or regional train or lift tickets (daily 8:30-12:00 & 13:15-17:00 except closed Mon-Tue in Oct-May; on the main street a few houses up from the train station, +41 33 856 8568, www.lauterbrunnen.swiss).

Arrival in Lauterbrunnen: The small, modern **train station** has a ticket office, a few small lockers (hiding just to the right of the ticket office; check larger bags at ticket desks), and free WCs. Across the main street is the cable-car station; up the ramp to the right is the stop for the PostBus up the valley to Stechelberg (generally parked and ready to depart shortly after each train arrives); and a giant parking garage is on the opposite side of the tracks. Go left as you exit the station to head up the main drag (toward the gushing waterfall) and find the TI and my recommended hotels and eateries.

For **drivers,** the cheapest parking option is the big outdoor lot by the church (1.50 CHF/hour, 14 CHF/24 hours). The multistory garage behind the station is more convenient if you're leaving a car here to take a train or lift higher up in the mountains (17 CHF/24 hours). Also, there's plenty of parking at the Schilthornbahn lift, farther up the valley toward Stechelberg.

HELPFUL HINTS

Medical Help: The **Care Mate clinic** (with pharmacy) is near the Jungfrau Hotel (look for *Arzt* sign, English spoken, +41 33 856 2626, answered 24/7).

Money: Several ATMs are along the main street, including one immediately across from the train station.

Laundry: The **Valley Hostel** has coin-op machines (daily 9:00-21:00, +41 33 855 2008).

Bike Rental: You can rent mountain bikes at **Imboden Bike** on the main street (reserving online can be smart, bikes—28 CHF/4 hours, 38 CHF/day; electric bikes—38 CHF/4 hours, 50 CHF/day; RS%, includes helmet, Mon-Fri 9:00-17:30, Sat-Sun until 17:00, possibly later in summer, +41 33 855 2114, www.imboden-bike.ch). Make a point to be well-fitted on your bike. **Intersport** (see next listing) has higher prices but will let you drop bikes in Interlaken for a 10 CHF surcharge.

Sports Gear: Rent summer hiking equipment (boots, poles, baby carriers, *via ferrata* kits) and winter sports gear (skis and snowboards) at the **Alpia Sports/Intersport** shop (daily 8:30-12:30 & 13:30-18:30, longer hours in winter, closes for a few weeks in spring and fall, at Hotel Crystal, +41 33 855 3292, www.alpiasport.ch).

Activities in and near Lauterbrunnen

For hikes and walks from Lauterbrunnen, including the "Cloudy-Day Lauterbrunnen Valley Walk" that links Lauterbrunnen to Staubbach and Trümmelbach falls, see page 220.

Staubbach Falls

The second highest waterfall in Switzerland (nearly 900 feet) is literally in Lauterbrunnen's backyard—just follow the side road past the church toward the sound of rushing water. Its spray looks like falling dust—*Staub*—hence the name. A short trail starting across

BERNER OBERLAND

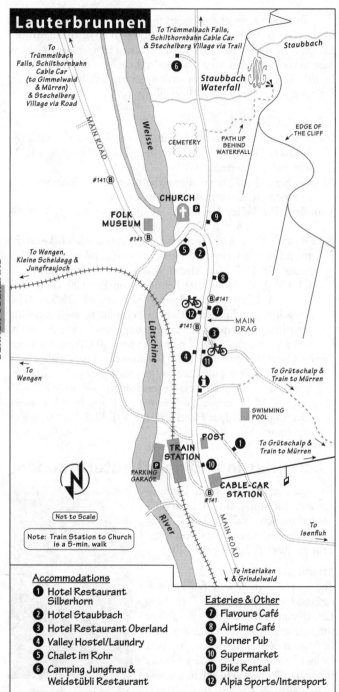

Lauterbrunnen

To Trümmelbach Falls, Schilthornbahn Cable Car & Stechelberg Village via Trail

To Trümmelbach Falls, Schilthornbahn Cable Car (to Gimmelwald & Mürren) & Stechelberg Village via Road

Staubbach

Staubbach Waterfall

MAIN ROAD

Weisse

CEMETERY

EDGE OF THE CLIFF

PATH UP BEHIND WATERFALL

#141 B

CHURCH

FOLK MUSEUM

#141 B

To Wengen, Kleine Scheidegg & Jungfraujoch

Lütschine

MAIN DRAG

#141 B

#141 B

To Wengen

To Grütschalp & Train to Mürren

SWIMMING POOL

POST

To Grütschalp & Train to Mürren

TRAIN STATION

PARKING GARAGE

CABLE-CAR STATION

#141 B

N

Not to Scale

Note: Train Station to Church is a 5-min. walk

River

MAIN ROAD

To Isenfluh

To Interlaken & Grindelwald

Accommodations
1 Hotel Restaurant Silberhorn
2 Hotel Staubbach
3 Hotel Restaurant Oberland
4 Valley Hostel/Laundry
5 Chalet im Rohr
6 Camping Jungfrau & Weidstübli Restaurant

Eateries & Other
7 Flavours Café
8 Airtime Café
9 Horner Pub
10 Supermarket
11 Bike Rental
12 Alpia Sports/Intersport

from the cemetery, by the tree-trunk benches, takes you up a few steep switchbacks to a path cut into the cliff and a delightful little perch behind the falls (there's a sturdy fence; the path is closed in winter).

▲Trümmelbach Falls

Sneak a behind-the-scenes look at the valley's most powerful waterfall, Trümmelbach Falls. Ride the elevator up through the

mountain, climb to the upper falls, and then hike down through several caves (wet, with lots of stairs, and claustrophobic for some). You'll see the melt from the Eiger, Mönch, and Jungfrau grinding like God's band saw through the mountain at the rate of up to 5,000 gallons a second. The upper area is the best; if your legs ache, skip the lower falls and ride down on the elevator. A café (with WC) is directly across from the bus stop. The ticket kiosk and falls are a short walk beyond the café.

Cost and Hours: 14 CHF, children under 4 not admitted, daily 9:00-17:00, July-Aug 8:30-18:00, closed Nov-March, opening date can vary with ice conditions, +41 33 855 3232, www.truemmelbachfaelle.ch.

Getting There: The falls are about halfway between Lauterbrunnen and the Schilthornbahn cable-car station; from either, it's about a 45-minute walk, or a short ride on the #141 PostBus (Trümmelbachfälle stop, pay driver in cash).

Hang Out with BASE Jumpers

The Lauterbrunnen Valley has become an El Dorado of BASE jumping (the name stands for the four fixed objects parachuters jump from: building, antenna, span, and earth—in this case, cliffs). The world BASE jumping championships are held here. BASE jumpers hike to the top of a cliff, leap off—falling as long as they can (this provides the rush)—then pull the ripcord to release a tiny parachute, hoping it will break their fall and a gust won't dash them against the walls of the valley. The Lauterbrunnen jumps are considered too tough for beginners—anyone considering BASE jumping should have extensive skydiving experience. Driving up the valley, you'll see windsocks in fields marking landing places. Unfortunately, several jumpers die here every year.

To learn more about this sport, search for "BASE jumping Lauterbrunnen" on YouTube, visit SwissBaseAssociation.org, or talk with the jumpers themselves. They congregate at the **Horner Pub,** at the upper end of Lauterbrunnen (near the waterfall). This is

BERNER OBERLAND

the grittiest place in town, providing cheap beds and filling meals for BASE jumpers, with five beers on tap. Locals, jumpers, and tourists gather here in the pub each evening—it's the town's only real after-dark scene (daily 12:00-late, dorm beds in 11 rooms, disco Fri-Sat from 22:00 upstairs, +41 33 855 1673, www.hornerpub.ch, mail@hornerpub.ch, run by Charlotte).

Lauterbrunnen Valley Folk Museum (Talmuseum Lauterbrunnen)

This interesting museum shows off the region's folk culture and two centuries of mountaineering from all the towns of this valley. You'll see lace, old tools, exhibits on cheese and woodworking, cowbells, classic old photos, and a brass bell—carried from the next valley in 1497—that rang at the church until 1952 (another bell is outside the neighboring village church). Request an English translation booklet.

Cost and Hours: 7 CHF, free with hotel Visitor Card, open limited hours—Wed and Fri 14:00-16:00, Sat 15:00-18:00, closed off-season, over bridge and below church at the far end of Lauterbrunnen town, +41 33 855 3586, www.talmuseum-sagenwelt-lauterbrunnen.ch.

Swimming Pool

Lauterbrunnen's cute little open-air pool has a great view and is just a minute's walk up the lane behind the TI.

Cost and Hours: 6 CHF, daily mid-May-June 10:30-18:00, July-Aug from 10:00.

Sleeping in Lauterbrunnen

The price ratings given are for high summer (July-Aug). Expect lower prices off-season (when many hotels close). As free parking is getting hard to find, request it with your hotel reservation. For more peace, choose Gimmelwald or Mürren.

$$ Hotel Silberhorn is a family-run, formal, 40-room hotel. It's in a very convenient location—a hundred yards uphill from the train station on a quiet side street. Almost every double room comes with a fine view and balcony; you can pay more for waterfall-view rooms clad in warm, knotty-pine woodwork (closed late Oct-mid-Dec, lots of stairs, free parking, dinner available, +41 33 856 2210, www.silberhorn.com, info@silberhorn.com).

$$ Hotel Staubbach, one of the oldest hotels in the valley (1890), is a big, creaky place that's been nicely upgraded. It has 33 rooms; the ones that face up the valley have balconies and fabulous waterfall views, though you may hear the church bells chiming on the hour. Rooms facing down the valley are a bit cheaper, with no balcony and an "A" rather than an "A-plus" view (family rooms, elevator, free parking, closed mid-Nov-March, 10-minute walk up from station on the left, +41 33 855 5454, www.staubbach.com, hotel@staubbach.com).

$$ Hotel Oberland is smack-dab in the center of town, with 28 tidy rooms, most with balconies and views of the Staubbach waterfall or Jungfrau (family rooms and one apartment, six rooms are in nearby Crystal Hotel annex, no elevator, pay parking, closes a few weeks in late fall, popular with my tour groups, five-minute walk up from station on the right, +41 33 855 1241, www.hoteloberland.ch, info@hoteloberland.ch, Stephen and Rubia).

¢ Valley Hostel is practical and comfortable, offering 92 inexpensive beds in two- to eight-bed rooms for quieter travelers of all ages, plus a pleasant garden (all rooms with shared bath, free parking, open all year, reception open 8:00-12:00 & 16:00-20:00—shorter hours off-season, five-minute walk up from train station, +41 33 855 2008, www.valleyhostel.ch, info@valleyhostel.ch, Abegglen family).

¢ Chalet im Rohr—a creaky, flower-draped, woody time-warp of a place—rents 23 rooms (each with a sink) that are about the cheapest in town. Showers and toilets are down the hall, and the building, while clean, is cheerfully unrenovated—you'll feel like nothing has changed since the 1970s. Lots of BASE jumpers stay here, and there's a memorial wall to jumpers who died

(cash only, family rooms, no breakfast, common kitchen, lots of stairs, free parking, across from church where main drag curves, +41 33 855 2182, www.chaletimrohr.ch, info@chaletimrohr.ch, Hans and Elsbeth von Allmen-Müller).

¢ Camping Jungfrau, a five-minute drive south of town or 15-minute stroll from the train station, rents two- to six-bed bungalows and cabins, a few dorm beds, and spots for campers. This can be a good deal for families (or small groups) traveling by car who want to stay a few days and cook for themselves. It's romantically situated along the small lane beyond Staubbach Falls, huge, and well-organized by Manuela. Ample facilities include a recommended restaurant and a grocery store (see listings below), communal kitchen, coin laundry, lounge, ATM, and playground (+41 33 856 2010, www.campingjungfrau.swiss, info@camping-jungfrau.ch).

BERNER OBERLAND

Eating in Lauterbrunnen

$$ Weidstübli Restaurant, at Camping Jungfrau past the waterfall, has earned a reputation in the valley as a great place to eat. Besides favorite Swiss standards, they do hearty meat and fish dishes, big salads, and vegan burgers. Reservations are wise; choose the bright interior or the attractive outdoor terrace (Wed-Sun 11:30-22:30, closed Mon-Tue and Nov-mid-Dec, +41 33 856 2010, www. weidstuebli.swiss).

$$ Hotel Restaurant Oberland serves good-value meals including traditional Swiss dishes and pizza. It's a high-volume place with lots of tourists and a huge, streetside front porch. Tables fill quickly, so reservations are a must (daily 11:30-14:00 & 18:00-21:00, dinner seatings at 18:00 and 20:00, +41 33 855 1241, www. hoteloberland.ch).

$$ Hotel Restaurant Silberhorn serves dinner in an elegant dining room with down-to-earth prices. They have all of the Swiss standards, plus good wood-fired pizzas. Call to reserve a view table (daily 18:00-21:00, outdoor seating too, above the cable-car station, +41 33 856 2210).

$$ Flavours, a café without a hint of yodeling or cowbells, serves up full breakfasts, burgers, focaccia sandwiches, fresh-squeezed juices, and gelato (takeaway available, daily 9:00-18:00, kitchen until 15:00, shorter hours off-season, closed Nov-April, +41 33 855 3652).

$ Airtime Café feels like a hipster alpine Starbucks with hot drinks, homemade treats, breakfast, and simple lunches—sandwiches, meat pies, soup, vegan options, and homemade sourdough bread (Fri-Sun 9:00-17:30, kitchen until 16:00, closed Mon-Thu and Nov, +41 33 855 1515, Annette and Fred).

$ Horner Pub, at the upper end of Lauterbrunnen near the waterfall, cranks out budget meals (like pasta, burgers, and raclette), serves breakfast, and has a few outside tables on a side street. It morphs into the town pub in the evenings, with several beers on tap (long hours daily, +41 33 855 1673).

Supermarket: The small but well-stocked **Co-op** is on the main street across from the train station (daily 8:00-19:00 in summer; Mon-Fri 8:00-18:30, Sat until 17:00, closed Sun rest of year). A smaller grocery is at **Camping Jungfrau** (daily 8:00-12:00 & 14:30-18:30; call +41 33 856 2010 to check before heading out).

Lauterbrunnen Valley Connections

The valley floor is connected by mountain train, bus, and cable car to the traffic-free villages, peaks, and hikes high above. Prices and trip durations given are one-way and per leg unless otherwise noted.

Getting from Lauterbrunnen to Gimmelwald or Mürren

To reach the mountain villages of Gimmelwald and Mürren, you have two options:

Schilthornbahn Cable Car: This is the most direct way to Gimmelwald, the easiest option if you're packing heavy, and the most sensible choice for drivers (parking at the cable-car station costs only 11 CHF/24 hours and practically never fills up). First, get to the Schilthornbahn valley station, near the village of Stechelberg at the top end of the valley, either by car (10 minutes) or by PostBus #141 (2/hour, 12 minutes from Lauterbrunnen station, departs five minutes after trains arrive, 4.40 CHF). Then ride up on the breathtaking Schilthornbahn cable car—first stop Gimmelwald (5 minutes), change there for Mürren (5 minutes more). The total bus-plus-cable car cost to Gimmelwald is 10.40 CHF; to Mürren it's 15.60 CHF.

From Stechelberg, the cable car runs at least twice hourly to Gimmelwald and Mürren (at :25 and :55 past the hour, more frequent during peak season). It runs late into the evening (Sun-Thu until 23:45, Fri-Sat until 24:55), but after 20:00 it's just once hourly. (The Mürren-Schilthorn route stops running much earlier. Also, be aware that the Schilthornbahn is closed for servicing for a week in April and three weeks in Nov-Dec, at least until a new cable-car lift is finished—see page 212. During these times, a cargo cable car from the valley floor goes up to Mürren, where a small bus shuttles travelers down to Gimmelwald.)

Grütschalp Cable Car and Mürren Train: This is a slightly quicker, cheaper, and more scenic way to get to Mürren. From the Lauterbrunnen train station, find the cable car station across the street and ride up to Grütschalp, where you'll immediately transfer to a tiny train. Sit on the left as the train rolls you along the cliffside to Mürren, looking across to the Eiger, Mönch, and Jungfrau panorama. The total trip from Lauterbrunnen to Mürren takes 20 minutes and a through ticket costs 11.20 CHF; if you continue from Mürren down to Gimmelwald on the Schilthornbahn, add 6 CHF. Getting to Gimmelwald this way takes longer and is less convenient (you'll have to walk across Mürren—about 15 minutes—then take the cable car down in 5 minutes, or hike down in 30).

BERNER OBERLAND

Trains to Interlaken, Wengen, Kleine Scheidegg, and Jungfraujoch

Lauterbrunnen's train station has trains to **Interlaken Ost** (1-2/ hour, 20 minutes, 7.60 CHF, covered by Swiss Travel Pass, 25 percent discount with Eurail Global Pass). Also from Lauterbrunnen, cute, old-fashioned, yellow-and-green Wengernalpbahn trains head up the steep cogwheel track twice hourly to **Wengen** (10 minutes, 6.80 CHF) and **Kleine Scheidegg** (40 minutes, 30.80 CHF; change here for the **Jungfraujoch**—see page 15). Note that the Swiss Travel Pass covers train travel only up to Wengen; buy any supplementary tickets before boarding the train in Lauterbrunnen (or pay a 10-CHF surcharge to buy on board; find the conductor before they find you to avoid a hefty fine). For the best views, sit on the right side—and be ready after the many short tunnels, just before Wengen, for grand views down over the Lauterbrunnen Valley. Feel the cogwheel gripping the tracks as you work your way up the steep incline. In Wengen, you can walk a few minutes up through town to the cable car up to **Männlichen,** where the spectacular hike to Kleine Scheidegg begins.

Gimmelwald

Saved from developers by its "avalanche zone" classification, Gimmelwald was (before modern tourism) one of the poorest places in Switzerland. Its traditional economy was stuck in the hay, and its farmers—unable to make it in their disadvantaged trade—survived on a trickle of visitors and Swiss government subsidies (and working the ski lifts in winter). For some travelers, there's little to see in such a village. Others (like me) enjoy a

fascinating day sitting on a bench and learning why they say, "If heaven isn't what it's cracked up to be, send me back to Gimmelwald."

Take a walk through the town. The huge, sheer cliff face that dominates your mountain views is the Schwarzmönch (Black Monk). The three peaks above (or behind) it are, left to right, the Eiger, Mönch, and Jungfrau. Although Gimmelwald's population dropped in the last century from 300 to about 100 residents, traditions survive. Most Gimmelwalders have one of two last names: von Allmen or Feuz. They are tough and proud. Raising hay in this

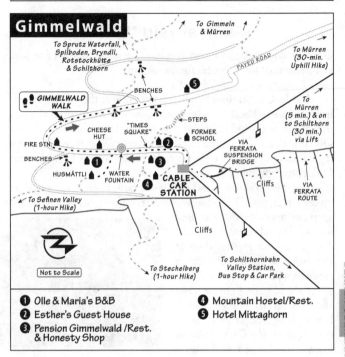

Gimmelwald

To Gimmeln & Mürren

To Sprutz Waterfall, Spilboden, Bryndli, Rotstockhütte & Schilthorn

To Mürren (30-min. Uphill Hike)

PAVED ROAD

BENCHES

GIMMELWALD WALK

To Mürren (5 min.) & on to Schilthorn (30 min.) via Lift

"TIMES SQUARE"

STEPS

CHEESE HUT

FORMER SCHOOL

VIA FERRATA SUSPENSION BRIDGE

FIRE STN

BENCHES

Cliffs

VIA FERRATA ROUTE

HUSMÄTTLI

WATER FOUNTAIN

CABLE CAR STATION

To Sefinen Valley (1-hour Hike)

Cliffs

Not to Scale

To Stechelberg (1-hour Hike)

To Schilthornbahn Valley Station, Bus Stop & Car Park

① Olle & Maria's B&B
② Esther's Guest House
③ Pension Gimmelwald / Rest. & Honesty Shop
④ Mountain Hostel/Rest.
⑤ Hotel Mittaghorn

rugged terrain is labor-intensive. One family harvests enough to feed only about 15 cows. But they'd have it no other way, and, unlike the absentee-landlord town of Mürren, Gimmelwald is locally owned. (When word got out that urban planners wanted to develop Gimmelwald into a town of 1,000, locals pulled some strings to secure the town's bogus avalanche-zone building code. Today, unlike nearby resort towns, Gimmelwald's population is the same all year.) Those same folks are happy the masses go to commercialized Grindelwald, just over the Kleine Scheidegg ridge. Don't confuse Gimmelwald and touristy Grindelwald—they couldn't be more different.

Tourist Information: Gimmelwald has a helpful little website (www.gimmelwald.ch) where you can check out photos of the town in different seasons, get directions for the best hikes from town (under "Summer Activities"), and see all the latest on activities and rooms for rent. For more on hikes from Gimmelwald, see page 221. And for a bit of Christmas-in-Gimmelwald fun, go to Classroom. RickSteves.com and search for "Christmas Gimmelwald."

Getting There: See "Lauterbrunnen Valley Connections," earlier.

Gimmelwald Walk

Gimmelwald, though tiny, with one zigzag street, offers a fine look at a traditional Swiss mountain community.

• *Start this quick self-guided walk at the...*

Cable-Car Station: When the lift came in the 1960s, the village's back end became its front door. As you walk out of the station, pause at the big Infopoint map to orient yourself. (You'll see a QR code that links to an interesting village tour that complements my walk; you can read or listen to its script now or later.) Ready? Let's turn right (uphill).

Gimmelwald was—and still is—a farm village. As you start up the street, you'll see a sweet little hut on the right. Set on stilts to keep out mice, the hut was used for storing cheese (the rocks on the rooftop are not decorative—they keep the shingles on through wild storms).

Behind the cheese hut stands a former village schoolhouse, long the largest structure in town. (In Catholic Swiss towns, the biggest building is the church; in Protestant towns, it's the school.) Gimmelwald's students now go to school in Lauterbrunnen, and the building is used as a chapel when the Protestant pastor makes his monthly visit. The little gray tower of loudspeakers on the roof is the town fire siren. Now turn around: On the other side of the street, next to the little playground, is a bench with a nice view, and just beyond it is the recommended Mountain Hostel.

• *Walk up the lane 50 yards to Gimmelwald's...*

"Times Square": The yellow alpine "street sign" shows where you are, the altitude (1,370 meters, or 4,470 feet), how many hours and minutes it takes to walk to nearby points, and which tracks are serious hiking paths (marked with red and white, and further indicated along the way with red and white patches of paint on stones). You're surrounded by buildings that were built as duplexes, divided vertically right down the middle to house two separate families.

Behind the street sign, the lettering high up on the post office building is a folksy blessing: "Summer brings green, winter brings snow. The sun greets the day, the stars greet the night. This house will protect you from rain, cold, and wind. May God give us his blessings." The yellow box is a reminder that, small as Gimmelwald is, it still has daily mail service. Someone comes down from Mürren's post office each day to deliver and pick up mail. The date on this building indicates when it was built—or maybe rebuilt (1911). Gimmelwald has a strict building code: For instance, shutters must be of wood and can only be painted certain colors.

Just down the lane to the left is the recommended Pension Gimmelwald (with rooms, a restaurant, and their wonderful Schwarz Mönch craft beer on tap). Look for the Honesty Shop featuring local crafts and little edibles for sale (summer only). Beyond is the Mountain Hostel, which welcomes all for a drink, pizza, or snack on its fine terrace.

• *From this tiny intersection, walk away from the cable-car station and follow the town's...*

Main Street: Head up the road about 30 yards to the next yellow sign post. Generations ago, Gimmelwald had more than twice the population and needed to produce more food. The scant remains of the terracing above was originally for post-WWII potato patches, now gone wild. All along this walk you'll also see private garden patches. Until recently, most locals grew their own vegetables, often enough to provide most of their family's needs. Today, while still widespread, most gardening is a hobby.

On the left (opposite the yellow signpost), notice the announcement board, with notifications such as deals on chainsaw sharpening, upcoming shooting competitions, local small business promotions, and news on community projects.

Walk about 30 yards farther to the big barn with a bovine orchestra of cowbells hanging on its wall, traditional milk canisters, and other farm implements. Just before that (on the right) is another big barn, dated 1995 and built in a modern style. At the far front corner is a cow-scratcher. Swiss cows have legal rights (for example, in the winter they must be taken out for exercise at least three times a week).

Traditionally, barns were small (like those on the hillside high above) and closer to the hay. But with trucks and paved roads, hay can be moved more easily, and farm businesses need more cows to be viable. Still, even a well-run big farm hopes just to break even. A century ago the village had 55 households, and 43 of them lived on farming. Today, just a few working farms survive.

• *A few steps farther up the lane, on your right, is a...*

Water Fountain/Trough: This is the site of the town's historic water supply (see photo on next page). Village kids love to bathe and wage water wars here when the cows aren't drinking from it.

BERNER OBERLAND

Swiss Cow Culture

Traditional Swiss cow farmers could make more money for much easier work in another profession. In a good year, farmers produce enough cheese to break even—they support their families on government subsidies. (Throughout the Alps, various governments support traditional farming as much for the tourism as for the cheese.) But these farmers have made a lifestyle choice to keep tradition alive and live high in the mountains.

The cows' grazing ground can range in elevation by as much as 5,000 feet throughout the year. In the summer (usually mid-June), the farmer straps elaborate ceremonial bells on his cows and takes them up to a hut at high elevation. These big bells weigh upward of 10 pounds and, while pricey, they are a proud investment for a humble farmer. When the cows arrive at their summer home, the ornamental bells are hung under the eaves and the cows get more practical bells.

These high-elevation summer stables are called "alps." Try to find some on a Berner Oberland tourist map (such as Wengernalp, Grütschalp, or Schiltalp). The cows stay at the alps for about

(Many locals drink this water, too, and live to be 100. It's perfectly drinkable.)

• *Detour left down a gravel path (along a wooden fence). First you'll pass (on your left) another lovingly tended pea-patch garden. With climate change, corn and pole beans are newcomers in the gardens here. Continue downhill along the path 50 yards or so to the corner. Notice the small barn ahead on the left. It's an 18th-century work of wooden art—cows downstairs and hay upstairs. Just to the right is another water trough in front of a house called...*

Husmättli: This is the oldest building in town, from 1658. (There are more 17th-century buildings on the road that zigzags down from Gimmelwald into the Sefinen Valley.) Study the log-cabin construction. Many old houses were built without nails. The wood was logged up the valley and cut on the still-working water-powered village mill (also in the Sefinen Valley).

From the water trough in front of Husmättli, look up to see a

100 days (roughly from June 10 to September 21). The farmers hire a team of cheesemakers to work at each alp—mostly hippies, students, and city slickers eager to spend three summer months in mountainous solitude. Each morning, the hired hands get up at 5:00 to milk the cows; take them to pasture; and make the cheese, milking the cows again when they come home in the evening. In the summer, all the milk is turned into alp cheese (it's too difficult to get it down to the market in liquid form). In the winter, with the cows at lower altitudes, the fresh milk is sold as milk.

Meanwhile, the farmers, glad to be free of their bovine responsibilities in summer, turn their attention to making hay. The average farmer has a few huts at various altitudes, each surrounded by small hay fields. The farmer follows the seasons up into the mountains, making hay and storing it above the huts. In the fall, the cows come down from the alps and spend the winter in the village, eating the hay the farmer spent the summer preparing for them.

Throughout the year you'll see farmers moving their herds to various elevations. If snow is in the way, farmers sometimes use tourist cable cars to move their cows. Every two months or so, Gimmelwald farmers bring together cows that aren't doing so well and herd them into the cable car to meet the butcher in the valley below.

BERNER OBERLAND

house with 10 solar panels on the roof—it's a B&B run by Olle and Maria, and we'll be passing there soon. As part of a green energy policy, a Swiss building code requires that new structures provide 30 percent of their own power. Switzerland is gradually moving away from nuclear power; its last reactor is supposed to close in 2034. The panels you see heat the water that Olle and Maria use for bathing and home heating; they fire up their furnace only from November to February.

• *Return up the gravel path to the main paved road, turn left, and continue.*

Although solar power is here, Gimmelwald still heats mostly with wood—and since the wood needs to age a couple of years to burn well, it's stacked everywhere.

Twenty yards along, on the left, look for the house with the *Self Service* sign. Climb the ramp, open the door, and you'll find a refrigerator with local cheese sold on the honor system by the Rubin family, with their woody portrait keeping an eye on the fridge. (Villagers generally see no need to lock their doors.) While inside, notice the lovingly stacked wall of kindling. Just outside the door, in the summer months, you may see a bunch of scythes hanging above a sharpening stone. Farmers pound, rather than grind, the blade to get it razor-sharp for efficient mowing on slopes too rocky or steep for machines or grazing animals. Feel a blade...carefully.

A few steps farther, notice the cute **cheese hut** on the right. This is where the cheese you saw on sale was aged (thousands of pounds turned and salted). The

hut's front wall is an alpine art gallery with nail shoes used as flowerpots. Nail shoes grip the steep, wet fields—this is critical for a farmer's safety, especially when carrying a sharp scythe. Even today, farmers buy metal tacks and fasten them to boots. The hut is full of strong cheese—up to three years old.

Look up. In the summer, a few goats are kept here behind the hut (rather than at a high alp) to provide families with fresh milk (about a half-gallon per day per goat). The farmers fence the goats in so they eat only this difficult-to-harvest grass.

See the *B&B* sign on the left? We've reached the solar-powered home and inn shared by Olle and Maria, who were the village schoolteachers for over three decades until the local school closed in 2010. (Check out Maria's cute "Amazing Window Store." It's mostly handmade giftables, and the proceeds support local charities.)

• *Fifty yards farther along on the right is the house called...*

Alpenrose: This is another old village school building, in use from about 1810 to 1930. Now it's a family home. You might see more ceremonial cowbells hanging under the eaves on the uphill side.

• *At the end of town, pause at the tiny viewpoint just before where a lane branches off to the left, leading into the dramatic...*

Sefinen Valley: At the bottom of this wild valley is a stream that rushes down toward Stechelberg. All the old homes in town are made from wood cut from the left-hand side of this valley (shady side, slow-growing, better timber) and milled in the water-powered sawmill farther down this road. The recommended hourlong hike down and then up to the head of Sefinen Valley and Kilchbalm starts from here.

• *A few steps ahead, the road switches back at the...*

Gimmelwald Fire Station *(Feuerwehrmagazin):* Peer through the cloudy windows in the bottom-floor door at the tractor-like engines. Then walk up around the hairpin bend to the notice board on the side of the building. The *Föhnwacht-Reglement* sheet explains rules to keep the village from burning down during the Föhn season, a period of fierce dry winds. During this time, there's a 24-hour fire watch, and even smoking cigarettes outdoors is forbidden. Mürren was devastated by a Föhn-caused fire in

the 1920s. Villagers in Gimmelwald—mindful of the safety of their volunteer fire department—are particularly careful. The town hasn't had a terrible fire in its history (a rare feat among alpine villages).

Check out the other posted notices. This year's Swiss Army calendar tells reservists when and where to go (in all four official Swiss languages). Every Swiss male is required to do a 22-week stint in the military, then serve three weeks a year in the reserves until age 34. The *Schiessübungen* poster details the shooting exercises required this year.

• *Unless you're really pooped, continue uphill along the road.*

High Road to More Views: High on the left, notice the hay field. It's a festival of alpine flowers in season (best at this altitude in May and June). On the right lives a legendary local gardener and her husband, who's fanatic about firewood ("trees tremble as he approaches").

• *In a couple of minutes, you'll reach a peaceful set of benches, through a break in the fence on the downhill side of the lane.*

Have a seat and take a moment to relax and savor the view. For decades, this has been a favorite place of mine to sit quietly, appreciate the Alps, and be thankful that I can travel and experience such wonders.

• *Continue about 100 yards until you see steps leading downhill on your right, just before Hotel Mittaghorn. Take these steps and you'll be back at the cable-car station in no time.*

Sleeping in Gimmelwald

Gimmelwald is my home base in the Berner Oberland. To inhale the Alps at 4,593 feet and really hold them in, you'll want to sleep high in Gimmelwald, too. Poor and pleasantly stuck in the past, the village has only a few accommodations options—all of them quirky and memorable. Note that the Visitor Card that comes with your hotel stay gives you free entry to the public swimming pool in nearby Mürren (at the Sportzentrum—described later in this chapter). Be warned: You'll meet a lot of my readers in this town.

BERNER OBERLAND

This is a disappointment to some; others enjoy the chance to be part of a fun extended family.

$$ Olle and Maria's B&B has Gimmelwald's most expensive and comfortable rooms. The Eggimanns' quirky but alpine-sleek house, where they raised three kids, offers visitors an intimate peek at this community. Two rooms with shared bath are upstairs in the house; there's also a ground-level studio apartment with its own bath, a kitchenette, and a private entrance (family room available, breakfast optional, three-night minimum, pay cash or with PayPal or Wise, nonrefundable 50 percent deposit required, pay laundry service; from cable car, continue straight for 200 yards along the town's only road, look for *B&B* sign on left; +41 33 855 3575, www.olleandmarias.ch, oeggimann@bluewin.ch).

$ Esther's Guest House rents seven clean, basic, and comfortable rooms. Three rooms have private bathrooms, the other four rooms share two bathrooms, and all share a generous lounge and kitchen (family rooms available—one sleeps up to six, breakfast extra, low ceilings, overlooking the village's main "intersection," +41 33 855 5488, www.esthersguesthouse.ch, info@esthersguesthouse.ch). Tobias and Franziska also rent three **apartments** with kitchenettes next door, sleeping four to eight people.

$ Pension Gimmelwald is an old, low-ceilinged farmhouse converted into a family-style inn, with 10 simple shared-bath rooms, two rooms with private bath, and a duplex apartment that sleeps up to seven at a pinch. There's a lively restaurant with nice old-style decor and a cozy bar. Its generous restaurant terrace, overlooking the Mountain Hostel, has gorgeous views across the valley (half-board available, open late May–mid-Oct and late Dec–March, two-minute walk up from cable-car station, +41 33 855 1730, www.hotel-pensiongimmelwald.ch, welcome@hotel-pensiongimmelwald.ch, Englishman David and Sabine).

¢ Mountain Hostel is a beehive of activity, as clean as its guests, cheap, respectable, and friendly. The 52-bed hostel has low ceilings and healthy plumbing, and it serves simple meals. There are three large dorm rooms, one reserved for women. They also have four

double rooms with shared bath. Janine Wenger runs this relaxed hostel and lines the porch with flowers. Read the signs, respect the house rules, and leave things tidier than you found them (closed Nov-mid-Dec and for about a month after Easter, from the lift station it's 20 yards up the path to the left, +41 33 855 1704, www.mountainhostel.com, info@mountainhostel.com).

Hotel Mittaghorn, one of my fond favorites, is another option after its renovation is complete (scheduled to reopen in 2024 with new owners; +41 33 855 1470, www.mittaghorn.ch, contact@mittaghorn.ch, Urs and Christine).

Eating in Gimmelwald

$$ Pension Gimmelwald Restaurant serves dinner to 30 people each night at 19:00 (reservations required). You get a three-course meal for 30 CHF (you have no choices, although there's a vegetarian option). Simple lunches (burgers, soup, nachos) are served 12:00-15:00. Eat in their rustic indoor dining room or on a terrace with a great view. David proudly pours their award-winning, very smooth Schwarz Mönch dark beer. The atmosphere here is jazz-and-blues mellow (daily late May-mid-Oct and late Dec-March 12:00-22:00, closed off-season, +41 33 855 1730).

$$ Mountain Hostel Restaurant specializes in pizza (served 12:00-21:00; the bar stays open later). They also serve breakfast from 7:30 to 9:30 (open daily in summer, weekends only in winter, closed Nov-mid-Dec and for about a month after Easter, +41 33 855 1704).

Picnics: If you can, pack in some supplies from the larger towns. Mürren has a grocery store and good restaurants (see "Eating in Mürren," later). If you need a few groceries and want to skip the hike to Mürren, you can buy the essentials—noodles, spaghetti sauce, and candy bars—at the little Honesty Shop at Pension Gimmelwald (closed off-season). Farmers post signs to sell their produce. The Rubin family sells cheese and eggs in their house on the town's main street (see "Gimmelwald Walk," earlier).

Nightlife: For after-dark entertainment in Gimmelwald, **Mountain Hostel** is the place. The bar is open until at least 23:00 nightly in season, and occasional live bands come to play (the website says what's on). **Pension Gimmelwald** offers a mellow scene with an old-time bar, cozy lounge, and view terrace. And from almost anywhere in Gimmelwald, you can watch the sun tuck the mountaintops into bed as the moon rises over the Jungfrau. If that's not enough nightlife, stay in Interlaken.

Mürren

Pleasant as an alpine resort can be, Mürren is traffic-free and filled with cafés, souvenirs, old-timers with walking sticks, and snap-happy tourists. Its chalets are prefab-rustic. With help from a cliffside train, a funicular, and a cable car, hiking options here are endless. Sitting on a ledge more than 2,000 feet above the Lauterbrunnen Valley (total altitude: just over a mile high), surrounded by a fortissimo chorus of mountains, the town has all the comforts of home without the pretense of more famous resorts.

Mürren has been settled for centuries, but its historic character has been overwhelmed by development (unlike Gimmelwald). Still, it's a peaceful town, with 400 permanent residents—and dropping. There's no full-time doctor, no police officer (they call Lauterbrunnen if there's a problem), and no resident priest or pastor. (The Protestant church—up by the TI—posts a sign showing where the region's roving pastor preaches each Sunday.) There's not enough business to keep a bank, butcher, or proper bakery open (the only place for provisions is the Co-op grocery store). Depending on the time of year, Mürren is either lively (winter and summer, when the population swells to 4,000) or completely dead (spring and fall).

Getting There: See "Lauterbrunnen Valley Connections" on page 191.

Orientation to Mürren

Mürren perches high on a ledge overlooking the Lauterbrunnen Valley. You can walk from one end of town to the other in 10 minutes.

Tourist Information: Mürren's TI, inconveniently located in the sports center uphill from the train station, is a wealth of information (June-Oct and mid-Dec-April daily 8:30-19:30; off-season Mon-Fri 8:30-12:00 & 13:00-17:00, closed Sat-Sun; free WCs, follow signs to *Sportzentrum* on the upper road—behind the giant old Hotel Alpin Palace, +41 33 856 8686, www.muerren.swiss). Pick up the flier that lists a slew of weekly activities, including a town walking tour (1/week June-Oct and Dec-April, free with your hotel's Visitor Card, otherwise 20 CHF).

HELPFUL HINTS

Money: There's no ATM in town, so plan ahead for any cash needs.

Laundry: Find a little self-service launderette in a shed by the side of **Hotel Bellevue** (open 24/7, but you must buy tokens at the hotel bar).

Bike Rental: You can rent mountain bikes at **Intersport** (30 CHF/half-day, 40 CHF/day, includes helmet, daily 9:00-12:00 & 13:00-18:00, closed off-season, in middle of town, +41 33 855 2355, www.intersport-muerren.ch). There's a bigger bike-rental place in Lauterbrunnen (Imboden Bike, described on page 185).

Sports Center: The slick **Sportzentrum** that houses the TI offers a world of indoor activities, including table tennis, a fitness room, sauna, hot tub, and steam bath (each with its own opening hours and price; most activities open same hours as TI—see above). The **indoor pool** (but not the other activities) is free with the Visitor Card given out by hotels and hostels (otherwise 12 CHF, daily 13:00-20:00, until 21:00 in winter, +41 33 856 8686, www.sportzentrum-muerren.ch). A **$ café** offers a reasonably priced, basic menu, with spacious indoor and outdoor seating (daily 9:00-17:30).

Yoga: Denise (proprietor of the recommended Chalet Fontana) offers yoga classes at the sports center on Wednesdays in summer (€15, RS%, +41 78 642 3485).

Skiing and Snowboarding: The Mürren-Schilthorn ski area is the Berner Oberland's best place for experts, especially those eager to tackle the famous, nearly 10-mile-long Inferno run. The runs on top, especially the Kanonenrohr, are quite steep and have predictably good snow; lower areas cater to all levels but can be icier. For rental gear, try the friendly, convenient **Ed Abegglen** shop (best prices, next to recommended Chalet Fontana, +41 33 855 1245), **Alfred's Sporthaus** (good selection and decent prices, between ski school and Sportzentrum, +41 33 855 3030), or **Intersport** (in the town center, +41 33 855 2355). For more info on snow sports, see the Switzerland in Winter chapter.

Mürren Walk

Mürren has long been a top ski resort, but a walk across town offers a glimpse into a time before ski lifts. This stroll takes you through town on the main drag, from the train station (where you'll arrive if coming from Lauterbrunnen) to the cable-car station.

• *Start at the...*

Train Station: The first trains pulled into Mürren in 1891. This is the "port" of Mürren. Goods are brought up from Laut-

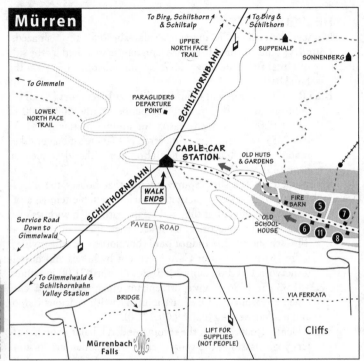

erbrunnen on the cable car to Grütschalp, then transferred to the train. Look inside the station for exhibits on the history of the rail line.

• *Wander into town along the main road (take the lower, left fork) for a stroll under the...*

Alpin Palace Hotel: This towering place was the "Grand Palace Hotel" until it burned in 1928. Today they're working on an ambitious renovation. The green meadow below the station on the left is a popular hangout for wild mountain goat and chamois (the animals, not the rags) that seem to understand that they can't be hunted so close to residences.

• *Carry on past the hotel for a...*

Cliffside Stroll: Just ahead, the small wooden platform cantilevered over the cliff is where snow-removal trucks dump their loads in the winter. Just beyond, on the right (across from Hotel Alpina), you can fill your water bottle with sweet spring water from the Alps high above. Farther down, Hotel Edelweiss' restaurant terrace comes with breathtaking views (overhanging a sheer cliff).

Hotels and restaurants crowd the cliff all along this side of town to enjoy views of the big three: Eiger, Mönch, and Jungfrau. Farther along, you'll pass the inviting outdoor seating of the recommended Café Liv—the closest thing to a Starbucks in town.

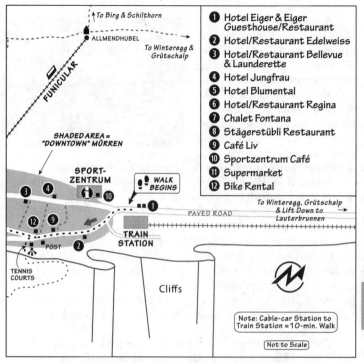

1. Hotel Eiger & Eiger Guesthouse/Restaurant
2. Hotel/Restaurant Edelweiss
3. Hotel/Restaurant Bellevue & Launderette
4. Hotel Jungfrau
5. Hotel Blumental
6. Hotel/Restaurant Regina
7. Chalet Fontana
8. Stägerstübli Restaurant
9. Café Liv
10. Sportzentrum Café
11. Supermarket
12. Bike Rental

To Birg & Schilthorn
ALLMENDHUBEL
To Winteregg & Grütschalp
FUNICULAR
SHADED AREA = "DOWNTOWN" MÜRREN
SPORT-ZENTRUM
WALK BEGINS
To Winteregg, Grütschalp & Lift Down to Lauterbrunnen
PAVED ROAD
TRAIN STATION
POST
TENNIS COURTS
Cliffs

Note: Cable-car Station to Train Station = 10-min. Walk

Not to Scale

BERNER OBERLAND

• *Just after the café, detour from the main street out to the cliff-hanging tennis court. Pause at the far corner of the first court, step up to the small arch, and look down.*

Via Ferrata: Directly below, at the base of the modern wall, is the start of the 1.5-mile *via ferrata*, a "trail" with a steel-cable guide that mountaineers use to venture safely along the cliff all the way to Gimmelwald (see "Activities in Mürren," later). The steel cable disappears over the cliff and ends at the Gimmelwald lift station (which you can see in the distance). On the hillside above and behind you may see parasailers taking off from above the Schilthorn lift station. Track their flight as they expertly catch the valley updraft (feel it on your face). Farther to the right, the Allmendhubel funicular trundles visitors up to some of the best views in the region—and the start of some glorious hikes (described later). Listen for the river, waterfalls, and avalanches on the far side.

• *Backtrack the way you came, then turn left at the Intersport shop onto the main street to reach...*

"Downtown" Mürren: At the main intersection, a small service road leads down to Gimmelwald. Stay right (following *Schilthornbahn* and *Mürren* signs) and enter the main drag. Here you'll find my favorite restaurant in town (Stägerstübli), the only grocery store (Co-op), and the best souvenir shop (Abegglen).

A bit farther on, past the faded old Hotel Regina, the tiny fire barn on the right (labeled *Feuerwehr*) has a list showing the leaders of the volunteer force and their responsibilities. The old barn behind it on the right evokes the time, not so long ago, when the town's barns housed cows. Imagine Mürren with

more cows than people, rather than more visitors than residents.

Across from the fire barn is the town bulletin board—with notices targeting both visitors and locals.

About 60 feet beyond the fire barn (across the street from and just before the old schoolhouse—*Altes Schulhaus*), detour right uphill a few steps into the oldest part of town. Explore the windy little lanes, admiring the ancient woodwork on the houses, 400-year-old timbers that could tell a story, Swiss precision in firewood stacking, and cute little pea patches. Arc your way up and around to the left, eventually returning to the main drag at the Hotel Alpenruh.

• *Back on the main drag, continue to the far end of Mürren, where you come to the...*

Cable-Car Station: The Schilthornbahn is the critical link connecting Mürren with the valley floor (via the village of Gimmelwald) and the reason most visitors are here—to summit the mighty Schilthorn peak. With ever-larger crowds of skiers in winter and tourists in summer blitzing from the valley floor to the Schilthorn and back, a new, bigger cable car is being built to better serve the town.

• *From here you can hike or catch the lift (five minutes) down to Gimmelwald. Or hike back into town along the high road, where you'll pass Mürren's two churches, the Allmendhubel funicular station, and the Sportzentrum (with swimming pool and TI).*

Activities in Mürren

During ski season and in the height of summer, the Mürren area offers plenty of activities ranging from mild to wild for those willing to seek them out. In spring and fall, Mürren is pretty quiet.

Allmendhubel Funicular (Allmendhubelbahn)

A surprisingly rewarding funicular (built in 1912, renovated in 1999) carries nature lovers in less than four minutes from Mürren up to Allmendhubel, a 6,257-foot perch offering a Jungfrau view that, though much lower, rivals the Schilthorn (without all of the James Bond kitsch). Consider mixing a mountain lift, grand views, and a hike with your meal by eating at the restaurant on Allmend-hubel (good chef, open daily until 17:00).

Allmendhubel, with a huge playground, is particularly good for families. This is also the departure point for the North Face hike and walks to Grütschalp (see page 222 for trails from Mürren). While at Allmendhubel, consider its flower trail, a 20-min-ute loop with nice mountain views and (from July through Sept) a chance to see more than 150 differ-ent types of alpine flowers

in bloom. At a minimum, simply climb the steep hill behind the playground to reach a stunning viewpoint, with benches looking out over the little restaurant facing all that big scenery.

Cost and Hours: 8.80 CHF one-way, 14 CHF round-trip, half-price with Swiss Travel Pass, 25 percent off with Eurail Global Pass, early June-mid-Oct daily 9:00-17:00, runs every 20 minutes, +41 33 855 2042 or +41 33 856 2141, www.schilthorn.ch.

Tandem Paragliding

If you've ever wondered what it's like to soar like an eagle, a tandem paragliding flight will give you a pretty good idea. Two companies offer guided flights that take off just above the Mürren cable-car station and end near the Stechelberg cable-car station. After your pilot rigs you into the tandem harness and gives you a few brief instructions, he'll take you on a short run downhill and then you're both up, up, and away—flying gracefully over the Lauterbrunnen Valley, along cliff faces, past waterfalls, and over treetops. Flights last around 15 to 20 minutes...God willing.

Cost: 180 CHF for Mürren-Stechelberg flight, transport to Mürren not included; other flight options available, no experience necessary. **Airtime Paragliding** is based at the recommended Air-time Café in Lauterbrunnen (+41 79 247 8463, https://airtime-paragliding.ch). **Paragliding Jungfrau** offers similar tandem flights at similar prices (+41 79 779 9000, www.paragliding-jungfrau.ch).

Mürren *Via Ferrata* (Klettersteig Mürren)

Mountaineers and thrill-seekers can test their nerves on this 1.5-mile trail along the cliff running from Mürren to Gimmelwald. A *via ferrata* ("way of iron" in Italian) or *Klettersteig* ("climbing path" in German) is a cliffside trail made of metal steps drilled into the mountainside with a cable running at shoulder height above it. Equipped with a helmet, harness, and two carabiners, you are clipped to the cable the entire way.

The journey takes about three hours (one-way only, dry weather only). While half of the route is easily walked, for several hundred yards (across what's called "The Hammer Corner") you are literally hanging over a 2,400-foot drop. I did it, and through the most horrifying sections, I was too scared to look down or take pictures. Along with ladders and steps, the trip comes with three thrilling canyon crossings—one by zip line (possible with guide only), another on a single high wire (with steadying wires for each hand), and a final stint on the terrifying suspension "Nepal Bridge" (which you can see from the Schilthorn cable-car—look for it just above or below Gimmelwald). For a peek at what you're considering getting yourself into, search for "*Via Ferrata* Mürren Gimmelwald" on YouTube.

On Your Own: Experienced mountaineers can rent gear locally and do it independently; others should hire a licensed mountain guide.

With a Guided Tour: The most practical way to experience the *via ferrata* is to join a guided group tour (149 CHF, includes gear and donation to the Mürren Via Ferrata Association, tours go daily from Intersport in Mürren, June-mid-Oct at 9:10 and 14:10, weather permitting, hiking shoes required—ask about rental, small groups of 4-8, reserve through Outdoor at +41 33 224 0701, www.klettersteig-muerren.ch and www.outdoor.ch).

Nightlife in Mürren

Mürren has several lively, atmospheric places for a drink after dinner (for details on these recommended spots, see "Sleeping in Mürren" and "Eating in Mürren," next). **Tächi Bar** at **Hotel Eiger** is a classy cocktail bar with dancing. For a simpler bar-and-view scene, **Hotel Bellevue** has elegant alpine-lounge ambience and a great terrace. In summer, you can enjoy occasional folkloric evenings (check with the TI for dates).

Sleeping in Mürren

Mürren is just over a mile high, so if you sleep here you may feel the altitude. These price rankings are based on summer room rates; they often rise during the ski season. Except where noted, all hotels and restaurants listed here close in spring (anywhere from Easter to early June) and again in fall (sometime between mid-Oct and mid-Dec). Half-board, if available, can be a good idea in Mürren.

$$$$ Hotel Eiger, a four-star hotel dramatically and conveniently situated just across from the tiny train station, is a good but expensive bet. Family-run for four generations, Adrian and Susanna Stähli offer all the services you'd expect in a big-city hotel (plush lounge, elegant dining rooms, original art on the walls, indoor swimming pool, exercise room, and saunas) while maintaining an Old World, woody elegance in its 50 business-class yet charming rooms. Their "unique" suites, while pricey, include two double rooms and can be a good value for groups of four or five (grand breakfast, discounts for stays of three nights or more, elevator, +41 33 856 5454, www.hoteleiger.com, info@hoteleiger.com).

$$$ Hotel Edelweiss is all about the location—convenient and literally hanging on the cliff with devastating views. It's a big, modern building with 42 straightforward rooms (most with balconies) and a busy, recommended restaurant that's well-run by hardworking Sandra and Daniel Kuster-von Allmen (family rooms, elevator, piano in lounge, self-serve pay laundry, closed Nov-mid-Dec, +41 33 856 5600, www.edelweiss-muerren.ch, info@edelweiss-muerren.ch).

$$ Hotel Bellevue feels country-upscale and authentically Swiss, with a homey lounge, solid woodsy furniture, a great view terrace, the recommended hunter-themed Jägerstübli restaurant, and 19 comfortable rooms—most with balconies and views. It may be under new management in the near future, so some details could change (discount if staying two nights or more in June or Oct, self-serve pay laundry, +41 33 855 1401, www.bellevuemuerren.ch, bellevue@muerren.ch).

$$ Hotel Jungfrau has a classic exterior and a modern interior, with 29 rooms plus two apartments for up to six people (elevator, pay laundry service, close to TI/Sportzentrum on the upper road, +41 33 856 6464, www.hoteljungfrau.ch, mail@hoteljungfrau.ch, Martin and Connie).

$$ Hotel Blumental, once family-run but now owned by the Schilthornbahn lift company, has 14 cozy but dated rooms with woody accents and down comforters, plus six rooms of equal quality in the chalet out back (half-board available; reception sometimes at Hotel Alpenruh, a three-minute walk away; +41 33 855 8856, www.blumental-muerren.ch, blumental@schilthorn.ch).

$ Eiger Guesthouse offers 21 good, small, budget rooms—including some great bunk-bed family rooms—across from the train station, above an easygoing ground-floor pub. Four of the rooms share three sets of bathroom facilities, while the rest are en suite. Ema—born in Portugal but a longtime Switzerland resident—is your host (RS%, closed Nov, +41 33 856 5460, www.eigerguesthouse.com, info@eigerguesthouse.com).

$ Hotel Regina, once a luxury hotel catering to posh English holiday-goers, may be a faded beauty but still has plenty of charm. It has 50 basic rooms (most with shared toilets and showers) and is conveniently located at the cable-car end of town. The owners continue to revive the place bit by bit. For solo travelers, the single

BERNER OBERLAND

rooms are a decent value (family deals, +41 33 855 4242, www.reginamuerren.ch, info@reginamuerren.ch).

$ Chalet Fontana, run by charming Englishwoman Denise Fussell, is a fine budget option, with five simple, crispy-clean, and comfortable rooms with shared bath (closed mid-Oct-April, fridge in common kitchen, across street from Stägerstübli restaurant in town center, +41 78 642 3485, www.chaletfontana.ch, chaletfontana@gmail.com). Denise also rents a family apartment with kitchen, bathroom, and breakfast (in a separate building with a mountain view).

Eating in Mürren

Outside of summer and ski season, only a few places remain open—so plan ahead if you visit during spring or fall.

$$ Stägerstübli, right in the town center, has a big menu, including all the Swiss standards plus some more adventurous meats (including goat, venison, wild boar, and rabbit), cheese *Spätzle,* and a couple of Asian options. It's in a 1902 building that was once a tearoom for rich tourists. Locals were limited to the room in the back—which is now the nicer indoor space (you might see grizzled regulars in the front room). Sitting on the broad terrace, you know just who's out and about in town (Thu-Mon 11:00-23:00, hot food served until 20:00, closed Tue-Wed, +41 33 855 1316, Lydia).

$$ Hotel Edelweiss offers lunch and dinner in the most cliff-hanging setting in town, with Swiss specialties, burgers, pizzas, and salads. It's family-friendly, the views are incredible, the dining spaces are attractive (despite the boxy exterior), and the prices are good (daily 11:00-20:30, +41 33 856 5600).

$$ Eiger Guesthouse Restaurant, a busy local hangout with a relaxed pub atmosphere, has long hours and a mostly Italian menu (pizzas, meal-sized salads). They also serve fondue, raclette, *Rösti,* inexpensive house wine, and local beers. A few outdoor tables have partial views (daily 11:30-14:00 & 17:30-22:00, closed Nov, +41 33 856 5460).

$$ Hotel Bellevue's restaurant is atmospheric, with three dining zones: a spectacular view terrace, a sophisticated indoor area, and the *Jägerstübli*—a cozy, well-antlered hunters' room guaranteed to disgust vegetarians. This is a good bet for game, as they buy chamois, wild boar, and deer directly from local hunters (meatless dishes available too; daily 11:30-14:00 & 18:00-21:00, +41 33 855 1401).

$$ Hotel Regina sets out a dinner buffet every day between 18:00 and 20:00. There are several options: soup and salad for 18 CHF; fill a plate with main dishes and salad for 30 CHF; or a full four-course meal for 42 CHF. Check the menu in the afternoon to see what they're serving (reservations appreciated, +41 33 855 4242).

$ Café Liv is a hip coffee shop with hot sandwiches, smoothies, homemade cakes, and quality coffee, including takeaway (daily 10:00-17:00, less off-season, in town center on the main street, across from tennis courts, +41 76 213 7305).

$ The breezy **café** at Mürren's Sportzentrum is good for a sandwich or an afternoon snack, and it is pleasantly away from the crowds (daily 9:00-17:30).

Supermarket: The **Co-op** has good picnic fixings and sandwiches (Mon-Fri 8:00-18:30, Sat-Sun until 18:00, sometimes closes Tue-Thu afternoons in off-season). This place is a godsend for those on a tight budget.

Activities in the Berner Oberland

Scenic Rides on Lifts and Trains

The Berner Oberland is famous for its high-altitude thrill rides. I've described the best of them here. A nice hot chocolate at 10,000 or even 11,000 feet on a sunny day surrounded by the heart of the Swiss Alps is pretty hard to beat. And those on a tight budget can enjoy the same majesty by taking advantage of much less expensive lifts and hiking (see "Hiking and Biking," later).

THE SCHILTHORN AND PIZ GLORIA

The Schilthornbahn cable car carries skiers, hikers, and sightseers effortlessly to the nearly 10,000-foot summit of the Schilthorn, where the Piz Gloria cable-car station awaits, with its solar-powered revolving restaurant, shop, and panorama terrace. At the top, you have a spectacular view of more than 100 peaks—starring the Eiger, Mönch, and Jungfrau mountains, all lined up just across the valley. The entire experience is worth ▲▲▲.

Cost: You can ride to the Schilthorn and back from three points—the cable-car station near Stechelberg on the valley floor (108 CHF), cliff-hanging Gimmelwald (97.60 CHF), or the higher Mürren (85.60 CHF).

Hours: Starting from Stechelberg, the ride requires three changes on the way up: at Gimmelwald (5 minutes), Mürren (5 minutes), and Birg; the entire ride, from valley floor to mountain-top, takes about 35 minutes (or about 25 minutes from Mürren). The first Schilthorn-bound lifts leave Stechelberg at 7:25, Gimmelwald at 7:30, and Mürren at 7:35; last lift from Stechelberg at 16:25, last return from Schilthorn at 17:55 (earlier in winter). Note that the Stechelberg-Gimmelwald-Mürren segment runs far longer hours (until about 24:00) than the Mürren-Birg-Schilthorn segment. Lifts run all year, except during maintenance closures (a week in April and three weeks in Nov-Dec). There will be no closures after the eventual opening of a new cable car; read on for details of this project.

Discounts: With a Swiss Travel Pass, you ride free to Mürren then pay half-price to the top; if you have a Eurail Global Pass, you get 25 percent off any ride. Special promotions can save you even more (including a good-value early-morning brunch deal)—check the website or ask when buying tickets.

Information: See Schilthorn.ch or call +41 33 826 0007 for more details and current weather conditions.

Avoiding Crowds: Crowds (mostly mass tourism groups coming up from Interlaken) are a big problem in peak season, especially on weekends (the worst bottleneck is in Mürren). Groups have priority access. Beat the Interlaken hordes by catching an early lift, preferably before 9:30, or a later one—it's quieter after about 14:30 and the mountains across the valley are bathed in late-day sunlight. You can also reserve a specific lift departure time online at least 24 hours in advance (5 CHF extra); you have the option to use the ticket at another time without a reserved spot.

Project 20XX and Construction Closures: To alleviate congestion at Mürren and get more tourists up and down quicker and easier, a bigger and better cable-car lift is under construction. The project, called "Project 20XX," may cause some closures (likely in 2024) before it is finished (likely in 2025). For the latest, visit Schilthornbahn20xx.ch.

Visiting the Schilthorn
Ascending the Schilthorn: As the cable car floats up the first

stage of the ascent, from Stechelberg to Gimmelwald, you'll see sweet little farms dotting the valley, the paved trail along the river, a line of tour buses foretelling how many groups are above you,

and the treacherous metal "Nepal Bridge" marking the end of the *via ferrata* cableway hike. On stage two—Gimmelwald to Mürren—you'll sail above the rooftops of Gimmelwald. You'll also see fields of wooden tripods, which serve two purposes: They stop avalanches and shelter newly planted trees. Made of wood, they're designed to eventually rot when the tree they protect is strong enough to survive the winter snowpack. On the third stage, just above Mürren on the way to Birg, look right to see a reservoir building that powers gray shower posts that make snow—a ski-industry necessity in these days of climate change. Keep an eye on the altitude meter. You'll change cable cars at Birg, midway between Mürren and the Schilthorn.

Birg Station (8,783 Feet)

If you're heading to the Schilthorn summit and the weather's good, skip Birg for now and go directly to your connecting cable car. On

the way back down, plan on 30 minutes here, which is plenty of time for Birg's two high-altitude attractions. Or linger longer and enjoy the Birg cafeteria (which I prefer to the Schilthorn's).

Birg's two activities are a viewing platform (called the **Skyline Walk**) and the **Thrill Walk**. Free to enter, the Thrill Walk is a 600-foot-long catwalk bolted to the cliffside. If walking the see-through metal catwalk seems tame to you, along the way you can choose to tightrope across a cable bridge (there's a net below), cross a section of glass flooring, and crawl through a chain-link tube—all with airy views to the valley far below.

Schilthorn Summit Sights (9,748 Feet)

Remember, you're here for the view—and it can disappear for the rest of the day in minutes. (The Schilthorn peak doubles as an ideal cloud-catcher.) So, if it's sunny when you arrive, ignore the indoor attractions—head outside on the deck and enjoy the vistas until you're satiated.

Upon arrival, head up two escalators to the **Skyline View Platform** (or go to the right out of the lift to zip up on the elevator). On this stark, often very cold, and scenic patio, information boards identify the peaks, and directional signs point hikers toward some seriously steep downhill climbs. There are plenty of James Bond-themed photo ops (this mountain was one of the major locations in the 1969 film *On Her Majesty's Secret*

Service). The big, round viewing scopes identify each peak as you survey the panorama; the pink scopes magnify. Note that the classic "Eiger, Mönch, Jungfrau" panorama is on the opposite side from the big platform. Watch paragliders set up, psych up, take off, and fly with the birds. In summer, live folk musicians often perform here (typically June-Aug 11:00-15:00). A highlight for travelers from arid lands is the "touch the snow" corner created by a hardworking little snowmaking machine.

Find the stairs near the view terrace to walk along the ridge out back—the **007 Walk of Fame,** where cast and crew members from the film have left their handprints and personal messages. At the end of this is the Piz Gloria view platform, offering great views back at the revolving restaurant with the mountains beyond. If you dare, let yourself through the gate by the platform and walk carefully along a gravelly, borderline scary trail (with no railings) to leave the crowds behind and really feel rugged. This is a great place for a photo of the mountain-climber you.

Piz Gloria Station: Once you've been outside, or if the weather is foul, consider a drink or a bite at the 360° **$$ Restaurant Piz Gloria** (top floor, up the stairs). In this revolving restaurant, you're invited to sit and slowly spin—viewing all the scenery from the comfort of your chair through cloudy windows. The restaurant serves drinks (including hot cocoa), salads, soups, and main dishes all day. Or consider the 35-CHF James Bond

Brunch, with breakfast items (8:00-11:00), then soups, salad bar, and warm dishes until 14:00 (after that, it's à la carte only). If you're heading up hungry in the morning, pay for brunch down below, where you'll get a discount. Reservations can be smart for Piz Gloria (+41 33 826 0007, or at www.schilthorn.com). A much less expensive **$ snack bar/cafe** is on the main level with tables inside and out on the view patio. (And remember, there is a better, equally scenic dining option at the Birg Station.)

Downstairs, follow the maze that leads to the **Bond World 007** exhibit and cinema. (Remember: Enticing and worthwhile as this is, don't spend time here until you've been outside to enjoy the actual views, as things can cloud up.) This interactive exhibit, well-explained in English, is worth a few minutes for even non-Bond fans. It takes you behind the scenes of the 1969 James Bond movie, *On Her Majesty's Secret Service,* which used the Schilthorn as one of its major locations (and helped finance the complex's completion). Step into the role of James Bond and try your hand at flying a helicopter to Piz Gloria or bobsledding down the Alps in the simulators. Even the prizewinning WCs are Bond-themed—a sign in the men's room urged me to "Aim Like James."

At the end of the exhibit, the Bond World 007 **cinema** shows a 20-minute, three-part video on a continuous loop that highlights the area's natural wonders and activities (including racing down the famous Inferno ski run), briefly shares the story of the Schilthorn-bahn lift itself and the Project 20XX work, and shows a substantial clip from *On Her Majesty's Secret Service.*

Hiking: You can hike down from the Schilthorn, but it's tough. (Hiking *up* is easier on your knees...if you don't mind a 5,000-foot altitude gain from Mürren.) Hiking down from Birg Station makes more sense for most. For information on **hikes** from lift stations along the Schilthorn cable-car line, see "Hiking and Biking," later. My favorite "hike" from the Schilthorn is simply along the ridge out back, to get away from the station and be all alone on top of an Alp. (But if you need company, both Birg and the Piz Gloria have Wi-Fi.)

JUNGFRAUJOCH

A literal high point of any trip to the Swiss Alps is the Jungfraubahn train ride through the Eiger mountain to the Jungfraujoch (the saddle between the Mönch and Jungfrau mountains)—an experience worth ▲▲▲. At 11,333 feet, it's Europe's highest train station. (If you have a heart or lung condition, you may want to check with your doctor before making this ascent.) Keep in mind that you can enjoy the Berner Oberland without taking this trip—it's long, slow, expensive, crowded, and cold. But if the weather's perfect and you have a spare day and spare cash, the views are exhilarating and it's fun to be on a snowy glacier in midsummer.

I've focused here on the train route up from Lauterbrunnen via Kleine Scheidegg to the Jungfraujoch. There's also an alternate approach, starting with the Eiger Express—a big new cable car from Grindelwald to Eiger-gletscher (above Kleine Schei-degg)—where you connect to the train for the last segment up (described later).

Cost and Hours: Round-trip fares are 236 CHF from Interlaken Ost, 222 CHF from Lauterbrunnen, 208 CHF from Wengen, and 156 CHF from Kleine Scheidegg. The train runs about twice hourly year-round. The last train back down departs the Jungfraujoch at 16:17 and Kleine Scheidegg at 17:14 (one hour later July-Aug).

Discounts: From May to late October, a "Good Morning Ticket" saves you 25 percent on the earliest departures of the day. To get the discount you must leave the top no later than 13:17. Eurail Global pass holders get 25 percent off and can't combine discounts, so they should go whenever they want. The same goes for Swiss Travel Pass holders, who travel free as far as Wengen (with a 25 percent discount beyond): Buy your supplementary ticket before boarding, or to avoid a steep fine—find the conductor before they find you and pay a 10-CHF surcharge to buy it on board. There's also the Jungfrau Travel Pass, but it's usually hard to make it pay off (see page 164 for details).

Information and Booking: Visit www.jungfrau.ch, stop by the ticket counters in Interlaken or Lauterbrunnen, or call +41 33 828 7233.

Crowd-Beating Tips: At peak periods (especially July-Aug), trains are standing-room only. During peak times, reserve a seat at a fixed time the day before (5 CHF extra for each leg—up and down; allow about two hours up top). The Jungfraujoch platforms can be jammed and chaotic. Without a reservation, you may have to wait in line (potentially an hour or more) both to get up and to get back down.

Weather: Don't bother coming all the way up here if it's cloudy. But be aware that even when it's socked in down in the valleys, it can be gloriously sunny up top—check the webcams and weather forecast at www.jungfrau.ch before committing.

Planning Your Trip: Visiting the Jungfraujoch takes most of a day. The trip up from Lauterbrunnen takes a little under two hours each way, with a change of trains at Kleine Scheidegg. If you're coming from Interlaken, Gimmelwald, or Mürren, add another half-hour. You'll want at least 1.5 hours at the top—more if you eat, hike, or frolic in the snow. Expect outdoor temperatures to be around freezing in summer—so if you plan to go outside, bring a hat and gloves, shoes with good traction, sunglasses, and sunscreen. Even if you stay inside, the train is chilly and you'll need a jacket. To minimize altitude sickness, local guides recommend drinking a half-liter of water as you ascend on the train.

Eiger Express: This new cable car, opened in 2020, runs from Grindelwald to Eigergletscher, where tourists switch to the train for the last segment up to Jungfraujoch. The 15-minute ride glides scenically along the bottom of the famed North Face of the Eiger in sleek 26-seat cable cars. This investment of about $500 million was designed to funnel masses of tourists up from Grindelwald and Interlaken. If you're staying in either town, the Eiger Express cuts about an hour off the time needed for the Jungfraujoch experience—but travelers from the Lauterbrunnen Valley still do better by taking the slow, scenic train to Kleine Scheidegg.

Ultimate Alpine Combo: For a thrilling day of alpine scenery, try this plan: From Lauterbrunnen, ride the train to Wengen, ride the cable car up to Männlichen, hike from there to Kleine Scheidegg (about 1.5 hours, easy), then catch the train up to the Jungfraujoch.

Eating: You'll find a variety of eateries in the main Jungfraujoch building (see "Shops and Services," later), but it's all overpriced and poor quality; I'd eat before or after my visit—or bring a picnic.

Visiting the Jungfraujoch
Ascending the Jungfraujoch: From Lauterbrunnen or Wengen, you'll board a characteristic little yellow-and-green Wengernalp-
bahn train to get as far as Kleine Scheidegg. There, you'll transfer to the Jungfraujoch train. The platform can be a bit hectic—take a calming breath and find your way to the end of the correct line: green if you've reserved, yellow if you haven't.

The 45-minute ride from Kleine Scheidegg to the top is mostly in a tunnel, but with a couple of stops. The first one, after five minutes, is at **Eigergletscher,** the high-altitude junction with the Eiger Express cable car. You'll then enter the tunnel in which you'll travel through the Eiger to the Jungfraujoch. After about 10 more minutes, you'll stop for five minutes at the **Eismeer** viewpoint, where you can get out of the train and enjoy glacier and mountain views from an amazing perch (10,368 feet). Look out the windows and marvel at how people could climb the Eiger—and how the Swiss built this train track more than a hundred years ago. (You can generally listen in as guides explain the views to their groups.) Notice how the once-solid ice mass is now broken by treacherous crevices as it melts. Back on your train, you'll ride up through darkness—watching video screens explaining your sightseeing options up top.

Jungfraujoch Sights (11,333 Feet)

Once you reach the top, breathe deep, take it easy, and move slow-ly—you're way high up and your body isn't used to such altitudes. Study the map to see your options. The big blue *TOUR* signs lead you on a loosely one-way route through the complex, with several numbered stops I've outlined below.

Jungfrau Panorama: To get ahead of the crowds, muscle your way through the congested shopping zone, bearing left for the *TOUR* signs (direction: Sphinx). You'll follow a tunnel to the Jungfrau Panorama, a 360-degree video that's pleasantly distract-ing while you wait in line for the elevator that rockets you up to the observation deck—and the highest Jungfraujoch viewpoint.

Sphinx Observation Deck: Head up the stairs and out onto the platform; at above 11,000 feet, the views are truly astound-ing. Use the **orientation pan-els** to get your bearings: You're between the Mönch and the Jungfrau (the Eiger is hidden, behind the Mönch). Looking toward the Mönch, notice the fun snow area below you, and the trail snaking across the snow to the Mönchsjochhütte (both described later). Looking left,

you're gazing (north) down on the Lauterbrunnen Valley area: Kleine Scheidegg, Gimmelwald, and in the distance, Interlaken. Try to spot the Schilthorn cable-car station. Farther to the left looms the giant Jungfrau. And left of that spreads the Aletsch Gla-cier—Europe's longest, at nearly 11 miles (or a bit less, by the time you read this). The silver-domed building above you is a scientific measurement station (from 1930). Scared of heights? Look down through the floor grates.

Ride the elevator back downstairs, where you'll find a small **exhibit** with interest-ing statistics on recent climate warming and the recovery of the ozone layer. From here, turn right to go outside to walk on the glacier (direction: Aletsch Glacier).

Aletsch Glacier: You'll find both outdoor and indoor attractions on the glacier. **Snow Fun Park** offers skiing and snowboarding (35 CHF), sledding (20 CHF), and a zip line (25 CHF—prices include equipment; 45 CHF for all three activities, mid-May-mid-Oct). The ticket desk also sells hot, cold, and hard drinks to enjoy in a sling-backed chair on the snow. To get away from the Jungfraujoch crowds, you can hike an hour across the ice to **Mönchsjochhütte** (a mountain hut with a small restaurant). While this can be a highlight, you need good shoes—when it's slushy, you'll end up with wet feet.

Back inside you'll head through a passage leading to and through several entertaining exhibits. **Alpine Sensation** is a fun zone draped in light-up edelweiss and Swiss kitsch. A **history exhibit** lines the tunnel, telling the story of the construction of the Jungfraujoch train line and station and memorializing the workers (mostly Italian) who died while working here. **Ice Palace** (Eispalast) is a slippery side trip off the main tunnel, with walls and floors made of ice and a few modest ice carvings.

The Plateau: Next you'll ride an elevator (or hike up a few flights of stairs) to the third and last outdoor experience: the Plateau, where you can walk out on the snow toward the Jungfrau and look back at the classic Jungfraujoch view—with the Sphinx's glittering silver dome capping a sheer cliff.

The Berghaus: Back in the main building (Berghaus) is a cluster of shops and eateries next to the train station. Consider departure times and lines, then you can peruse several levels of shops (including the **Lindt Swiss Chocolate Heaven,** a candy store with a brief exhibit about Swiss chocolate making); the pricey **$$$ Restaurant Crystal;** the self-service **$ Aletsch** cafeteria; and a basic **$ coffee bar,** near the doors to the train station. Indian tourists appreciate the Bollywood restaurant nearby.

Return Trip: Trains depart twice hourly; unless you've reserved a seat, you may have to wait in line to board a train back down to earth. In Kleine Scheidegg, you'll change to the Wengernalpbahn line back down to Lauterbrunnen. Remember, you can connect from the first stop (Eigergletscher) directly to Grindelwald in 15 minutes on the new Eiger Express cable car (described earlier).

Hiking and Biking

The Berner Oberland offers days of possible hikes. Many are a fun combination of trails, mountain trains, and cable-car rides. The information below can help you decide which hike to tackle but isn't intended as a turn-by-turn guide. Good hiking maps and more detailed trail descriptions are essential, and they're available from area TIs and hotels. Before setting out on any hike, check locally to be sure you've made the best match between your skills, gear, and trail conditions (snow can persist on trails even into summer). Every year, tourists die doing stupid things in the Alps. Respect the risks or you could end up as a sad memory marked by a cross at the side of a trail. (For tougher hikes, do what you can to buy, rent, or borrow hiking poles.)

EASIER HIKES
On the Valley Floor
▲▲Cloudy-Day Lauterbrunnen Valley Walk

Try the easy trails and pleasant walks along the floor of the Lauterbrunnen Valley. You don't ever need to (and shouldn't) walk along the main road, which parallels the river. A fine, paved, mostly vehicle-free farm lane (great for walkers, runners, bikers, and people with strollers) goes all the way along the valley on the opposite side of the river from the main road, from the town of Lauterbrunnen to the top of the valley (Stechelberg). Small bridges let you cross from the lane to the main road at various points. PostBus #141 runs the entire length, with stops along the way, twice an hour.

For a smell-the-cows-and-flowers lowland walk—ideal for a cloudy day, weary body, or tight budget—try this three-mile, basically level ramble from Lauterbrunnen to Stechelberg. While you could go either way, I'd go upstream (very gradually uphill) to walk toward the grandest mountain views.

Leaving Lauterbrunnen town, take the side road to the right, past the Horner Pub). Just beyond that, with the cemetery on your left, climb up the path on your right to the free and slippery gallery that runs under the **Staubbach waterfall,** one of 72 waterfalls in the valley. Fact-filled information posts accompany each one. Here, notice the cone-like mound of earth piled against the side of the cliff—formed by centuries of rocks hurled by the water. You'll see mounds like this (and often "ice caves" formed by the constant mist) all along the valley.

Follow the river up the valley. Along the way, you may see **BASE jumpers**—parachutists who leap from cliffs—or helicopters looking for their bodies. Windsocks in fields mark landing spots. Lauterbrunnen Valley is a mecca for BASE jumpers. Keep your eyes open for people looking up in the sky as if spotting Superman. (It's a bird, it's a plane...no, it's a BASE jumper!)

About 45 minutes after leaving town, you can cross the river for an optional side trip to **Trümmelbach Falls** (it's signposted; see page 187). After seeing the falls, you can catch the PostBus in either direction—back to Lauterbrunnen or on to Stechelberg. (Or keep walking: From the falls, walk uphill on the main road about five minutes, then cross through the Breithorn Campsite and over the river to return to the trail.)

After walking about half an hour farther upstream, you come to a fine picnic stop at the base of **Mürrenbach Falls,** where the water enjoys a 1,400-foot free fall. Just beyond is the **Schilthornbahn cable-car station.** From here you can ride the lift up; catch the PostBus back to Lauterbrunnen; or walk another half-hour to the top of the valley. Just before the end of the trail, a five-minute side trip takes you over a bridge and to one final waterfall, **Sefinenfall.** Next to Hotel Stechelberg, where the road ends, you'll find another stop for the PostBus back to Lauterbrunnen.

Alternate Route via Gimmelwald: If you're staying in Gimmelwald, try this plan: Take the Schilthornbahn lift down to the station near Stechelberg (five minutes), then walk 1.5 hours along the river to Lauterbrunnen (with the possible side-trip to Trümmelbach Falls about halfway). To return to Gimmelwald from Lauterbrunnen, take the cable car up to Grütschalp and transfer to the train to Mürren (20 minutes total). From Mürren, it's a downhill walk (30 minutes) to Gimmelwald. You can also walk from Grütschalp to Gimmelwald (1.5 hours). This loop trip can be reversed or started at any point along the way—such as Lauterbrunnen or Mürren.

From Gimmelwald
▲Sefinen Valley to Kilchbalm

The trail from Gimmelwald up the Sefinen Valley (Sefinental) is easy and a good rainy-weather hike. After about an hour and a gain of about a thousand feet, you hit the end of the trail at Kilchbalm, a dramatic bowl of glacier fields. There's no food or drink along the way. While the trail—downhill on a service road for half an hour and then uphill along a trail for half an hour—is just a hike through a forest, the payoff at the end is great.

From the Gimmelwald fire station, walk about 100 yards down the paved road, following *Stechelberg* signs. Turn onto the dirt Sefinental road, which becomes a lane, then a trail. Follow signs to Kilchbalm through a forest, along a river, and finally to a big rocky meadow with the river running through it to where the trail ends. (Notice the intriguing cave on the right where shepherds are said

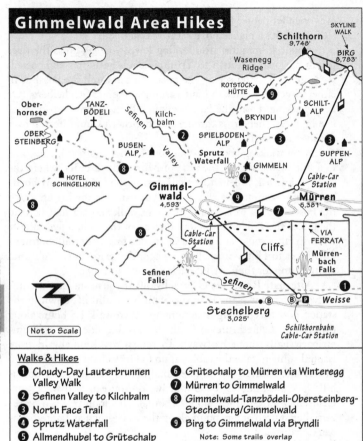

Gimmelwald Area Hikes

Walks & Hikes

① Cloudy-Day Lauterbrunnen Valley Walk
② Sefinen Valley to Kilchbalm
③ North Face Trail
④ Sprutz Waterfall
⑤ Allmendhubel to Grütschalp
⑥ Grütschalp to Mürren via Winteregg
⑦ Mürren to Gimmelwald
⑧ Gimmelwald-Tanzbödeli-Obersteinberg-Stechelberg/Gimmelwald
⑨ Birg to Gimmelwald via Bryndli

Note: Some trails overlap

to have slept.) From here, surrounded by a powerful amphitheater of glaciers, you'll enjoy an unforgettable setting.

From Mürren

▲▲▲North Face Trail (with Sprutz Waterfall Option)

This pleasant, fairly easy, 2.5-hour, four-mile hike offers excellent views, flowery meadows, mountain huts, and a dozen information boards describing the fascinating climbing history of the great peaks around you. You'll also pass a few farms (technically "alps," as they are only open in the summer) that serve meals and drinks. You'll begin at 6,257 feet (Allmendhubel) and finish at 5,381 feet (if you end in Mürren); while it's mostly downhill, there's one uphill stretch that can be challenging if you're not in shape. The trail is well-signed and easy to follow.

The signed route loops counterclockwise from Allmendhubel around to Mürren; near the end, at Spielboden, you can go directly

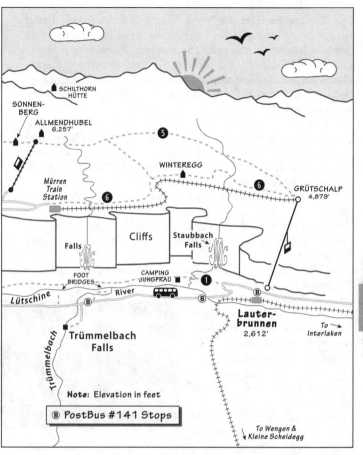

SCHILTHORN
HÜTTE

SONNEN-
BERG
ALLMENDHUBEL
6,257'

5

WINTEREGG

6

GRÜTSCHALP
4,879'

Mürren
Train
Station

6

Cliffs

Falls

Staubbach
Falls

FOOT
BRIDGES

CAMPING
JUNGFRAU

1

Lütschine

River

B

B

B

Trümmelbach
Falls

Lauter-
brunnen
2,612'

To
Interlaken

Trümmelbach

Note: Elevation in feet

B PostBus #141 Stops

To Wengen &
Kleine Scheidegg

into Mürren or opt to extend the hike and descend into Gimmel-wald via the Sprutz waterfall. This final, optional stretch is the most challenging—it goes very steeply downhill, with un-even footing, behind the waterfall, and then steeply down again into Gimmel-wald. To keep things easy, skip Sprutz and circle back to Mürren.

To begin the hike, ride the Allmendhubel funicular up from Mürren (good restaurant at top). Leaving the funicular, follow the path uphill, skirting around the alp-themed play area. From here, follow the trail or service road down into the valley toward Sonnenberg.

You can navigate the North Face trail from Allmendhubel simply by following yellow directional signs connecting these farms or hamlets in this order: Sonnenberg, Suppenalp, Schiltalp (Im Schilt), Gimmeln, and Mürren. For the harder finish that includes the waterfall and skips Mürren, from Gimmeln go through Spielbodenalp, downhill to Sprutz, and steeply through the forest to Gimmelwald.

Here's a more detailed description of the route: From All-mendhubel, head over a little ridge and drop into lovely **Blumental** ("Flower Valley," under the Schilthornbahn cable-car line), which is hopping with marmots (see the "Hiking in the Berner Oberland" sidebar for more on these rodents and other animals you may see).

Follow the gravelly service road down into the valley. At the intersection just before pension/restaurant **Sonnenberg** (where they were allowed to break the all-wood building code with concrete for protection against avalanches), turn right to the quainter Suppenalp.

Follow the paved trail across the meadow, then hook left to **Suppenalp.** Lean against the house with a salad, soup, or sand-wich, and enjoy the view (closed Mon-Tue). Notice how older huts are built into the protected side of rocks and outcroppings, in anticipation of avalanches.

From here, head uphill on the gravel path—directly toward the looming, craggy Schwarz-mönch peak. You'll gain alti-tude as you curve around the ridge (called **Schiltgrat**), directly under the tourists gliding in cable cars up to the Schilthorn. In spots where the path is not clear, look for white-and-red stripes painted on rocks. Watch for great views down over Mürren. Going through a small alpine forest, more peaks come into view. You'll emerge at a broad, grassy meadow high over Gimmelwald, where the views open up. Look high on the right for both the Birg and Piz Gloria stations on the Schilt-hornbahn.

After strolling blissfully through high alpine meadows (enjoying grand views of the Eiger with boards describing historic ascents), you'll finally come to a group of huts called **Schiltalp** (with a romantic farm setting and food and drink for sale). At Schiltalp, if the poles

under the eaves have bells, the cows are up here. If not, the cows are at the lower farms. Half the cows in Gimmelwald (about 100) spend their summers here. In July, August, and September, you can watch cheese being made. Thirty years ago, each family had its own hut. Labor was cheap and available. Today, it's a communal thing, with several families sharing the expense of a single cow herder. Cow herders are master cheesemakers and have veterinary skills, too.

From Schiltalp, the trail winds gracefully downhill to the hamlet of Gimmeln, then back to Mürren.

Or—for a more dangerous and demanding option—from Gimmeln, hike to **Spielbodenalp** and descend steeply through a thick forest and under the dramatic Sprutz waterfall into Gimmelwald.

Sprutz Waterfall

The forest above Gimmelwald hides a powerful waterfall with a trail snaking behind it, offering a fun gorge experience. The waterfall itself is not well-signed, but it's on the Spielboden-Gimmelwald trail. It's steep, through a forest, requires climbing up and down stairs that are carved into the rock without handrails, and can be very slippery when wet—but the actual crossing under the waterfall is just misty.

The hike up to Sprutz from Gimmelwald isn't worth the trip in itself, but the trail is handy when combined with the hike down from Birg and Bryndli (described later) or the North Face trail (described above).

From the waterfall you'll climb back into the thick forest and continue your steep descent until you pop out at the meadows high above Gimmelwald. From here, you'll follow narrow, rutted trails cut into the grass as you descend very steeply to Gimmelwald.

▲Allmendhubel to Grütschalp (a.k.a. Mountain View Trail)

For a not-too-tough two-hour walk with great Jungfrau views, ride the funicular from Mürren to Allmendhubel and walk to Grütschalp (a drop of about 1,500 feet), where you can catch the train back to Mürren. You'll see this route clearly marked as the "Mountain View trail" on maps and brochures.

Hiking in the Berner Oberland

This region is a wonderful place to hike. I've listed my favorite excursions in this chapter. The super-scenic walk from Männlichen to Kleine Scheidegg is the best of all worlds: It's both dramatic and relatively easy (gently downhill, but doesn't open until June). Other relatively easy hikes include the North Face trail from All-mendhubel; various walks from Mürren or Allmendhubel to Grüt-schalp; the Sefinen Valley hike from Gimmelwald; and the stroll along the Lauterbrunnen Valley floor. More challenging routes include the spectacular hike from Schynige Platte to First and the hike from Gimmelwald to Tanzbödeli to Obersteinberg to Stech-elberg.

For easy hikes, it's usually enough to use the 3-D maps in the free brochures (called *Wandern/Hiking*) published by the Schilt-hornbahn (for the west side of the valley) and the Jungfrau-bahn (for the east side); they're available at stations, hotels, and TIs. These overview maps of the mountainsides also make attractive souvenirs. But for more demanding hikes, get a more detailed map and check trail conditions before departing.

Don't forget a water bot-tle and some munchies. In addition to a good map, for serious hikes it's wise to carry sun protection, an extra layer of clothing, basic first-aid supplies, and hiking poles. Know when the last lifts run in the afternoon. Trails are well-marked, with yellow signs list-ing destinations and the estimated time it'll take you to walk there; some trails are also marked with red-and-white stripes painted on rocks and trees.

Electric Fences: The many working farms in this area con-tain their livestock with solar-powered electric fences (which look

▲Grütschalp to Mürren

For a family-friendly, super-easy panorama stroll with grand views, walk either direction between Mürren (5,381 feet) and Grütschalp (4,879 feet)—roughly following the scenic train line between the same points. You'll enjoy the best vistas walking from Grütschalp to Mürren.

Aside from the dramatic views of the Eiger, Mönch, and Jungfrau, a highlight of this trail is the wonderful restaurant/play-ground/cheese farm midway at Winteregg. (The Grütschalp-Mür-ren train also stops at Winteregg.) Here, the Alpkäserei Staubbach lets you peer into the cheese-making action through a window (belike plastic tape strung between thin metal poles). You can't tell if they're turned on without touching a wire—but it's much better not finding out. On certain trails (for example, at several points on the North Face trail), hikers may need to let themselves through gates in the electric fences. In some, a long, plastic, pointy pole sticks out horizontally and pivots like a door—just walk on through (if there's tape on the pole, touch it only on the tape). At other gates, you'll need to grab a plastic handle, unhook it, and rehook it—again, being careful not to touch the wires.

Weather Concerns: Clouds can roll in anytime, but on warm summer days, skies are usually clearest in the morning. Locals always seem to know the weather report (as much of their income depends on it). All over the region, TV sets are tuned to the local weather station, with real-time views from all the famous peaks. You can also check weather reports and view live webcams at Jungfrau.ch and Schilthorn.ch. For more detailed weather reports in English, visit Meteoswiss.admin.ch.

Snow can curtail your hiking plans, even in July. Before setting out on any hike, get advice from the TI or a knowledgeable local. The high trails (Männlichen to Kleine Scheidegg, Schynige Platte to First, and anything from Schilthorn or Birg) are typically passable only from June into October.

Wildlife: As hunting is not allowed in the vicinity of any lifts, animals find safe havens in places you're likely to be. Keep an eye out for chamois (called *Gemsen* here)—the sure-footed "goat antelopes" that live at the top of the tree line and go a little lower when hungry. Spotting an ibex—a wild goat with horns, scrambling along the rocky terrain—is another Berner Oberland thrill. You'll also encounter marmots—big alpine rodents that get fat each summer, then sleep underground for six months through the winter. These burrowing critters are fun to watch, and if you sit still, they don't see you. You'll hear them whistle. The best viewing place is above Allmendhubel, in the meadow above the highest hut in Blumental.

fore 11:00) and buy fresh yogurt and cheese. The Berg-Restaurant Winteregg has a dramatic view terrace and an extensive alp-happy playground (www.restaurant-winteregg.ch).

The trail from the tiny station at Grütschalp to Winteregg (5,177 feet) is the best part: a 30-minute scenic walk mostly through cow country with an accompaniment of tinkling bells on a gravelly lane. The trail between Winteregg and Mürren mostly parallels the train track—also scenic and gravelly, but less interesting.

▲Paved Downhill Bliss from Mürren to Gimmelwald

This super-easy, super-scenic stroll brings you down on a paved road from Mürren to Gimmelwald in about 30 minutes. While there's a 900-foot elevation drop, it's all smooth and easy—doable for any fitness level, or even with a stroller (and more interesting than the five-minute cable-car ride). It's simple—just stay on the same paved path the whole way down—but I've noted a few things to look out for.

In **Mürren,** follow the *Gimmelwald* signs, which lead down through the lower levels of town. You'll end up on the paved road that runs between the two vil-  lages—and though it's closed to casual car traffic, watch out for service vehicles (like mini trucks and tractors) and for bikes blazing downhill. Crossing under the first set of overhead cables (for the service lift from the valley floor up to Mürren), look high on the right for the Birg cable-car station. As the road bends left, you'll pass some "tripods" on your right—these provide structure for new trees being planted as an avalanche barrier.

Enjoy the grand alpine views across the valley. You'll cross the little **Mürrenbach stream** as it churns downhill; on the right, look for the flood gates used to control its flow, and on the left, watch it tumble down into the valley. Continuing farther, down in the valley below you'll see some of the houses of Stechelberg—the end-of-the-valley community. Crossing under the second set of cable-car cables, visually trace them downhill toward Gimmelwald's station—the end point of this walk, and the starting point of my self-guided "Gimmelwald Walk" (see page 194).

A bit farther along, you'll see steep **switchbacks** snaking down below you. Head on down. At the second switchback are more of those avalanche tripods. After the third switchback, the road straightens out, following the cable cars all the way into town. You'll pass through a small forest, cross the little Wyenbach waterfall, then reach the outlying houses of **Gimmelwald.** One of the first buildings you'll pass is Hotel Mittaghorn; just past this, a stepped lane leads directly into the village center and the cable car station. Or, for a commanding "aerial view" over Gimmelwald, carry on farther to the four benches positioned perfectly over town. Lounge here as long as you like, with alpine cliffs in your face, a real Swiss mountain farming community all around you, and a charming village at your feet. (You could also follow my "Gimmelwald Walk" in reverse as you stroll through the town to the lift station.)

From Lauterbrunnen/Wengen
▲▲▲Männlichen-Kleine Scheidegg Hike

This is my favorite easy alpine hike (2.5 miles, about 1.5 hours, 900-foot altitude drop to Kleine Scheidegg). It's entertaining all the way, with glorious mountain views. If you missed the plot, it's the Monk (Mönch) protecting the Young Maiden (Jung-

frau) from the Ogre (Eiger). The trail usually opens sometime in June and closes due to snow in October. Ask about conditions and get a map at lift stations or at TIs; there are also useful webcams at Maennlichen.ch and Jungfrau.ch.

Ascending to Männlichen: If the weather's good, start off bright and early. From the Lauterbrunnen train station, take the little mountain train up to **Wengen.** Sit on the right side of the train for great valley and waterfall views. In Wengen, buy a picnic at the Co-op grocery across the square from the station, walk a couple of blocks into town, and catch the lift to Männlichen, located on top of the ridge high above you (26 CHF one-way, half-price with Swiss Travel Pass, 3/hour, six-minute trip, late May-late Oct first ascent at 8:50, last descent at 16:50, longer hours July-mid-Sept, different hours in winter, closed in spring and fall, +41 33 855 2933, www.maennlichen.ch). Couch potato thrill-seekers can pay 5 CHF extra for the "Royal Ride" to climb the spiral stairs and enjoy an open-air rooftop perch. This lift may run even when the trail is closed; if the weather is questionable, confirm that the Männlichen-Kleine Scheidegg trail is open before ascending. If it's sunny, don't waste time in Wengen—you can linger back here after your hike.

Riding the gondola from Wengen to **Männlichen,** you'll go over the old lift station—built in 1978, then inundated by a 1999 avalanche that buried a good part of Wengen (notice there's no development in the "red zone" above the tennis courts). Farms are built with earthen ramps on the uphill side in anticipation of the next slide. The forest of avalanche fences near the top was re-inforced after that 1999 avalanche. As you ascend, you can also survey Wengen—the bright red roofs mark new vacation condos, mostly English-owned and used only a few weeks a year.

When you get to the station at the top of the Wengen-Männlichen lift (7,317 feet), check inside to see if they have any free "king for a day" Männlichen Experience envelopes; these fun sou-

BERNER OBERLAND

venirs open to make a panoramic crown that names the mountains you're seeing.

At Männlichen there are two gondola stations, an inviting and economic cafeteria (indoor and outdoor seating), a playground, and a panoramic summit a short hike away.

Männlichen Gipfel Detour ("The Royal Walk"): Before your easy hike, consider a steeper detour: From the Wengen-Männlichen lift station, hike uphill to the little peak, topped with a crown-shaped viewpoint (Männlichen Gipfel, 7,687 feet). Marked as "The Royal Walk," this paved path gains more than 350 feet of elevation; if you're in decent shape, it takes about 20 minutes up, then 10 minutes back down. The last stretch is

thin-air-sucking steep, with ropes you can grab onto for added confidence. Once at the **summit**, you're rewarded with 360-degree views. Beneath you, look for avalanche barriers—both directly below the viewpoint, and striping the cliffs across the valley. Looking back at the cable car, you'll see the Eiger, Mönch, and Jungfrau; in front of them, the pointy Tschuggen peak indicates the location of the Jungfraujoch station. Stretching to the right of those peaks is the Lauterbrunnen Valley; on the far ridge, try to spot the Birg and Schilthorn cable-car stations. On the left side of the three big peaks is the Grindelwald Valley, a parallel universe of alpine villages, lifts, and hikes. And in the opposite direction from the big peaks, the knobby ridge straight ahead is Schynige Platte, with Interlaken on the valley floor beyond and below.

Easy Männlichen to Kleine Scheidegg Hike: Back at the lift station, enjoy the walk—facing spectacular alpine panorama views—to Kleine Scheidegg. From the Männlichen lift station, just head downhill. Ahead of you in the distance, left to right, are the north faces of the Eiger, Mönch, and Jungfrau; in the foreground is the Tschuggen peak, and just behind it, the Lauberhorn. This hike takes you around the left (east) side of this ridge. Simply follow the signs for *Kleine Scheidegg*, and you'll be there in about 1.5 hours—allowing extra time for gawking, picnicking, and photography. (Speed walkers can make it in an hour.)

Walk a few minutes to the second Männlichen lift station (with free WCs; these lifts go to Grindelwald, the touristy town in the valley to your left). Nearby is the Berghaus Männlichen restaurant and cafeteria, a great kids' play area, and a landing pad for helicopter sightseeing flights.

From here, carry on along the path as it curls around the left

(Grindelwald-facing) side of the ridge. From time to time, you might have to tiptoe through streams of melted snow—or some small snowbanks (with ropes to hang onto for safety), even well into the summer—but the path is well-marked, well-maintained, and mostly level all the way to Kleine Scheidegg.

About two-thirds of the way through the hike, you'll arrive at a cluster of benches and a shelter with incredible unobstructed views of all three peaks—the perfect picnic spot.

About 15 minutes later, you'll reach the first sign of civilization: the recommended **Restaurant Grindelwaldblick** (the best lunch stop up here—less crowded, more Swiss and friendlier than Kleine Scheidegg options; it's described on page 239). Hike to the restaurant's fun mountain lookout to survey the Eiger and look down on the Kleine Scheidegg (rated ▲▲ for its spectacular panoramic mountain view).

From the Grindelwaldblick, it's a steep five-minute hike down to the Kleine Scheidegg train station where, since 1893, two lines from the world's longest rack railway meet up at the foot of the Eiger, Mönch, and Jungfraü. From Kleine Scheidegg, you could catch this train up to the Jungfraujoch.

To return to the valley, take the train back down from Kleine Scheidegg (25 minutes to Wengen, then another 15 minutes to Lauterbrunnen). If you have a Swiss Travel Pass, it doesn't cover your fare until Wengen, though it does give a discount; buy a supplementary ticket before boarding or pay a 10-CHF surcharge to buy on board (but find the conductor before they find you, or you may have to pay a steep fine). If you're up for it, hike part of the way downhill (gorgeous 30-minute hike to the Wengernalp station, a little farther to the Allmend stop; 60 more steep minutes from there into Wengen—not dangerous, but requires a good set of knees). The alpine views might be accompanied by the valley-filling mellow sound of cow bells, alphorns, and distant avalanches. If the weather turns bad or you run out of steam, catch the train at any of the stations along the way. The boring final descent from Wengen to Lauterbrunnen is steep—catch the train instead.

MORE DIFFICULT HIKES

From Schynige Platte

▲▲Schynige Platte to First

The best day I've had hiking in the Berner Oberland was on this demanding all-day ridge walk, with Lake Brienz on one side and all that Jungfrau beauty on the other. You pay for, rather than earn, the high-country thrills (riding a lift up to the start and down from the finish).

Wilderswil to Schynige Platte Train Ascent: From the Wilderswil train station (just outside Interlaken), catch the charming old time train up to Schynige Platte (6,454 feet; 32 CHF one-way, goes every 40 minutes and takes about an hour, runs late May-late Oct). Catch the early 8:05 train to have time at Faulhorn (trail's high point) and to get to the First gondola before it stops running. (Or sleep at the mountain hotel at the top; see listing below.) The TI produces a helpful Schynige Platte map/guide narrating the train ride up and describing various hiking options from there (available at Wilderswil train station).

Schynige Platte to First Hike: Allow at least seven hours for this hike (six hours of hiking plus stops for photo fun and picnicking). The trail is nearly all above the tree line and without shelter or water until the gondola station at First. While powerfully beautiful from start to finish, the best hour is the first hour—the Panorama Way.

From the Schynige Platte train station do not take the direct route to First. Add 30 minutes to the hike by walking past the mountain hotel and climbing to a peak called Daube. From that lookout, follow a ridge until you meet the Schynige Platte-First trail. From there (assuming you're not looping back to your starting point), just follow the signs to *Faulhorn* and *First*. Along the way you'll pass a solitary mountain hut squatting on a ridge saddle (strictly no WC or water for non-customers) and then pass under Faulhorn (capped by the highest old time mountain hotel in Switzerland), the high point of the trail at 8,790 feet. From there, it's all downhill, hiking past an alpine lake (Bachsee) and down to First (7,106 feet). You'll be alone for most of the trail, but the last hour from Bachsee is busy with Grindelwald tourists taking a walk from the First gondola.

First Gondola Descent: This gondola takes you from the end of the trail down into Grindelwald town (32 CHF; runs continuously—until at least 17:00 in summer, 30 minutes). From there you can catch a train back via Zweilutschinen to wherever you're staying (2/hour).

The First station comes with the **First Cliff Walk,** a scenic catwalk popular with the Grindelwald crowd (free and a fascinating chance to imagine a rock climber hanging by their fingers onto the craggy face you're strolling under). While you'll avoid the 2.5-hour hike down by catching the gondola from First, you can make the descent a little more fun (and a little more expensive) with a trio of activities. Two stops break the long cable-car ride into thirds, and each third can be swapped for a thrill ride: the **First Flyer** and **First Glider** (two versions—like a zipline for four, 800 meters long from First to Schreckfeld); the **Mountain Cart** (three-wheeled cart on a 3-km track from Schreckfeld to Bort); and the **Trottibike Scooter** (on a 4.5-km paved lane from Bort to Grindelwald). Each segment costs around 20 SF (depending on your lift pass) and can come with a long wait.

Hiking in Reverse (from First to Schynige Platte): You can also do this hike in reverse, which means less climbing, from First (7,106 feet) to Schynige Platte (6,454 feet, last train down at 17:53).

Sleeping in Schynige Platte: For an early start on the Schynige Platte to First hike, sleep at the **$ Berghotel Schynige Platte,** a rustic and well-run mountain inn offering simple rooms and good food (open July-late Oct, +41 33 828 7373, www.hotelschynigeplatte.ch, hotel.schynigeplatte@jungfrau.ch, Jasmin and Thomas Willem).

▲▲▲Panorama Way Loop Trail

To enjoy the best of the Schynige Platte-First hike without the demanding six-hour hike, simply ride the Schynige Platte train round-trip and take your choice of two scenic "Panoramaweg" loop hikes, which include the Daube lookout and the scenic ridge walk.

For each of these walks, start from the station by walking past the hotel and then climbing 20 minutes to the Daube lookout. From there the Panorama Way stretches along an incredibly scenic ridge. In my lectures to illustrate the wonder of the Swiss Alps, I've long described it this way: "Imagine tight-roping high above the valleys on a ridge, with lakes on one side stretching all the way to Germany, cut-glass peaks—the Eiger, Mönch, and Jungfrau—on the other. And ahead of you, the long legato tones of an alphorn announcing that the helicopter-stocked mountain hut is open, it's just around the corner, and the coffee schnapps is on."

With the help of the simple tourist map and signposts, you can decide which version of the Panoramaweg you want to take—1.5 hours or 2.5 hours, each looping back to Schynige Platte.

Back at the Schynige Platte station, an **alpine flower park** offers a delightful stroll through several hundred alpine flowers, including a chance to see edelweiss growing in the wild (free, late May-late Oct daily 8:30-18:00, www.alpengarten.ch).

From Gimmelwald

▲Gimmelwald-Tanzbödeli-Obersteinberg-Stechelberg/ Gimmelwald

This six-hour, 11-mile hike can be extremely rewarding, offering perfect peace, very few people, traditional alpine culture, and spectacular views. It's one long trail with two one-hour side trips. Allow eight hours if you include both the Busenalp and Tanzbödeli excursions.

This demanding hike requires serious shoes and is best done with poles. There's no food or water along the way, so pack accordingly. For either of the side trips, I'd hide my bag in the bushes to lighten my load (especially for Tanzbödeli, which finishes with a scramble).

About 100 yards below the Gimmelwald firehouse, take the **Sefinental** dirt road (described earlier, in the Sefinen Valley to Kilchbalm hike). As the dirt road switches back after about 30 minutes, take the right turn across the river and start your long ascent, following signs to *Obersteinberg.*

Busenalp Side Trip: After two hours of hard climbing, you have the option of this 30-minute (each way) side trip. Busenalp, a working farm, lies at the end of a scant trail (just follow the cow pies uphill, arcing to the right). As the farm comes into view, there's a welcome picnic bench with grand views. At Busenalp, friendly Elisa works hard all summer minding 55 cows, three horses, six goats, and a variable number of chickens—and enjoying the tranquility.

Tanzbödeli: Farther along the main trail, at the *Obersteinberg 50 Min/Tanzbödeli 20 Min* signpost, is the steep trail to the Tanzbödeli ("Dancing Floor"). This grassy plateau (about the size of a football field) is a favorite alpine perch—great for a little romance or a picnic with breathtaking views of the upper and lower Lauterbrunnen Valley. I found the last 100 yards a frightening scramble—too steep for hiking poles, which I stowed—but very rewarding. (From a distance, throughout the region, the Dancing Floor is marked by the shark-fin-shaped Spitzhorn peak that towers over the perch.)

Obersteinberg: From Tanzbödeli, you return to the main trail (there's no other way out) and continue to Obersteinberg. You're entering a natural reserve, so you're likely to see chamois and other alpine critters. You'll eventually hit the Mountain Hotel Obersteinberg (see below; they can normally serve you a meal or drink, and might let you look at their cheese cellar).

Sleeping in Obersteinberg: Two romantic yet rustic **$** mountain hotels are side by side (at about 6,000 feet in altitude, a 20-minute walk from each other), accessible only to hikers via a steep 2.5-hour hike above Stechelberg. They each charge about 100 CHF a night per person with dinner and breakfast in simple double rooms and are open from June through September. Both serve lunches to hikers.

Mountain Hotel Obersteinberg is a classic working alpine farm run by Julian and his family. They rent 12 primitive double rooms and 30 less-expensive loft beds. There's no shower, no hot water, and no electricity. Candles light up the night. Ask for a hot-water bottle to warm your bed (cash only, reserve by phone only, +41 33 855 2033, www.stechelberg.ch; look under "Accommodation & Dining").

Berggasthaus Tschingelhorn Steinberg, 20 minutes below Obersteinberg, is more comfortable with good food, a little electricity, and showers (+41 33 855 1343, www.tschingelhorn.ch, info@tschingelhorn.ch; run by Rudi, Stephanie, and team).

Stechelberg/Gimmelwald: From Obersteinberg, the trail leads to another mountain hotel at Tschingelhorn, then back down to Stechelberg and the Schilthornbahn cable car valley station (1.5 hours total). Or branch off before reaching Stechelberg and hike back up to Gimmelwald (2 hours total).

From Mürren

To arrange a guide for the white-knuckle, cliff-hugging *via ferrata* trail near Mürren, see page 207.

From the Schilthorn

Several tough trails lead down from the Schilthorn (there's a reason that virtually all visitors take the cable car down). Only a serious, experienced hiker should consider walking all or part of the way back to Gimmelwald. Proper shoes and clothing (weather can change quickly) and good knees are required. Don't attempt to hike down unless you've confirmed that the trail is clear of snow. While it's possible to make the steep descent directly from the top of the Schilthorn, I prefer the less strenuous (but still challenging) hike from the intermediate cable-car station at Birg.

▲▲Birg to Gimmelwald via Bryndli

You can combine this difficult downhill hike (4-5 hours) from the Birg cable-car station with a visit to the Schilthorn by buying the round-trip excursion early-bird fare (it's cheaper than the Gimmelwald-Schilthorn-Birg ticket). Visit the summit first, then descend to Birg to hike down.

The most interesting trail from Birg to Gimmelwald is the high one via Grauseeli lake and Wasenegg Ridge to **Bryndli,** then down to Spilboden and the Sprutz waterfall. Warning: This trail drops 4,500 feet, is quite steep and slippery in places, and can take over four hours. Locals take their kindergarteners on this hike, but Americans unused to alpine hikes shouldn't attempt it.

From the **Birg lift station,** hike toward the Schilthorn, taking your first left down and passing along the left side of the little Grauseeli lake. From the lake, a gravelly trail leads down rough switchbacks (including a stretch where the path narrows and you can hang onto a guide cable against the cliff face) until it levels out. When you see a rock painted with arrows pointing to Mürren and Rotstockhütte, follow the path to **Rotstockhütte** (traditional old farm with light meals and drinks), traversing the cow-grazed mountainside.

The safer, well-signposted approach to Bryndli is to drop down to Rotstockhütte then climb back up to Bryndli. Thrillseekers instead follow **Wasenegg Ridge,** which is more scary than dangerous if you're sure-footed and can handle the 50-foot-long "tightrope-with-handrail" section along an extremely narrow ledge with a thousand-foot drop. This trail gets you to Bryndli with the least altitude change. A barbed-wire fence leads you to Bryndli's knobby little summit, where you'll enjoy an incredible 360-degree view and a chance to sign your name on the register stored in the little wooden box.

From **Bryndli,** a steep trail winds directly down toward Gimmelwald and soon hits a bigger, easier trail. The trail bends right (just before the farm/restaurant at Spielboden), leading to Sprutz. Walk under the Sprutz waterfall, then follow a steep, wooded trail that deposits you in a meadow of flowers at the top side of Gimmelwald. (For details on the hike from Spielboden down to Sprutz and Gimmelwald, see page 222.)

MOUNTAIN BIKING

Mountain biking is popular and accepted, as long as you stay on clearly marked mountain-bike paths. You can rent bikes in Mürren, Lauterbrunnen, or Interlaken (see listings under each section). You may save time and avoid disappointment by reserving your bike online in advance. Wherever you rent your bike, take a few minutes to be sure it's properly fitted to your size. Rentals come with helmets. Locks, while not considered necessary, are available on request. Some hotels and B&Bs also rent or loan mountain bikes.

While there is a world of more demanding mountain bike routes for serious bikers, I've outlined a couple of the most popular and easy bike rides here.

Lauterbrunnen Valley

From top to bottom, Lauterbrunnen Valley seems made to order for a bike ride. Using Lauterbrunnen town as a springboard, you can pedal to the top of the valley, down the valley to Interlaken, or both. It's two totally different rides: top of the valley is sweet and romantic; down to Interlaken is more intense and less scenic. Except in Lauterbrunnen town, you'll never need to share the road with cars

since you'll be on a bike path. Here are
tips for both ends of the valley. Lacing
the two rides together (including a visit
to Interlaken) makes for a great day.

Top of the Valley (Lauterbrunnen
Town to Stechelberg): From Lauterbrunnen town it's gently uphill, always
on the right (traffic-free) side of the
river. Along the way you can explore a
typical European campground, stop at
Trümmelbach Falls (signposted across
the river), and maybe even see a BASE
jumper. Eventually (near the top of the
valley) the paved lane turns left over the
river to the regular road. Don't follow it; instead, stay on the gravelly
lane, which becomes a path all the way to the top. At the top you'll
reach a "rainbow bridge"; carry your bike over it to get to the hamlet
of Stechelberg. For more descriptions see "Cloudy-Day Lauterbrunnen Valley Walk" (page 220), which follows the same route.

Bottom of the Valley (Lauterbrunnen Town to Interlaken):
While the top of the valley is more idyllic, it's fun to spend an
hour charging downhill on the gravelly eight-mile path along the
river from Lauterbrunnen to the "big city" of Interlaken. Immediately below the Lauterbrunnen station, turn right, pass the big
parking garage, go downhill over the river, and look for a hard left
onto a tiny riverside lane. You're on your way, and except for at the
very start, the trail is marked for bikes. Staying on the right side of
the river, follow signs downhill to *Zweilütschinen,* then *Wilderswil,*
then into *Interlaken* (with plenty of things to see and do). Do not
bike back uphill—it's hard and dull. Instead, return to Lauterbrunnen from the Interlaken Ost train station (2/hour, evenings 1/hour,
20 minutes; you can take your bike on for half the ticket price).

Mürren-Winteregg-Grütschalp and Back

This fairly level route takes you not along the peaceful valley floor
but through high country, with awesome mountain views (see the
"Grütschalp to Mürren" hike description on page 226).

More Berner Oberland Towns

I'd sleep in Gimmelwald, Mürren, or Lauterbrunnen, but you
could also consider overnighting in the following places.

Sleeping and Eating in Wengen

Wengen—a bigger, fancier Mürren (pop. 1,300) on the east side of the valley at 4,180 feet—has plenty of grand hotels, restaurants, shops, diversions, and terrific views...though it lacks the soul of the towns I've described earlier. This mostly traffic-free resort is an easy train ride above Lauterbrunnen and halfway up to Kleine Scheidegg and Männlichen. From Wengen, you can catch the Männlichen lift (www.maennlichen.ch) up to the ridge and take the rewarding, view-filled, mostly downhill Männlichen-Kleine Scheidegg hike (described earlier, under "Hiking and Biking").

Wengen's **TI** is a two-minute walk from the station. When you get off the train, look for the big map and bear left up to the main drag (Dorfstrasse). This strip is lined with big hotels on the left; on the right are a playing field, the bottom station for the Männlichen cable car, and the **TI** (Tourist Center Wengen, daily 9:00-18:00, sometimes later in summer, closed Sat-Sun off-season, +41 33 856 8585, https://wengen.swiss).

The good-sized **Co-op grocery,** across the square from the train station, is great for picnic fixings (daily 8:00-18:30; closed Sun off-season). The small **Dorflade Wengen** grocery store on the main street (near the cable-car station) opens a little earlier and later.

Above the Train Station: $$$ Hotel Schönegg, at the top end of Wengen's main road, is a centrally located splurge exuding a warm and woody ski-lodge ambience, with a generous view terrace out front. Its 20 rooms are designed in a cozy alpine style, almost all with balconies and great views (family room with fireplace, elevator, sauna, half-board in good restaurant with big terrace available, +41 33 855 3422, www.hotel-schoenegg.ch, mail@hotel-schoenegg.ch).

$$ Hotel Berghaus, in a quiet area facing a pasture, is a five-minute uphill walk from the main street (about 10 minutes from the station). This sedate old place offers 19 rooms above a fine restaurant specializing in fish (family room, elevator, open June-Sept and mid-Dec-early April, +41 33 855 2151, www.berghaus-wengen.ch, info@berghaus-wengen.ch, Fontana family). From the main drag, head up the street across from Hotel Bernerhof, bear right at the fork, go 200 yards more (past the church), and it's on the left.

Below the Train Station: Friendly Therese and Willy Brunner run the **$$$ Bären Hotel,** which offers 17 tidy rooms with modern bathrooms. To save money, opt for one of the three rooms without a balcony (half-board available in their restaurant, family rooms, elevator, kids' playroom, table tennis, closed mid-April-mid-May and mid-Oct-mid-Dec, +41 33 855 1419, www.baeren-wengen. ch, info@baeren-wengen.ch). Their **$$$ restaurant** is a bright, inviting option for a memorable dinner with sharp, professional service. They source many ingredients locally and enjoy crafting seasonal specials (dinner reservations wise, breakfast available to non-guests, daily 8:00-10:30 & 18:00-22:00). From the station, cross the street to the Co-op grocery, turn right and go under the rail bridge, and follow the road down the hill—the hotel will be on your right.

Sleeping and Eating at or near Kleine Scheidegg

This high settlement above the timberline (6,762 feet) is as close as you can stay to the Jungfraujoch. All these places serve meals and let you sleep face-to-face with the Eiger. Confirm prices and availability before ascending.

$$$$ Hotel Bellevue des Alpes, lovingly maintaining a 1930s elegance, is a very expensive but potentially worthwhile splurge. Since the 1840s, five generations of von Almens have run this classic old 60-room alpine hotel. Every detail has been preserved, and filmmakers often use the hotel as a set for pre-WWII period shoots. The hallway is like a museum lined with old photos (breakfast and sumptuous four-course dinner included, four floors and no elevator, no TVs, closed mid-April-mid-June and mid-Sept-mid-Dec, +41 33 855 1212, www.scheidegg-hotels.ch, welcome@scheidegg-hotels.ch).

$$ Bergrestaurant Kleine Scheidegg is a handy, basic lodge in the train-station building. It has 17 rooms with shared bath, plus **$** dorm beds (breakfast and dinner included for all guests, lodge closed off-season, +41 33 828 7828, www.bergrestaurant-kleine-scheidegg.ch). The **$$ restaurant** (open year-round) has a predictable menu of basic Swiss and international food.

$ Restaurant Grindelwaldblick, a 10-minute hike up along the path toward Männlichen and visible from the train station, is more charming, romantic, and remote than **Bergrestaurant Kleine Scheidegg** (private rooms, family room, closed Nov and May, +41 33 855 1374, www.grindelwaldblick.ch, info@grindel-waldblick.ch). The **$$ restaurant,** with a great sun terrace and a cozy interior, sells good three-course lunches and dinners, including a cheesy *Rösti* (food served daily 11:00-20:00, drinks until 22:00).

Sleeping in Stechelberg

Stechelberg, at 3,025 feet, is the hamlet at the end of the road up the Lauterbrunnen Valley; it's about a mile beyond the Schilthornbahn lift. From the lift station to Stechelberg, it's a five-minute ride on the same PostBus #141 that comes from Lauterbrunnen (2/hour, get off at "Stechelberg, Hotel") or a 20-minute walk. Beyond Stechelberg lies the rugged upper end of the Lauterbrunnen Valley, which is mostly a nature reserve with only a few scattered huts and a narrow service road.

$$ Hotel Stechelberg, at road's end, is surrounded by waterfalls and vertical rock, with a garden terrace, a good restaurant, and 16 quiet rooms—half with shared bath in a functional old building, half with private bath in a concrete, no-character new building (free parking, bus stops right in front, hotel closed mid-Nov-Christmas, restaurant closed Mon-Tue off-season, +41 33 855 2921, https://hotel-stechelberg.ch, hotel@stechelberg.ch, Marianne and Otto).

¢ The **Alpenhof** fills a former "Nature Friends' Hut" with 44 cheap beds in rooms of two to six beds with bathrooms down the hall. Creaking like a wooden chalet built in 1926 should, and surrounded by a broad lawn, it provides a good, inexpensive base for drivers and families (each group gets a private room, breakfast optional, open nearly year-round, kitchen, no Wi-Fi, free parking, reception staffed 8:00-12:00 & 17:00-18:30, +41 33 855 1202, www.alpenhof-stechelberg.ch, alpenhof@stechelberg.ch, Diane from Australia and Marc from England). It's 300 yards from the Stechelberg Hotel bus stop: Continue up the road, stay right at the fork, cross the river, and it's on your left.

ZERMATT & THE MATTERHORN

There's just something about the Matterhorn, the most recognizable mountain on the planet. Anyone who says, "You've seen one mountain, you've seen them all" hasn't laid eyes on this pointy, craggy peak. And hiking with that iconic pinnacle as a backdrop is even more exciting.

Oh, and there's a town, too. Zermatt, a bustling burg of about 5,800 people, might well be the most touristy resort in Switzerland. While the village has pockets of traditional charm, virtually everyone you meet in Zermatt earns a living one way or another from those who flock here for a peek at the peak. Aside from the stone quarries you'll pass on the way into town, tourism is Zermatt's only industry.

With the first ascent of the Matterhorn in 1865 and the arrival of trains, Zermatt found itself on the Grand Tour of Europe. Over time, its residents learned it was easier to milk the tourists than the goats, and mountain tourism became the focus. Today the town is a collection of over a hundred modern chalet-style hotels with a well-organized and groomed infrastructure for summer and winter sports with no gas engines—only electric cars slalom between the pedestrians. Sure, there are fabulously wealthy visitors, but locals like to say that the "traffic-free" nature of the town is a great equalizer. With only pedestrians and the golf-cart-style shuttles on the lanes, "you have no idea who owns a Ferrari."

Zermatt has some disadvantages. Many find it quite touristy, and its location—at the dead-end of a long valley in the southwest corner of the country—is not on the way to anything (though it links up with the Glacier Express). And if you make the long journey here only to find cloudy weather, you may end up shopping for a T-shirt that reads, "I went all the way to Zermatt and didn't even see the lousy Matterhorn." But in sunny weather, riding the high-mountain lifts, poking through lost-in-time farm hamlets, and ambling along on scenic hikes are even more enjoyable with that triangular summit nodding its white head in the background.

GETTING TO ZERMATT

Zermatt is barely two hours from Bern and Interlaken by train, thanks to the Lötschberg Base Tunnel. It's also easy to reach from Zürich or Lausanne (about three hours). Another popular way to reach Zermatt is from the St. Moritz area on the Glacier Express, an all-day ride on a historic narrow-gauge line that cuts across the country (see the Scenic Rail Journeys chapter). You can also do just half of this route by connecting Zermatt with Luzern or Lugano (changing in Andermatt).

PLANNING YOUR TIME

High summer into early fall is the best time to come to Zermatt. On a two-week trip in Switzerland, I'd suggest two nights and the better part of two days here—if the weather's good. The first half of September can be a sweet spot: Europe's summer vacation season is over, so it's no longer "high season" (making it easier and more affordable to find a room). But things are still up and running, and you can often catch the last few days of sunny weather. Spring is a bad time to visit: Most trails, lifts, and restaurants are closed. Before June, I'd skip it.

Zermatt has earned its reputation for untrustworthy weather—the valley can get completely socked in at any time of year. While two good-weather days are enough to experience the highlights, add at least one buffer day, if you can, as insurance against rain. For the latest weather report, check the webcams and forecast at www.zermatt.ch. In clear weather, you'll want to spend your daylight hours up above town.

With One Day: If you have just one good day in Zermatt in high season (when all the lifts are running), follow this plan, which connects the Gornergrat and the Klein Matterhorn (buy the Peak2Peak ticket, which includes the necessary lifts). Start the day by taking the first train up to the high Gornergrat ridge. On the way down, do the gentle-but-gorgeous Rifelseeweg hike that connects the Rotenboden and Riffelberg train stops. From Riffelberg (on the Gornergrat hillside), take a gondola over and down to the stop called Furi, on the Klein Matterhorn (runs July-Aug only). Depending on your timing and interest, ride all the way up to the Matterhorn Glacier Paradise station at the Klein Matterhorn summit, then return via the Schwarzsee ridge (and perhaps hike part of the way back to Zermatt). Outside of peak summer, when the

Which Lift?

There are three main lift experiences from Zermatt. All are well worth your time in good weather (for suggestions on weaving these together, see the "Planning Your Time" section). But if

you need to choose among them, here are the key differences:

Gornergrat Railway: If you can fit only one high-mountain excursion on your trip to Zermatt, make it this one. This pleasant and easy cogwheel train ride departs immediately across the street from Zermatt's train station and summits the Gornergrat ridge in just over 30 minutes. The train runs above ground the entire time, with great scenery the whole way. The top offers Matterhorn vistas as well as the best glacier views. One of the main reasons to ascend the Gornergrat ridge is for access to the dramatic, fairly easy but steeply downhill Riffelseeweg hike between two stations, with great Matterhorn views. The Gornergrat Railway also runs later in the day, making this a good choice if you're trying to squeeze an extra activity into a sunny afternoon.

Rothorn Lift: This is your short-and-sweet option. The first stretch of this ascent is to Sunnegga via a funicular inside the mountain (with no views). When you emerge at Sunnegga, you're rewarded with *the* classic Matterhorn view. From here it's a relatively quick gondola-and-cable car ascent to the Rothorn summit. The views here are less striking than from the Gornergrat and Klein Matterhorn summits, but the journey is relatively easy and affordable (five-minute walk from Zermatt train station to base station, then 30 minutes to summit). Another big draw is the wonderful hike from the Blauherd station (partway up) to the alpine lake Stellisee, with grand Matterhorn views. This is the area's only truly "easy" high-mountain walk (under an hour) beyond simply wandering around a lift station.

Matterhorn Glacier Paradise Lift: This lift, to the Klein Matterhorn summit, is the longest, priciest high-altitude option (in fact, it's the highest lift station in Europe). From the base station, which is a 10- to 15-minute walk from the center of Zermatt, a series of gondolas and cable cars take you up, up, up, over glaciers to the summit (about 50 minutes). While extremely expensive, this lift gives you that top-of-the-world feeling. Klein Matterhorn is the only accessible place in the Zermatt region with snow year-round, allowing for summer skiing. There are no hikes at the top, but the moderately difficult Matterhorn Trail hike, from the midway Schwarzsee station, is one of the area's most satisfying.

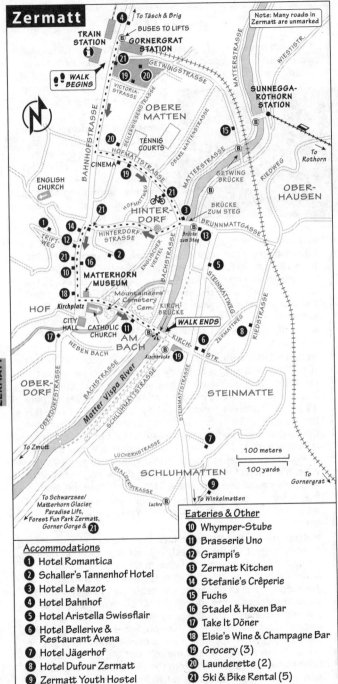

Zermatt

Note: Many roads in Zermatt are unmarked

WALK BEGINS

WALK ENDS

TRAIN STATION

BUSES TO LIFTS

GORNERGRAT STATION

GETWINGSTRASSE

VICTORIA-STRASSE

BAHNHOFSTRASSE

SEILERWIESENSTRASSE

OBERE MATTEN

TENNIS COURTS

HOFMATTSTRASSE

CINEMA

ENGLISH CHURCH

TRIFTWEG

HINTER-DORF

HOFMATTWEG

HINTERDORF STRASSE

ENGLISCHER VIERTEL

MATTERHORN MUSEUM

BACHSTRASSE

Mountaineers' Cemetery Cem.

KIRCH-BRÜCKE

Kirchplatz

CITY HALL

CATHOLIC CHURCH

NEBEN BACH

AM BACH

Kirchbrücke

OBER-DORF

OBERDORFSTRASSE

BACHSTRASSE

SCHLUHMATTSTRASSE

Matter Vispa River

LUCHERNSTRASSE

SCHLUHMATTEN

STALDENSTRASSE

Luchre

To Zmutt

To Schwarzsee/ Matterhorn Glacier Paradise Lift, Forest Fun Park Zermatt, Gorner Gorge &

MATTERSTRASSE

WIESTISTR.

SUNNEGGA-ROTHORN STATION

To Rothorn

OBER-HAUSEN

OBERE MATTENSTRASSE

MATTERSTRASSE

GETWING BRÜCKE

RIEDWEG

BRÜCKE ZUM STEG

BRUNNMATTGASSE

Brücke zum Steg

STEINMATTWEG

RIEDSTRASSE

ZERMATTWEG

KIRCH-STR.

STEINMATTE

STEINMATTSTRASSE

To Winkelmatten

To Gornergrat

100 meters

100 yards

Accommodations
1 Hotel Romantica
2 Schaller's Tannenhof Hotel
3 Hotel Le Mazot
4 Hotel Bahnhof
5 Hotel Aristella Swissflair
6 Hotel Bellerive & Restaurant Avena
7 Hotel Jägerhof
8 Hotel Dufour Zermatt
9 Zermatt Youth Hostel

Eateries & Other
10 Whymper-Stube
11 Brasserie Uno
12 Grampi's
13 Zermatt Kitchen
14 Stefanie's Crêperie
15 Fuchs
16 Stadel & Hexen Bar
17 Take It Döner
18 Elsie's Wine & Champagne Bar
19 Grocery (3)
20 Launderette (2)
21 Ski & Bike Rental (5)

ZERMATT

Riffelberg-Furi connector is not running, this plan still works—you'll just need to connect the two lifts through Zermatt, which takes a bit longer. To visualize this plan, see the "Zermatt Area" map, later.

With a Second Day: If it's clear, I'd head up to the Rothorn summit, or at least to the midpoint lift station at Blauherd for the easy walk to the alpine lake Stellisee (and consider the restaurant at Fluhalp). With the rest of your day, consider one of the hikes from the Sunnegga ridge, or relax in Zermatt.

Arriving on a Sunny Afternoon: If you arrive in Zermatt in the midafternoon with a few hours of clear daylight, I'd get a head start and ascend the Gornergrat, then hike the Riffelseeweg on your way back down. The Gornergrat train runs into the early evening in high season, but confirm the exact schedule.

Alternative for Serious Hikers: If the Rothorn excursion sounds more appealing than the Matterhorn Glacier Paradise, start with the two-hour Naturweg hike from Sunnegga to Riffelalp (better Matterhorn views than if done in reverse). Then take the train to Gornergrat and, on the way back down, get off at Rotenboden and hike to Riffelberg. From there, you can either keep walking or take the train back to town. If Mother Nature cooperates, you can do the Matterhorn Glacier Paradise and/or hikes from Schwarzsee on a second day.

Orientation to Zermatt

Zermatt (elevation 5,265 feet) lies at the end of the Nikolaital valley, in the shadow of the mighty Matterhorn (14,690 feet, "Cervin" in French, "Cervino" in Italian).

The train station is at the north end of the town's shopping zone, a few steps from the main drag, Bahnhofstrasse. As you stand in front of the station, facing the parking lot with the tracks at your back, the heart of the village is to your right. Lifts to thrilling Matterhorn viewpoints leave from near the train station: The cog railway up to Gornergrat leaves from directly across the street; the Sunnegga-Rothorn station for the lift to Rothorn is a few blocks ahead (along the Gornergrat tracks, then across the river); and the lift up to the Matterhorn Glacier Paradise (at the Klein Matterhorn peak) is at the upper (southern) end of the village (about three-quarters of a mile away).

Zermatt bans cars within the town limits and brags that its streets are traffic-free. Well, not quite. Electric cars (resembling big golf carts) buzz around the streets like four-wheeled Vespas. Half of these cars are owned by hotels, which use them to shuttle guests and luggage to the train station; the other half operate as taxis. As

Zermatt at a Glance

In Zermatt

▲▲**Matterhorn Museum** Underground museum resembling archaeological dig covers history of Zermatt and its magic mountain. **Hours:** Daily 14:00-18:00 in summer, from 15:00 in shoulder season, closed off-season. See page 253.

▲**Zermatt Walk** Orientation stroll, from the train station, through the attractive old Hinterdorf quarter, with antique chalets and traditional *mazots* (shacks on stone stilt), to the cemetery. See page 249.

Lifts and Trains

▲▲▲**Matterhorn Glacier Paradise** Europe's highest cable-car station (12,739 feet), with jaw-dropping Alps view, year-round snow, and a "palace" carved into ice (but no hikes). See page 261.

▲▲▲**Sunnegga Viewpoint** Best mountain destination for budget travelers, offering the ultimate Matterhorn views from partway up Rothorn (7,506 feet). See page 268.

▲▲**Gornergrat Top Station** Viewpoint (10,270 feet), reached by a cogwheel train, hovering above the Gorner glacier with fantastic views of the Matterhorn and Switzerland's tallest mountain—Monte Rosa (15,200 feet). See page 264.

▲▲**Rothorn Summit** Cable-car station at 10,180 feet with sweeping views of the Matterhorn and its valley. See page 267.

these cars are silent and weave speedily between pedestrians, stay alert on any street wide enough for traffic.

In this small town, locals don't bother much with street names and house numbers. To find your hotel, use a map (the TI has a free detailed one).

TOURIST INFORMATION

Zermatt's TI is at the train station, facing the big e-car parking lot (daily 8:00-18:00, +41 27 966 8100, www.zermatt.ch). The unstaffed lobby stays open later and has maps and brochures.

The TI sells lift passes/tickets and is well-versed in helping visitors weigh their options given current weather, time constraints, budgets, and hiking interests. They also offer several free resources: an extremely detailed village map, lift schedules/prices, and a panoramic hiking map. The region's trail signs can be confusing; the hiking map, which outlines the distance and difficulty level of the

▲**Schwarzsee Ridge** Hillside midpoint (8,474 feet) of Matterhorn Glacier Paradise ascent; directly under the Matterhorn, with a lovely picnic spot and a jumping-off point for hikes. See page 262.

Walks and Hikes

▲▲▲**Riffelseeweg Hike** Easy, mostly downhill walk with nonstop scenery between two stations on the Gornergrat line. See page 265.

▲▲▲**Blauherd-Fluhalp Hike** Mostly level walk from the Blauherd lift station (partway up Rothorn) past a picturesque glacial lake (and great Matterhorn views). See page 267.

▲▲**Matterhorn Trail Hike** Deservedly popular trail from the Schwarzsee gondola station back to Zermatt. See page 262.

▲▲**Hikes from Sunnegga** Choice of long, mostly gentle trail (Gourmetweg) from Rothorn's lowest lift station back down to Zermatt, mixing hillside hamlets and lush forest, or a moderately strenuous walk (Naturweg) across to the Gornergrat's Riffelalp station. See page 268.

▲**Furi to Zermatt Hike** Steep hour-long hike from lowest lift station on Klein Matterhorn past cute hamlets and down into town. See page 263.

ZERMATT

most popular hikes, can help you avoid taking a longer or steeper route than you intended. More detailed maps are available for free on the TI's website.

ARRIVAL IN ZERMATT

Zermatt's small **train station** is in the middle of town. The ticket office is beside the tracks; a free WC and pay lockers are downstairs. The TI is straight ahead from the head of the tracks and on the right. Lines of electric taxis wait in the big parking lot out front.

All the hotels I list are within walking distance of the train station (provided you're packing light). However, the places across the river are far enough away that you might want to take a hotel shuttle (ask about this when you book), a taxi, or the bus. There are also free airport-style luggage carts at the train station (5-CHF deposit)—useful if it's a fairly level walk to your hotel (or if your car is parked at Täsch, you can use them to wheel your baggage onto the shuttle train—see below). Look for racks of carts just behind the head of the tracks or along the back wall of the station.

Because cars are not allowed in Zermatt, **drivers** can park in the huge lot at Täsch, a few miles before Zermatt (16 CHF/day), then take the shuttle train into town (runs every 20 minutes until about 22:00, less frequent after that, 8.20 CHF one-way, www.matterhornterminal.ch). Täsch has many parking options, but the big modern lot at the station is most convenient. With 4,000 spots, it's rarely full (look for the big sign: *Matterhorn Terminal Täsch*). Park (you'll pay when you leave) and hop on the next shuttle train—it's very slick.

GETTING AROUND ZERMATT

Even though Zermatt is "traffic-free," your feet aren't your only transportation option. Buses (basically oversized electric cars) are useful for hauling luggage to more distant lodgings or for saving the 20-minute walk between the station and the Matterhorn Glacier Paradise lift station at the top of town. These free buses depart across from the train station and make several stops along the way to the Matterhorn Glacier Paradise station, including at the Sunnegga-Rothorn lift (about 3/hour, last buses

leave around 18:00 or 19:00). The green Bergbahnen line goes more directly; the red line takes a roundabout route via the Winkelmatten neighborhood. Ask the TI for a timetable or check www.e-bus.ch.

You can also hire a **taxi** from in front of the train station (12 CHF for a short ride in the heart of town; extra charge for greater distances, luggage, and rides at night or that are more uphill).

HELPFUL HINTS

Festivals: Folk troupes from all over western Switzerland converge on Zermatt for the **Folklore Festival,** usually on the second weekend in August.

Blackneck Goat Parade: The local Valais Blackneck goat, unique to this region (with a black head and shoulders, a white rear end, and long horns), is being heavily promoted as a sort of mascot for the Zermatt area. (Baby goats that don't fit the proper color scheme are immediately butchered, ensuring the herd evolves as expected.) Every day in summer (July-mid-

Aug, at about 9:00 and again at 16:30), a small flock of these furry goats are herded through the center of town (down the length of Bahnhofstrasse) on the way to and from the pasture. Keep an eye out for this charming and unusual parade.

Laundry: Two launderettes provide drop-off service only. **Waschsalon Doli** is nice and central (Mon-Sat 8:30-12:00 & 14:00-19:00, closed Sun, a block off the main drag at Hofmattstrasse 3—look for the concrete stairs leading down to a basement across from the tennis courts, +41 27 967 5100). **Womy Express** is in the Viktoria Center mall across from the train station (Mon-Fri 8:30-12:00 & 14:00-18:00, closed Sat-Sun, +41 27 967 3242).

Cinema: The **Vernissage Cinema,** oddly located in the Backstage Hotel, plays a rotating schedule of historical Matterhorn-centric films and some first-run features in the evening during peak season (Hofmattstrasse 4, +41 27 966 6970, www.backstagehotel.ch).

Ski and Mountain Bike Rental: For equipment rental in town, try **Matterhorn Sport** (Bahnhofstrasse 78, +41 27 967 2956, www.matterhornsport.ch), **Bayard Sports & Fashion** (branches on Bahnhofplatz and at Bahnhofstrasse 35, +41 27 966 4960, www.bayardzermatt.ch), **Bike Arena** (near the Migros at Hofmattstrasse 30, +41 27 510 25 11, www.bikearenazermatt.ch), and **Dorsaz-Sport** (near Matterhorn Glacier Paradise lift station, +41 27 966 3810, www.dorsaz-sport.ch).

Zermatt Walk

At first glance, Zermatt appears to be single-minded about catching the tourist dollar. The streets may be lined with chalet after chalet, but all the dark wood and overflowing flower boxes lend this super-touristy town a pleasant realness. This walk, worth ▲ and only about 30 minutes, orients you to the town while exploring some back streets and more authentic spots that many visitors miss.

Train Station Square (Bahnhofplatz): Zermatt entertains two million guests a year...and they all arrive here. While skiing is the big draw in winter, this is a popular terminal in summer for the scenic Glacier Express—the daily eight-hour train ride connecting Zermatt and the St. Moritz area in the Upper Engadine (see the Scenic

Rail Journeys chapter). The first train arrived here in 1891 (and the first winter train in 1928).

Across the street is the station for the **cogwheel train to Gornergrat** (at an altitude of more than 10,000 feet), which opened in 1899. If you walked alongside that train station—following its tracks for a few short blocks—then crossed the river and turned left, you'd reach the base station for the **funicular to Rothorn** in about five minutes.

The town is committed to its car-free environment. Listen to the sounds of a traffic-free city. Locals who own cars have to park them at a garage at the south end of town. E-cars—like oversized golf carts—move people to and from hotels and serve as taxis. (The first Zermatt bus ran on gas...it lasted about one day after locals put sugar in the tank. City leaders got the message.)

Here at Bahnhofplatz, you'll find the TI and the big Co-op supermarket (a budget-friendly depot for most shopping needs).
• *Now stroll up...*

Bahnhofstrasse and Hofmattstrasse: Zermatt strives to be a high-class mountain resort for active guests. The town's main street, Bahnhofstrasse, is lined with hotels, souvenir shops, après-ski bars, and fondue restaurants. You'll notice even bikes are forbidden—this street is only for people, the occasional e-car, and the twice-daily parade of goats in summer.

After 250 yards, turn left just before Hotel Pollux and stroll down Hofmattstrasse. Between here and the river, this practical street has a sports arena (its tennis courts freeze over and become ice rinks for curling and hockey in the winter), a handy laundry service (see "Helpful Hints," earlier), indoor golf, a cinema (tucked in the back of a hotel, on your right), and the Migros supermarket.
• *Continue along the street until you reach the little bridge.*

Brücke zum Steg and the River: For centuries, the bridge called Brücke zum Steg has crossed the Matter Vispa River. Two hundred years ago, this was a humble wooden crossing just strong enough to support a cow. The embankment containing the river was built after World War II to contain floods (once common with the spring and summer melts). This is the practical spine of Zermatt, with a shuttle bus running along the riverbank. Higher buildings are connected to this street by a clever system of tunnels and elevators (handy in the snowy winter).

Notice the many **small hotels.** Hotels in Zermatt are generally family owned and run. Local inheritance laws—which require that all relatives who own a stake in a plot of land agree to any sale—have prevented big chains from infiltrating the town.

While hotel owners may be local, hotel staffers are typically not Swiss. Zermatt may look quintessentially Swiss, but most of the workers who keep the hotels, restaurants, and lifts going are from other parts of Europe, particularly Portugal. In Täsch, the next village down the valley (with more affordable housing than Zermatt), most residents are Portuguese. While some Swiss feel that the current policy of free movement between Switzerland and the rest of Europe should be curtailed, immigrants are hard at work in Switzerland's hospitality industry.

• *Now look toward the Matterhorn at the far end of the valley and imagine standing on the old wooden bridge in 1800. To get an even better taste of those days, head into the...*

Hinterdorf Quarter: Once the core of the Zermatt village, this small but very atmospheric area is worth a ▲▲ stroll. To reach it from the bridge, head slowly up **Hinterdorfstrasse**—the tight, cobbled lane just to the right of the Matterhorn—and take a slight right turn at the fountain, which honors mountaineering legend Ulrich Inderbinen (for more on Inderbinen, see the Matterhorn Museum listing, later). Walk up the street.

The narrow lanes through here are lined with traditional wooden buildings called *mazots*, built between the 16th and 18th centuries. As you explore, you'll notice several buildings labeled according to their former purpose. Before the tourism boom, you'd have seen houses built with hand-hewn larch trees. Foundations were made by stacking local quarried stone, set on stilts with "plate stones" to keep rodents out of storage huts (filled with tasty corn, cheese, and meat). Staircases were on the outside to save space on the heated inside.

Elsewhere in town, you'll see several *mazots* perched around Hotel Romantica, and on the walk up to—and around—the Winkelmatten area. The valley's best and most scenically situated clusters of *mazots* are in the hamlets of Blatten and Zum See, just below the Furi gondola station, and in Zmutt below the Schwarzsee gondola station (see the "Zermatt Area" map, later).

• *Walk uphill on Hinterdorfstrasse until you reach busy Bahnhofstrasse again. Turn left on this main drag as the street narrows, and pass through Zermatt's nightlife district until the street opens up into a big square (with a church at its far end).*

Church Square (Kirchplatz): As you enter the square, notice the two grand 19th-century hotels. **Monte Rosa Hotel,** on your right, was Zermatt's first (1838). The **Grand Hotel Zermatterhof,** facing it on the left in the small park, was built a few decades later. Locals thought early tourists would appreciate big, modern, city-type buildings like these. Only later did they realize people came here to escape the urban environment and enjoy woody chalet-type hotels, as is now the standard.

The plaque on Monte Rosa honors the Englishman **Edward Whymper.** He fell in love with the Matterhorn and, in 1865, set out from this hotel for the first ascent of that mountain. On the way down, four of Whymper's party of seven fell to their deaths. (You'll see their names listed on bronze markers along Bahnhofstrasse.) The news put Zermatt on the map and mountain lovers soon began flocking here. Now, each year several thousand attempt to climb the iconic mountain. While most make it, about a dozen die trying.

Now walk to the far end of the square. The **Matterhorn Museum** fills the sunken building at the corner of the square, under an angled glass roof (see listing under "Sights in Zermatt," later). Just above that, at street level, enjoy Zermatt's beloved **marmot fountain.**

Straight ahead is the **Parish Church (Pfarrkirche) of St. Mauritius.** Built in 1913, this replaced an earlier church that dated back to the 13th century. Its central location makes it a hub of local activity—from weddings to concerts. Inside, the ceiling features a cheerful painting of Noah's Ark, by Paolo Parente.

Beyond the church stands the **City Hall** *(Gemeindehaus).* And just beyond that are three community information boards that illustrate how, behind the crowds of tourists, a real community lives and works here. They list everything from report dates for military reserve training to upcoming ballot measures (the Swiss love participating in their democracy) to childcare services. While it's a little old-fashioned, it's a far cry from the days when such news would be hollered from the steps of the City Hall by the local herald.

Backtrack to the marmot fountain. Nearby, in front of the church, notice the standard **yellow signpost**—which you'll find at every trail intersection in the high country—telling the altitude (1,616 meters) and how long it takes to hike to nearby points.

Walk downhill on **Kirchstrasse,** between the side of the church and the museum. You'll pass a park on your left with several "sister cities" plaques.

• *Turn right immediately behind the church to reach the...*

Mountaineers' Cemetery: This is dedicated to great climbers and mountain guides, many of whom died on the mountain (and many of whom were English). It's worth a thoughtful wander. The lovingly tended graves are adorned with flowers and lit by glowing votive lanterns at night. Look for "the tomb of the unknown climber" (bottom corner, nearest the fence).

• *For our walk's grand finale, keep going downhill. Pause when you get to the middle of...*

Church Bridge (Kirchbrücke): On your left, you'll see a much larger **cemetery.** Space here is very limited; notice the several compact rows of available space, all ready for future occupants. While an unusual use of valuable real estate in the heart of such a touristy city, this is a poignant reminder that this is also a place where people spend their lives.

Now turn 180 degrees and enjoy a fantastic, famous view of the **Matterhorn**—with the Matter Vispa River trickling down from those foothills and gushing under your feet. The bridge even has a special platform that allows more people to crowd in for the ultimate Matterhorn selfie.

• *There's one more landmark worth knowing about: It's the multistage lift to* **Matterhorn Glacier Paradise,** *about a 10-minute walk farther up the valley (see listing under "High Mountain Activities in Zermatt," later). You can follow the river partway, or—for the most direct route—cross the bridge, turn right at the Spar Express grocery, and follow Schluhmattstrasse past a couple dozen hotels. Buses and taxis also go there from the town center.*

Sights in Zermatt

Consider the following options for when the weather is not cooperating with an alpine adventure—or for when you return from a busy morning high in the Alps. Besides the sights listed below, other bad-weather options include walking up and out of town until you hit the cloud cover (the hamlet of Winkelmatten is a pleasant 20-minute stroll from the Catholic church), catching a movie, and/or taking a dip in one of the big hotel pools (nonguests can enjoy for a fee; get advice from TI).

▲▲Matterhorn Museum
This fun and interesting museum is the town's best indoor activity, and worth at least an hour of your time, especially on a rainy day. Most of the museum is underground—the idea is that it's like an archaeological dig where you can unearth the history of Zermatt and its famous mountain. There are also reproductions of an old hotel and church from Zermatt's past. Exhibits show off typical village furnishings, tools, and stuffed alpine fauna, and detail the local prehistory and geology. The museum brings you back to the 19th century, when Zermatt saw the advent of mountaineering and the golden age of tourism. Quite suddenly, what had been a tiny, backwater village became a major destination, known worldwide.

Cost and Hours: 10 CHF, covered by Swiss Travel Pass, includes audioguide download for your smartphone; hours vary but likely open daily 14:00-18:00 in summer, 15:00-18:00 in shoulder season, closed off-season; under glass dome at Kirchplatz 11, across from Catholic church, +41 27 967 4100, www.zermatt.ch/museum.

Visiting the Museum: Pick up the free English flier and head downstairs. The museum's main hall is filled with little *mazots* (those stone-roofed huts you've seen all around town). Each hut houses an exhibit, and throughout, you'll pass taxidermied mountain animals. Circling the huts roughly clockwise, you'll see:

The Mule Driver's House features a relief map of Zermatt's valley, offering a helpful topographic overview.

In the **Mountain Guides' House,** press the buttons to see the different routes up the Matterhorn. Consider that even now, only about half the people who attempt this climb make it to the top. Find the picture (a rare one in color) of local hero Ulrich Inderbinen, who climbed the Matterhorn more than 370 times, the last when he was—no kidding—90 years old. (Inderbinen died in 2004 at age 104; a fountain in the Hinterdorf area of town honors him.)

The **Alpine Museum** displays artifacts found after deadly accidents, with a room dedicated to July 14, 1865—the day the Matterhorn was finally conquered by a team of seven climbers. (Four of them died on the descent, when the least-experienced among them fell, dragging three others to their deaths; you can see the snapped rope in a glass case.)

In the mockup of the belle-époque **Monte Rosa Hotel,** short movies play. Just beyond that is a corridor with WCs; don't miss the display case in this hall that holds a collection of Matterhorn memorabilia and products.

The **Alpine Dairy** captures life for summer cheesemakers on the high Alps. From here, circle back through more huts. The Living Area shows how people cohabitated in a very small space. You'll then cut through a replica chapel and peek inside the Priest's House—which doubled as a sort of guesthouse for the very first visitors (scientists and scholars) to Zermatt.

Finally, go back into the hotel and head upstairs. More exhibits wrap around the space on an upper walkway, which eventually brings you back to the entrance/exit.

Forest Fun Park Zermatt

This high-ropes park has zip lines and a good range of ropes courses at various difficulty levels. Since it's open in all weather, the park is a great way to enjoy active fun on a rainy day. It's located right under the gondola line to Furi, about 10 minutes past the lift station—you'll hear people screaming through the trees below you on your way up the mountain.

Cost and Hours: 37 CHF, 21 CHF for kids, daily 10:00-19:00, shorter hours or closed off-season, Zen Stechenstrasse 110, +41 27 968 1010, www.zermatt-fun.com.

Gorner Gorge (Gornerschlucht)

This deep, narrow, and dramatic gorge is lined with a skinny wooden walkway over its river so hikers can enter at one end and walk about 15 minutes (past a waterfall and whirlpools) to the other. You can enter and leave at either end or just go in and out from the bottom. It's about 15 minutes beyond the top end of Zermatt and on the path down from the Furi gondola station. This is especially worth considering if you're hiking to or from Furi (well signed, right under the gondola). Wear sturdy shoes as the visit (allow 15-20 minutes) involves steep stairs and potentially slippery walkways.

Cost and Hours: 5 CHF, daily 9:15-17:45, closed off-season, +41 27 967 2096, www.gornergorge.ch.

High-Mountain Activities in Zermatt

Think of the Zermatt region's many lifts and hikes in terms of the three high-mountain summit stations to which they're linked: **Matterhorn Glacier Paradise** (the highest and closest to the Matterhorn), **Gornergrat** (the historic train that goes to 10,000 feet), and **Rothorn** (farthest up the valley from the Matterhorn). For a quick comparison of these three summit experiences, see the "Which Lift?" sidebar near the beginning of this chapter. While prices are steep, the community has invested hundreds of millions of dollars in their mountain lifts. They're state of the art, they manage crowds well, and experiencing them is unforgettable. Strategies for enjoying each of these are laid out below.

Weather Watch: Whichever excursions you opt for, pay close attention to the weather—the lifts aren't cheap, and none of them is worth it if the Matterhorn is completely socked in. If the weather's iffy, confirm that the entire route is open before you buy a summit ticket—upper segments can close if it's too windy (though the Gornergrat train and some Klein Matterhorn lifts usually keep running).

That said, don't wait for perfectly clear skies to head into the

The Lowdown on High-Altitude Hiking

Here are some tips for staying safe and getting the most out of your Swiss mountain adventure:

- A waterproof/windproof outer layer will protect you from the Alps' unpredictable weather, and hiking boots are a must for rocky terrain. No matter how warm it might be in the valley, take extra layers for cold weather at the top.
- June through September are the best months for hiking in the Alps, though at high altitudes snow can make hiking difficult any time of year.
- The weather can be unpredictable, but locals can give you a general idea of what to expect. You can find weather reports in English at www.meteoswiss.admin.ch. It's also smart to check live webcams such as the ones at www.zermatt.ch.
- Consider renting (or bringing from home) hiking poles for steep or uneven trails. European hikers swear by these.
- Know the symptoms of altitude sickness: shortness of breath, headaches, fatigue, and—in serious cases—confusion and ataxia (not being able to walk straight). Having plenty of water is a must, and ibuprofen, acetaminophen, or aspirin can combat headaches.
- A network of huts throughout the Swiss Alps provides meals and a place for hikers to sleep (see www.sac-cas.ch). Be aware these can be pricey.
- Many trails cross through fields of cattle. Hikers are expected to close gates after passing through. Keep your distance from cows, especially if calves are nearby. If they're in your way, try to pass without making any sudden movements or loud noises.

hills—even in bright, sunny weather, the Matterhorn loves playing peek-a-boo behind the clouds, and often wears a puffy crown. (It's shaped like a hook and grabs onto passing clouds.) As long as some part of the Matterhorn is visible, local hoteliers like to say, "Clouds add drama!" If it's at least sunny-ish, get up the mountainside.

Be Prepared: Even when it's balmy in the valley, take cold-weather gear if you're heading up the mountainside. It's chilly and often windy (even at the lower elevations).

Passes and Tickets: It can be tricky figuring out the best ticketing option for your excursion. Consult the TI to determine whether you should buy a pass covering multiple lifts, or individual tickets.

A **Peak Pass** gives you unlimited access to all lifts in the area, bike transport, and use of the local bus (July-Aug: 216 CHF/1 day, 241 CHF/2 days, longer versions available; prices are about 10 percent cheaper in June and Sept-Oct and about 20 percent cheaper

Nov-May; 25 percent discount on any pass with Swiss Travel Pass; 5-CHF refundable card deposit, www.matterhornparadise.ch). You can purchase the pass online or in person at the Zermatt TI, the train station in Täsch, or the base stations for all three lifts/trains.

Another pass option—available July-Aug—is the **Peak2Peak** ticket: a one-day pass covering the trains/lifts for the Matterhorn Glacier Paradise and the Gornergrat, as well as the Riffelberg Express gondola that connects them (197 CHF, half-price with Swiss Travel Pass; slightly cheaper version available Dec-April; this ticket is not sold—and Riffelberg Express does not run—May-June or Sept-Nov).

Even with the freedom and ease of a pass, it pays to consider **individual tickets** (lift prices are listed later). Keep in mind that Swiss Travel Pass holders pay half-price on full-fare individual tickets and the Peak2Peak ticket but get only a 25 percent discount on the Peak Pass. While they don't like to advertise it, all three mountain excursions offer discounted prices if you're ascending later in the afternoon—always ask. (They don't stack discounts, and the Swiss Travel Pass half-price is better than the afternoon deal.)

Connecting the Mountainsides: I've described the three main excursions as separate experiences, but you could connect them to make the most of a sunny day. In the peak of summer, the Gornergrat railway connects to the Klein Matterhorn hillside and lifts via the **Riffelberg Express** gondola, running between Riffelberg and Furi (26.50 CHF, half-price with Swiss Travel Pass, also covered by Peak2Peak ticket—see above; runs July-Aug only from 8:30 to 16:30, last descent at 16:45).

Hikers can connect the Gornergrat hillside with Sunnegga, on the slopes of the Rothorn, via the moderately strenuous two-hour **Naturweg hike** (described later, under "Hikes from Sunnegga").

MATTERHORN GLACIER PARADISE

An excursion to what's branded as Matterhorn Glacier Paradise (the summit station for the Klein—"Little"—Matterhorn) has several highlights: the summit (with views across the top of the Alps and a few fun indoor/outdoor activities), the halfway point at Schwarzsee (a nice spot to bask in Matterhorn views), hikes down the mountainside (including my favorite, the Matterhorn Trail from Schwarzsee), and the multistage lift ride itself, which takes you from the valley floor to dizzying heights...with Matterhorn views most of the way. (Note that by the time you visit, the lift may extend all the way over the border and down into Italy.)

The Matterhorn Glacier Paradise is impressive but expensive. If you've visited the Berner Oberland's Schilthorn and/or Jungfraujoch (or France's Aiguille du Midi) in clear weather, the trip up

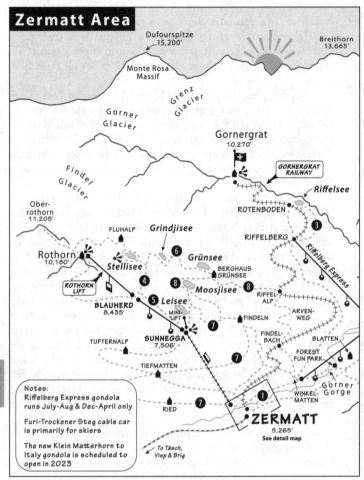

Zermatt Area

Dufourspitze
15,200'

Breithorn
13,665'

Monte Rosa Massif

Grenz Glacier

Gorner Glacier

Findel Glacier

Gornergrat
10,270'

GORNERGRAT RAILWAY

Riffelsee

ROTENBODEN

Ober-rothorn
11,205'

FLUHALP

Grindjisee

❻

RIFFELBERG

Riffelberg Express

❸

Rothorn
10,180'

Stellisee

Grünsee

BERGHAUS GRÜNSEE

ROTHORN LIFT

❹

❽

Moosjisee

RIFFEL-ALP

❽

ARVEN-WEG

BLAUHERD
8,435'

❺ *Leisee*

MINI-LIFT

FINDELN

TUFTERNALP

SUNNEGGA
7,506'

❼

FINDEL-BACH

BLATTEN

FOREST FUN PARK

TIEFMATTEN

❼

WINKEL-MATTEN

Gorner Gorge

Notes:
Riffelberg Express gondola runs July-Aug & Dec-April only

Furi-Trockener Steg cable car is primarily for skiers

The new Klein Matterhorn to Italy gondola is scheduled to open in 2023

❼

RIED

ZERMATT
5,265'
See detail map

To Täsch, Visp & Brig

to this summit may not be as worthwhile for the high price tag. But you could still consider riding partway up to the Schwarzsee midpoint.

Lift Stages: There are several stages (six to eight minutes each, all run continuously). The entire journey—from the **Glacier Paradise lift station** in Zermatt to the top station at Klein Matterhorn—takes approximately 50 minutes.

The lift trip starts with a gondola ride. You'll stay in the same gondola as it passes through several stations: First you'll ascend over glacier-carved foothills to **Furi.** Then you'll go above the tree line, and with smashing glacier views on your left, up to **Schwarzsee,** with its point-blank Matterhorn views, a humble restaurant with a big terrace, and trails leading back down the mountain. From

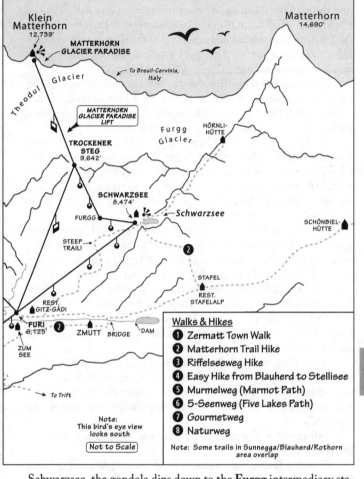

Walks & Hikes
1. Zermatt Town Walk
2. Matterhorn Trail Hike
3. Riffelseeweg Hike
4. Easy Hike from Blauherd to Stellisee
5. Murmelweg (Marmot Path)
6. 5-Seenweg (Five Lakes Path)
7. Gourmetweg
8. Naturweg

Note: Some trails in Sunnegga/Blauherd/Rothorn area overlap

Note: This bird's eye view looks south

Not to Scale

Schwarzsee, the gondola dips down to the **Furgg** intermediary station, then soars up to Trockener Steg—where you'll disembark.

Trockener Steg has free WCs and the Info Cube, a free attraction with hands-on exhibits and a virtual-reality journey over the glacier. When you're ready to continue your trip, board the sleek cable car up to the **Klein Matterhorn summit.** As you ascend, you'll enjoy great views on the left side over glaciers and across to the Gornergrat train station. (For even more thrills, you can pay extra for a "crystal ride" in a special cabin with see-through glass panels in the floor; 10 CHF one-way, 15 CHF round-trip—purchase either at the base station or before boarding the cable car at Trockener Steg.)

Note: At certain times of year, there's a **direct cablecar from Furi to Trockener Steg.** As this is designed for skiers heading up first thing in the morning, it typically only runs very early and can be crowded (often stops running by 8:00 or 9:00). I'd rather stay on the multistage gondola to relax and enjoy the ride, but if your timing is right and you're trying to pack a lot into one day, this shortcut may be a good option.

Returning to the valley the way you came, consider hopping off at Schwarzsee for a hike, or at Furi for a hike or meal (all described later). From the base station, the elevators across the street lead to a taxi stand and bus stop to return to town.

Cost: A peak-season (July-Aug) round-trip ticket between Zermatt and the Matterhorn Glacier Paradise summit costs 120 CHF; Zermatt to Schwarzsee is 61 CHF round-trip (40 CHF one-way). All tickets are about 10 percent less in spring and fall, and half-price with the Swiss Travel Pass. If heading up in the afternoon, ask about discounts.

Hours: The Klein Matterhorn lifts are open daily year-round. In summer (May-mid-Oct) they generally start running at 8:30, with the last ride up between 16:00 and 16:30, and the last ride down at 16:15-16:30 (from the summit) and 17:00-18:00 (from Furi). Note that the two stretches of gondola (from Furi to Schwarzsee, and from Schwarzsee to Trockener Steg) only run June to mid-Oct. The direct cable car between Furi and Trockener Steg keeps its own schedule—check times carefully if planning to take this shortcut.

Remember, the **Riffelberg Express** gondola—a spur line connecting Furi up to Riffelberg, on the Gornergrat hillside—runs only in July and August, and during the winter ski season, but not May-June or Sept-Nov (see "Connecting the Mountainsides," on page 257).

Information: For detailed schedule and price info, go to www.matterhornparadise.ch.

Getting There: The base station for the gondola to Furi (and Schwarzsee) is about three-quarters of a mile upriver from the Zermatt train station: Walk up Bahnhofstrasse to the Catholic church, cross the bridge, and follow the river from there. The gradually uphill walk takes 10 to 15 minutes from the town center. Otherwise, you can catch an e-bus (see "Getting Around Zermatt," earlier).

Trip Tips: It's always frigid and often windy at the summit—bring cold-weather gear no matter how pleasant it might be in the valley. Consider packing a lunch, as the summit's restaurant is expensive and crowded. Save money by using the free WCs at the Schwarzsee or Trockener Steg stations rather than the 2-CHF WCs at the summit.

Since the area around the summit stays snow-covered all year long, there are no real hiking opportunities up top (but there are some great hikes on your way down—especially at Schwarzsee, described later). However, all that snow means that you can usually get in some summer skiing (rent gear in town—there are no rentals up top—and get an early start, before the snow turns slushy).

▲▲▲Matterhorn Glacier Paradise Summit (12,739 feet)

The highest cable-car station in Europe perches near the pointy top of the Klein Matterhorn. Be warned: Some visitors are disappointed by the view of the "real" Matterhorn from the summit, because it's not the classic postcard profile. (For views of the Matterhorn you imagined, visit the intermediate Schwarzsee stop.)

Exiting the cable car, you step into a long tunnel carved out of granite—similar to the surface on which climbers hang. Go ahead and grip it. To the left is a "cinema lounge," with cozy pod seats suspended from the ceiling and several short films about high adventure in the area (skippable unless you're killing time waiting for clouds to clear). Most attractions are to the right: First, the elevator to the observation deck; then the **$$$** "Ice" restaurant and shop (with pricey WCs); and finally the entrance to the Glacier Palace and the exit to the snow fields, where shivering tourists venture out to walk under ski lifts.

Observation Deck (Panorama-Plattform): The undisputed highlight of the Matterhorn Glacier Paradise, this perch offers 360-degree views of the Alps. On a clear day, you can see Italy and France (including Mont Blanc, the Alps' highest peak), as well as the "back" of the Berner Oberland's Jungfrau and Mönch peaks. To get here, ride the elevator, then climb up the 42 metal steps.

Here's a quick spin-tour of the view from the top. Begin by facing the large **cross,** with a reminder to "Be More Human" (*mehr Mensch sein*)—a humbling thought when you're surrounded by nature's majesty. To the left of the cross is the Matterhorn, with a little bit of Zermatt poking out in the valley far below. To the right of the cross, you can see the **Gornergrat** (look for the building with silver turrets on the corners). If you've ridden the cogwheel train up there already, follow your route, and notice how the main, upper part of the Gorner glacier is tucked just out of view from this vantage point. It's hidden behind the pointy peak called **Breithorn** (13,661 feet). Notice intrepid mountain climbers scaling its back, like ants climbing a snowy anthill. Pan right to look out over a vast snow field (with the concrete elevator shaft in the middle). Looking in this direction, you're surrounded on three sides—virtually your entire field of vision—by Italy. (Zermatt fills a small nub of Switzerland that pokes into its neighbor.) Farther to the right, in the distance, is the **Testa Grigia** lift station. From here, lifts descend all the way to the village of Breuil-Cervinia—Italy's Zermatt doppelgänger. (By the time you visit, the cable car connecting this lift station to that one may be up and running.) Spinning farther right, look for the **Trockener Steg** lift station, which connects the place where you're standing to Zermatt in the valley far below. And finally, of course, is the giant triangular **Matterhorn.**

Glacier Palace (*Gletscher-Palast*): A tunnel carved 50 feet below the glacier surface, this attraction brags that it's the "highest glacial grotto in the world." You'll walk deep into the tunnel, where a maze of corridors hides some fun ice sculptures (including one of the Matterhorn—handy if the real one's socked in). This area, with some low-impact information boards, is fun to explore but not exactly thrilling. Look for the small Hindu shrine and the ice tube that you can slide down

(find the pads at the bottom end to sit on as you go down).

Matterhorn Glacier Ride II
A tri-cable gondola continuing the Klein Matterhorn journey may be open by the time you visit. It goes over the Theodul glacier as it descends 1,190 feet to Testa Grigia (11,345 feet), just over the border in Italy. From here, lifts descend to the Italian town of Breuil-Cervinia. This is not intended for through passengers—in fact, luggage will likely be forbidden—so the gondola will function mainly as an international extension of the existing Klein Matterhorn day trip from Zermatt.

▲Schwarzsee Ridge (8,474 feet)
Roughly halfway to the Klein Matterhorn summit is the gondola station of **Schwarzsee** (named for the alpine lake nearby). Though much lower in elevation than the top station, this area is the closest you can get to the Matterhorn by lift. A short walk below the station is a **$$** restaurant with rustic mountain food and a big view terrace, plus a lovely picnic spot near the station—making this a great pit stop on your way up or down the mountain. It's also the starting point for one of the best hikes in the area, the Matterhorn Trail (described next). Shorter walks back to town from the gondola station at Furi are also worthwhile (described later).

▲▲Matterhorn Trail Hike (2-3 hours)
This moderately strenuous hike (#29 on local signs and maps) goes from Schwarzsee via Stafel to either Furi (2 hours), where you can ride the gondola back into town, or all the way to Zermatt (3 hours total), either via Zmutt or Furi. (From Schwarzsee, avoid the trail that leads directly down to Furi—it's much steeper than it is fun.)

From the Schwarzsee station, head down to the lake, then follow *Matterhorn Trail* signs to Stafelalp (the name of the hillside and the restaurant). A little farther down the path, ignore the red signs pointing to Stafelalp—red signs are for skiers—and stay on the main road. At the first major fork, about 30 minutes into your hike, a wooden sign off to the right points to the shortest path to Restaurant Stafelalp (20 minutes from here, near the mini village of Stafel), which takes you through a fascinating pocket of mossy hillocks, ponds, and bubbling streams.

From the restaurant, follow signs to *Furi* and *Zmutt*. After about 30 minutes you'll need to make a choice: Head downhill to cross over a dam and on to the cute hamlet of Zmutt (25 minutes); or stay on the path to the gondola at Furi (which becomes hike #29a after the fork; about 40 mostly level minutes). I recommend taking the Zmutt fork, as it is a joy—an almost tourist-free time warp (with a restaurant or two as well as a fine cluster of traditional *mazot* buildings); from there, it's about an hour down to Zermatt.

Furi (6,125 feet)

There's not much to see at this lift station—it's in a wooded area, with the Matterhorn out of view—but it offers an opportunity for a hike back down to Zermatt (described next). It also has a fine restaurant, worth considering on your way back down.

Eating in Furi: There are a couple of straightforward restaurants, with sunny terraces, next to the Furi lift station. But for a better meal, it's worth a 10-minute, gently uphill walk to $$$ **Restaurant Gitz-Gädi.** Attached to an upscale ski hotel, this restaurant has attentive service and excellent regional dishes, plus creative spins on *cordon bleu* (some using local raclette cheese). There's delightful seating both inside and outside on the terrace. It's popular, so during peak season, call ahead before hiking up here (daily 8:00-19:30, +41 27 966 28 00). Another foodie destination in Furi—closer to the lift station—is $$$$ **Aroleid,** expected to reopen in 2023 (www.aroleid-kollektiv.ch).

▲Furi to Zermatt Hike (1 hour)

If returning to Zermatt via Furi, you can either take the gondola from Furi or hike a pleasant hour, past the adorable hamlets of Zum See and Blatten (and its restaurant) and the Gorner Gorge (see listing under "Sights in Zermatt," earlier). The trail is steep, stony, and stepped at times.

GORNERGRAT

The Gornergrat has been wowing visitors since 1899. Located between the Klein Matterhorn and the Rothorn, it's not inherently better than the neighboring peaks, but it's a best-of-all-worlds experience. It's a simple half-hour cogwheel train ride from downtown Zermatt to the summit. The ride itself is spectacular, with

Matterhorn views most of the way. And the summit comes with two main highlights: the views from the top station, and the Riffelseeweg hike between the Rotenboden and Riffelberg stops partway up. Because the train runs relatively late, the Gornergrat can be a good choice for travelers who want to squeeze in a lift before dinner (though things get quieter up top after about 16:00, and trains run less frequently later in the day—see "Hours," below).

Train Stations: A cogwheel train takes you from Zermatt steeply up to the Gornergrat summit (10,270 feet) with stops at Findelbach, Riffelalp, Riffelberg, and Rotenboden. On the way up, sit on the right side for great Matterhorn vistas.

Cost: Peak-season (June-Aug) trips up to the Gornergrat station cost 126 CHF round-trip (110 CHF in May and Sept-Oct; no round-trip discount). If combining a Gornergrat trip and a Matterhorn Glacier Paradise visit on the same day via the Riffelberg Express, consider the Peak2Peak ticket (described earlier, under "Passes and Tickets").

Hours: Trains run daily year-round, departing 2-3/hour from early June to mid-Oct, with the first ascent at about 7:00 and the last descent around 20:00 (after 17:30, trains run only hourly); off-season, there are fewer departures and the last descent is around 19:00. The Riffelberg Express gondola runs only in July-Aug and Dec-April; see "Connecting the Mountainsides," earlier.

Information: +41 848 642 442, www.gornergratbahn.ch.

Getting There: The Gornergrat train station is right across the street from Zermatt's train station.

▲▲Gornergrat Top Station (10,270 feet)

From the train platform, head up to the large hilltop building with the silver turrets—either follow the serpentine path, or ride the elevator, located in the first building you come to. (For an even better view, you can hike up to the stone terrace up above.) The sweeping panorama includes excellent views of the Matterhorn (though it's not *quite* the perfect profile that you see from the Rothorn). You're also up close to the *other* big mountain in the neighborhood, Monte Rosa, the highest point in Switzerland

(15,200 feet). And from here you have the best possible look at the Gorner glacier, a thousand-foot sheer drop below the platform. Observe the slow-motion rivers of ice that flow across the mountaintops between here and the Matterhorn.

The main building houses shops, a hotel, and—upstairs—a **$$$$ restaurant** and a **$$$ self-serve buffet.** Nearby is a small chapel and, just below, the **Zoom the Matterhorn** attraction. It features hands-on exhibits (such as a mini rock-climbing wall and a station where you can smell various mountain flowers and herbs); a wrap-around movie about the Matterhorn in all four seasons; and a virtual paraglider flight (all included in your train ticket, daily 9:45-16:15).

▲▲▲Riffelseeweg Hike (1.5 hours)

Perhaps my favorite hike in the entire Zermatt region is the Riffelseeweg path (hike #21 on local signs and maps), which usually opens in late June and connects the Rotenboden station to the Riffelberg station. Overall it's an easy hike—for those with good knees—though there's lots of downhill walking (with an elevation loss of 700 feet) on occasionally steep, rocky terrain. But your effort is rewarded with beautiful topography and spectacular Matterhorn views almost the entire way.

Take the train from the Gornergrat summit back down to the Rotenboden station. From there, follow the official Riffelseeweg trail, which is clearly marked at each signpost. (It's not the Swiss Topwalk labeled *#23* toward Riffelalp—don't confuse your Riffels!)

Just down the hillside from the Rotenboden station, you'll pass the pretty lake called Riffelsee—and, if you're lucky, catch the Matterhorn's reflection on its surface. Farther along, you'll pass another little lake and head more steeply downhill. When you reach a fork, take the left/downhill option, marked as *35 minutes to Riffelberg* (don't continue straight ahead for 20 minutes to Riffelberg, which cheats you out of some of the best scenery). From here, you'll descend steeply through a dramatically rocky and rugged landscape with head-on views of the Matterhorn. At the next fork, stay straight (still marked for *Riffelberg*). You'll curl around the side of a hill, then head up a brief uphill stretch, cresting at a meadow. Walk across the meadow and soon the Riffelberg station comes into view.

While most stops on the Gornergrat train line have few services, Riffelberg has WCs, a small shop, and nearby restaurants. From Riffelberg, you can continue by train back into Zermatt, disembark at any point to hike down, or cross over from Riffelalp to Sunnegga, on the Rothorn side, via the Naturweg hike (described later). Or, in summer (July-Aug), you can head over to the Matterhorn Glacier Paradise station via the Riffelberg Express gon-

ZERMATT

dola, which whisks you efficiently to the gondola station at Furi (described on page 257, under "Connecting the Mountainsides").

ROTHORN

Of the main mountain options in the area, the Rothorn (ROTE-horn) hillside offers *the* classic Matterhorn view. It's also less crowded than the Gornergrat. There's

plenty to see and do on an ascent up Rothorn: Its first stage, at Sunnegga, offers the cheapest ride into the mountains—and arguably the best Matterhorn vantage point anywhere. Several hiking trails extend from Sunnegga (described later). Beyond Sunnegga, highlights include the view from the Rothorn summit and the easy loop hike from Blauherd to Stellisee (and on to Fluhalp, if you choose).

The view from Rothorn is fantastic, but it's not that much better than what you see from Blauherd—if you don't have a Peak Pass, you might want to skip the summit and save your time and money for the lower stations.

Lift Stages: The lift system up to Rothorn has three parts: a frequent funicular up to **Sunnegga** (3-6/hour, 8 minutes), a five-minute gondola ride to **Blauherd,** and, finally, a cable car to **Rothorn** (at least 3/hour). If you catch all the connections, you get to the top in about 30 minutes.

Cost: A peak-season (July-Aug) ticket between Zermatt and the Rothorn costs 74 CHF round-trip (49 CHF one-way); Zermatt to Blauherd is 53 CHF round-trip (33 CHF one-way), and Zermatt to Sunnegga is 26 CHF round-trip (18 CHF one-way). All full-fare tickets are about 10 percent cheaper in spring and fall, and half-price with the Swiss Travel Pass. If going in the afternoon, ask about discounts.

Tip: If you intend to tackle the Naturweg hike but don't have a Peak Pass, you'll save money by getting the **Naturweg combo-ticket** in advance to cover your one-way rides between Zermatt and Sunnegga, and between Riffelalp and Zermatt (43 CHF; half-price with Swiss Travel Pass).

Hours: Daily lifts to the summit operate seasonally: The lower-elevation Sunnegga funicular operates late May-late Oct; the middle lift (Sunnegga-Blauherd) stops running in early Oct; and the top lift (Blauherd-Rothorn) runs July-early Oct. From July to mid-Sept, the lifts start running at 8:00, with the last ride to the summit from Blauherd at 16:40, and the last ride down between

16:50 (from Rothorn) and 18:00 (from Sunnegga). Lifts operate on shorter schedules outside those months. Everything is open again for skiers in winter but closes entirely in the shoulder season.

Information: For detailed schedules and pricing, go to www.matterhornparadise.ch.

Getting There: The base station for the Sunnegga-Rothorn funicular is across the river from the Zermatt train station, just downstream from the Gornergrat train tracks—about a five-minute walk from the heart of town.

▲▲Rothorn Summit (10,180 feet)

Atop the Rothorn, there's less to do than at some of the other lift summits, but it's peaceful being immersed in the scenery of the entire Matterhorn massif.

Facing the Matterhorn and looking just to the left, in the foreground you'll see Gornergrat—look for the stations of the cogwheel train marking the route to the top. (The hiking trail called Naturweg connects Blauherd—just below you—with the Riffelalp station on that parallel ridge—see later.) Far below you'll see the Grünsee, a lake with a restaurant (more easily hikeable from Sunnegga than from here). Higher up, the pointy peak marks the Klein Matterhorn summit; you can see the lift stations connecting its Glacier Paradise station to the valley below. And finally, over your left shoulder, check out the giant Findel glacier. The gravelly area behind the restaurant offers better views of this glacier and serves as the launching point for paragliders stepping into thin air. Also up top is a fancy **$$$$ pizzeria,** and some spots where you can picnic on the rocks.

▲▲▲Easy Hike from Blauherd to Stellisee (1 hour)

Probably the best hike on this mountainside is the mostly level walk from the Blauherd station (8,435 feet) to the scenic mountain lake called Stellisee. If you're looking for an "easy" hike in this vertical region, this is about the best you'll do. While the lake itself is modest, it provides a dramatic foreground for Matterhorn photos. The hike to Stellisee, around it, and back again takes less than an hour; you can extend the walk by continuing gradually uphill to the restaurant at Fluhalp, then back again (adds about 20 minutes each way).

From the Blauherd station (with WCs and a small lounge with exhibits on local ecology), head for the giant heart-shaped photo-op cutout on a nearby ridge. From here, turn 180 degrees and follow the path along the ridge under the cables for the Hublot-Express lift (marked for *5-Seenweg* and *Murmelweg*). Just beyond, the path forks; either route gets you there, but the upper one is more interesting and scenic.

After about 15 minutes, you reach the lake called **Stellisee.**

It's pretty in its own right, but on calm days it becomes a reflecting pool for the Matterhorn—walk around to the far end to take in the view. On a nice day, the lakeside boulders make for a picturesque picnic spot.

From here, you could head back the way you came to Blauherd. The return is an utter delight, with head-on Matterhorn views the entire way. (Returning along this upper path, it's easy to get diverted to the gravel road just below, which also leads back to the lift station.)

Or, if you're up for more of a hike, continue to the restaurant hut at **Fluhalp**—the path climbs gently but steadily from here.

Hikes from Blauherd to Sunnegga

Murmelweg (40 minutes): This 1,000-foot descent along the Murmelweg ("Marmot Path") to Sunnegga is a disappointment—just steep enough so you can't enjoy the view, and with no guarantee you'll see the elusive rodents.

5-Seenweg (2.5 hours): Of more interest to hardy hikers is the moderately strenuous, up-and-down 5-Seenweg ("Five Lakes Path"; #11 on local maps). The trail zigzags across the Findelbach valley as it connects five alpine lakes: Stellisee (described earlier), Grindjisee, Grünsee (with the appealing Berghaus Grünsee restaurant), Moosjisee, and Leisee. The 5-Seenweg covers much of the same ground as the Naturweg hike described later, but in reverse (overall downhill, rather than up from Sunnegga), and looping between Blauherd and Sunnegga rather than continuing all the way across to Riffelalp on the Gornergrat side.

▲▲▲Sunnegga Viewpoint (7,506 feet)

This stop, just uphill from Zermatt at the end of the in-mountain funicular (just an eight-minute ride), is the cheapest of all the lifts from Zermatt, but it's quite possibly the best spot anywhere to enjoy the classic Matterhorn view. (It's also the starting point for several great hikes, described next.)

From the Sunnegga lift station, you can go through the tunnel (following the *Wolli* sheep signs) to take a free mini-lift down to a lakeside picnic-and-play area with nice views. Or you can eat at the self-service **$$$ buffet**. The outdoor terrace is ideal for a hot drink with just about the best view you can get.

▲▲Hikes from Sunnegga

Gourmetweg Hike (Sunnegga-Zermatt, 2.5 hours): This popular hike is mostly gentle, taking you through deserted villages, among larch forests, and past several restaurants. If you follow the official #6 path via the hamlet of Ried, it takes about 2.5 hours. You can cut the walk shorter by following signs off the route to steeper paths back to Zermatt.

The first part, leading through several sleepy hamlets, has fantastic Matterhorn views but is confusingly signed. Near the start of the hike, a fork points left (signed *Paradies*), but either path will take you to the same spot farther down the Gourmetweg trail. A little farther along (with the village of Findeln below you), a sign shows the Gourmetweg going downhill on a low road and also on a higher path—take the low road.

Not long after Findeln, with the ravine on your left, there are two spots where you can cut the walk short and hike steeply down into town via the Winkelmatten neighborhood (about 50 minutes to reach central Zermatt). If you continue on the Gourmetweg toward Ried, be warned that the trail turns into a relatively tedious forest walk, albeit over soft, fragrant pine needles. You have one last chance at a more direct route (via Tiefmatten) into town but after that, resist the urge to follow downhill paths off the main trail—some of these seeming shortcuts are knee killers, and ultimately won't save time.

Naturweg Hike (Sunnegga-Riffelalp, 2 hours): With enough up and down to get your heart pumping, the #19 Naturweg trail connects Sunnegga with Riffelalp. From the cute lake called Leisee, just under the Sunnegga station, go crosswise via the unremarkable Moosjisee, then up-up-up toward Grünsee. The path doesn't lead to the lake itself (though it's just a short detour off the trail), but rather to the pleasant Berghaus Grünsee restaurant and mountain refuge—perfectly placed for a well-earned break. From the refuge you're rewarded with an extra-scenic final stretch through forests and on to Riffelalp.

From Riffelalp you can either take the Gornergrat train back to town, or follow one of two good, relatively easy trails all the way into Zermatt (1.5 hours via the Arvenweg, hike #14, or 2 hours via the poorly signed Riffelalpweg, hike #20).

Note that the Naturweg trail overlaps substantially with the 5-Seenweg (hike #11, described earlier) that connects Sunnegga with Blauherd. If you'd like much of the same scenery, but without switching over to the Gornergrat side of the valley (and a different mountain-lift zone), consider that hike instead.

OTHER MOUNTAIN ACTIVITIES
Paragliding
Tandem paragliding down the mountainside is an expensive but unforgettable experience. You pick the altitude of your takeoff point and land back in Zermatt (about 170 CHF from Blauherd

or Riffelberg, 220 CHF from Gornergrat or Rothorn; contact Air Taxi Paragliding, +41 27 967 6744, http://airtaxi-zermatt.ch; or FlyZermatt, +41 27 967 2100, www.flyzermatt.com).

Mountain Biking

The hills above Zermatt are laced with great mountain-bike paths, ranging from moderate to difficult. Bikers can buy day passes or single-ride tickets for riding lifts and transporting bikes. For more information on trails and passes, or to connect with local guides, visit the TI and pick up the helpful bike map. Detailed info on individualized bike tours is available for free on the TI's website (www.zermatt.ch/en/bike).

Summer Skiing

Zermatt's high elevation and variety of runs—and, in winter, the chance to actually ski or snowboard from Switzerland to Italy—make this a popular skiing destination. Summer skiing is usually an option at Matterhorn Glacier Paradise (see listing, earlier, for lift times). A one-day summer lift ticket will run you about 95 CHF; for specifics, see www.matterhornparadise.ch. However, due to extreme temperatures caused by global climate change, 2022 was the first year in recent memory when summer skiing was impossible; it remains to be seen whether this was a fluke...or if the days of summer skiing at the Matterhorn are numbered.

For equipment rental in town, see "Helpful Hints," earlier. For more tips, see the Switzerland in Winter chapter.

Sleeping in Zermatt

Little Zermatt has more than a hundred hotels. This is a resort town, plain and simple, where building after building is for guests (many who rent by the week). You'll pay less at most places early and late in the season (June and Oct), and more during ski season (Dec-late March/early April). Most hotels close in the off-season (early spring and late fall) and many listed below don't have a night reception. Let your hotel know if you plan to arrive after 19:00. For hotel locations, see the "Zermatt" map, earlier.

Town Center

$$$ Hotel Romantica, a flower-dappled, four-story chalet located one scenic (and steep) block up from the main street, offers 13 cozy, traditional alpine rooms with balconies. It's lovingly run and decorated by the Cremonini family—Thor and Michele—who make you feel at home and provide all the modern conveniences. They also rent two tiny alpine cottages (family room, some minimum-stay requirements, elevator, closed May and Nov, Chrum 21,

+41 27 966 2650, www.romantica-zermatt.ch, info@romantica-zermatt.ch).

$$ Schaller's Tannenhof Hotel is ideally located near the main drag, tucked away in tranquil back streets. Its 16 rooms are slick and modern, and its restaurant, in a sunken atrium, surrounds an old cogwheel train car (includes breakfast, elevator, Englischer Viertel 3, +41 27 966 2690, www.tannenhofzermatt.ch, info@tannenhofzermatt.ch).

$ Hotel Le Mazot has nine cozy-if-basic budget rooms with spacious bathrooms, in a quiet location next to the river. The four rooms with stunning Matterhorn-view balconies make this a good value (some shared baths, closed May and Oct, Hofmattstrasse 23, +41 27 966 0606, www.mazot-zermatt.ch, info@mazot-zermatt.ch).

¢-$ Hotel Bahnhof is a respectable budget hotel and hostel in a remodeled building with four floors (but no elevator) across the street from the train station. There are 17 tidy, alpine-style rooms (those without bath have Matterhorn-view balconies) and three dorm rooms. The basement features a relaxing lounge, a dining room, and a large guests' kitchen. It's well-run, but management is offsite at night—so if the younger crowd comes back late after partying, you're on your own (family rooms, no breakfast, nice showers, closed May and Oct-Nov, Bahnhofplatz 54, +41 27 967 2406, www.hotelbahnhofzermatt.com, welcome@hotelbahnhofzermatt.com, Lauber family).

Across the River

These places are only slightly farther from the train station—still walkable, but more comfortable by e-car. Ask your hotel if they can provide a transfer (either free, or for a fee), or consider a taxi at the station. On foot, follow Bahnhofstrasse all the way up to the Catholic church and take a left onto Kirchstrasse. Cross the river and walk up Kirchstrasse one more block to the intersection with Steinmattstrasse. All of these places are within a few minutes' walk from here.

$$$ Hotel Aristella Swissflair, filling a modern chalet-style building, has 28 welcoming rooms (some with Matterhorn views), a staff that works hard to provide extra touches, and an especially nice spa/sauna/wellness center (Steinmattweg 7, +41 27 967 2041, www.aristella-zermatt.ch, info@aristella-zermatt.ch, Perren-Tenisch family).

$$$ Hotel Bellerive feels more stylish and hip, with 25 rooms, a nice lounge, an inviting terrace, and a spa right in the heart of a bustling hotel-and-restaurant zone (elevator, Riedstrasse 3, +41 21 966 7474, www.bellerive-zermatt.ch, info@bellerive-zermatt.ch, Noti family).

ZERMATT

$$ Hotel Jägerhof has 48 homey rooms and seven apartments with a mix of rustic charm and modern comfort. The lounge and restaurant—complete with mounted deer heads—are cozy, and there's a fine winter garden and cute little private fondue chalet. The rooms with balconies are worth the extra cost. They'll pick you up at the train station for no extra fee—use the designated phone at the station (family rooms, elevator, fitness room, Steinmattstrasse 85, +41 27 966 3800, www.jaegerhofzermatt.ch, info@jaegerhofzermatt.ch, Perren family).

$ Hotel Dufour Zermatt, a block higher up from the others, fills a classic chalet that feels like old Zermatt. It has 17 rooms in the original, woody building, plus six more in a newer annex. Rooms are traditional, but with a few modern touches. The winter garden is a fine place to relax (Riedstrasse 35, +41 27 966 2400, www.dufourzermatt.ch, info@dufourzermatt.ch).

¢ $ Zermatt Youth Hostel looks over town from a perch high above the river and offers views of the Matterhorn. The super-modern hostel offers dorm beds and private rooms, most with bathrooms—travelers of all ages will feel comfortable here (no curfew, reception open 7:00-10:00 & 16:00-21:00, Staldenweg 5, +41 27 967 2320, www.youthhostel.ch/zermatt, zermatt@youthhostel.ch). From the station, take the red-line bus marked *Winkelmatten* to the Luchre stop; the hostel is 50 yards uphill from there (follow signs with international hostel symbol).

Eating in Zermatt

Zermatt's restaurants are very expensive. But affordable takeout-type places aren't too hard to find, and you can easily assemble a picnic at one of the town's bakeries or supermarkets.

$$$ Whymper-Stube, named for the first brave soul to conquer the Matterhorn, specializes in raclette and fondue (traditional cheese, as well as meat—which they call "Chinese-style"). It's also a rare place that lets you order a single portion of cheese fondue, rather than for the entire table. This cozy space with a friendly staff attracts mainly tourists, but local regulars warm six barstools in the corner. On evenings in peak season, reservations are smart (kitchen open daily 11:00-21:00 except no lunch service in winter, closed May and mid-Oct-mid-Nov, Bahnhofstrasse 80, in the cellar of the Monte Rosa Hotel, across from the huge Grand Hotel Zermatterhof, +41 27 967 2296, www.whymper-stube.ch).

$$$$ Brasserie Uno is the best of Zermatt's many high-cuisine restaurants. Rising-star chef Luís Romo prioritizes locally sourced ingredients and respects Valais cuisine, but injects his Mexican heritage and other international influences. The result: delicious, thoughtfully prepared meals that balance creativity and tradition. The ambience is casual and inviting, with attentive yet easygoing service. Reservations are essential (Tue-Sat seatings 19:00-19:45, closed Sun-Mon, Kirchstrasse 38, +41 79 851 1768, www.brasserieuno.com).

$$ Grampi's, tucked upstairs a few steps off the main drag, is a bustling restaurant serving Italian specialties. Try a pizza baked in their wood-fired oven or a healthy salad (daily 18:00-24:00, Bahnhofstrasse 70, +41 27 967 7775).

$$$ Restaurant Avena, in the heart of the hotel zone just across the river, has a cozy, country-cutesy interior and a big, covered and heated terrace with some Matterhorn-view tables. The menu is an eclectic mix of traditional Swiss and modern international dishes; they enjoy cooking local game, and the "surprise fixed-price menu" is a hit for adventurous big eaters (Wed-Mon 16:00-24:00, closed Tue, Steinmattstrasse 53, +41 27 967 8333).

$$ Zermatt Kitchen, facing the river right at the old bridge, feels like it could be a trendy big-city café...but the Matterhorn is right out the front door. There's limited indoor seating, tables outside facing the river, and an appealing menu of coffee, cakes, brunch, and lunch dishes (Thu-Mon 9:00-19:00, may also be open for dinner on weekends, closed Tue-Wed, Uferweg 1, +41 766 414 644).

$ Stefanie's Crêperie is understandably popular—sometimes marked with a long line. This little walk-up window in a cellar along Bahnhofstrasse cranks out fresh sweet and savory crêpes that make for a light meal or dessert (no seating, Sun-Fri 13:00-19:00, Sat until 20:00, Bahnhofstrasse 60).

$$ Stadel, although right along the main street, can easily be overlooked—it's unpretentious and nondescript. But this small restaurant with indoor/outdoor seating dishes up homemade Swiss specialties with a smile and at fair prices (daily 12:00-22:00, closed Nov, Bahnhofstrasse 45, +41 27 967 3536).

Bakery: $-$$ Fuchs is a bakery with outposts all over town. They have good pastries and decent sandwiches. Some locations are takeout-only, while the branch along the Gornergrat tracks, just a short walk from the train station, has a little outdoor terrace and table service (daily 7:00-18:30, Getwingstrasse 24).

Kebabs: $ Take It Döner is tucked away just uphill from the Catholic church (daily 11:00-21:00, Oberdorfstrasse 24, cash only).

Supermarkets: A large **Co-op** is in the little mall across from the train station, and **Migros** is across from the tennis courts on Hofmattstrasse. The small **Spar Express,** along the river at the corner of Kirchstrasse and Schluhmattstrasse, is convenient if you're staying at the upper end of town. All are open daily about 8:00-19:00.

Pre- or After-Dinner Drinks: There are only a few parts of town dishing up after-dinner action. **Hexen Bar** caters to a crowd looking for something a bit more traditional. **Elsie's Wine and Champagne Bar** oozes with character; the extensive list of wine and cocktails can be enjoyed inside or out, with views of the Catholic church and Grand Hotel Zermatterhof.

Zermatt Connections

Zermatt is at the end of the Nikolaital valley, which is reached on the narrow-gauge Matterhorn Gotthard Railway (MGB, www. mgbahn.ch). This scenic ride—which follows rivers and waterfalls along the lip of a canyon—is described on page 428 of the Scenic Rail Journeys chapter. **Swiss Rail info:** www.sbb.ch.

By Train: All these trains from Zermatt transfer in Visp. Some have multiple transfers. Trains from Zermatt go to: **Bern** (1-2/hour, 2 hours), **Zürich** (1-2/hour, 3.5 hours), **Montreux** (1-3/hour, 2.5 hours), **Lausanne** (2/hour, 3 hours), **Interlaken Ost** (1-2/hour, 2.5 hours, 2 transfers), **Luzern** (hourly, 3 hours, 2 transfers).

By Glacier Express to Eastern Switzerland: This scenic train departs Zermatt (at least once daily through most of the year, more in summer) and arcs scenically on high-altitude tracks over the middle of Switzerland to the east. All of these Glacier Express trains go through **Chur** (6 hours), then continue either to **Davos** or **St. Moritz** (8 hours total to either). For details, see the Scenic Rail Journeys chapter.

APPENZELL

Appenzell • Ebenalp • Liechtenstein

Welcome to cowbell country. In the moo-mellow and storybook-friendly Appenzell region, you'll find the warm, intimate side of the land of staggering, icy Alps. With just one percent of Switzerland's territory and one percent of its population, the little canton of Appenzell stubbornly celebrates its way of life. You'll see its symbol everywhere: a scary bear walking upright, wielding its sharp claws and teeth. And yet the people here are welcoming. You'll savor Appenzell's cozy, small-town atmosphere—and if there's time, you can stop by one of Europe's smallest nations, Liechtenstein.

Appenzell is one of Switzerland's most traditional regions... and the butt of jokes because of it. Entire villages meet to vote in town squares such as Appenzell town's Landsgemeindeplatz (an event featured on postcard racks). Until 1990, the women of Appenzell were barred from voting on local issues. But in a break from convention, in 2000 Appenzell's schools were the first in Switzerland to make English—rather than distant French—the mandatory second language.

A gentle beauty blankets this region of green, rolling hills, watched over by the 8,200-foot peak of Mount Säntis, Appenzell's highest point. As you travel, you'll enjoy an ever-changing parade of finely carved chalets, colorful villages, and cows mooing, "Milk me." While farmers' daughters make hay, older women with scythes walk the steep roads, looking as if they just pushed the Grim Reaper down the hill. When locals are asked about Appenzeller cheese, they clench their fists as they answer, "It's the best." (It is, without any doubt, the smelliest.)

If you're here in late August or early September, there's a good

Appenzell Region

GERMANY

To Munich

A-96

Lindau

10 Kilometers

10 Miles

Lake Constance

Romans-
horn

13

Rorschach

Bregenz

202

A-14

Gossau

St.
Gallen

St. Marg.

A-1

A-13

Dornbirn

Herisau

Teufen

Altstätten

Stein

Stoss

13

Oberriet

A P P E N Z E L L

Jakobsbad
(LUGE)

Gonten-
bad

Gais

Rankswell

Urnäsch

(BAREFOOT
TRAIL)

Appenzell Town

AUSTRIA

Helmberg

Ebenalp

Brülisau

See Ebenalp
detail map

Wasserauen

Feldkirch

SCHWÄGALP-
STRASSE

Mt.
Säntis

13

191

To Innsbruck
via Arlbergpass

A-14

16

Buchs

Schaan

S W I T Z E R L A N D

Vaduz

LIECHTEN-
STEIN

Sevelen

To Zürich
& Luzern

A-3

A-13

Sargans

Baby
Rhine

A-3

To Chur &
Pontresina

Bern
SWITZ.

To
Winterthur
& Zürich

A-1

E-60

8

8

To
Rapperswil
& Luzern

⚑ Appenzeller Bahnen
⚑ Other Rail
Note: Not all rail lines are shown

chance you'll get to watch (or at least have to slow down for) the ceremonial procession of flower-bedecked cows and whistling herders in formal folk costumes. The festive march down from the high pastures is a spontaneous move by the herding families, and when they finally do burst into town, locals young and old become children again, running joyously into the streets.

PLANNING YOUR TIME

On a two-week trip through Switzerland, save a day for the Appenzell region. This pastoral area has its subtle charms—but it can be anticlimactic after the rugged Berner Oberland or Matterhorn. In the Appenzell region, I prefer overnighting in Appenzell town, which is a more efficient base for getting around the region; however, those up for a mountaintop retreat and rustic accommodations should consider Ebenalp. If you have only a week or less in Switzerland, skip the Appenzell region and head instead for the high mountains.

GETTING AROUND THE APPENZELL REGION

This area is a breeze by **car**—you could see everything in this chapter in one (very busy) day. Notice that the attractions in Stein and Urnäsch and the Kronberg luge ride form a handy little loop to the west of Appenzell town. The lift up to Ebenalp is just to the south.

The regional narrow-gauge **trains** are run by a private operator (Appenzeller Bahnen—Eurail Global Pass and Swiss Travel Pass are valid). A very handy train generally runs twice an hour (except after 19:00, when it's hourly), taking about 50 minutes to connect almost all the destinations I describe. Starting up at Wasserauen (at the base of the Ebenalp lift), it runs through Appenzell town, stopping at Gontenbad (one end of the Barefoot Trail), Jakobsbad (luge ride and other end of the Barefoot Trail), and Urnäsch (folk museum), and then going north to Herisau (change here to reach Luzern) and Gossau (change here to reach Zürich). A separate line runs from Appenzell to the city of St. Gallen.

The one destination in this chapter not well covered by public transportation is Stein (with its folk museum and tourable cheese factory). It is reachable by taxi (for details, see the listing later in this chapter).

Appenzell Town

The center of this authentically Swiss town is a painfully cute pe-

destrian zone lined with colorful, patterned house fronts (rather than the white-painted or wooden facades favored elsewhere). This is a great spot to simply let your pulse slow and enjoy Swiss small-town life. The big square of Landsgemeindeplatz— near many of my recommended restaurants—is where residents gather on the last Sunday of each April to vote on local issues by show of hands. (The rest of the year, it's a parking lot.) A fountain on the square shows an Appenzeller raising his hand to be counted.

Appenzell town is touristy, sure. But from watching the locals robustly greet each other in the streets or laugh over a local beer in the pubs, it's clear this is also a real, living town.

Orientation to Appenzell Town

Appenzell town (pop. 6,000) clusters along its main street, Hauptgasse, which runs from the bridge over the Sitter River to the biggest square, Landsgemeindeplatz. From the middle of this colorful drag, Postgasse (which turns into Poststrasse) heads south to the train station. You can walk from one end of town to the other in about 10 minutes.

TOURIST INFORMATION

The helpful TI is on the main street at Hauptgasse 4 (generally Mon-Fri 9:00-12:00 & 13:30-18:00, Sat-Sun until 17:00, +41 71 788 9641, www.appenzell.ch). Stop by on arrival to ask about special events.

If you stay at least three nights in the region, your hotel or pension will give you an **Appenzell Card.** This card is a great moneysaver, as it covers all local train trips (on trains operated by Appenzeller Bahnen, as far as St. Gallen), rides on three different cable cars, admission to local museums, a ride on the Kronberg luge, a day's bike rental, and more, and it gets you a discount on PubliCar taxi service. It can be well worth extending a two-night stay to three just to get the card.

ARRIVAL IN APPENZELL TOWN

The cute **train station** has a ticket office (Mon-Fri 7:30-18:00, Sat-Sun 8:00-12:15 & 13:15-17:00), WCs, small lockers (the ticket office and TI can store larger bags), and a handy, well-stocked Shop Mercato minimart (daily 6:00-20:00).

If arriving by **car,** ask your hotel about parking. If you're just day-tripping here, leave your car in the pay lot by the brewery just across the river from downtown. Walk across the bridge and veer right onto the main drag, Hauptgasse; the TI is just past the church, on your right.

HELPFUL HINTS

Blue Monday: Some of the region's museums are closed on Monday, but hiking and biking are good any day the sun shines. The folk museum in Urnäsch and the cheese factory in Stein are other good Monday options—and, spring through fall, so are the folk museum in Appenzell town and the Kronberg luge in Jakobsbad (unless it's raining).

When the Cows Come Home: If you're here at the right time of

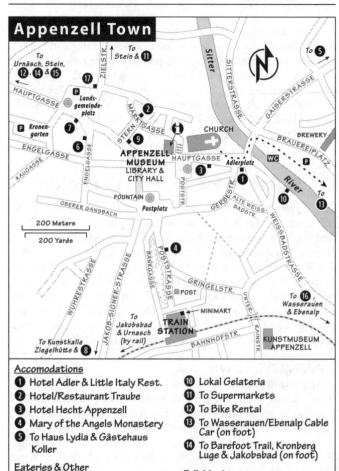

Appenzell Town

Accomodations

1 Hotel Adler & Little Italy Rest.
2 Hotel/Restaurant Traube
3 Hotel Hecht Appenzell
4 Mary of the Angels Monastery
5 To Haus Lydia & Gästehaus Koller

Eateries & Other

6 Gasthaus Hof
7 Café-Hotel Appenzell
8 To Panorama Hotel Freudenberg
9 Drei Könige

10 Lokal Gelateria
11 To Supermarkets
12 To Bike Rental
13 To Wasserauen/Ebenalp Cable Car (on foot)
14 To Barefoot Trail, Kronberg Luge & Jakobsbad (on foot)

Folk Music

15 To Kapuzinerkloster
16 To Hotel Hof Weissbad
17 Romantik-Hotel Säntis

year, you might luck into seeing the festive procession of cows heading up to the high-mountain pastures (*Alpfahrt*, generally late May-early June) or returning from a summer high in the Alps (*Alpabfahrt*, generally late Aug-early Sept). Unfortunately, the cows don't give much advance notice—announcements of the event pop up around town just a few days ahead. There's also the one-day Appenzell cattle show in early October.

Bike Rental: The **train station** has a few electric bikes that can be reserved through the national rail system (see page 491), but don't forget that the Appenzell Card (described earlier) includes a day's free bike rental from several shops in the area (the rail system's bikes are not part of the free program). Some hotels rent bikes or can help you arrange a rental.

For mountain bikes, go to **Neff Zweirad,** a five-minute walk beyond Landsgemeindeplatz (40 CHF/day, e-bike-50 CHF/day; Mon-Fri 7:30-12:00 & 13:15-18:30, Sat until 16:00, closed Sun, shorter hours off-season; Hauptgasse 58, +41 71 787 3477, www.neff-zweirad.ch).

Sights in the Appenzell Region

The Appenzell region has three folk museums—one in Appenzell town, another in Stein, and a third in Urnäsch. All are good, and they're different enough that it's worth considering visiting all three if you have ample time and interest. To be more selective, weigh these differences: Stein's is the biggest, most modern, and probably the best presented (but also the most difficult to reach without a car); Urnäsch's is the most atmospheric, as it's in a creaky old house; and Appenzell town's is the most convenient, giving a good all-around look at the region (it's especially strong on local costumes), but lacking a bit of the charm of the other two.

APPENZELL TOWN
▲Appenzell Museum

This folk moo-seum above the TI provides a fine and efficient look at the local cow culture. Note that its name is similar to the larger Appenzell Folklore Museum in nearby Stein.

Cost and Hours: 7 CHF, covered by Swiss Travel Pass; Mon-Fri 10:00-12:00 & 13:30-17:00, Sat-Sun 11:00-17:00; Nov-March Tue-Sun 14:00-17:00, closed Mon; Hauptgasse 4, +41 71 788 9631, http://museum.ai.ch.

Visiting the Museum: Buy your ticket, borrow the English translations, and ride the elevator all the way up (push button 6). From there, take the stairs to the attic for a collection of coins, measurement instruments, and torture devices. Descend the stairs to check out the excellent collection of traditional costumes, then work your way down through the rest of the exhibits. As you wander, you'll see old flags and banners, reconstructed rustic rooms, woodcarvings, 19th-century peasant art, tools, handmade embroidery, religious art, and (oddly) an Egyptian coffin. One thought-provoking room displays boards called *Rebretter,* which were used to lay out the body of a recently deceased loved one. The boards were painted with the name and information of the deceased and, after the burial, displayed on the family's house.

▲Folk Music

The accordion never really caught on here, making Appenzell's folk music—which still uses older instruments (violin, dulcimer)—unique in Switzerland. Free concerts take place every Thursday (early June-mid-Oct) at 18:30 in the **Kapuzinerkloster** (Capuchin monastery) at the far end of Hauptgasse, at #49; every Wednesday at 20:00 at the ritzy **Hotel Hof Weissbad** (about two miles out of town); and every Saturday (July-Aug) at the **Romantik-Hotel Säntis** (Landsgemeindeplatz 3). The hotel venues require a reservation if you plan to eat dinner. If not, try to persuade the staff to let you have a drink within earshot of the music. You can also ask the TI (or check their website) about other live music options.

Modern Art Museums

Appenzell showcases modern and contemporary art in a museum with two branches: **Kunstmuseum Appenzell** is a silver-clad modern building right behind the train tracks (Unterrainstrasse 5, +41 71 788 1800), and **Kunsthalle Ziegelhütte** is a bit farther out (Ziegeleistrasse 14, +41 71 788 1860).

Cost and Hours: 15 CHF combo-ticket covers both; also covered by Swiss Travel Pass; Tue-Fri 10:00-12:00 & 14:00-17:00, Sat-Sun 11:00-17:00, shorter hours Nov-March, closed Mon year-round; www.h-gebertka.ch.

HIKING

Appenzell makes a good home base for hiking, with gentle hills and pastoral scenery all around. The TI can suggest several easy walks in the region. I recommend two possibilities here.

Appenzell to Wasserauen

This two-hour walk, which takes you to the foot of the Ebenalp cable car (described later), begins near the parish church in Appenzell and leads you along a creek through meadows and forests. The path is well marked. Once you reach Wasserauen, you can take the cable car up to Ebenalp, or simply hop on the train back to Appenzell.

Barefoot Trail (Barfussweg)

This 1.5-hour walk between Jakobsbad and Gontenbad offers a surprising and unusual experience...yes, with your shoes off. The trail leads over meadows, through creeks, and on stretches of asphalted road, in a tranquil valley roughly parallel to the Appenzell-Urnäsch road and rail line. Two specially designed fountains along the way will refresh your feet. The path was inspired by the philosophy of 19th-century therapist Sebastian Kneipp, who sought to treat medical conditions with water of different temperatures and pressures.

To get from Appenzell to the trailhead, take the train to Jakobsbad (1-2/hour, 8 minutes, trailhead right across the street from the train station and the Kronberg luge ticket office—described later), stow your shoes in your pack, and do the barefoot walk to Gontenbad. From Gontenbad, you can ride the train back to Appenzell (4 minutes) or put on your shoes and keep on walking back to town (about another hour).

NEAR APPENZELL TOWN
▲Stein

The unassuming, hill-capping village of Stein has two worthwhile attractions side by side: a cheese-production facility with a visitors center and what's arguably the region's best folk museum. If you don't have a car, use the subsidized taxi service **PubliCar,** which takes passengers to Stein and other locations not serviced by buses (each passenger pays a distance-dependent fare plus a flat fee—about 12 CHF from Appenzell to Stein). To reserve, ask at the TI, call +41 848 553 060, or download the PubliCar app (more info at www.postauto.ch/publicar-appenzell).

Appenzeller Dairy (Appenzeller Schaukäserei)

This is one of several dozen dairies in the area where the well-known Appenzeller cheese is made, and it's set up to explain the process to curious visitors. It's fast, a little smelly, and user-friendly.

Cost and Hours: 12 CHF (includes a small box of cheese containing five samples of various ages), 15 CHF combo-ticket also covers Appenzell Folklore Museum; daily 9:00-18:30, off-season until 17:30; +41 71 368 5070, www.showcheese.ch.

Visiting the Dairy: As you enter, scan the QR code for an English audioguide to the exhibits and ask about the next English showing of the 10-minute video (which treads a fine line between being informative and promotional).

Large, colorful displays trace the cheesemaking process, and you can peer down into the production facility (cheese is generally made 9:00-15:00—most interesting when they pour the contents of the giant vat into the long line of wheel molds). You'll learn how the special pungent flavor of Appenzeller cheese comes from an age-old, secret-recipe herbal brine mixture that's lovingly rubbed on each wheel as it ages. Nibble your cheese samples as you explore, noting how the different ages affect the aroma and taste. Head down the long hallway, where you can watch hundreds of wheels of cheese silently age (and occasionally see them turned by an automated cheese-wheel flipper). You can also collect and keep samples of the herbs used in making the secret brine. The dairy shop sells yogurt, meats, and cold drinks, and the restaurant serves powerful cheese specialties, including fondue.

Appenzell Folklore Museum (Appenzeller Volkskunde Museum)

This fine museum offers a modern, well-presented look at the folk culture in these parts.

Cost and Hours: 7 CHF, 15 CHF combo-ticket also covers Appenzeller Dairy, covered by Swiss Travel Pass; Tue-Sun 10:00-17:00, closed Mon; +41 71 368 5056, www.appenzeller-museum.ch.

Demonstrations: A visit to this museum is best on Saturdays and summer Wednesdays, when cheesemaking demonstrations are

going on (starts at 13:00, most interesting around 15:00). Other craft demonstrations happen daily during the summer starting at 13:30 (Sun at 10:30). Call ahead to confirm the schedules.

Visiting the Museum: Borrow the essential English translations at the entry, then explore the three floors of exhibits. The ground floor is dedicated to local customs and lifestyles. The replica of the alpine cheesemaking hut is used for live demonstrations. There's a huge collection of cowbells, which, according to the explanation, are used for various purposes: to scare off evil spirits, to make the lead cow easier to follow in processions, to more easily find a lost cow..."and anyway, cows like them."

Upstairs is an art collection titled "Peasant Painting 1600-1900," with everything from huge murals from the sides of barns to delicate oil paintings to miniature wood carvings—virtually all featuring pastoral countryside scenes of cheesemaking huts, cows, and rolling meadows. Each of the "naive" (untrained) artists who

created these works is explained in a short bio, which brings the collection to life. You'll see great examples of the brightly painted traditional regional furniture (also easy to find in local hotels and restaurants).

The basement shows off more furniture pieces (in the replica of a traditional bedroom, notice how the colorful paint makes the furniture stand out from the plain wooden walls). But the focus here is local weaving and embroidery. The exhibit explains how embroidery gradually evolved from being simple and handmade to machine-made, as it went from a craft to an industry. The rustic loom and the giant embroidery machine are sometimes used for demonstrations.

Urnäsch

This sleepy one-street town is worth the trip to see what could be one of Europe's cutest museums. It's a 15-minute train ride from Appenzell.

▲Museum of Appenzell Customs (Appenzeller Brauchtumsmuseum)

Located on the town square across from the church, this thoroughly enjoyable museum brings this region's folk traditions to life.

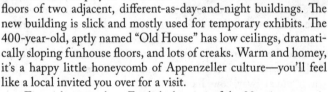

Cost and Hours: 8 CHF, covered by Swiss Travel Pass; Mon-Sat 9:00-11:30 & 13:30-17:00, Sun from 13:30; shorter hours off-season; +41 71 364 2322, www.museum-urnaesch.ch.

Visiting the Museum: Exhibits are displayed on four floors of two adjacent, different-as-day-and-night buildings. The new building is slick and mostly used for temporary exhibits. The 400-year-old, aptly named "Old House" has low ceilings, dramatically sloping funhouse floors, and lots of creaks. Warm and homey, it's a happy little honeycomb of Appenzeller culture—you'll feel like a local invited you over for a visit.

First ask to watch an English showing of the 20-minute movie that explains four of the major regional festivals. The most memorable is Silvesterchläus—the Appenzell New Year, celebrated on January 13 per the old Julian calendar. On this date, local men celebrate by putting on gigantic, cartoonish headdresses and giant cowbells. You'll see some of those costumes—and others—then twist your way up through the tiny halls and staircases, pausing to look at replicas of local rooms, collections of handicrafts and tools, and other slices of Appenzell life. On the top floor of the new building, don't miss the music room, where you can try your hand at traditional musical instruments, including a hammered dulcimer and a coin-in-a-bowl (which, in the right hands, is more musical than you might think). There's no English and barely any German, but it's still fun to explore.

Kronberg Luge Ride (Bobbahn)

Between Appenzell and Urnäsch, in the village of Jakobsbad, you can enjoy a bobsled ride that runs on steel rails spring through fall. Each sled has seatbelts and can carry two people. Two side handles allow you to control the speed: Respect the *Bremsen!* signs—which suggest when to brake. The same entertainment zone includes a chairlift for hikes, as well as a high-ropes course.

Cost and Hours: 9 CHF per sled for adults—two adults can share one sled, 6 CHF per sled for kids—ditto, multiple-ride cards available and shareable; daily 9:00-18:00, shorter hours in spring and fall, closed Nov-March; no rides in rainy weather, +41 71 794 1289, www.kronberg.ch.

Getting There: The luge is just across the tracks from the Jakobsbad station, which is an 8-minute train trip from Appenzell.

Sleeping in Appenzell Town

Sleep in touristy Appenzell town if you want comfort—or for a rustic, high-altitude thrill, opt for the low-tech, no-shower dorms at Ebenalp (listed later). Appenzell town is small and the hotels are central. The B&Bs are a 10- to 20-minute hike from the town center.

HOTELS

$$ Hotel Adler rents 20 rooms in a building that dates from 1562 and boasts a historic fondue cellar (winter only) where you can see a stone floor from an even earlier structure. The hotel has two types of rooms: modern or traditional Appenzeller. Franz Leu, a sixth-generation innkeeper, decorates the halls with fun memorabilia while sons Matjaz and Clemens handle day-to-day business (family rooms, elevator, pleasant garden lounge, small free parking lot, closed Nov and Feb, Weissbadstrasse 2, between TI and bridge on Adlerplatz, +41 71 787 1389, www.adlerhotel.ch, info@adlerhotel.ch). The Adler is also home to the recommended Little Italy restaurant.

$$ Hotel/Restaurant Traube rents seven cozy, tastefully decorated, modern rooms in a very pretty building right in the center of town (**$$$** restaurant with balcony seating, Marktgasse 7, +41 71 787 1407, www.traube-appenzell.ch, info@traube-appenzell.ch).

$$ Hotel Hecht Appenzell rents 38 bright, updated rooms on the main drag, but without the family-run feel (quieter rooms in back, elevator, spacious breakfast room, Hauptgasse 9, +41 71 788 2222, www.hecht-appenzell.ch, info@hecht-appenzell.ch).

¢ Mary of the Angels Monastery offers 19 simple yet appealing rooms a block from the train station. If you're looking for a quiet yet central location, and a way to save some francs, this is a good bet (breakfast extra, family rooms, bathrooms down the hall, Poststrasse 7, +41 71 787 1845, www.kloster-appenzell.ch, gaestehaus@kloster-appenzell.ch).

B&Bs

To experience a pleasant Swiss residential neighborhood, consider the following B&Bs, just east of Appenzell's pedestrian zone. To reach them from the town center (TI/town church), cross the bridge and take a right on Eggerstandenstrasse. You'll reach Gästehaus Koller first (just a few houses down), then—after another 500 yards or so—Haus Lydia. To reach Haus Lydia by public transit, take the train to the Hirschberg station (2 minutes from Appenzell on the line to St. Gallen). From the station, it's a three-minute downhill walk following the tracks.

$ **Haus Lydia** has four guest rooms on the upper floors of a large, traditional home filled with tourist information and a woodsy folk atmosphere, plus a garden with lounge chairs and a view of Ebenalp. The crisp, nicely decorated rooms have a mountain-lodge feel, and are a good value if you have a car or don't mind a 20-minute walk from the town center (great breakfast, Eggerstandenstrasse 53, +41 71 787 4233, www.hauslydia.ch, contact@ hauslydia.ch, friendly Lydia Mock-Inauen). She also rents two roomy apartments by the week (no breakfast).

$ At **Gästehaus Koller,** Stefan and Karin rent four comfortable rooms on the upper floor of their home. Stefan is a carpenter and did much of the woodwork, and his wife, Karin, makes traditional costumes (Eggerstandenstrasse 9, +41 71 787 0222, www. gaestehaus-koller.ch, info@gaestehaus-koller.ch).

Eating in Appenzell

MEALS WITH TABLE SERVICE

Most of the restaurants in Appenzell's old town cater to locals and day-trippers with classic Swiss-German menus and elaborate desserts. Almost every menu features (surprise) the heavenly but oh-so-smelly Appenzeller cheese. The Appenzeller beer is tasty, famous, and about the only thing cheap in the region. Many top restaurants cluster around the big main square (Landsgemeindeplatz). All these places are open until about 22:00-23:00.

$$$ **Gasthaus Hof,** which feels particularly local, has a pleasant beer garden out back. The menu features a bewildering variety of specials, but they are most proud of their cheese dishes—the cozy dining room is filled with the unforgettable aroma of Appenzeller cheese (daily, Engelgasse 4, +41 71 787 4030).

$$$ **Café-Hotel Appenzell** serves from a large menu (in-

cluding salads and vegetarian dishes) in a genteel dining room and at a host of inviting outdoor tables. They also run a pastry shop in one corner of the building (daily, at corner of Landsgemeindeplatz closest to TI, +41 71 788 1515).

$$ Little Italy, at the recommended Hotel Adler, dishes up authentic Italian fare at reasonable prices. Run by Calabria native Stefano and his friendly crew, the restaurant offers a delightful selection of *antipasti*, homemade pastas, pizzas, and gelato. Dine in the bright and cheery dining room or outside on the people-watching terrace on Adlerplatz (open Wed-Sun, closed Mon-Tue, +41 71 787 1389).

With a View over Town: A steep 15-minute uphill walk or short drive from the town center, **$$$ Panorama Hotel Freud-enberg** serves beef, pork, and vegetarian dishes, plus more reasonably priced small plates. You'll get sweeping vistas over Appenzell's rooftops from the outdoor tables. If you'd like to dine with a view, it's worth the effort, but wear appropriate footwear for the steep climb (closed Wed and Nov; go under train station, turn right, and follow yellow *Freudenberg* signs through a residential zone, then up through the hills; Riedstrasse 57, +41 71 787 1240). Drivers can follow the yellow *Freudenberg* signs from near the train station.

CHEAP EATS AND TREATS

$$ Drei Könige is clearly the local favorite serving coffee, delicious cakes, and light food in a cozy interior or on a sunny terrace (Wed-Mon 8:00-18:30, Sat-Sun until 17:00, closed Tue; Hauptgasse 26, +41 71 787 1124).

$ Lokal Gelateria is a low-key café serving homemade gelato (made with milk produced just a few miles away), coffee, and alcoholic beverages. Their location, tucked behind an old sawmill along the banks of the Sitter River, makes this a nice place to retreat (usually Wed-Sun 13:30-18:00; closed Mon-Tue, in bad weather, and in winter; Weissbadstrasse 3a, +41 71 787 0115).

Supermarkets and Cafeterias: The **Migros** (with a self-service cafeteria) and **Co-op** supermarkets face each other along Zielstrasse, a five-minute walk downhill from Landsgemeindeplatz (both generally open Mon-Sat 8:00-19:00, closed Sun).

Appenzell Connections

For details on taking the train to nearby destinations, see "Getting Around the Appenzell Region," earlier. For connections beyond the Appenzell region, you'll generally change in either Herisau or Gossau.

From Appenzell Town by Train to: Zürich (3/hour, 2 hours, change in Gossau), **Chur** (2/hour, 2.5 hours, 1 or more changes),

St. Moritz (1-3/hour, 4 hours, several changes), **Luzern** (2-3/hour, 3 hours, change in Herisau; more with additional changes), **Bern** (hourly, 3 hours, change in Gossau), **Interlaken** (3/hour, 4 hours, 1-3 transfers), **Lausanne** (2/hour, 4.5 hours, change in Gossau), **Munich** (2-3/hour, 4.5-6 hours, 1 change, more with additional changes). **Train info:** www.rail.ch.

Ebenalp

This mountain features wonderful views and a cliff-hanging hut, providing a lofty "hills-are-alive" alternative to Appenzell town.

From Wasserauen—five miles south of Appenzell town by road or rail line—ride the lift to Ebenalp (5,380 feet), a high, rocky ridge that drops off to vertical cliffs on the southern side. On the way up, you'll get a sneak preview of Ebenalp's cave church and the cliffside boardwalk that leads to the restaurant (near the top, left side). From the top you'll enjoy a sweeping view north all the way to Lake Constance (Bodensee). Though this excursion is doable in so-so weather, clear skies really enhance the Ebenalp experience—ask in Appenzell before you head up to the mountain or check the webcam at www.ebenalp.ch. In any weather, sturdy shoes and rain gear are recommended—the weather can change in the blink of an eye.

Getting There: First, a train takes you from Appenzell to Wasserauen (1-2/hour, 12 minutes). Then, across the road from the Wasserauen station, the Ebenalp lift carries hikers to the summit and back every 15 minutes (22 CHF one-way, 34 CHF round-trip, half-price with Swiss Travel Pass, 6-minute trip, daily July-Aug 7:30-19:00, June and Sept until 18:00, May and Oct 8:00-17:30, mid-Dec–March 9:30-17:00, usually closed April and Nov-mid-Dec—check website or call ahead, free parking, pick up free hiking map before you ascend, +41 71 799 1212, www.ebenalp.ch).

Hiking from the Lift Station to Aescher-Gasthaus am Berg: Leaving the lift, look for *Wildkirchli* and *Aescher* signs pointing to the 15-minute hike down to the mountain hut. First you'll hike steeply down under the cables, then you'll hook right and venture downhill through a good-sized natural cave where archaeologists once found the bones of prehistoric bears. It's slippery, so watch your step and use the railing—trust me, you'll soon return to daylight. As you emerge into the light, you'll pass a tiny **museum** (free and always open; scan barcode with phone for English descriptions) in a hut built on the site where hermit monks lived from 1658 to 1853. Don't miss the 400-year-old **Wildkirchli church,** a few yards farther along the cliff, in a separate cave.

Next you'll follow the cliff-hugging path (not for those afraid of steep drop-offs, though there's a sturdy railing) to a 170-year-old, weathered-shingle hut sitting snugly against the mountain. Originally built to house farmers, goats, and cows, it evolved into a lodge for pilgrims coming to the monks for spiritual guidance. Today, the recommended **Aescher-Gasthaus am Berg** caters to overnighters, and its restaurant welcomes hordes of tourists in search of a decent meal and great views (see listing, later).

From the guesthouse's sunny cliffside perch, you can almost hear the cows munching on the far side of the valley. Only the paragliders tag your world as 21st century. In the distance, nestled below Säntis peak, are the isolated Seealpsee (Lake-Alp Lake) and the recommended Berggasthaus Seealpsee.

Map: Ebenalp

To Gais
To Stein
APPENZELL TOWN
To Gontenbad, Jakobsbad & Urnäsch
STEINEGG
WEISSBAD
Ebenalp 5,380'
To Säntis
To Brülisau & Hoher Kasten
STEEP TRAIL!
CAVE
WASSERAUEN
Seealpsee
Not to Scale
Note: Appenzell Town to Wasserauen = 5mi / 8km

❶ Aescher-Gasthaus am Berg
❷ Berggasthaus Seealpsee
❸ Berggasthaus Ebenalp

Returning to the Ebenalp Lift: Retrace your steps through the cave (allow 25 minutes for this uphill hike). Or, for a different and more strenuous yet less-crowded return, you can hike up around the back of the mountaintop: As you leave Aescher-Gasthaus am Berg, continue straight on the path. At the fork, the path winds you steeply uphill, among goats and wildflowers, eventually arriving back at the top of the Ebenalp lift (allow 40 minutes).

Hikes from Aescher-Gasthaus am Berg: The trail beyond Aescher-Gasthaus am Berg leads to a pair of rugged hikes that are worth considering: down to the alpine lake called Seealpsee (and

APPENZELL

eventually all the way down to
Wasserauen), or up for a steep-
but-scenic route back to the Ebenalp lift (described above).

The hike down to **Seealpsee,** which takes a little over
an hour, is steep but rewarding: Take a left at the first fork
beyond Aescher-Gasthaus am
Berg. After some initial knee-jarring switchbacks, the trail gets
easier, and as it flattens out, a fork to the right leads in about 10
minutes to the lake. To reach Wasserauen (45 minutes) and the
train back to Appenzell, retrace your steps until you reach the nearest fork, but this time take the other path (to the right), which turns
into a narrow road.

Sleeping and Eating on Ebenalp

Sleeping: Although Appenzell town offers all the predictable
comforts, hardy travelers enjoy overnighting on Ebenalp instead.
The facilities are limited (only rainwater) and reaching any of these
accommodations involves some steep hiking. Beyond these three
options, the entire region is a hit with hikers, who can trek between
as many as 24 mountain hotels, each a day's hike apart. All originated as alpine farms.

$$$ Aescher-Gasthaus am Berg offers rustic cliffside ac-
commodations bundled with alpine vistas in their historic guest-
house and in the "Hermit Hut" just up the path. The guesthouse,
a wonderland of knotty wood, contains one double, one four-bed
room, and a bunkroom; the Hermit Hut sleeps 2 (book well ahead;
bunkroom sleeps 6-15—price based on number of guests, bring
sleeping sack; no shower or Wi-Fi, +41 71 799 1142, www.aescher.
ch, info@aescher.ch).

$ Berggasthaus Seealpsee is on the idyllic alpine Seealpsee,
most easily reached by an hour-long hike up a private road from
the Wasserauen train station (private rooms available, includes
sheets and showers, closed Nov-mid-April, +41 71 799 1140, www.
seealpsee.ch, info@seealpsee.ch, Parpan-Dörig family).

$ Berggasthaus Ebenalp perches just a couple of minutes'
steep walk up from the upper lift station (200-foot elevation gain).
There's a bumpy paved path up, and it's doable with sturdy wheeled
luggage. Its bunkroom and private rooms are booked long in ad-
vance for Saturdays, but are otherwise empty (restaurant, coin-op
rainwater shower, closed April and mid-Nov-mid-Dec, +41 71 799
1194, www.gasthaus-ebenalp.ch, infos@gasthaus-ebenalp.ch).

Eating: Built in 1805, **$$ Aescher-Gasthaus am Berg** is a memorable place to eat. The hut is actually built into the cliff; its back wall is the rock itself (see photo at the start of the Ebenalp section). The outdoor terrace and comfortable dining room are filled with happy hikers and plenty of tourists drawn by *National Geographic* publicity that labeled this a "destination of a lifetime." For a strenuous 45-minute pre-dinner hike, copy the goats: Take the high trail toward the lake, circle clockwise up toward the peak and the lift, then hike down the way you came (closed Dec-early May, 15 minutes by steep trail below top of lift, +41 71 793 9223, www.aescher.ch).

You can also eat at the restaurant of the **Berggasthaus Ebenalp,** listed earlier.

Liechtenstein

Appenzell is just an hour away by car from the tiny, pricey, and touristy country of Liechtenstein. This quirky remnant of medieval feudal politics is truly landlocked, without a seaport or even an airport. Liechtensteiners—who number about 38,000—speak German, are mostly Catholic, and have a stubborn independent streak. Women were barred from voting until 1984.

Liechtenstein is certainly not worth going out of your way for (unless you collect stamps—postal or passport), but a detour here is something to consider if you have time to kill and happen to be driving south from Appenzell toward Chur or the Upper Engadine (Pontresina/St. Moritz).

Vaduz

Low-key Vaduz, with about 5,000 people, feels basically like a mid-size Swiss town. Its pedestrianized main drag is lined with modern art and hotels bordering a district of slick office parks. Like other "micro-countries," Liechtenstein offers businesses special tax and accounting incentives. Many European companies establish their official headquarters here to take advantage of its low taxes.

Getting There: Heading south on the A-13 expressway from Appenzell, the road actually skirts Liechtenstein just across the Rhine River (the border). For a 30-minute detour, exit at Buchs and turn toward Schaan. After crossing the border (without stopping, or likely even noticing), you'll wind up in the town of Schaan. Follow signs (south/right) toward Vaduz, the capital of the Principality of Liechtenstein (Fürstentum Liechtenstein, or FL for short on its sleek black license plates).

Visiting Vaduz: Various parking lots and garages are along the main street, Äulestrasse. Try to park directly under the looming castle. If you park at the Marktplatz garage, you can simply walk one block up to the pedestrian zone called Städtle, where you'll run right into the **TI** (at #39, daily 9:00-17:00, +423 239 6363, www. tourismus.li). The TI, which comes off more as a souvenir shop, will stamp your passport for a small fee.

Go for a stroll along enjoyable Städtle street. Use Swiss francs or euros to buy a postcard and some Liechtenstein stamps to send to the collector in your life (but be sure to write and send it before leaving the country).

The prince's striking castle, a 20-minute hike above Vaduz, is closed to the public, but there's a fine view from the grounds (find the trail near **$$ Café Burg**). The billionaire prince, who looks down on his six-by-twelve-mile country, wields more real political power in his realm than any other member of European royalty. The Liechtenstein family purchased this piece of real estate from the Holy Roman Emperor. In 1719, the domain was granted principality status, answering only to the emperor. In 1806, during the age of Napoleon, Liechtenstein's obligations to the Habsburg emperor disappeared, and the country was granted true independence.

The Liechtenstein princes, who lived near Vienna, saw their country merely as a status symbol and at first didn't even bother to visit. In fact, it wasn't until the 20th century that a Liechtenstein prince actually lived here. Later, after World War I, tough times forced the principality to enter an economic union with Switzerland. To this day Liechtenstein enjoys a very close working relationship with its Swiss neighbors—functioning in some ways like just another Swiss canton, with the same currency, international diplomacy, bus system, and even soccer league.

Leaving Vaduz: After visiting the castle grounds, you'll quickly run out of things to do. No problem—just head back to Switzerland. Continue south through town on Äulestrasse, turn right at the well-marked *Schweiz* sign, cross back over the Rhine, and you're back in Switzerland (and on the A-13 expressway)... having checked another country off your list. Or, if you're headed northeast toward Austria, drive back north through Schaan, then up to Feldkirch.

LAKE GENEVA & FRENCH SWITZERLAND

Lausanne • Château de Chillon • Montreux • Gruyères

Lake Geneva, in the southwest corner of the country, is the Swiss Riviera. Separating France and Switzerland, the lake is surrounded by Alps and lined with a collage of castles, museums, spas, resort towns, and vineyards. The elegant French-style villas that grace the lakeshore—with pastel colors, frilly balconies, and characteristic mansard roofs—give it an air of gentility. And compared to the high mountains, this part of Switzerland (like Lugano and Italian-speaking Ticino) tends to be hazy and languid, with hints of a Mediterranean climate...even a few palm trees. The area is so beautiful that Charlie Chaplin and Idi Amin both chose it as their second home.

French is the predominant language at Lake Geneva ("Lac Léman" in French, "Genfersee" in German). To establish a better connection with the locals, see the "French Survival Phrases" in the appendix, *s'il vous plaît.*

Skip the big, dull city of Geneva; instead, sleep in fun, breezy Lausanne. Explore the romantic Château de Chillon and stylishly syncopated Montreux. It's also worth

taking a day to delve into the French Swiss countryside, which offers up rolling green foothills topped with castles; chocolates, vineyards, and Gruyère cheese galore; a high-mountain excursion to

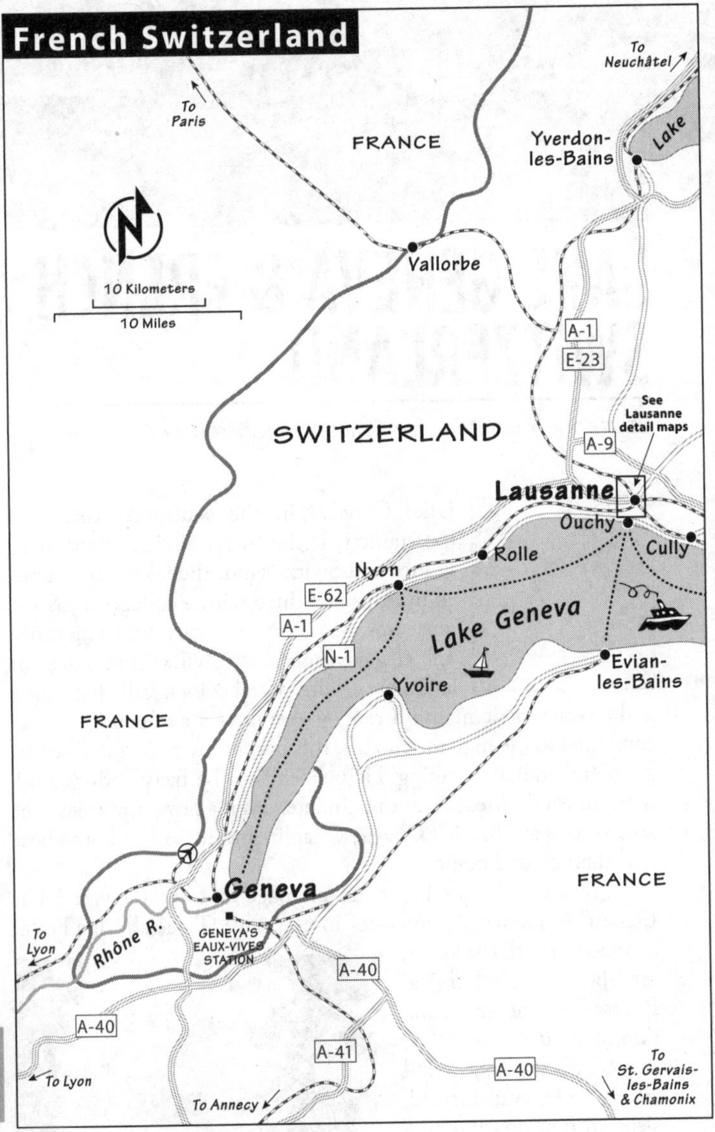

French Switzerland

FRANCE

To Paris

To Neuchâtel

Yverdon-les-Bains

Lake

Vallorbe

10 Kilometers

10 Miles

SWITZERLAND

A-1
E-23

A-9

See Lausanne detail maps

Lausanne

Ouchy

Cully

Nyon

Rolle

E-62

A-1

N-1

Lake Geneva

Evian-les-Bains

Yvoire

FRANCE

Geneva

GENEVA'S EAUX-VIVES STATION

Rhône R.

To Lyon

A-40

A-40

A-41

A-40

To Lyon

To Annecy

To St. Gervais-les-Bains & Chamonix

FRANCE

LAKE GENEVA

give you a quick dose of the Alps; and picturesque towns tucked into the folds of the hillsides.

PLANNING YOUR TIME

On a quick trip, you can get a good overview of Lake Geneva's highlights in one very busy day. Lausanne makes the best home base. In the morning, get oriented with my self-guided Old Laus-

anne Walk; dip into the cathedral and, if you have time and interest, the outstanding Art Brut and/or Olympic museums; and make
sure you side-trip to Château de Chillon well before closing time.

With more time, linger longer at Lausanne's great museums;
lazily float your way between Lausanne and Chillon (2 hours) or
other lakeside towns on a scenic boat cruise; stroll Montreux's

Lake Geneva and French Switzerland at a Glance

▲▲▲**Château de Chillon** Medieval castle perched romantically on eastern shore of Lake Geneva, with climbable ramparts, damp dungeons, and literary history. See page 319.

▲▲**Lausanne** Twisty, 3-D city stretching up a steep hill from the lakefront, with pleasant old town, plenty of sights—most notably the Olympic and Art Brut museums—and easy boat and train connections to the surrounding area. See page 297.

▲▲**Gruyères** Storybook small town overlooking dreamy countryside, with worthwhile nearby sights, including a folk museum, cheese- and chocolate-making factories, and a mini mountain with views of the Lake Geneva basin. See page 328.

▲**Montreux** Relaxed lakeside resort offering few sights—just sublime views of the misty lake and cut-glass peaks, and immediate access to the Golden Pass and Chocolate Train scenic rail lines. See page 325.

breezy promenade; or consider day trips into the surrounding vineyards and villages.

Beyond Lausanne and Chillon, the French Swiss countryside to the east is lower on the list of priorities. Gruyères is a fine (if touristy) village; while workable as a day trip by public transportation, it's most efficient with the Chocolate Train excursion from Montreux. Otherwise, I'd skip this area without a car. Drivers who are connecting Lake Geneva and the Berner Oberland can carve out some time for the Gruyères region en route, or consider a longer detour via Les Diablerets.

GETTING AROUND LAKE GENEVA

By Train: You can easily connect towns along Lake Geneva via train. The faster IR (interregional) trains efficiently zip between larger cities, such as Lausanne and Montreux. Slower, regional "S" trains connect smaller destinations—most notably Château de Chillon. The regional trains, while a bit slower, spend more of their journey time down along the lakefront—making them more scenic.

By Boat: This region offers a dizzying array of boat routes. Daily boat trips connect Lausanne with Vevey (21 CHF, 1 hour), Montreux (26 CHF, 1.5 hours), Château de Chillon (29 CHF, 2 hours), and points in between. In the summer (late June-early Sept), these run about four times per day in each direction (fewer in shoulder season, virtually none mid-Oct-mid-April). Some of the boats are historic, belle époque paddlewheel steamers, which feel just right in this romantic setting.

For just a quick hop on the water—on the most scenic stretch of the lake—the 15-minute cruise between Montreux and Château de Chillon is fun. The pretty town of Vevey, between Montreux and Lausanne, is enjoyable for a short stop and a visit to Charlie Chaplin's former home. A different route runs from Lausanne directly across the lake to Evian-les-Bains, the French spa town famous for its mineral water (hourly, 35 minutes, passport required).

To find a cruise that appeals to you, study the schedule (at www.cgn.ch, at TIs, and at boat ticket windows; or call CGN at +41 848 811 848). First class costs about 40 percent more and gets you passage on the deck up top, where you should scramble for the first-come, first-served chairs. You can sail free with a Swiss Travel Pass (using a travel day of a flexipass—ideally do this on your day of arrival or departure) or get 50 percent off with a Eurail Global Pass (does not use a day of a pass).

Lausanne

Lausanne is the most interesting city on the lake, proudly dubbing itself the "Olympic Capital" (it's been home to the International Olympic Committee since 1915). Amble along the serene lakefront promenade, stroll through the multilevel and characteristic old town, explore the sculptures at Olympic Park, and visit the remarkable Art Brut museum. Take a peek at the Gothic cathedral, and climb its tower for the view.

The Romans founded Lausanne on the lakefront—but with the fall of Rome and the rise of the barbarians, the first Lausanners fled for the hills, establishing today's old town. Over time, the city covered its rivers and spanned its valleys with beefy bridges. Later, as Lake Geneva became part of the Grand Tour of European tourism during the Romantic age, the waterfront—a district called Ouchy—was revived. The city thus has a design problem that goes back 1,500 years: two charming zones separated by a nondescript residential/industrial section. Thankfully, the waterfront and the old town are easily linked by a steep, handy Métro line. This helps somewhat, but Lausanne is undeniably challenging to navigate: It's next to impossible to avoid going uphill or downhill (or both) when walking between any two points. The city is a joy to explore...but it makes you work for it.

Orientation to Lausanne

Lausanne has the energy and cultural sophistication of a larger city, but is home to only about 130,000 people (350,000 in the greater area). A progressive city govern-

ment that subsidizes art and culture and a university with plenty of foreign students carbonate the place with a youthful spirit.

The tourist's Lausanne has two parts: the lakefront **Ouchy** (oo-SHEE), with a breezy resort ambience and the Olympic Museum; and the **old town,** with creaky Old World charm and fine museums, directly uphill from the lake. The old town district is divided roughly into two parts: The true old town, or *vieille ville* (vee-yay veel), near the cathedral, is staid and sleepy; more interesting is the city center, or *centre-ville,* located on an adjacent hillock where you'll find my favorite hotels and restaurants.

A third zone—around the **train station**—is located between Ouchy and the old town, but you'll likely spend time there only when in transit, or possibly to visit nearby art museums. These three zones—and much more—are all connected by the slick Métro.

Walking around Lausanne's old town feels like a life-size game of Chutes and Ladders. Two-dimensional maps don't do justice to the city's bridges, underpasses, stairways, hills, and valleys. Even the Métro trains and platforms are on an incline. Expect to be confused by the street plan at first. The model of old Lausanne in the City History Museum helps you understand how it developed.

Be careful to pronounce Lausanne correctly (loh-zahn), and don't confuse it with Luzern.

TOURIST INFORMATION

Lausanne's helpful TI is at the **train station's** main entrance (daily 9:00-19:00, +41 21 613 7373, www.lausanne-tourisme.ch). A second branch is inside the **cathedral,** at the welcome desk for the tower climb (Mon-Sat 9:30-12:30 & 13:30-18:30, Sun 13:00-17:30, shorter hours off-season). Another good (unofficial) resource—especially for recent reports on the restaurant scene—is

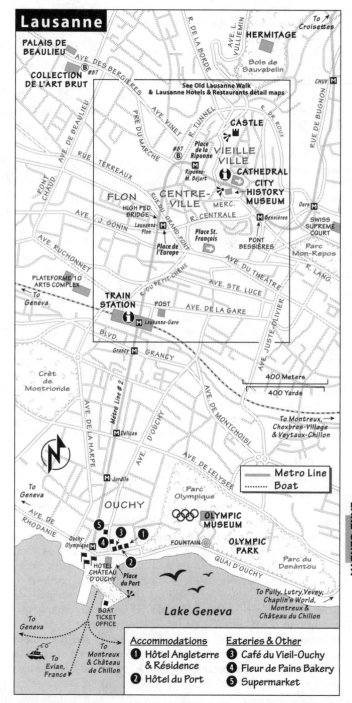

Lausanne

PALAIS DE BEAULIEU

COLLECTION DE L'ART BRUT

HERMITAGE

Bois de Sauvabelin

To Croisettes

CHUV

AVE. DES BERGIÈRES

B #87

AVE. DE BEAULIEU

RUE TERREAUX

AVE. RUCHONNET

PONT CHAUD.

PRÉ DU MARCHÉ

AVE. VINET

R. TUNNEL

R. DE LA BORDE

AVE. L. VULLIEMIN

R. DR. ROUX

RUE DU BUGNON

RUE DE BUGNON

CASTLE

VIEILLE VILLE

Place de la Riponne

#87 B

Riponne-M. Béjart

CATHEDRAL

CITY HISTORY MUSEUM

Ours M

SWISS SUPREME COURT

FLON

CENTRE-VILLE

MERC.

RUE DU GRAND PONT

J. GÖNIN

HIGH PED. BRIDGE

Lausanne-Flon M

Place de l'Europe

R. CENTRALE

Place St. François

M Bessières

PONT BESSIÈRES

Parc Mon-Repos

R. LANG.

AVE. DU THÉÂTRE

AVE. STE. LUCE

R. DU PETIT-CHÊNE

See Old Lausanne Walk & Lausanne Hotels & Restaurants detail maps

PLATEFORME 10 ARTS COMPLEX

To Geneva

TRAIN STATION

POST

Lausanne-Gare

AVE. DE LA GARE

AVE. JUSTE-OLIVIER

BLVD.

Grancy M

GRANCY

400 Meters

400 Yards

Crêt de Montriond

AVE. DE LA HARPE

Metro Line #2

M Délices

AVE. D'OUCHY

AVE. DE MONTCHOISI

To Montreux, Chexbres-Village & Veytaux-Chillon

AVE. DE L'ELYSÉE

M Jordils

OUCHY

Parc Olympique

Metro Line
Boat

To Geneva

AVE. DE RHODANIE

5

Ouchy-Olympique M

3 **1**

4

OLYMPIC MUSEUM

FOUNTAIN

OLYMPIC PARK

Parc du Denàntou

HOTEL CHÂTEAU D'OUCHY

2

Place du Port

QUAI D'OUCHY

To Pully, Lutry, Vevey, Chaplin's World, Montreux & Château du Chillon

BOAT TICKET OFFICE

Lake Geneva

To Geneva

To Evian, France

To Montreux & Château de Chillon

Accommodations
1 Hôtel Angleterre & Résidence
2 Hôtel du Port

Eateries & Other
3 Café du Vieil-Ouchy
4 Fleur de Pains Bakery
5 Supermarket

LAKE GENEVA

The Lausanne Guide, a blog written by two American expats (www.thelausanneguide.com).

Lausanne has a variety of **walking tours,** but they are usually offered in multiple languages—and English sometimes doesn't make the cut. Ask for details at the TI. Most are run by Lausanne à Pied (15 CHF, Mon-Sat usually at 10:00 and 14:30, 2 hours, no tours Sun or Oct-April, meet in front of Town Hall at Place de la Palud, www.lausanne-a-pied.ch). The TI also runs its own town walks (20 CHF, typically Sat at 14:00).

Be sure to ask about concerts (free and otherwise)—especially organ concerts at the cathedral. There are ample cultural events from about mid-June through mid-September (check out www.lausanne.ch/agenda).

ARRIVAL IN LAUSANNE

By Train: The train station—with lockers, WCs, ATMs, ticket office, TI, pharmacy, and late-night groceries—is midway between the old town and the lakefront. The station area will be torn up for many years to come as the area is modernized. But here's the gist:

The simple way to get either up to the old town or down to the lake—in about five minutes—is by Métro. If you arrive at track 1, head straight out the main door, cross the street, and look for the blue *Métro* sign. From other tracks, you'll descend into a pedestrian underpass; follow this past track 1 (and under the street) to surface across from the station, near the Métro stop. The Métro runs every few minutes; to go up (old town), look for direction: *Croisettes* (at street level); to go down (lakefront), look for direction: *Ouchy-Olympique* (below street level). You'll find ticket machines standing by (Métro also covered by Swiss Travel Pass; for more on riding the Métro, see "Getting Around Lausanne," later).

Taxis can be hard to find in the torn-up station area (exit to the right and go to the end of the station, near the post office). And they're fairly expensive, charging about 15-20 CHF to most of my recommended hotels. But this may be a worthwhile investment if you're packing heavy in this disorienting, hilly city.

By Car: Driving is tricky—especially in the twisty old town. Consider leaving your car at a park-and-ride (labeled *P+R*); several surround the city center and are well connected by Métro to the old town. If you're coming on the freeway from the north (such as from Bern), exit at *Vennes* and use the covered park-and-ride garage by the Vennes Métro stop (20 CHF/day covers parking and transit into the center). Or stay on the freeway as it loops down to *Lausanne Sud,* ending near the Bellerive park-and-ride, about a 15-minute walk from the Ouchy-Olympique Métro station (16 CHF/day). If you're approaching on the lakeside road from the east (such as from Montreux), follow blue signs along the lakeshore directly to Ouchy. For more information, go to www.lausanne.ch/stationnement.

By Boat: From the dock, veer left toward the plaza with the flagpoles. Across the street is the Métro station.

By Plane: Lausanne and the Lake Geneva area are served by the Geneva airport, at the lake's southwest corner. The airport sits on the western edge of Geneva, straddling the French border. For more on the airport, and how to get to town from there, see "Lausanne Connections," later.

HELPFUL HINTS

Sunday Closures: Sundays are pin-drop quiet; many shops and restaurants are closed.

Market Days: On Wednesday and Saturday mornings, produce stands fill the pedestrian streets of the old town.

Laundry: Quick-Wash, well-run and handy, is just behind the train station (self-service, daily 8:00-22:00, Boulevard de Grancy 44, +41 79 449 3761).

Bike Rental: A bike is worthless in this steep city, but can be great for exploring the lakefront, vineyards, and nearby villages. It's a three-hour waterfront pedal from Ouchy to Montreux and back. Your best bet is the city's PubliBike program (requires registering online; details at www.publibike.ch). Or, you can rent a more serious bike at the train station's ticket office, then bring it down to Ouchy on the Métro.

GETTING AROUND LAUSANNE

By Public Transport: Lausanne's nifty **Métro** and **bus** network makes it easy to get around. For transit info, visit www.t-l.ch.

The Métro has two lines (converging at the Lausanne-Flon stop in the city center), with a third line under construction. But only line #2 is useful for travelers. Using it is simple: up (direction: Croisettes) or down (direction: Ouchy-Olympique). This inclined 14-stop line climbs up from the lakefront to the old town, then all the way up to the freeway. The key stops are Ouchy-Olympique (at the lakefront); Lausanne-Gare (at the train station); Lausanne-Flon (at the bottom of the old town—exit into Place de l'Europe, ride the elevator up to the pedestrian bridge on Rue du Grand-Chêne, then stroll straight into the town center); and Riponne-M. Béjart (at the top end of the old town, on Place de la Riponne). You're unlikely to need the bus, except to reach the Art Brut museum.

If you're sleeping in Lausanne, your hotel should give you a **Lausanne Transport Card,** which covers local transit and is paid for by your hotel tax. Otherwise, unless you have a Swiss Travel Pass, you'll need to buy tickets from the machines. Tickets are valid on both Métro and buses (short-ride ticket-2.30 CHF, valid 30 minutes, up to three stops; single ticket-3.70 CHF, valid one hour; all-day ticket-9.30 CHF, valid 6:00-24:00). Almost everything in this chapter is in the central zone 11.

By Taxi: Cabs are pricey—figure 15-20 CHF for even a short ride.

Old Lausanne Walk

There's no way to see this town without lots of climbing. Locals are used to it (try to keep up). This self-guided stroll introduces you to both parts of Lausanne's charming old town, starting in *centre-ville* near the Church of St. Francis and ending in *vieille ville* near the cathedral.

❶ Lausanne-Flon Métro Station
This is where you're most likely to arrive in town.

• *From the Métro stop, ride the elevator up to the high pedestrian bridge (Passerelle du Flon). Orient yourself from midway across the bridge, which leads to the city's main thoroughfare. Start by looking west (toward the solitary gray skyscraper).*

❷ Passerelle du Flon View
Below you stretches Flon (the "Quartier du Flon")—once a ravine of the Flon River, then a down-and-dirty industrial zone, and

now—so typical of post-industrial 21st-century Europe—a thriving people zone. Its old warehouses come alive at night with trendy bars and nightclubs. The only reminder of the mills that once churned here is the name of the hottest nightclub in town: MàD (which stands for "Moulin à Danse" or "Dance

at the Mill"; it's just out of sight at Rue de Genève 23). The Art Deco-ish Bel-Air Tower (to the right) is famous as the country's first skyscraper (1932). The more elegant building, far to the left in the trees, was the 19th-century home of the Swiss Supreme Court.

Turn around and look down on the green rooftop of the Métro station (where different local plants grow all year). Scan this human coral reef of a city. Look for the viaduct, built in the 19th century as a double set of arches to cross the ravine. Now, as the city has evolved, only the top set of arches is visible.

• *Walk to where the pedestrian bridge hits the busy street, Rue du Grand-Pont. Head right toward the green copper spire of the Church of*

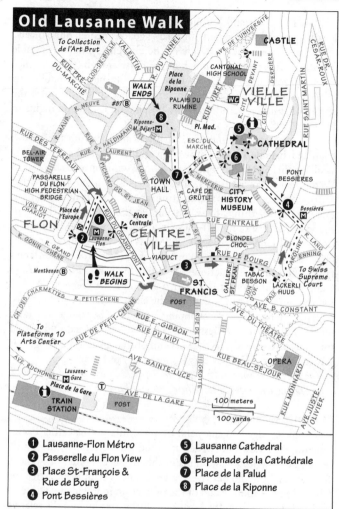

Old Lausanne Walk

1. Lausanne-Flon Métro
2. Passerelle du Flon View
3. Place St-François & Rue de Bourg
4. Pont Bessières
5. Lausanne Cathedral
6. Esplanade de la Cathédrale
7. Place de la Palud
8. Place de la Riponne

St. Francis. As you walk along Rue du Grand-Pont, enjoy lovely views of the cathedral on your left and the grassy Métro station on the right, with its vertical garden. You'll soon reach...

❸ Place St-François & Rue de Bourg

The **Church of St. Francis** marks the town's center and transportation hub. Across the busy street stands the grand post office, a belle époque building from the days when post offices were a big deal. It's flanked by two also-grand banks (still a big deal in Switzerland). The church is Gothic, founded by Franciscans in the 13th century. But in 1536, it went Protestant—and was gutted of decorations. Later, a grand Baroque organ was installed. The church's locally quarried stones, laid 500 years ago, cleaned up quite nicely.

Circle around the left side of the church to find the humble **fountain.** This replaced a much larger horse trough (this was once where wagons entered town). Look for a fun piece of public art: Brass plaques, embedded in the surrounding cobbles, feature the names of children born in the city hospital on full-moon nights in the year 1998.

As you face the fountain, turn left and head up the pedestrianized **Rue de Bourg.** Stow your guidebook and simply enjoy strolling this pretty shopping street, lined with top-end shops. (On Wednesdays and Saturdays, this street is also filled with market stalls.) Notice the fine architecture above the noisy storefronts. Here are a few things to watch for: At the first corner (Rue St. François), glance downhill—it's lined with circa-1960 St. Francis signposts. Blondel (on the left, at #5) has been hand-making chocolate in Lausanne for more than 150 years. (Much of Switzerland's famous chocolate production—including big names like Nestlé and Cailler—got their start in the area around Lake Geneva.) At #12 (on the right), you can look down the elegant Galerie St. François, which stretches to a busy shopping street. Just beyond at #22 (also on the right) is Tabac Besson, a classic wood-grained Old World tobacco store. Finally, at the very top of the street at #28 (right) is Läckerli Huus, selling sweets from the city of Basel.

• *When the street ends, turn left (onto Rue Caroline), continuing uphill, then bearing left over the large bridge toward the cathedral.*

❹ Pont Bessières

Pause mid-bridge and enjoy the view—similar to the earlier Passerelle du Flon view but higher up. Find the skyscraper, the courthouse, and the Jura Mountains in the distance (border of France). And notice how the old river valley below is built over. After the fall of Rome—and the end of the protection it provided—vulnerable locals moved from the lakefront Ouchy area up into the relative safety of adjacent hilltops between river valleys. Looking out over the landscape, appreciate what a terrible location this was for building a modern city. Imagine the headaches this location has caused for urban planners, who've had to figure out some way to turn Lausanne into a cohesive, well-connected metropolis. Two rivers have been covered over; bridges and viaducts run every which way; and elevators, funiculars, and a uniquely vertical Métro attempt to tame the undulating land. And yet, somehow, it works...if you don't mind a little exercise. By the way, the oversized railing you may be leaning on is designed to discourage suicidal people from leaping.

Walking toward the cathedral, you'll notice that Lausanne's true old town (*vieille ville*, where we're headed)—filling the highest hill in town with administration buildings, offices, schools, and apartments—is subdued compared with the commercial center (*centre-ville,* which we just left).

• *Once across the bridge, bear right and curve on up (with the patch of grass on your left—or use the stairs straight up through the park) to the upper level around the giant cathedral. Walk alongside the massive building, passing the City History Museum on your left (we'll circle back here soon) to the big, leafy terrace in front of the cathedral. We'll enjoy the view in a bit. But first, check out the biggest church in the country.*

❺ Lausanne Cathedral (Cathédrale de Lausanne)

Lausanne's cathedral is an Evangelical Reform Church, meaning that it belongs to the tradition of the early Protestant reformer John Calvin. Iconoclasm, the removal of religious symbols, suited the Calvinists well. The once-ornate cathedral, originally dedicated to Mary, was cleared of all its statues and decorations. Its frescoes were plastered over, and its colorful windows were trashed and replaced

by plain ones. But, thankfully, there's still a lot to see.

Cost and Hours: Free, daily 9:00-19:00, Oct-March until 17:30; www.cathedrale-lausanne.ch.

Concerts: Organ concerts take place on some Friday evenings in peak season, usually at 20:00 (look for posted schedules, check online at www.grandesorgues.ch, or ask at the cathedral welcome center/TI).

Visiting the Church: Enter through the main doors, facing the view terrace. (If the door's closed...open it.) Walk partway down the nave and look back.

The **pipe organ** above the main door is American-made (by Boston-based company Fisk) and was installed in 2003. Locals love their organ and figure its cost (4 million CHF) was money well spent. Look back at its 7,000 pipes: The "stiletto in Oz" design represents the wings of angels. Notice that the pews in this part of the nave have "reversible" seats—they can either face the pulpit, or be switched to face the organ.

As you continue down the nave, admire the **stained glass.** In the south (right) transept, the **rose window** has the church's only surviving 13th-century glass. The rest of the glass dates from the early 1900s. Don't miss the bold and clearly labeled scenes in the

LAKE GENEVA

apse. The north (left) transept has some dreamy blue Art Nouveau scenes.

The **Mary Chapel,** below the rose window (and just to the left), was the most elaborate chapel in the church. In 1536, it was scraped clean of anything fancy or hinting of the Virgin Mary. Look at the bits of surviving original paint, and imagine the church in all its colorful glory six centuries ago. Also notice the stamp for the "pilgrims' passport." This church is a stop on one of the many Camino de Santiago pilgrimage routes across Europe that funnel hikers to Santiago de Compostela in northernwestern Spain. Pilgrims mark their passport with a stamp at each stop.

The church's highlight is on the way back out: Head up the aisle the way you came and watch on the left for the door that leads to the light-bathed **painted portal.** This was the church's main entrance in the Middle Ages. Today, it's glassed in to protect its remarkable painted Gothic statuary. Imagine being a pilgrim approaching this beautifully painted main entrance to one of the great churches of Europe: On the left are six Old Testament prophets and on the right are six apostles—all standing upon symbols of evil and welcoming you with benevolent smiles. High above you, Jesus is about to crown Mary "Queen of Heaven." And then you step inside.

Tower: In the back-right corner of the church, you'll find a **TI/welcome center** and gift shop, and the entrance to the tower climb (224 steps, grand lake views, lots of Alps, 5 CHF, Mon-Sat 9:30-12:30 & 13:30-18:30, Sun 13:00-17:30, shorter hours off-season).

Since the Middle Ages, a **night watch** has lived in the church's tower. As the city was originally built of wood, fire was a constant fear. The job: to watch for fires and to call out the hours. The city is made of stone today—so there's little danger of fire—and people wear their Swiss timekeepers on their wrists. Nevertheless, Lausanne retains this 600-year-old tradition—the only Swiss city to do so. (Even in this "progressive" city, it took until 2022 to hire a female night watch.) Every night on the hour, from 22:00 to 2:00 in the morning, the night watch steps onto the balcony and hollers. Their first announcement: "I am the watchman. I am the watchman. We just had 10 o'clock. We just had 10 o'clock."

• *Back outside, belly up to the fine viewpoint immediately in front of the cathedral.*

❻ Esplanade de la Cathédrale

On a clear day, look beyond the spire of the Church of St. Francis to see the French Alps (Chamonix and Mont Blanc, over there somewhere, are just out of sight). Evian-les-Bains, the famous French spa town, is immediately opposite Lausanne. On the right, the soft, rolling Jura Mountains, which mark the border of France and Switzerland, stretch all the way from Lake Geneva to Germany.

• *On the left side of the terrace (as you face the view) is the **City History Museum** (described later, under "Sights in Lausanne"). Now's a good time to visit.*

A covered wooden staircase called **Escaliers du Marché** leads down from the cathedral's front door. When you're two-thirds of the way down the stairs, notice the blue plaque with the stylized seashell icon, marked *Chemin de St. Jacques* ("Way of St. James"—another name for the Camino de Santiago.

Just beyond, head through the tunnel marked *1975* under the busy road. Continue down the covered steps along a row of funky businesses, bear right to pass the recommended Café du Grütli, and land on a long and narrow cobbled square.

❼ Place de la Palud

This square is marked by its colorful Fountain of Justice. Since 1585 this blindfolded figure of Justice, holding her sword and scales, has commanded fairness as she stands triumphantly over kings and bishops. Imagine the neighborhood moms sending kids here to fetch water in the days before plumbing. Behind the fountain is a mechanical clock, with animated figures that perform with recorded French narration every hour, on the hour (daily 9:00-19:00). The Town Hall at the bottom of the square dates from 1685.

• *Uphill from Town Hall, Rue de la Madeleine leads to the vast and modern...*

❽ Place de la Riponne

The Palais du Rumine (former university), overlooking the square, now houses a collection of museums (all of which are skippable). The recommended **Great Escape,** a fun hamburger bar with a nice selection of beers, fills the terrace a few flights of stairs above you (between the square and the cathedral tower). There's a free WC on the first floor of the Palais du Rumine.

• *Our tour is over. To reach the **Collection de l'Art Brut**, walk northwest about 15 minutes. Or—much easier—catch bus #87 from this square (the stop is across the street, in front of La Vaudois café).*

*Or, to head down to the lakefront **Ouchy district**, ride the Métro from this square (the Riponne-M. Béjart stop) all the way down to the end of the line, Ouchy-Olympique.*

Or...simply enjoy poking around more of the old town's twisty lanes.

Sights in Lausanne

IN AND NEAR THE OLD TOWN

▲City History Museum (Musée Historique de Lausanne)

This museum, housed in what was the bishop's residence (facing the cathedral), has nicely presented displays that trace life in Lausanne from Roman times to the present.

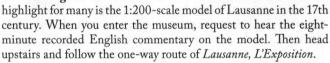

Cost and Hours: 12 CHF, covered by Swiss Travel Pass, Tue-Sun 11:00-18:00, closed Mon except July-Aug, bags must be checked in lockers, Place de la Cathédrale 4, +41 21 315 4101, www.lausanne.ch/mhl.

Visiting the Museum: The highlight for many is the 1:200-scale model of Lausanne in the 17th century. When you enter the museum, request to hear the eight-minute recorded English commentary on the model. Then head upstairs and follow the one-way route of *Lausanne, L'Exposition*.

The **model,** in the first room, is based on an engraving from 1638 (see copy on wall). It will give you a feel for how this hilly city and its quirky street plan developed. You're viewing the town from the perspective of the lakefront district of Ouchy, with the Church of St. Francis in the foreground. You can see river valleys that have since been built over by the modern city. The little water mills mark the birthplace of industrial Flon. Though the city's walls are long gone, its vineyards survive.

From here, the mild-mannered but interesting exhibits tell the rest of Lausanne's story. You'll see a variety of exhibits on how, as Lausanne grew, city leaders and engineers attempted to tame this unruly landscape—including for example, the construction of the Grand-Pont.

On the lower levels, you'll find exhibits on city transportation and religious life, as well as rooms dedicated to the economic, social, and cultural history of Lausanne: the Enlightenment (when Lausanne was a printing center), high society, commerce, and industry (including chocolate-making, which remains a big business in this part of Switzerland). The grand finale is an endearing exhibit called "From Lausanne with Love," recalling Lake Geneva's arrival on the world tourism stage as part of the Grand Tour of 19th-century aristocrats (who brought money and fame to Lausanne). The final display features holograms of locals describing what their hometown means to them.

LAKE GENEVA

▲▲Collection de l'Art Brut

This well-displayed, evocative collection shows art produced by untrained artists, many labeled (and even locked up) by society as "criminal" or "insane." It's a beautiful testament to the fragility and resilience of the human spirit. Many of the featured artists had a history of war, illness, and/or abandonment—and yet created something unique, moving, and worthy of thoughtful contemplation. It's tragic and uplifting at the same time—in other words, utterly human.

Cost and Hours: 12 CHF, covered by Swiss Travel Pass, Tue-Sun 11:00-18:00, closed Mon except July-Aug, bags must be checked in lockers, Avenue des Bergières 11, +41 21 315 2570, www.artbrut.ch.

Getting There: From the old town, the museum is a dull 15-minute walk or an easy ride on the frequent bus #87 (from Place de la Riponne, direction: Désert, get off at Beaulieu stop and backtrack a short block). From the train station, take bus #3 or #21 (also very frequent, direction: Bellevaux or Blécherette, get off at Beaulieu stop for bus #21, or Beaulieu-Jomini stop for bus #3).

Visiting the Museum: In 1945, artist Jean Dubuffet began collecting art he called *brut* ("raw" or "crude")—created by untrained, highly original individuals who weren't afraid to ignore rules. In the 1970s, he donated his huge collection to Lausanne, and it has now expanded to 60,000 works by hundreds of artists—loners, mavericks, fringe people, prisoners, and 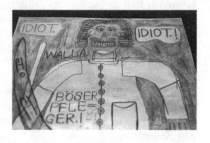 mental-ward patients. Dubuffet said, "The art does not lie in beds ready-made for it. It runs away when its name is called. It wants to be incognito."

About 800 works are displayed at a time, (perhaps fittingly) without much rhyme or reason on four floors. Rooms with black walls are part of the permanent collection; white walls indicate temporary exhibits. Read the posted thumbnail biographies of these outsiders, and then enjoy their unbridled creativity.

Here's just a sampling of the artists you'll see in the permanent collection: Emile Ratier, a blind farmer who made rudimentary statues out of wood; Madge Gill, an Englishwoman who drew portraits of a grieving mother; Sylvain Fusco, a cabinetmaker who went to war, stopped talking, and began drawing; August Walla, a psychiatric hospital inmate who painted boldly colorful murals; Pascal-Désir Maisonneuve, who created portraits of monarchs and politicians using seashells; Philippe Dereux, whose favored media were fruit and vegetable peels and various grains; David Braillon, from a family of railway workers, who crayoned long, detailed illustrations of trains; and Paul Amar, who assembled elaborate dioramas using brightly painted shells from the seafood he consumed.

As you tour the thought-provoking collection and learn about the artists, ponder the fine line that separates "sanity" and "insanity" when it comes to creative output. The thoughtful visitor ponders what "normal" really means, and why some innovators become cultural icons...while others get ridiculed, ignored, or locked up.

NEAR THE TRAIN STATION
▲Plateforme 10 Arts Complex
Just a five-minute walk from the train station on Place de la Gare, this arts district consolidates three museum collections. Art aficionados will find a visit here worth ▲▲, but casual visitors may find the collections less satisfying and more challenging to appreciate than some of Lausanne's (and Lake Geneva's) bigger thrills. **Lausanne Cantonal Museum of Fine Arts** (Musée Cantonal des Beaux-Arts Lausanne, or **MCBA**), in a large, white-brick building, combines works of local artists with lesser works by big names (as well as frequent temporary exhibits), all beautifully displayed in a vast, open, custom-built space. A boxy building houses two more museums: Upstairs is the **Museum for Contemporary Design and Applied Arts (MUDAC)** and downstairs is the **Musée de l'Elysée** photography collection.

Cost and Hours: 15 CHF each; 25 CHF for 3-museum combo-ticket; all are covered by the Swiss Travel Pass; MCBA closed Mon, MUDAC and Musée de l'Elysée closed Tue, otherwise all are open 10:00-18:00, Thu until 20:00; +41 21 318 44 00, www.plateforme10.ch.

IN OUCHY, LAUSANNE'S WATERFRONT
The lazy resort charm of Lausanne lies on its lakefront. The place is lively from Easter through October, and dead otherwise. Start at the **Ouchy-Olympique** stop, connected by Métro with the train station and the old town every few minutes.

Before you leave the Métro, notice the parade of Olympic athletes literally hanging from the ceiling. Walk straight out to the main road, **Quai d'Ouchy.** Several restaurants are a block to the left. Also to the left, notice the grand Hotel Château d'Ouchy. It was built around a 13th-century tower—a reminder of Lausanne's importance in the Middle Ages. Before the hotel gates is an Olympic countdown clock (marking the days, and even seconds, remaining until the next winter and summer games). Continuing past the hotel, you'll pass an elaborate kids' playground on the left and a sprawling festival zone on the right before reaching the **lakefront.** Environmentalism is popular in this city, which boasts 300 square feet of green space per inhabitant—more than nearly any city in Europe.

Straight ahead, the big C-shaped **weathervane** stands on the breakwater, indicating to sailors if the wind is *vaudaire* (roughly southeast, over the lake from Montreux), *bise* (northerly), *joran* (northwest), or *vent* (southwest). It's a puzzle, as the "C" is designed to line up with the semicircle cutouts in the four strangely placed stone pillars. Crouch down, match the "C" with the pillar that creates an "O," then look down at the pavement for the corresponding name of today's wind.

At the **harbor**—to the left from the weathervane—you'll find the departure docks for boat cruises (see next). A five-minute stroll farther along the lake takes you to Ouchy's main attraction, the Olympic Museum and Park (described later).

Boat Rides

Lake Geneva **cruise boats** operated by CGN leave from the piers just to the left (see "Getting Around Lake Geneva," earlier). Stop by dock 3, next to the main boat-ticket office, for information on the lake's still-steaming historic paddleboats (1904-1927).

▲▲▲Olympic Museum and Park
(Le Musée et Parc Olympique)

This museum celebrates the colorful history of the Olympic Games. It's set in a beautiful lakeside park where the Olympic flame flickers between editions of the games.

The exhibits and park celebrate the ideals of Pierre de Coubertin, who in 1894 founded the International Olympic Committee and restarted the games after a 1,500-year lapse. Coubertin acknowledged that to ask nations to love one another was naive, but to ask them to respect one another was a realistic and worthy goal.

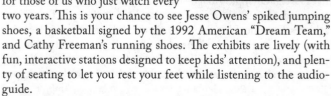

The museum is a thrill for Olympics buffs—and plenty of fun for those of us who just watch every two years. This is your chance to see Jesse Owens' spiked jumping shoes, a basketball signed by the 1992 American "Dream Team," and Cathy Freeman's running shoes. The exhibits are lively (with fun, interactive stations designed to keep kids' attention), and plenty of seating to let you rest your feet while listening to the audioguide.

LAKE GENEVA

Cost and Hours: 20 CHF, family deals, free with Swiss Travel Pass; Tue-Sun 9:00-18:00, closed Mon, Quai d'Ouchy 1, +41 21 621 6511, www.olympic.org/museum.

Getting There: From the Ouchy-Olympique Métro stop, turn left and walk five minutes along the water to the big, white fountain, then walk up the stairs. On the way, you'll pass the Beau-Rivage Palace, Lausanne's venerable belle époque hotel that, since 1857, has hosted a glamorous guest list including Winston Churchill, Charlie Chaplin, Dizzy Gillespie, Liz Taylor, and, uh, Richard Nixon and Woody Allen.

Visiting the Museum: As you approach the building—perched on a grassy hill above the lakefront—appreciate the statue-studded park, filled with Olympics symbolism. Just before the entrance, look left to see a high-jump bar set at the current Olympic record level. Imagine trying to clear it yourself—these are no average feats. Just beyond is a full-scale track on which you can measure your pace against the performance of Olympic athletes.

Inside, buy your ticket at level 0, then head up the spiral ramp to enter at level 1 and follow the one-way route. First up, **The Olympic World** covers the history of the games and their organization. You'll learn how the Olympics were born in ancient Greece, then reconceived by French aristocrat Pierre de Coubertin (1863-1937). Coubertin, a progressive thinker with socialist leanings, believed that strict French schools needed more physical education. He looked to British traditions as a model, and worked with British and Greek educators to hold the first modern games in Athens in 1896. Fourteen nations participated (more than 200 have competed in recent summer games). The exhibit covers the different host cities since then, the complex politics involved, the tradition of the torch, and the games' planning and organizational challenges. You'll see past Olympic flags, stadiums, and mascots; an example of every single torch from each modern Olympics; and an audiovisual display of opening ceremonies across the years.

One level down, **The Olympic Games** covers the winter, summer, and Paralympic games, displaying uniforms, shoes, and other memorabilia of competitors through the decades. A circular projection theater serves up a riveting medley of dramatic replays of competition highlights.

The basement exhibit, **The Olympic Spirit,** is about athletes' lives in the Olympic village—what they eat, where they live, drug tests and anti-cheating measures, and the "Olympic Truce" that athletes from hostile nations commit to observe. Interactive displays allow you to try your hand at Olympic sports and a thought-provoking body-image wall shows the diverse bodies of Olympic athletes and how little they resemble fashion-model stereotypes.

The exhibit concludes with a room of shiny replica medals from each of the modern games.

The museum's top-floor **$$ Tom Café** has nice views and decent prices.

LAKESIDE AND VINEYARD EXCURSIONS NEAR LAUSANNE

The countryside immediately surrounding Lausanne—with farms and villages, winding lanes, picturesque vineyards, and glorious mountain and lake views—is enticing, and those with plenty of time may be tempted to get out of the city and explore. Here are a few ideas (ask local TIs for details):

Hike: A delightful promenade stretches in both directions from the Ouchy-Olympique Métro stop; it's fun to stroll about one hour east to Pully (left as you face the lake), then catch the train back to Lausanne.

Wine Country Visit: Beyond Pully are the terraced vineyards of the Lavaux wine country. Of the hiking trails that snake from Pully to Montreux, the best stretch is between Lutry and Vevey. One short, easy, rewarding walk is the hike from Chexbres-Village down to St-Saphorin (both with train stations).

Bike Ride: Pedal east from Ouchy along the road for about a half-mile, then follow the bike path that hugs the shoreline for about six miles to Morges (easy return by boat or train). You'll pass Vidy (with its scant Roman ruins), the headquarters of the International Olympic Committee, and lots of sports facilities.

Nightlife in Lausanne

Trendy **Quartier du Flon,** Lausanne's old industrial district, is a dull commercial zone by day and thriving entertainment area in the evening. This is where hardworking Lausanners come for an après-work cocktail with colleagues and friends. While a vibrant scene, it's mainly bars with afterthought food rather than a dining destination; come here for the lively al fresco ambience and a stylish cocktail rather than a memorable meal. From the Flon Métro station, the main drag Voie du Chariot leads to the central Flon square (following what was the original train line serving the warehouses). Convivial cocktail bars lead to the area's central square, which has a cinema (multiplex; "VO" means it's playing in the original language), bowling, and **MàD** (an iconic nightclub with four floors of dancing and pricey cover, starting well after my bedtime).

Sleeping in Lausanne

Lausanne hotels are priciest between April and October, but with a summer lull in July and August. At many places, prices also fall on weekends, as the city gets more business than leisure travelers. Courtesy of Lausanne's tourist tax, along with your hotel room you'll get a Lausanne Transport Card, which gives you free access to the city's public transportation (plus discounts at many recommended museums) for the duration of your stay.

If you're arriving by car, ask for parking advice from your hotel (many offer discounted rates at a nearby garage, or have parking on site). Otherwise, leave your car at a park-and-ride and arrive by Métro.

IN THE OLD TOWN

$$$ Hôtel de la Paix is an enticing splurge, a short walk beyond the old town. This classic, classy hotel—built in 1910 and run by the same family since the 1930s—has more than 100 rooms, including some with Lake Geneva views (for an extra charge). It comes with Old World charm and the professional predictability of a well-run business-class hotel (elevator, air-con, fitness room, restaurant, pay parking immediately in front of hotel, 5 Avenue Benjamin-Constant, +41 21 310 71 71, www.hoteldelapaix.net, info@hoteldelapaix.net).

$$ Hôtel des Voyageurs rents 35 classy, if nondescript, Swiss-modern rooms. It feels comfortable and well run, with a good breakfast served in a bright, open, and cheery space. Streetside rooms overlook a picturesque pedestrian lane but can by noisy; rooms in back face a quiet courtyard (elevator, air-con in some rooms, Rue Grand Saint-Jean 19, +41 21 319 9111, www.voyageurs.ch, hotel@voyageurs.ch). To find the hotel, take the Métro to the Lausanne-Flon stop, ride the elevator up to the pedestrian bridge, cross Rue du Grand-Pont, walk up Rue Pichard, and take the first right.

$$ Fassbind Hotels: This Swiss chain operates several straightforward, moderately priced hotels around Lausanne, many with kitschy themes. The rooms are functional with midrange charm and can be a decent value in this pricey city. Their **Hôtel Swiss Wine** has 62 rooms—and, of course, a wine cellar—just across the bridge from the cathedral (cathedral-facing rooms are quieter and pricier than street-facing rooms in the back, Rue Caroline 5, +41 21 320 21 41). **Hôtel Swiss Chocolate** has 54 rooms a bit farther from the old town (some with views of Lake Geneva or the cathedral, a few minutes' walk from the Bessières and Ours Métro stops at Rue Marterey 15, +41 21 601 80 00). Both have elevators but no air-con (www.byfassbind.com).

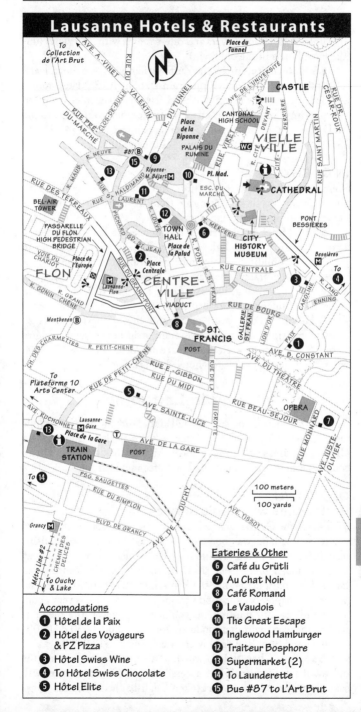

Lausanne Hotels & Restaurants

LAKE GENEVA

Accomodations
1 Hôtel de la Paix
2 Hôtel des Voyageurs
   & PZ Pizza
3 Hôtel Swiss Wine
4 To Hôtel Swiss Chocolate
5 Hôtel Elite

Eateries & Other
6 Café du Grütli
7 Au Chat Noir
8 Café Romand
9 Le Vaudois
10 The Great Escape
11 Inglewood Hamburger
12 Traiteur Bosphore
13 Supermarket (2)
14 To Launderette
15 Bus #87 to L'Art Brut

NEAR THE TRAIN STATION

This hotel is easier for drivers and offers rooms with lake views (unlike most hotels in the old town).

$$ Hôtel Elite, run by the Zufferey family, is on a quiet, leafy, residential street just above the train station. Its 33 dated rooms are pleasant without being plush—a few have balconies (elevator, free parking; from station, cross the street and go uphill around McDonald's, take first right to Avenue Sainte-Luce 1; +41 21 320 2361, www.elite-lausanne.ch, info@elite-lausanne.ch).

IN OUCHY

Scenic, great for a waterfront stroll, and close to the Olympic Museum, Ouchy is a short Métro ride from the more interesting dining and nightlife zones higher up.

$$$$ Hôtel Angleterre & Résidence is a luxurious splurge across the street from Lake Geneva. The 75 rooms are spread through four buildings—some more traditional, others contemporary—around a grassy lawn (air-con, elevator, outdoor pool, gym, restaurant, pay parking, Place du Port 11, +41 21 613 34 34, www.angleterre-residence.ch, ar@brp.ch).

$ Hôtel du Port, your "cheap and cheery" option, rents 22 basic rooms right along the restaurant strip near Ouchy's Métro station (breakfast extra, elevator, Place du Port 5, +41 21 612 04 44, www.hotel-du-port.ch, info@hotel-du-port.ch).

Eating in Lausanne

By Swiss standards, you can eat well and affordably here. Lausanne restaurants typically offer a weekday lunch deal for about 20-25 CHF (sometimes on Saturday, too). This usually just means a main course, perhaps with a side salad or coffee included.

OLD TOWN

Restaurants with Table Service

$$$ Café du Grütli, named for the meadow south of Luzern where Switzerland was born, offers typical French Swiss cuisine near Place de la Palud. While they have outside tables on a cozy cobbled lane, I prefer their 1849 dining room, with century-old tables. It's a bit touristy, but the Prutsch family (Willi, Heike, and Vanessa) is hands-on, the food's fresh, and the service is very good. The family is into hunting, so you'll find game on the menu as well as an award-winning fondue (Mon-Sat 10:00-14:30 & 18:00-23:30, closed Sun, Rue de la Mercerie 4, +41 21 312 9493).

$$$$ Au Chat Noir is worth a 10-minute walk beyond the old town for an upscale yet accessible brasserie experience with scarcely a tourist in sight. In broken English, cheery waiters translate the chalkboard menu, which changes frequently—but everything's delicious. It's worth reserving before you make the walk here (Mon-Fri 12:00-14:00 & 19:00-22:00, closed Sat-Sun, tucked down a side street near the opera house at Rue Beau-Séjour 27, +21 312 95 85).

$$ Café Romand is a venerable, simple brasserie filled with locals enjoying hearty Swiss home cooking, and comes with tables out on the square facing St. Francis Church. It feels like a city hangout—students, pensioners, and professionals sit under old-time photos like they own the place (Swiss wines by the glass, Mon-Sat 11:45-23:00, closed Sun, Place St-François 2, +41 21 312 6375).

$$$ Le Vaudois, facing lively Place de la Riponne, is a modern brasserie with charming seating inside and out, serving all the traditional French and Swiss dishes (daily 7:00-24:00, food from 11:30, Place de la Riponne, +41 21 331 2222).

Affordable Eats

$$ The Great Escape is a happening spot in good weather. The fun-loving crew cranks out great burgers and bar-type food on nights and weekends (order inside), but offers a few nicer options and table service for lunch (weekdays only). The restaurant is like a big woody pub (with classic rock playing, one screen showing sports, and a long bar), but I prefer the rickety tables outside on the gravelly square. When it's busy, people perch throughout the small park with their little Great Escape trays (you'll pay a 2-CHF deposit for your tray—turn it in to get your coin back). While quiet early, it gets loud and crazy late—but remains welcoming for all ages (daily 11:00-23:00, Place de la Madeleine, above the Métro stop on Place de la Riponne—head up three flights of stairs to reach it, +41 21 312 3194).

$$ Inglewood Hamburger is a thriving joint with friendly service in the old center near Place de la Palud. Happy locals munch creative burgers on the small terrace or within the quaint interior (beer on tap, Mon-Sat 11:30-14:00 & 18:30-21:30, closed Sun, Rue St. Laurent 14, +41 21 323 6388).

$$ PZ Pizza, on a serene pedestrian street in the heart of the old town, has good wood-fired pizza on super-crispy thin crusts. Choose from a variety of toppings, order at the counter, then find a table—either in the pleasant, split-level, modern interior or out on the lane (Mon-Sat 11:30-22:30, closed Sun, Rue Grand Saint-Jean 5, +41 21 312 8282).

$ Traiteur Bosphore, a brighter-than-average kebab shop, is a good option for a quick and inexpensive takeaway lunch or early dinner. There's no seating—stand at the back counter or walk to the nearby Place de la Louve and find a bench (Mon-Fri 10:00-18:45, Sat 9:00-17:00, closed Sun, Rue de la Louve 7).

Supermarket: The **Co-op** department store in the center has a big supermarket in the basement (there's also a lunch cafeteria upstairs; store open Mon-Fri 8:00-19:00, Sat until 18:00, closed Sun, Rue St-Laurent 24).

OUCHY

The lakeside Ouchy district is the place to relax. Immediately in front of the Métro stop is a fun zone with fountains, parks, playgrounds, promenades, and restaurants.

$$$ Café du Vieil-Ouchy, charming and reasonably priced, seems a bit out of place among all the fancy, expensive restaurants. It offers traditional Swiss cuisine, including the local filet of perch, cheese fondue, and various versions of *Rösti* (outdoor seating, main courses listed on chalkboard, daily 12:00-22:00, Place du Port 3, +41 21 616 2194).

Picnics: The most affordable option is a picnic with the local office gang on any of the many inviting benches or scenic lakeside perches. Leaving the Métro station, head left one block to Avenue d'Ouchy, where you'll find several eateries including a **Co-op** supermarket (at #70, daily 6:00-22:00) and **$ Fleur de Pains,** a bakery offering sandwiches, quiche, tarts, and a few humble tables (daily 6:00-19:00, at #73).

Lausanne Connections

By Plane: If arriving by plane, you'll land at the manageable Geneva airport (code: GVA, www.gva.ch). Exiting from baggage claim, you're met by various local TI desks and ATMs. Turn left to reach the airport's train station, with handy connections to points all over Switzerland. Trains leave for Lausanne about every 20 minutes (27 CHF, 50 minutes). Geneva's city-center train station is the first stop on any train departing from the airport (3 CHF for this short hop). If you'll be buying a train ticket, you can save time by using the ticket machine in the baggage claim area while waiting for your bag (there can be lines at the ones in the station). It's possible to take a taxi to Lausanne, but it's very pricey (170 CHF or more) and takes longer than the train.

From Lausanne by Train to: Montreux (5/hour, 30 minutes), **Château de Chillon** (hourly, 35 minutes, station name: Veytaux-Chillon, more with change in Montreux or Clarens), **Gruyères** (2/hour, 1.5 hours, 2 changes), **Geneva** (7/hour, 45 minutes), **Geneva Airport** (at least 4/hour direct, 50 minutes), **Bern** (3/hour, 1.5 hours), **Murten** (hourly direct, 1.5 hours, more with changes), **Interlaken** (at least 2/hour, 2 hours, change in Bern and sometimes Spiez; or go by Golden Pass scenic route—see the Scenic Rail Journeys chapter), **Luzern** (3/hour, 2.5 hours; or go by Golden Pass scenic route—see the Scenic Rail Journeys chapter), **Zürich** (2/hour direct, 2 hours, more with change in Bern or Yverdon-les-Bains), **Zermatt** (2/hour, 3 hours, change in Visp), **Lyon** (hourly, 3 hours, 1-2 changes), **Chamonix** (hourly, 2.5 hours, 3 changes), **Paris** (5/day direct, 4 hours, more with changes). **Train info:** www.rail.ch.

By Boat: For boat connections from Lausanne, see "Getting Around Lake Geneva" near the beginning of this chapter.

ROUTE TIPS FOR DRIVERS

If connecting the Lake Geneva sights by car, note the various routes. The expressway high above the lake zips you quickly between Lausanne and Montreux; although slower, the lakeside road provides great lake-and-vineyards views for about half of the drive (but also passes through several congested towns along the way).

For an even slower but more scenic approach, consider detouring to the **Corniche de Lavaux.** This rugged, sometimes frightening Swiss Wine Road swerves through picturesque towns and the stingy vineyards that produce Lake Geneva's tasty but expensive wine. It lies roughly between Lausanne and Montreux; to get a taste, detour from the lakeside road between Cully (near Lausanne) and Vevey (near Montreux). Going in either direction, follow signs for *Chexbres* to find the wine road. The Route de la Corniche between Chexbres and Cully is particularly well known. Note that this isn't a tidy, straightforward route; expect lots of exploring on twisty vineyard roads. Getting lost is the point.

Château de Chillon

This medieval castle, set wistfully at the edge of Lake Geneva on the outskirts of Montreux, is a ▲▲▲ joy. Because it's built on a rocky island, it has a uniquely higgledy-piggledy shape that combines a stout fortress (on the land side) and a residence (on the lake side).

Remarkably well-preserved, Château de Chillon (shee-yohn) has never been damaged or destroyed—always inhabited, always maintained. Today it's Switzerland's best castle experience. Enjoy the château's tingly views, dank prison, battle-scarred weapons, simple Swiss-style mobile furniture, and 800-year-old toilets. Stroll the patrol ramparts, then curl up on a windowsill to enjoy the lake.

GETTING THERE

The castle sits at the eastern tip of Lake Geneva, about 20 miles east of Lausanne and about 2 miles east of Montreux. From Lausanne, you can connect to the castle using a combination of methods. For a memorable outing, consider mixing and matching these options. For instance, if the timing works out, consider this plan: Ride the regional train straight to Veytaux-Chillon for the short walk to the castle. Then take the boat (ideally an antique steamer) to Montreux, wander that city's lovely embankment back to the train station, and ride a fast train back to Lausanne.

By Train Plus a Short Walk: The S5 regional train (14.80 CHF one-way, hourly, 30 minutes, direction: Villeneuve) takes you to the station at Veytaux-Chillon, a five-minute walk along the lake from the castle.

By Train Plus a Bus Ride or Hike: The faster, more frequent IR (interregional) train whisks you to Montreux (13 CHF one-way, 2/hour, 20 minutes), where you transfer to a bus that takes you straight to the castle. Exiting the Montreux station, cross the street and go down the stairs to Grand-Rue (or take the elevator down, marked *Ascenseur public Grand-Rue*). Cross the street and find the blue bus stop on your right, where you can hop bus #201 to Château de Chillon (3.50 CHF, 6/hour, less frequent on Sun, 10 minutes, direction: Rennaz Village, stop: Chillon, ticket machines on board, covered by Swiss Travel Pass, www.vmcv.ch). You can also walk the two miles from Montreux to Château de Chillon (figure about 45 minutes one-way).

To return to Lausanne, simply reverse the above directions: Catch the regional S5 train from the Veytaux-Chillon station back to Lausanne (hourly), or hop the more frequent bus from Château de Chillon to Montreux's train station (direction: Vevey, stop: Escaliers de la Gare and ride the escalator up to the station).

By Boat: A slower but more scenic route to Château de Chillon is to cruise there from Montreux (15 minutes), Vevey (30-60 minutes), or even Lausanne (2 hours). For details, see "Getting Around Lake Geneva," near the beginning of this chapter.

ORIENTATION TO CHATEAU DE CHILLON

Cost and Hours: 13.50 CHF, free with Swiss Travel Pass, 35-CHF family ticket, daily 9:00-18:00, Nov-March 10:00-17:00, last entry one hour before closing, +41 21 966 8910, www.chillon. ch.

Parking: There's free, easy parking along the road above the castle, but you'll need a blue cardboard clock (the ticket desk can give you one).

Tours: My self-guided tour hits all the highlights, but for more depth, rent the excellent 1.5-hour audioguide (6 CHF, leave ID as deposit) or download the audioguide app (3 CHF) from the château's website.

Baggage Storage: The castle has free lockers, and pay lockers are at the Montreux train station. There are no lockers at the Veytaux-Chillon train station or the Chillon boat dock.

Eating: Consider bringing a picnic to enjoy outside the castle on benches by the lake. Food at the garden **$$ Byron Café** next to the castle is on the pricey side, but there are few other options nearby.

BACKGROUND

The Savoy family—who later ruled a newly united Italy from 1860 through World War II (their seal is the skinny red cross on the towers)—enlarged Château de Chillon to its current state in the 13th century. From the outside, the castle has looked pretty much the same for 800 years. The only major difference: In the Middle Ages, it gleamed with a bright whitewash.

This was the Savoys' fortress and residence, with four big halls (a major status symbol) and impractically large lake-view windows (because their powerful navy could defend against possible attacks from the water). But when the Bernese invaded in 1536, the castle was conquered in just two days, and the new governor made Château de Chillon his residence (and a Counter-Reformation prison). With the help of French troops, the French-speaking Swiss on Lake Geneva finally kicked out their German-speaking Bernese oppressors in 1798. The castle became—and remains—the property of the canton of Vaud. It's been used as an armory, warehouse, prison, hospital, and tourist attraction. Jean-Jacques Rousseau's writings first drew attention to the castle, inspiring visits by Romantics such as Lord Byron, Goethe, and Victor Hugo, plus other notables, including Dickens and Hemingway. During the Grand Tour of aristocratic tourism, the castle became a major draw.

LAKE GENEVA

● SELF-GUIDED TOUR

Before entering the castle, go for a little **lakeside stroll** beyond it (to the south); just five minutes takes you past the boat dock, to where you can look back for classic views of the mighty little fort poking out into the lake, with jagged peaks beyond. (If an old-fashioned steamboat happens to pull up to the dock while you're snapping photos, so much the better.) This view helps you understand why the Romantics fell in love with Chillon.

Walking back to the castle, you can detour down into the little garden below the drawbridge. From here, you can see how the château is built on an island, so the lake creates a natural "moat" that enhanced its fortifications.

When you buy your ticket, ask for the free English brochure and map (there's also a kids' version). The numbers in my tour correspond to those in the brochure, on the audioguide, and posted at the site.

Now enter the château: You'll cross a bridge and enter the **first courtyard** (#3, with handy fountains for your water bottle). In the room marked #4, you can pick up an audioguide and get oriented with a good model of the castle (if the audioguide desk isn't open, check the gift shop—Room 2). Also in this area, you'll find a room with vending machines and lockers; a bit farther along are WCs.

• *Start by heading down the stairs marked 5/9 to a series of...*

Cellars: You can see how the castle was built upon a foundation of jagged natural stone. In Room 8, find the hidden water gate—a secret escape route for the castle lord, who could (and did, in 1536) hightail it into a waiting boat when the Bernese invaded. Room 9 is **Bonivard's Prison,** named for a renegade Savoyard who was tortured here for six years (lashed to the fifth column from the entrance). When the Romantic poet Lord Byron came to visit, Bonivard's story inspired him to write *The Prisoner of Chillon,* which vividly recounts a prisoner's dark and solitary life ("And mine has been the fate of those / To whom the goodly earth and air / Are bann'd, and barr'd—forbidden fare"; full text available in the gift shop). You can still see where Byron scratched his name in a column (third from entrance, covered by glass).

• *Head back out the way you came in and turn left through the big gate into the **second courtyard** (#12), dominated by the towering keep (more on that later). Just before the keep, on the left, go into the...*

Constable's Dining Room (#13): This is one of the château's finest halls. Look up to the six-centuries-old wooden ceiling. The gigantic fireplace was used to roast large animals (including bears and boars) for feasts. The opposite wall has the first of many grand lake-view windows you'll see in the castle. From here the lords of Savoy had a view of all their land holdings.

• *Climb up the spiral staircase to the...*

Aula Nova (#14): This room has a striking barrel-vaulted ceiling that was restored in the 1920s. The collection of mobile furniture recalls a time when nobility traveled throughout their realm (and took their belongings with them) to keep an eye on things and collect taxes. In fact, in many European languages, the word for "furniture" implies that it's mobile—German *Möbel*, French *mobilier*, and so on. Enjoy the ornate decorations on each traveling chest.

• *Continue up to the...*

Private Quarters (#15-17): The **bedroom** (#16) has a short bed—only about five and a half feet long. Not only were people shorter back then, but they also slept half-upright, propped up on pillows. The **coat-of-arms hall** (#18) is usually filled with temporary exhibits. The walls are lined with the family crests of some 50 "bailiffs" who governed this territory during Bernese rule. Capping this hall is another great wooden ceiling reminiscent of a waffle.

• *Exit at the far end of the hall, and turn right into the...*

Camera Domini (#19): This was the bedroom of the master of the house. Its location—at the farthest end of the castle from the entrance—was particularly secure.

In the corner, notice the spiral stairs (closed to the public) that the lord could use to scamper down to Mass in his private chapel, or up to the ramparts. Under a sumptuous fleur-de-lis ceiling, wall paintings (imitating tapestries) illustrate various animals, including a camel, lion, griffin (with the body of a lion and the head and wings of an eagle), and the trademark Bernese bear. Study the model in the middle of the room, which helps you imagine what this room looked like in all its original colorful splendor.

• *Exit the room and turn right (following the 20/24 sign). In Room 21, make sure to see the **medieval latrines,** which take a looooong drop straight down into the lake—a feature that aims to please a certain class of traveler. Take the narrow stairs down and pass through Room 22. You'll end up in a **small courtyard** (#23), where stairs lead up to an observation post with good views. From the courtyard, squeeze into that **private chapel** (#24) where the lord's staircase ended up. Leave this room following the signs for 26, and you'll wind up in the...*

Third Courtyard (#25): Notice that the courtyard's irregular shape causes the angled walkways to focus your attention on the grand window of the master's bedroom—the *camera domini* we visited earlier. There's no question who was king of this castle.

• *Go in the door marked 26/33. The **aula magna** (#26) is yet another*

grand hall—this one for ban-
quets—with spectacular (for their
time) lake-view windows. Proceed
through a few more rooms (includ-
ing more latrines, #29) to the...

Domus Clericorum (#31):
In this "house of the clerks," the
castle bean-counters kept metic-
ulous records of all money and
goods that passed through here, creating an invaluable historical
record. In Room 32 a series of **models and illustrations** explain the
gradual construction of the château over time.

• *Follow signs for 34 to climb back up into the third courtyard again,*
then hook left to find the...

Fourth Courtyard (#34): From this vantage point you can see
how the entire defensive system of the castle developed over the
years. The first phase was the steep ramp, followed by the thick
walls, and finally the semicircular towers with just enough of an
opening to attack invaders below. This is quite a contrast to the
grand windows on the other side of the castle, where the lake
served as a natural defense.

• *Now's the time to scramble along the...*

Sentry Walk: As you pass through various indoor rooms and
outdoor galleries (marked *38/46*), pretend that you're defending the
château from invaders. Enjoy the castle courtyard and lake views.
Circle all the way around, finally squeezing through the archway
(rather than going down the wooden stairs) into the...

Keep (#42): This was the
last line of defense and final refuge in the event of a siege. To
climb to the top of the eight-sto-
ry tower, you can scale 76 claustrophobic steps (marked *42/46*)
for views over the castle, lake,
and surrounding mountains.
From here you can see France
(across the lake) as well as three
different Swiss cantons.

• *Our tour is over. You may scramble the ramparts, enjoy the lake views,*
and play king (or queen) of the castle at will.

Montreux

This expensive resort—primarily famous for its jazz festival each July—doesn't offer much to see. But its laid-back vibe and lakev-iew accommodations help you remember that you're on vacation. Montreux is also a major rail junction; it's both a terminus for the Golden Pass (described in the Scenic Rail Journeys chapter), and the starting and ending point for the Chocolate Train, which choo-choos travelers into

the green interior of French Switzerland (described on page 328). About five miles to the northwest, the town of Vevey is home to the worthwhile Chaplin's World museum.

The Montreaux **train station**—one steep block uphill from the main waterfront road—has lockers both at track 1 and at tracks 3-4. Tickets for most journeys are sold in the main part of the station, facing the lake; however, the Chocolate Train and Golden Pass are operated by MOB, which has its own ticket office and tracks at the back of the station.

To get to the lakefront promenade, exit the station via the escalator down to Avenue des Alpes, cross the street, and continue down the escalator to the lake. Cross busy Grand-Rue, turn left, and stroll along the promenade about 200 yards to reach the TI and boat dock.

The Montreux **TI** has extensive information about the region and possible excursions (Mon-Fri 9:00-18:00, Sat-Sun 10:00-15:00, Place de l'Eurovision, +41 848 868 484, www.montreuxriviera.com).

Visiting Montreux: The lakeside promenade takes you along parks, palm trees, *crêperies*, ice-cream stands, and modern sculptures. Starting below the train station, stroll along the lovely waterfront promenade (with the lake on your right). You'll reach the TI, then the dock for boats to other lakefront communities. Farther along is the town's main landmark: the gigantic lakefront canopy *(marché couvert)* that's filled with a produce market each Friday. Nearby, close to the water, stands a beloved statue of Freddie Mercury, with one arm raised triumphantly. His band, Queen, bought the local Mountain Recording Studios here in 1978, and the late singer has strong ties to Montreux.

Montreux Connections: Trains go from Montreux to **Lau-**

sanne (4-5/hour, 30 minutes), **Vevey** (5/hour, 10 minutes), **Gruyères** (2/hour, 1-2 hours, 1-3 changes), **Bern** (3/hour, 2 hours, change in Lausanne, more with additional changes), **Geneva** (2-3/hour direct, 70 minutes, more with change in Lausanne), **Zermatt** (1-2/hour, 2.5 hours, change in Visp). For trips to **Interlaken** or **Luzern,** you can take either the slower Golden Pass trains (see the Scenic Rail Journeys chapter); or faster, less scenic normal trains, which change in Visp (for Interlaken) or Lausanne (for Luzern).

Bus #201 goes from Montreux to Chillon and Vevey (for the Chaplin's World museum). Catch it on Grand-Rue; facing the lake, the Chillon bus (direction: Rennaz Village) is headed to the left, and the Vevey bus to the right (6/hour, fewer on Sun, 10 minutes to Chillon, 20 minutes to Vevey). The **boat** connecting Montreux to Lausanne, Château de Chillon, and several other Lake Geneva destinations departs from the big park next to the TI (see "Getting Around Lake Geneva," earlier).

NEAR MONTREUX
▲▲Chaplin's World

This museum explores the colorful life of actor and filmmaker Charlie Chaplin (1889–1977), who relocated here in 1952 after being denied re-entry into the US for his outspoken political beliefs. Although a bit out of the way, Chaplin's World is worth a visit—even for those with no prior interest in Chaplin or his films. The museum (and Chaplin's former home) sit on 10 acres surrounded by landscaped gardens with expansive views. With film clips, re-created film sets, and tons of memorabilia, the three-part visit (studio/museum, house, and gardens) celebrates Chaplin's groundbreaking career and provides insight into the man behind *The Tramp.*

Cost and Hours: 29 CHF; daily 10:00-18:00, Nov-March until 17:00; Route de Fenil 2, +41 842 422 422, www.chaplinsworld. com.

Getting There: From the Vevey train station, take bus #212 (departs in front of the post office, 3 CHF, 2/hour, 15 minutes, direction: Fenil, stop: Chaplin, buy tickets from machines). Drivers should take the A9 to the Vevey exit. There is easy pay parking at the museum.

Eating: The estate's former barn is now **$$ The Tramp** café, a nice place for a light snack or drink.

Visiting the Museum: Your visit starts just beyond the gift shop with a short biographical film. Then, you're invited into the studio-like "Chaplin's World." The first room covers Chaplin's early years in Victorian-era London (after his father's death, his mother was committed to a psychiatric hospital). Young Charlie and his brother took odd jobs to survive, and at age nine, Chaplin joined a dance and comedy troupe, touring the UK and eventually the US.

His big break came in 1912 when he was "discovered" by a US film producer. Film set re-creations highlight Chaplin's rise to stardom, from *The Immigrant* (1917) to *Gold Rush* (1925; be sure to test the movable cabin—constructed on rockers to make it sway). By 1923 Chaplin had starred in more than 70 films and started his own movie company (United Artists, based in the heart of Hollywood). The final room houses treasures from Chaplin's career, including an Honorary Academy Award (bestowed in 1929, at the inaugural award ceremony) and the oversized shoes, signature derby hat, and cane he used in character as the mustachioed, sure-footed Tramp.

Next you can walk through Chaplin's former **home,** the Manoir de Ban, for a closer look at his life in Vevey and his role as a husband and father. The first floor focuses on the controversies that led Chaplin to settle in Switzerland at age 63. You'll explore memorabilia-strewn reconstructions of Chaplin's library, living room, and dining room, where you can imagine Chaplin's bilingual family gathering for dinner (while his eight children primarily spoke French, Chaplin insisted they speak English at dinner). The second floor highlights Chaplin's encounters with celebrities from Albert Einstein to Mahatma Gandhi. You'll see Chaplin's bedroom, with numerous family photos. The last room—wife Oona's bedroom—displays home movies filmed here.

Outside, the manicured **gardens** are great for roaming. Picture Chaplin and Oona playing with their children on the lawn. You're encouraged to do the same.

French Swiss Countryside

The sublime French Swiss countryside is sprinkled with crystal-clear lakes, tasty chocolates, fragrant cheese, and sleepy cows. Those with a car will enjoy twisting and turning through this idyllic corner of the Swiss Alps. (For most, it's not worth

the trouble by public transit—though the Chocolate Train from Montreux offers an efficient, well-organized all-day excursion taking in some of this area's best bits.)

LAKE GENEVA

The Gruyères area, just north of Lake Geneva, is particularly handy if you're traveling between Lake Geneva and points north (such as Bern, Murten, or the Berner Oberland). The town of Gruyères, famous for cheesemaking, is charming but touristy; nearby, you can visit two very different cheesemakers, a chocolate factory, an appealing little mountain with surprisingly big views, a workaday town with a fine folk museum, and more. East of Lake Geneva are even more cute villages that can be laced together with a scenic drive.

Southeast of the lake is the mountainous Diablerets region, highlighted by a picturesque hillside village and a lift up to an icy peak.

GETTING AROUND THE FRENCH SWISS COUNTRYSIDE: THE CHOCOLATE TRAIN

The misnamed "Chocolate Train"—it's more about cheese than chocolate, and the route's mostly by bus—is nevertheless a fun, efficient way to connect several French Swiss countryside sights on a day out from Lake Geneva. It's worth ▲▲.

The excursion begins in **Montreux** (with easy connections from Lausanne) in the morning, shortly before 10:00. The first leg is a narrow-gauge train ride in old-time belle époque coaches that twist up through vineyards over Lake Geneva (note that this trip is described—in the opposite order—at the end of the Golden Pass route in the Swiss Rail Journeys chapter). You'll transfer to a bus in **Montbovon,** which takes you first for a visit to the Maison du Gruyère cheese factory, then up to the town center of **Gruyères.** Here you'll have about two and a half hours—plenty of time for lunch and to see the town's few sights. Then the bus brings you downhill to **Broc** for a visit/tasting at the Cailler Chocolate Factory, before returning you to **Montreux** around 17:15. A "guide" offers very little commentary but ensures that nobody gets lost. While a bit pricey, the excursion is a good value when you consider how efficiently it uses your time to combine a cross-section of worthwhile sights and scenery (90 CHF second class or 99 CHF first class, discounts with Swiss Travel Pass; runs July-Aug daily, May-June and Sept Tue and Thu only, none Oct-April; +41 21 989 8190, www.mob.ch).

Gruyères

This ultratouristy town, a household name because of its cheese, fills its fortified hilltop like a beautiful bouquet—but when you get up close, you realize the flowers are fake. But even a hardened cynic has a tough time dismissing the town's undeniable charm. Gruyères' quaint, cobbled main square, which blankets its hilltop, sags in the middle around its flower-bedecked fountain, with sharp mountain peaks rising on the horizon. The town ramparts are now a park, offering grand views from a lofty perch.

There's no doubt you'll be sharing Gruyères: Its ancient buildings serve only tourists; everything is expensive, from museums to food to its *other* culinary claim to fame, merengues; and it seems the local cafés conspire to ensure there's nowhere free to sit. And yet somehow, even with those downsides, Gruyères is still worth a visit.

GETTING TO GRUYÈRES

By Train: The Chocolate Train, described earlier, makes things easy. But if you're coming on your own, the larger town of Bulle is the area's transit hub, with direct trains from Bern and easy connections from Lausanne (both about an hour away). From Bulle, local trains and buses connect easily to Gruyères (trains run hourly, 7 minutes).

Orientation to Gruyères

Tourist Information: The TI is at the entrance to town just above the main parking lot, where drivers and bus passengers arrive (daily 9:30-17:30, May-June and Sept-Oct closed for lunch 12:00-13:00, shorter hours Nov-April, Rue du Bourg 1, +41 26 919 8500, www. la-gruyere.ch/gruyeres).

Arrival in Gruyères: The town's **train station** *(gare)* is at the foot of the hill, a steep 15-minute hike up to the village itself (as you face town, take the path that angles up to the left through the field; you'll enter town via the old ramparts). To make things easier, a bus meets each train (stops at curb just outside station shack, 3 CHF, covered by Swiss Travel Pass, 3-minute ride, get off at first stop: Gruyères Ville).

Drivers: Follow signs up to town and shoot for a spot in the handy P1 lot (2 CHF/hour, 5-hour max). On your way uphill, you'll pass two other lots (P3 on the right, then P2 on the left)—parking in either saves you a few francs but requires a longer walk up into town. On busy days, when P1 is full, the road may be blocked—forcing you to use the lower lots.

Festivals: The town center hosts a one-day cheese festival on the first Sunday in May, and over a weekend in late June the castle

LAKE GENEVA

goes full medieval with the midsummer festivities of La Saint-Jean. The region's most colorful autumn cow processions *(désalpes)* are in nearby Charmey, Albeuve, and Jaun (www.la-gruyere.ch). If you're here on a summer weekend, you might happen to catch a free alphorn concert on the main square (about a dozen performances a year, mostly Sat or Sun, some on Thu, always 14:30-16:30).

Sights in Gruyères

All of the town center sights are covered by the Swiss Travel Pass. Combo-tickets can save money if you visit more than one sight.

▲▲Old Town and Main Square

Gruyères' main attraction is the charming town itself—especially the big square that dominates the town center, which feels like a movie set. You'll see the town symbol—the crane *(grue* in French)—everywhere. While overtaken by tourism, Gruyères still offers hints of the hard life of centuries past. Imagine the jubilation in 1755 when the fountain (with its wooden pipes) first brought the town running water. If you head down the steep lane to the left of the fountain, you'll find a small area of surviving ramparts that you can climb on.

Back on the main square, carry on uphill about 40 yards past the fountain and look right to find a big stone block with hollowed-out holes in the top. These were once measuring bins used by merchants when a lively market occupied this square.

Just beyond is the Calvaire, a former guardhouse now converted into a gallery that displays works by local artists (April-Oct only); a picturesque, trough-like fountain gurgles along its left side.

If you bear left around the Calvaire and continue uphill, you'll pass the H. R. Geiger Museum and the Tibet Museum on your way up to the town's castle—built in the 13th century and once the fortified home of a leading medieval Swiss noble family, the counts of Gruyères.

Even if you're skipping the castle interior, don't miss its garden and ramparts, which are free to enter—you can walk all the way around to enjoy sweeping views of the surrounding countryside.

▲Castle

Gruyères' castle is nicely restored and works to illustrate its long history. A one-way route takes you through rooms that cover three eras: the 13th century (counts of Gruyères), the 16th century ("bailiffs" period, when financial ruin put the castle under the control of a neighboring state), and the 19th century (the Romantic Age). You'll climb up and down through several levels, from the hardworking kitchens to beautifully decorated salons and halls. The finest rooms were restored during the Romantic 1800s, when Gruyères' picturesque townscape put it on the Grand Tour of traveling aristocrats. Two of the highlights, dating from this period, are on the top floor. First is a small exhibit on vintage guidebooks from the Grand Tour age (dating as far back as the early 19th century)—plus a balcony with smashing views over the manicured gardens, ramparts, and mountains beyond. And second is the Knights' Room, which in the 1850s was slathered with Romantic scenes from the town's history and illustrious residents. At the end, you'll be funneled down into the ramparts and idyllic gardens.

Cost and Hours: 12 CHF, covered by Swiss Travel Pass, daily 9:00-18:00, Nov-March 10:00-17:00, +41 26 921 2102, www. chateau-gruyeres.ch.

H. R. Giger Museum

A spooky contrast to idyllic Gruyères, this museum is dedicated to the Swiss artist (1940-2014) best known for designing the gruesome "xenomorphs" in the *Alien* mov-

ies. Not for young kids or the easily creeped out, this museum shares those movies' dark aesthetic. In this deceptively large space, you'll climb through three floors of dark rooms filled with dark images, ranging from Geiger's designs for the films (including life-size models and costumes) to thematically adjacent works that are even more unsettling. Then, on the top floor, you'll find selections from Geiger's personal collection of his fellow surreal artists; this feels almost like a mini-Art Brut museum. Most visitors leave with an obvious question: Why Gruyères? Years ago, Geiger came to the castle—just uphill—to present an exhibit of his works. He got a kick out of the juxtaposition between his boldly challenging art and cutesy, traditional Gruyères...so he wanted this to be the home of his legacy.

Cost and Hours: 12.50 CHF, covered by Swiss Travel Pass, daily 10:00-18:00, Sat-Sun until 18:30; Nov-March closed 12:00-13:00 and all day Mon; below the castle in the Château St. Germain, +41 26 921 2200, www.hrgigermuseum.com.

Tibet Museum

This museum displays an offbeat but genuinely interesting collection of art and artifacts—statues, paintings, and other objects—

from the top of the world. These prized Tibetan possessions of a Swiss collector are thoughtfully displayed inside a former church, making it feel as though the Tibetan deities are squatting in Jesus' old house. Dim lighting and mood music add to the mellow ambience. It's very small—especially considering its high price—but might interest anyone who enjoys Tibetan culture. You can use the free Wi-Fi to access English descriptions.

Cost and Hours: 10 CHF, covered by Swiss Travel Pass; daily 11:00-18:00, Nov-Easter shorter hours and closed Mon; 4 Rue de Château, +41 26 921 3010, www.tibetmuseum.ch.

NEAR THE TRAIN STATION
▲La Maison du Gruyère Cheese Factory

Gruyères is justifiably famous for its Gruyère cheese (no "s" at the end when it's the cheese itself). The cheese is an A.O.C. *(appellation d'origine controlée)* product, meaning that to be called Gruyère, it must be made right here, according to exacting standards. This modern cheese-production center at the foot of Gruyères is handy for train travelers (it's right across from the station). To see the same cheese made in a more traditional setting, head to the hillside *fromagerie* in Moléson (described later). Admission here includes a sample of three varieties of Gruyère cheese (aged 6, 9, and 12 months), plus a cheesy cow-narrated audioguide, essential for understanding the otherwise sparse exhibits.

Cost and Hours: 7 CHF, 12-CHF family ticket, covered by Swiss Travel Pass, daily 9:00-18:00, restaurant, well-stocked gift shop also serves as a decent minimart for picnic fixings and travel essentials, across the street from the train station—or straight ahead as you come down the road from Gruyères' hilltop, +41 26 921 8400, www.lamaisondugruyere.ch.

Visiting the *Fromagerie*: A cow consumes 220 pounds of grass and 22 gallons of water each day to produce 6 gallons of milk, while 100 gallons of milk goes into making one 77-pound wheel of cheese. You'll come across these fun cheese facts and more en route to the viewing area. Smell the various alpine flowers and plants— see if you can discern the subtle flavors they lend the cheese—and hold some cheesemaking tools in your hands. Above the production floor, big windows give you a view down into the milky vats (most interesting when cheese production is going on, generally 9:00-12:30)—watch as the curds are pulled from the vats. Even if cheesemakers aren't working during your visit, videos show the process. The finale is the cellar (near the ticket desk), where long rows of cheese wheels age. Watch a robot cheesemaker move up and down the aisles, lovingly flipping and rubbing each wheel just right.

Sleeping and Eating in Gruyères

Sleeping: $ Hotel le Saint-Georges is ideal if you want to sleep right on the main square. It has 14 comfortable, traditionally out-fitted rooms above a restaurant (Rue du Bourg 22, +41 26 921 8300, info@lesaintgeorges.ch, www.lesaintgeorges.ch).

$ La Ferme du Bourgoz, a quaint farmhouse midway between the walled town and the train station, is a B&B with three home-spun rooms and a big family room (Chemin du Bourgo 14, +41 79 252 7451, www.lafermedubourgoz.ch, info@lafermedubourgoz.ch, Eliane).

Eating: Gruyères' **main square** is surrounded by **$$$** eateries serving (guess what?) all manner of Gruyère cheese dishes. These places are more or less interchangeable; pick the spot with the view that strikes your fancy. (Note that many of them, especially on the right side of the square as you enter town, also have terraces out back with views over the countryside.)

A less romantic but perhaps more practical option: the **$$** cafeteria/restaurant at the **cheese factory** down by the train station. It has a cheery, open, and airy dining hall, some outdoor seating, and good, reasonably priced cheese specialties (same hours as museum—see earlier).

Near Gruyères

The following worthwhile sights are just a short hop from Gruyères in the towns of Moléson-sur-Gruyères, Bulle, and Broc. Bulle and Broc have train stations; Moléson is served by bus. The sights are just minutes apart by car and clearly sign-posted. Drivers can link them with one of my scenic countryside drives through this region, both of which include a stop to summit 10,000-foot Les Diablerets.

Moléson-sur-Gruyères

The sleepy vacation-home village of Moléson-sur-Gruyères, about five miles from Gruyères, is basically a big parking lot with a bundle of condos on one side and three attractions on the other: a mountain lift, the luge ride, and an old farmhouse that offers a cheesemaking demo. The village has a **TI** (+41 26 921 8500, www.moleson.ch), plenty of free parking, and hourly bus service from Gruyères.

▲▲Le Moléson Mountain

The verdant hills and pastures immediately surrounding Gru-yères are beautiful but relatively undramatic, with one exception: the rocky-headed Moléson massif, which stretches up into the air over the hills behind Gruyères. At 6,678 feet, it's not much by

Swiss standards, but its solitary prominence makes for impressive 360-degree views from its summit.

From the parking lot, a funicular takes you to the Plan-Francey transfer point (4,987 feet), where you can catch a cable car to the mountaintop perch. From the top of the lift, you can climb to its rooftop viewing platform—or, for a grand king-of-the-mountain climax, hike 10 minutes up a long set of stairs to the actual summit. From there (weather permitting) you can see Lake Geneva, Mont Blanc, and even some peaks of the Berner Oberland.

The mountain's hiking options include the 2.5-hour, not-as-steep-as-it-looks Panoramic Trail from the summit to Plan-Francey via Gros-Plané—get details and free hiking maps from the Moléson TI before heading up. There's a good self-service restaurant at the top of the lift.

Cost and Hours: 35 CHF round-trip to summit, 46 CHF day-ticket covers unlimited funicular and cable-car rides plus the summer luge (described later), no discounts with Swiss Travel Pass or Eurail Global Pass; lifts run daily 3/hour until 18:00 (last descent at 17:40), also Fri-Sat June-Oct 2/hour 18:00-23:00 for stargazing from observatory, and Sat-Sun Nov-Dec 3/hour until 18:00, closed April-mid-May, www.moleson.ch.

▲Fromagerie d'Alpage du Moléson

Each morning at 9:45, the traditional old Fromagerie d'Alpage du Moléson hosts a small group of visitors for a cheesemaking demonstration. In stark contrast to the sterile Maison du Gruyère's cheese factory, this rustic 17th-century farmhouse gives you an intimate look at the traditional, smelly method of crafting cheese in a huge cauldron over an open fire.

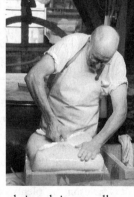

Cost and Hours: 5 CHF for 45-minute cheesemaking demonstration, daily at 9:45, closed Oct-April, lunches served in restaurant; at Place de l'Aigle 12—from the main Moléson parking lot, hike about 5 minutes up to the *fromagerie*.

Reservations: Space at the demos is limited to 50 people, so it's wise to reserve a slot the day before. Use the email link from their website, or call (+41 26 921 1044, www.moleson.ch, Isabelle).

Visiting the *Fromagerie*: A slow-moving video (with some English captions) traces the entire process. Then they repeat the whole thing in the flesh: First the milk is brought to the proper temperature and consistency. Then the cheesemaker skims out the curds with a cloth and packs it into a frame to drain and compress.

Finally, they chop it into blocks and separate it into smaller circular frames that will turn it into wheels of cheese. Visitors are offered cups of the cheesemaking leftovers (milk minus curds, a.k.a. whey) to taste—it's like sweet skim milk. Then the cheesemaker takes buckets of whey out to feed to the pigs. Unfortunately, there's not a word of English during the presentation, but even for non-Francophones, it's still memorable.

Summer Luge

On the hillside next to the *fromagerie* is a low-key luge ride—not Switzerland's best, but worthwhile for kids, luge fans, and anyone with the Moléson day-ticket, which covers unlimited rides (6 CHF/ride, daily 11:00-17:00, closed Nov-May and in bad weather).

▲Musée Gruèrien

Bulle's refreshing, cheery folk museum teaches you all about life in these parts and leaves you feeling good. A two-minute walk behind the castle, the museum is located in the basement of the modern library, with thoughtfully displayed cheesemaking and cow-culture artifacts and fine 19th-century photographs of village and folk life. In this cheese-crazy region, cows are key—notice the many cowbells and the panels from barns painted with murals of the cows' twice-yearly procession up and down the Alps.

Cost and Hours: 12 CHF, covered by Swiss Travel Pass; Tue-Sat 10:00-17:00, Sun from 13:30, Oct-May closes Tue-Fri 12:00-13:30, closed Mon year-round; Rue de la Condémine 25, +41 26 916 1010, www.musee-gruerien.ch.

Broc

The sweet-smelling town of Broc (pronounced "broh") is 30 minutes from Gruyères by an hourly train—which takes you right to the chocolate factory (use the Broc-Fabrique stop; they may instead be using a bus if the train line is being worked on). By car, just follow the signs once you get to Broc and park for free in the big square, a five-minute walk from the factory entrance. The Chocolate Train—ahem, bus—brings you right here.

Cailler Chocolate Factory

This giant factory fills Broc's otherwise tranquil meadow. And the factory's fun "Maison Cailler" visitors center is an engaging, if ex-

LAKE GENEVA

pensive, way to learn about Swiss chocolate. It features a tries-to-be-high-tech presentation, followed by the chance to sample several types of chocolate, peek into a working factory, and peruse a gigantic shop. (Note that you only get a glimpse of the production process; for a more in-depth education on how chocolate is made, consider the Alprose factory near Lugano—see page 355.)

Cost and Hours: 15 CHF, covered by Swiss Travel Pass, daily 10:00-18:00, Nov-March until 17:00, last entry one hour before closing, at Rue Jules Bellet 7, follow signs to *Chocolaterie Maison Cailler*, +41 26 921 5960, www.cailler.ch. Try to visit in the morning, when it's less busy. On weekends and in summer, book a time slot in advance online—otherwise the wait can be up to three hours.

Visiting the Factory: Tours depart every five minutes. You'll be given a "choco-guide" and, with a small group, you walk through a series of eight rooms that pres-
ent a goofy history of chocolate, from the Aztecs to the present day. You'll learn how a chocolate-making industry thrived along the shores of Lake Geneva and in the surrounding countryside, and how, over time, several big names—Cailler, Kohler, Peter, and of course Nestlé—in-

crementally merged into one giant Swiss *chocolaterie*.

After this 20-minute "tour," you enter a zone where you learn about Switzerland's chocolate industry. You'll smell almonds and hazelnuts, crumble a cocoa bean in the palm of your hand, and touch a block of cocoa butter. Peek into the actual working factory, as video screens explain the process, then taste a variety of Cailler chocolates. Your tour ends in the choc-full gift shop. There's also a small café with hot chocolate, coffee, and basic sandwiches, and a great playground for kids.

▲▲Scenic Drives in Les Alpes Suisses

Many rent a car in Switzerland simply to better experience the country's dramatic scenery. And the French-speaking Alps put the "joy" in joyride. In this part of the Swiss Alps east of Lake Geneva, narrow but smooth roads wind past grand old working farms, antique shops, cheesemakers, hilltop churches, lots of lumber industry, and romantic covered wooden bridges. I've outlined two scenic driving routes that offer a taste of the area's remote and pristine landscape. While you can rely on GPS or buy a map, most tourist offices have a free "Grand Tour de Suisse" map that provides the same detail. Before setting out, plot your route by the series of towns and villages you'll lace together. A highlight of both drives is the most impressive Glacier 3000 mountain lift up Les Diablerets.

Valley Loop Drive from Gruyères (or Bulle)

To see how your car does on steep inclines—and how your travel partner does with carsickness—consider this half-day (3-hour) loop from Gruyères through the Simmental Valley to the town (and cable car) of Les Diablerets. You'll cover about 80 miles in all, making a tidy little loop around this scenic region. You can also do this loop from Bulle; just follow signs to Broc, then pick up my driving route below.

From **Gruyères,** head northeast, following signs to *Broc* (with its chocolate factory, described earlier), then *Charmey.* The stretch between Gruyères and Broc has fantastic views back to Gruyères town (on the right). From **Broc,** you'll follow a tiny road over 4,951-foot Jaun Pass, leaving the French-speaking region for the German-speaking zone. Then you'll descend scenically into the **Simmental Valley** (famous for its cows and richly ornamented farmhouses). About 45 minutes into your drive, you'll reach a fork in the town of Boltigen. Turn right (following the sign to *Zweisimmen*) to head south on highway 11 through **Zweisimmen** and Saanen. (From here you could cut the loop short by staying on highway 11 and going directly to Château-d'Œx.) For the full loop, leave highway 11 at **Saanen,** head straight through two roundabouts, and follow the smaller road south. Continue to resorty **Gstaad,** pass through idyllic farm country to the cute little hamlet of Gsteig, go over the 5,072-foot pass at Col du Pillon (consider stopping here for its famed **Glacier 3000** lift), and arrive at the town of **Les Diablerets.** Continue west for about six miles to **Le Sépey,** then head north over the pass called Col des Mosses. At **Château-d'Œx,** head west and then north (perhaps side-tripping to the scenic village of Grandvillard) back to Gruyères.

From Interlaken to Montreux, Chamonix, or Zermatt

The touristy town of Interlaken (see the Berner Oberland chapter) is a handy base for joyriding through the mountains to other Swiss and French alpine destinations. Drivers leaving Interlaken for Zermatt (with its crowd-pleasing Matterhorn), Montreux (on Lake Geneva), or Chamonix (in France), can spend a couple of hours exploring the region en route. Though most of the drive is the same for all three destinations, expect a total drive time of 2.5 hours to Montreux (80 miles), 3 hours to Chamonix (115 miles), and 3.5 hours to Zermatt (150 miles). (There's a faster, 70-mile, 2.5-hour route from Interlaken to Zermatt but it misses the charming towns and sights I describe below.)

From **Interlaken,** head southwest on highway 11, hugging the south side of Lake Thun. When you reach the town of **Spiez,** take exit 19 (continuing on highway 11) and drive for about 30 miles (roughly an hour) through the pastoral **Simmental Valley.** At **Saanen,** head straight through two roundabouts and drive about 12 miles (20 minutes) on a smaller road south through the famed mountain resort of **Gstaad,** the cute village of Gsteig, and on to Col du Pillon (with the fun **Glacier 3000** lift). Next, you'll pass through **Les Diablerets,** where you'll take the fork south (signed *Rue des Ormonts*) and drive 33 miles (about an hour), climbing over the 5,833-foot pass at Col de la Croix to the delightful little village of **Gryon** before winding down about 25 minutes to the autobahn (A9/E62) that cuts across southwest Switzerland. From the autobahn, it's an easy drive to **Montreux** (20 minutes), **Chamonix** (1 hour), or **Zermatt** (1.5 hours).

▲▲▲Diablerets Summit (Glacier 3000)

For a grand alpine trip to the tip of a 10,000-foot peak, take a cable car from Col du Pillon pass to the top of the Diablerets massif, high above the town of Les Diablerets. Up top you'll enjoy views of peaks all around, a vast glacier slowly oozing down below, and some fun mountaintop diversions. While similar lifts in the Lauterbrunnen Valley and Zermatt area are more thrilling, this is French Switzerland's answer to high-altitude fun. Allow two hours to get your money's worth.

Cost and Hours: 85 CHF round-trip, 43 CHF with Swiss Travel Pass or Eurail Global Pass; 3/hour 9:00-16:50, closed mid-Oct-early Nov, +41 24 492 3377, www.glacier3000.ch.

Getting There: It's about a 1.5-hour drive from Gruyères to the pass called Col du Pillon, where you'll find free parking at the base of the Les Diablerets cable car. By public transit, catch the train to the town of Les Diablerets; from here public buses connect to the lift (hourly, 15 minutes).

Ascending Diablerets: At **Col du Pillon** you'll load into the cable car, ride five minutes up, switch to another car (follow *Glacier 3000* signs), then ride another five minutes to the summit. In just 15 minutes total, you're standing on a perch overlooking a glacier, with panoramic alpine views.

The top of the lift is called **Glacier 3000**—it's at nearly 3,000 meters elevation (over 9,800 feet). At your feet sprawls a glacier filled with skiers from fall through spring. I remember summer skiing here—but, with climate change, those days are over. From the top of the cable car you'll find an elevator (the air is thin so you'll appreciate the lift), gift shop, view terrace, cafeteria, and restaurant.

To summit the peak called Scex Rouge (which is actually two peaks), climb 100 steps to a viewing platform. From there, walk the thrilling Peak Walk suspension bridge, which stretches 100 yards to the second peak (with the best viewpoint). Free telescopes have built-in labels identifying the peaks. You can see the Matterhorn, Jungfrau, and a bit of Mont Blanc, the Alps' highest peak.

High-Altitude Luge: From the top of the lift you can ride the "alpine coaster"—the world's highest summer luge course, perched on a rocky bluff (9 CHF/ride). You'll sit on a plastic sled and shoot down a 3,000-foot-long metal rail, with twists and turns that feel like they're about to send you over the edge (pull back on your handles to brake). At the end, you and your sled are pulled safely back up to the top.

Chairlift: A chairlift (included in your lift ticket) takes you down to the glacier. From here, a level but slushy walk across the ice field leads (for about an hour) to a bowling-pin-like rock called Quille du Diable ("pin of the devil"), where you'll find a restaurant with a terrace and more grand views.

Town of Les Diablerets

The pleasant if scruffy and modern-feeling town of Les Diablerets is 10 minutes from the base of the cable car. It's a good overnight stop for drivers seeking an evening surrounded by dramatic and snowy mountain views (**TI** open daily, +41 24 492 0010, www.alpesvaudoises.ch/en/stories/les-diablerets-summer). For public-transit travelers just passing through, Les Diablerets offers bus connections for destinations not served by trains.

My favorite place to stay is **$ Auberge de la Poste,** offering 10 comfortable rooms with plenty of rustic flavor despite its location in the center of town. Alex Pichard is the latest in a line of Pichards since the French Revolution who've run this creaky, low-ceilinged coaching inn (two blocks from the station, just past the TI at Rue de la Gare 8, +41 24 492 3124, www.aubergedelaposte.ch, info@aubergedelaposte.ch). Their **$$ restaurant** is a reliable choice for an affordable dinner (daily 18:30-21:00).

LAKE GENEVA

LUGANO

Lugano, the leading city of the Italian-speaking Swiss canton of Ticino, gives you Switzerland with an Italian accent. The town—which feels bigger than its population of 60,000 (metropolitan area 140,000)—sprawls luxuriously along the shores of Lake Lugano. Just a short, scenic train ride over the Alps from the German and French regions of Switzerland, Lugano has a splashy, zesty, Mediterranean ambience. It attracts vacationers from the rainy north with its sunshine, lush vegetation, inviting lake, and shopping. (When the Swiss couldn't travel abroad due to Covid restrictions, Lugano boomed as their very own exotic, good-weather escape.) While many travelers come here for the fancy boutiques, others make this a base for hiking, cruising the lake, and passing lazy afternoons in its many gardens. Its mountains aren't mighty, its beaches are lousy, and the cityscape is nothing thrilling. But Lugano is the best spot to enjoy palm trees in Switzerland, and its charm merits at least a short visit.

PLANNING YOUR TIME

Lugano lies conveniently at the intersection of the Gotthard Panorama Express and the Bernina Express—two of Switzerland's famous scenic train rides. Blitz sightseers arrive along the Gotthard Panorama route one day and take off on the Bernina Express the next.

If relaxing is on your itinerary, spend two nights and a full day here, arriving and departing on the scenic trains. With a day, spend the morning exploring the old town with my self-guided walk, then do a boat cruise and ascend a mountain lift in the afternoon. For something a bit more active, consider my half-day Gandria and

Monte Brè plan. Any extra time you have can be spent relaxing in the gardens and along the lakefront.

Orientation to Lugano

The old town is on Lake Lugano, which is bordered by promenades and parks. A funicular connects the old town with the train station above. Nearly everything in this chapter (with the exception of the mountain lifts and other excursions) is within a five-minute walk of the base of the funicular. The town of Lugano fades into other, smaller waterfront communities all around the lake (much of which lies in Italy).

Italian is the language of Lugano and its region (Ticino), which is surrounded on three sides by Italy (see "Italian Survival Phrases" in the appendix). In this corner of Switzerland, a *Strasse* (street) becomes a *Via,* and a *Platz* (square) becomes a *Piazza.*

TOURIST INFORMATION

Lugano's main TI is in the **City Hall** building facing the main square (Mon-Fri 9:00-18:00, Sat until 17:00, Sun 10:00-16:00, shorter hours and closed Sun off-season, Palazzo Civico, Piazza della Riforma 1, +41 58 220 6506, www.luganoregion.com). There's also a branch at the **train station,** at the far end of the old, pink station hall (Mon-Fri 9:00-18:00, Sat until 13:00, closed Sun, shorter hours off-season). Stop by either one to pick up a city map, a bus and boat schedule, and to inquire about any special events.

The TI offers a free **city walk** (Mon from the main TI, Sat from the train station branch, departs at 10:00, 2 hours) as well as various **excursions,** such as to the fishing village of Gandria; to the top of San Salvatore; and to the top of Monte Brè, including a short boat ride (all tours well described on the website). As each of these costs just 15 CHF and includes transport or lift tickets worth much more, it can be an exceptional value. The catch: Excursions run in two languages at the same time, and depending on who signs up, the commentary may lean much more heavily toward one or the other (excursions run about once weekly, reservations required, all tours leave from the TI).

Ticino Ticket: All Lugano hotel guests get a free Ticino Ticket, which covers all public transit in the city and entire Ticino region for the duration of your stay. Note that this does not include the lake boats, and lifts are discounted just 20-30 percent. Still, this opens up some fun options for exploring the area.

ARRIVAL IN LUGANO

The train station is on a hill above downtown. You'll find lockers near the escalators in the underground passage. As you exit toward the city, you'll enjoy a grand view (across the street) of rooftops and bell

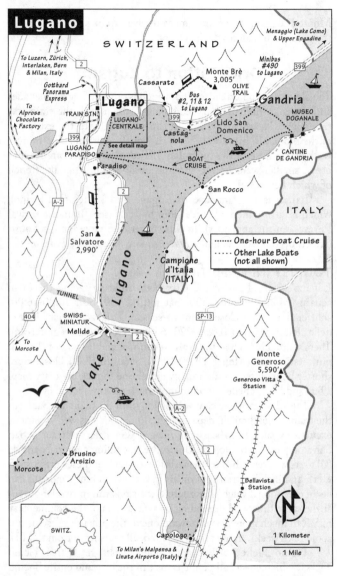

Lugano

To Menaggio (Lake Como) & Upper Engadine

SWITZERLAND

To Luzern, Zürich, Interlaken, Bern & Milan, Italy

Gotthard Panorama Express

To Alprose Chocolate Factory

TRAIN STN.

Lugano

LUGANO CENTRALE

See detail map

LUGANO-PARADISO

Paradiso

San Salvatore 2,990'

TUNNEL

SWISS-MINIATUR

Melide

To Morcote

Cassarate

Monte Brè 3,005'

OLIVE TRAIL

Minibus #490 to Lugano

Bus #2, 11 & 12 to Lugano

Castagnola

Lido San Domenico

Gandria

MUSEO DOGANALE

CANTINE DE GANDRIA

BOAT CRUISE

San Rocco

ITALY

Campione d'Italia (ITALY)

Lake Lugano

······· One-hour Boat Cruise
······ Other Lake Boats (not all shown)

SP-13

Monte Generoso 5,590'

Generoso Vitta Station

Brusino Arsizio

Morcote

Bellavista Station

N

SWITZ.

1 Kilometer

1 Mile

Capolago

To Milan's Malpensa & Linate Airports (Italy)

towers, the lake, and the mountains beyond. To the right you'll find a long-hours grocery, with a taxi stand in the little park just beyond. To the left is the old, pink station building—with ticket offices, the TI, and a surprisingly genteel restaurant (Buffet della Stazione, with affordable pizzas and a salad bar). Beyond this end of the building, you'll find long-distance buses (such as the Bernina Express bus to Tirano; note that this area may be torn up due to construction).

The easiest way to get to the town below is by **funicular** (look for *funicolare* sign—it's in the lower level, near the escalators leading up to street level; 1.30 CHF, free with Ticino Ticket or Swiss Travel Pass, daily 5:00-24:00, departs every 5 minutes). The funicular deposits you right in the heart of the old town, at Piazza Cioccaro, also the start of my self-guided Lugano walk. You can also **walk** (but not with wheeled luggage) down the hill.

HELPFUL HINTS

Laundry: Self-service launderette **Il Girasole** has English instructions. It's a 15-minute walk away from the lake—or take bus #7 (direction: Pregassona) three stops from Lugano Centro to Piazza Molino Nuovo, then walk a block onward (daily 7:00-22:00, Via Giuseppe Bagutti 8, +41 76 503 7964, www.lavanderiaselfservice.ch).

Local Guide: Lovely **Christa Branchi** teaches enthusiastically about her city and its history (200 CHF/1-3 hours, 250 CHF/half-day, 370 CHF/day, +41 79 413 6402, christabranchi@hotmail.com).

GETTING AROUND LUGANO

The town center is easily walkable, and the two nearby hilltop excursions, San Salvatore and Monte Brè, start from funicular stations that are each a 20-minute lakeside stroll (in opposite directions) away from the center.

Buses can save time, though. All lines converge at the Lugano Centro terminal on the north edge of downtown. Bus #2 (2-4/hour) is the one to know: It conveniently links the Paradiso neighborhood (for San Salvatore), the train station, Lugano Centro, Cassarate (for Monte Brè), and Castagnola (where the path to Gandria starts). Buses are free with the Ticino Ticket or Swiss Travel Pass; otherwise, buy tickets from machines at most bus stops (2.30-CHF regular "Area 100" ticket valid for one hour; 4.60-CHF day pass—to buy, choose "Further Tickets," then "Day Pass," then select "Lugano"; www.tplsa.ch).

Lugano Walk

Resorty Lugano hides some interesting history, but let's face it: You're here to relax. Consider taking this short self-guided stroll to get yourself oriented...or just grab a gelato and wind your own way through the city center's arcades and lakeside promenade.

Start on Piazza Cioccaro, at the base of the funicular that connects the train station with the town center.

• *With your back to the funicular, go down the narrow street that angles to the right of the building at the bottom of the square.*

Via Pessina: In this tangled, colorful little corner are several small delicatessen-type shops run by Signor Gabbani. Venture in if you'd like to be tempted by some of the best local cheese, bread, salami, and/or wine.

• *Bear right (at the Gabbani salamis), and about a block down on your right, at Via Pessina 3, find the...*

Grand Café al Porto: This venerable, elegant institution is the most historic café in town. Inside, the *1803* above the fireplace is the date it opened—and also when Ticino joined the Swiss Federation. Once a convent (notice the fine *sgraffito* facade), the café evokes the 19th-century days when Giuseppe Mazzini and fellow Italian patriots would huddle here—safely over the border—planning their next move to unify Italy. Much later, as World War II wound down, US intelligence officer Allen Dulles (future head of the CIA) met right here with Nazi and Italian representatives to organize a graceful end to the war and prevent the Germans from ruining Italy with a scorched-earth retreat. And in more carefree times, this is where Clark Gable and Sophia Loren dipped cookies in their coffee.

• *Just past Grand Café al Porto, take a left at the fountain into...*

Piazza della Riforma: This square is Lugano's living room. With geraniums cascading on all sides, the square hosts an open-air cinema, markets (Tue and Fri mornings), and local festivals. The stately yellow building is the City Hall (*municipio*, with the **TI** at its right corner).

• *Facing the City Hall, make a 90-degree left turn and walk (between the* farmacia *and the white bank building) down...*

Via Canova: This pedestrianized street leads directly to the city park. Follow it for a few blocks, watching for the elegant gallery that burrows through a block (on your left after the second crosswalk). Just after that, on your right, you'll pass the **Lugano Art Museum of Italian Switzerland** (one of several

MASILugano venues), which displays ever-changing exhibits of primarily 19th- and 20th-century art (main collection-8 CHF, covered by Swiss Travel Pass, Tue-Fri 11:00-18:00, Thu until 20:00, Sat-Sun 10:00-18:00, closed Mon, Via Canova 10, www.masilugano.ch).

Next is the creamy little **Church of San Rocco.** Inside, its rich frescoes celebrate the saint responsible for protecting the city from the plague. In Switzerland, you grow accustomed to stark, austere, Protestant church interiors. But Lugano has some exuberant Baroque decor, like this one (and another church we'll see later on this walk)—thanks, in part, to the influence of nearby Italy.

A block beyond the church on your left is the parklike **Piazza Indipendenza.** The giant head on its side is the work of Polish sculptor Igor Mitoraj, who has decorated squares all over Europe with similar sculptures. On your right is the vast, sterile **casino** building.

• *Continuing straight across the street from Piazza Indipendenza, pass through the gate to come face-to-face with the pink palace in the...*

City Park (Parco Civico Villa Ciani): Lugano lacks the over-the-top villas and gardens that people flock to see just over the border at Lake Como. But this park captures some of that lakefront elegance. The park's centerpiece is the Villa Ciani, now an events venue. Sprawl-

ing from here along the lake is a lush park filled with modern art and exotic trees from around the world. Its water gate—a stony gateway that leads nowhere—evokes the 19th century, when this was the private domain of aristocrats. Farther along are fine, yellow pavilions on a little island, with a wonderful statue nearby depicting Socrates taking a snooze. Throughout the park, the flower beds are organized to show off maximum color all year long. If the weather's nice, stow your guidebook and remember you're on vacation as you explore this ingeniously landscaped, people-friendly space. Go ahead—walk all the way

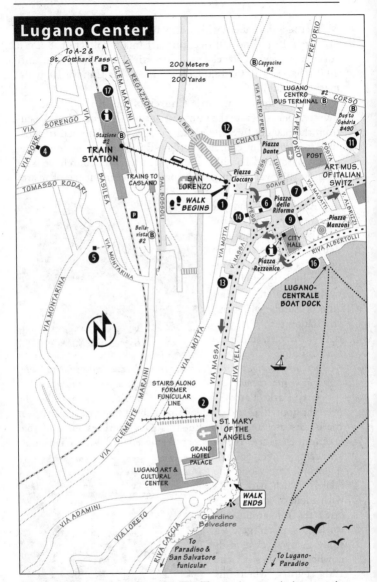

Lugano Center

To A-2 &
St. Gotthard Pass

200 Meters
200 Yards

Cappucine #2

LUGANO CENTRO
BUS TERMINAL

Bus to Gandria #490

Stazione #2
TRAIN STATION

TRAINS TO CASLANO

Piazza Dante

POST

ART MUS. OF ITALIAN SWITZ.

SAN LORENZO

Piazza Cioccaro

WALK BEGINS

Piazza della Riforma

Piazza Manzoni

Bellavista #2

CITY HALL

Piazza Rezzonico

LUGANO-CENTRALE BOAT DOCK

STAIRS ALONG FORMER FUNICULAR LINE

ST. MARY OF THE ANGELS

GRAND HOTEL PALACE

LUGANO ART & CULTURAL CENTER

WALK ENDS

Giardino Belvedere

To Paradiso & San Salvatore funicular

To Lugano-Paradiso

LUGANO

to the little beach near the marina. The park is nicely lit at night and particularly good for a late, romantic stroll (open long hours daily).

• *From the city park, walk back to the town center along the...*

Waterfront: This lovely promenade gets even nicer on Friday and Saturday evenings from June through August (after 20:30), when the busy street is closed off to traffic and you'll find concerts and other events in full swing.

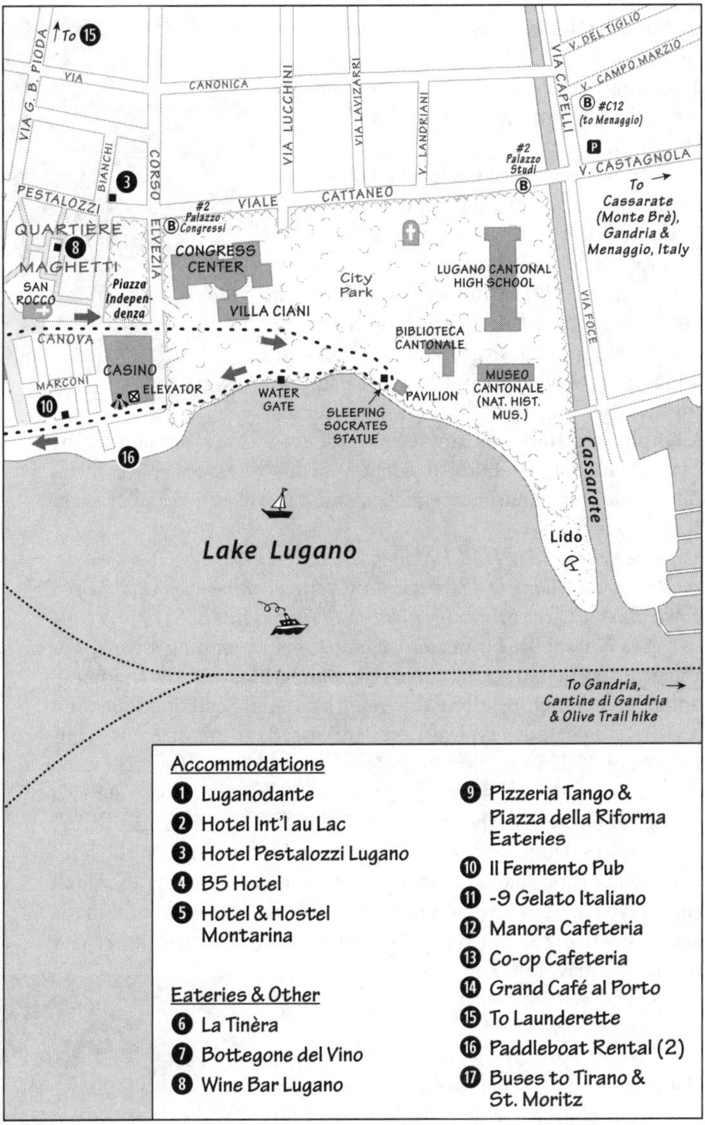

Accommodations
1. Luganodante
2. Hotel Int'l au Lac
3. Hotel Pestalozzi Lugano
4. B5 Hotel
5. Hotel & Hostel Montarina

Eateries & Other
6. La Tinèra
7. Bottegone del Vino
8. Wine Bar Lugano

9. Pizzeria Tango & Piazza della Riforma Eateries
10. Il Fermento Pub
11. -9 Gelato Italiano
12. Manora Cafeteria
13. Co-op Cafeteria
14. Grand Café al Porto
15. To Launderette
16. Paddleboat Rental (2)
17. Buses to Tirano & St. Moritz

On the right, the casino's top-floor restaurant overlooks the lake. If it's open, ride the glass *elevatore* up and down for a fun and free view. Then continue strolling through the arcade (passing **Il Fermento,** a fun spot with Ticino craft beers) or under the mulberry trees (a favorite of silkworms, dating from the time when silk was a local industry). Slow down and saunter—remember, you're in Italian Switzerland—and do the *passeggiata*. You'll pass a couple of places where you can rent paddleboats, and eventually you'll come to the **boat dock,** where you can peruse options for a lazy lake cruise (for details, see "Cruising Lake Lugano," later). Just beyond, a small lakefront park has sand and inviting slingback chairs.

Look across the lake for the village clustered around a huge, blocky, sand-colored building (lit up in bright colors at night; it's just to the left of the pointy San Salvatore hill). That's the **Casinò di Campione,** the largest casino in Europe, which enjoys special legal privileges, granted by Mussolini when he saw what casino tourism had done for nearby Lugano. The casino dominates **Campione d'Italia**—a tiny enclave of Italy that's surrounded by Switzerland on all sides; residents use Swiss francs, have Swiss phone numbers and license plates, and pay Swiss taxes...but carry Italian passports.

• *At the yellow City Hall building, use the crosswalk to cross the busy road. A block inland is Piazza della Riforma again—you've come full circle. But let's keep going. The first left off the square is...*

Via Nassa: This is one of Lugano's main shopping streets. For the next several blocks, just enjoy the wandering, window shopping, and people-watching along this gauntlet of high-end boutiques and jewelry shops under typical Lombardi arcades. This street is reminiscent of Milan's fashion drags. You'll see Hermès, Gucci, Prada, Rolex, and Louis Vuitton. But it's not all luxury goods. After a couple of blocks, on the right at #22, the Co-op department store has a good selection of chocolates (just inside the door on the left), a basement supermarket, and a handy top-floor cafeteria. The small square you pass between Via Nassa and the lake has a dramatic statue honoring Carlo Battaglini, an influential 19th-century city president (mayor) of Lugano.

• *Follow Via Nassa until it dead-ends at the small but historic...*

Church of St. Mary of the Angels (Chiesa Santa Maria degli Angioli): This lakefront church, which dates from 1499, was part of a monastery (next door). Inside the church are the city's best frescoes—worth ▲ and a quick look.

The Passion and Crucifixion of Christ, the artistic highlight of all Ticino and the finest Renaissance fresco in Switzerland, is on the wall that separates the nave from the altar area. Milanese Bernardino Luini, who painted it in 1529, is sometimes called the "Raphael of the North" for the gentle expressions and calm beauty of his art. Follow the action as the scenes from Christ's passion are played out, from Jesus being crowned with thorns (left) to the doubting apostle Thomas touching Jesus' wound after his Resurrection (right). The dominating theme is the Crucifixion. The work is full of symbolism. For instance, at the base of the cross, notice the skull and femur of Adam, as well as his rib (from which Eve was created). Worshippers saw this and remembered that without Adam and Eve's first sin, none of the terrible action in the rest of the fresco would have been necessary. Luini spent a decade working on this fresco, applying his paints day by day, a section at a time, over thin layers of wet plaster.

Facing the giant fresco, look to your left to find the three smaller frames. This is Luini's *Last Supper,* which was sliced off a wall of the monks' dining hall and put on canvas to be hung here.

Finally, wander up to the front of the church. The altar is rich and unusual with its wooden inlay work.

Near the Church: Back outside, notice the old funicular track running up the right side of the church, alongside a long staircase (and next to the Hotel International au Lac). This was built in 1913 to connect two burgeoning hotel zones—high on the hill and here on the lakefront. It ran until 1987.

The building just beyond the church was once a monastery, then the Grand Hotel Palace. This first grand hotel on the lake was radical in that it actually faced the lake.

Just beyond the former hotel, you can't miss the big and bold **Lugano Art and Cultural Center** (LAC). Featuring a changing array of contemporary art exhibits, this is a magnet for art lovers and helps raise the cultural bar in this already very proud city (20 CHF, Tue-Fri 11:00-18:00, Thu until 20:00, Sat-Sun 10:00-18:00, closed Mon, www.masilugano.ch).

• *Along the lakefront across from the church is the...*

Giardino Belvedere: This delightful little garden park is an open-air modern-art museum. From here, survey the scene. Paradiso, the big hotel zone with its 80-foot-high fountain, is a 15-minute walk along the lakeside. From there, the San Salvatore lift zips sightseers to the summit. The ridge across the lake marks the border of Italy.

• *Our walk is finished. If you've got energy left, continue along the lakefront on the pleasant path to Paradiso; there you can summit San Salvatore, hop on a lake cruise, or do both.*

The Story of Lugano

Lugano's history is tied to its strategic position: where the Italian world is pressed up against the Alps, and just below the most convenient alpine passes. The Celts crossed the Alps here and left their mark. The ancient Romans were here, too—the oldest sacred building in Switzerland is an early Christian baptistery on Lake Lugano.

In 1220, when the first road over the Gotthard Pass was built, the Swiss took an interest in acquiring the Italian-speaking region of Ticino, leading to a three-century-long battle for control. Several castles in the nearby town of Bellinzona recall a pivotal Swiss victory in 1513. With this success, the Swiss gained a toehold south of the Alps. At first, Ticino was ruled from farther north, as a sort of colony. But in 1798, after French troops invaded Switzerland and proclaimed the Helvetic Republic, locals stood up to Napoleon by creating an independent Republic of Ticino. The Ticinese couldn't rule themselves peacefully, though, and five years later (in 1803) they joined the reestablished Swiss Federation as a regular canton, on the same footing as the rest of Switzerland.

In the 19th century, Lugano—Italian-speaking, just a short trip from Milan, yet safely over the border in Switzerland—provided a refuge and staging ground for intellectual Italian revolutionaries. They'd meet here to plan the Risorgimento, the struggle for Italian unification (c.1840-1869). Later in the 19th century, tourism arrived, and the grand lakefront hotels were built.

Today, Lugano is second among Swiss cities only to Zürich in its number of banks. It's easy for Italians and others with suitcases of hard cash—black money—to swing by and take advantage of the secret bank accounts. But the mentality here remains Italian. Rather than the Zürich model ("live to work"), the people of Lugano brag that they work to live.

Sights near Lugano

MOUNTAIN LIFTS

Two handsome mountains (San Salvatore and Monte Brè) flank Lugano's city center, and you can conquer either one, sweat-free, by lifts. At about 3,000 feet, Lake Lugano's mountains are unimpressive compared with the mightier Alps farther north; if you've done some of the higher lifts in the Berner Oberland, Zermatt, or Upper Engadine regions, nothing here will thrill you. Still, the commanding mountaintop views over the lake are enjoyable. Doing more than one is overkill. San Salvatore is best and relatively handy to Lugano town; Monte Brè works better with a Gandria visit. Monte Generoso is a higher mountain that's a little farther from town.

▲San Salvatore

The easiest and most rewarding peak on the lake, thanks to its fine panoramic views, San Salvatore (2,990 feet) rockets up from the Lugano suburb of Paradiso. You can reach it by funicular.

Cost and Hours: 30 CHF round-trip, half-price with Swiss Travel Pass; daily mid-July-Aug 9:00-23:00; rest of year until 17:00 or 18:00, Fri-Sat until 23:00, closed Nov; these are last-ascent times—last descent generally 30 minutes later; 2/hour—departs on the hour and the half-hour, 12-minute ride, transfer to another funicular midway up; +41 91 985 2828, www.montesansalvatore.ch.

Getting There: To reach the base of the funicular, either walk along the water (about 20 minutes south of the city center; keep your eye out for brown *funicolare* signs), or take bus #2 (direction: Paradiso, get off at Paradiso/Geretta stop, rather than staying on until the Funicolare San Salvatore stop). Alternatively, bus #1—which stops near Piazza della Riforma—runs along the lakefront to the Scuole Paradiso stop.

At the Summit: You'll find good viewpoints, a playground, and a restaurant (reasonably priced if you buy the daily special with your funicular ticket—menu posted at valley station, food served 11:00-15:00, in high season also 19:00-23:00).

From the lift, be sure to climb five more minutes to the actual summit. On the way up, pop into the Salvatore Museum, with its small collection of religious art and exhibits on local geology (included in funicular ticket, closed Mon-Tue). At the top of the mountain, there's a small church surrounded by a view terrace. For the best panorama, climb to the rooftop of the church (entrance around the right side) for a sweeping, nearly 360-degree view. Unfortunately, the bay directly in front of Lugano is just about the only thing you can't see from up here.

▲Monte Brè

Departing from the other end of Lugano, in the suburb of Cassarate, this funicular takes you to arguably the best view down on Lugano itself (3,005 feet).

Cost and Hours: 25 CHF round-trip, 16 CHF one-way, discount with Ticino Ticket, half-price with Swiss Travel Pass; runs daily 9:00-19:00 plus July-Aug Fri-Sat until 23:00, off-season until 18:00 or 17:00, closed Jan-Feb; these are last-ascent times—last descent gener-

ally 30 minutes later; first stage from Cassarate to Suvigliana runs 4/hour and takes 5 minutes, you may wait a bit for the second stage to Monte Brè, which runs 2/hour and takes 10 minutes; +41 91 971 3171, www.montebre.ch.

Getting There: From Lugano's old town, you can take bus #2 (direction: Castagnola) to the Cassarate/Monte Brè stop. Getting off the bus, walk a little farther along the water, then follow brown *funicolare* signs uphill to the right. Don't dawdle—the automatic turnstile gate closes with little warning shortly before the funicular departs. You can also reach Cassarate via the lake boat from downtown Lugano.

At the Summit: You'll find two restaurants good for a drink or a snack up top. Ristorante Vetta, farther down from the lift station, has better views and a nice shaded playground nearby (daily 10:00-19:00, until 23:00 Fri-Sat—reservations required, +41 91 971 2045, www.vetta.ch).

Monte Generoso

The tallest mountain but farthest from Lugano, Monte Generoso (5,590 feet) is high enough that you can see some of the more distant cut-glass peaks. Enjoy the striking panorama as a cogwheel train climbs up from the station at Capolago (at the south end of Lake Lugano) in 40 minutes, leaving you at Generoso Vetta, a 10-minute walk below the summit. You'll be right on the Italian border, with great views of Lugano in one direction and Lake Como in the other.

Cost and Hours: 68 CHF round-trip, half-price with Swiss Travel Pass, roughly hourly 9:25-16:35, off-season until 15:35, few or no trains Nov-March, restaurant and cafeteria, +41 91 630 5111, www.montegeneroso.ch.

Getting There: From Lugano, take a regular train (15 minutes) to Capolago. You can also get there by boat, though it's slower and only runs once a day at 9:55.

CRUISING LAKE LUGANO WITH A STOP IN GANDRIA

Lake Lugano is made to order for a boat trip. In fact, getting out on the water here is a ▲▲ experience (and makes up for the lack of other big-league sightsee- ing in this sleepy city). The lake boats serve as regular public transport to a cou- ple of car-free spots on the lake. You can either ride the boat around the lake or hop on and off the boat to explore. There's also a diz- zying array of more elabo-

rate excursions to choose from (such as a lunch trip, a grand tour, a shopping excursion into Italy, and an evening dinner cruise).

Boats and Schedules

The basic one-hour boat cruise does a loop from Lugano. It stops at a few desolate restaurants and hamlets along the far side of the lake, visits Gandria (a peaceful and picturesque little fishing town with several romantic view restaurants), then returns to Lugano (27.40 CHF round-trip including stopovers, 16.60 CHF for one segment, free with Swiss Travel Pass).

You can get off at any point, look around, and wait for a later boat; from Gandria, you can also return to Lugano by foot or bus (explained later). Note that if you're hopping on and off the boat, you'll actually cobble together the trip from various longer cruises, each with different itineraries. Some circle the lake clockwise, oth- ers counterclockwise, and not every boat makes every stop (the boat serves only parts of the lake within Swiss borders). Pick up the boat schedule *(orario)* or find it online or with the SBB Mobile app. Note when the next boat comes and exactly where it stops. The sched- ule can be confusing, so ask at the TI or one of the boat docks if you need planning help. If you plan to spend all day on the water, consider the day pass (49 CHF, 20 percent discount with Ticino Ticket, +41 91 222 1111, www.lakelugano.ch).

Stops on the Lake

The following stops make memorable excursions off the boat.

On the Far Side of the Lake: Cantine di Gandria and Museo Doganale

One good place to break your journey is at the adjacent stops of **Cantine di Gandria** and **Museo Doganale,** which are a quick walk from each other (boats dock at just one of these stops, not both). Cantine di Gandria has two traditional trattorias and wine grottos—great for a rustic meal or just a snack and a drink (daily, closed Oct-April, Grotto Teresa: +41 91 923 5895, Grotto Descanso: +41 91 922 8071). A five-minute walk from Cantine di Gandria takes you to the bright orange **Museo Doganale,** right on the Italian border, with underwhelming exhibits on customs and smuggling (free, no English but worth a quick visit, daily 13:30-17:30, closed mid-Oct-March, +41 79 512 9907, www.zollmuseum.ch).

▲Gandria

This town on the Lugano side of the lake is the most popular stop. A dense cluster of houses hangs over the lake with a few lazy, ro-mantic hotels and several invit-ing restaurants. The approach by water is simply dramatic: As you cruise toward sheer alpine peaks, the cluster of rooftops and a church bell tower slowly come into view around a wooded bluff. Once off the boat here, the only "streets" are stairways and cool, narrow passageways be-

tween the lake below and the road above. Go for a circular stroll, climbing up, up, up through town. Eventually you'll find your way to the church; the little parking lot just beyond it has WCs and the bus stop for the minibus back to Lugano.

Eating in Gandria: This is a popular spot to have a lunch break. Either of the two restaurants by the boat dock will do for a meal or drink (**$$ Ristorante Roccabella:** +41 91 971 2722; and just up the stairs to the left, **$$ Ristorante Antico:** +41 91 971 4871). For something more memorable, try **$$$ Locanda Gandriese,** which has better food and a smaller, quieter terrace (pasta and polenta dishes, a short walk farther into town past Ristorante An-tico, just below the church; +41 91 971 4181).

Reaching Gandria by Bus: You can also connect Gandria and downtown Lugano by minibus (#490, 4.60 CHF, free with Ticino Ticket, about hourly Mon-Fri—but there are gaps so check sched-ule carefully, fewer on weekends, timetables at www.lakelugano.ch). The bus stop in Lugano, called Al Forte, is across the street from Lugano Centro bus station, in front of Via Giovanni Nizzola 2. In Gandria, buses stop in the small parking lot just beyond the church. Note that this bus also stops in Cassarate, at the base of the Monte Brè funicular.

Returning to Lugano from Gandria: You can **walk** back to Lugano along the scenic, mostly lakeside Olive Trail, through restored olive groves, with multilingual signposts telling you all about olive cultivation. Exploring Gandria, you'll see green *Sentiero dell'Olivo* signs posted throughout town. When you're ready to leave town, follow these to the left to find the trail (also marked for the town of Castagnola). It's about a 45-minute walk to Castagnola and your bus back to Lugano. Along the way you'll pass the inviting **Lido San Domenico**—a nice place for a swim and a snack. Eventually you'll stray from the lake and intersect with a parking lot. Take the stairs up, up, up past some private homes to the town of Castagnola, a suburb of Lugano. From the Castagnola post office, catch **bus #2, #11, or #12** back into Lugano. It's also possible to **walk** another 40 minutes back to town and the Monte Brè **funicular**—simply continue down busy Via Rivera. After crossing a bridge, you'll see brown signs pointing to the *funicolare* on the right.

You can also return from Gandria to Lugano via **boat** or the **minibus** described above. Note that the last boat and bus depart from Gandria around 18:05 (boat runs later in high season; confirm locally). If you miss these, you'll have to walk or pay about 50 CHF for a **taxi**.

▲▲Half-Day Gandria and Monte Brè Plan

A pleasant way to spend half of your Lugano day is this fun, active circuit: Catch the boat to Gandria and have lunch. Then hike from there on the Olive Trail (*Sentiero dell'Olivo,* 1.5 hours) back to Lugano's Monte Brè funicular (described above). Ride the lift to Monte Brè, where you can enjoy the summit and an *aperitivo* at the terrace restaurant. Then, with the playground to your left and the lake to your right, follow the wooden fence into the shaded forest—within 20 minutes you'll reach the tiny village of Brè. Wander through the town and then ride bus #12 from the parking lot next to the church back to Lugano Centro (20 minutes).

CHOCOLATE EXCURSION
Alprose Chocolate Factory

A visit to this factory in Caslano, a small town near Lugano, makes a fun excursion. Alprose is one of Switzerland's smaller, less-well-known chocolate producers, but their factory is geared up for visitors and generous with free samples.

Cost and Hours: 5 CHF, daily 9:00-17:00, Via Rompada 36, Caslano, +41 91 611 8856, www.alprose.ch.

Getting There: The S60 suburban train runs from Lugano to

Caslano (covered by rail passes, Mon-Fri 4/hour, Sat-Sun 2/hour, 20 minutes, direction: Ponte Tresa). The train leaves from the cute yellow antique train station across the street from Lugano's main station (marked *Ferrovie Luganesi*; go down the stairs). Machines and windows sell tickets. From Caslano station, cross the tracks and go one block downhill along Via Stazione, then turn right on Via Rompada (passing *Museo del Cioccolato* signs).

Visiting the Factory: The machines are in operation Monday to Friday from 9:00 to 14:00, but you're always allowed a look at

the factory. An elevated, enclosed, air-conditioned walkway lets you watch as big dollops of chocolate are dropped into plastic molds, cooled and popped out onto a conveyor belt, wrapped (mechanically), and packed (manually) into boxes. Next to the factory is a modest museum. A 10-minute film describing the chocolate-making process runs continuously (ask for the English soundtrack). The shop sells fresh factory seconds for a reduced price.

MORE LAKE LUGANO EXCURSIONS

If you have a Ticino Ticket (and a little surplus energy), take advantage of its free transportation privileges to explore the region. Ask about your options at the TI: trains, buses, and boats make it easy to get around.

One popular choice is a side trip to the charming town of **Morcote,** which was voted "Switzerland's most beautiful village" in 2016 (www.visitmorcote.ch). Similar to Gandria, but even more appealing and fun to explore, it has a row of historic houses along the lakefront. On the hilltop above is the Church of Santa Maria del Sasso and a terraced cemetery, and Parco Scherrer has some fine lakeview gardens. The bus from Lugano to Morcote takes about 30 minutes; it's also reachable, more slowly, by lake boat (50-90 minutes).

Other options include visiting the charming village of **Montagnola** and its Hermann Hesse museum (www.hessemontagnola.ch); touring the **Swissminiatur** park in Melide (www.swissminiatur. ch); side-tripping to the city of **Locarno** on the shores of Lake Maggiore (www.ascona-locarno.com); or venturing even farther north to hike or mountain bike in the picturesque, rugged **Valle Verzasca.**

LUGANO

Sleeping in Lugano

Lugano's hotel rooms are even more in demand than in other Swiss destinations; prices are generally highest between April and October. Hotels in the city center are easily reachable by a funicular from the train station to Piazza Cioccaro.

IN THE CITY CENTER

$$$ Luganodante, a sleek, trendy-feeling hotel with 84 stylish, well-equipped rooms, sits right at the base of the train station funicular on Piazza Cioccaro (air-con, elevator, pay parking garage, Piazza Cioccaro 5, +41 91 228 0429, www.luganodante.com, info@luganodante.com).

$$ Hotel International au Lac is a classic, elegant hotel with 74 rooms, old-school furnishings, some Lake Lugano views, and relics from the hotel's Victorian past. It's conveniently and scenically located where pedestrian-only Via Nassa hits the lake. Four generations of Schmids have maintained the early-20th-century ambience since 1906, with old photos, inviting lounges, antique furniture, and, it seems, many of their original guests (family-friendly, air-con, elevator, cozy bar with fun view seats on balcony, swimming pool, pay parking, closed Nov-March, Via Nassa 68, +41 91 922 7541, www.hotel-international.ch, info@hotel-international.ch). From the train station take the funicular down and walk (5 minutes), or take bus #4 from the station (direction: Lugano Centro) to Piazza Luini, right at the hotel's front door.

$$ Hotel Pestalozzi Lugano, near the city park, is plain and vaguely institutional (it's run by a nonprofit foundation), but a good value. It offers 54 fresh but somewhat sterile rooms (family rooms, some rooms with lake view and/or air-con—ask when you reserve, elevator, +41 91 921 4646, www.pestalozzi-lugano.ch, info@pestalozzi-lugano.ch). From the station, you can reach the hotel quickly by taking bus #2 (direction: Castagnola) four stops to Palazzo Congressi.

NEAR THE TRAIN STATION

$$$ B5 Hotel, a wonderful little oasis that should be reopen after renovation by the time this book is in print, sits between office buildings just behind the train station. It has 20 rooms, a garden, and an emphasis on sustainability. Owners Daniel and Alexandra Hahne are caring, hands-on, and committed to giving guests a great experience. The name is a play on words—both an abbreviation of the address, and the idea that this is the fifth track *(binario)* of the train station (RS%, air-con, elevator, Via Francesco Borromini 5, +41 91 966 3370, www.b5hotel.ch, info@b5hotel.ch). From the station, find track 4 and walk to the end of the platform (keep-

LUGANO

ing the station building on your right), turn left to cross the street by the big willowy tree, head uphill for a few yards, then turn left up Via Francesco Borromini.

$ Hotel & Hostel Montarina, a creaky pink mansion in a palm garden overlooking the lake, has to be one of Europe's most

appealing hostels, with 124 ¢ dorm beds. It's a great hotel option as well, with 24 private rooms; half of these are antique rooms with classic furniture and shared bathrooms, and the other half are modern "comfort" rooms, with private bathrooms and air-conditioning. Surrounded by lush tropical gardens and an extremely inviting swimming pool, and with a helpful staff, this place is well worth considering, even for those who usually don't stay in hostels (breakfast buffet extra, reception open 7:00-23:00, late-night train noise, lockers, small kitchen, pay laundry, free parking, closed Nov-Feb, Via Montarina 1, +41 91 966 7272, www.montarina.com, info@montarina.com). At the train station, head to track 4, then walk along the platform with the station and lake on your left, and go through the parking lot toward the *Continental Parkhotel* sign. Just before the sign and a stone wall, take the sharp uphill turn to the right; halfway up the hill, go left through the gate marked *#1*.

Eating in Lugano

My recommended restaurants are all in the old town. You'll pay a premium to dine on Piazza della Riforma, but it can be worth the expense. Lugano is not the best place for lakeside dining—instead, cross the lake to the remote little grotto restaurants, or visit the town of Gandria (both options described earlier, under "Cruising Lake Lugano").

Lugano is a good place to sample Swiss wines. And, conveniently, most places let you order a little one-deciliter glass (about 3.5 oz) for the same price, per liter, as the big half-liter (about 17 oz) carafes—so go with a succession of small glasses and try several different wines. Experiment. The Ticino merlot is great.

This is the only corner of Switzerland that embraces the Italian *aperitivo* ritual, where a predinner drink comes with heavy snacks—so keep an eye out for places with that happy-hour tradition of offering a small plate of meats and cheeses with your drink in the early evening.

LUGANO

IN THE OLD TOWN

$$ La Tinèra, in an old wine cellar decorated with wine bottles and antique copper cookware, is filled with locals and a few tourists enjoying big portions of rustic, traditional Ticinese cuisine. The presentation is basic, but the food—including seasonal and nightly specials (such as *bollito misto,* a beef stew offered every Tuesday)—is simply satisfying (Mon-Sat 11:30-15:00 & 18:30-23:00, closed Sun, Via dei Gorini 2, just a block behind Piazza della Riforma, +41 91 923 5219).

$$$ Bottegone del Vino is a quality wine bar with indoor and outdoor ambience and a small but enticing menu (just a few top-end dishes). Sitting here, you feel in the know—but order carefully, as prices really add up (Mon-Sat 11:30-24:00, closed Sun, a block off Piazza della Riforma at Via Magatti 3, +41 91 922 7689).

$$ Wine Bar Lugano is a low-key place to sample wines both from this part of Switzerland and from international wineries. They have a huge variety of bottles, but the staff enjoys talking you through the chalkboard list of what they're pouring today. They also have a few straightforward food items, including a selection of *salumi* (cold cuts) and cheeses from around Switzerland. The bar is hidden in a fun and very local-feeling indoor/outdoor shopping zone a five-minute walk from the touristy core (Mon-Sat 11:00-23:00, closed Sun, Quartiere Maghetti 10, +41 91 921 0186).

Around Piazza della Riforma: Various restaurants offer decent but pricey food and great people-watching from outdoor tables on Lugano's main piazza. The ambience here is delightful at twilight. At **$$$ Pizzeria Tango,** a helpful waitstaff serves Italian cuisine with a Ticino influence. While many of its tables face the busy main piazza, its interior and the tables facing a

quiet little square in the back are also inviting (daily 11:00-23:00, +41 91 922 2701).

Microbrews and Pub Grub Facing the Lake: Named the best bar in Switzerland a few years back, **$$ Il Fermento Pub** has a fun and welcoming ambience that's more rock n' roll than hip-hop. The staff enjoy their work, and the seven Ticino craft beers on tap are great. Peanuts in the shell are free, or if you're here for a meal it's *Flammkuchen* (German-style pizzas, both savory and sweet), burgers, and salads (daily 12:00-24:00, ask for a quieter table outside, facing the lake at Via Marconi 91, +41 91 923 4545).

Ice Cream: Find a nice variety of creamy gelato at **-9 Gelato**

Italiano (that's "Minus Nine"). The interesting flavors are served from covered metal tins—which, any gelato aficionado will tell you, is a sign of fresh-made quality. It's across the street from the Quartiere Maghetti shopping zone (and the Lugano Wine Bar, described above), offering another excuse to wander to this relatively untouristed part of town (daily 11:00-23:00, Via al Forte 4).

CHEAP EATS

Self-Service Cafeterias: Part of a chain, **$$ Manora** offers affordable, healthy food—a salad bar, pasta bar, main-dish counter where meat or fish is cooked in front of you, and lots more. Sit inside or outside on the covered terrace (with a playground). As it has its own entrance (on Salita Chiattone, up the stairs 100 yards from the bottom of the train-station funicular), it stays open later than the Manoras in other Swiss cities. During Manor department store business hours, you can also enter via the bridge from its third floor (Mon-Sat 7:30-22:00, last orders at 21:00, closed Sun, Piazza Dante 2).

The **Co-op's fourth-floor cafeteria,** midway along the Via Nassa pedestrian mall, has a pretty rooftop terrace but is otherwise a poor second to Manora, with a smaller selection and shorter hours (Mon-Sat 8:00-17:00, closed Sun, Via Nassa 22).

Supermarkets: Try the midrange **Co-op** on Via Nassa, or the more upscale **Manor** off Piazza Dante. Both share the same hours (Mon-Fri 8:00-19:00, Thu until 20:00 or 21:00, Sat 8:00-18:30, closed Sun) and are in the basements of their similarly named department stores. On Sunday, your only option is the small **Piccobello** at the train station.

Lugano Connections

The opening of the world's longest railway tunnel—the over-35-mile-long **Gotthard Base Tunnel**—has shortened travel times between Lugano and Zürich, Luzern, and the rest of northern Switzerland.

If you're not in a hurry, though, knit Lugano into your Swiss itinerary with **scenic trains**—take the 5.5-hour **Gotthard Panorama Express** train-and-boat combination to Luzern, or the **Bernina Express** bus-and-train combination to eastern Switzerland. More details about these trips are in the Scenic Rail Journeys chapter. **Train info:** www.rail.ch.

Long-distance **buses**—including Bernina Express and St. Moritz buses—generally leave Lugano from a parking lot beyond the north end of the train station (that's to the right, as you face it). However, this area may be under construction, so ask around if you can't find it—and allow extra time when departing.

From Lugano by Train to: Luzern (every 2 hours direct, 1.75 hours), **Zürich** (1-2/hour, 2 hours), **Interlaken Ost** (1-2/hour, 4 hours, 2 changes, more with additional transfers), **Bern** (hourly, 3 hours, change in Zürich or Luzern), **Milan** (1-2/hour, 1.5 hours).

From Lugano by Bus and Train to the Upper Engadine: The **Bernina Express** bus (#731) leaves from outside Lugano's train station at 10:00 (daily April-late Oct only), connecting in Tirano with trains heading over the scenic Bernina Pass to Pontresina, Samedan, St. Moritz, and Chur (reservations required, +41 81 288 6565, www.berninaexpress.ch; see the Scenic Rail Journeys chapter). A less scenic but quicker option with no changes is the **Palm Express** bus to St. Moritz (#631), which leaves Lugano's train station at 15:31 (daily mid-June-late Oct, Fri-Sun only off-season, 4 hours to St. Moritz; reservations required by 8:30 the same day, +41 58 341 3492, www.postauto.ch). You can always reach St. Moritz from Lugano via **regular train** to Bellinzona, then bus to Thusis, then train to St. Moritz (almost hourly, 4 hours total).

From Lugano by Bus to Italy's Lake Como: An Italian-run local bus (#C12) goes from Lugano to Menaggio on Lake Como (nearly hourly, fewer on Sun, 1 hour, www.asfautolinee.it). From Menaggio, you can take a ferry across the lake to Varenna. This bus leaves Lugano from Stazione Nord near the train station and, less frequently, from a stop on Via Campo Marzio, by the corner of Via Pietro Capelli. This is near the Lido stop of bus #2, in the Cassarate neighborhood a little east of downtown. Tickets are sold at the Lucini Store a few minutes' walk from the park (at Viale Carlo Cattaneo 21) or by the driver for a surcharge.

From Lugano to Milan's Airports: The closest major airports to Lugano are actually in Italy, near Milan: Malpensa Airport and the smaller Linate Airport (www.milanomalpensa-airport.com and www.milanolinate-airport.com). A handy train runs from Lugano's train station to **Malpensa** (hourly, 1.5 hours, www.rail.ch). To reach **Linate**, take the train to Milano Centrale train station, then catch a shuttle bus from there (€5, roughly hourly, 30 minutes, www.airportbusexpress.it). At Milano Centrale, buses for Linate leave from the east side of the station (Piazza Luigi di Savoia).

LUGANO

UPPER ENGADINE

Pontresina • Samedan • St. Moritz

Pontresina, Samedan, and St. Moritz are a trio of towns that anchor the Upper Engadine region—tucked away in an intriguing and picturesque fringe of Switzerland. Here you can ride a vintage funicular to a scenic hike along a mountain ridge, explore the unique townscapes of a remote mountain valley, gaze on a local virtuoso's paintings that capture the region's grandeur, and catch enticing snippets of the rarely heard Romansh language.

Nestled in the southeast corner of the country, the time-passed Upper Engadine (Engiadin Ota in Romansh, Oberengadin in German) is arguably less thrilling—and certainly more difficult to reach—than the mountain resorts of the Berner Oberland and Zermatt. But that's precisely its charm: This region, wedged in the Alps between Italy and Austria, offers rough-around-the-edges mountain culture that feels far from Germanic influence, and closer to the Latin roots that run deep beneath this part of Switzerland. It's also a more rugged landscape—less groomed by humanity, with more wildlife than you'll see elsewhere in Switzerland (the area is home to the largest colony of ibex in the Alps). And for train travelers riding the scenic Bernina Express or Glacier Express, or drivers keen to experience the country's most exciting roads, this area is an easy stopover.

Celtic people inhabited this region centuries before Christ, and the hillsides are still terraced, recalling the hard work that came with farming up here in ancient times. Like French and Spanish, the Romansh language evolved from the Latin that arrived with Roman soldiers and settlers, who moved here as Rome expanded. Town names date back to various invaders. For instance, "Pontresina" comes from "Bridge of the Saracens."

UPPER ENGADINE

Two valleys meet in the Upper Engadine, carving out a picturesque region dominated by three very different towns that form a convenient little triangle, each about 10 minutes apart by train or bus. The most famous—but perhaps least visit-worthy—is the ritzy ski resort of **St. Moritz.** To settle into the region, I prefer **Pontresina,** a lower-key resort town where high-mountain activities are valued more than high society. Pontresina's relatively reasonable prices and proximity to my favorite hike make it an ideal base for the region. Humble **Samedan,** with its cobbled lanes and lovingly painted facades, is worth a lazy walk to learn about traditional Engadine architecture, but offers little else besides pure village relaxation.

The towns are fine, but the mountains (accessed by easy lifts) are the big draw: **Piz Nair** over St. Moritz offers a bird's-eye overview of the Upper Engadine; **Muottas Muragl** features stately valley views and the chance to hike along a super-scenic ridge; and

Alp Languard, over Pontresina, is accessed by a fun, breezy chairlift (and is the endpoint of that glorious hike).

If you can ignore the jet set comparing tans in St. Moritz, the Upper Engadine feels like a place where normal Swiss people go to find some high-altitude fun. And with the Engadin guest card—which covers all area lifts and transit and is free at most hotels if you stay at least two nights—it's extremely affordable, too.

PLANNING YOUR TIME

Compared with the other high-mountain areas I recommend in this book (especially the Lauterbrunnen Valley and Zermatt), the Upper Engadine is pretty ho-hum. On a one- or even a two-week trip around Switzerland, it's probably not worth going out of your way to spend time here...unless you're seeking to get well off the beaten path.

But for those linking two of Switzerland's top scenic rail journeys—the Glacier Express and the Bernina Express—the Upper Engadine is a logical overnight stop (and far more appealing than Chur). With just one night, you'll get only a fleeting glimpse of the Upper Engadine's charms (maybe you'll have time to ascend the Muottas Muragl funicular for sunset). Consider spending a second night here, hope for nice weather, and use that time for riding lifts, hiking, and town-hopping. The chance to experience Switzerland's overlooked Romansh corner is a cultural bonus.

Lingering in the Upper Engadine may also work well for drivers: The valley lies right at the end of the stunning Julier Pass, a high-alpine wonderland of waterfalls and green ridges (take routes via Tiefencastel).

The Upper Engadine in One Full Day: If staying two nights, with one full (good-weather) day, I'd rise early to do the Muottas Muragl panoramic hike to Alp Languard (above Pontresina) in the morning, then head over to St. Moritz for a joyride up to Piz Nair. In the afternoon, consider visiting the Segantini Museum in St. Moritz and detouring to Samedan for a quick town stroll. If it's still nice out, maybe head back up to Muottas Muragl to watch the sunset. (If the weather's bad, hit the Bellavita spa in Pontresina.)

With More Time: With two full days, spread these activities out. Do the Muottas Muragl hike one day, maybe combined with the Morteratsch Glacier trail near Pontresina (especially if it's cloudy). On day two, hike around on Piz Nair, tour the Segantini Museum or walk around St. Moritz's lake, and take a leisurely wander in Samedan.

Seasonal Closures: Like other mountain resort areas, this region has two distinct tourist seasons: summer (June-mid-Oct) and winter (Dec-March). In spring and fall many places are closed and the area can feel dead.

Allegra (Welcome) to Graubünden

Pontresina, Samedan, St. Moritz, and the rest of the Upper Engadine belong to Switzerland's biggest canton, Graubünden (sometimes English-speakers use its French name, Grisons). Isolated by high mountain ranges, this canton is also one of the country's most conservative. The name Graubünden goes back to 1395, when a group of farmers wearing drab clothing organized themselves in the "Gray League" to fight for autonomy. This fiercely independent region didn't join the Swiss Confederation until 1803.

People in Graubünden are passionate about their environment, and purify all dirty water before returning it to the rivers. Engineers are currently going through the expensive process of removing canals (built to direct streams and rivers) and once again allowing the water to choose its own course. The Graubündners love their beautiful countryside and cherish their customs—consistently voting against EU membership, immigration, and other issues that might compromise Swiss neutrality and self-determination. (Many urban Swiss see this conservatism as narrow-minded and harmful to the country's economy, and support a more open, European Switzerland.)

Graubünden cuisine is hearty. Try *Pizokel*, a *Spätzle*-like creation of cheesy flour dumplings. In fall you might find *Pizokel* made from chestnut flour and served with wild mushroom stew. Dishes with *pizzoccheri*—a buckwheat pasta that originated in Italy—are also common here. Graubünden's air-dried beef, *Bündnerfleisch*—very expensive and sliced paper-thin—is popular throughout Switzerland. *Capuns* are cabbage leaves stuffed with a mix of dough, leeks, bacon, onion, and air-dried beef. *Bündner Gerstensuppe* is a creamy barley-and-vegetable soup. For dessert, it's got to be *Nusstorte*, a rich walnut cake.

Graubünden has three official languages: German, Italian, and Romansh (a descendant of Latin with its own independent history). You'll overhear conversations where one person speaks Italian, the other replies in German, a third butts in with Romansh...and everybody understands each other. On trains and buses, the announcements are in German and Romansh (which sounds a bit like Italian).

Most tourists here speak German (others Italian, others English), but if you'd like to please your Romansh hosts, try these phrases:

English	Romansh
Welcome.	*Allegra.* (ah-LEY-grah)
Hello (Good day).	*Bun di.* (boon dee)
Good evening (after 17:00).	*Buna saira.* (BOO-nah SIGH-rah)
Please.	*Per plaschair.* (pehr plah-ZHAIR)
Thank you very much.	*Grazcha fich.* (GRAHTS-chah feech)
Goodbye.	*Arevair.* (ah-reh-VAIR)

GETTING AROUND THE UPPER ENGADINE

Pontresina, Samedan, St. Moritz, and Punt Muragl (the base of the funicular to Muottas Muragl) are all less than 10 minutes apart and well connected by **bus** (about 2/hour, 5.60 CHF per trip, 11.20 CHF for 24-hour ticket). You can also take the **train** between towns (runs about hourly, same price), but the more frequent buses take you up into each village center and save you time and the walk up from the train station down below. Bus rides within a town (such as between St. Moritz Bad and St. Moritz Dorf) cost 3 CHF. All local transport is covered by the Engadin guest card and Swiss Travel Pass.

You can pick up the bus schedule *(Fahrplan/Urari)* at a TI, but the Switzerland-wide SBB Mobile transport app works great here: Just punch in where you're heading and it will list your upcoming options by both bus and train. Bus info: +41 81 837 9595, www.engadinbus.ch.

When checking bus schedules, pay close attention to which stop you're using. For example, Pontresina Bahnhof is at the bottom of town, while Pontresina Post is up in the town center, near my recommended hotels and restaurants. St. Moritz's most useful stops are Schulhausplatz (town center, near the Piz Nair funicular station) and Bahnhof (train station). The Samedan Chesa Planta and Samedan Central stops—a few blocks apart in the town center—are more central than Samedan Bahnhof.

Even if you have a **car,** when you consider the cost of parking, the value of the Engadin guest card, and the frequency of buses and trains, it makes little sense to drive between towns.

HELPFUL HINTS

Altitude Alert: Even the valley floor here is at a high elevation (more than 6,000 feet), and you might feel dizzy and tired, especially on your first day. Top athletes from all over the world come here for altitude training.

Hiking Tips: Hikers should have appropriate gear, including solid shoes, sun protection, a windbreaker, a hat, plenty of water, and maybe hiking poles (for more hiking tips, see the sidebar on page 256). Even in summer, chilling winds blow down from the snow-capped mountains, and it can get cold—especially on chairlifts. Trails are marked according to their difficulty. Yellow signs indicate easy hikes and walks. White-and-red signs signal more demanding hikes, where real hiking boots are in order. Blue signs are for alpine routes that require serious gear (these trails can be treacherous and include rock climbing and glacier crossings).

Keep in mind that in the Alps, some flowers are protected; pick one, and you may be fined. Some meadows are also

Free Transport and Lifts for Hotel Guests

The Upper Engadine offers summer visitors a guest card that covers all transportation in the region, including the pricey mountain lifts. It's hard to overstate what a screamin' deal this card is. Elsewhere in Switzerland, the price of a lift ticket is a major factor in your alpine planning, even with a Swiss Travel Pass. Here, with an Engadin guest card, you can ride lifts to your heart's content...for free.

The card is free (with a refundable 10-CHF deposit) for anyone who stays at least two nights in a participating hotel in summer (May-Oct). The most common version is the "mountain railways inclusive" card, which covers local public trains and buses, mountain lifts, and even some guided hikes (see www.engadin.ch; select "Mountain Railways Included"). Most hotels in the region offer the card, including those I recommend in Pontresina. However, before you book, it's worth asking whether the card is included, and which version you'll get. One version of the card covers local transit but not lifts (rendering it essentially useless); the "mountain railways all-inclusive" card lets you take a bike on board at no extra cost; another version covers lifts but not public transit between towns (not a big deal since local transit is pretty reasonable).

protected for haymaking. Signs ask you to stick to the trails, as trampled grass is hard to cut.

Winter Activities: If you want to ski some of the most famous slopes in the world, head for Corviglia, the largest ski area in the region. It offers varied terrain, mostly intermediate runs, and good snowboarding (convenient from St. Moritz, or a bus ride from Pontresina). Other areas to consider are Corvatsch-Furtschellas (great views) and Diavolezza-Lagalb (smaller, less crowded, great for nonskiers who want views). Both cater mainly to intermediate and expert skiers. See www.engadin.ch/en/bergbahnen for more information and to buy lift tickets in advance. The area also has more than 100 miles of cross-country skiing trails, great sledding, Nordic walking, and spectator sports such as polo in the snow (horses and all). Ask at any TI for information; for more tips, see the Switzerland in Winter chapter.

Essential Brochures: Any TI can give you the local bus schedule *(Fahrplan/Urari)* and a panoramic foldout map showing the lifts and hiking trails.

Pontresina

A popular winter and summer mountain resort with about 2,000 residents, Pontresina ("Puntraschinga" in Romansh) makes a good Upper Engadine home base. At 6,000 feet above sea level on a wind-protected terrace overlooking the Bernina Valley, Pontresina faces southwest and enjoys plenty of sunshine. Popular trails through its larch forests offer spectacular views of the 13,000-foot Piz Bernina peak and the immense Morteratsch Glacier.

Pontresina's first tourists, mostly German and British, arrived in the 1850s. For a while, it was a summer-only destination. But by the early 1900s, the Muottas Muragl railway was inaugurated, the first grand hotels were built, and tourists began showing up in winter, too.

The town feels a bit sterile and resorty, with not quite enough local charm or character. (For more rusticity, wander the steep streets up toward the town church on the hillside. This area has more of a neighborhood feel, with some traditional Engadine architecture.) But Pontresina offers more activities and services than Samedan, without being as glitzy as St. Moritz. This makes it the best compromise home base in this region.

Orientation to Pontresina

Pontresina sits on a ledge overlooking the confluence of two mountain streams, which then flow together across the valley to join the Inn River as it heads north to Innsbruck. Virtually everything of interest is along Via Maistra (may-strah)—Romansh for "Main Street." My recommended hotels are at the top end of Via Maistra, and the TI is near the bottom end. The train station sits in the valley floor a 10-to-15-minute walk below.

Tourist Information: The TI is in the heart of town in the big, round, landmark Rondo Culture and Congress Center, right on Via Maistra. The staff is happy to suggest hikes and mountain lifts (Mon-Sat 8:30-18:00, closed Sat 12:00-15:00 for lunch, Sun

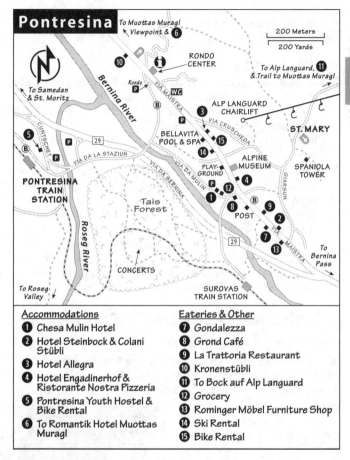

Accommodations
1. Chesa Mulin Hotel
2. Hotel Steinbock & Colani Stübli
3. Hotel Allegra
4. Hotel Engadinerhof & Ristorante Nostra Pizzeria
5. Pontresina Youth Hostel & Bike Rental
6. To Romantik Hotel Muottas Muragl

Eateries & Other
7. Gondalezza
8. Grond Café
9. La Trattoria Restaurant
10. Kronenstübli
11. To Bock auf Alp Languard
12. Grocery
13. Rominger Möbel Furniture Shop
14. Ski Rental
15. Bike Rental

16:00-18:00, shorter hours and closed Sun off-season, +41 81 838 8300, www.pontresina.ch).

ARRIVAL IN PONTRESINA

The train station lies at the foot of the town and has lockers and a ticket office. You can walk about 15 minutes steeply uphill to the town center, following the white signs to *Pontresina*. Or take bus #1 or #2 to Pontresina Post, near my recommended hotels (2-3/hour, buy ticket at counter inside train station or on bus, free with Swiss Travel Pass). To get straight to the TI, get off at Pontresina Rondo or Pontresina Punt Ota Sur. Walking the 10 (easier) minutes from Pontresina back down Via da Mulin to the train station offers dramatic gorge views.

All my recommended hotels (except the hostel) offer free or discounted parking, but drivers who aren't spending the night should head for one of the hourly pay garages: either near the uphill end of Via da Mulin or near the TI, at the Rondo Center.

HELPFUL HINTS

Music: Free summer classical music concerts are offered in the Tais Forest across the river, and (on rainy days) in the Rondo Center or in the church next door (daily at 11:00, mid-June-mid-Sept, confirm and get details at TI).

Ski Rental: Try **Gruber Sport** (at Via Maistra 190, across from Hotel Schweizerhof, +41 81 842 6236, www.gruber-sport.ch).

Shopping: Furniture and housewares store **Rominger Möbel** has an upstairs showroom that's like a modern Engadine home show: Walking among hand-carved beds, tables, and dressers—all made from the fragrant Swiss pine unique to this region—gives you a sense of good living high in this remote corner of Switzerland. You can find good souvenirs here (Mon-Fri 9:15-12:00 & 14:00-18:30, Sat until 17:00, closed Sun, Via Maistra 246, at the top end of town 5 minutes past Pontresina Post bus stop, +41 81 842 6263, www.rominger.ch).

Sights and Activities in Pontresina

CHURCHES AND MUSEUMS

▲Church of St. Mary (Begräbniskirche Sta. Maria)

Above town, just beyond the five-sided, 13th-century Spaniola Tower, stands this remarkable little church. Inside, the wooden ceiling is entirely original. Faded 13th-century, Byzantine-inspired frescoes survive on the west wall (to the left as you enter). The other walls and ceiling were richly decorated by an Italian workshop (1497). The frescoes depict the legend of Mary Magdalene and (above) the story of Lazarus' resurrec-

tion. Imagine this church five centuries ago, packed with illiterate villagers who worshipped by following along with the pictures.

Cost and Hours: Free entry, but limited hours: in summer generally open Mon-Fri 15:30-17:30, closed Sat-Sun; in shoulder season open only Mon, Wed, and Fri; closed off-season. For information, contact the Pontresina TI.

Hiking Back to Town: For a quick (10-minute) hike, walk down from the church a different way: Follow the yellow sign for *Las Blais,* which takes you along the hillside under the chairlift. Signs along the way share interesting facts on ibex, which you may see from here if you look up the mountain. Eventually, head down to the left following the *Puntraschigna-Laret* sign; you'll come back into town near the TI.

Alpine Museum (Museum Alpin)

This little museum, founded by the local mountain guides association, is worth a quick visit. The exhibits fill three floors of an old Engadine town house. Be sure to pick up the brief English descriptions when you enter, then explore.

Cost and Hours: 8 CHF, covered by Swiss Travel Pass; Mon-Sat 15:30-18:00, closed Sun and off-season; Via Maistra 199, +41 81 838 8349, www.pontresina.ch/museumalpin.

Visiting the Museum: The ground floor has replicas of traditional rooms (bedroom, kitchen, living room) as well as good temporary exhibits. The small basement features hunting (with antique rifles and stuffed animals) and alpine wildlife.

The heart of the collection is upstairs, covering the development of alpine climbing and skiing, the regional mining industry (with plenty of mineral samples), and traditional costumes. You'll find a relief map of the entire valley, and models and replica interiors of mountain huts. Look for the chunk of 10,000-year-old wood, which was pulled out of a glacier. One room is devoted to birds: About 130 of the 250 bird species found in the Upper Engadine are shown here. Listen to the recorded songs of 60 different birds on the primitive aviary jukebox. In the room with the mineral samples, you can choose from four mellow slideshow themes (mountains, flowers, butterflies, and a changing theme)—the mountain slides will make you feel like a wimp.

LIFTS AND HIKES

Pontresina is a hiker's paradise. The town boasts one of Switzerland's largest mountaineering schools and has a good reputation for adventure sports. Shops lining Via Maistra rent and sell all kinds of sports gear. The TI will help you find the right hike. Their great, free foldout *Wandern* map is marked with hiking trails and lists details about each one; QR codes link to websites with more information. (Most hikers agree that the Muottas Muragl-Alp Languard panoramic route is tops.) For a fee, you can hire an English-speaking mountaineer through the TI.

▲▲Muottas Muragl Viewpoint (8,105 feet)

The impressive alpine perch of Muottas Muragl (pronounced MWOH-tas moo-RAY) isn't as high as other spots mentioned in this chapter (Piz Nair, Diavolezza), but it's my favorite for its spectacular views over Pontresina, Samedan, and far away to the valleys and lakes beyond St. Moritz. To reach the viewpoint, ride the cute 1907 funicular from the Punt Muragl valley station about 10 minutes to the summit. At the top of the funicular, you can rent a deck chair, have a meal, do an easygoing loop hike, or start a hike over to Alp Languard (described later). And since the funicular runs until late in the evening, Muottas Muragl is the perfect place to watch the sunset (the funicular is discounted after 18:00). A pricey-but-good **$$$** restaurant on the terrace is open late daily and a fine spot to sip a sunset *aperitivo*.

Cost and Hours: Catch the funicular from the **Punt Muragl** valley station: 28 CHF one-way, 39 CHF round-trip, 15 CHF after 18:00, covered by Engadin guest card; runs early June–mid-Oct 2/hour 8:00-23:00, typically departs at :15 and :45 past each hour; round-trip ticket lets you return on this funicular or on the Alp Languard lift described later; also runs late Dec-March; +41 81 842 8232, www.muottasmuragl.ch.

Getting There: To reach the valley station from Pontresina, take bus #1 (in either direction—the bus stops at Punt Muragl both on the way into and out of town) or #2 (direction: Maloja). You can also catch the train between Pontresina and Samedan and get off at Punt Muragl (by request only—press the green button, or the train won't stop). You can park here for free—but if you're hiking to Alp Languard, it makes more sense to take the train or bus, as the hike ends back at Pontresina.

▲▲▲Muottas Muragl Panoramic Hike

This fantastic hike over to Alp Languard, directly above Pontresina, comes with grand views the entire way and a gradual descent of about 400 feet (follow the *Panoramaweg* trail, #10). Midway, at Unterer Schafberg, there's a great soup or coffee-and-cakes stop (ask for the WC key for a fun alpine memory). Keep your eyes open for ibex, bighorn stags, and marmots. It's about four hours round-trip from Pontresina, including three hours of easy to moderately strenuous  hiking. Leave Pontresina by 13:30 if you want to reach Alp Languard in time to catch the chairlift down to Pontresina (otherwise, you just bought yourself 45 minutes more of hiking).

For extra credit, consider the more challenging upper route that climbs the mountainside above the main route via the Chamanna Segantini hut (trail #20, adds about an hour to the hike).

▲▲Alp Languard Viewpoint (7,710 feet)

Pontresina has its own scenic, charming, and easy-to-reach mountaintop lift station, accessed by a fun 15-minute chairlift ride from the town center. If you'd like to enjoy an affordable Upper Engadine viewpoint with grand views for minimal effort, plus a tempting restaurant...this is the place.

Cost and Hours: 18.50 CHF one-way; 26.50 CHF round-trip—or, if coming from Muottas Muragl, use the return part of the round-trip ticket you bought there; covered by Engadin guest card, runs continuously early June-late Oct 8:30-17:30, +41 81 842 6255.

Getting There: To find the chairlift station, go up the ramp across from the Bellavita pool, between the Allegra and Schweizerhof hotels.

Visiting Alp Languard: The trip itself is a joy, as you float silently for about 15 minutes high above the treetops. Up top, the view is outstanding as you look out over St. Moritz (with Piz Nair overhead) and the village of Celerina, across the valley. From here, you can head out on a loop hike, bask in a lounge chair, unwind after your hike from Muottas Muragl, let the kids loose in the play area, and enjoy an affordable lunch with unbeatable views at the **$$ Bock auf Alp Languard** chalet (early June-mid-Oct daily 9:00-17:00, +41 79 719 7810).

If you'd like to **hike down** (or if you make it here too late to catch the chairlift), the descent takes about 45 minutes. Where the path splits, take the left fork (the "Röntgenweg") for an easier descent on a zigzag path through the trees.

▲▲Bernina Railway Joyriding

If you enjoy scenic rail journeys but aren't up for the full Bernina Express train-plus-bus trip to Lugano, there's good news: The best, most scenic part of the Bernina Express is the one-to-two-hour stretch from Pontresina to the Bernina Pass or beyond to Poschiavo. You can take any regional train, or pay extra for a panoramic Bernina Express seat. The train trip is covered by a Swiss Travel Pass (panoramic seat reservations cost extra); the Engadin guest card covers you as far as the viewpoint at Alp Grüm, so if going beyond that, you'll need to buy a separate ticket.

From Pontresina, trains leave at least hourly heading south, toward Tirano. Along the way, you'll enjoy dramatic scenery as you head up and over the Bernina Pass—the highest rail crossing in Europe, accomplished with a twisting track so that it can be done with a standard (non-cogwheel) locomotive. Designated Bernina Express trains (marked *PE* on schedules) run about five times daily and make fewer stops; regional trains (marked *R*) stop at more points of interest. Two of the activities listed next—**Morteratsch Glacier** and the **Diavolezza** cable car—are on this train line. Other intriguing stops, farther along the same line, include **Ospizio Bernina** (at the summit, with the dramatic Lago Bianco);

Alp Grüm (with views over the Palü Glacier); the charming, tidy, and fun-to-explore small town of **Poschiavo; Brusio,** for a closer look at the Bernina Railway's famous circular viaduct; and the end of the line, the Italian town of **Tirano.** The most scenic and efficient half-day plan may be to simply ride the train about two hours to Poschiavo, stroll the town, maybe grab lunch, then ride back the way you came.

For complete descriptions of all these options, see the Bernina Express section of the Scenic Rail Journeys chapter.

Morteratsch Glacier Walk

A popular, inexpensive excursion from Pontresina is by train to Morteratsch, partway up the Bernina Pass. From Morteratsch, an easy trail leads up-valley for 50 minutes to the tongue of the Morteratsch Glacier, with signposts marking the glacier's reach in past decades. It's also a pleasant walk on a cloudy day. The whole round-trip from Pontresina is about two hours by train.

Following the glacial stream gently uphill, you first pass a field of dramatically lumpy glacier-hewn rocks. Farther along, you get the sense you're hiking on the bottom of a drained swimming pool—it's amazing (and alarming) to see, high up on the hillsides, the obvious former extent of the glacier (it hit the upper line in 1850). At the top of the trail, you're eye-to-eye with the snout of the glacier. Keep in mind that much of what looks like rock here is actually dirty ice. To extend the hike, you can scramble over the rock field past the end of the official path for a more up-close look, but be careful—the ground is very unstable beyond the groomed path.

Back at the trailhead, you can eat at the restaurant near the train stop, and also visit a traditional cheesemaker (mid-June–early Oct only, +41 81 842 6273, www.alp-schaukaeserei.ch).

Getting There: The train drops you off right at the foot of the trail (hourly, 8 minutes from Pontresina). From the highway, drivers should follow signs for *Morteratsch* to the large parking lot at the end of the road (pay at machine). Walk from the lot toward the white Morteratsch Hotel, and then past it (with the hotel on the right) to the trailhead.

Diavolezza Peak (9,930 feet)

The 15-minute cable-car ride up to the peak called Diavolezza—the "she-devil"—takes you over an otherworldly green landscape of babbling brooks, then past stark rock and ice to a ridgetop station. There you'll find a restaurant and terrace with expansive views of the top of the Morteratsch Glacier. To turn this into a hiking excursion, return to the valley on foot (2 hours on a moderately difficult trail via Lake Diavolezza, or 3.5 hours on an easier trail past Lake Collinas).

Getting There: To reach the lift station from Pontresina, either take the train 10 minutes beyond Morteratsch to the Bernina Diavolezza stop or drive 12 minutes toward the Bernina Pass (free parking). The cable car is covered by the Engadin guest card (otherwise 31 CHF one-way, 44 CHF round-trip, 3/hour, daily 8:30-17:00, +41 81 838 7373, www.diavolezza.ch).

Roseg Valley Stroll

You can hike two easy hours up the Roseg Valley, directly opposite Pontresina (look for the trailhead behind the Pontresina train station), and marvel at its glacier (from a distance). Consider taking the fun **horse-drawn omnibus** back to Pontresina—or take the omnibus up and hike back (reservations required, mid-June-late Oct departures at fixed hours, 25 CHF one-way, 37 CHF round-trip, +41 78 944 7555, www.engadin-kutschen.ch). You can also rent a private carriage (several coachmen offer this—try the Costa family, +41 81 842 6057, www.stalla-engiadina.ch, office@stalla-engiadina.ch).

OTHER ACTIVITIES

▲Bellavita Pool and Spa

This delightful pool is an ideal place to relax in any weather. The fun complex includes a big indoor lap pool, an enclosed 250-foot-long spiral waterslide, an outdoor pool that stays at 93 degrees Fahrenheit year-round, and an indoor water playground for kids. There's also a spa (nudity required) with a series of saunas, steam baths, and more. (The spa is usually mixed-gender and adults-only, but it's women-only Mon 13:00-17:00 and Thu after 17:00; kids ages 6-15 allowed with parents Sat-Sun 12:00-16:00.) Taken together, this is an ideal place to wind down after a long day hiking (or on a train)—it's affordable and open fairly late.

Cost and Hours: Pool only—11 CHF, pool and spa—26.50 CHF; pool open Mon-Fri 10:00-22:00, Sat-Sun until 21:00, spa open similar hours; in the middle of town at Via Maistra 178, +41 81 837 0037, www.pontresina-bellavita.ch. You can rent a swimsuit for a few francs, or buy one in the shop.

Biking

Several sports stores rent bicycles, e-bikes, in-line skates, tennis rackets, and other gear. Riding the train to the Bernina Pass and biking nine miles back into town is just one of many fun biking options. In the town center, **Fähndrich Sport** rents good mountain bikes and e-bikes (Via Maistra 169, +41 81 842 7155, www.faehndrich-sport.ch). Across the street from the train station, in the lower level of the big youth hostel building, **Bikezentrum Pontresina** rents a huge selection of bikes (+41 81 544 6550, www.pontresina-sports.ch).

Sleeping in Pontresina

These hotels are all within steps of Pontresina Post, the town's most convenient bus stop. All of these hotels, including the hostel, offer the Engadin guest card free to guests staying at least two nights (see the "Free Transport and Lifts for Hotel Guests" sidebar, earlier).

$$ Chesa Mulin Hotel, below the main street, has 30 modern, bright, and comfortable rooms, most with nature themes. This functional, well-designed place attracts serious hikers who want a good night's sleep more than luxury digs. The inviting sitting area with open fireplace and library makes bad weather tolerable, and the breakfast buffet is a delight. The friendly Isepponi-Schmid family takes good care of their guests (discounts sometimes available in shoulder season for guests over age 60, elevator, sauna, sundeck, free access to Bellavita pool and spa with 2-night stay, limited free parking, Via da Mulin 15, +41 81 838 8200, www.chesa-mulin.ch, info@chesa-mulin.ch).

$$ Hotel Steinbock, situated in an old Engadine house, blends a respect for tradition with modern comfort and conveniences. Its 32 smallish rooms are woody and traditional, but the excellent restaurant, charmingly decorated lounges, access to an indoor pool at the big hotel next door, and other touches give it real class (Via Maistra 219, +41 81 839 3626, www.hotelsteinbock.ch, info@hotelsteinbock.ch).

$$ Hotel Allegra feels a bit more modern, snazzy, and hotelesque than others I recommend, with 54 businesslike rooms located in the heart of town (elevator, Via Maistra 171, +41 81 838 9900, www.allegrahotel.ch, info@allegrahotel.ch).

$ Hotel Engadinerhof, while less cozy, can be a good value. The hotel preserves a pre-WWII ambience, and its 88 rooms gather around a sprawling and classic Old World lounge. The three-night minimum is waived when business is slow. Cheaper sink-only "budget" rooms are clean and have well-preserved furniture from the 1930s. "Standard" rooms are similarly old-fashioned but add antique bathrooms, and "comfort" rooms are modern (family deals, elevator, free pickup from train station if staying at least 3 nights, pay parking, Via Maistra 203, +41 81 839 3100, www.engadinerhof.com, info@engadinerhof.com).

¢ Pontresina Youth Hostel, across the street from the train station, rents 120 beds (24-hour access, though check-in times are limited; includes sheets and lockers, discount at Bellavita spa, dinner available, pay laundry service, game and TV room, limited pay parking, closed early April-early June and late-Oct-early Dec, Via da la Staziun 46, +41 81 842 7223, www.youthhostel.ch/pontresina, pontresina@youthhostel.ch).

High in the Mountains: Perched on a ledge above town, **$$$ Romantik Hotel Muottas Muragl** offers a secluded overnight high in the Alps. Its 16 elegant-rustic rooms are furnished in local Swiss pinewood. When the funicular takes the last tourist down, things become as peaceful as the Alps can be (cheaper for 3 or more nights, price includes funicular ticket, open mid-June-mid-Oct and mid-Dec-March only, free parking at base of funicular, +41 81 842 8232, www.muottasmuragl.ch, info@muottasmuragl.ch).

Eating in Pontresina

Virtually all restaurants in Pontresina are part of a hotel, apart from a few bakeries that serve reasonably priced meals. Except for the Grond Café, all the restaurants listed below are closed off-season, generally from early April to early June and again from mid-October to mid-December. The Muottas Muragl and Alp Languard viewpoints (both described earlier) also have good eating options (though Alp Languard's closes before dinnertime).

$$$ Colani Stübli, a cozy yet elegant eatery, is an inviting place to relax over a meal of beautifully presented local fare, with an emphasis on meat and fish. This is a great spot for traditional, hearty Upper Engadine specialties—such as *Krautpizokel* and *Capuns*—executed at a high level. They have a variety of dining areas, ranging from time-warp to modern elegance (daily 12:00-14:00 & 18:00-21:00, at Hotel Steinbock, Via Maistra 219, +41 81 839 3626).

$$ Ristorante Nostra Pizzeria serves wood-fired pizzas as well as some local dishes in two pleasantly low-key rooms on the ground floor of Hotel Engadinerhof (pastas, meat dishes, fondue for two, daily 11:00-14:00 & 18:00-22:00, Via Maistra 203, +41 81 839 3333).

$$ Gondolezza is a fun spot when the weather's good. Huddled around a namesake, antique gondola cabin on a grassy lawn, it has cozy seating inside the gondola plus sprawling outdoor tables and chairs, with plenty of cushy seating to nurse a drink or have a meal with a grand view across the valley. They serve pricey fondue and raclette dishes and more affordable light meals, plus snacks and cocktails (hours are weather dependent, generally Wed-Mon 15:30-22:00, closed Tue; at the far end of town—just beyond the Pontresina Post bus stop—in front of the grand Hotel Walther; +41 81 839 36 96).

$ Grond Café is a bakery with great desserts, plus sandwiches and takeaway lunches (daily 7:00-18:30, Via da Mulin 29, +41 81 838 8030).

$$ Pontresina Youth Hostel, by the train station, welcomes nonguests for its hearty, affordable, four-course self-serve dinner (includes soup, salad, main course with vegetarian option, dessert, and tap water; daily 18:00-19:30, reservations appreciated, Via da la Staziun 46, +41 81 842 7223, www.youthhostel.ch/pontresina). They also serve breakfast year-round and a three-course lunch in winter.

Elegant Five-Star Hotel Dining Rooms: Pontresina's two top hotels have wonderful restaurants in sumptuous dining rooms. **$$$ La Trattoria,** in the fanciful faux-castle Hotel Walther at the top end of town, serves inventive, well-executed Italian cuisine (hours variable, but typically daily 18:30-20:00 in summer, off-season closed Sun-Mon, Via Maistra 215, +41 81 839 3636). **$$$$ Kronenstübli** is in the Grand Hotel Kronenhof, which dominates the bottom end of town and has public rooms fit for a Viennese palace. It's less accommodating to anyone concerned about price, but if you've got francs to burn, its multicourse fixed-price meal is a memorable splurge (Tue-Sat 19:00-21:30, closed Sun-Mon, Via Maistra, +41 81 830 3030, www.kronenhof.com).

Supermarket: Picnickers seek out the **Co-op** grocery, just below Via Maistra on Via da Mulin (Mon-Fri 8:00-19:00, Sat-Sun until 18:00).

Samedan

Tiny Samedan (sah-MAY-den, population 3,000) is the prettiest—and sleepiest—town of the three described in this chapter.
The historic capital of the valley, it's stuffed with traditional Engadine architecture, and Romansh remains strong here. Though charming, Samedan is also humble, workaday, and even a bit rough around the edges. Aside from the grand Hotel Bernina, the town seems almost untouched by the era of  belle époque tourism. It was primarily the region's transportation hub back then, when horse-drawn carriages met arriving train passengers to cart them off to fancy hotels in St. Moritz and Pontresina—and today it still feels like the backwater cousin of its ritzy neighbors.

There's not much to do here after an hour or two, but it's worth popping over from Pontresina for a quick taste of untouched Engadine-village beauty.

Orientation to Samedan

Samedan is gently spread along the slope of a hill that rises from the Inn River. The train station is at the bottom of town; the town center clusters just above. The main street, called Plazzet, runs through the middle of town parallel to the river (it's closed off on market day—Tue, June-early Oct). All the streets seem to converge at the main square (*Plaz*, in Romansh), with its tall Protestant church.

Tourist Information: Samedan's TI is at Plazzet 3, by the Chesa Planta bus stop (Mon-Fri 8:30-12:00 & 15:00-18:00, Sat 15:00-17:00, closed Sun year-round and Sat off-season, +41 81 851 0060, www.engadin.ch/en/samedan).

Arrival in Samedan: Whether you come by **bus or train,** you'll stop at the train station, which has lockers, ticket windows, and a free WC. Most buses do go up into the town itself after a short wait (ask the driver); if you stay on, you'll want to get off in two stops, at Samedan Chesa Planta, then backtrack a short block to the main square. Or, from the train station, just hike up the hill: Go straight ahead out of the station, hook left around the Terminus Hotel, then take the next left up Via Mulin. You'll walk through a small square, then pass the TI on your right, before emerging at the main square. **Drivers** who are here for just a quick visit can park free for one hour in the big garage just off the roundabout into town (past the Co-op and before the station). Pay parking is also available at the train station.

Sights in Samedan

Samedan Town Walk

Samedan offers few activities other than relaxing and enjoying the town. For a start, follow this pleasant, uphill, self-guided stroll with nice views. The route described here takes you steeply up through town (you'll feel the altitude) to a perch overlooking Samedan's magnificent setting, and offers a look at the local architecture.

Begin at the **main square** (Plaz), where Samedan's cobbled streets meet. A giant church tower soars overhead, and a functional fountain quietly gurgles in the middle of the square. At the corner of the church, notice the stone block marking distances to other places, including Pontresina and the Italian border (*Grenze*, in German). Notice that the town name is spelled *Samaden*—as it appeared when the town was first mentioned in writing, in 1130.

Just behind the church tower, the blocky, modern building with the colorful tiled window frames is Samedan's **"vertical spa,"** with several levels of pools (more expensive and purely therapeutic than Pontresina's spa, www.mineralbad-samedan.ch).

From the square, walk uphill on Surtuor (leaving the steeple behind you on the left) to the fork in the road, and take the lane on the left, following the white sign for *Kath. Kirche*. Continue straight up the hill for a block to find (tucked back on the right) a 13th-century, castle-like **stone tower** that belonged to a noble family. From its wooden balcony, they'd oversee festivities in their little domain. It's now used for changing museum exhibits (www. latuor.ch).

Next door, the house at **#12** dates from 1656. The extended roof beams form an X-shaped St. Andrew's cross. This was a pop-

ular way to bless homes here. Notice the sturdy beam ends— roofs were built to support heavy stones and snow. Houses in the region are known by Romansh names: For example, you'll see houses marked *Chesa Juzi* (Juzi's House) and *Chesa dals 3 Frers* (House of the Three Broth- ers). A little farther up, across the street, look between Chesa Manzoni and Chesa Sleim to see a strikingly modern house that's influenced by old local styles.

Continue uphill to the **Catholic Church** (Neo-Romanesque from 1910, with a bell dating back to 1505), at the top of the town. Looking uphill from here, survey the surrounding slopes and their ancient terracing, a vestige from Celtic peoples.

Now carry on uphill, passing the ski lift. Yes, you can do it. Where the road swings right, pause at the wooden bench for the gorgeous **view.** Samedan overlooks the point where the Inn River (coming from St. Moritz) is joined by the Flaz (coming from Pontresina and the Bernina Pass). From here, the Inn continues through Innsbruck in Austria before joining the Danube. The val- ley on your right leads to Pontresina (you can even see a few of its rooftops) and, beyond that, the Bernina Pass. The white building capping the hill directly ahead is the **Muottas Muragl viewpoint** with its hotel and restaurant.

Huff and puff the thin air (you're at 6,000 feet) to the dramat- ically situated Protestant **Church of St. Peter.** The Romanesque

Traditional Engadine Architecture

Samedan and Pontresina both have fine old Engadine houses. A short stroll in either town shows plenty of traditional elements and medieval ingenuity intended to keep inhabitants warm in the harsh mountain weather. Walls are thick—typically

two feet—for insulation. Notice how windows are like the narrow end of a funnel; they were originally covered with animal skin rather than glass. Bay windows gathered maximum precious light and came with built-in seats where women sat to do handwork.

Even though they're thoroughly modernized, the structural essence of these grand farmhouses survives. You can still see the big lower door for animals and the big upper door for hay and the carriage—with a smaller door built into it for people to get in and out while minimizing heat loss. People had the animals sleep below in the hope their rising body heat would warm the living space above. Proud noble-family coats of arms still decorate buildings; many local families can trace their heritage to the Middle Ages.

Look for the traditional Engadine *sgraffito* ornamentation on exterior walls. To make *sgraffito,* facades are covered with a layer of dark plaster, which is then covered with white or colored plaster. Before the white plaster dries, decorative designs are scratched into it, so that the dark background appears. These rustic and crude decorations—much more durable than painted facades—look modern, but have a long history.

bell tower (c. 1100) predates today's late-Gothic church (c. 1480; now a burial church, generally closed to tourists). Benches line the cemetery walls and offer sunny, wind-protected picnic spots. To the right of the church stands a monument marked *Gemeinschaftsgrab*—a "community grave" honoring all members of this region who have passed on. The plaque lets you read some Romansh; if you speak German, there's a handy translation. Now appreciate the view: Beneath

you stretches the highest-altitude airport in Europe, a favorite place to fly gliders (launched by a yellow truck with a huge winch).

When you've had your fill of this panorama, continue around the far side of the church, where the paved path leads quickly back down into town—steer for the tall steeple. (The first residential street you come to, on the right, says "dead end," but a footpath lets you get through.)

Chesa Planta

This interesting old mansion, just a block from the main square, shows off upper-crust lifestyles of the 18th and 19th centuries. This

former residence of the wealthy local Planta family is preserved just as it was when they lived here. It's rarely open, but the fascinating interior makes it worth considering if you happen to be here at the right time. You'll see some gorgeous wood-carved rooms, a beautifully painted dining room, original granite slab floors, and fancy ceramic stoves. Upstairs, the same building houses a Romansh library *(biblioteca rumauntscha),* where scholars collect Romansh literature. A copy of any new book published in the Romansh language is sent to this library.

Cost and Hours: 15 CHF, covered by Swiss Travel Pass, 1.5-hour tour in German and usually also English runs Thu at 15:30 in early June-late Oct; may open other weekdays, at least partly for temporary exhibits—check; +41 81 852 1272, www.chesaplanta. ch.

St. Moritz

The oldest and perhaps best-known winter resort in the world, St. Moritz has long been the snowy haunt of Europe's rich and famous. It's said that in 1864, St. Moritz hotel pioneer Johannes Badrutt invented winter tourism in the Alps. To allay his British guests' skepticism, he offered them free accommodations if the winter weather was bad. They came and enjoyed fine weather. He liquored them up, they had fun...and they brought their friends along the next year. St. Moritz added to its fame when it hosted the Winter Olympics in 1928 and 1948.

Although St. Moritz might have been a real town once, today it's little more than a charmless cluster of luxury hotels and designer boutiques. (Think of it as the anti-Gimmelwald.) For the jet set, winter is prime time in St. Moritz, when celebrity-spotting and prices are at their peak. In summer, however, it's pretty quiet and mostly attracts sporty Swiss vacationers of means who come for active recreation (in-line skating, polo, golf, paragliding, horseback riding, lake strolling, etc.).

For the rest of us, the town has little to offer—I don't recommend overnighting here (though nightlife seekers will find it far livelier than surrounding towns). But in good weather, it's worth a visit for the funicular-and-cable-car ride up to Piz Nair (free with Engadin guest card), a hike or bike on the mountainside above town, and a visit to the Segantini Museum.

Orientation to St. Moritz

The older section of St. Moritz (known as the "Dorf") sits on a steep slope above the lake. The train station *(Bahnhof)* is next to the lake at the base of the hill.

The main bus stop (Schulhausplatz) is at the top. From the center of town, the busy Via dal Bagn runs downhill to the modern suburb of St. Moritz Bad, which sprawls on a level plain at the far end of the lake. St. Moritz Bad has sports facilities (covered pool, tennis courts, ice-skating hall, horseback riding, and so on), a big Co-op supermarket, and a one-block shopping district (Via Salet), but it's mostly a characterless concrete town. Aside from its proximity to the lake, St. Moritz Bad is pretty, well, bad.

Tourist Information: The TI is along the main drag in the old center, a couple of short, meandering blocks below the central bus stop at Schulhausplatz (Mon-Sat 9:00-18:30, closed Sun, shorter hours off-season, Via Maistra 12, +41 81 837 3333, www.stmoritz.ch). There's also a tiny branch TI next to the ticket office at the train station (similar hours, plus Sun 10:00-13:30 & 14:30-18:30).

ARRIVAL IN ST. MORITZ

The most straightforward approach from Pontresina is by **bus,** since it takes you directly to St. Moritz's town center (Schulhaus-platz stop, a short walk below the Piz Nair lift and above the TI).

St. Moritz's **train station** is near the lake, just below the Dorf. The station has lockers, ticket windows, a baggage-storage desk, and a branch TI. To get into town, you can simply **walk** uphill for 15 minutes, but it's more fun (and less work) to head up via the Ser-letta parking garage: Exit the station to the left (look for *Zentrum/Dorf* signs with an escalator icon) and cross the footbridge into the garage. Inside, find the art-lined escalator (Switzerland's longest) that zips you up next to the Palace Hotel. Even ritzier, to enjoy your own private Swiss mountain lift for a couple of minutes, ride the angled elevator—which feels like a mini-funicular—that runs next to the escalators (enter underneath the first stage). From the top, it's a relatively quick walk up to the center (head uphill and to the left). You can also take a **bus** from the station up to Schulhausplatz.

If arriving by **car,** you can pay to park at the Serletta garage near the train station (see above) or at the more central Quadrellas garage, right on Schulhausplatz. Street parking is a little cheaper.

HELPFUL HINTS

Bike Rental: Try **Skiservice Corvatsch** (Via Stredas 11, +41 81 838 77 88), or ask at the TI for tips.

Winter Activities: Ender Sport is one of many ski-rental shops (just uphill from TI at Via Maistra 26, +41 81 833 3536, www.endersport.com). For a thrilling splurge, you can take a ride—between a professional pilot and brakeman—on the mile-long Olympic **bobsled** course from St. Moritz to Celerina...in 75 seconds (270 CHF, open mid-Jan-early March, reserve ahead, www.olympia-bobrun.ch).

Posters: St. Moritz's tourist board offers pre-WWII tourism posters for 5-10 CHF each. Buy one at the main TI or order online (https://shop.stmoritz.ch).

Sights and Activities in St. Moritz

ST. MORITZ DORF (TOWN CENTER)

While not without its charms, the old town center of St. Moritz feels rather sterile and soulless—surrounded by high-rise, high-price development.

The most natural entry point is the square called **Schulhaus-platz,** named for the landmark schoolhouse, now a city library, that dominates it. Schulhausplatz is officially called "Plazza da Scou-la" in Romansh (but you won't hear much Romansh in German-speaking St. Moritz). Here you'll find St. Moritz's most central bus stop and parking garage, and a handy Co-op grocery (to the right of the library). The Piz Nair lift departs from just uphill, roughly behind the library (follow signs up the stepped lane around its left side).

On the downhill side of Schulhausplatz sprawls the tight and tidy **historical center,** with the TI more or less in its middle, on Plazza Mauritius. On the street in front of the TI sits Hanselmann, a venerable cafè/*Bäckerei/Confiserie.* Directly behind the TI is the Chesa Veglia, a house dating from 1658, offering a good look at rustic Engadine architecture (described on page 381; also houses a traditional restaurant). Just beyond is the Kulm Hotel—one of the city's many grand hotels—and downhill (on Via Serletta) you'll find the entrance to the escalator and elevator/mini-funicular leading all the way down to the lake. If you ride to the bottom, you'll pop out at a view platform that extends over the calm turquoise waters.

Hemming in the bottom of the historical center (above the train station and lake) is **Via Serlas,** famed for its high-end shopping. This is dominated by Badrutt's Palace, a grand hotel that opened in 1896 and has been hosting VIPs ever since (including Marlene Dietrich, Audrey Hepburn, Alfred Hitchcock, and John Lennon...though not all in the same room).

There's only one real museum in the town center: the **Berry Museum,** dedicated not to delicious little fruits but to local painter Peter Robert Berry (1864-1942). While Berry enjoyed neither the talent nor the fame of Segantini, and the entry price is steep, this is a suitable rainy-day activity for art lovers (15 CHF, covered by Swiss Travel Pass; Mon-Fri 14:00-18:00, closed Sat-Sun; closed in shoulder season, open in winter; just below the center of the pedestrian zone at Via Arona 32, +41 81 833 3018, www.berrymuseum.com).

The two museums listed below—while a bit farther from the town center—are more worthwhile.

MUSEUMS JUST OUTSIDE CENTRAL ST. MORITZ
These are a 10-to-15-minute walk from the center, with the Segantini Museum perched directly uphill from the Engadiner. A steep, woodsy path connects the two—look for the path directly across the street from the Segantini; leaving the Engadiner, head to the right to start the walk up.

▲▲Segantini Museum
This museum is dedicated to the ultimate painter of alpine life, Giovanni Segantini (1858-1899). The tiny museum, which looks like a Neo-Byzantine church, is based on Segantini's design for the Swiss Pavilion at the 1900 World's Fair in Paris—but made

of local stone rather than the originally intended steel. Segantini's vision—both his pavilion and his life's major work—lives on here, near where he settled in his 30s.

Cost and Hours: 15 CHF, Tue-Sun 11:00-17:00, closed Mon and off-season, Via Somplaz 30, +41 81 833 4454, www.segantini-museum.ch.

Getting There: To reach the museum on foot you can simply follow signs along Via Somplaz, but for a nicer stroll, look for the "Segantiniweg" path that cuts through the woods just above the road. (Or take bus #2 one stop from Schulhausplatz to the Segantini Museum stop.) Drivers will find metered roadside parking just before the museum.

Background: Segantini came to these mountains to get away from the misty air of his native Milan and to live more cheaply (in those days, Switzerland was a low-budget destination—I know, hard to imagine). The crisp alpine atmosphere was great for capturing the bright, sharp, crystal-clear mountain light. Painting in the open air with brushstrokes that invigorated his fascinating scenes, Segantini created works reminiscent of the French Impressionists. Segantini died young (at age 41), and money ran out before this grandiose pavilion could be built. Segantini's masterpiece, the *Alpine Triptych*, was also intended for the World's Fair but never completed.

Visiting the Museum: The paintings are displayed on two floors. Begin by climbing the stairs to the round room on the top floor, where you can view the haunting *Alpine Triptych:* three paintings representing (left to right) life, nature, and death. Notice how, even in the death scene—as the body of a newly deceased loved one is brought out to a horse cart while mourning women look on—there's a glimmer of hope and faith in the swirling clouds above. Segantini even designed the *Triptych*'s frames, ornamented with the local five-needled Swiss pine.

Then head back to the entry level, and spend some time with the many smaller canvases here. Particularly notable is *Ave Maria at the Crossing,* where a man rowing a simple boat—laden with a flock of sheep and a mother and baby—pauses to pray at sunset as the church bells toll.

Engadiner Museum (Museum Engiandinais)

This four-story Engadine-style house, built in 1905 to house this museum, displays a collection of lovingly reassembled living areas *(stüvas)* from the region's surviving patrician houses of centuries past. Most of these interiors are entirely paneled in wood, much of it elaborately carved (especially in the Stüa de Gros). Following the well-done tablet guide (included with entry), you can also peek at a smoky farm kitchen and a nightmare-inducing four-poster bed that's overseen by a painted skeleton, just in case life in medieval Switzerland didn't provide enough reminders of one's mortality.

Cost and Hours: 15 CHF, covered by Swiss Travel Pass; open Thu-Sun 11:00-17:00, closed Mon-Wed and off-season; walk 10 minutes downhill from town center to Via dal Bagn 39, +41 81 833 4333, www.museum-engiadinais.ch.

LIFTS AND HIKES
▲▲▲Corviglia Funicular and Cable Car to Piz Nair (10,030 feet)

A trip up to the Piz Nair summit is the best reason to visit St. Moritz in the summer. The ride up is a treat, and from the top you get a sprawling, nearly 360-degree view across the Upper Engadine's rugged mountain rooftop and down to the strangely colorful lakes and valleys below. (This is especially appealing if you have an Engadin guest card, which makes it free. Without the card, your money's better spent on a visit to Muottas Muragl and Alp Languard.)

Cost: 12.60 CHF for each leg, 69-CHF round-trip ticket, covered by Engadin guest card, +41 81 83 5020, www.mountains. ch.

Lift Stages: The ride up to Piz Nair has three stages: two funiculars, then a cable car, all of which leave every 20 minutes. The entire trip to the top, from the center of St. Moritz, takes about half an hour.

The departure station is just uphill from Schulhausplatz, in the middle of St. Moritz Dorf. From here, ride the first funicular just five minutes up to **Chantarella** (6,578 feet; this leg runs 8:20-17:00, last ascent to Piz Nair at 16:00, last descent at 17:20). There's not much to see here, but you can follow "Heidi's Flower Trail," a relatively level one-hour loop through wildflower fields.

At Chantarella, change to a second funicular up to **Corviglia** in about seven minutes (aim for a seat on the left; runs 8:30-16:50, last descent at 17:10). Corviglia (8,156 feet) is a lovely spot to pause on your way back down. Next to the lift station, the swanky, crassly promotional **$$$ Quattro Bar** (hyping the Audi model) perfectly captures the whole St. Moritz vibe. For something a little more rustic, you can hike steeply 10 minutes uphill to the **$$ Alpina Hütte,** which also serves food.

At Corviglia, switch to the cable car for the last leg—about seven more minutes—up to Piz Nair (8:45-16:25, last descent at 16:45).

At the **Piz Nair** summit station (10,030 feet), you'll find a panoramic **$$$** restaurant with a small outdoor terrace *(Sonnenterrasse)*. Nearby, wander the metal walkway to enjoy spine-tingling views straight down. Looking in the direction the cable car runs, you can just barely see the St. Moritz train station on the edge of the big, turquoise lake. Directly above that, the long town at the base of a sharp ridge is Pontresina. And just to the

left, up the valley, is Samedan. (You can't quite see the town itself, but you can see the Samedan airstrip for private jets that give the "jet set" their name.) Look at the sharp pinnacle the cable car runs next to; immediately above it, on a high plateau, is the station for the Muottas Muragl mountain lift, reached by funicular from near Pontresina.

Now pan to the right. Of the cut-glass peaks along the horizon, the tallest is Piz Bernina (13,284 feet), which gives this mountain range (and the Bernina Express) its name. In the foreground and just to the right, the emerald alpine lake is one of a chain that leads all the way to Italy (the biggest one is Silvaplana).

Before leaving, circle around back behind the lift station. The view is less striking, but the statue of an ibex makes for great photos. Hardy visitors scramble up the rocky trail to the communications tower for even bigger views.

Hikes: The mountain's footpaths and bike trails are well maintained. Experienced hikers up for a steep challenge can walk back to town in four to five hours. For a much easier descent, ride the cable car down to the Corviglia ridge, then enjoy great views while hiking from there back into town (2 hours via Marguns—which also has eating options, fairly easy walk most of the way but with steep parts at the start and end).

Walk Around the Lake

The charming lake below St. Moritz is a delightful place for a stroll—especially on sunny summer days, when it's filled with sailboats. It takes about an hour to walk all the way around.

Eating in St. Moritz

As in Pontresina, most of St. Moritz's restaurants are in hotels.

$$$ Restaurant Hauser is the standard stop for locals who know where to find a good-value sit-down restaurant meal. Centrally located, this place has everything—restaurant, café, pastry shop, indoor and outdoor seating, and a vast menu—and you'll find everyone here (also sandwiches to go, daily 7:00-21:00, below Hotel Hauser at Via Traunter Plazzas 7, +41 81 837 5050). To shop for a snack or a picnic, a small, basic **Co-op** grocery is right on the main square (Mon-Fri 8:00-19:00, Sat-Sun until 18:00, Schulhausplatz/Plazza da Scoula 12).

Upper Engadine Connections

BY TRAIN
From Pontresina to: Chur (hourly, 2 hours, change in Samedan), **Zürich** (hourly, 3.5 hours, change in Samedan and Chur or Landquart), **Luzern** (hourly, 4.5 hours, 3 changes), **Appenzell** (hourly, 5 hours, 3 changes), **Zermatt** (every 2 hours, 7 hours, several changes).

From St. Moritz and Samedan to: Chur (hourly direct, 2 hours, more with change), **Zürich** (1-2/hour, 3.5 hours, change in Chur or Landquart), **Luzern** (1-2/hour, 4.5 hours, several changes), **Appenzell** (1-3/hour, 4 hours, several changes), **Zermatt** (1-2 direct Glacier Express trains/day, 8 hours), **Tirano** (hourly, 2.5 hours), **Milan** (hourly, 5 hours, 1-2 changes).

For details on the **Bernina Express** to Tirano and Lugano, and the **Glacier Express** to Zermatt, see the Scenic Rail Journeys chapter.

Train info: www.rail.ch.

BY BUS
While the Bernina Express connects this area to Lugano, it's a very roundabout (if scenic) journey. Much speedier, the **Palm Express** bus (#631) offers a connection-free trip over the Maloja Pass to Lugano (departs St. Moritz train station at 10:25, stops at Menaggio on Italy's Lake Como en route, arrives at Lugano's train station at 14:16; daily mid-June-late Oct, Fri-Sun only off-season, reservations required by 8:30 the same day, +41 58 341 3492, www.postauto.ch). Otherwise, connect via train to Thusis, then bus to Bellinzona, then train to Lugano (hourly, 4 hours). To **Milan,** the quickest route is by bus from St. Moritz to Chiavenna in Italy, then onward by train (every 2 hours, 4.5 hours).

SCENIC RAIL JOURNEYS

Golden Pass • Gotthard Panorama Express •
Bernina Express • Glacier Express • Chur

Switzerland has one of the world's best rail networks, and many of its tracks run through dramatic and beautiful scenery. While just about any train ride in Switzerland is photogenic, four are aggressively marketed as the most spectacular: the Golden Pass, Gotthard Panorama Express, Bernina Express, and Glacier Express. If you're looking for a scenic day enjoying the Alps from the window of your train, and would like to do it in a "panoramic" car (with huge windows that sweep halfway across the ceiling), these journeys can be great experiences. Though they aren't quite as "fantastic with countless highlights" as they're advertised to be (the high lifts in the mountains themselves are much higher and more breathtaking), the trains are a fun way to do some sightseeing while getting from point A to point B.

This chapter provides you with all the logistical, nuts-and-bolts information you'll need to splice each journey into your itinerary. Keep this in mind as you plan: You don't need to take a special train to enjoy the routes described in this chapter. Regular, nonpanoramic trains also run along all these scenic routes. They go more frequently and cost less. The branded journeys are a premium service available on a handful of regular departures each day, which add meals and souvenirs, and seat guests in special rail cars with expansive windows.

I've described highlights along each route, written in the direction that most travelers are likely to go. If you travel in the opposite direction, the same information still applies—just hold the book upside down. Of course, these descriptions also apply to those who have bought a regular ticket along the route rather than the premium package.

This chapter also includes information about Chur, a town that's not really worth a visit, except that it lies on both the Bernina Express and Glacier Express routes and can be handy for a pit stop or an overnight (especially if you're connecting to or from Zürich or Appenzell). Pontresina (covered in the Upper Engadine chapter), is an additional—and more appealing—place where these routes overlap.

TICKETS

Verify Schedules: Though I've listed some specific departure and arrival times, schedules are always subject to change. It's essential to confirm times before you travel. You'll find timetables and prices on the Swiss rail system's website (www.rail.ch) and on their excellent SBB Mobile app. Any train station in Switzerland can provide free schedules. Each scenic rail line also operates its own website, with even more details.

Buying Tickets: You can purchase tickets and reservations for all these scenic rail lines at any train station in Switzerland. At larger stations, staffers are familiar with the scenic routes and can help you sort through your options. However, in peak season, premium seats on the famous routes can sell out far in advance—it's better to book online well ahead, either on the Swiss Rail website, on each scenic rail website, or through the SBB Mobile app. You can also book via the North American-friendly RailEurope.com (online or through your travel agent)—but you'll pay a substantial markup.

Seat Reservations: Some scenic trains require seat reservations (including for rail-pass holders—see below). Be warned that these can sell out several days, or even weeks, ahead in high season. Reservations are required for all classes of the Glacier Express and Gotthard Panorama Express, the panoramic cars in all classes on the Bernina Express, and the bus segment of the Bernina Express. They are strongly recommended for the Golden Pass Express train between Interlaken and Montreux during peak season (and mandatory for Prestige class). These options are explained in each section, later.

If you're set on taking a panoramic train and your itinerary is already fixed, it makes sense to book your scenic-train seats as soon as you can. However, individual travelers may be able to book just a few days in advance to maximize their chances of traveling in clear weather. If your itinerary is flexible, keep an eye on the weather, pick a good travel day, and then reserve your seats. You're taking a bigger risk from mid-July to mid-August, when trains (especially the über-promoted Glacier Express) fill up faster.

Rail Passes: Swiss Travel Passes and the Eurail Global Pass cover travel on all four scenic trains. Seat reservations, though, always cost extra. You can skip reservations if traveling scenic routes on standard regional trains, rather than on the designated tourist departures.

When buying your ticket or making reservations, be sure the ticket agent understands what type of rail pass you have and exactly what trip you're taking. (Pass coverage varies on boats, buses, and mountain lifts, and is subject to change.) Confirm that you've purchased all the reservations and other tickets you need to complete your trip.

TRAIN TYPES

Various types of trains, with various types of cars, run these routes. Here are the key distinctions to look for:

Classes: Most trains have both first- and second-class cars. On both tourist and standard trains, first class has somewhat wider seats, a little more legroom, and fewer passengers; second-class cars offer the same scenery, go just as fast, and usually still have plenty of room. Some train cars on scenic routes have an additional premium class (see "Panoramic vs. Standard Cars," later).

If you have a second-class rail pass, you can always pay extra to sit in first on any given train (though reservations may be necessary). In bigger train stations, a digital panel on the tracks indicates departure time, destination, and at which part of the platform you'll find the first- and second-class cars.

Standard vs. Tourist Trains: Used by local commuters, standard trains may stop at more stations along the route than the designed-for-tourists panoramic trains. Many travelers enjoy the flexibility of following the scenic route on standard trains, enabling them to hop off and explore a village, then hop on the next standard train that comes through (reservations are not necessary on standard domestic trains).

Panoramic vs. Standard Cars: All the tourist trains on the routes in this chapter offer special panoramic cars, usually in both first and second class, so there's no need to splurge for first class. Panoramic cars have huge windows that curve back into the roof of the train car, allowing you to view high mountains from a wider angle than in a normal train car.

The windows in the panoramic cars generally can't open, and there are no window shades, so the interior can heat up on sunny days even with air-conditioning. Bring sunglasses and a hat.

Since nonpanoramic cars have a smaller field of vision than the panoramic

cars, these require a little more bobbing and weaving to enjoy the views. Aside from being cheaper, the chief advantage of standard cars is that the windows generally can be opened, for cool air and better photos.

Some trains have even fancier carriages. For instance, the Glacier Express has a super-pricey "Excellence" class, which is very roomy (only one row of seats on each side of the car) and adds lots of food en route. And the Golden Pass Express has a more affordable "Prestige" class, with cushier seats that can swivel to face oncoming scenery.

Caveat for Shutterbugs: Panoramic windows have lots of glare, and the famous bridges and viaducts used to advertise these trips are not actually visible. For clearer shots, look for openable windows in standard train cars or in passages between cars; the Gotthard Panorama Express has a "photo coach" in the middle of the train. Or, consider just sitting back, relaxing, and enjoying the scenery.

Golden Pass

The exceptionally picturesque Golden Pass train route cuts a swath diagonally across the pristine center of the country, connecting Luzern, the Berner Oberland, and Lake Geneva—and German Switzerland with French. Of all the scenic routes in this chapter, it's the one you're most likely to travel along, as it's central and laces together many of Switzerland's top sights.

ROUTE OVERVIEW

The classic Golden Pass route connects Luzern with Lake Geneva, by way of the Berner Oberland, in about five hours. The first section, from Luzern to Interlaken, is covered by the Luzern-Interlaken Express (departs hourly, 2 hours). The second, more scenic section, from Interlaken to Montreux, is covered by the new panoramic Golden Pass Express (4/day direct, just over 3 hours)—with no further train changes required. This is a bigger feat than it sounds, because the rail gauge changes midway through. (More on this later, under "Self-Guided Tour.")

SCENIC RAIL JOURNEYS

Splicing the Golden Pass into Your Itinerary

Because it connects so many knockout Swiss destinations, the Golden Pass route can fit into your itinerary in many different ways.

To enjoy the best stretch, use the Golden Pass Express between Interlaken and Montreux to connect the **Berner Oberland** with **Lake Geneva** in just over three hours—either as a long day trip or en route to an overnight on the lake (ideally in Lausanne).

For a roundabout, scenic route from **Lake Geneva to Zermatt** (about 5 hours), ride the Golden Pass Express north from Montreux to Spiez, then change to head back south to Visp on the Zermatt line. To go to **Bern** instead (3.5 hours), head north from Spiez.

The Luzern-Interlaken Express is the quickest way between those two towns, as well as the natural way to connect Interlaken with **Lugano** and **Italian Switzerland.** You can also ride from **Interlaken** to **Zürich** this way, via Luzern, in three hours (the less scenic route, via Bern, takes 2 hours).

You can also take standard trains between Interlaken and Montreux, but they have nonpanoramic windows, take a bit longer, require two additional changes, and save you only about 20 CHF.

PLANNING YOUR TIME

To go all the way from **Luzern** to **Lake Geneva,** here's a sample day plan: Take the 8:06 Luzern-Interlaken Express train to Interlaken Ost (arriving at 9:55), wander Interlaken and have a quick lunch, then catch the 14:08 Golden Pass Express train that arrives in Montreux at 17:20.

From Montreux, **Lausanne** (a more substantial and appealing town with many places to stay) is only another 20-30 minutes by train. And to make an even fuller day of the Golden Pass, you could begin in **Zürich** and ride the train 40 minutes to Luzern.

For onward train connections from major Golden Pass stops, see the Connections sections for Luzern (page 94), Interlaken Ost (page 183), and Montreux (page 325).

ORIENTATION TO THE GOLDEN PASS

Cost: The full, classic Golden Pass trip from Luzern to Montreux costs 86 CHF second class; the Golden Pass Express segment from Interlaken to Montreux is 53 CHF for second class (93 CHF for first class). Reservations (20 CHF extra) are optional but strongly recommended. The entire journey—not counting reservations—is covered by Swiss Travel or Eurail Global passes.

Schedule: Regular **Luzern-Interlaken Express** trains with semi-panoramic windows run hourly (trip takes about 2 hours). On the **Interlaken-Montreux** leg, panoramic Golden Pass Express trains run four times daily (trip takes a bit longer than 3 hours). If you take standard trains on this leg, two changes are required: in Spiez and again in Zweisimmen. There may be a brief lag between trains, so the total journey can take longer.

Information: For the **Luzern-Interlaken** leg, visit www.zentralbahn.ch/en/interlaken-express or call +41 58 668 8000. For the Golden Pass Express, visit www.gpx.swiss or call +41 21 989 8190. **Switzerland-wide rail information** is at www.rail.ch or on the SBB Mobile app.

Seats: On the **Golden Pass Express** between Interlaken and Montreux, all the carriages are panoramic. There are three classes: second class, first class, and "Prestige" class. It's always smart to reserve a seat (20 CHF in either second or first class). The fancy "Prestige" seats are cushy, heated, and can swivel to face the direction of travel (35 CHF extra with a first-class ticket or rail pass).

If you're taking **standard trains** between Interlaken and Montreux, the seats are...well, standard, in nonpanoramic carriages. However, on the Zweisimmen-Montreux leg, twice daily you can pay extra to ride in an elegant belle époque coach with a wood-paneled interior (not available on Express trains; see www.mob.ch).

Eating: The Luzern-Interlaken stretch is the only section with a restaurant car, but it may be closed on trains running early or late in the day. On Golden Pass Express trains (Interlaken to Montreux), pricey drinks and snacks are available (best to pre-order). Otherwise, Interlaken is a good spot for lunch or for picnic shopping.

❂ SELF-GUIDED TOUR

The most heavily promoted stretch is the Golden Pass Express, between Interlaken and Montreux—and it's certainly the most visually exciting part of the trip. But the classic Golden Pass trip starts in Luzern.

Part 1: Luzern to Interlaken

As you leave Luzern (sit on the right side), you'll go along the lake to **Alpnachstad,** the starting point for the cogwheel train that climbs to the top of Mount Pilatus (the massive bulk on the right). Then the train follows the **Sarner Aa River** through farmland, passing through the town of Sarnen and running along Lake

Sarnen. Beyond the end of the lake is the town of Giswil, where the train begins its gradual ascent to the **Brünig Pass.**

Eventually the train runs above the beautiful turquoise waters of the **Lungernsee** reservoir. After passing the resort of Lungern, the train climbs gradually through the forest to the summit station of Brünig-Hasliberg (keep an eye out for fake animal cutouts—lynx, ibex, deer—placed whimsically in the woods at eye level).

After cresting the pass, the train descends to the **Aare River valley,** with its sheer cliffs and waterfalls. The arrow-straight river channel, straightened by the ever-efficient Swiss, slices through the broad valley and on to Meiringen. (Sir Arthur Conan Doyle chose Meiringen and nearby Reichenbach Falls as the setting for the death of Sherlock Holmes.)

The train then follows the river to beautiful **Lake Brienz** (Brienzersee; a bus runs from the town of Brienz to the remarkable open-air museum at Ballenberg).

Beyond Brienz, the train follows the lakeshore to **Interlaken** ("between the lakes"), where the town sits between the big lakes of Thun and Brienz.

Here you'll change trains. If you're taking the Golden Pass Express train onward to Montreux, you'll need to change at the **Interlaken Ost** station (that train's departure point). If you're taking standard trains, you can change at either Interlaken Ost or Interlaken West for the next leg, to Spiez. If you have a layover, Interlaken is a handy place to grab lunch or shop for a picnic.

Part 2: Interlaken to Montreux

Lake Thun to Zweisimmen: As the train pulls out of Interlaken, you cruise along the south bank of **Lake Thun** (Thunersee). Enjoy watching the sailboats and lazy lake cruises under soaring alpine peaks. Soon you'll pull into the town of **Spiez,** overlooking the lake. (If you're taking standard trains, you'll change here.)

From Spiez, you'll head southwest toward Zweisimmen—squeezing between two mountainsides and into the rolling, cow-speckled valley called Simmental.

Rail Gauge Change in Zweisimmen: A small commotion surrounds the Golden Pass Express train at the Zweisimmen station, where the gauge (width) of the track changes. You may hardly notice what is happening, but it represents a major achievement of rail-carriage engineering. Historically, changing gauges required changing to a different train. (And, over time, other countries have come up with creative solutions. At the Spanish-French border, for decades, the entire carriage would be hoisted up by a winch and moved to a new set of wheels.) To make this express line possible, with limited hassle to passengers, engineers created a "variable gauge bogie" (a bogie is the set of wheels at the bottom of the carriage) that adjusts seamlessly to the new gauge. The process requires adjusting not only the gauge but the height of the train above the tracks (to match the new platform height). It also requires a locomotive switch to one with a different electrical voltage.

There are early discussions about extending the Golden Pass Express to Luzern, eliminating the need to switch trains at all. However, that would require yet another rail gauge change...so don't hold your breath.

If you're taking a standard train, you'll make yet another change here in Zweisimmen to reach Montreux.

Simmental: Leaving Zweisimmen, you'll continue through the Simmental, famous among American farmers for its top-end cows. Big farmhouses lie scattered in the lush meadows—an indication that the farmland is good here. The large wooden buildings are typical of Bernese farm architecture: housing the barn, sheltering the crops, and storing agricultural machines, all under one huge roof. Farming is heavily subsidized in Switzerland, and farmers form the strongest economic lobby. Trying to increase their income, many farmers have added exotic crops (like melons) or animals. Ostriches, yaks, bison, and highland cattle have become a common sight in the Swiss Alps.

Gstaad: Between Saanenmoser and Schonried, the train reaches its highest point (about 4,000 feet) and stops at the famous resort town of Gstaad. Although known as a favorite hangout for well-known rustic mountain folk such as Julie Andrews, Monaco's Princess Caroline, and Roman Polanski, the town doesn't offer much in the way of sights. In winter, its modest ski slopes are less crowded than the town's flashy nightspots. Sipping their cocktails, the *après*-skiers eye each other and discuss the latest trends in ski fashion. In summer, Gstaad hosts the Swiss Open tennis, polo, and golf tournaments, as well as high-quality music festivals.

French Switzerland: Just south of Gstaad, say *auf Wiedersehen* to the German-speaking part of Switzerland and *bonjour* to French Switzerland. The mountains are jagged. In fact, many are called *dents,* French for "teeth." With the change in language comes a change in culture and architecture. French-style gray stone houses start to replace half-timbered, woody, German-style chalets. The mountain airstrips—generally made for the Swiss Air Force during World War II—are used today for sightseeing flights around the Alps. The cute village of Rougemont, with its fine church and traditional houses, is famous among the Swiss as the place where the wealthy send their girls to boarding school.

Happy **cows** spend their summers on the Alps, wandering freely and munching the fragrant herbs of these lush alpine meadows. The resulting milk is the secret ingredient for tasty Gruyère cheese. On steep hillsides here, the grass is still cut by hand. It dries in the summer sun, then is collected and stored in the barns to serve as cow salads through the winter.

Château-d'Œx: This charming alpine village may tempt you to interrupt your journey. It's known for its Hot-Air Ballooning Week (last week of Jan). Bertrand Piccard and Brian Jones took off from here on March 1, 1999, and sailed their balloon all the way around the world. Below the train station, Le Chalet restaurant gives insight on Gruyère cheese production.

South of Château-d'Œx, the valley narrows to a deep gorge. The hillsides above were devastated by the 1999 **Lothar** winter storm. Entire forests were leveled, aggravating an already precarious avalanche situation. Trees on steep slopes stop snow from sliding down and burying the villages, but once the trees are gone, artificial avalanche barriers need to be erected. Landslides and floods have been relatively common in recent years—an unfortunate consequence of deforestation and the construction of vacation homes in areas that traditionally served as pastures and forestlands.

The small lake, **Lac du Vernay,** is dammed and used for hydroelectric power. Switzerland makes good use of its Alps, with their fast-flowing streams. Although it has some nuclear power plants, 60 percent of Switzerland's energy is hydroelectric. The country exports its electricity to France and Italy.

Montbovon: This small town is the place to change trains if you're going to Bulle or Gruyères (see page 328). After the first tunnel, an inscription on the barn to the right welcomes you to the Gruyère region: *La Gruyère vous salue.* From here, the train winds its way uphill with more curves and tunnels than before.

Bienvenue to the "Swiss Riviera": The Jaman Tunnel engulfs you in nearly two miles of darkness. When you emerge, you're in another world—you've left the feudal Middle Ages and entered the 19th-century belle époque. At the village of Les Avants, one of Switzerland's oldest winter resorts, the first glimpses of Lake Geneva sprawl deep underneath you. Beginning a steep descent, the train passes through a series of sharp bends in tunnels before delivering you from the mountains to lake level.

The architecture has even more of a French flair now that you've entered the **"Swiss Riviera."** Palm trees, grapevines, and many sanatoriums indicate that this is a warmer climate. You're surrounded by the vineyards of the **Lavaux** region, famous for its white wine. The view broadens to include the French Alps of Savoy across the lake, the lakeshore of the Swiss Riviera to the west, and the broad Rhône Valley to the east. As you approach Montreux—with its grand hotels—the train meanders its way intimately through private gardens.

Montreux: Stepping off your train here, notice that this is one of the only train stations in Europe with three different rail gauges: regular, narrow, and very skinny (for the Rochers de Naye train, taking sightseers to a nearby peak with views less exciting than those you've just enjoyed).

From here, it's an easy train trip to Lausanne, or a quick bus ride or about a two-mile lakefront hike to Château de Chillon (covered in the Lake Geneva & French Switzerland chapter).

Gotthard Panorama Express

The Gotthard Panorama Express is half by boat and half by train, from Luzern to Lugano in the Italian-speaking region of Ticino. The boat ride passes the place where the first Swiss cantons pledged "all for one and one for all," the birthplace of the Confoederatio Helvetica in 1291. Then, at Flüelen, you switch to a train that climbs up to the town of Göschenen (3,600 feet), then plunges through the old Gotthard Tunnel into Italian Switzerland.

Don't go out of your way to do this trip. The boat ride is more pastoral than thrilling, and the train ride is more interesting as a lesson in Swiss engineering than impressive for its views. But if you're connecting Luzern and Italian Switzerland in high season and have the time, this 5.5-hour boat-train combination is undeniably scenic. If you've already taken a boat trip on Lake Luzern, you won't see much more by taking the Gotthard Panorama Express boat. Conversely, if you're planning on doing the whole Gotthard Panorama trip, don't bother doing a boat trip while in Luzern.

Alternatives: If you're in a hurry to get between Luzern and Lugano, you can do it by train in less than two hours via the 35-mile-long **Gotthard Base Tunnel,** which lets trains burrow through the Alps at full speed. Or, to make the trip to Lugano a little more scenic (without doing the full-blown Gotthard Panorama Express), you can take a slower regional **"Treno Gottardo"** from Luzern through the old Gotthard Tunnel (this also skips the boat and takes just over three hours, with a change of trains in Bellinzona). To find the more scenic routes through the old tunnel, search for trains that go through Airolo.

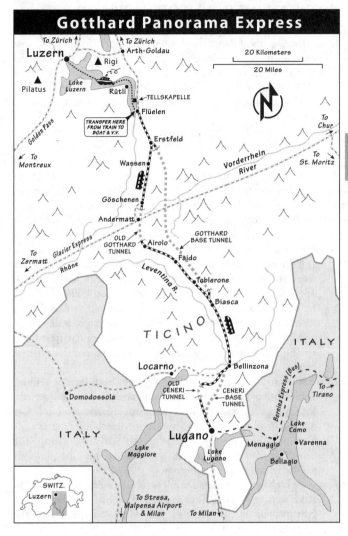

ROUTE OVERVIEW

The Gotthard Panorama Express begins with a very pretty three-hour boat trip along the length of Lake Luzern from the city of Luzern to Flüelen. As the traditional steamer blows its old-time horn, you glide by idyllic lakeside resort towns and under mighty peaks. In Flüelen, you leave the boat and board the train, which crosses the Alps and cuts down into the Italian-speaking canton of Ticino (2.5 hours).

For onward train connections, see the Connections sections under Luzern (page 94) and Lugano (page 360).

ORIENTATION TO THE GOTTHARD PANORAMA EXPRESS

Cost: The Gotthard Panorama Express trip costs 153 CHF for first class all the way, or 93 CHF for second class on the boat and first class on the train (second class is not available). You'll also pay an obligatory train seat reservation fee of 16 CHF. The boat doesn't have reserved seats, though you can reserve a table.

First-class rail passes cover the train part of the journey but not the seat reservation fee. With a second-class pass, you'll have to pay the reservation fee plus a 20 CHF upgrade to sit in the first-class train cars. The Swiss Travel Pass covers the lake segment; the Eurail Global Pass gives you half off, so you'll pay 24 CHF for the second-class boat trip.

Schedule: The official Gotthard Panorama Express package is available once daily except Mon in each direction between mid-April and mid-October. Going from north to south, you'll leave Luzern on the 11:12 boat (board at pier 1, across from the train station); after the boat docks in Flüelen at 13:55, you have about 15 minutes before the 14:09 train leaves for Lugano, arriving at 16:41. Going from south to north, you leave Lugano at 9:18 to make a Flüelen-Luzern boat departing at 12:00 and arriving at 14:47. Off-season, regular trains still run between Luzern and Lugano via Flüelen, but there are no boat sailings.

Information: The boat and train companies both have brochures and websites about the Gotthard Panorama Express (general information: www.gotthard-panorama-express.ch; boat: +41 41 367 6767, www.lakelucerne.ch). Switzerland-wide rail information is at www.rail.ch or on the SBB Mobile app. The Gotthard Panorama Express also has live, multilingual tour guides who narrate the journey.

Luggage Delivery Service: Travelers from Luzern to Lugano can have luggage delivered to the platform in Lugano (free, no access to bags while traveling). Ask when you check in at the Luzern boat pier.

◒ SELF-GUIDED TOUR

Here's what you'll see if you're doing the entire Gotthard Panorama Express route. If you're taking only the train, skip to that section.

Boat Trip

Departing Luzern: The boat crisscrosses the **Vierwaldstättersee** (the "Lake of the Four Forest Settlements"—let's call it Lake Luzern). The trip is popular with the older generation of European tourists, who eat and drink their way through the lazy route. On a sunny day, you can sit on the deck and enjoy the mountain views. Survey the boat before you settle on a seat—consider sun, shade, and wind.

After two hours, you sail into the **canton of Uri,** and the landscape gets rougher, the slopes steeper, and the villages fewer and more rustic.

Rütli: Swiss patriots get excited as the boat approaches **Rütli.** The meadow above is the birthplace of the Swiss Confederation. In 1291, representatives of the three founding cantons met here and swore allegiance to each other, against their oppressive neighbors. More than 700 years later, Switzerland is still a confederation—but now its cantons number 26.

You may see hikers disembark at Rütli and head for the mystical meadow marked by a big Swiss flag. Then they follow the **Weg der Schweiz** ("Path of Switzerland"), a trail leading around the lake. Along the way, they contemplate stone signs representing each of the 26 cantons in the order they joined the union. The canton markers are spaced according to each canton's population (the 20-mile-long trail was designed to have exactly 5 millimeters for each Swiss citizen).

Tellskapelle: The boat stops at this 16th-century frescoed chapel, marking the spot where, according to legend, Swiss hero William Tell jumped ship on the way to prison and swam to freedom.

Flüelen: This is the boat's last stop, where the panoramic train awaits.

Train Trip

Above Flüelen: Soon after departure, the train climbs from 1,540 feet up toward its maximum of 3,600 feet. You enter a classic alpine world of snowcapped mountains towering above wild valleys, with narrow gorges carved over eons by angry white water. Wooden chalets, pine forests, and lush meadows dotted with munching cows complete this picture-perfect image of Switzerland.

The train tracks are protected from avalanches, landslides, and waterfalls by concrete galleries. Gazing out the window, you'll see some of the greatest accomplishments of Swiss road-and-railroad engineering.

Wassen: Keep an eye out for the striking chapel. At first, the chapel is on your right. Then the train loops around the tiny town, and the chapel is on your left. Your train disappears into a tunnel, and when you emerge, the same chapel is still there. The train actually spirals up the slopes. Bring a compass and you can watch it spin 360 degrees.

Gotthard Pass: After Göschenen, your train approaches the famous **Gotthard Pass,** which—since the 13th century—has been *the* major trade route over this part of the Alps, connecting northern and southern Europe. Today, trade—and your train—rumbles under rather than over the pass. You'll be taking the original **Gotthard Tunnel.** Completed in 1882, this 9.5-mile-long engineering marvel was the primary north-south train link through the Swiss Alps until 2016. That's when they opened the much longer Gotthard Base Tunnel—where express trains zip at top speed, 2,000 feet below you.

When you enter that original tunnel, your train slows down and the lights dim as a video is projected on the tunnel walls. And then, after about 10 minutes of click-clacking through darkness, you emerge in a whole different world—a different climate (warmer), language (Italian), and canton (Ticino).

Ticino: Welcome to Ticino, Switzerland's botanical garden. While the weather around Lake Luzern is often iffy, Ticino feels Mediterranean—warm and southern—making it a favorite weekend destination for the Swiss. Rather than cuckoo-clock-like chalets, the houses are now plain, square, and made of stone. Instead of conifers, the forests are full of chestnut trees. You'll see vineyards, oleander, and even palm trees. And the upcoming train stops are announced in Italian now: *"Prossima fermata..."*

While life seems almost too good in the pristine and touristic Lake Luzern region, in this valley south of the mountains the economy is tougher. There are few local jobs, and young folks commute or move into the cities farther south. Houses and roads aren't as well maintained, and window boxes no longer come with so many flowers.

On either side of **Faido,** the train goes through several more tunnels. Past **Bellinzona,** the train zooms through the 10-mile-long Ceneri Base Tunnel, which opened in 2020. And before you know it...you're pulling into **Lugano.**

Bernina Express

The Bernina Express is one of the more exciting rides through the Swiss Alps, thanks to its diversity: starting with the sunny, palm-tree ambience of Lugano; getting a taste of Italy along beautiful Lake Como; climbing up and over the twisting Bernina and Albula passes; and seeing mountain towns like Pontresina before finishing up in eastern Switzerland. The first half of the trip is by bus; the second by rail. The little red train with panoramic cars spirals up to 7,380 feet, passing steep mountains and cliffs, glaciers, waterfalls, and a wild, rugged landscape.

ROUTE OVERVIEW

The Bernina Express combines a bus trip through Italy with a train ride up into the mountains. The bus begins in Lugano but soon crosses the border to run along the west side of Italy's Lake Como and up the vineyard-draped valley called Valtellina, eventually arriving at Tirano. Here passengers change to a train that crosses back into Switzerland, stops in the sleepy and charming town of Poschiavo, then  twists north up the mountainside—mastering a very steep grade on regular tracks (no cogwheels) en route to the most spectacular stretch: over the Bernina Pass. Then the train winds back down the other side and finally deposits you in one of several eastern Swiss towns, such as Pontresina, St. Moritz, Samedan, or—farther north, via the Albula Pass—Chur. (In summer, you can also finish in the resort town of Davos.)

As with other scenic rail journeys, the route can be reversed (Chur or Pontresina to Tirano by train, then bus to Lugano).

PLANNING YOUR TIME

The trip between Lugano and Pontresina takes about six hours—or longer, if you linger en route at Poschiavo or Tirano (see next). Finishing or starting in Chur makes for a very long day (8-9 hours). If you want to travel the whole route, split it up and do the two-hour Pontresina-Chur stretch on the way to destinations such as Zürich or Appenzell, or as part of the Glacier Express (which overlaps with the Bernina Express on this segment). If you're being selective, the most scenic and rewarding stretch is the two hours over the Bernina Pass between Poschiavo and St. Moritz/Pontresina.

As you're sorting through schedules, consider a brief stopover in Tirano (Italy), Poschiavo (Switzerland), or both. Depending on your train and travel direction, you could spend up to an hour and a half in either (or both). Of the two, Poschiavo is more charming, compact, and easier to appreciate. Tirano, on the other hand, is...*in*

SCENIC RAIL JOURNEYS

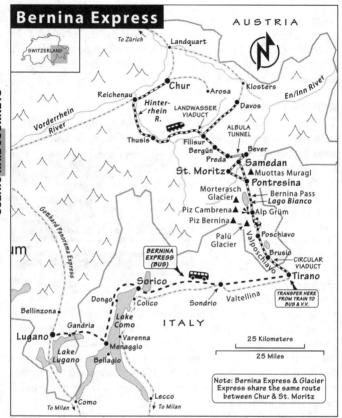

Italy, with all the good and bad that entails (lively street life, shabbier, great food, more traffic, more chaos).

If you have more time, consider taking a standard regional train along the Pontresina-Tirano route (rather than the official Bernina Express train, with panoramic cars). The regional train makes more stops en route, so you can get off as you like to hike and explore (see "Skipping the Official Panorama Train," later).

Also remember that you don't have to start or end the trip in Lugano. You could use the Pontresina-Tirano train as a way of connecting to Milan or Lake Como (see "Connecting to Towns in Italy," later in this section).

Given how long (and relatively uncomfortable) the bus leg is, here's another possibility: Make a day trip out of the Bernina Express, leaving Pontresina in the morning, exploring over the pass to Poschiavo (2 hours) or Tirano (2.5 hours), then heading back—perhaps stopping en route for a glacier hike or a lift.

And finally, don't worry too much about which of the Upper

Engadine towns your train stops in (Pontresina, St. Moritz, or Samedan)—the three towns are within 10 minutes of each other by local bus or train.

For onward train connections from the major Bernina Express stops, see the Connections sections for Lugano (page 360) and Chur (at the end of this chapter).

ORIENTATION TO THE BERNINA EXPRESS

Cost: The total cost for a one-way trip on the Bernina Express from Lugano to Pontresina is about 100 CHF second class or 120 CHF first class; continuing to Chur raises the price to 130 CHF second class or 180 CHF first class. St. Moritz is a few francs more expensive than Pontresina. These prices include reservations for the bus (10-16 CHF depending on season) and the panoramic Bernina Express train (20-26 CHF depending on season); in summer, the total reservation fee, first or second class, is 42 CHF. The entire trip (including the bus) is covered by the Swiss Travel and Eurail Global passes, but passholders have to pay for reservations.

If you don't have a reservation for the bus, you may be allowed to board and pay if there's room, but there are no guarantees (and the bus is typically full, so have a plan B in mind). If you don't have a reservation for the panoramic cars on the train, no worries: Every train on this route also has nonpanoramic cars, accessible without a reservation.

Schedule: I've provided sample departure times; confirm schedules before your trip.

The bus from Lugano to Tirano leaves daily at 10:00 (mid-May-Oct only) from outside Lugano's train station. The departure point may be in flux while this area is under construction, but it's likely in the big parking lot to the right as you face the train station building (look for yellow signs saying *Tirano, St. Moritz,* and *#731*). Give yourself plenty of time to find it...or scout it the night before.

About 13:00, you'll arrive in Tirano. Here, you'll board a panoramic train that continues north over the mountains. In summer, one train leaves Tirano almost immediately, at 13:17 (arrives in Pontresina at 15:34 and St. Moritz at 15:45; change here to continue to Chur for a regional train, arriving at 18:04). For those wanting a little more time for lunch in Tirano, there's another train at 14:24 (arrives in Pontresina at 16:22—change here for St. Moritz; then in Chur at 18:20). All trains follow the same tracks for most of the trip before fanning out at the end to different destinations.

If you're doing it the other way around, the train from St. Moritz leaves at 9:17, stops in Pontresina at 9:28, and arrives in Tirano at 11:32. From Chur, the train departs at 8:32 and stops in Pontresina at 10:22, arriving in Tirano at 12:49. (Note that if you're starting in Pontresina, you can take the first train to Poschiavo, spend about an hour there, then hop on the second train onward to Tirano. Otherwise you may have more time than you really want in Tirano.) There's just one bus from Tirano, which departs at 14:20 and arrives in Lugano around 17:30.

Service is reduced off-season. Generally, the bus still runs daily from April through October; weekends only in November and mid-February through March; and not at all from December through mid-February. The Bernina Express panoramic trains continue to run over the pass to Tirano once or twice a day.

Information: The Bernina Express is operated by the Rhätische Bahn (RhB, +41 81 288 6565, www.berninaexpress.ch). They hand out a free leaflet on board explaining the key stops. You can use the Wi-Fi on the train and the bus to access the "InfoT(r)ainment" website, which tracks your route and offers both text and audio commentary. For major points of interest, recorded English commentary plays on the train's loudspeaker.

Bring Food: For those traveling west to east, the connection time between bus and train in Tirano may be brief (especially if the bus is running late), so it's smart to pack a lunch. No food is available on the bus, and there's no dining car on Bernina Express trains. In a pinch, buy a takeaway lunch during your bathroom break on the bus ride. If the timing works out, get lunch in Poschiavo (see "Eating in Poschiavo," later).

Bus Tips: Be warned that this is not a luxurious tour bus. Seats are extremely tight, there's limited space for day bags under seats (and no over-seat storage), and the bus is typically jam-packed. Large bags can be stored under the bus. There are no WCs on the bus, but it stops for a WC break about halfway through, near the north end of Lake Como. The bus trip is almost entirely through Italy. If many people reserve the trip, a second bus may be added. For the best Lake Como views, sit on the right side of the bus going westbound (from Lugano), or the left side going eastbound (to Lugano).

Train Tips: Tirano is where the bus and train meet. Heading north, for the first part of the ride, views are somewhat better on the right (though the left is better for seeing the train curve around the famous spiral viaduct at Brusio). After Poschiavo, views are better on the left.

Topless Trains: If traveling in July and August, ask about sitting in the yellow "convertible" train cars—called *carrozze pan-*

oramiche—with flip
seats and no roof (but
be aware that these go
only on certain seg-
ments of the trip). The
railway decides the
day before—depend-
ing on the weath-
er—whether to add
these cars to the train
(available in both first
and second class). Bring a jacket, hat, and sunscreen. If you
get cold, you can move into a regular car when the train stops.

Skipping the Official Panorama Train: The train segment of the
Bernina Express can be done on a standard regional train (with
smaller windows that open, and possibly a car with larger-view
windows). These trains stop at all stations along the line, giving you more options to hop off and walk around in the beautiful surroundings. (The "official" Bernina Express only stops at
three important stations—Poschiavo, Alp Grüm, and Ospizio
Bernina.) On a standard train, you can get off at Poschiavo for
a quick visit, at the Bernina Pass for hiking, at Diavolezza to do
a cable-car trip, or at Morteratsch for a glacier hike. Alp Grüm
and Ospizio Bernina are also starting points for several great
high-mountain hikes. Take advantage of the frequent and easy
train connections to make as many short stops as time and interest allow. Not only do you save yourself the panoramic train
supplement, but you have the flexibility of traveling without a
seat reservation. The panoramic cars are indeed lovely—and
this stretch is particularly well suited for a panoramic car—but
the trip is still very rewarding on a standard train.

Connecting to Towns in Italy: There are many other ways to reach
Tirano than by bus from Lugano. For example, inexpensive,
direct, hourly trains run to Tirano from both Milan (2.5
hours) and Varenna, a favorite stop on Lake Como (1.5 hours).

History Exhibit in St. Moritz: A small, free exhibit on the history
of the Bernina Express rail line, including an English film, is
in the St. Moritz train station. It's worth a look if you're killing
time there, though not a special trip.

❂ SELF-GUIDED TOUR

I've narrated this journey going westbound: starting in Lugano,
taking the bus around Lake Como to Tirano, then taking the Bernina Express train north (via Poschiavo) to the Upper Engadine
and Chur.

SCENIC RAIL JOURNEYS

Bus Trip: Lake Lugano, Lake Como, and Valtellina to Triano

The bus trip is more scenic than relaxing. Lakes Lugano and Como are almost fjord-like, lined with little Italian getaways. For the best views, sit on the right-hand side (if your reserved seat is on the left and seats are available, change once the bus is under way).

Lake Lugano: At first, the bus takes you around Lake Lugano on narrow, winding roads—often in tunnels, sometimes with peek-a-boo views over the lake—frequently honking its horn to warn oncoming traffic at tight passages. Leaving Lugano, you'll pass the town of **Gandria** (fun to visit from Lugano by boat and described in the Lugano chapter).

Shortly after Gandria, you cross the border into **Italy** (no need to show passports, or even stop). You may notice changes in architecture and design: Whereas the Swiss love meticulously manicured gardens, painstakingly renovated houses, and clean, uncluttered lines, the Italians generally take things a bit easier. One exception is well-tended little Porlezza—the last lakefront village you'll pass through—which has a picture-perfect square with a fountain.

Lake Como: Once the bus leaves Lake Lugano, the road broadens and takes you through modern Italian villages before reaching picturesque Lake Como, above the town of Menaggio. First you'll see the lake from a distance, then you'll wind down through a confusing (and shockingly tight) series of switchback roads and interchanges, until you're driving along the lakeside.

The village across the lake on the right (by the funny hump of land) is the *real* Bellagio. Along the lakeside road, you'll pass through several more villages: In unassuming **Dongo,** the Italian fascist dictator Mussolini was captured at the end of World War II. In **Gravedona,** the street narrows, and getting the bus through is a tight squeeze. Posh private villas and gardens line the street; look for the 12th-century Romanesque Church of Santa Maria del Tiglio. From here, the trip takes you to the tiny harbor town of **Domaso,** a touristy area with plenty of campgrounds, hotels, and swimming pools.

The Y-shaped lake is huge; your drive along the northern finger takes about as long (30 minutes) as each of the two southern fingers. Somewhere around the northern end of the lake (likely in or near Sorico—but without a view), the bus stops for 15 dull minutes for the trip's sole WC break. Here you can also buy a snack or drink (Swiss francs and credit cards accepted).

The bus then crosses the Mera River and the **"Pian di Spagna"**—today a nature reserve, but famous as the site of a tense stand-off between Spanish and Swiss troops during the religious wars of the Counter-Reformation.

Valtellina: The trip continues up the fertile valley called Valtellina, where some of northern Italy's best white wine is produced. The sunny slopes on the left side are reserved for vineyards, the right lower slopes are for woodland, and the bottom of the valley is occupied by apple plantations. For centuries (from 1512 until Napoleon in 1797) this region belonged to Switzerland's largest canton, Graubünden. The region is Italian today, but many Swiss are still nostalgic for the valley (called the *Veltlin* in German) and its wines. The white Grüner Veltliner grape is named after the valley, though it isn't actually grown here.

While famous for its food and wine, Valtellina is pretty drab from the bus, which follows the same rail line that eventually crosses the Bernina Pass and is the lifeline of commerce in the region. Through the main town of Sondrio—and the other towns that flow into it—you'll drive by hardworking industry, punctuated with occasional vineyards and apple orchards.

In **Tresivio** (just after Sondrio, toward the end of the bus ride) you'll notice the creamy white, brown-trimmed 17th-century Baroque pilgrimage church of Santa Casa on the hill to your left.

Eventually the bus pulls into **Tirano**—our last stop in Italy.

Tirano

This town of about 9,000 people is defined by its position as the "end of the road" of the Valtellina (and Italian territory) and the base station for the Bernina Pass railway line.

On your way into town, watch on the left as the bus passes an impressive Renaissance pilgrimage church, **Madonna di Tirano.** (You'll see this again, even closer, as the train passes right next to it on the way out of town.) If you have plenty of time here, you could consider walking about 15 minutes from the train station to see it up close.

You'll arrive at the back of the Italian Railways train station (on the far side of the tracks). Now you'll need to cross under the tracks to the separate, narrow-gauge, Swiss rail station. Go down the ramp or the stairs and through the tunnel.

You'll emerge at a little piazza where two rail systems come together. On your left is the boxy, handsome **Swiss Railways terminal**—this is where you'll catch the train onward to the Bernina Pass. Entering this station, you'll actually pass by a customs office, which normally shows no interest in you. Inside are free WCs. If you need to leave your bags here, ask at the ticket desk; you can pay an exorbitant 8 CHF per bag to store them in the luggage room. (There is no bag storage at the Italian train station, or anywhere else nearby.)

While Tirano is pleasant, the Swiss town of Poschiavo (described later)—just over the border—is arguably more appealing. To cram in more sightseeing, consider taking an earlier departure from Tirano on a regional train to gain time for a stopover in Poschiavo, then catch another train onward from there.

Visiting Tirano: If you have some time to spend here between your bus and train connections, here are some tips:

There's a small **TI** at the Italian train station (at the corner closest to the Swiss station) where you can get a free map and advice.

From the station piazza, walk straight out—past some cafés, bars, restaurants, and souvenir stands—to the busy main road, **Viale Italia.** Following this left for about 15 minutes will take you to the Madonna di Tirano church; about 10 minutes to the right will take you to the humble old town.

Eating in Tirano: On the left where the train-station road hits the main road, **$$ Merizzi** is a good choice for interesting local pastas and other dishes—either out on the leafy sidewalk or in the retro-mod interior. Or head right on the main road to find other options: **$ El Trigo** is simpler and cheaper, selling fresh pasta dishes. Across the street, **$ Profumo di Pizza** has takeout pizzas. And farther along past El Trigo, you'll find a welcoming café, a Valtellina products shop, and a *gelateria*. Note that most of these places don't take Swiss francs—but they accept credit cards.

Train Trip
Part 1: Tirano to Poschiavo
Tirano: Leaving the Swiss station in Tirano, the train rolls street-car-style through the center of town. You'll pass right by the Madonna di Tirano church; notice that the area surrounding it acts as a sort of secondary town square for the whole community.

Valposchiavo: After Tirano, your train crosses the Italian-Swiss border (in Campocologno), and then climbs uphill. Now you're traversing the Valposchiavo ("Valley of Poschiavo"), the southernmost valley of Switzerland's largest canton, Graubünden (Grigioni, in Italian). The rest of the Bernina Express journey—from here all the way to the end of the line in Chur—is in Graubünden.

Brusio Viaduct: Just before **Brusio,** be ready: The train swirls up a **circular viaduct**—an ingenious construction allowing the train to reach higher altitudes without the help of a cogwheel mechanism. As the train spirals up, you can see the front and back cars curving in front of and behind you, riding over the viaduct. In the very center of the circle of rails, you'll see a few statues—and, often, trainspotters here to take videos of the train maneuvering the loops. (There's another 360-degree loop later on this trip, but it's entirely in tunnels—so passengers barely notice.)

Upper Valposchiavo: As you gain altitude, sit back and enjoy the gentle beauty of this part of the trip, where you leave the flat-

ter, broader valleys behind and head higher and higher up the Valposchiavo. You'll pass dark old pine forests with needle-and-moss-covered boulders. Chestnut forests, tobacco plantations, and vineyards contribute to the lush tableau. Wildflowers along the track include bright-orange lilies and mountain azaleas.

Lago di Poschiavo: Soon the train runs along the beautiful emerald waters of the mile-and-a-half-long Lago di Poschiavo. You'll pass through a resort town on each end—first **Miralago** (ahem, *not* Mar-a-Lago), then **La Prese.** Notice how, in La Prese (as in Tirano), the track runs along city streets, as if it's a streetcar rather than an intercity scenic train. Then your train pulls into **Poschiavo** (if you're not stopping here, skip the next section).

Poschiavo

This extremely pleasant town of 3,500 people is a delight to explore if you have the time. (Confirm the time of your onward train carefully

before leaving the station.) The station has free WCs on the platform. Inside the hall, the local **TI** hands out a free map with a short orientation walk; if you ask nicely, they'll also let you leave your bags here for free (TI +41 81 839 0060, www.valposchiavo.ch).

Eating in Poschiavo: A big, handy **Co-op** is just down the tracks (toward Italy) from the station, and there's a small **$ pizzeria**

directly outside the station's front door that sells pizzas after 11:30. Or take my town walk (see next), where you'll find some nicer restaurants on and near the main square, plus a sprinkling of bakeries, butchers, and small grocery stores.

Visiting Poschiavo: The best quick visit to Poschiavo includes a stroll to the main square (Piazza Comunale), with the Museo Casa Console and near the town's main church (St. Ignazio). From the station, walk straight out and down the main street until it ends at the river, then turn left, following signs for *Museo Casa Console*. Cross the river over the pedestrian bridge and continue left. Follow this street for a few blocks through town. When the road narrows, turn right (again following brown *Museo Casa Console* signs) to reach the main piazza.

The main square, **Piazza Comunale,** is lined with Neoclassical and Neo-Gothic buildings. Two big hotel restaurants face each other (worth considering for a sit-down meal if time allows).

To the right stands the impressive Catholic church, **Chiesa di San Vittore Mauro.** A church stood here as early as 703, but the building has been rebuilt and renovated several times: The bell tower dates from 1202, and the Baroque front door was carved in the 1700s. Circle around the back of the church (up a few steps to the elevated terrace) for a better look at the tower. Directly opposite the tower's base is an orange building with intricate wrought-iron grills. Have a peek inside, and don't be startled by the skulls lining the walls—you're standing in front of the local ossuary.

Now circle back around to the main square. Find the rustic-looking 12th-century tower, and head up the little street in front of it (Via da Mez). You'll pass the old Town Hall, then the tiny **Museo Casa Console.** It has a nice collection of Romantic-era paintings of this region—the sort that helped kick off the tourism boom and, in a sense, brought you here. Before becoming glamorized in the Romantic era, mountains were seen more as obstacles than objects of beauty (free with Swiss Travel Pass, otherwise overpriced at 10 CHF, Tue-Sun 11:00-16:00, closed Mon and Nov-mid-Dec, +41 81 844 0040, www.museocasaconsole.ch).

Carry on a few more steps up this same street to find the **Church of St. Ignazio.** It's ironic that this Protestant church's namesake, St. Ignatius of Loyola, was the founder of the militant Jesuit order, whose main purpose was to fight "heretic" Protestants. For confirmation that it's Protestant indeed, head into the austere interior. Notice the inscription above the central pulpit, which is fervently Protestant: *Chiesa cristiana vangelica riformata da gli errori e superstizioni umane* ("Christian evangelical church, reformed from human errors and superstitions").

But you've got a train to catch! For a slightly more interesting return to the station, take the street that goes straight south from the main square, alongside the old church tower. After a few blocks through sleepy streets, turn right (next to Hotel Suisse) and find the footbridge that leads back to your train.

Part 2: The Bernina Pass, from Poschiavo to Pontresina

Above Valposchiavo: Leaving Poschiavo, it takes only a few minutes before you begin your ascent—probably the most dramatic stretch of this entire journey. The train slaloms up the steep mountain—making four switchback turns—and offers more and more views of waterfalls, steep cliffs, and the Poschiavo valley and lake far below.

Bernina Railway: As you gain altitude, remember why the Bernina Pass (and this journey) is famous: This is the highest rail crossing over the Alps. More impressive, it accomplishes this feat without rack-and-pinion or cogwheel systems; the tracks are simply engineered to curve just so, allowing a standard locomotive to make the ascent at up to a 7 percent grade. Completed in 1910, the Bernina Railway was a follow-up to another remarkable engineering feat, the Albula Pass (described later). The Albula Railway, completed just a few years earlier, connected Graubünden to the Swiss mainstream, and the Bernina Railway completed the connection to Italy. (The two lines meet in St. Moritz.) Taken together, these two ambitious projects revolutionized transportation, trade, and culture in this part of Switzerland.

Cavaglia: Just before Cavaglia, keep an eye out the window to see the Glacier Garden—a series of walkways that offer an up-close view of fascinating circular shafts carved out of the rock by glaciers. Cavaglia's rustic, chalet-like station marks the bottom of another big ascent. As you twist up and up, notice many places where you go under avalanche shelters—little roofed sections that protect the most vulnerable stretches of the line from fierce winter weather.

Palü Glacier: Thirty minutes after leaving Poschiavo, you'll glimpse the trip's first glacier, the **Palü** (above the little lake called Palüsee). As you twist up through tunnels, you'll see it on both the left and the right side of the train. It lies nestled between the peak of Piz Varuna (11,330 feet) on the left and the eastern summit of Piz Palü on the right (12,790 feet).

Alp Grüm: At the top of this section of curves, the train stops at the Alp Grüm station. You may be given a few minutes outside to appreciate the sweeping views of the glacier. Looking back, you'll also enjoy hazy views over the narrow, lush Valposchiavo.

Alp Grüm is the first stop in German-speaking Switzerland; ascending this mountain, you've left Italian behind. (Most of Italian-speaking Switzerland is the canton of Ticino. But the finger of Graubünden occupied by Poschiavo also speaks Italian.)

The screeching of the wheels as you leave Alp Grüm is another reminder that this is the only train that crosses over the Alps without any tunnels. It goes right over the top.

Ospizio Bernina and Lago Bianco: This station marks the Bernina Pass and the highest point of this trip (7,380 feet, above the tree line). Next to the station, you'll see **Lago Bianco** ("White Lake"), which gets its color from the snowmelt, also called glacier milk. At the end of the lake, look to the left for a watershed sign that explains that this is a European continental divide: From here, rivers flow either north (toward the Inn and Danube rivers, and finally to the Black Sea) or south (to the Adriatic Sea via the Adda and Po rivers).

Behind Lago Bianco, you can see the glaciers of **Sassal Masone** and **Piz Cambrena**. This mountain pass separates not only European drainage basins but also cultures. In earlier decades, the train line was more susceptible to bad-weather closures. The Valposchiavo was often cut off from Switzerland in the winter, and better connected to the valleys across the border in Italy.

Engadine: Now the train crosses the barren landscape and descends into the Engadine valley. Tourists and convalescents discovered this part of Switzerland at the end of the 19th century. Imagine the gorgeous skiing here in the winter, which still attracts the rich and famous. After the railroad opened this secluded valley to the world, the first hotels and sanatoriums were built (the air and sunshine supposedly helped cure diseases like tuberculosis). Poets found their muse in the wild, romantic landscape, while painters flocked in, attracted by the quality of the light. Keep an eye out for typical Engadine architecture—small windows set in thick walls, etched *sgraffito* decorations, and carved wooden doors. (For more on this topic, see page 381.)

Start watching on the left for snow-capped peaks peering over the bald, jagged, brown and gray cliffs—we'll get a better view of these soon, at the Montebello curve. At the **Bernina Diavolezza** station, a cable car ascends to the top of this peak ("She-Devil," 9,930 feet, described on page 374).

Montebello Curve: This stretch offers you the best views over the **Morteratsch Glacier** on the left, with impressive peaks in the background. From left to right: the Bellavista Range (12,770 feet), Crest Agüzza (12,690 feet), and the highest peak in the canton, Piz Bernina (13,280 feet).

Piz Bernina was first climbed in 1850 by a team led by rangers from the village of Schanf. Their gear consisted only of thick woolen pants, a shirt and jacket, hobnailed shoes, and a hat with a black veil to shade them from the strong sunshine. Others followed: Lucy Walker (1836–1916), a Canadian-born Liverpudlian who suffered from rheumatism, was recommended by her doctor to take up hiking. She took this advice very seriously, traveled to Switzerland, and became addicted to mountaineering. Wearing a flannel skirt, she became the first woman to conquer the Eiger (1864), the Matterhorn (1866), Piz Bernina (1869), and many other peaks.

Morteratsch: At the base of the curve, you'll pass through the Morteratsch station. If staying in the area, consider backtracking here for a fine one-hour hike to the edge of the glacier, past posts tracking the glacier's recent retreat (described on page 374).

As you continue, the tracks are lined by more and more larch trees. The milky-white waters from Lago Bianco and the Morteratsch Glacier run wild in a broad riverbed alongside the tracks, as satisfied cows chew away in the meadows while waterfalls tumble down the cliffs.

Pontresina: This town is a good place to break the journey (see the Upper Engadine chapter). Consider spending a night or two in Pontresina, exploring the quaint village of Samedan, visiting the glitzy resort of St. Moritz, and maybe doing some hiking before continuing on your way.

If you're going to **St. Moritz,** your train trip is nearly over (about 10 minutes after Pontresina). If you're continuing to **Chur** (or, in summer, to Davos), there's more to see.

Part 3: The Albula Pass, from Pontresina to Filisur

Although you're leaving the glaciers behind, your trip will still lead you through magnificent mountain scenery, with steep cliffs and deep gorges. (Note that from here on, the journey overlaps with the Glacier Express.)

Upper Engadine: First, you'll slide through the broad and mellow valley around Samedan, following the "shortest river in Switzerland," the Flazbach. On the right, look for the funicular heading up to **Muottas Muragl,** a viewpoint overlooking the valleys that come together in Samedan (described in the Upper Engadine chapter). **Samedan** is home to Europe's highest airport. It serves glider enthusiasts and vacationers in St. Moritz.

After Samedan, in **Bever,** the train leaves the Inn River valley and climbs to another spectacular leg of its journey.

Albula Railway: The section between Bever and Bergün boasts amazing engineering work. Technicians from all over the world come here to admire the diversity of spiral tunnels, looping viaducts, galleries, and bridges that span the Albula Gorge.

The train works its way up along a cheerfully splashing mountain creek, between the Swiss pine and larch trees and some isolated farmhouses. The **Albula Tunnel,** the highest subterranean alpine crossing in Europe, takes you up to 5,970 feet.

It's difficult to overstate the importance of this tunnel and rail line—opened in 1903—to the fate of Graubünden. Just a generation earlier, a north-south transalpine route was very nearly built through here. Instead, the Gotthard Tunnel was built to the west (see "Gotthard Panorama Express," earlier). As trade shifted away from this pass—which still required a complicated, meandering route over the high mountains—to that slick new tunnel, Graubünden's economy collapsed. So Graubündners decided to build their own tunnel. Over the four-year construction of this tunnel, more than 1,300 workers toiled in hazardous conditions. (While some died because of accidents, even more were claimed by a worm infection caused by contaminated wastewater.) With the completion of the Albula Railway, the journey from St. Moritz to Chur that took twelve hours by horse and carriage could be done in four; today it takes just two. The population of the Upper Engadine grew tenfold, and it's because of this tunnel that St. Moritz was transformed from a humble farming village into a glitzy resort and Winter Olympics host.

A **new Albula Tunnel,** under construction since 2014, is finally nearing completion. The length of time it has taken—more than twice as long as the first tunnel, built more than a century earlier—is both a testament to the original feat of engineering and construction, and an indication of modern safety standards and environmental considerations.

The pass you're conquering right now is another barrier between cultures and climate—it takes you from the valley of the Inn River (part of the Danube watershed) to the valley of the Albula, a tributary of the Rhine, and the weather is often quite different on either side of the tunnel.

Preda: After this village, the train loops down through five spiral and two straight tunnels, crosses nine viaducts, and goes under two galleries—more reminders of why the Albula Railway is considered the most ingenious ever built. It covers almost eight miles and descends more than 1,365 feet. The village of **Bergün** will be visible three separate times as you loop around the valley.

Bergün: This town greets you with a modern, public open-air swimming pool and an onion-shaped 17th-century "Roman tower." When the Albula Railway was completed, there were high hopes that Bergün might become a big resort—like Pontresina, or even St. Moritz. They built an elaborate spa to wow visitors. But those dreams were never realized, and the village remains as sleepy as it is remote. Even so, it has a certain offbeat charm. Every winter, the street along the tracks above Bergün is closed to cars, and 100,000 sled enthusiasts enjoy the ride of their lives on a winding three-mile stretch.

Below Bergün: As the train continues winding down the pretty valley, you may be able to see other parts of the track below or next to you. Just before Filisur, the train does a 360-degree spin inside a tunnel. In **Filisur,** summer Bernina Express trains to Davos split off. If you're continuing to Chur, read on.

Part 4: Filisur to Chur

Landwasser Viaduct: After Filisur, the train enters a tunnel, and an announcement reminds you to ready your camera and position yourself on the left side. Just after the tunnel, you'll cross the famous Landwasser viaduct. (The train might pause here—mid-bridge—for a brief photo op.) A masterpiece of engineering, the viaduct's pillars were built without scaffolding. Iron towers, which formed the center of each pillar, were built first. With the help of cranes set up atop each pillar, materials were hoisted up and the brick was laid. The 425-foot-long viaduct curves elegantly in a radius of 330 feet. Notice how nicely the dark limestone masonry matches the surrounding landscape (it was quarried right here).

Albula River Gorge: After the viaduct, you continue through a gentle valley—with picturesque towns—to Tiefencastel. As you leave that town, the **Albula River** runs far beneath you. In Solis, watch on the left for the dramatic Solis Viaduct, which rises high above the gorge. Between here and Thusis, the wild Albula River carves the dramatic gorge; above, your train's panoramic windows allow you to see the steep, rugged cliffs looming over the tracks.

Domleschg Valley: Thusis is the commercial hub of the broad and lush Domleschg valley, which stretches from here to Reichenau. The trip takes you down along the Hinterrhein ("Back-Rhine") River. Notice the many fortresses, castles, towers, and ruins along the river—a reminder that taxes were levied on the traders who traveled this major route between northern and southern Europe. The 13th-century castle above Thusis now belongs to a local chemical company.

Reichenau: Surrounded by wide waters, this town marks the confluence of two arms of the Upper Rhine (the Hinterrhein and the Vorderrhein—"Front-Rhine"). Reichenau became wealthy from the taxes it got from the passing merchants. The 17th-century Reichenau Castle, right where the rivers converge, was once used as a school, but now it's a hotel. From here, the Upper Rhine flows to Lake Constance (Bodensee), then follows the German-Swiss border to Basel.

The train follows the Rhine at the foot of Calanda Mountain to our final stop.

Chur: The area around Chur is Heidi country. This was the home of Johanna Spyri (1827-1901), who lived on an alp high above Maienfeld, just 12 miles north of here. Her Heidi novels were semi-autobiographical: Spyri was an orphan who lived with her grandfather and a goatherd named Peter, and came to know the majesty of the Alps.

For more on Chur, see the end of this chapter. You can catch the Glacier Express (explained next) from Chur or from St. Moritz. Or, from Chur, you can transfer to destinations elsewhere in Switzerland.

Glacier Express

This most promoted of the Swiss scenic rail routes travels between Zermatt in the southwest of Switzerland and the best-known resort towns in eastern Switzerland (St. Moritz and Davos). If you stay on for the whole ride, you'll spend more than eight hours crossing 291 bridges, going through 91 tunnels, and reaching an altitude of 6,670 feet.

While it's an impressive and famous journey, the Glacier Express is not necessarily the be-all and end-all of Swiss rail trips. Much of the journey is down in valleys (as opposed to along the sides of cliffs), meaning that high-altitude views are a little lacking. And doing the whole route makes for a long day. But the stark landscape, carved by the glaciers that gave the train its name, is striking. The trip offers a dramatic way to connect eastern Switzerland with tucked-away-in-the-mountains Zermatt.

ROUTE OVERVIEW

"Glacier Express" is a misnomer—you'll only glimpse glaciers at the two ends of the route, and it's hardly an express. Not only does it take its time (traveling at about 20 mph to make the full trip in 8 hours), but it also makes plenty of stops along the way. The route cuts along the southern part of Switzerland, between St. Moritz/Davos (in the east) and Zermatt (in the west). You can ride in either direction.

One two-hour stretch of track—the Albula Pass between Chur and the St. Moritz area—is on both the Glacier Express and Bernina Express routes.

PLANNING YOUR TIME

Eight hours on a winding, jolting narrow-gauge train is a long time. If you don't want to commit to the whole journey, keep in mind that the most distinctive stretch of the trip is the high-moun-

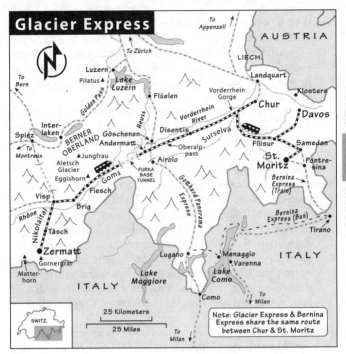

tain pass between Disentis and Brig. The trip over the Albula Pass between St. Moritz and Filisur (which is also part of the Bernina Express route) is also a highlight.

There are several ways of doing just a part of the route, though none is an obvious winner. Consider doing just St. Moritz to Chur (2 hours), then continuing to Zürich or Appenzell; St. Moritz to Brig (6.5 hours), then branching off to Interlaken, Bern, or Lausanne; Luzern or Lugano to Zermatt, connecting at Göschenen (6 hours); Luzern to St. Moritz, connecting at Andermatt (6.5 hours, see "**Luzern to St. Moritz Option**" later); or Lugano to Bern, via Göschenen and Brig (5.5 hours).

ORIENTATION TO THE GLACIER EXPRESS

Cost: You'll pay 152 CHF for second class, or 268 CHF for first class, between St. Moritz and Zermatt (prices include seat reservation fees). The entire trip is covered by the Swiss Travel and Eurail passes except the required reservation fee (29-49 CHF, price depends on the season, cheaper if you don't do the whole route). Those with a second-class rail pass will need to pay an additional fee to upgrade to first class. If you're riding the full length of the Glacier Express *sans* rail pass, the cost is high enough to warrant a look at the Swiss Half-Fare Card, which can quickly pay for itself (see page 487).

All Glacier Express trains have panoramic first- and second-class cars with air-conditioning and the option of an in-seat meal. Second-class seating can get extremely crowded in summer, so consider splurging on first class.

For the crème de la crème, step up to the **"Excellence Class,"** with much roomier cabins (one row of seats on each side of the train—all window seats), a full-service bar, and lots of drinks and food—including a seven-course lunch and afternoon tea (420 CHF extra).

Schedule: The Glacier Express train runs at least once daily in each direction, *except* from late October to mid-December (when local trains are your only option). Going from east to west, the train begins in St. Moritz at 8:51 and arrives in Zermatt at 17:10. Going from west to east, the train departs Zermatt at 8:52 and arrives in St. Moritz at 16:38. Those overnighting in Davos need to change trains in Filisur. In summer, one or two extra departures per day are added, an hour earlier and later than the times above. Confirm all times before your trip.

Information: The Glacier Express is operated jointly by the Matterhorn Gotthard Bahn (MGB), based in Brig (+41 84 864 2442, www.glacierexpress.ch or www.matterhorngotthardbahn.ch), and the Rhätische Bahn (RhB), based in Chur (+41 81 288 6565, www.rhb.ch). Trains have free Wi-Fi with access to their "InfoT(r)ainment" multimedia guide, providing insightful tidbits about towns and natural attractions along the way.

Seats: For most of the trip—including the most dramatic stretch, between Disentis and Brig—it's much better to sit on the south-facing side of the train (generally seat numbers ending in 1 or 2 in both classes face south on this stretch; in second class, seats ending in 3 or 8 are along the aisle on the south-facing side). Coming from the east, even-numbered seats face forward for

most of the trip. Keep in mind that trains change directions in Chur—so if you start on the right side facing backward in Davos, Samedan, or St. Moritz, you'll be on the (preferable) left side facing forward for most of the trip. Conductors take

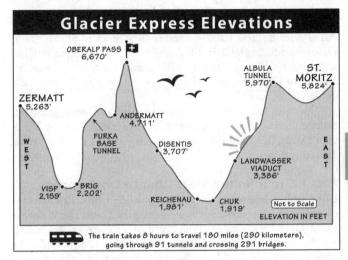

Glacier Express Elevations

OBERALP PASS
6,670'

ALBULA
TUNNEL
5,970'

ST.
MORITZ
5,824'

ZERMATT
5,263'

ANDERMATT
4,711'

FURKA
BASE
TUNNEL

DISENTIS
3,707'

LANDWASSER
VIADUCT
3,386'

W E S T

E A S T

VISP
2,159'

BRIG
2,202'

REICHENAU
1,981'

CHUR
1,919'

Not to Scale

ELEVATION IN FEET

The train takes 8 hours to travel 180 miles (290 kilometers),
going through 91 tunnels and crossing 291 bridges.

SCENIC RAIL JOURNEYS

reserved seat numbers seriously but may allow you to switch into an unoccupied seat.

Luggage: You'll keep your luggage with you (they don't check it through, except in Excellence Class)—just slip it between the backs of the seats.

Taking Regular Trains: This is one scenic route where regular trains are not a good option. While they do save you the seat reservation fee, they require changing trains three times. Regular trains are, however, the only option in late fall, when the express doesn't run.

Luzern to St. Moritz Option: An alternative, convenient way to connect visits to the Berner Oberland and the Upper Engadine regions is to go by train from Luzern to St. Moritz on a route that covers some of the nicest portions of the Glacier Express trip. Two trains leave Luzern every morning for St. Moritz with changes in Erstfeld, Göschenen, and Andermatt (see www.rail.ch for schedules).

Connecting to Pontresina: Pontresina, on the Bernina Express route, is easy to connect to the Glacier Express route—it's less than a 10-minute train ride away from St. Moritz or (somewhat simpler) in little Samedan.

Eating: A fancy restaurant car offers a **$$$$** lunch, which is handy if you're in for the full trip. A plate of the day costs 34 CHF, or you can pay more for a two-, three-, or four-course fixed-price meal (drinks cost extra).

Most seats have tables—perfect for a bring-your-own grocery-store feast. Each table has a rail in the middle with bumpers built in, to prevent drinks from sliding around too much on the twisty tracks.

⊙ SELF-GUIDED TOUR

All Glacier Express trains—whether they begin in St. Moritz or Davos—go through Chur. I'll describe the route starting at Chur and heading toward Zermatt. (For details on the trip **from St. Moritz to Chur,** see parts 3 and 4 of the Bernina Express self-guided tour, earlier.)

Note: In Chur, the train changes directions, resupplies, and changes locomotives. If you've started out your journey in St. Moritz or Davos, this is a great time to stretch your legs (be clear on the departure time).

Part 1: Graubünden, from Chur to Oberalppass

Chur and Reichenau: A few miles outside Chur, Reichenau—roughly 2,000 feet above sea level—marks the lowest altitude of the route. From here, the big climb begins. (For more on Reichenau, see the Bernina Express section, earlier.) This is also where the Chur line hits the St. Moritz line, so if you're riding the full Glacier Express route, your train will backtrack on this short stretch.

Vorderrhein Gorge: Leaving Reichenau, you'll begin following the river called **Vorderrhein** (in Romansh, Rein Anterieur). This "Front-Rhine"—an early tributary of the Rhine River—carved the **Vorderrhein Gorge,** nicknamed "the Swiss Grand Canyon," through which you'll soon be traveling. While this gorge is significantly less dramatic than its namesake, the chalky, jagged, white cliffs that rocket up from the river's surface  are certainly picturesque. (Watch for rafters and kayakers frolicking (or at least attempting to stay alive) in the rapids.

Surselva: After exiting the gorge, the train enters a pastoral region called Surselva, centered on the town of **Ilanz.** This is Romansh country, where the fourth official language of Switzerland is kept alive—barely. Even in innocuous, idyllic small towns like this one, Switzerland is prepared for war. Tucked under small brown roofs along the bottom of the hillside are loads of explosives. They're part of Switzerland's military defenses; access to this pass can be blown up on short notice.

As you approach **Disentis,** the tracks begin to twist along the edge of a canyon—making the scenery more dramatic (a taste of what's to come). Thirty years ago, those mountains above you were covered in snow year-round—but no longer. The Swiss, so in touch with nature, are painfully aware of their changing, ever-hotter climate. In Zermatt—where this journey terminates—2022 was the first time in living memory that summer skiing was not possible up at the Klein Matterhorn summit. It was just too slushy.

Disentis: You'll pull into Disentis, with its big 17th-century Benedictine monastery looming in your window. At the Disentis station, you may get a brief break to stretch your legs as a cogwheel engine (a.k.a. rack-and-pinion drive) is attached to the train. If you're on board, you'll feel it jiggle, but trainspotters enjoy hopping out to watch them make the switch. This locomotive has gears that can lower to latch onto the cogs of an extra rail with grippable teeth. At a 10 percent incline (that's 100 meters of gain per kilometer, or about 500 feet per mile), conventional train wheels start to slip.

Disentis is also where the eastbound and westbound Glacier Express runs cross. The trains don't just swap engines; they swap some members of the crew—allowing them to head home for the evening rather than spend the night stranded all the way across the country.

All aboard! We're moving on.

Above Disentis: You'll work your way up the mountain alongside the Vorderrhein River. Appreciate the glorious views of farmhouses and hamlets climbing up grassy green hills on the far side of the valley. Just west of the larger town of **Sedrun** was the staging ground for the excavation of the Gotthard Base Tunnel (completed in 2016), which runs for 35 miles under the mountain from the Lake Geneva area to Lake Lugano in Ticino. (We'll cross over the other, original, Gotthard Tunnel farther along in Andermatt.)

Beyond **Rueras,** the track steepens and the train slows to allow its gears to latch into the cog rail. After Tschamut, the last inhabited place before Oberalppass, you enter a long series of snow sheds—designed to protect the tracks (and trains) in case an avalanche strikes. If you hadn't noticed, you're now entering the most dramatic stretch of this entire trip.

Part 2: Uri Canton, from Oberalppass to Furka Tunnel

Oberalppass: You'll emerge from the sheds at **Oberalppass,** the literal high point of this journey (6,670 feet). Keep an eye out for the red lighthouse, which seems extremely out of place high in the Alps. It's not functional but symbolic: The lighthouse matches a much larger one at Rotterdam, Netherlands, where the Rhine River empties into the North Sea after traveling through Switzerland, Germany, and Holland. This lighthouse marks the source of that river. (Well, almost. The official Rhine source is Lake Toma, downhill from here in Graubünden. But technically that water must begin as snow, up in these mountains.)

The train glides along **Lake Oberalp**—like many alpine lakes, this is controlled by a dam, making it larger than it might naturally be. This water is used to generate snow for nearby ski areas in winter.

The scenery up here is stark. Notice the extensive network of **avalanche fences** high above you—a reminder of the many generations of Swiss farmers who have learned to live on the land. The reddish streaks you might see on the snow? Believe it or not, that's sand from the Sahara Desert. It gets caught up in high-altitude winds and carried all the way to the Swiss Alps.

Oberalp also marks your departure from Graubünden and your entrance to the **canton of Uri,** with just 37,000 people and no cities. This canton, birthplace of the legendary William Tell, stretches along the Reuss River valley to the southern shores of Lake Luzern. While this train line feels remote, Uri is in the very heart of Switzerland and was one of the original eight cantons that united to create the Old Swiss Confederacy in the 14th century.

Over Andermatt: After the little station at Nätschen, you'll twist under a gondola line into the valley around Andermatt. First you'll get a high, wide overview of the entire valley; then you'll curl down four switchbacks, partly through tunnels, into the town itself. (If you miss the view the first time around, no worries—you'll see it a few more times, from each side of the train.)

Andermatt: This fairly dreary, hardworking mountain town is making a supreme effort to rebrand itself as a luxury ski resort. (While it isn't quite Davos or St. Moritz, it certainly enjoys some wonderful scenery.) Running directly beneath Andermatt is the junction for the nearly 10-mile-long Gotthard Tunnel (not visible from here), which takes trains unscenically from Göschenen to Airolo. While still used by the Gotthard Panorama Express train (described earlier in this chapter), the tunnel has been made nearly obsolete by another corridor: the 35-mile Gotthard Base Tunnel, which speedily connects Luzern with Lugano in just two hours.

Reuss River: Leaving Andermatt, the scenery opens up again. You'll (very briefly) follow the Reuss River, which from its source near here runs north through the mountains to the Vierwaldstättersee (a.k.a. "Lake Luzern") and through downtown Luzern. The huge boulders seen throughout this desolate terrain were deposited by—what else?—glaciers.

Furka Pass: As you approach a high, bald peak, notice the roads snaking up the hillside. They're headed to the Furka Pass...

but you don't have to. Instead, you're headed into the nearly 10-mile-long **Furka Base Tunnel.** While it might seem like a view killer, realize that this tunnel—finished in 1982—makes it possible for the Glacier Express to continue running through the winter. Automobiles are allowed onto the train to ride smoothly and safely between Realp and Oberwald. This is especially handy in the winter, when the road is closed. (The train picks up speed here, zipping through the tunnel before you know it.)

Part 3: Valais Canton, from Furka Tunnel to Brig and Visp

Goms and Rhône River Valley: Exiting the tunnel, things feel different. While you were underground, you left Uri and entered the **canton of Valais** (Wallis, in German). This vast region—which stretches from here south to the Italian border, and west all the way to the shores of Lake Geneva (and France)—is where you'll spend the rest of this journey. Notice how the terrain has changed: less bald, rugged, and arid; more bucolic and green-rolling-hills...classic "Switzerland."

Specifically, we're in the region called **Goms.** The river we're following through this relatively flat valley is the **Rhône,** whose source is the glaciers just overhead. From here, the Rhône flows into, and back out of, Lake Geneva before coursing through southern France, under the bridges of Lyon, Avignon, and Arles, to where it meets the Mediterranean at the Camargue delta—famous for its pink flamingoes and precious *fleur de sel* salt deposits. Just imagine: Over the last few miles of track, we passed the sources of the Rhine (which powers industry on its way north to the Atlantic at Rotterdam), the Rhône (which courses through idyllic Provence to *Le Med*), and the Reuss (which flows under the famous wooden bridges of Luzern). And that's what they mean by "continental divide."

As we travel through this valley, you may see ongoing work to channel and control this upper stretch of the powerful river, which has a long history of flooding the valley.

Reckingen: About 20 minutes after exiting the tunnel, be ready for the up-close view of the village of Reckingen, which is particularly fun as the train snakes through a narrow passage between the houses made of local larch wood that darkens naturally in the sun.

Eggishorn: As the valley gets rockier, consider that you're on the "back" side of the Berner Oberland. (As the crow flies, you're less than 20 miles from Gimmelwald.) In fact, farther along in the town of Fiesch, notice the cable car running overhead. This runs up to Eggishorn, which—on clear days—boasts views of the Eiger, Mönch, Jungfrau, and Matterhorn, plus Mont Blanc (not to mention the Aletsch Glacier—more on that later). Imagine...you're at the very center of many of Europe's most famous Alps, spanning three countries.

Grengiols Tunnel: About 10 minutes after Fiesch, just before the village of Grengiols, the train does a 360-degree loop-de-loop inside a darkened tunnel, then descends to a valley floor. We're getting close to the junction city of Brig. But first...

Aletsch Glacier: While this is called the "Glacier Express," have you noticed that we haven't seen too many, you know, *glaciers*? Here's another unseen glacier to add to the list: The Alps' biggest glacier, the 14-mile-long, up to 3,000-feet-thick Aletsch Glacier, stretches overhead on your right, just out of sight. From here, it runs all the way to the Berner Oberland; if you ride the lift up to the Jungfraujoch, you can walk on it.

Brig and Visp: Finally, you'll arrive at **Brig,** an ugly industrial town with good connections to other train lines (some key connections are listed at the end of this section). While not much to look at, Brig acts as a sort of linguistic and cultural hinge of Switzerland: You're in the German-speaking Valais, but straight ahead, the Rhône River leads to Lake Geneva and French Switzerland. Keep an eye out for vineyards—the highest in Europe. We're out of milk country and into wine country. The Simplon Pass, near here, is one of the main crossings (and historic trade routes) to Italy—to Domodossola, Lake Maggiore, and eventually Milan and Torino.

Visp, the next town you'll reach (just a few minutes down the track), is another common transit point. If you're staying on the train here, you'll feel the tug as the train's cogwheel attaches again for another steep climb...toward Zermatt.

Part 4: Nikolaital Valley, from Visp to Zermatt

Visp marks the entrance to the Nikolaital Valley, which follows the Matter Vispa upriver through a narrow canyon to Zermatt and the Matterhorn.

Matter Vispa River: Leaving Visp, as you get deeper into the mountains, you'll be following the Matter Vispa River. At Neubrück, just after a giant factory, you'll pass two dramatic, stone bridges arching elegantly over the water. Later, as things get steeper, the river has a particularly scenic stretch of rapids that churns over chunky white boulders on the right side of the train (soon after the village of Kalpetran).

From there, you'll be going through the **Mattertal**—Switzerland's deepest valley, and the steepest stretch of the entire Glacier Express.

Shortly before the village of Randa, you pass a cone of rubble left by a huge avalanche that wiped out two miles of road and track here in 1991.

Randa: This town is known to adventure seekers as the site of what was, for a time, the world's longest suspension footbridge, at 1,621 feet. (It has since been surpassed by several longer bridges.) If you'd like to go for a bounce and a swing on the bridge, the Zermatt TI has tips.

Täsch: Vast parking lots mark the end of the road for drivers. From here it's train-only into the traffic-free terminus of this line, Zermatt. Think about how much the terrain has changed since you started the trip: from remote valleys to fertile farmlands, to tundra above the tree line, to this rough and rocky terrain.

The Matterhorn: As you continue along the valley lined with quarries, you'll get your first glimpses (provided the weather's clear) of the unmistakable shape of the **Matterhorn**—a fitting exclamation point marking the end of this long journey. **Zermatt**—with its bunker-like, avalanche-proof train station—lies just around the bend.

GLACIER EXPRESS CONNECTIONS

If you're not going all the way to St. Moritz or Zermatt, Chur and Brig are handy places to bail out of the Glacier Express.

From Brig by Train to: Bern (2-3/hour, 1-2 hours direct), **Lausanne** (2/hour, 2 hours direct), **Interlaken Ost** (1-2/hour, 70 minutes, change in Spiez), **Luzern** (1-2/hour, 2.5 hours, change in Bern and sometimes Olten), **Zürich** (hourly, 2 hours, more with change in Bern).

For Chur connections, see the next section.

Chur

The routes of the Glacier Express and the Bernina Express both pass through Chur—supposedly Switzerland's oldest and warmest town. Fanning out over the foothills from the Rhine River, filling its broad valley with industry and commerce, Chur is a handy transportation hub for these two scenic train lines and has a charming-enough old town. Overall, Chur (pronounced "khoor") is just a typical Swiss burg—fine for passing through, but not worth a detour.

Visiting Chur: Chur's train station is at the bottom (north end) of the town center, where it sits atop a long underground concourse housing the

TI (+41 81 252 1818, https://chur.graubuenden.ch), a ticket office, the handy Bahnhofplatz parking garage, and a Co-op supermarket. To get to the old town, follow *Stadtzentrum* signs up the escalator, then walk straight up Bahnhofstrasse. In two blocks, you'll reach the big roundabout at Postplatz. The old town is straight ahead.

Public **WCs** are next to the cathedral. If you've got time to kill, you can wander up through the cobbled old town to two big churches (the Romanesque cathedral and the Gothic Church of St. Martin), some remains of the medieval city wall, and the town museum (Rätisches Museum, https://raetischesmuseum.gr.ch). Follow the handy red signs pointing you toward the attractions.

Sleeping in Chur: Sleep in Chur only if you must, in order to connect to one of the scenic rail lines. (If you're connecting both the Glacier and Bernina Express routes, note that they also overlap farther south, in St. Moritz; nearby Pontresina is a more enjoyable place to overnight than Chur—see page 376.) Here are three moderately priced places in the atmospheric old town, an easy 10-to-15-minute walk from the train station: **$ Hotel Restaurant Rebleuten** (overlooking a quiet little square a block off Kornplatz at Pfisterplatz 1, +41 81 255 1144, www.rebleutenchur.ch); **$$ Hotel Freieck** (with a mod lobby and 41 rooms over a low-key café, Reichsgasse 44, +41 81 255 1515, www.freieck.ch); and charming **$$ Hotel Franziskaner** (with rooms above a popular restaurant, Kupfergasse 18, +41 81 252 1261, www.hotelfranziskaner.ch).

Chur Connections: In addition to being a key stop for the Glacier Express and the Bernina Express, Chur also offers speedy, frequent connections to **Zürich** (3/hour, 2 hours), **Luzern** (2/hour, 2.5 hours, 1-2 changes), and **Appenzell** (3/hour, 2.5 hours, 1 or more changes).

SWITZERLAND IN WINTER

One of my favorite Swiss memories happened one winter night on the snowy slopes of the Berner Oberland. My friend Walter (who ran the old Hotel Mittaghorn in Gimmelwald) and I, warmed by hot chocolate laced with schnapps, decided to go sledding between mountain-high villages. We strapped flashlights to our heads, miner-style, and zoomed through the crisp, moonlit night.

That said, this is a summertime book. I've included plenty of tips on hiking, while mostly ignoring the winter-sports scene. But winter activities are an important part of the Swiss culture (and tourist industry).

Just a century ago, clever entrepreneurs in the Swiss Alps realized that skiing (which began as a method of wintertime transportation in Scandinavia 4,000 years ago) could be a profitable extension of their resorts' spring and summer seasons. Telemark (cross-country) skiing came first, then alpine (downhill) skiing, and, more recently, snowboarding. Generations of Swiss skiers have honed their skills on these slopes. Big names include Erika Hess, Vreni Schneider, Wendy Holdener, Carlo Janka, and the venerable 1948 Olympic champion Karl Molitor.

You don't have to be a skier or snowboarder to enjoy Switzerland in the winter. Ski resorts offer plenty of other activities, including snowshoeing, sledding, ice skating...and shopping. Or just ride up a lift, rent a chair in the sun, and warm up with a glass of *Pflümli* (plum liqueur).

TOP WINTER DESTINATIONS

The winter-sports season begins in early December and runs through Easter. Peak time hits at Christmas and New Year's—during this period, hotel prices in resort towns surpass summer highs.

While Switzerland's resorts vary greatly, they share a rich ski culture, an astounding variety of terrain, relatively mild temperatures (compared to many American destinations), and a lively *après*-ski scene. For those who can afford them, the best winter activities are in the Berner Oberland (Mürren, Wengen, Grindelwald, and Gstaad); the southern canton of Valais (Zermatt, Saas-Fee, Crans-Montana, and Verbier); and the eastern canton of Graubünden (St. Moritz, Davos, Klosters, and Arosa).

The **Berner Oberland** offers the ultimate diversity of terrain and character, as well as great sledding and stellar views (see the Berner Oberland chapter). The cliff-hanging town of Mürren is relatively uncrowded and a good home base for expert skiers, with the 10,000-foot Schilthorn peak as the backbone of its ski area. Across the valley, Wengen offers skiing for all skill levels, fine accommodations, and shopping, with a complex lift system  connecting it to Kleine Scheidegg, Männlichen, and Grindelwald. Grindelwald, a little closer to Interlaken, is a bit pricier but has the world's longest sled run and easy access to more than 100 miles of downhill trails, including the area's best range of beginners' runs. For more on these ski regions, see the Jungfrau Region tourism website (www.jungfrauregion.swiss).

The canton of **Valais** is known for its excellent winemaking (in the Rhône River valley) as well as its ski slopes (www.valais.ch). Connected to Italy by several high-mountain passes, Valais is home to Switzerland's best-known sight: the Matterhorn (see the Zermatt & the Matterhorn chapter). The area around the Matterhorn, including the villages of Zermatt and Saas-Fee, enjoys high elevation and good skiing.

The canton of Graubünden (www.graubuenden.ch) is home to **St. Moritz,** a resort town so well known that it's a registered trademark (see the Upper Engadine chapter). St. Moritz offers designer boutiques, luxury accommodations, a natural mineral-spring spa... oh, and ski slopes, too (www.stmoritz.ch). In addition to skiing, winter visitors to St. Moritz play polo and cricket on snow, go bobsledding on natural ice, or try "skijoring"—skiing while being pulled by riderless horses.

TIPS FOR WINTER SPORTS

Expect to spend 70-90 CHF a day on lift tickets. You may find cheaper prices in the off-peak season (before mid-Dec and after Easter), if you buy a mul-

tiday pass, or if you have a Swiss Travel Pass. Prices may also be lower for seniors, teenagers, and kids (exact age cutoffs vary). Most ski areas offer half-day afternoon passes.

Rental prices are a bit higher than what you'd find in the US. Depending on the fanciness of the gear, you'll pay 50-80 CHF per day for skiing or snowboarding equipment. If you haven't packed ski wear, you'll pay about 50 CHF per day to rent ski pants, a jacket, and gloves.

Many rental shops in Switzerland belong to the Intersport rental network (www.intersportrent.ch), which sets fairly high standards for its member shops. Places outside this network can be cheaper, but Intersport shops are generally a safe bet and offer useful bonuses: You can reserve gear online at a discount, and many network shops let you pick up rental gear at one ski area and drop it off at another in the region for no charge (an especially handy option in the Berner Oberland).

Always ask your hotelier if they've arranged any special rental deals through local shops. Rental prices don't vary much (since so many shops are part of the Intersport network), so choose a place that's close to your hotel or convenient for getting up the mountain.

Swiss ski resorts are deservedly popular, and slopes can get crowded. Peak crowd times are Christmas, New Year's, mid-February to mid-March (when European school holidays hit), and Easter. The Berner Oberland also fills up in mid-January for world-class racing. Hit the slopes as soon as they open—the hordes don't usually arrive until 10:00 or later. This is especially true in swankier resorts, where well-heeled tourists enjoy long nights and short ski days.

For more in-depth information on the winter scene, see the winter sports section of the Swiss tourism website (www.myswitzerland.com).

CHRISTMAS CELEBRATIONS

Switzerland is an ideal place to celebrate the winter holidays. Imagine spending your days exploring Christmas markets in cozy Swiss cities, sipping hot mulled wine *(Glühwein)*, picking out your favorite handmade ornaments, then relaxing at night in a warm little chalet, making figure-eights with your cube of bread through a steaming pot of cheese fondue.

Swiss Christmas markets are a treat, whether in big cities (such as Bern, Zürich, and Basel) or smaller towns (Interlaken, Appenzell, Chur, and many others). While some of the bigger markets start at the beginning of December and run through Christmas Eve, smaller towns host markets for just one week or weekend. Check the Swiss Tourist Board's website for dates (www.myswitzerland.com/experiences/winter/christmas).

You'll find all cities festively decorated, but Zürich's remarkable display of tasteful, twinkling lights is arguably Switzerland's best. This being the land of Cal-

vin—the most austere of Protestant Reformers—most Christmas decorations are relatively understated here, but they're still charming.

In the village of Gimmelwald, residents in each home decorate a window for Advent. Just as children open a different little paper window each day on an Advent calendar, Gimmelwald residents reveal a new decorated window on a different house each day.

The debut of a new Advent window often comes with a party. Under a cold sky, with stars reflecting off the snow and the moon inside a halo, the village gathers. In a kind of roving block party, neighbors emerge to meet friends and enjoy grilled sausages, hot mulled wine, and folk music on the accordion. Men take sections of logs (the size of a four-foot chunk of telephone pole), cut the ends into a point, and plant them upright in the snow. Coated with tar, they're set ablaze—torches to light and warm the cozy yet frigid occasion. In the distance, children ride old-time wooden sleds, going up and down, up and down.

For the Swiss, a communal pot of fondue is purely a winter specialty. Invitations to a cozy

Swiss party include the Swiss-German word *FIGUGEGL* (fee-GOO-geck-ul), which stands for *Fondue isch guet und git e gueti Luune*—"Fondue is good and gives a good mood." According to tradition, if you drop your bread into the pot, you must kiss the person to your left.

Each Christmas season, usually on St. Nicholas Day (December 6), Swiss children receive a visit from Samichlaus—that's Swiss German for St. Nicholas. With his black-clad, soot-faced henchman, Schmutzli, by his side, Samichlaus goes door to door, visiting the town's children. He knocks on the door, and when the frightened-but-excited kids answer, Samichlaus consults his big book of sins—co-authored by parents—and does some lighthearted moralizing. Schmutzli stands by as a menacing enforcer, traditionally holding either a stick or switch for beating bad children, and a sack for carrying them away to be eaten (nowadays he eats only the really bad children).

Then Samichlaus asks the kids to earn a little forgiveness by reciting a poem. After the poems and assurances of reform, Samichlaus allows them to reach deep into his bag for a smattering of tangerines, nuts, gingerbread, and other treats. (Schmutzli—whose name means "the little dirty one"—usually smears his face with ashes, rather than the problematic, full-on blackface worn by his Dutch counterpart, Zwarte Piet.)

Cutting and decorating the Christmas tree—traditionally on December 24—is a family affair. Real candles, kept upright by dangling ornamental counterbalances, are attached, then lit by the children. (Locals are bold with their candles; to me, it feels as if their pine houses, with open beams, are ready to go up in flames.) Presents are opened while the candles burn. The tree stays up after Christmas; candles are lit again on New Year's Eve for good luck. Some traditional rural Swiss churches also light candles on their trees for Christmas Eve services.

OTHER FESTIVITIES

Second only to Christmas is *Fasnacht*, the Germanic equivalent of Mardi Gras or Carnival. Traditionally celebrated in the days before or after Ash Wednesday, *Fasnacht* festivities often include a parade with floats and locals in traditional masks and garish, larger-than-life costumes. Quirky traditions vary from town to town (for example, in Basel—home to Switzerland's most outlandish *Fasnacht*—celebrations begin promptly at 4:00 in the morning and feature roving fife-and-drum bands). This pre-Christian cer-

emony likely dates from a pagan tradition to frighten away evil winter spirits and welcome the renewal of springtime. The most famous *Fasnacht* celebrations in Switzerland occur in Basel (www.fasnacht.ch), Bern (www.fasnacht.be), and Luzern (www.luzerner-fasnacht.ch). If you'll be in Switzerland at this time of year, it's worth the effort to catch one of these weird and wonderful celebrations.

SWITZERLAND: PAST & PRESENT

Switzerland has a unique and impressive story, forging unity from diversity and somehow remaining above the fray when Europe goes ballistic. Despite four languages, diverse geography, ill-defined borders, and many religious sects—and despite being surrounded by continental Europe's four big powers (France, Germany, Austria, and Italy)—the Swiss cantons banded together to form an independent federal system that still works today.

Even if you're not going to Switzerland for the history (who would?), you'll encounter it. You can play gladiator inside a fighting arena from Roman times or tour medieval castles and battlegrounds, left over from when the Swiss wrested their independence from foreign rulers. Stripped-down cathedrals attest to the religious violence of the Reformation, which almost tore the country apart. You'll ride the ingenious cogwheel trains and cliff-climbing funiculars of Switzerland's progressive 19th century, when the country was at the forefront of the emerging Industrial Age. The specters of Nazi Germany and the Soviet Union arise in underground fortresses and bomb shelters now open to the public. And finally, you'll see the Switzerland of today—gleaming cities, state-of-the-art transportation, and happy citizens. I love to go a-wandering along the history path, so strap on your rucksack, and let's go.

EARLY HISTORY: CELTS AND ROMANS
(c. 500 BC-AD 500)

The Alps—Switzerland's star attraction—were born 500 million years ago, when the ocean floor was rocked by earthquakes that folded the earth's crust upward and created this long range of peaks (see the "Understanding the Alps" sidebar). The rugged landscape shaped the history and character of the Swiss people. It kept early

Switzerland Almanac

Official Name: The Confoederatio Helvetica, or Switzerland, has a different name in each of its four official languages: *Schweizerische Eidgenossenschaft* (German), *Confédération Suisse* (French), *Confederazione Svizzera* (Italian), and *Confederaziun Svizra* (Romansh). Locals shorten those to "die Schweiz," "la Suisse," "la Svizzera," and "la Svizra."

Size: 16,000 square miles (twice the size of New Jersey), with a population of 8.5 million (similar to Virginia).

Geography: Switzerland sits at the crossroads between northern and southern Europe. The Alps are Europe's high point and continental divide, from which the major rivers flow—Rhine, Rhône, Danube, and Po. Switzerland's highest point is the 15,200-foot Monte Rosa (specifically, the summit called Dufourspitze), along the Italian border. Though Switzerland is mostly mountainous, the center of the country consists of rolling hills and large lakes.

Latitude and Longitude: 47°N and 8°E, similar latitude to Quebec, Canada.

Major Cities: Zürich (pop. 430,000 in the city, 1.4 million in the metropolitan area), Geneva (192,000), Basel (167,000), and Bern (the capital, 129,000).

Economy: The gross domestic product is $731 billion. Its per-capita GDP of $68,400 is among Europe's highest. The franc is strong and unemployment is less than half the EU average. Blessed with hydropower and using nuclear technology, Switzerland generates 99 percent of its electricity with virtually no oil.

Government: Founded in 1291 as a confederation of cantons, balancing the needs of its different linguistic/ethnic groups. No single political party (or two or even three parties) dominates. The president, chosen by the legislature, serves for just one calendar year. The two-house Federal Assembly consists of the 46-seat Council of States and the 200-seat National Council, elected for four-year terms.

Flag: Switzerland's distinctive square flag is a white cross on red background.

The Average Swiss: On average, they have 1.5 children and will live to be 83. A typical Swiss man serves at least 245 days of compulsory military service. The average Swiss woman earns over 20 percent less than her male counterparts (similar to the US). The Swiss travel an average of 1,400 miles a year on a train, the equivalent of crossing the country six times. They consume a monthly average of about a quart of alcohol and more than a pound and a half of chocolate.

populations physically isolated, leading to still-present cultural divisions and fostering an ethos of independence. Switzerland's location at the heart of Western Europe forced it to be international in outlook, yet the impregnable mountains allowed it to remain apart and neutral.

The first Swiss to appear in written records (c. 500 BC) were a Celtic tribe called the Helvetii. Their name survives today in the country's official title, Confoederatio Helvetica. "Helvetia," the female symbol of Switzerland, appears dressed in robes and armed with a spear and shield on coins, stamps, and statues.

In 58 BC, the Helvetii were defeated by Julius Caesar, the Roman general and future ruler. The Romans established a capital at Avenches, near Murten (where evocative ruins remain); built the cities of Zürich, Geneva, Basel, and Lausanne; and assimilated the Helvetii into their Europe-wide empire. Roman culture thrived in Switzerland for almost 500 years.

As Rome fell (c. AD 400), the Alemanni and other Germanic tribes swarmed in from the north, snuffed out Roman culture, and established the German language. In the west, the Burgundians adopted Latin, which eventually evolved into French. But these tribes never penetrated the nooks and crannies of the most remote mountain areas, and in these regions, particularly in the southeast, people still converse in Romansh, a language that descends independently from the colloquial Latin spoken by Roman-era occupiers. South of the Alps, Latin gradually developed into modern-day Italian. These linguistic and cultural divides remain today.

THE MIDDLE AGES: THE HOLY ROMAN EMPIRE (c. 500-1291)

Like most of Europe during the dark medieval centuries, Switzerland was poor, feudal, and swept by barbarian invasions. The mostly pagan Swiss were slowly converted to Christianity by traveling Irish monks, including St. Gallus (seventh century), who gave his name to the canton of St. Gallen. Swiss lands became part of Charlemagne's empire (c. 800) and then of its successor to the east—the Holy Roman Empire.

Around the turn of the first millennium, Switzerland began to prosper. Cities such as Bern and Luzern were founded, welcoming skilled craftsmen and traders. High in the Alps, clever engineers built bridges and catwalks to open a vital north-south highway

Understanding the Alps

Switzerland's snowy, rugged mountains are its claim to fame—and most likely a main reason for your visit. Fortunately, you don't have to be a mountain climber to see the Alps up close, as the Swiss transportation system is as remarkable as its mountains. Its cog railways, gondolas, and cable cars whisk you up into the type of scenery that's only accessible in some countries by ropes, pitons, and crampons.

The Alps were formed by the collision of two continents. About 100 million years ago, the African plate began pushing north against the stable plates of Europe and Asia. In the process, the sediments of the ancient Tethys Ocean (which once occupied the general real estate of the modern Mediterranean) became smooshed between the landmasses. Shoving all this material together made the rocks and sediments fold, shatter, and pile on top of each other; over millennia this growing jumble built itself up into today's Alps. Up in the mountains, look for folds and faults in the rocks that hint at this immense compression, which is still happening today: The Alps continue to rise by at least a millimeter each year (while erosion wears them down at about the same rate).

The current shape of the mountains and valleys is the handiwork of at least five ice ages over the last two million years. Glaciers flowed down the mountain valleys, scooped out Switzerland's beautiful alpine lakes, and carried rocks far away from where they had formed. The Alps were the first mountains extensively studied by geologists, and many of the geological terms that describe mountains originated here. Once you learn how to recognize a few of the landforms shaped by glaciers, you can easily spot these features when you visit other alpine areas. Study glacier exhibits to train your eye to recognize what you're seeing.

Glaciers are big and blunt, so they make simple, large-scale marks on the landscape. If a valley is U-shaped (with steep sides and a rounded base), it likely was scoured out by a glacier. Switzerland's Lauterbrunnen Valley and California's Yosemite Valley are classic examples.

A **cirque** (French for "circus") is the amphitheater-like depression carved out at the upper part of a valley by a glacier. If two adjacent cirques erode close to each other, a sharp steep-sided ridge forms, called an **arête** (French for "fishbone"). Cirques and arêtes are common in mountains with glaciers. More rarely, when three or more cirques erode toward one another, a pyramidal peak is created, called a **horn.** The Matterhorn is the world's most famous example. Glaciers flowed down all sides of this mountain, scooping material away and creating the distinctive sharp peak.

A common feature left behind by retreating glaciers is a **moraine,** a pile of dirt and rocks carried along on the glacier as it advanced, then dumped as the glacier melted. The Lindenhof in Zürich, a hilltop square once crowned with forts to defend the town, perches on a moraine.

Alpine glaciers can only originate above the snowline, so if you see any of these landforms (U-shaped valleys, cirques, horns, or moraines) in lower elevations, you know that the climate there used to be colder. The warming climate has profoundly affected the glaciers of Switzerland, which have lost more than half their total volume since the early 1930s, according to the latest research. Some studies project that most glaciers in Switzerland will virtually disappear by the end of the century, affecting water storage and hydroelectric power generation.

In higher elevations, mountainsides have become less stable due to the melting of permafrost. Major landslides and rockfalls are increasingly common as warming accelerates the weathering and erosion process on slopes. Some communities, including the ski resort of Pontresina, have built dams to protect areas from potential landslides from nearby mountains; some towns have installed alarm systems. Experts report that the unprecedented heat wave of 2022 shrunk Swiss ice volume by 6 percent in just one year.

Another consequence of the warming climate is that winter weather no longer reliably produces snow at altitudes that it did in the past—which is bad news for Switzerland's huge ski industry. Seeing a future of ever-warmer winters, the Swiss are putting their ingenuity to the test. This goes beyond snow machines: Many resorts are investing hugely in new spas, convention centers, and other attractions that don't require snow.

With their acute awareness of their alpine climate's fragility, the Swiss are especially keen to explore green technology—even high up in the Alps. Now when they build mountain refuges, the favored design isn't necessarily a rustic stone-hut chalet, but a high-tech building that depends on solar power. Switzerland's technological innovation can help keep its mountains white and its valleys green.

through the St. Gotthard Pass. Merchants bought luxury goods in Venice and shipped them over the high mountains to northern Europe. This trade route proved so lucrative that the Holy Roman Emperor ensured access to it by granting the Swiss a measure of independence. Switzerland got a taste of freedom, and when the emperor (a member of the powerful Habsburg family) later tried to bring the country under tighter control, the Swiss had had enough.

THE OLD CONFEDERACY (1291-1500)

On August 1, 1291 (celebrated today as the country's national day), representatives of Switzerland's three original cantons (Uri, Schwyz, and Unterwalden) gathered together and swore an oath. "We will be a single nation of brothers..." they asserted, and joined together to oppose Habsburg rule. According to a famous legend, a Swiss man named William Tell refused to bow to the Habsburg hat, a symbol of their power. As punishment, he was forced to shoot an apple off his own son's head. His son lived to see another haircut, and Tell led the rebellion. (Sadly, historians say that Tell probably never actually existed.)

The Swiss had to battle the powerful Habsburg family for two full centuries to completely drive them out. Meanwhile, in the west, the Swiss fought Burgundy, trouncing them at the pivotal Battle of Murten. One by one, other cantons and cities (Luzern, Zürich, Bern) joined the confederacy. By around 1500, Switzerland's territory had grown to become roughly similar to its current bounds.

During these centuries of warfare, the Swiss earned a reputation as Europe's fiercest warriors. Swiss mercenaries became a valuable export, hired by foreign kings to fight their wars and defend their palaces (think of the Swiss Guards, who still protect the Vatican today). During the French Revolution in 1792, when crowds stormed the king's palace in Paris, it was Swiss mercenaries who went through with the hopeless defense. Six hundred of them were killed—

an event memorialized in Luzern's famous Lion Monument to fallen Swiss Guards.

REFORMATION AND ENLIGHTENMENT (c. 1500-1700)

The Protestant Reformation split Switzerland in two. Huldrych Zwingli preached Protestantism in Zürich (see sidebar on page

46), John Calvin brought his French flock to Geneva, and the Dutch humanist Desiderius Erasmus taught at Basel. While the cities went Protestant, the more rural cantons stayed true to the Catholic faith, plunging the country into religious warfare (1529-1531). Angry rioters stormed Catholic cathedrals, stripping them of their "graven images" and leaving the austere interiors travelers see today (including Zürich's Grossmünster, Bern's Münster, and Lausanne's cathedral). This destruction of religious symbology is known as "iconoclasm."

While Europe suffered through a century of religious wars, Switzerland's struggles were relatively short-lived. Swiss mercenaries fought other countries' wars more than their own. When peace came to Europe with the Treaty of Westphalia (1648), the agreement also officially recognized Switzerland as a fully independent nation.

1700s AND 1800s

Through the Age of Enlightenment, Switzerland bucked the European trend toward absolute monarchs. As the country steadily advanced economically and technologically, it moved in a firmly democratic direction. However, internal conflict about how to organize the country's government made for a rocky transition. Swiss Protestants generally favored a strong central government and were more open to new political and social ideas. The more remote, more Catholic cantons wanted to keep power in local areas and preserve traditional ways of life. This tension continues in Swiss politics to this day.

Riding the wave of the French Revolution, Napoleon Bonaparte occupied Switzerland (1798) and tried (unsuccessfully) to establish a unified central government—called the Helvetic Republic—which fell apart within five years. With Napoleon's defeat (and the 1815 Congress of Vienna), the European powers restored Switzerland's old status. They also set it on its future political course: neutrality in all conflicts.

In 1847, the Swiss fought a four-week, not-very-bloody civil war that ended in a victory for the advocates of centralization. In 1848, amid a Europe-wide wave of liberal reforms, Switzerland crafted a constitution that struck a balance between the two camps. The constitution created a strong central government but also allowed each canton much more autonomy than the regions in other European countries. (It was partly modeled on America's, as the Swiss struggles with centralism and federalism mirror American debates over states' rights.) The country's seat of government was established in the low-key town of Bern, at the boundary of the German- and French-speaking parts of Switzerland.

Around this time the country began to welcome hordes of

PAST & PRESENT

tourists, beginning with French, English, and German aristocrats on the Grand Tour, who passed through Switzerland on their way to Italy. Next came the British mountaineers, whose reverence for the Alps was part of the Romantic outlook on nature: For the first time, Europeans looked at mountains as objects of beauty and inspiration, rather than as frustrating obstacles. Visitors marveled at the mountain scenery and the "sublime" rush it gave them. The new technology of rail travel made trips more comfortable and affordable.

In this heyday of European travel, Switzerland virtually invented mass tourism as we know it—pioneering ways of marking its mountains, offering the first organized vacations, investing in a well-oiled infrastructure, and establishing a reputation for efficiency, cleanliness, quality, and ease (even inventing new names for places that had local names that were considered too intimidating for foreign visitors). Switzerland's system of high-altitude trains, funiculars, and mountain lifts was built to carry 19th-century tourists to previously unheard-of heights. Today's visitors stay in the same resort towns (Interlaken, Zermatt, Luzern, St. Moritz), ride the same kind of lifts, and see echoes of themselves in the stylized travel advertisements from that Romantic Age.

As a neutral country, Switzerland fostered its reputation as a leader in international relations. Like tourists, politicians loved to meet amidst its clear air and alpine vistas. The world's diplomats descended on Geneva in 1863 and 1864, producing two landmark institutions: the International Red Cross (still run from Geneva) and the Geneva Conventions war treaties. The United Nations and other international organizations still maintain a large presence in Geneva. And when the modern Olympic Games were founded by a French aristocrat in 1894, nearby Lausanne became the movement's world headquarters.

20TH CENTURY: WORLD WARS

Switzerland entered the 20th century on the cutting edge of progress. Its trains and communications systems were top-notch. The artist Paul Klee (1879-1940), with his playful, eccentric style, con-

tributed to the Modernist movement (see his works at the Rosengart Collection in Luzern and at the
Paul Klee Center in Bern). Europe's
rich flocked to visit Swiss doctors
at alpine sanatoriums. Carl Jung
(1875-1961) pioneered the blossom-
ing field of psychoanalysis. And in
the quiet city of Bern, an anony-

mous patent clerk named Albert Einstein (1879-1955) was rewrit-
ing humankind's understanding of how the universe worked (see
sidebar on page 124).

In World War I (1914-1918), Switzerland declared itself neutral and escaped the devastation that hit the rest of Europe. After
the war, Geneva served as the seat of the League of Nations, a
short-lived forerunner to the United Nations.

When World War II broke out (1939-1945), Swiss neutrality was not taken for granted. As Nazi Germany and fascist Italy
flanked the country, 850,000 Swiss men grabbed their rifles and
mobilized to protect the borders. They had an ambitious plan, in
case of invasion, to assemble the country's leadership and military
into the innermost, mountainous core of the country—sealing off
a fortified Swiss National Redoubt. Switzerland avoided invasion
through both "militarized neutrality," and by trading with (some
would say "appeasing") the Nazis. Switzerland sheltered some refugees—and turned others away—and acted as a mediator between
the Allies and the Axis.

Today, critics charge that, though neutral in the war, Switzerland actually helped the Nazi effort by continuing to do business
with them. (It's no secret that a significant number of German-
speaking Swiss weren't all that opposed to the Nazi regime.) They
exchanged Swiss francs (the only currency accepted throughout
Europe) for Nazi gold—knowing full well that the gold had been
stolen from other nations and Holocaust victims. In the 1990s,
lawsuits called Swiss banks to account for the ill-gotten bullion in
their vaults. A 2002 commission formed by the Swiss government
agreed that Switzerland could have done more to resist the Nazis
and to help Jewish refugees...but restitution has been slow in coming.

After the war, Switzerland's policy of neutrality led the country to refuse membership in various international alliances and
organizations, including the United Nations, NATO, and the European Union.

SWITZERLAND TODAY

Switzerland maintains a delicate balance between its traditional, neutral past and the high-tech, global future.

As it has been for 700 years, the government is a federalist democracy that gives considerable autonomy to each canton.

On the national level, the executive branch is steered by a seven-member committee, and the presidency is just a figurehead position that rotates between the seven members. There's a strong bicameral parliament, in which no single political party has more than about a fourth of the seats. Since World War II, legislative power has been held by an ever-changing array of coalitions. No single point of view dominates, and collaboration is essential.

The federal government handles foreign affairs, national defense, currency, and the federal courts—and leaves most everything else to the 26 cantons. Similar to US states, each canton has its own political concerns, dialect, and cultural heritage. Just as we debate "states' rights," the Swiss wrangle with just how much autonomy to allow cantons. The person-on-the-street can always make their voice heard thanks to frequent referendums, held when citizens gather enough signatures to require a public vote on an issue. Unlike in most modern democracies, Swiss citizens have a direct say in many political matters and leave fewer decisions to elected representatives.

In business, Zürich continues to be a global center of banking and finance. And Swiss-made equipment helps produce everything from clothing to ballpoint-pen tips to space-bound rocket parts.

Stability is enhanced by strong social security and a collaborative approach to settling labor disputes between unions and employers. The Swiss have also chosen (at great cost) to protect their agricultural sector against competition from imports, and the government subsidizes families who raise cows and make cheese the old-fashioned way.

In foreign affairs, Switzerland remains neutral...but ever-vigilant. Every able-bodied man serves in the army and stays in the reserves. Each house has a gun and a fully stocked bomb shelter. (Swiss vacuum-packed emergency army bread, which lasts two years, is also said to function as a weapon.) Altogether, the country bristles with 600,000 rifles in homes and 12,000 heavy guns in place. Airstrips are hidden inside mountains, accessed by  camouflaged doors. With the push of a button, all road, rail, and bridge entries to Swiss territory can be destroyed, sealing off the country from the outside world. Sentiments are changing, though, and Switzerland has come close to voting away its entire military. Today, you can visit once-hidden military installations, now open to the public as museums (for example, Fortress Fürigen—covered in the Luzern & Central Switzerland chapter).

The question of how closely to integrate with Europe has dominated political discussion in Switzerland for the past few decades. In 2002, the Swiss made a big step away from total neutrality when voters approved a referendum to join the United Nations. In 2008, Switzerland joined the Schengen Agreement, opening its borders to its neighboring countries and most of the EU. Is EU membership next? Probably not. In referendum after referendum the Swiss have strongly rejected the idea of full economic and political integration with the EU, judging the costs to be more significant than the huge potential gains. Still, they've seen benefits in collaborating with Europe on practical matters such as scientific research. For example, Switzerland is home to Europe's high-tech particle accelerator laboratory, called CERN (the place where the World Wide Web was invented by a British scientist).

While it's nice to think of Swiss neutrality as born of pacifism, many realists argue that it's more about money: Switzerland's neutrality policy was key to one of its main sources of income. Traditionally, many Swiss banks allowed foreigners to deposit money with few questions asked. Critics charge that these secret bank accounts have harbored the dirty money of mobsters, terrorists, dictators, guidebook authors, tax evaders, and sleazy businessmen. Switzerland also has a reputation as a safe haven from prosecution, harboring a long list of foreigners (from Hollywood sex offender Roman Polanski to Ugandan dictator Idi Amin). But times are changing. Swiss politicians and bankers responded to outside pressure and introduced legislation that went into effect in 2018, requiring banks to share information on clients with tax authorities in other countries.

Another big issue in Switzerland is how to deal with the rising tide of immigrants. The country's high standard of living makes it an appealing place to live, and Switzerland has more noncitizen residents than most countries (about 24 percent, compared with 7 percent in the US). Many of those immigrants are wealthy Europeans enjoying the country's easy tax laws. Others are young Germans, Italians, or Portuguese who have taken jobs in the hospitality industry. Still others are the Swiss-born, Swiss-raised children of an earlier generation of immigrants (called "Secondos")—who still don't have Swiss citizenship due to the complicated application requirements. It's the "less-desirable" immigrants who have drawn fire—those who arrive with little wealth and then rely on generous social services—but it's not clear that there are really that many immigrants in this category.

Opinions on this and many other issues are generally divided along geographic/linguistic lines. City dwellers, along with French and Italian speakers, tend to favor immigrants' rights, EU membership, and other progressive issues; rural German speakers are more likely to be conservative. In 2009, when Switzerland voted to ban the construction of new minarets—sparking controversy across Europe—only four cantons opposed the initiative, all of them in French-speaking areas.

Climate issues also loom large in Swiss politics. Swiss people are keenly aware of the widespread impact of climate change. In 2019 elections, the balance of parliamentary power was tipped not toward right-wing nativist parties (as in many other European nations), but toward environmental movements. Switzerland's various "green" parties took 20 percent of seats—one of the highest ratios in Europe.

With 2,500 years of history, Switzerland has seen many shifts—from Celts to Romans to Habsburgs, from wars to neutrality to technological progress.

But what's striking is how little Switzerland has changed. The Alps are still there, and they're still big and rugged (even if the glaciers are smaller than ever). The government, after 700 years in existence, remains a model of democracy and international cooperation. Switzerland is fully modern, but you'll also encounter quaint pockets of the past. Take time to see Swiss history alive today—from the cow parades of Appenzell to the Roman ruins in Avenches, and from the turrets of Château de Chillon to the farmers of Gimmelwald, who still make hay while the sun shines.

NOTABLE SWISS PEOPLE

William Tell (c. 1280-1354): On November 18, 1307, William (Wilhelm) Tell, a Swiss peasant, refused a bailiff's order to bow to a symbol of the Habsburg emperor. As punishment, Tell was forced to fire his crossbow at an apple resting on his son's head. He shot cleanly through the apple without injuring his son, and later ambushed and killed the bailiff—launching a revolt for Swiss independence. Though historians say the famous hero is fictional (a similar Danish legend predates the Swiss one), don't "tell" the Swiss—up to 60 percent still believe there was a real William Tell.

Huldrych Zwingli (1484-1531): The son of a farmer, Huld-

rych Zwingli started out as a Catholic true believer, but under the influence of Renaissance humanists,
turned into a religious revolutionary. Known as the "third man of
the Protestant Reformation" (the
other two were Martin Luther and
John Calvin), he used his position
as the top pastor in Zürich to challenge Rome, insisting that Christians study the Bible to guide their
beliefs. Many Protestant faiths, including the United Church of
Christ and the Presbyterian Church, trace their theology back to
Zwingli.

Jean-Jacques Rousseau (1712-1778): One of the most influential writers of the 18th century, Jean-Jacques Rousseau ran
away from his humble Geneva home for France when he was 16,
but he always considered himself Swiss, not French. His writings
celebrated nature and human passion (over cold reason), unleash-
ing forces that would result in the French Revolution, Romantic
literature, and even a return to breastfeeding. Publishers couldn't
print his books fast enough, so they rented them out by the day.
Rousseau's descriptions of the Swiss countryside helped start the
19th-century craze for visiting the Alps.

Madame Tussaud (1761-1850): An entertainment empire
began when Swiss-born Anna Maria Grosholtz moved to Paris and
learned how to sculpt wax. It was an auspicious time and place—
she was able to create figures of Voltaire, Jean-Jacques Rousseau,
and Benjamin Franklin. Later, during the French Revolution, she
made death masks from decapitated heads. After marrying François Tussaud (becoming "Madame Tussaud"), she moved to London and eventually opened a museum of wax figures, which still
shows some of her original work.

Henri Dunant (1828-1910): In 1859, Geneva businessman
Henri Dunant witnessed one of the bloodiest battles of the 19th
century—the Battle of Solferino in northern Italy, where about
40,000 soldiers were killed or wounded. He wrote a book that not
only described the carnage, but also proposed a neutral organization that would care for those wounded in wartime. His leadership
led to the founding of the International Red Cross and the Geneva
Conventions, which put humanitarian limits on the waging of war.
He won the first Nobel Peace Prize in 1901.

Carl Jung (1875-1961): After Freud, Carl Jung had the greatest impact on modern psychology; there probably wouldn't be a
New Age movement or the Myers-Briggs personality test without
him. The Zürich psychologist popularized such terms as "introvert/

extrovert," "personality complex," and "collective unconscious." He once said that the Swiss are a "primitive" people (their love of cows reminded him of African animism), and that under their legendary efficiency is a deeply buried "earth mysticism."

Hermann Hesse (1877-1962): German-born Hesse, who became a Swiss citizen in 1923, was into psychoanalysis, India, and Buddhism before they were cool. His writing was banned by the Nazis and later beloved by 1960s hippies for its themes of self-discovery and enlightenment. His best-known works—among them *Steppenwolf, Siddhartha,* and *Narcissus and Goldmund*—are still widely read today. He was particularly publicity-shy—upon winning the Nobel Prize for Literature in 1946, he wrote to a friend, "To hell with this damn business."

Paul Klee (1879-1940): Paul Klee's mastery of color and tone created highly individual art that critics have described as "musical" and "childlike." Born and raised in Bern, Klee became a teacher at the famous Bauhaus school in Weimar, Germany, but when Hitler came to power in 1933, he was fired. He returned to Switzerland as the Nazis stripped his paintings from museums and classified them as "degenerate." You can see his work at museums in Bern and Luzern—then decide for yourself.

Le Corbusier (1887-1965): "The house is a machine for living in." With this and other edicts, architect Charles-Edouard Jeanneret-Gris, better known as Le Corbusier, changed the shape of 20th-century cities. His plan for Paris' Marais district was emblematic—rows of identical towers set between freeways, replacing public squares and winding streets. The Parisians turned him down, but many office and housing projects in Europe and America followed his precepts. Le Corbusier was one of the most influential architects of his time, though today many regard his International Style as sterile and socially destructive.

Jean Piaget (1896-1980): According to *Time* magazine, Geneva psychologist Jean Piaget was "the first to take children's thinking seriously." Before the publication of his groundbreaking work, parents and teachers regarded children as empty vessels into which they poured knowledge. By studying his own three kids, Piaget deduced that children are constantly testing their own theories of how the world works, asserting that "children have real understanding only of that which they invent themselves."

Alberto Giacometti (1901-1966): The son of a Post-Impressionist painter, sculptor/painter Alberto Giacometti was born in a Swiss alpine valley near the Italian border. Best known for his stylized, elongated figures, he was an important Surrealist sculptor in the 1930s, while his later work explored existentialism, evoking the melancholy and alienation of a post-WWII world.

Elisabeth Kübler-Ross (1926-2004): She grew up in a strict,

Protestant family, but Elisabeth Kübler-Ross defied tradition and got her MD in 1957. A year later, she left Zürich for the US, where she was appalled by the way doctors and hospitals treated the dying. The five stages of grief she first explained in *On Death and Dying*—denial, anger, bargaining, depression, and acceptance—have become a modern touchstone, now commonly applied to any catastrophic personal loss.

Ursula Andress (born 1936): When the bikini-clad Andress walked out of the ocean in the first James Bond movie, *Dr. No*, the indelible image of the "Bond heroine" was born. Tough, smart, and outrageously beautiful, Andress was a great match for Sean Connery's 007, even though the producers dubbed her voice to mask her Swiss-German accent. Though many of her subsequent films were subpar, the list of her leading men is not: Laurence Olivier, Frank Sinatra, Marcello Mastroianni, Peter Sellers, and even Elvis Presley.

Roger Federer (born 1981): This Swiss ace was born and raised near Basel. By the age of 29, Federer had won a record 16 Grand Slam tennis titles, including all four majors. Retired from the sport in 2022, Federer is considered one of the greatest tennis players of all time. He holds a record eight Wimbledon titles, 20 Grand Slam singles titles, and more than 1,200 career wins. The Swiss are justifiably proud of their tennis pro: You can find his face on some 20- and 50-franc coins.

PRACTICALITIES

This chapter covers the practical skills of European travel: how to get tourist information, pay for things, sightsee efficiently, find good-value accommodations, eat affordably but well, use technology wisely, and get between destinations smoothly. For more information on these topics, see RickSteves.com/travel-tips.

Travel Tips

Travel Advisories: Before traveling, check updated health and safety conditions, including restrictions for your destination, on the travel pages of the US State Department (www.travel.state.gov) and Centers for Disease Control and Prevention (www.cdc.gov/travel). The US embassy website for Switzerland is another good source of information (see below).

Covid Vaccine/Test Requirements: It's possible you'll need to present proof of vaccination against the coronavirus and/or a negative Covid-19 test result to board a plane to Europe or back to the US. Carefully check requirements for each country you'll visit well before you depart, and again a few days before your trip. See the websites listed above for current requirements.

ETIAS Registration: The European Union may soon require US and Canadian citizens to register online with the European Travel Information and Authorization System (ETIAS) before entering Switzerland and other Schengen Zone countries (quick and easy process). For the latest, check www.etiasvisa.com.

Tourist Information: The Swiss national tourist office in the US is a wealth of information (+1 800 794 7795, MySwitzerland. com). Before your trip, download brochures (including regional and city maps, festival schedules, and hiking information).

In Switzerland, a good first stop in every town is generally the tourist information office (abbreviated TI in this book). While you can get plenty of information online, I still swing by to pick up a city map and get info on public transit, walking tours, special events, and nightlife. Throughout Switzerland, you'll find TIs are usually well organized and always have an English-speaking staff. Most TIs are run by the government, which means their information isn't colored by a drive for profit.

Some TIs have information on the entire country or at least the region, so you can pick up maps for other destinations you'll be visiting later in your trip.

Emergency and Medical Help: For any emergency service—ambulance, police, or fire—call **112** from a mobile phone or landline (operators typically speak English). If you get sick, do as the locals do and go to a pharmacist for advice. Or ask at your hotel for help—they'll know the nearest medical and emergency services.

Theft or Loss: To replace a passport, you'll need to go in person to the US embassy (see next). If your credit and debit cards disappear, cancel and replace them (see "Damage Control for Lost Cards" on page 459). File a police report, either on the spot or within a day or two; you'll need it to submit an insurance claim for lost or stolen items, and it can help with replacing your passport or credit and debit cards. For more information, see RickSteves. com/help.

US Embassy in Bern: Dial +41 31 357 7011, services by appointment only; Mon-Fri 9:00-11:30, closed Sat-Sun—after-hours +41 31 357 7777; Sulgeneckstrasse 19, Ch.usembassy.gov/embassy/bern.

Canadian Embassy in Bern: Dial +41 31 357 3200, services by appointment only; Mon-Fri 8:30-11:30, closed Sat-Sun; Kirchenfeldstrasse 88, Switzerland.gc.ca.

Borders: Although Switzerland isn't in the European Union, it does belong to the Schengen Zone, which means border controls are a wave-through. Even so, remember that when you change countries, you also change currencies, country dialing codes, and *Unterhosen*. (You'll still go through a full passport control when flying to or from non-Schengen countries, including the UK.)

PRACTICALITIES

Time Zones: Switzerland, like most of continental Europe, is generally six/nine hours ahead of the East/West Coasts of the US. The exceptions are the beginning and end of Daylight Saving Time: Europe "springs forward" the last Sunday in March (two weeks after most of North America), and "falls back" the last Sunday in October (one week before North America). For a handy online time converter, use the world clock app on your phone or download one (see www.timeanddate.com).

Business Hours: In large cities, shops are generally open Monday through Friday 9:00-18:30 (later on Thursday) and Saturday 8:00-17:00. Smaller shops, and all shops in villages, typically close for one or two hours at lunchtime—often from 12:00 to 14:00. Sundays have the same pros and cons as they do for travelers in the US: Sightseeing attractions are generally open, while shops and banks are closed, public transportation options are fewer, and there's no rush hour. Many sights are closed on Monday (head for the hills).

Watt's Up? Europe's electrical system is 220 volts, instead of North America's 110 volts. Most electronics (laptops, phones, cameras) and newer appliances (newer hair dryers, CPAP machines) convert automatically, so you won't need a converter, but you will need an adapter plug with two round prongs, sold inexpensively at travel stores in the US.

Switzerland uses its own style of electrical plugs, not shared with any other country in Europe: three slim round prongs arranged in a triangular shape:

Don't buy an adapter with the thicker ("Schuko" style) prongs—it won't work. You'll often see wall sockets with a three-plug cloverleaf pattern. If you already have an adapter for European plugs, you may not need another adapter for Switzerland—European plugs will fit in Swiss sockets if the prongs are of the slimmer type and ungrounded, and if the body of the adapter is small enough to fit in a recessed outlet. If your adapter doesn't work in your hotel room's sockets, ask your hotelier if they have one you can borrow, or buy one locally.

Rip up this book! Turn chapters into mini guidebooks: Break the book's spine and use a utility knife to slice apart chapters, keeping gummy edges intact. Reinforce the chapter spines with clear wide tape; use a heavy-duty stapler; or make or buy a cheap cover (see the Travel Store at RickSteves.com), swapping out chapters as you travel.

Discounts: Discounts for sights are generally not listed in this book. However, seniors (age 65 and over), youths under 18, and students and teachers with proper identification cards (www.isic. org) can get discounts at many sights—always ask. Some discounts are available only to European citizens.

Online Translation Tips: Google's Chrome browser instantly translates websites; Translate.google.com and DeepL.com are also handy. The Google Translate app converts spoken or typed English into most European languages (and vice versa) and can also translate text it "reads" with your phone's camera.

Going Green: There's plenty you can do to reduce your environmental footprint when traveling. When practical, take a train instead of a flight within Europe, and use public transportation within cities. In hotels, use the "Do Not Disturb" sign to avoid daily linen and towel changes (or hang up your towels to signal you'll reuse them). Bring a reusable shopping tote and refillable water bottle (Europe's tap water is safe to drink). Skip printed brochures, maps, or other materials that you don't plan to keep—get your info online instead. To find out how Rick Steves' Europe is offsetting carbon emissions with a self-imposed carbon tax, see RickSteves.com/about-us/climate-smart.

Money

Here's my basic strategy for using money wisely in Europe. I pack the following and keep it all safe in my money belt.

Credit Card: You'll use your credit card for purchases both big (hotels, advance tickets) and small (little shops, food stands). Some European businesses have gone cashless, making a card your only payment option. A "tap-to-pay" or "contactless" card is the most widely accepted and simplest to use.

Debit Card: Use this at ATMs to withdraw a small amount of local cash. Wait until you arrive to get francs (European airports have plenty of ATMs); if you buy francs before your trip, you'll pay bad stateside exchange rates. While most transactions are by card these days, cash can help you out of a jam if your card randomly doesn't work, and can be useful to pay for things like tips and local guides. But don't take out too much, or you may find you can't use it all.

Backup Card: Some travelers carry a third card (debit or credit; ideally from a different bank) in case one gets lost or simply doesn't work.

Stash of Cash: I carry $100-200 in US dollars as a cash backup, which comes in handy in an emergency (for example, if your debit card gets eaten by the machine).

Exchange Rate

Switzerland, which isn't a member of the European Union, has retained its traditional currency, the Swiss franc. The international abbreviation for the Swiss franc is "CHF."

1 Swiss franc (CHF) = about $1

One Swiss franc is broken down into 100 rappen (or centimes in French Switzerland). There are coins for one, two, and five francs, plus several coins for very small denominations of rappen. The small coin with real value is the 50-rappen (marked with "½" rather than "50"). It looks like a tiny dime, but is equivalent to a half-dollar. In a handful of change, it's easy to identify as the only one with ridges.

Check www.oanda.com for the latest exchange rates.

BEFORE YOU GO

Know your cards. For credit cards, Visa and MasterCard are universal while American Express and Discover are less common. US debit cards with a Visa or MasterCard logo will work in any European ATM.

Go "contactless." Get comfortable using contactless pay options. Check to see if you already have—or can get—a tap-to-pay version of your credit card (look on the card for the tap-to-pay symbol—four curvy lines), and consider setting up your smartphone for contactless payment (see next section for details). Both options are widely used in Europe and are more secure than a physical credit card: Instead of recording your credit card number, a one-time encrypted "token" enables the purchase and expires shortly afterward.

Know your PIN. Make sure you know the numeric, four-digit PIN for each of your cards, both debit and credit. Request it if you don't have one, as it may be required for some purchases. Allow time to receive the information by mail—it's not always possible to obtain your PIN online or by phone.

Report your travel dates. Let your bank know that you'll be using your debit and credit cards in Europe, and when and where you're headed.

Adjust your ATM withdrawal limit. Find out how much you can withdraw daily and ask for a higher daily limit if you want to get more cash at once. Note that European ATMs will withdraw funds only from checking accounts, not savings accounts.

Find out about fees. For any purchase or withdrawal made with a card, you may be charged a currency conversion fee (1-3 percent) and/or a Visa or MasterCard international transaction fee (less than 1 percent). If you're getting a bad deal, consider getting a new card. Reputable no-fee cards include those from Capital One, as well as Charles Schwab debit cards. Most credit unions and some airline loyalty cards have low or no international transaction fees.

IN EUROPE
Using Credit Cards and Payment Apps

Tap-to-Pay or **Contactless Cards:** These cards have the usual chip and/or magnetic stripe, but with the addition of a contactless symbol. Simply tap your card against a contactless reader to complete a transaction—no PIN or signature is required. This is by far the easiest way to pay and has become the standard in much of Europe. Some small businesses (such as market stalls or food stands) accept *only* tap cards, and sometimes don't accept cash.

Payment Apps: Just like at home, you can pay with your smartphone or smartwatch by linking a credit card to an app such as Apple Pay or Google Pay. To pay, hold your phone near a contactless reader; you may need to verify the transaction with a face scan, fingerprint scan, or passcode. If you've arrived in Europe without a tap-to-pay card, you can easily set up your phone to work in this way.

Other Card Types: Chip-and-PIN cards have a visible chip embedded in them; rather than swiping, you insert the card into the payment machine, then enter your PIN on a keypad. **Swipe-and-sign** credit cards—with a swipeable magnetic stripe, and a receipt you have to sign—are increasingly rare.

Will My US Card Work? Usually, yes. On rare occasions, at self-service payment machines (such as transit-ticket kiosks, tollbooths, or fuel pumps), some US cards may not work. Usually a tap-to-pay card does the trick in these situations. Just in case, carry cash as a backup and look for a cashier who can process your payment if your card is rejected. Drivers should be prepared to move on to the next gas station if necessary. (In some countries, gas stations sell prepaid gas cards, which you can purchase with any US card). When approaching a toll plaza or ferry ticket line, use the "cash" lane.

Using Cash

Cash Machines: European cash machines work just like they do at home—except they spit out local currency instead of dollars, calculated at the day's standard bank-to-bank rate. In most places, ATMs are easy to locate—in Switzerland, ask for a *Bankomat* or *Geldautomat* in German, or a *distributeur* in French. When possible, withdraw cash from a bank-run ATM located just outside that bank.

If your debit card doesn't work, try a lower amount—your re-

Why No Swiss Euros?

Though surrounded by countries enjoying the convenience of a shared currency, the Swiss have hung on to their old franc. They would have to be part of the European Union to join the euro zone—and compliance with European Union regulations would mean the end of Switzerland's fortress identity and subsidized agricultural system. Most Swiss are horrified by the idea of having to square their fiscal, military, and foreign policies with the cacophonous EU.

But it's not just fear of instability and loss of sovereignty that's kept the Swiss clinging to their francs. Having a separate currency helps bring business to Switzerland. A huge part of the Swiss economy is based on providing a safe and secret place for wealthy people from around the world to stash their money. When bank fees are figured in, people who "save" in Swiss banks actually earn negative interest—they pay the Swiss to keep their money. Switzerland's separate currency also means that residents enjoy lower mortgage interest rates than the rest of Europe.

Even though Switzerland hasn't adopted the euro, some Swiss hotels, restaurants, and shops (especially in touristy areas) accept smaller euro bills. Most of these businesses will not take euro coins or larger bills, and you'll usually get bad rates (and your change in Swiss francs). But unless this is your last chance to use up leftover euros, spend francs in Switzerland instead—you'll save money, and they're prettier.

quest may have exceeded your withdrawal limit or the ATM's limit. If you still have a problem, try a different ATM or come back later.

Avoid "independent" ATMs, such as Travelex, Euronet, Moneybox, Your Cash, Cardpoint, and Cashzone. These have high fees, can be less secure, and may try to trick users with "dynamic currency conversion" (see next).

Dynamic Currency Conversion: When withdrawing cash at an ATM or paying with a credit card, you'll often be asked whether you want the transaction processed in dollars or in the local currency. Always refuse the conversion and *choose the local currency*. While DCC offers the illusion of convenience, it comes with a poor exchange rate, and you'll wind up losing money.

Exchanging Cash: Minimize exchanging money in Europe; it's expensive (you'll generally lose 5 to 10 percent). In a pinch you can find exchange desks at major train stations or airports. Banks generally do not exchange money unless you have an account with them.

Security Tips

Pickpockets target tourists. Keep your cash, credit cards, and passport secure in your money belt, and carry only a day's spending money in your front pocket or wallet.

Before inserting your card into an ATM, inspect the front. If anything looks crooked, loose, or damaged, it could be a sign of a card-skimming device. When entering your PIN, carefully block other people's view of the keypad.

Avoid using a debit card for purchases. Because a debit card pulls funds directly from your bank account, potential charges incurred by a thief will stay on your account while your bank investigates.

To access your accounts online while traveling, be sure to use a secure connection (see the "Tips on Internet Security" sidebar, later).

Damage Control for Lost Cards

If you lose your credit or debit card, report the loss immediately to the respective global customer-assistance centers. With a mobile phone, call these 24-hour US numbers: Visa (+1 303 967 1096), MasterCard (+1 636 722 7111), and American Express (+1 336 393 1111). From a landline, you can call these US numbers collect by going through a local operator.

You'll need to provide the primary cardholder's identification-verification details (such as birth date, mother's maiden name, or Social Security number). You can generally receive a temporary card within two or three business days in Europe (see RickSteves. com/help for more).

If you report your loss within two days, you typically won't be responsible for unauthorized transactions on your account, although many banks charge a liability fee.

TIPPING

Tipping in Switzerland isn't as automatic and generous as it is in the US. For special service, tips are appreciated, but not expected. As in the US, the proper amount depends on your resources, tipping philosophy, and the circumstances, but some general guidelines apply.

Restaurants: You don't need to tip if you order your food at a counter. At Swiss restaurants that have a wait staff, it's common to tip by rounding up (about 5-10 percent) after a good meal. If paying with a credit card, be prepared to tip separately with cash or coins; credit card receipts don't often have a tip line. For more details on tipping in restaurants, see the "Eating" section, later.

Taxis: For a typical ride, round up your fare a bit (for instance, if the fare is 13 CHF, pay 15 CHF). If the cabbie hauls your bags and zips you to the airport to help you catch your flight, you might want to toss in a little more.

PRACTICALITIES

Services: In general, if someone in the tourism or service industry does a super job for you, a small tip of a franc or two is
appropriate...but not required. If you're not sure whether (or how
much) to tip, ask a local for advice.

GETTING A VAT REFUND

Wrapped into the purchase price of your Swiss souvenirs is a value-
added-tax (VAT) of about 8 percent (one of the lowest in Europe).
You're entitled to get most of that tax back if you purchase more
than 300 CHF worth of goods at a store that participates in the
VAT-refund scheme. Typically, you must ring up the minimum at a
single retailer—you can't add up your purchases from various shops
to reach the required amount. (If the store ships the goods to your
US home, VAT is not assessed on your purchase.)

Getting your refund is straightforward...and worthwhile if
you spend a significant amount.

At the Merchant: Have the merchant completely fill out the
refund document (they'll ask for your passport; a photo of your
passport usually works). Keep track of the paperwork and your
original sales receipt. Note that you're not supposed to use your
purchased goods before you leave Europe.

At the Border or Airport: Process your VAT document at
your last stop in Switzerland (such as the airport) with the customs
agent who deals with VAT refunds (allow plenty of extra time to
deal with this process). At some airports, you'll have to go to a customs office to get your documents stamped and then to a separate
VAT refund service (such as Global Blue or Planet) to process the
refund. At other airports, a single VAT desk handles the whole
thing. (Note that refund services typically extract a 4 percent fee,
but you're paying for the convenience of receiving your money in
cash immediately or as a credit to your card.) Otherwise, you'll
need to mail the stamped refund documents to the address given
by the merchant.

CUSTOMS FOR AMERICAN SHOPPERS

You can take home $800 worth of items per person duty-free once
every 31 days. Many processed and packaged foods are allowed, including cheeses, dried herbs, jams, baked goods, candy, chocolate,
oil, vinegar, condiments, and honey. Fresh fruits and vegetables
and most meats are not allowed, with exceptions for some canned
items. As for alcohol, you can bring in one liter duty-free (it can
be packed securely in your checked luggage, along with any other
liquid-containing items).

To bring alcohol (or liquid-packed foods) in your carry-on bag
on your flight home, buy it at a duty-free shop at the airport. You'll
increase your odds of getting it onto a connecting flight if it's pack-

aged in a "STEB"—a secure, tamper-evident bag. But stay away from liquids in opaque, ceramic, or metallic containers, which usually cannot be successfully screened (STEB or no STEB).

For details on allowable goods, customs rules, and duty rates, visit https://help.cbp.gov.

Sightseeing

Sightseeing can be hard work. If you're spending time in urban Switzerland, use these tips to make your museum visits meaningful, fun, efficient, and painless.

MAPS AND NAVIGATION TOOLS

A good map is essential for efficient navigation while sightseeing. The maps in this book are concise and simple, designed to help you locate recommended destinations, sights, hotels, and restaurants. In Europe, simple maps are generally free at TIs and hotels.

You can also use a mapping app on your mobile device, which provides turn-by-turn directions for walking, driving, and taking public transit. Google Maps, Apple Maps, and CityMaps2Go allow you to download maps for offline use; ideally, download the areas you'll need before your trip. For certain features, you'll need to be online—either using Wi-Fi or an international data plan.

PLAN AHEAD

Set up an itinerary that allows you to fit in all your must-see sights. Since the Covid-19 pandemic, hours for museums and sights have been unstable. Both before and during your trip, confirm the latest opening days and times with the TI or on a museum or sight's official website (listed throughout this book).

Don't put off visiting a must-see sight—you never know when a place will close unexpectedly for a holiday, strike, or restoration. Many museums are closed or have reduced hours at least a few days a year, especially on holidays such as Christmas and New Year's. A list of holidays is in the appendix; check for possible closures during your trip. In summer, some sights may stay open late. Off-season hours may be shorter.

Going at the right time helps avoid crowds. This book offers tips on the best times to see specific sights. Try visiting popular sights very early or very late. Evening visits (when possible) are usually more peaceful, with fewer crowds. Late morning is usually the worst time to visit a popular sight.

If you plan to hire a local guide, reserve ahead by email. Popular guides can get booked up.

Study up. To get the most out of the sight descriptions in this book, read them before your visit.

SWISS TRAVEL PASS AND SWISS MUSEUM PASS

The Swiss Travel Pass (described on page 485) doubles as a Swiss Museum Pass while your pass is valid; the sights described in this book that are covered are listed below. The Museum Pass on its own costs about $180, covers admission to more than 500 museums, and is good for a year. For a full list of covered sights, see Museumspass.ch.

- **Zürich:** National Museum Zürich and Rietberg Museum
- **Luzern:** Rosengart Collection, History Museum, Luzern Museum of Art, Bourbaki Panorama, Glacier Garden, Richard Wagner Museum, and Fortress Fürigen Museum in nearby Stansstad; 50 percent off Swiss Transport Museum
- **Bern:** Museum of Fine Arts, Paul Klee Center, and Einstein Museum/Bern Historical Museum
- **Murten and Nearby:** Town Museum in Murten and Roman Museum in Avenches
- **Near Interlaken:** Museum of Tourism in Unterseen and Ballenberg Open-Air Museum in Brienz
- **Zermatt:** Matterhorn Museum
- **Appenzell Region:** Appenzell Museum, Appenzell's two modern art museums, and folk museums in Stein and Urnäsch
- **Lausanne:** City History Museum, Collection de l'Art Brut, Lausanne Cantonal Museum of Fine Arts, Musée de l'Elysée, Museum for Contemporary Design and Applied Arts, and Olympic Museum
- **Lake Geneva Region:** Château de Chillon
- **French Swiss Countryside:** La Maison du Gruyère Cheese Factory, Musée Gruèrien, Gruyères Castle, H. R. Giger Museum, Tibet Museum, and Cailler Chocolate Factory
- **Upper Engadine:** Alpine Museum in Pontresina, Chesa Planta in Samedan, and Berry Museum and Engadiner Museum in St. Moritz
- **Other Scenic Rail Journey Stops:** Museo Casa Console in Poschiavo

AT SIGHTS

Here's what you can typically expect:

Entering: You may not be allowed to enter if you arrive too close to closing time. And guards start ushering people out well before the actual closing time, so don't save the best for last.

Many sights have a security check. Allow extra time for these lines. Some sights require you to check day packs and coats. (If you'd rather not check your day pack, try carrying it tucked under your arm like a purse as you enter.)

Photography: If the museum's photo policy isn't clearly posted, ask a guard. Generally, taking photos without a flash or tripod is allowed. Some sights ban selfie sticks; others ban photos altogether.

Audioguides and Apps: Some sights offer audioguides with recorded descriptions in English. In some cases, you'll rent a device to carry around (if you bring your own plug-in earbuds, you'll enjoy better sound). Increasingly, museums and sights instead offer an app you can download with their audioguide (often free; check websites from home and consider downloading in advance as not all sights offer free Wi-Fi).

Temporary Exhibits: Museums may show special exhibits in addition to their permanent collection. Some exhibits are included in the entry price, while others come at an extra cost (which you may have to pay even if you don't want to see the exhibit).

Expect Changes: Artwork can be on tour, on loan, out sick, or shifted at the whim of the curator. Pick up a floor plan as you enter and ask museum staff if you can't find a particular item.

Services: Important sights usually have a reasonably priced on-site café or cafeteria (handy and air-conditioned places to rejuvenate during a long visit). The WCs at sights are free and generally clean.

Before Leaving: At the gift shop, scan the postcard rack or thumb through a guidebook to be sure you haven't overlooked something that you'd like to see. Every sight or museum offers more than what is covered in this book. Use the information I provide as an introduction—not the final word.

Sleeping

Extensive and opinionated listings of good-value rooms are a major feature of this book's Sleeping sections. Rather than list accommodations scattered throughout a town, I choose hotels in my favorite neighborhoods that are convenient to your sightseeing.

My recommendations run the gamut, from dorm beds to luxurious rooms with all the comforts. I like places that are clean, central, relatively quiet at night, reasonably priced, friendly, small enough to have a hands-on owner or manager, and run with a respect for Swiss traditions. I'm more impressed by a handy location and a fun-loving philosophy than oversized TVs and a fancy gym. Most of my recommenda-

PRACTICALITIES

Sleep Code

Hotels in this book are categorized according to the average price of a standard double room with breakfast in high season.

$$$$	**Splurge:** Most rooms over 325 CHF
$$$	**Pricier:** 250-325 CHF
$$	**Moderate:** 175-250 CHF
$	**Budget:** 100-175 CHF
¢	**Backpacker:** Under 100 CHF
RS%	Rick Steves discount

Unless otherwise noted, credit cards are accepted, hotel staff speak basic English, and free Wi-Fi is available. Comparison-shop by checking prices at several hotels (on each hotel's own website, on a booking site, or by email). For the best deal, *book directly with the hotel.* Ask for a discount if paying in cash; if the listing includes **RS%,** request a Rick Steves discount.

tions fall short of perfection. But if I can find a place with most of these features, it's a keeper.

Book your accommodations as soon as your itinerary is set, especially if you want to stay at one of my top listings or if you'll be traveling during busy times. See the appendix for a list of major holidays and festivals in Switzerland.

Some people make reservations a few days ahead as they travel. This approach fosters spontaneity, and booking sites make it easy to find available rooms, but—especially during busy times—you run the risk of settling for lesser-value accommodations.

RATES AND DEALS

I've categorized my recommended accommodations based on price, indicated with a dollar-sign rating (see sidebar). Room prices can fluctuate significantly with demand and amenities (size, views, room class, and so on), but relative price categories remain constant. Part of the room price is a local tax (about $2-6 per person per night). In return, you get perks such as free local transport or museum discounts. In a few towns (and some types of accommodations) the tax is included in quoted room rates; in most others, it's broken out.

Booking Direct: Once your dates are set, compare prices at several hotels. You can do this by checking hotel websites and booking sites such as Hotels.com or Booking.com. After you've zeroed in on your choice, book directly with the hotel itself. This increases the chances that the hotelier will be able to accommodate special needs or requests (such as shifting your reservation). And when you book on the hotel's website, by email, or by phone, the owner avoids the commission paid to booking sites, giving them wiggle room to offer you a discount, a nicer room, or a free breakfast (if it's not already included).

Getting a Discount: Some hotels extend a discount to those who pay cash or stay longer than three nights. And some accommodations offer a special discount for Rick Steves readers, indicated in this guidebook by the abbreviation **"RS%."** Discounts vary: Ask for details when you reserve. Generally, to qualify for this discount, you must book direct (not through a booking site), mention this book when you reserve, show this book upon arrival, and sometimes pay cash or stay a certain number of nights. In some cases, you may need to enter a discount code (which I've provided in the listing) in the booking form on the hotel's website. Rick Steves discounts apply to readers with either print or digital books. Understandably, discounts do not apply to promotional rates.

TYPES OF ACCOMMODATIONS
Hotels

Swiss hotels are, generally speaking, clean, comfortable, and efficiently run by English-speaking staff. Plan on spending about $180-300 for a double room in a hotel or $120-175 for a double (with the bathroom down the hall) in a small guesthouse. Double rooms with bath for less than $175 are rare. Even dormitory beds are expensive.

Some hotels can add an extra bed (for a small charge) to turn a double into a triple; some offer larger rooms for four or more people (I call these "family rooms" in the listings). If there's space for an extra cot, they'll cram it in for you. In general, a triple room is cheaper than the cost of a double and a single. Three or four people can economize by requesting one big room.

Arrival and Check-In: Hotels and B&Bs are sometimes located on the higher floors of a multipurpose building with a secured door. In that case, look for your hotel's name on the buttons by the main entrance. When you ring the bell, you'll be buzzed in.

Hotel elevators are common, though small, and some older buildings still lack them. You may have to climb a flight of stairs to reach the elevator (if so, you can ask the front desk for help carrying your bags up).

Swiss law requires hotels to collect your name, nationality, and passport number. At check-in, the receptionist might ask for your passport and may keep it for several hours. If you're not comfortable leaving your passport at the desk, bring a copy to give them instead.

Smoking is prohibited in many Swiss hotels, sometimes by law (depending on the region) and sometimes by choice. Nearly all the hotels I list are completely nonsmoking, and all of them offer nonsmoking rooms. If it's important to you to have a nonsmoking room, ask for one.

PRACTICALITIES

Using Online Services to Your Advantage

From booking services to user reviews, online businesses play a greater role in travelers' planning than ever before. Take advantage of their pluses—and be wise to their downsides.

Booking Sites

Booking websites such as Booking.com and Hotels.com offer one-stop shopping for hotels. While convenient for travelers, they're both a blessing and a curse for small, independent, family-run hotels. Without a presence on these sites, small hotels become almost invisible. But to be listed, a hotel must pay a sizable commission...and promise that its own website won't undercut the price on the booking-service site.

Here's the work-around: Use the big sites to research what's out there, then book directly with the hotel by email or phone, in which case hotel owners are free to give you whatever price they like. Ask for a room without the commission markup (or ask for a free breakfast if not included, or a free upgrade). If you do book online, be sure to use the hotel's own website. The price will likely be the same as via a booking site, but your money goes to the hotel, not agency commissions.

As a savvy consumer, remember: When you book with an online service, you're adding a middleman who takes a cut. To support small, family-run hotels whose world is more difficult than ever, book direct.

Short-Term Rental Sites

Rental juggernaut Airbnb and other short-term rental sites allow travelers to rent rooms and apartments, often providing more value, space, and amenities than a cookie-cutter hotel. Airbnb fans appreciate feeling part of a real neighborhood and getting into a daily routine as "temporary Europeans." Some places are run by thoughtful hosts, allowing you to get to know a local and keep your money in the community; but beware: others are impersonally managed by large, absentee agencies.

If you're arriving in the morning, your room probably won't be ready. Check your bag safely at the hotel and dive right into sightseeing.

In Your Room: Most hotel rooms have a TV and free Wi-Fi, which can vary in strength and quality. Simpler places rarely have a room phone.

Breakfast and Meals: Swiss hotel breakfasts are usually excellent: fruit, eggs, muesli, cheese, fresh bread, and yogurt. Some places give you the option of skipping breakfast and paying less; you can buy breakfast items easily and cheaply at a bakery or supermarket—the savings add up, especially for families. Some places offer "half-board," which means that dinner is included in the room

Critics of Airbnb see it as a threat to "traditional Europe." Landlords can make more money renting to short-stay travelers, driving rents up—and local residents out. Traditional businesses are replaced by ones that cater to tourists. And the character and charm that made those neighborhoods desirable to tourists in the first place goes too. Some cities have cracked down, requiring owners to obtain a license and to occupy rental properties part of the year (and staging disruptive "inspections" that inconvenience guests).

As a lover of Europe, I share the worry of those who see residents nudged aside by tourists. But as an advocate for travelers, I appreciate the value Airbnb can provide in offering the chance to stay in a local building or neighborhood with potentially fewer tourists.

User Reviews

User-generated review sites and apps such as Yelp and TripAdvisor can give you a consensus of opinions about everything from hotels and restaurants to sights and nightlife. If you scan reviews of a restaurant or hotel and see several complaints about noise or a rotten location, you've gained insight that can help in your decision-making.

As a guidebook writer, my sense is that there is a big difference between the uncurated information on a review site and the vetted listings in a guidebook. A user review is based on the limited experience of one person, who stayed at just one hotel in a given city and ate at a few restaurants there. A guidebook is the work of a trained researcher who forms a well-developed basis for comparison by visiting many restaurants and hotels year after year.

Both types of information have their place, and in many ways, they're complementary. If something is well reviewed in a guidebook and it gets good online reviews, it's likely a winner.

price. This is often a good deal and gets you a hassle-free, value-priced three-course meal, but limits your choices.

Checking Out: While it's customary to pay for your room upon departure, it can be a good idea to settle your bill the day before, when you're not in a hurry and while the manager's in.

Hotelier Help: Hoteliers can be a good source of advice. Most know their city well and can assist you with everything from public transit and airport connections to finding a good restaurant, the nearest launderette, or a late-night pharmacy.

Hotel Hassles: Even at the best places, mechanical breakdowns occur: Sinks leak, hot water turns cold, toilets may gurgle or smell, the Wi-Fi goes out, or the air-conditioning dies when you

Making Hotel Reservations

Reserve your rooms as soon as you've pinned down your travel dates. For busy national holidays, it's wise to reserve far in advance (see the appendix).

Requesting a Reservation: For family-run hotels, it's generally cheaper to book your room directly via email or phone. For business-class and chain hotels, or if you'd rather book online, reserve directly through the hotel's official website (not a booking website). Almost all of my recommended hotels take reservations in English.

Here's what the hotelier wants to know:

- Type(s) of rooms you want and number of guests
- Number of nights you'll stay
- Arrival and departure dates, written European-style as day/month/year (for example, 18/06/25 or 18 June 2025)
- Special requests (such as en suite bathroom, cheapest room, twin beds vs. double bed, quiet room)
- Applicable discounts (such as a Rick Steves discount, cash discount, or promotional rate)

Confirming a Reservation: Most places will request a credit-card number to hold your room. If the hotel's website doesn't have a secure form where you can enter the number directly, share this info via a phone call.

Canceling a Reservation: If you must cancel, it's courteous—and smart—to do so with as much notice as possible, especially for

need it most. Report your concerns clearly and calmly at the front desk.

If you think that night noise might be a problem (if, for instance, your room is over a nightclub or facing a busy street), ask for a quieter room in the back or on an upper floor. To guard against theft in your room, keep valuables out of sight. Some rooms come with a safe, and other hotels have safes at the front desk. I've never bothered using one and in a lifetime of travel, I've never had anything stolen from my room.

For more complicated problems, don't expect instant results. Above all, keep a positive attitude. Remember, you're on vacation. If your hotel is a disappointment, spend more time out enjoying the place you came to see.

Pensions

Compared to hotels, pensions (small guesthouses) and rooms in private homes give you double the cultural intimacy for half the price. While you may lose some of the conveniences of a hotel—such as lounges, in-room phones, daily bed-sheet changes, and

From: rick@ricksteves.com
Sent: Today
To: info@hotelcentral.com
Subject: Reservation request for 19-22 July

Dear Hotel Central,

I would like to stay at your hotel. Please let me know if you have a room available and the price for:
• 2 people
• Double bed and en suite bathroom in a quiet room
• Arriving 19 July, departing 22 July (3 nights)

Thank you!
Rick Steves

smaller family-run places. Cancellation policies can be strict; read the fine print before you book. Many discount deals require pre-payment and can be expensive to change or cancel.

Reconfirming a Reservation: Always call or email to reconfirm your room reservation a few days in advance. For B&Bs or very small hotels, I call again on my arrival day to tell my host what time to expect me (especially important if arriving late—after 17:00).

Phoning: For tips on calling hotels overseas, see page 482.

credit-card payments—I happily make the tradeoff for the lower rates and personal touches.

Small guesthouses go by several inexact German names: *Pension, Gasthaus, Gästezimmer,* even "B&B" (in French, it's also *pension*). In many parts of Switzerland, people rent out rooms *(Zimmer)* in their homes to travelers. Look for *Zimmer Frei, Zimmer mit Frühstück,* or *Privatzimmer* signs in German-speaking areas and *chambres d'hôte* in French Switzerland.

Don't confuse *Privatzimmer* with the *Ferienwohnung,* which is a self-catering apartment rented out by the week or fortnight.

Camping and Other Budget Beds

Campers can manage with listings at EuroCampings.co.uk or with help from the local TI (ask for a regional camping listing). Your hometown travel bookstore should also have guidebooks on camping in Europe. You'll find campgrounds just about everywhere you need them. Look for *Campingplatz* signs. You'll meet lots of Europeans, as camping is a popular, middle-class-family way to go.

Campgrounds are cheap ($10 per person), friendly, safe, more central and convenient than rustic, and rarely full.

A fluffy straw bed awaits you at a number of farms that have opened their haylofts to sleepy tourists. It's a fun hostel alternative and more comfortable than you'd think (for details, visit www.myfarm.ch, and search for "Sleeping on Straw").

Many hotels and campsites provide dormitory-style accommodations in bunk-bedded rooms. These slumber mills may be less charming than cozy hostels, but they're cheap and convenient.

Mountain Hotels: For hikers, the grand-but-rustic mountain hotels, many of which date back to the 19th century, are fine options. For many, the best part is sharing the tranquility and powerful remoteness with like-minded hikers who all are motivated to make the most of it. These hotels can be a hike of several hours from the nearest paved road or mountain lift, and generally have both double rooms and *Matratzenlagers* (lofts lined with mattresses). As there is no alternative, most expect visitors to get half-board (breakfast and dinner) with their reservations; food is good if simple (helicopter services deliver groceries weekly). Electricity can be limited or nonexistent—as can hot or even running water. A woody double room with half-board runs about $100 (dorm beds are cheaper). See www.sac-cas.ch for a map and database of Swiss mountain huts.

Short-Term Rentals

A short-term rental—whether an apartment, a house, or a room in a private residence—is a popular alternative, especially if you plan to settle in one location for several nights. For stays longer than a few days, you can usually find a rental that's comparable to—and cheaper than—a hotel room with similar amenities. Plus, you'll get a behind-the-scenes peek into how locals live.

Many places require a minimum stay and have strict cancellation policies. And you're generally on your own: There's no reception desk, breakfast, or daily cleaning service.

Finding Accommodations: Websites such as Airbnb, FlipKey, Booking.com, and VRBO let you browse a wide range of properties. Alternatively, rental agencies such as InterhomeUSA.com and RentaVilla.com can provide a more personalized service (their curated listings are also more expensive).

Before you commit, be clear on the location. I like to virtually "explore" the neighborhood using Google Street View. Also consider the proximity to public transportation, and how well connected the property is with the rest of the city. Ask about amenities (elevator, air-conditioning, laundry, Wi-Fi, parking, etc.). Reviews from previous guests can help identify trouble spots.

Think about the kind of experience you want: Just a key and an affordable bed...or a chance to get to know a local? Some hosts offer self check-in and minimal contact; others enjoy interacting with you. Read the description and reviews to help shape your decision.

Confirming and Paying: Many places require payment in full before your trip, usually through the listing site. Be wary of owners who want to take your transaction offline; this gives you no recourse if things go awry. Never agree to wire money (a key indicator of a fraudulent transaction).

Apartments or Houses: If you're staying in one place for several nights, it's worth considering an apartment or rental house, called *Ferienwohnung* in German. Apartment or house rentals can be especially cost-effective for groups and families. European apartments, like hotel rooms, tend to be small by US standards. But they often come with laundry facilities and small, equipped kitchens, making it easier and cheaper to dine in.

Rooms in Private Homes: Renting a room in someone's home is a good option for those traveling alone, as you're more likely to find true single rooms—with just one single bed, and a price to match. These can range from air-mattress-in-living-room basic to plush-B&B-suite posh. While you can't expect your host to also be your tour guide—or even to provide you with much info—some are interested in getting to know the travelers who pass through their home.

Other Options: Swapping homes with a local works for people with an appealing place to offer (don't assume where you live is not interesting to Europeans). Good places to start are HomeExchange.com and LoveHomeSwap.com. To sleep for free, Couchsurfing.com is a vagabond's alternative to Airbnb. It lists millions of outgoing members, who host fellow "surfers" in their homes.

Hostels

Switzerland has a wonderful network of official hostels (*Jugendherberge* in German, *auberge de jeunesse* in French) that charge under $100 per night for beds (for a full list, see www.youthhostel.ch). Choose your hostel selectively: They can be cozy mountain chalets, serene lakeside villas—or antiseptic spaces overrun by noisy school groups. While official hostels are clean and predictable, they can also have an institutional feel.

Travelers of any age are welcome if they don't mind dorm-style accommodations and meeting other travelers. Most hostels offer kitchen facilities, guest computers, Wi-Fi, and a self-service laundry. Hostels almost always provide bedding, but the towel's up to you (though you can usually rent one). Many hostels offer inexpensive evening meals (about 17-20 CHF), but there are also posh boutique hostels with in-house restaurants that are significantly more expensive. Expect youth groups in spring, crowds in the summer, snoring, and variability in quality from one hostel to the next. Family and private rooms are often available.

Independent hostels tend to be easygoing, colorful, and informal (no membership required; www.hostelworld.com or www.swissbackpackers.ch). You may pay slightly less by booking directly with the hos-

tel. **Official hostels** are part of Hostelling International (HI) and share an online booking site (www.hihostels.com). HI hostels typically require that you be a member or else pay a bit more per night.

Eating

For listings in this guidebook, I look for restaurants that are convenient to your hotel and sightseeing. When restaurant-hunting, choose a spot filled with locals, not the place with the big neon signs boasting, "We Speak English and Accept Credit Cards." Venturing even a block or two off the main drag leads to higher-quality food for a better price.

The Swiss eat when we do and enjoy a straightforward, no-nonsense cuisine. Specialties include delicious fondue, rich chocolates, a melted cheese dish called raclette, *Rösti* (hash browns), fresh dairy products (try *Birchermüesli* for breakfast or an afternoon snack), 100 varieties of cheese, and Fendant—a good, crisp white wine.

The exorbitant prices at Swiss restaurants—up to double what you'd pay in neighboring Germany—mean that eating here demands some different strategies if you're on a budget. Think of restaurants with table service as a luxury for special occasions, and self-service cafeterias and supermarkets as your everyday options. Bakeries also sell sandwiches, quiches, and the like. A night on the town can be a major splurge. Locals call sitting on the pavement around a bottle of wine "going out."

If breakfast is included in your room price, don't miss it. But if your hotel gives you the option to skip an expensive breakfast and pay a lower rate, consider saying yes and eating more cheaply on your own.

Tipping: If you buy food at a counter, don't tip. Service is included at Swiss restaurants with table service, but it's customary to round up the bill (5-10 percent; for a 19-CHF meal, pay 20 CHF. (Rounding up isn't required, though, and no one will come running after you if you don't.)

PRACTICALITIES

Restaurant Code

Eateries in this book are categorized according to the average cost of a typical main course. Drinks, desserts, and splurge items can raise the price considerably.

$$$$	**Splurge:** Most main courses over 40 CHF
$$$	**Pricier:** 30-40 CHF
$$	**Moderate:** 20-30 CHF
$	**Budget:** Under 20 CHF

In Switzerland, a kebab stand or other takeout spot is **$**; a self-service cafeteria or casual café is **$$**; a restaurant with table service is **$$$**; and a swanky splurge is **$$$$**.

When paying, the Swiss tell the server how much they'd like the bill to be. For example, if paying for an 8.10-CHF drink with a 20-CHF bill, say "Nine francs" or *("Neun Franken")*. The server will keep a .90-CHF tip and give you 11 CHF in change. With a card, just ask the server to round up the total to include the tip. (While uncommon in most of Europe, this is standard practice in Switzerland.) It's unlikely that you'll be given a receipt with a tip line to fill in, though a few restaurants may be adding these.

RESTAURANT PRICING

I've categorized my recommended eateries based on the average price of a typical main course, indicated with a dollar-sign rating (see sidebar). Obviously, expensive specialties, fine wine, appetizers, and dessert can significantly increase your final bill.

The categories also indicate the personality of a place: **Budget** eateries include street food, takeaway, order-at-the-counter shops, and bakeries selling sandwiches. **Moderate** eateries are nice (but not fancy) sit-down restaurants, ideal for a pleasant meal with good-quality food.

Pricier eateries are a notch up, with more attention paid to the setting, presentation, and (often inventive) cuisine. **Splurge** eateries are dress-up-for-a-special-occasion swanky—typically with an elegant setting, polished service, and pricey and refined cuisine.

BUDGET OPTIONS

Grocery Stores: The midrange Migros and Co-op grocery stores are the hungry hiker's best budget bet. Larger stores have a great selection of prepared foods and picnic fixings. These include a huge variety of salads (green, potato, pasta, or meat—sometimes sold with a plastic fork), decorated hard-boiled eggs (called *Picknickeier*), premade sandwiches, delicious cheese, single portions of cake and ice cream, inexpensive chocolate bars, and sometimes, a hot-meal counter. You'll also see Manor ("mah-NOR"), a more elegant supermarket chain, and Aldi, a discount grocery store with a limited range. Manor is actually a department store (and many Migros and Co-ops are as well), with the supermarket typically hiding in the basement.

By law, most supermarkets are required to close on Sunday, with exceptions for stores in train stations and in some towns where grocery stores are allowed to open for a few hours on Sunday afternoons (a controversial issue in Switzerland). In larger cities, supermarket chains have skirted the law by building big stores in malls attached to train stations.

In larger cities such as Bern, Co-op and Migros also have smaller outlets that focus on prepared foods for takeout. You'll find many locals here, picking up lunch to enjoy on a park bench, at the office, or on a train ride.

Self-Service Cafeterias and Buffets: Cafeterias have good food at much lower prices than restaurants with table service. You'll find them in most cities, usually at downtown branches of Manor, Co-op, and Migros supermarkets (in descending order of fanciness). In cities, some are on the top floor or even the rooftop—giving you a great view at budget prices.

Manor's cafeterias (called "Manora") feature lush salad bars, tasty entrées, and fresh-squeezed juices (I've listed several specific Manora locations in this book). Co-op and Migros cafeterias are only a little more modest. A main course at a cafeteria is usually cooked to order in front of you and will cost 14-19 CHF; drinks and dessert run about 3-4 CHF each. Some self-service cafeterias have free tap water, often hidden in an inconspicuous place to encourage diners to pay for bottled drinks.

While cafeteria food may not be inventive, it is typical, fresh, and high quality (these are supermarkets, after all); they're also popular with locals. Eating some of your meals at cafeterias can free up money for splurges on traditional dishes at fine restaurants with table service.

Another common type of self-service eatery is a gourmet buffet (often vegetarian) that is charged by weight. Look for Hiltl (in Zürich) and the Tibits chain (in Zürich, Bern, and Luzern).

Hostels: Swiss hostels that belong to the Hosteling International network usually offer a fine four-course dinner for around 20 CHF, with free tap water—a great deal for guests. In a few cases this is open to nonguests, too, at a slightly higher price (call to reserve).

Global Food: Asian and Middle Eastern restaurants abound, but are generally not as much of a bargain as in neighboring countries (a *döner kebab* costs around 10 CHF and a main course at an Asian restaurant about 20 CHF). The same goes for pizzerias, which are often upscale places with table service and 20-CHF pies; takeout orders are often slightly cheaper than the sit-down price.

RESTAURANTS

The cheapest main courses at Swiss restaurants start at around 20 CHF—typically starchy dishes topped with meat or cheese (pasta, pizza, and potato dishes) or sausages with kraut or potato salad. Meat courses (served with a starch and vegetable) will run you 28-45 CHF at an average restaurant. Many restaurants offer a daily special—a main course for about 25 CHF (at least Mon-Fri at lunch, sometimes weekends and evenings, too). High-priced drinks can quickly run up the cost of a meal.

Different kinds of restaurants offer different experiences. Hotels often serve fine food. A *Gaststätte* is a simple, less expensive restaurant. A *Weinstübli* (wine bar) or *Bierstübli* (tavern) usually serves food, too. Mountain huts—called *Hütte*—generally have hot chocolate and hearty meat-and-potato meals. Smoking is no longer allowed inside Switzerland's eateries (though a few places skirt the laws with enclosed verandas for smokers). If you're not too hungry, order from the *kleine Hunger* (small hunger) section of the menu.

Most restaurants tack a menu onto their door for browsers and have an English menu inside. If you ask for the *Menü* (or *menu* in French), you won't get a list of dishes; you'll get a fixed-price meal of several courses. If you simply want a list of what's cooking, ask for *die Speisekarte* (dee SHPIE-zeh-kar-teh; *la carte* in French).

Only a rude server will rush you. Good service is relaxed (slow to an American). To wish others "Happy eating!" offer a cheery *"En Guete!"* When you want the bill, request *"Die Rechnung, bitte."* (See the survival phrases in the appendix for more tips.)

SWISS CUISINE

Here at this meeting point of European cultures, a region's food is heavily influenced by the cuisine of neighboring countries. You'll find heavy wurst-and-kraut fare in German-speaking areas; delicate, subtle French cuisine in the west; and pasta and polenta dishes *all'Italiana* in Ticino. In alpine regions, most meals are still built on the hardy ingredients that can be produced and stored in the mountains: cheese, potatoes, onions, cheese, cabbage, sausage, cheese, cured meat...and more cheese.

Traditional Dishes

Aside from clocks and banks, Switzerland is known for its cheese. Gruyère cheese is hard, with a strong flavor; Emmentaler is also hard, but milder (and looks like what we call "Swiss cheese"). Appenzeller is the incredibly pungent cheese from the northeast of

Swiss Chocolate:
The Souvenir that Disappears

Of Switzerland's well-known icons—watches, banks, gadgety knives, booze-bearing mountain dogs—only one makes would-be visitors salivate in anticipation: chocolate. But why does Swiss chocolate hold such cachet? The answer dates back to 1819, when François-Louis Cailler figured out how to mechanize chocolate production and set up a factory near Lake Geneva. The Swiss also invented milk chocolate (in 1875) and conching, the process that makes solid chocolate smooth (1879).

The 1890s golden age of Swiss tourism spurred a golden age of Swiss chocolate, when vacationers returned home with a chocolate habit and chocolatey gifts for friends and family. By the 1910s, about 75 percent of the chocolate produced here was being exported. Today, Swiss chocolate is still a popular souvenir, what had been a small collection of "manufactories" has become a billion-dollar industry, and the Swiss people are among the world's top chocolate consumers.

When looking for high-quality chocolate, notice the way the chocolate breaks (a clean break with no crumbles is best), how it melts (like butter?), how it feels in your mouth (the smoother the better), and whether it leaves any gritty, unchocolatey aftertaste.

Of course, the only way to know what you like best is to try lots of different kinds (in the name of science!). The big-name brands—such as Lindt, Toblerone, and Cailler—are everywhere;

Switzerland, with a smell that verges on nauseating...until you taste it.

Two of Switzerland's best-known specialties are cheese-based. (Swiss people typically eat these at home, so restaurants featuring them tend to cater to tourists.) *Käsefondue* is usually Emmentaler and Gruyère cheese melted with white wine, garlic, nutmeg, and other seasonings. You use a long fork to dip cubes of bread into it. The price for fondue is calculated per person (about 25-30 CHF), and most restaurants have a two-person mini-

mum. While the Swiss consider fondue a winter-only meal, it's served year-round in touristed areas, and there's nothing silly about eating it "out of season." Note that "meat fondue," in which you cook raw meat in broth at your table, is not typically Swiss. Sometimes called *fondue chinoise* (Chinese fondue), this is an Asian-style hot pot.

keep your eyes peeled for lesser-known hometown brands like Villars and Camille Bloch. In his book *Swiss Watching,* Diccon Bewes reports on a blind taste test in which Prix Garantie, the Co-op house brand, came in a close second to Cailler—despite costing only a fraction of Cailler's price.

If you prefer milk chocolate, look for bars marked *Vollmilch* or *Alpenmilch;* dark chocolate fans want the *dunkle* stuff (often called *Edelbitter*), and *weisse Schokolade* is white chocolate. Bars with percentages printed on them are boasting their high cocoa content (the higher the number, the more bitter the chocolate). Common additions include *Haselnüsse* (hazelnuts), *Mandeln* (almonds), *Trauben* (grapes/raisins), and *Joghurt* (guess). Connoisseurs watch for seasonal flavors. And it's worth trying Ovo (or Ovomaltine) chocolate—in an orange wrapper—that has an addictive malted flavor.

Switzerland offers a few worthwhile sights for the choco-curious. Factories that you can visit and/or tour include the big Cailler operation in Broc, in the hills above Lake Geneva (see the Lake Geneva & French Switzerland chapter); the Alprose chocolate factory just outside Lugano (see the Lugano chapter); the Lindt factory near Zürich; or the Camille Bloch factory in Courtelary (an hour from Bern). But my favorite Swiss chocolate experience is simply nibbling a bar on a high-mountain hike.

Raclette is cheese slowly melted on a special appliance; as it softens, scrape a mound off and eat it with potatoes, pickled onions, and gherkins. (In restaurants, raclette sometimes comes as little slices of cheese already melted.)

Another must-try dish, most typical in the mountains of the German-speaking areas, is **Rösti**—sort of like hash browns. The potatoes are grated coarsely, then often molded into a loose, round patty. Try *Rösti* topped with alpine cheese, a bit of bacon or ham, or with an egg cracked over it...yum.

Each region has its own specialties. In French-speaking Switzerland, white wine and heavy cream are used in many dishes, and you'll occasionally see horsemeat on the menu. The cuisine in eastern Switzerland (Pontresina, St. Moritz) uses chestnuts in many forms, wild mushrooms, and air-dried beef. Southwestern Switzerland (Zermatt area) specializes in all kinds of cheese, and their favorite white wine is Fendant.

Despite all the cheese and potatoes, the Swiss tend to be health-conscious; after all, they invented **muesli.** While the dry muesli served at breakfast buffets is unremarkable, *Birchermüesli*— a yummy mixture of fresh yogurt, fresh fruit, nuts, and juice- or milk-soaked oats—is worth trying. Restaurants often feature a *Fitnessteller* ("fitness plate")—usually a large mixed salad that comes with steak, chicken, or fish. *Bio* means organically grown (a *Biolädeli* is a store that sells organic products).

Of course, on the other end of the health spectrum, there's the famous **Swiss chocolate.** The vast variety of chocolate flavors available in any Swiss supermarket—let alone a specialty chocolate shop—is staggering. Only chocolate actually produced in the country is granted the honor of being called Swiss. Stroll the chocolate aisle of a grocery store and take your pick.

Beverages

Wine: Swiss wine is good, but expensive because of high production costs and mostly small vineyards. The Swiss certainly have plenty of winemaking experience—they've been growing grapes since Roman times. Since Swiss wine is not well known outside of the country, and very little is exported, this is your chance to try the local *Wein/vin/vino*. About two-thirds of the production is white, and much of that is made from the Chasselas (a.k.a. Fendant) grape. Swiss specialties include the red Dole (a light-bodied blend of pinot noir and gamay grapes), Gutedel (or Chasselas; full, fruity, dry white); Fendant (a dry white that pairs well with cheese dishes), St. Saphorin (lovely, fruity white from Lake Geneva), and Merlot del Ticino (full-bodied red from Italian-speaking Switzerland).

Menus list drink size by the "deci"—a deciliter (dl, tenth of a liter). In German-speaking areas, order wine by the *Glas* (glass) or *Viertel* (quarter liter, or 8 ounces). Order it *süss* (sweet), *halb trocken* (medium), or *trocken* (dry); *weiss* (white), or *rot* (red). To order white wine, for instance, you can say, *"Ein Viertel Weisswein, bitte."* For fun, try ordering the same thing in colloquial Swiss German: *"Ä Viertel Wiisewyy, bitte"* (ih FEER-tehl VEE-seh-vee, BIT-teh).

In French Switzerland, wine comes either by *le verre* (a glass, 1-2 dl), *la carafe* (3 dl or 5 dl), or *la bouteille* (bottle). Order by requesting *"Un verre de vin blanc, s'il vous plaît"* (or *"vin rouge"* if you prefer red). In the Ticino region, *un boccalino* is a small, decorated 8-ounce ceramic jug filled with the local red wine.

Beer: Swiss beer is surprisingly good and inexpensive. Most of the beer is light, golden-colored lager, but you'll also find other types, such as *Hefeweizen* and *Dunkel* (dark) beers. Each pub has one brand of a local beer on tap, with others available in bottles. Feldschlössen is the largest brewery in the country, and you'll see its red-castle logo all over. But the Swiss are loyal to their local brews; for example, in the Appenzell region, Appenzeller is the beer of choice. The standard size, measured in centiliters (cl), is a *Stange* (33 cl); the smaller size is called a *Herrgöttli* (20 cl). Beer mixed with lemon-flavored soda or *Citro* (lemonade) is called a

Panaché. In summer, this lightly sweet, sudsy drink is more refreshing than straight beer.

Water: Switzerland has a tradition of **free fountains,** with fresh, mountain-chilled water, in squares and other central points around cities and towns. I assume I can fill my bottle from any well-maintained public fountain unless I see a sign saying otherwise (*kein Trinkwasser* means it's not potable). At restaurants, tap water, which many servers aren't eager to bring you, is *Leitungswasser* (*l'eau du robinet* in French). Ask for it by name, or you'll receive—and be charged for—*Mineralwasser* (*mit/ohne Gas,* with/ without carbonation).

Other Nonalcoholic Drinks: Instead of Coke, try the local favorite, Rivella, a carbonated, vitamin-rich soft drink made with 35 percent whey (called "milk serum" on the label). Its unusual— but not unpleasant—taste isn't milky at all; it's more like chewable vitamins. It comes in several color-coded varieties: Red is regular; blue is low-calorie; green is mixed with green tea. *Süssmost* is apple juice.

As an alternative to hot chocolate, try Ovomaltine. The Swiss have a fondness for this hot drink powder—the main ingredient is barley malt, flavored with chocolate so kids will drink it, and fortified with vitamins. (In the US and Britain, Ovaltine is a variation on this drink.) Crispy, Ovomaltine-flavored chocolate bars are also popular for their malted-milk-ball taste.

If you're hiking or skiing, and you stop at a mountain hut for a hot cocoa or Ovomaltine, a key word to know is *Mélange*—which tops the drink with whipped cream.

Staying Connected

One of the most common questions I hear from travelers is, "How can I stay connected in Europe?" The short answer? More easily and affordably than you might think.

The simplest solution is to bring your own device—phone, tablet, or laptop—and use it much as you would at home, following the money-saving tips below, such as getting an international plan or connecting to free Wi-Fi whenever possible. Another option is to buy a European SIM card for your mobile phone. Or you can use European landlines and computers to connect. More details are at RickSteves.com/phoning.

USING YOUR PHONE IN EUROPE

Here are some budget tips and options.

Sign up for an international plan. To stay connected at a lower cost, sign up for an international service plan through your carrier. Most providers offer a simple bundle that includes calling,

Hurdling the Language Barrier

Switzerland has four official languages: German, French, Italian, and Romansh (a Romance language spoken in far-flung corners of Graubünden). Most of the destinations in this book are in the German-speaking territory. No matter where you are, most young or well-educated people—especially those in larger towns and the tourist trade—speak at least some English. Still, you'll get more smiles by using the local pleasantries. See the German, French, and Italian survival phrases at the end of the appendix.

In German-speaking Switzerland, locals speak singsongy *Schwyzerdütsch* (Swiss German), but they usually write in the same standard German used in Germany and Austria (called "High" German, *Hochdeutsch*—though many Swiss prefer to call it *Schriftdeutsch*, "Written German"). If you speak standard High German, Swiss German speakers will switch over smoothly to accommodate you, then revert to Swiss German when you leave the conversation.

In Swiss German, the standard greeting is a hearty *Grüezi* (GREWT-see). "Thank you" is derived from French, but pronounced a little differently: *Merci* (MUR-see). They also sometimes use the more German-like *Dankche* (DAHN-kheh, with a guttural "kh," as in the Scottish "loch"). Swiss German pronunciation varies substantially by region, and there's no standard spelling.

English is a Germanic language (along with Dutch, Danish, Swedish, and Norwegian), making standard German easier on most American ears than Romance languages (such as Italian and French). High German is spelled phonetically—its pronunciation rules are regular, and there are no silent letters.

These tips will help you pronounce German words: The letter *w* is always pronounced as "v" (e.g., the word for "wonderful" is *wunderbar*, pronounced VOON-dehr-bar). The vowel combinations *ie* and *ei* are pronounced like the name of the second letter—so *ie* sounds like the letter *e* (as in *hier* and *Bier*, the German words for "here" and "beer"), while *ei* sounds like the letter *i* (as in *nein* and *Stein*, the German words for "no" and "stone"). The vowel combination *au* is pronounced "ow" (as in *Frau*). The vowel combinations *eu* and *äu* are pronounced "oy" (as in *neu*, *Deutsch*, and *Bräu*, the words for "new," "German," and "brew"). To pronounce *ö* and *ü*, purse your lips when you say the vowel; the other vowel with an umlaut, *ä*, is pronounced the same as the *e* in "men." (In written German, these can be depicted without an umlaut as the vowel followed by an *e: oe*, *ue*, and *ae*, respectively.) Written German always capitalizes all nouns.

Give it your best shot. The locals will appreciate your efforts.

For more tips on hurdling the language barrier, consider the *Rick Steves French, Italian & German Phrase Book* (available at RickSteves.com).

messaging, and data. Your normal plan may already include international coverage (for example, T-Mobile's covers data and text, but not voice calls).

Before your trip, research your provider's international rates. Activate the plan a day or two before you leave, then remember to cancel it when your trip's over.

Use free Wi-Fi whenever possible. Unless you have an unlimited-data plan, save most of your online tasks for Wi-Fi. Most accommodations in Europe offer free Wi-Fi. Many cafés (including Starbucks and McDonald's) offer hotspots for customers; ask for the password when you buy something. You may also find Wi-Fi at TIs, city squares, major museums, public-transit hubs, airports, and aboard trains and buses.

Minimize the use of your cellular network. The best way to make sure you're not accidentally burning through data is to put your device in "airplane" mode (which also disables phone calls and texts) and connect to Wi-Fi as needed. When you need to get online but can't find Wi-Fi, simply turn on your cellular network (or turn off airplane mode) just long enough for the task at hand.

Even with an international data plan, wait until you're on Wi-Fi to Skype or FaceTime, download apps, stream videos, or do other megabyte-greedy tasks. Using a navigation app such as Google Maps over a cellular network can require lots of data, so download maps when you're on Wi-Fi, then use the app offline.

Limit automatic updates. By default, your device constantly checks for a data connection and updates app content. Check your device's settings menu for ways to turn this off, and change your email settings from "auto-retrieve" to "manual" (or from "push" to "fetch").

Use Wi-Fi calling and messaging apps. Skype, WhatsApp, FaceTime, and Google Meet are great for making free or low-cost calls or sending texts over Wi-Fi worldwide. Just log on to a Wi-Fi network, then connect with friends, family members, or local contacts who use the same service.

Buy a European SIM card. If you anticipate making a lot of local calls, need a local phone number, or your provider's international data rates are expensive, consider buying a SIM card in Europe to replace the one in your (unlocked) US phone or tablet. SIM cards are sold at department-store electronics counters and some newsstands (you may need to show your passport), and vending machines. If you need help setting it up, buy one at a mobile-phone shop.

Since Switzerland is not part of the EU, you'll often pay high roaming charges when you use a SIM card from another European country here. To be on the safe side, remove any other European cards from your phone unless you know they include a reasonably

How to Dial

Here's how to dial from anywhere in the US or Europe, using the phone number of one of my recommended Gimmelwald hotels as an example (033 855 3575). If a number starts with 0, drop it when dialing internationally (except when calling Italy).

From a US Mobile Phone

Phone numbers in this book are presented exactly as you would dial them from a US mobile phone. For international access, press and hold 0 (zero) to get a + sign, then dial the country code (41 for Switzerland) and phone number.

▶ To call the Gimmelwald hotel from any location, dial +41 33 855 3575.

From a US Landline

Replace + with 011 (US/Canada access code), then dial the country code (41 for the Switzerland) and phone number.

▶ To call the Gimmelwald hotel from your home landline, dial 011 41 33 855 3575.

From a European Landline

Replace + with 00 (Europe access code), then dial the country code (41 for Switzerland, 1 for the US) and phone number.

▶ To call the Gimmelwald hotel from a German landline, dial 00 41 33 855 3575.

▶ To call my US office from a Dutch landline, dial 00 1 425 771 8303.

From One Swiss Phone to Another

To place a domestic call (from a Swiss landline or mobile), drop +41 and dial the phone number (including the initial 0).

▶ To call the Gimmelwald hotel from Bern, dial 033 855 3575.

More Dialing Tips

Local Numbers: European phone numbers and area codes can vary in length and spacing, even within the same country. Mobile phones use separate prefixes (for instance, in Switzerland, mobile numbers begin with 07).

Toll and Toll-Free Calls: It's generally not possible to dial European toll or toll-free numbers from a US mobile or landline (although you can sometimes get through using Skype). Look for a direct-dial number instead.

Calling the US from a US Mobile Phone, While Abroad: Dial +1, area code, and number.

More Phoning Help: See HowToCallAbroad.com.

priced Switzerland plan. Visit a store run by one of the major Swiss phone operators (Swisscom and Sunrise) and ask about their talk, text, and data options.

WITHOUT A MOBILE PHONE

It's less convenient but possible to travel in Europe without a mobile device. You can make calls from your hotel and check email or get online using public computers.

Most **hotels** charge a fee for placing calls. You can use a pre-

---

Tips on Internet Security

Make sure that your device is running the latest versions of its operating system, security software, and apps. Next, ensure that your device and key programs (like email) are password-protected. On the road, use only secure, password-protected Wi-Fi. Ask the hotel or café staff for the specific name of their network, and make sure you log on to that exact one.

If you must access your financial info online, use a banking app rather than accessing your account via a browser, and use a cellular connection, not Wi-Fi. Never log on to personal finance sites on a public computer. If you're very concerned, consider subscribing to a VPN (virtual private network).

---

paid international phone card (usually available at newsstands, tobacco shops, and train stations) to call out from your hotel.

Some hotels have **public computers** in their lobbies for guests to use; otherwise you may find them at public libraries (ask your hotelier or the TI for the nearest location). On a European keyboard, use the "Alt Gr" key to the right of the space bar to insert the extra symbol that appears on some keys. If you can't locate a special character (such as @), simply copy and paste it from a web page.

MAIL

You can mail one package per day to yourself worth up to $200 duty-free from Europe to the US (mark it "personal purchases"). If you're sending a gift to someone, mark it "unsolicited gift." For details, visit www.cbp.gov, select "Travel," and search for "Know Before You Go." The Swiss postal service works fine, but for quick transatlantic delivery (in either direction), consider services such as DHL (DHL.com).

Transportation

Because Switzerland's train network is excellent, I recommend using public transportation here. Only a few areas—like the Appenzell region and the French Swiss countryside—are better by car. Cars are an expensive headache in the bigger cities. For more detailed information on transportation throughout Europe, see RickSteves.com/transportation.

TRAINS

Trains in Switzerland are generally slick, speedy, and punctual, with synchronized connections. They're also clean, roomy, and nonsmoking. Few places in Switzerland are out of reach of the train system—but those that are can be reached by bus (in rural areas, the yellow PostBuses usually run in sync with trains).

Virtually all Swiss stations have luggage lockers. In smaller towns, lockers are sometimes too small to fit larger bags, but if asked nicely the ticket office will usually store bigger luggage for the same price.

Many Swiss trains and stations are marked "SBB CFF FFS." All those letters mean the same thing ("Swiss Federal Railways"), in three different languages: German, French, and Italian. Quite a few of Switzerland's trains are, however, run by small private companies—particularly in mountain areas. Though private, these companies all take part in the same website with schedule and pricing information.

Schedules

For timetables and online tickets, visit the official SBB website (www.sbb.ch; www.rail.ch gets you straight to the English version). Better yet, download and use the **SBB Mobile app,** which includes up-to-the-moment departure information on trains, buses, and even many funiculars and boats throughout Switzerland. This is a great tool whether you're using public trams in a big city, or traveling across the country. (For in-city transit, Google Maps has similar information and may be easier to use.) Note: Prices shown on the SBB website and app look deceptively low, as by default, it assumes you have a Swiss Half-Fare Card (as most Swiss do). To see the full price, select "No Discount." Germany's excellent all-Europe timetable, www.bahn.com, also covers Switzerland, but doesn't always give fare information. Although Switzerland has a 24-hour train-info number, it's so expensive that using it is a last resort (+41 848 44 66 68).

In stations, yellow posters show departures, but not arrival times at destinations. At the cost of waiting in line, ticket-office staff will print out a step-by-step itinerary for you, free of charge. It can help to know that most routes follow a regular schedule, with the same pattern usually repeated every hour or half-hour.

Intercity trains (IC, ICN, and EC) are the fastest, interregional trains (IR) come next, "regional expresses" (RE) skip minor stops, and most other trains (including those beginning with S) stop at all stops. Knowing these codes can help you save time by zeroing in on the fastest train available.

Tickets

If you're traveling without a rail pass, get train tickets online, on the SBB Mobile app, or at the station—either at the ticket windows, or at the easy-to-use machines. You're not normally allowed to buy your ticket on board the train. The penalty for boarding a train without a ticket is 90 CHF—which Swiss conductors strictly enforce.

When buying point-to-point train tickets in Switzerland, watch for "supersaver" fares that give you a discount off the regular price, but restrict you to one departure time and aren't changeable. Regular undiscounted fares are tied to a given route on a particular day, but not a specific departure time. Tickets on fast trains often cost the same or only a little more than tickets on slower trains.

At larger stations, ticket offices may have separate windows for international travel, which close earlier than the regular domestic sales windows.

The Swiss rarely make seat reservations on trains. Reservations are important only on certain special or international trains (for example, they're required on the Glacier Express, the Gotthard Panorama Express, and on TGV trains to France). They can also provide peace of mind at busy travel times (the Rail.ch website helpfully indicates how crowded a train is expected to be). Buy seat reservations at any ticket counter, online, or via the SBB Mobile app.

If you're waiting on the platform for your train, and you have a reserved seat or are planning to sit in first class, look for blue diagrams or monitor displays that show the sector of the platform where the various cars in the train will stop (usually A through F). Stand in the appropriate sector to avoid a last-minute dash to your car or a long walk through the train to your seat.

Rail Passes

Because of high ticket prices, rail passes are a good deal in Switzerland, often even for just a three-day trip. For such a little country, Switzerland has a dizzying array of train passes and deals—but for most travelers, the Swiss Travel Pass is the way to go. For more detailed advice on figuring out the smartest rail pass options for your train trip, visit RickSteves.com/rail.

Swiss Travel Pass: If you're going to Switzerland to relax, this pass may be overkill, but if you're hoping to pack a lot in, the convenience and likely cost savings of the Swiss Travel Pass are huge. While not cheap, it includes rail travel throughout Switzerland, lake boats, buses, in-city transit, most museums in the country, and a half-price discount on most high-mountain trains and lifts. And it's super-convenient: Rather than nickel-and-diming as you go,

PRACTICALITIES

Rail Pass or Point-to-Point Tickets?

Will you be better off buying a rail pass or point-to-point tickets? It pays to know your options and choose what's best for your itinerary.

Rail Passes

A Swiss Travel Pass lets you travel by train in Switzerland for three to fifteen days (consecutively or not) within a one-month period. This pass also covers boats, buses, many museum admissions, and gives discounts on mountain trains and lifts.

Switzerland is also covered (along with most of Europe) by the classic Eurail Global Pass. It's generally cheaper to buy one pass for your whole trip than separate, single-country passes. But since Eurail passes don't cover all the same extras that a Swiss Travel Pass does, different combinations are worth considering.

Switzerland's many travel options also include a one-month Half-Fare Card for discounts on individual point-to-point tickets and various local or regional passes.

While most rail passes are sold electronically by international agents like Rick Steves' Europe, the Swiss Travel Pass and related products are also sold at train stations in Switzerland and at www.rail.ch (search for "Swiss Travel Pass"). For more on rail passes, including current prices and purchasing, visit RickSteves.com/rail.

Point-to-Point Tickets

Use this map to add up approximate pay-as-you-go train fares for your itinerary and compare that to the price of a rail pass. A pass can help with expensive lift tickets and other bonuses in Switzerland, so remember to include these in your comparison.

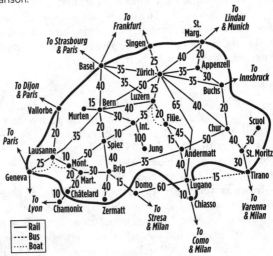

Map shows approximate costs, in US dollars, for one-way, second-class tickets.

Comparing Swiss Pass Coverage

All passes that include Switzerland cover national network trains and many sightseeing and private rail and boat discounts.

Route or Bonus	Eurail Global Pass	Swiss Travel Pass
Swiss Museum admission	No	Covered
Postal buses	No	Covered
Urban buses and trams	No	Covered
Mt. Rigi above Vitznau, Arth-Goldau, or Weggis ($25–40 per leg)	50% off	Covered
Mt. Pilatus above Kriens or Alpnachstad ($70 for 2 legs)	50% off	50% off
Mt. Schilthorn lifts from Stechelberg ($105 roundtrip)	25% off	50% off above Mürren
Jungfrau Region Railways from Interlaken (e.g. $10 to Lauterbrunnen, $11 to Grindelwald, $15 to Wengen; $200 round-trip Jungfraujoch)	25% off above Interlaken	25% off above Grindelwald or Wengen
Glacier Express scenic train	Covered	Covered
Brig-Zermatt private train to see Matterhorn ($40 2nd class)	Covered	Covered
Le Châtelard, Switzerland, to Chamonix, France ($14)	Covered	Covered

All "covered" and discounted services start use of a travel day on a Swiss Travel Pass flexipass. Eurail Global flexipasses allow discounts without using a counted travel day.

flashing your Swiss Travel Pass instantly opens doors all over the country.

The pass comes in both consecutive-day and flexipass versions. Both versions cover the cost of most transportation options for a specified number of days (but do not cover seat reservations). Second class is 35 percent cheaper than first class. They are phasing out the paper pass in favor of an electronic version, which you'll show on your phone (or you can print it out).

Swiss Half-Fare Card: This card gives you a 50 percent discount off all national and private trains, PostBuses, boats, and many lifts ($125 for one month). This can save you money if your Swiss travel adds up to more than $250 in point-to-point tickets.

Swiss Family Card: This card allows children ages 6-15 to travel free with their parents who are using a Swiss Travel Pass or one-month Half-Fare Card for visitors (kids are free even on high-mountain routes where the parents may pay extra). If parents are not buying a pass, the similar Swiss Junior Travelcard costs 30 CHF/1 child or 60 CHF/2 or more children at Swiss stations, valid for one year. A Children's Co-Travelcard works for non-parents (30 CHF/each child). Children under 6 always travel free.

Eurail Global Pass: This pass covers most European railways for as few as three travel days within a month or as long as three months continuously in either first or second class. They can make sense if Switzerland is part of a multicountry trip. All Eurail passes allow up to two kids (ages 4-11) to travel free with each adult, and rates are discounted for youths under 28 or seniors age 60 or older.

Rail Pass Bonuses and Discounts: If you buy a rail pass, know what extras are included—for example, Swiss Travel Passes can get you free entry to many museums and discounts on many mountain lifts. Always ask. The Eurail Global Pass also includes some deals in Switzerland beyond simple trains (such as discounts on lake boats and some mountain lifts), but the coverage and discounts aren't as extensive as the Switzerland-only passes. (For example, lifts in Zermatt are discounted and PostBuses nationwide are free with a Swiss Travel Pass, but both are full price with a Global Pass.)

If your rail pass is a flexipass (covering a certain number of days spread over a longer span, rather than consecutive days), it pays to maximize the benefits you use on a single calendar day. With a flexi version of a Swiss Travel Pass, all coverage and discounts are offered only on the counted travel days. Even if you use the pass just for a short bus ride, a museum entrance, or a discounted ticket, you start the use of a flexi-day. If you don't have more travel planned on the same day, it can make sense to pay out of pocket rather than using a valuable day of your flexipass.

With a Eurail Global Pass, discounted (but not free) trips—most notably many mountain lifts—are still offered at the lower price anytime within the validity window (not just on a flexi-day).

Train Tips

Scenic Rail Journeys: In addition to being convenient for transportation, many of Switzerland's trains are also breathtakingly scenic. Several trips are particularly beautiful and billed as special "theme" routes for tourists. For many visitors, these are a Swiss highlight, and I've devoted an entire chapter to them (see the Scenic Rail Journeys chapter).

Using Rail Passes on Private Lines: Switzerland has some privately owned train lines. Most notably, the private Jungfrau Railway operates the trains from Interlaken up the Lauterbrunnen Valley and to the Jungfraujoch. In this region, Swiss Travel Pass coverage switches to just a discount above Wengen, Grindelwald, or Mürren, but Eurail Global Pass coverage switches to a discount once you board a Jungfrau Railway train at Interlaken. If your rail pass doesn't cover an entire journey, pay for the "uncovered" portion at the station before you board the train.

Check Your Bags: If you're town- or mountain-hopping

Public Transportation

Rail
Boat
Bus

Note: Not all transportation routes shown.

50 Kilometers
50 Miles

PRACTICALITIES

Lift Lingo

The Swiss have come up with an impressive variety of ways to conquer peaks and reach the best viewpoints and trailheads with minimum sweat. Known generically as "lifts," each of these contraptions has its own name and definition. Use the right terms, and impress your new Swiss friends.

Cogwheel Train: A train that climbs a steep incline using a gear system, which engages "teeth" in the middle of the tracks to provide traction. Also known as "rack-and-pinion train" or "rack railway." In German, it's a *Zahnradbahn* (*train à cremaillère* in French and *ferrovia a cremagliera* in Italian).

Funicular: A car that is pulled by a cable along tracks up a particularly steep incline, often counterbalanced by a similar car going in the opposite direction (which you'll pass halfway through the ride). Funiculars, like cogwheel trains, are in contact with the ground at all times. In German, it's a *Standseilbahn* (*funiculaire* in French and *funicolare* in Italian).

Cable Car: A large passenger car, suspended in the air by a cable, which travels between stations without touching the ground. A cable car holds a large number of people (sometimes dozens at a time), who generally ride standing up. When a cable car reaches a station, it comes to a full stop to allow passengers to get on and off. In German, it's a *Seilbahn* (*téléphérique* in French and *funivia* in Italian).

Gondola: Also suspended in the air by a cable, but smaller than a cable car—generally holding fewer than 10 people, who are usually seated. Gondolas move continuously, meaning that passengers have to hop into and out of the moving cars at stations. Generally, gondolas have many smaller cars strung along the same cable. In German, it's a *Gondel* (*télécabine* in French and *telecabine* in Italian). Confusingly, the "car" compartment of a cable car is sometimes referred to as a "gondola."

through Switzerland by train, a great way to lighten your load is by sending your baggage ahead (drop it off at the station before 19:00, pay 12 CHF with ticket or rail pass, maximum 55 pounds). Your bag will show up at the designated station within 36 hours of your arrival (usually faster) and will be held for four days for free (after that, it's a few francs a day). Door-to-door delivery is available with an additional flat fee of 40 CHF per travel group and offers a same-day express upgrade in some locations for another 30 CHF per group. See www.rail.ch for details.

Bike 'n' Rail: You can rent a bike at more than 80 Swiss rail stations, usually at the baggage counter, for 38 CHF per day (33 CHF with rail pass; 27 CHF/half-day, 22 CHF with rail pass, helmets included). You may be able to return the bike at another station (10 CHF extra, no half-day discount). They also have electric bikes, tandem bikes, and kids' bikes. For more information, see www.rail.ch under "Station & Services." Though not required, online reservations are encouraged. For suggested bike routes in Switzerland, visit www.veloland.ch.

TAXIS AND RIDE-BOOKING SERVICES

While most European taxis are reliable and cheap, Swiss taxis are expensive (Zürich's were recently ranked among the priciest in the world). Public transit is extremely efficient; using it to get to outlying sights or an airport is still the best option. If you like ride-booking services such as Uber, their apps work in Zürich, Lausanne, and Geneva just like they do in the US: Request a car on your mobile phone (connected to Wi-Fi or data), and the fare is automatically charged to your credit card.

RENTING A CAR

It's cheaper to arrange most car rentals from the US, so research and compare rates before you go. Most of the major US rental agencies (including Avis, Budget, Enterprise, Hertz, and Thrifty) have offices throughout Europe. Also consider the two major Europe-based agencies, Europcar and Sixt. Consolidators such as Auto Europe (AutoEurope.com or the often cheaper AutoEurope. eu) compare rates at several companies to get you the best deal.

Wherever you book, always read the fine print. Check for add-on charges—such as one-way drop-off fees, airport surcharges, or mandatory insurance policies—that aren't included in the "total price."

Rental Costs and Considerations

If you book well in advance, expect to pay roughly $350-500 for a one-week rental for a basic compact car. Allow extra for supplemental insurance, fuel, tolls, and parking.

Manual vs. Automatic: Almost all rental cars in Europe are manual by default—and cars with a stick shift are generally cheaper. If you need an automatic, reserve one specifically. When selecting a car, don't be tempted by a larger model, as it won't be as maneuverable on narrow, winding roads or when squeezing into tight parking lots.

Age Restrictions: Some rental companies impose minimum

and maximum age limits. Young drivers (25 and under) and seniors (69 and up) should check the rental policies and rules section of car-rental websites.

Choosing Pick-Up/Drop-off Locations: Always check the hours of the locations you choose: Many rental offices close from midday Saturday until Monday morning and, in smaller towns, at lunchtime. When selecting an office, confirm the location on a map. A downtown site might seem more convenient than the airport but could actually be in the suburbs or buried deep in big-city streets. Pedestrianized and one-way streets can make navigation tricky when returning a car at a big-city office or urban train station. Wherever you select, get precise details on the location and allow ample time to find it.

Have the Right License: If you're renting a car in Switzerland, bring your driver's license. If you're also planning to drive in Austria or Italy, you're also technically required to have an International Driving Permit—an official translation of your license (sold at AAA offices for about $20 plus the cost of two passport-type photos; see AAA.com). How this is enforced varies: I've never needed one.

Picking Up Your Car: Before driving off in your rental car, check it thoroughly and make sure any damage is noted on your rental agreement. Rental agencies in Europe tend to charge for even minor damage, so be sure to mark everything. Find out how your car's gearshift, lights, turn signals, wipers, radio, and fuel cap function, and know what kind of fuel the car takes (diesel is common in Europe). When you return the car, make sure the agent verifies its condition with you.

Car Insurance Options

When you rent a car in Europe, the price typically includes liability insurance, which covers harm to other cars or motorists—but not the rental car itself. To limit your financial risk in case of damage to the rental, choose one of these options: Buy a Collision Damage Waiver (CDW; also called "loss damage waiver" or LDW by some firms) with a low or zero deductible from the car-rental company (roughly 30-40 percent extra), get coverage through your credit card (free, but more complicated), or get collision insurance as part of a larger travel-insurance policy.

Basic **CDW** costs $15-30 a day and typically comes with a $1,000-2,000 deductible, reducing but not eliminating your financial responsibility. When you reserve or pick up the car, you'll be offered the chance to "buy down" the deductible to zero (for an additional $10-30/day; this is sometimes called "super CDW" or "zero-deductible coverage").

If you opt for **credit-card coverage,** you must decline all cov-

Driving in Switzerland

Note: Your times may vary based on traffic, cows, fondue spills, construction and road conditions

erage offered by the car-rental company—which means they can place a hold on your card to cover the deductible. In case of damage, it can be time-consuming to resolve the charges. Before relying on this option, quiz your card company about how it works.

If you're already purchasing a **travel-insurance policy** for your trip, adding collision coverage can be an economical option. For example, Travel Guard (TravelGuard.com) sells affordable renter's collision insurance as an add-on to its other policies; it's valid everywhere in Europe except the Republic of Ireland, and some Italian car-rental companies refuse to honor it, as it doesn't cover you in case of theft.

For more on car-rental insurance, see RickSteves.com/cdw.

Navigation Options

If you'll be navigating using your phone or a GPS unit from home, remember to bring a car charger and device mount.

Your Mobile Phone: The mapping app on your mobile phone works fine for navigating Europe's roads. To save on data, most apps allow you to download maps for offline use (do this before you need them, when you have a strong Wi-Fi signal). Some apps—including Google Maps—also have offline route directions, but you'll need mobile data access for current traffic. For more on using a mapping app without burning through data, see "Using Your Phone in Europe," earlier.

PRACTICALITIES

GPS Devices: If you want a dedicated GPS unit, consider renting one with your car (about $20/day, or sometimes included—ask). These units offer real-time turn-by-turn directions and traffic without the data requirements of an app. The unit may come loaded only with maps for its home country; if you need additional maps, ask. Make sure you know how to use the device—and that the language is set to English—before you drive off.

Paper Maps and Atlases: Even when navigating primarily with a mobile app or GPS, I always have a paper map—ideally a big, detailed regional road map. It's invaluable for getting the big picture, understanding alternate routes, and filling in if my phone runs out of juice. The free maps you get from your car-rental company usually don't have enough detail. It's smart to buy a better map before you go, or pick one up at a local gas station, bookshop, newsstand, or tourist shop.

DRIVING

You can get anywhere quickly on Switzerland's fine road system, the world's most expensive per mile to build.

Road Rules: By law, you must use your headlights day and night in Switzerland (driving without them on will earn you a 40-CHF fine). Seat belts are required, and two beers under those belts are enough to land you in jail. Children under 12 (yes, 12) need to ride in a child-safety seat. Be aware of typical European road rules; for example, like many other European countries, Switzerland forbids handheld mobile-phone use. Ask your car-rental company about these rules, or check the "International Travel" section of the US State Department website (www.travel.state.gov, search for your country in the "Learn About Your Destination" box, then click on "Travel & Transportation").

Tolls: Drivers pay an annual 40-CHF fee for a permit to use Swiss autobahns. Check to see if your rental car already has one of these windshield stickers, called a "vignette"—if you picked it up in Switzerland, it most likely does. If not, buy it at border crossings, gas stations, post offices, or car-rental agencies. Anyone caught driving on a Swiss autobahn (indicated by green signs with a white expressway symbol) without this tax sticker is likely to be stopped and slapped with a steep fine (200 CHF plus the 40-CHF fee).

Fuel: Gas and diesel are both expensive—often around $8 per gallon. US credit and debit cards may not work at pay-at-the-pump stations, but are generally accepted (with a PIN code) at staffed stations. Diesel rental cars are common; make sure you know what type of fuel your car takes before you fill up. Some pumps are color-coded: Unleaded pumps are green and labeled "E," while diesel pumps (often yellow or black) are labeled "B."

Signage: Know the universal road signs (shown in this chap-

AND LEARN THESE ROAD SIGNS

Speed Limit (km/hr) · Yield · No Passing · End of No Passing Zone

One Way · Intersection · Main Road · Expressway

Danger · No Entry · Cars Prohibited · All Vehicles Prohibited

No Through Road · Restrictions No Longer Apply · Yield to Oncoming Traffic · No Stopping

Parking · No Parking · Customs or Toll Road · Peace

ter and explained in charts in most road atlases and at service stations). *Dreieck* (literally, "three corners") means a Y in the road; *Autobahnkreuz* is an intersection (*carrefour* in French). Exits are spaced about 20 miles apart and often have a gas station (*bleifrei/sans plomb* are German/French for "unleaded"), a restaurant, a minimart, and sometimes a tourist information desk. Exits and intersections refer to the next major city or the nearest small town. Look at your map and anticipate which town names to watch out for. Know what you're looking for—miss it, and you're long autobahngone. When navigating, you'll see *Nord, Süd, Ost, West,* or *Mitte* (*nord, sud, est, ouest,* or *centre* in French).

To get to the center of a city, follow signs for *Zentrum* or *Stadtmitte* (*centre-ville* in French). Ring roads go around a city.

Parking: Even in small towns, prime parking spots usually require payment. But it's easy to find free short-term parking in relatively central "blue zone" spaces, which require a blue cardboard "parking disc" clock (*Parkscheibe*, available free at TIs, gas stations, police stations, and *Tabak* shops). It's easy: Display your arrival time on the clock (you can scoot it up to the nearest full hour or half-hour) and put it on the dashboard, so parking attendants can see how long you've been there. Unless the sign indicates otherwise, you can park for free for an hour past the time set on your clock. If you arrive after 11:30, you can leave your car till 14:30, and if you arrive after 18:00, you're good until 9:00 the next day. Blue zones aren't patrolled overnight (19:00-8:00) or on Sundays, so you don't need to display a disc during those times.

FLIGHTS

To compare flights, begin with an online travel search engine: Kayak is the top site for flights to and within Europe, easy-to-use Google Flights has price alerts, and Skyscanner includes many inexpensive flights within Europe. To avoid unpleasant surprises, before you book be sure to read the small print about refunds, changes, and the cost for "extras" such as reserving a seat, checking a bag, or printing a boarding pass.

Flights to Europe: Start looking for international flights about four to six months before your trip, especially for peak-season travel. Depending on your itinerary, it can be efficient and no more expensive to fly into one city and out of another. If your flight requires a connection in Europe, see my hints on navigating Europe's top hub airports at RickSteves.com/hub-airports.

Flights Within Europe: Flying between European cities is surprisingly affordable. Before buying a long-distance train or bus ticket, check the cost of a flight on one of Europe's airlines, whether a major carrier or a no-frills outfit like EasyJet and Ryanair. Be aware that flying with a discount airline can have drawbacks, such as minimal customer service, time-consuming treks to secondary airports, and a larger carbon footprint than a train or bus.

Flying to the US and Canada: Because security is extra tight for flights to the US, be sure to give yourself plenty of time at the airport (see www.tsa.com for the latest rules).

Resources from Rick Steves

Begin Your Trip at RickSteves.com

My mobile-friendly **website** is *the* place to explore Europe in preparation for your trip. You'll find thousands of fun articles, videos, and radio interviews; a wealth of money-saving tips for planning your dream trip; travel news dispatches; a video library of travel talks; my travel blog; our latest guidebook updates (RickSteves.com/update); and the free Rick Steves Audio Europe app. You can also follow me on Facebook, Instagram, and Twitter.

Our **Travel Forum** is a well-groomed collection of message boards where our travel-savvy community answers questions and shares their personal travel experiences—and our well-traveled staff chimes in when they can be helpful (RickSteves.com/forums).

Our **online Travel Store** offers bags and accessories that I've designed to help you travel smarter and lighter. These include my popular carry-on bags (which I live out of four months a year), money belts, totes, toiletries kits, adapters, guidebooks, and planning maps (RickSteves.com/shop).

Our website can also help you find the perfect **rail pass** for your itinerary and your budget, with easy, one-stop shopping for rail passes, seat reservations, and point-to-point tickets (RickSteves.com/rail).

Rick Steves Tours, Guidebooks, TV Shows, and More

Small Group Tours: Want to travel with greater efficiency and less stress? We offer more than 40 itineraries reaching the best destinations in this book...and beyond. Each year about 30,000 travelers join us on about 1,000 Rick Steves bus tours. You'll enjoy great guides and a fun bunch of travel partners (with small groups of 24 to 28 travelers). You'll find European adventures to fit every vacation length. For all the details, and to get our tour catalog, visit RickSteves.com/tours or call us at +1 425 608 4217.

Books: This book is just one of many books in my series on European travel, which includes country and city guidebooks, Snapshots (excerpted chapters from bigger guides), Pocket Guides (full-color little books on big cities), "Best Of" guidebooks (condensed, full-color country guides), and my budget-travel skills handbook, *Rick Steves Europe Through the Back Door.* A complete list of my titles—including phrase books, cruising guides, and travelogues on European art, history, and culture—appears near the end of this book.

TV Shows and Travel Talks: My public television series, *Rick Steves' Europe,* covers Europe from top to bottom with over 100 half-hour episodes—and we're working on new shows every year (watch full episodes at my website for free). My free online video library, Rick Steves Classroom Europe, offers a searchable database of short video clips on European history, culture, and geography (Classroom.RickSteves.com). And to raise your travel I.Q., check out the video versions of our popular classes (covering most European countries as well as travel skills, packing smart, cruising, tech for travelers, European art, and travel as a political act—RickSteves.com/travel-talks).

Audio Tours on My Free App: I've produced dozens of free, self-guided audio tours of the top sights in Europe. For those tours and other audio content, get my free **Rick Steves Audio Europe app,** an extensive online library organized by destination. For more on my app, see page 26.

Radio: My weekly public radio show, *Travel with Rick Steves,* features interviews with travel experts from around the world. It airs on 400 public radio stations across the US. An archive of programs is available at RickSteves.com/radio.

Podcasts: You can enjoy my travel content via several free podcasts. The podcast version of my radio show brings you a weekly, hour-long travel conversation. My other podcasts include a weekly selection of video clips from my public television show, my audio tours of Europe's top sights, and live recordings of my travel classes (RickSteves.com/watch-read-listen/audio/podcasts).

APPENDIX

Holidays and Festivals

This list includes selected festivals in major cities, plus national holidays observed throughout Switzerland. Many sights and banks close on national holidays—keep this in mind when planning your itinerary. Not every canton celebrates all holidays (particularly religious ones); if you find yourself in a town closed down for an unexpected holiday, consider going on to your next stop (call ahead), where everything may well be in full swing. Before planning a trip around a festival, verify the dates with the festival website, the Switzerland tourist office (www.myswitzerland.com), or my "Upcoming Holidays and Festivals in Switzerland" web page at RickSteves.com/europe/switzerland/festivals.

Jan 1	New Year's Day
Jan 2	Berchtoldstag (St. Berchtold's Day); Harder-Potschete, Interlaken (parade)
Jan 6	Epiphany
Mid-Jan	Lauberhorn ski race, Wengen (www. lauberhorn.ch); Inferno ski race, Mürren (www.inferno-muerren.ch)

Mid-Late Jan	Light Festival, Murten (www.murtenlichtfestival.ch)
Feb/March	Fasnacht (Carnival), especially celebrated in Luzern, Zürich, Bern, and Basel
March 19	Josefstag (St. Joseph's Day)
March-May	International Jazz Festival, Bern (www.jazzfestivalbern.ch)
Early April	Lucerne Festival at Easter, Luzern (classical and sacred music, www.lucernefestival.ch)
Early to Mid-April	Sechseläuten, Zürich (Spring Festival, www.sechselaeuten.ch)
March/April	Easter Sunday-Monday: April 9-10, 2023; March 31-April-1, 2024
Last Sun in April	Open-Air Parliament, Appenzell (public selection of delegates)
May 1	Labor Day
May	Ascension (Christi Himmelfahrt): May 18, 2023; May 29, 2024
May/June	Pentecost and Pentecost Monday (Pfingsten and Pfingstmontag): May 28-29, 2023; May 19-20, 2024
May/June	Corpus Christi (Fronleichnam): June 8, 2023; May 30, 2024
June	Fête de la Musique, Geneva (www.ville-ge.ch/fetedelamusique)
June-Sept	William Tell Performance, Interlaken (open-air theater, www.tellspiele.ch)
June-July	Montreux International Jazz Festival (www.montreuxjazz.com)
Early July	City Festival, Lausanne (www.festivalcite.ch)
Mid-July	Gurten Open-Air Rock Festival, Bern (www.gurtenfestival.ch)
July or August	Estival Jazz, Lugano (free open-air festival, www.estivaljazz.ch), Lugano
Aug	Street Parade, Zürich (citywide rave, www.streetparade.ch)
Aug 1	Swiss National Day (parades and fireworks)
Aug 15	Assumption of Mary (Maria Himmelfahrt)
Mid-Aug-Mid-Sept	Lucerne Festival in Summer, Luzern (classical music, www.lucernefestival.ch); Murten Classics (classical music, www.murtenclassics.ch)

Early Oct	Festa d'Autunno, Lugano (food and wine festival, https://luganoeventi.ch)
Nov 1	All Saints' Day
Late Nov	Zibelemärit, Bern (traditional onion market festival)
Dec	Christmas markets
Dec 6	St. Nicholas Day
Dec 8	Immaculate Conception
Dec 25	Christmas
Dec 26	St. Stephen's Day (Boxing Day)

Books and Films

To learn more about Switzerland past and present, check out a few of these books or films.

Nonfiction

Eiger Dreams (Jon Krakauer, 1990). In this collection of essays, Krakauer explores the trials and triumphs of mountaineering, including his attempt on the Eiger's north face.

La Place de la Concorde Suisse (John McPhee, 1983). Following a mountain unit of the Swiss Army, this book explores how mandatory military service (for men) keeps Switzerland from breaking apart.

Scrambles Amongst the Alps (Edward Whymper, 1871). This mountaineering classic recounts adventure and tragedy in the life of the first climber to summit the Matterhorn.

Swiss History in a Nutshell (Gregoire Nappey, 2010). Nappey delivers information that's concise and enjoyable, yet not dumbed down.

Swiss Watching (Diccon Bewes, 2010). This fun yet well-researched book covers all the basics in an easy-to-digest look at 21st-century Switzerland.

Target Switzerland: Swiss Armed Neutrality in World War II (Stephen P. Halbrook, 1998). Halbrook posits that Switzerland's robust preparation for armed resistance against the Nazis was a key to its success in maintaining neutrality.

A Tramp Abroad (Mark Twain, 1880). Twain humorously recounts his 1878 "walking tour" through the Alps.

The White Spider (Heinrich Harrer, 1959). This book chronicles the first successful ascent of the Eiger's north face in 1938.

Why Switzerland? (Jonathan Steinberg, 1976). Steinberg explains how a country with four official languages can still have a common culture.

APPENDIX

Fiction

Einstein's Dreams (Alan Lightman, 1992). A young Albert Einstein wrests with his theory of relativity in turn-of-the-century Bern.

A Farewell to Arms (Ernest Hemingway, 1929). Two lovers struggle through the horrors of World War I, finding brief peace in Switzerland in the last act.

Frankenstein (Mary Shelley, 1818). Set partially in Geneva, this novel explores the nature of humanity when scientist Victor Frankenstein creates a monster and brings it to life.

Hotel du Lac (Anita Brookner, 1995). A writer of romance novels attempts to recover from her own misguided love affair by fleeing to Switzerland.

I'm Not Stiller (Max Frisch, 1954). In an attempt to reclaim his true identity, a prisoner in a small Swiss town recounts his adventurous life.

The Magic Mountain (Thomas Mann, 1924). An exclusive sanatorium high in the Alps is a microcosm for European society in the days before World War I.

The Night Manager (John le Carré, 1993). The fussy manager of a Swiss hotel is recruited by British intelligence to bring down a millionaire gunrunner.

The Watchers (Jon Steele, 2011). Three strangers in Lausanne must solve the mysteries haunting their town.

William Tell (Friedrich Schiller, 1804). William Tell, legendary Swiss marksman, fights for Swiss independence from the Habsburg Empire in the 14th century.

Films and TV

The Bourne Identity (2002). This action movie, set mostly in Prague, pits an amnesiac spy against his pursuers in the heart of Zürich.

Clouds of Sils Maria (2014). Largely set (and filmed) in the Upper Engadine valley, this coming-of-middle-age drama stars Juliette Binoche as an aging actress and Kristen Stewart as the personal assistant who poses a subtle threat (as does the Engadine's unique weather patterns).

Dilwale Dulhania Le Jayenge (1995). In the longest-running film in Indian cinema (600 weeks in the movie theaters), two young people fall in love on a trip to Switzerland.

The Eiger Sanction (1975). A mountain climber (Clint Eastwood) joins an expedition on the Eiger's north face intending to expose a murderer among his climbing team. The film includes scenes from Kleine Scheidegg and on the Eiger itself.

Five Days One Summer (1982). Sean Connery stars in the tale of an incestuous love triangle, offset by breathtaking climbing sequences in the Swiss Alps.

Jonah Who Will Be 25 in the Year 2000 (1976). A group of student activists living in Geneva face disillusionment during the late 1960s.

Journey of Hope (1990). Three members of a Kurdish family search for a better life in Switzerland.

North Face (2008). Inspired by a true story, this adventure chronicles a 1936 attempt by two German soldiers to be the first to scale the Eiger's daunting north face.

On Her Majesty's Secret Service (1969). James Bond (George Lazenby) goes undercover in the Swiss Alps, with action sequences on the Schilthorn.

The Swissmakers (1978). The most popular Swiss movie ever made showcases a group of foreigners trying to get Swiss citizenship.

Three Colors: Red (1994). In the Oscar-nominated final film of the acclaimed *Three Colors* trilogy, a young model living in Geneva forms an unlikely bond with a cynical old judge.

For Kids

And Both Were Young (Madeleine L'Engle, 1983). In a tale for teens, Philippa struggles to find her place at a Swiss boarding school until she starts a secret romance and gains new friends.

Asterix in Switzerland (René Goscinny, 1970). Asterix and Obelix have adventures in Switzerland during Roman times in book number 16 of this beloved French cartoon series.

Banner in the Sky (James Ramsey Ullman, 1954). Young Rudi Matt tries to climb one of the world's most forbidding Alpine peaks in this Newbery Honor book.

A Bell for Ursli (Selina Chönz, 2007). High in the Alps, a boy named Ursli hikes alone into the snowy mountains to find a big bell with which to lead the spring procession.

Count Karlstein (Philip Pullman, 2000). Two girls escape the sinister plot of their uncle—an evil count—in this humorous middle-grade thriller set in a Swiss village in 1816.

Dear Alexandra: A Story of Switzerland (Helen Gudel, 1999). This charming picture book takes the form of letters from a grandmother who awaits her granddaughter's visit in a Swiss mountain village.

Heidi (Johanna Spyri, 1880). In the most famous novel about Switzerland, an orphan girl is sent to live with her grandfather in the Alps. A popular film version starring Shirley Temple was released in 1937.

Pitschi (Hans Fischer, 1947). In this Swiss children's classic, a kitten named Pitschi sets out to find her place among the animals on Old Lisette's farm.

A Tale of Two Brothers (Eveline Hasler, 2006). This Swiss-Italian folk tale of two brothers with vastly different worldviews delivers a moral about the power of positive thinking.

William Tell: One Against an Empire (Paul D. Storrie, 2008). This dynamic retelling of the legendary Swiss hunter's story is presented in graphic-novel format.

Conversions and Climate

Numbers and Stumblers

- Europeans write a few of their numbers differently than we do. 1 =1, 4 =4, 7 =7.
- In Europe, dates appear as day/month/year, so Christmas 2024 is 25/12/2024.
- Commas are decimal points and decimals are commas. A dollar and a half is $1,50, one thousand is 1.000, and there are 5.280 feet in a mile.
- When counting with fingers, start with your thumb. If you hold up your first finger to request one item, you'll probably get two.
- What Americans call the second floor of a building is the first floor in Europe.
- On escalators and moving sidewalks, Europeans keep the left "lane" open for passing. Keep to the right.

Metric Conversions

A **kilogram** equals 1,000 grams (about 2.2 pounds). One hundred **grams** (a common unit at markets) is about a quarter-pound. One **liter** is about a quart, or almost four to a gallon.

A **kilometer** is six-tenths of a mile. To convert kilometers to miles, cut the kilometers in half and add back 10 percent of the original (120 km: 60 + 12 = 72 miles). One **meter** is 39 inches—just over a yard.

1 foot = 0.3 meter	1 square yard = 0.8 square meter
1 yard = 0.9 meter	1 square mile = 2.6 square kilometers
1 mile = 1.6 kilometers	1 ounce = 28 grams
1 centimeter = 0.4 inch	1 quart = 0.95 liter
1 meter = 39.4 inches	1 kilogram = 2.2 pounds
1 kilometer = 0.62 mile	32°F = 0°C

Clothing Sizes

When shopping for clothing, use these US-to-European comparisons as general guidelines (but note that no conversion is perfect).

Women: For pants and dresses, add 30 in Switzerland (US 10 = Swiss 40). For blouses and sweaters, add 8 for most of Europe (US 32 = European 40). For shoes, add 30-31 (US 7 = European 37/38).

Men: For shirts, multiply by 2 and add about 8 (US 15 = European 38). For jackets and suits, add 10. For shoes, add 32-34.

Children: Clothing is sized by height—in centimeters (2.5 cm = 1 inch), so a US size 8 roughly equates to 132-140. For shoes up to size 13, add 16-18, and for sizes 1 and up, add 30-32.

Switzerland's Climate

First line, average daily high; second line, average daily low; third line, average days without rain. For more detailed weather statistics for destinations in this book (as well as the rest of the world), check Wunderground.com. For specific weather forecasts by city or town, visit Meteo.search.ch.

	J	F	M	A	M	J	J	A	S	O	N	D
Bern												
	38°	42°	51°	59°	66°	73°	77°	76°	69°	58°	47°	40°
	29°	30°	36°	42°	49°	55°	58°	58°	53°	44°	37°	31°
	20	19	22	21	20	19	22	20	20	21	19	21

Fahrenheit and Celsius Conversion

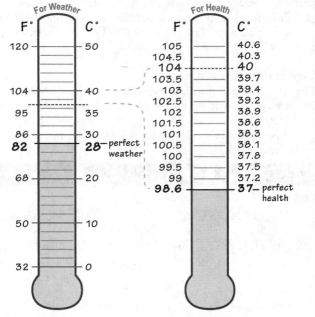

Europe takes its temperature using the Celsius scale, while we opt for Fahrenheit. For a rough conversion from Celsius to Fahrenheit, double the number and add 30. For weather, remember that 28°C is 82°F—perfect. For health, 37°C is just right. At a launderette, 30°C is cold, 40°C is warm (usually the default setting), 60°C is hot, and 95°C is boiling. Your air-conditioner should be set at about 20°C.

Packing Checklist

Whether you're traveling for five days or five weeks, you won't need more than this. Pack light to enjoy the sweet freedom of true mobility.

Clothing

- ❑ 5 shirts: long- & short-sleeve
- ❑ 2 pairs pants (or skirts/capris)
- ❑ 1 pair shorts
- ❑ 5 pairs underwear & socks
- ❑ 1 pair walking shoes
- ❑ Sweater or warm layer
- ❑ Rainproof jacket with hood
- ❑ Tie, scarf, belt, and/or hat
- ❑ Swimsuit
- ❑ Sleepwear/loungewear

Money

- ❑ Debit card(s)
- ❑ Credit card(s)
- ❑ Hard cash (US $100-200)
- ❑ Money belt

Documents

- ❑ Passport
- ❑ Other required ID: Vaccine card/Covid test, entry visa, etc.
- ❑ Driver's license, student ID, hostel card, etc.
- ❑ Tickets & confirmations: flights, hotels, trains, rail pass, car rental, sight entries
- ❑ Photocopies of important documents
- ❑ Insurance details
- ❑ Guidebooks & maps

Electronics

- ❑ Mobile phone
- ❑ Camera & related gear
- ❑ Tablet/ebook reader/laptop
- ❑ Headphones/earbuds
- ❑ Chargers & batteries
- ❑ Phone car charger & mount (or GPS device)
- ❑ Plug adapters

Toiletries

- ❑ Basics: soap, shampoo, toothbrush, toothpaste, floss, deodorant, sunscreen, brush/comb, etc.
- ❑ Medicines & vitamins
- ❑ First-aid kit
- ❑ Glasses/contacts/sunglasses
- ❑ Face masks & hand sanitizer
- ❑ Sewing kit
- ❑ Packet of tissues (for WC)
- ❑ Earplugs

Miscellaneous

- ❑ Daypack
- ❑ Sealable plastic baggies
- ❑ Laundry supplies: soap, laundry bag, clothesline, spot remover
- ❑ Small umbrella
- ❑ Travel alarm/watch
- ❑ Notepad & pen
- ❑ Journal

Optional Extras

- ❑ Second pair of shoes (flip-flops, sandals, tennis shoes, boots)
- ❑ Travel hairdryer
- ❑ Picnic supplies
- ❑ Disinfecting wipes
- ❑ Water bottle
- ❑ Fold-up tote bag
- ❑ Small flashlight
- ❑ Mini binoculars
- ❑ Small towel or washcloth
- ❑ Inflatable pillow/neck rest
- ❑ Tiny lock
- ❑ Address list (to mail postcards)
- ❑ Extra passport photos

German Survival Phrases

In the phonetics, ī sounds like the long i in "light," and bolded syllables are stressed.

Hello.	Grüetzi.	**grewt**-see
Do you speak English?	Sprechen Sie Englisch? **shprehkh**-ehn zee **ehng**-lish	
Yes. / No.	Ja. / Nein.	yah / nīn
I (don't) understand.	Ich verstehe (nicht).	ikh fehr-**shtay**-heh (nikht)
Please. / Thank you.	Bitte. / Merci	**bit**-teh / **mur**-see
You're welcome.	Prego.	**preh**-go
I'm sorry. / Excuse me.	Es tut mir leid. / Entschuldigung. ehs toot meer līt / ehnt-**shool**-dig-oong	
No problem.	Kein Problem.	kīn proh-**blaym**
Goodbye.	Ciao.	chow
(Very) good.	(Sehr) gut.	(zehr) goot
one / two / three	eins / zwei / drei	īns / tsvī / drī
four / five / six	vier / fünf / sechs	feer / fewnf / zehkhs
seven / eight	sieben / acht	**zee**-behn / ahkht
nine / ten	neun / zehn	noyn / tsayn
How much is it?	Wieviel kostet das?	**vee**-feel **kohs**-teht dahs
Write it?	Schreiben?	**shrī**-behn
Is it free?	Ist es umsonst?	ist ehs oom-**zohnst**
Is it included?	Inklusive?	in-kloo-**zee**-veh
Where can I buy / find...?	Wo kann ich kaufen / finden...? voh kahn ikh **kow**-fehn / **fin**-dehn	
I'd like / We'd like...	Ich hätte gern / Wir hätten gern... ikh **heh**-teh gehrn / veer **heh**-tehn gehrn	
...a room.	...ein Zimmer.	īn **tsim**-mer
...a ticket to _____.	...eine Fahrkarte nach _____. ī-neh **far**-kar-teh nahkh _____	
Is it possible?	Ist es möglich?	ist ehs **mur**-glikh
Where is...?	Wo ist...?	voh ist
...the train station	...der Bahnhof	dehr **bahn**-hohf
...the bus station	...der Busbahnhof	dehr **boos**-bahn-hohf
...tourist information	...das Touristeninformationsbüro das too-**ris**-tehn-in-for-maht-see-**ohns**-bew-roh	
...the toilet	...die Toilette	dee toy-**leh**-teh
men / women	Herren / Damen	**hehr**-ehn / **dah**-mehn
left / right	links / rechts	links / **rehkhts**
straight	geradeaus	geh-**rah**-deh-**ows**
When does this open / close?	Um wieviel Uhr ist hier geöffnet / geschlossen? oom **vee**-feel oor ist heer geh-**urf**-neht / geh-**shloh**-sehn	
At what time?	Um wieviel Uhr?	oom **vee**-feel oor
Just a moment.	Moment.	moh-**mehnt**
now / soon / later	jetzt / bald / später	yehtst / bahld / **shpay**-ter
today / tomorrow	heute / morgen	**hoy**-teh / **mor**-gehn

In a German-Speaking Restaurant

I'd like / We'd like...	Ich hätte gern / Wir hätten gern...
	ikh **heh**-teh gehrn / veer **heh**-tehn gehrn
...a reservation for...	...eine Reservierung für...
	ī-neh reh-zehr-**feer**-oong fewr
...a table for one / two.	...einen Tisch für eine Person / zwei Personen.
	ī-nehn tish fewr ī-neh pehr-**zohn** / tsvī pehr-**zoh**-nehn
...the menu (in English),	...die Speisekarte (auf Englisch), bitte.
please.	dee **shpī**-zeh-kar-teh (owf **ehng**-lish) **bit**-teh
service (not) included	Trinkgeld (nicht) inklusive
	trink-gehlt (nikht) in-kloo-**zee**-veh
cover charge	Eintritt **īn**-trit
to go	zum Mitnehmen tsoom **mit**-nay-mehn
with / without	mit / ohne mit / **oh**-neh
and / or	und / oder oont / **oh**-der
menu (of the day)	(Tages-) Karte (**tah**-gehs-) **kar**-teh
set meal for tourists	Touristenmenü too-**ris**-tehn-meh-new
specialty of the house	Spezialität des Hauses
	shpayt-see-ah-lee-**tayt** dehs **how**-zehs
breakfast / lunch /	Frühstück / Mittagessen / Abendessen
dinner	**frew**-shtuhk / **mit**-ah-geh-sehn / **ah**-behn-deh-sehn
appetizers	Vorspeise **for**-shpī-zeh
bread / cheese	Brot / Käse broht / **kay**-zeh
sandwich	Sandwich **zahnd**-vich
soup / salad	Suppe / Salat **zoo**-peh / zah-**laht**
meat / poultry	Fleisch / Geflüge flīsh / geh-**flew**-gehl
fish / seafood	Fisch / Meeresfrüchte fish / **mee**-rehs-**froysh**-teh
fruit / vegetables	Obst / Gemüse ohpst / geh-**mew**-zeh
dessert	Nachspeise **nahkh**-sh pī-zeh
tap water	Leitungswasser **lī**-toongs-**vahs**-ehr
mineral water	Mineralwasser meen-eh-rahl-**vahs**-ehr
milk	Milch milsh
(orange) juice	(Orangen-) Saft (oh-**rahn**-zhehn-) zahft
coffee / tea	Kaffee / Tee kah-**fay** / tay
wine / beer	Wein / Bier vīn / beer
red / white	rot / weiß roht / vīs
glass / bottle	Glas / Flasche glahs / **flah**-sheh
Cheers!	Prost! prohst
More. / Another.	Mehr. / Noch eins. mehr / nohkh īns
The same.	Das gleiche. dahs **glīkh**-eh
The bill, please.	Rechnung, bitte. **rehkh**-noong **bit**-teh
Do you accept credit	Akzeptieren Sie Kreditkarten?
cards?	ahkt-sehp-**teer**-ehn zee kreh-**deet**-kar-tehn
tip	Trinkgeld **trink**-gehlt
Delicious!	Lecker! **lehk**-er

For more user-friendly German phrases, check out *Rick Steves German Phrase Book*.

French Survival Phrases

When using the phonetics, try to nasalize the n sound.

Good day.	Bonjour. bohn-zhoor
Mrs. / Mr.	Madame / Monsieur mah-dahm / muhs-yuh
Do you speak English?	Parlez-vous anglais? par-lay-voo ahn-glay
Yes. / No.	Oui. / Non. wee / nohn
I understand.	Je comprends. zhuh kohn-prahn
I don't understand.	Je ne comprends pas. zhuh nuh kohn-prahn pah
Please.	S'il vous plaît. see voo play
Thank you.	Merci. mehr-see
I'm sorry.	Désolé. day-zoh-lay
Excuse me.	Pardon. par-dohn
No problem.	Pas de problème. pah duh proh-blehm
It's good.	C'est bon. say bohn
Goodbye.	Au revoir. oh ruh-vwahr
one / two / three	un / deux / trois uhn / duh / trwah
four / five / six	quatre / cinq / six kah-truh / sank / sees
seven / eight	sept / huit seht / weet
nine / ten	neuf / dix nuhf / dees
How much is it?	C'est combien? say kohn-bee-an
Write it?	Ecrivez? ay-kree-vay
Is it free?	C'est gratuit? say grah-twee
Included?	Inclus? an-klew
Where can I buy / find...?	Où puis-je acheter / trouver...? oo pwee-zhuh ah-shuh-tay / troo-vay
I'd like / We'd like...	Je voudrais / Nous voudrions... zhuh voo-dray / noo voo-dree-ohn
...a room.	...une chambre. ewn shahn-bruh
...a ticket to ___.	...un billet pour ___. uhn bee-yay poor ___
Is it possible?	C'est possible? say poh-see-bluh
Where is...?	Où est...? oo ay
...the train station	...la gare lah gar
...the bus station	...la gare routière lah gar root-yehr
...tourist information	...l'office du tourisme loh-fees dew too-reez-muh
Where are the toilets?	Où sont les toilettes? oo sohn lay twah-leht
men / women	hommes / dames ohm / dahm
left / right	à gauche / à droite ah gohsh / ah drwaht
straight	tout droit too drwah
pull / push	tirez / poussez tee-ray / poo-say
When does this open / close?	Ça ouvre / ferme à quelle heure? sah oo-vruh / fehrm ah kehl ur
At what time?	À quelle heure? ah kehl ur
Just a moment.	Un moment. uhn moh-mahn
now / soon / later	maintenant / bientôt / plus tard man-tuh-nahn / bee-an-toh / plew tar
today / tomorrow	aujourd'hui / demain oh-zhoor-dwee / duh-man

In a French Restaurant

I'd like / We'd like...	Je voudrais / Nous voudrions... zhuh voo-dray / noo voo-dree-ohn
...to reserve...	...réserver... ray-zehr-vay
...a table for one / two.	...une table pour un / deux. ewn tah-bluh poor uhn / duh
Is this seat free?	C'est libre? say lee-bruh
The menu (in English), please.	La carte (en anglais), s'il vous plaît. lah kart (ahn ahn-glay) see voo play
service (not) included	service (non) compris sehr-vees (nohn) kohn-pree
to go	à emporter ah ahn-por-tay
with / without	avec / sans ah-vehk / sahn
and / or	et / ou ay / oo
breakfast / lunch / dinner	petit déjeuner / déjeuner / dîner puh-tee day-zhuh-nay / day-zhuh-nay / dee-nay
special of the day	plat du jour plah dew zhoor
specialty of the house	spécialité de la maison spay-see-ah-lee-tay duh lah may-zohn
appetizers	hors d'œuvre or duh-vruh
first course (soup, salad)	entrée ahn-tray
main course (meat, fish)	plat principal plah pran-see-pahl
bread / cheese	pain / fromage pan / froh-mahzh
sandwich / soup	sandwich / soupe sahnd-weech / soop
salad	salade sah-lahd
meat / chicken	viande / poulet vee-ahnd / poo-lay
fish / seafood	poisson / fruits de mer pwah-sohn / frwee duh mehr
fruit / vegetables	fruit / légumes frwee / lay-gewm
dessert	dessert day-sehr
mineral water	eau minérale oh mee-nay-rahl
tap water	l'eau du robinet loh dew roh-bee-nay
(orange) juice	jus (d'orange) zhew (doh-rahnzh)
coffee / tea / milk	café / thé / lait kah-fay / tay / lay
wine / beer	vin / bière van / bee-ehr
red / white	rouge / blanc roozh / blahn
glass / bottle	verre / bouteille vehr / boo-tay
Cheers!	Santé! sahn-tay
More. / Another.	Plus. / Un autre. plew / uhn oh-truh
The same.	La même chose. lah mehm shohz
The bill, please.	L'addition, s'il vous plaît. lah-dee-see-ohn see voo play
Do you accept credit cards?	Vous prenez les cartes? voo pruh-nay lay kart
tip	pourboire poor-bwahr
Delicious!	Délicieux! day-lees-yuh

For more user-friendly French phrases, check out *Rick Steves' French Phrase Book* or *Rick Steves' French, Italian & German Phrase Book*.

Italian Survival Phrases

Hello. (informal)	Ciao.	chow
Good day.	Buongiorno.	bwohn-**jor**-noh
Do you speak English?	Parla inglese?	**par**-lah een-**gleh**-zay
Yes. / No.	Si. / No.	see / noh
I (don't) understand.	(Non) capisco.	(nohn) kah-**pees**-koh
Please.	Per favore.	pehr fah-**voh**-ray
Thank you.	Grazie.	**graht**-see-ay
You're welcome.	Prego.	**preh**-go
I'm sorry.	Mi dispiace.	mee dee-spee-**ah**-chay
Excuse me.	Mi scusi.	mee **skoo**-zee
No problem.	Non c'è problema.	nohn cheh proh-**bleh**-mah
Goodbye.	Arrivederci.	ah-ree-veh-**dehr**-chee
one / two / three	uno / due / tre	**oo**-noh / **doo**-ay / tray
four / five / six	quattro / cinque / sei	**kwah**-troh / **cheeng**-kway / **seh**-ee
seven / eight	sette / otto	**seh**-tay / **oh**-toh
nine / ten	nove / dieci	**noh**-vay / dee-**ay**-chee
How much is it?	Quanto costa?	**kwahn**-toh koh-**stah**
Write it?	Me lo scrive?	may loh **skree**-vay
Is it free?	È gratis?	eh **grah**-tees
Is it included?	È incluso?	eh een-**kloo**-zoh
Where can I buy / find...?	Dove posso comprare / trovare...?	**doh**-vay **poh**-soh kohm-**prah**-ray / troh-**vah**-ray
I'd like / We'd like...	Vorrei / Vorremmo...	voh-**reh**-ee / voh-**reh**-moh
...a room.	...una camera.	**oo**-nah **kah**-meh-rah
...a ticket to ___.	...un biglietto per ___.	oon beel-**yeh**-toh pehr ___
Is it possible?	È possibile?	eh poh-**see**-bee-lay
Where is...?	Dov'è...?	doh-**veh**
...the train station	...la stazione	lah staht-see-**oh**-nay
...tourist information	...informazioni turisti	een-for-maht-see-**oh**-nee too-**ree**-stee
...the bathroom	...il bagno	eel **bahn**-yoh
men / women	uomini, signori / donne, signore	**woh**-mee-nee, seen-**yoh**-ree / **doh**-nay, seen-**yoh**-ray
left / right / straight	sinistra / destra / sempre dritto	see-**nee**-strah / **deh**-strah / **sehm**-pray **dree**-toh
What time does this open / close?	A che ora apre / chiude?	ah kay **oh**-rah **ah**-pray / kee-**oo**-day
At what time?	A che ora?	ah kay **oh**-rah
Just a moment.	Un momento.	oon moh-**mehn**-toh
now / soon / later	adesso / presto / tardi	ah-**deh**-soh / **preh**-stoh / **tar**-dee
today / tomorrow	oggi / domani	**oh**-jee / doh-**mah**-nee

In an Italian Restaurant

I'd like / We'd like...	Vorrei / Vorremmo... voh-**reh**-ee / voh-**reh**-moh
...to reserve a table for one / two.	...prenotare un tavolo per uno / due. preh-noh-**tah**-ray oon **tah**-voh-loh pehr **oo**-noh / **doo**-ay
...the menu (in English).	...il menù (in inglese). eel meh-**noo** (een een-**gleh**-zay)
Is this seat free?	È libero questo posto? eh **lee**-beh-roh **kweh**-stoh **poh**-stoh
service (not) included	servizio (non) compreso sehr-**veet**-see-oh (nohn) kohm-**pray**-zoh
cover charge	(pane e) coperto (**pah**-nay ay) koh-**pehr**-toh
to go	da portar via dah **por**-tar **vee**-ah
with / without	con / senza kohn / **sehnt**-sah
and / or	e / o ay / oh
breakfast / lunch / dinner	(prima) colazione / pranzo / cena (**pree**-mah) koh-laht-zee-**oh**-nay / **prahn**-zoh / **chay**-nah
fixed-price meal (of the day)	menù (del giorno) meh-**noo** (dehl **jor**-noh)
specialty of the house	specialità della casa speh-chah-lee-**tah deh**-lah **kah**-zah
appetizer	antipasto ahn-tee-**pah**-stoh
first course	primo (piatto) **pree**-moh (pee-**ah**-toh)
main course	secondo (piatto) seh-**kohn**-doh (pee-**ah**-toh)
side dishes	contorni kohn-**tor**-nee
cold cuts / bread / cheese	salumi / pane / formaggio sah-**loo**-mee / **pah**-nay / for-**mah**-joh
sandwich	panino pah-**nee**-noh
soup / salad	zuppa / insalata **tsoo**-pah / een-sah-**lah**-tah
meat / chicken	carne / pollo **kar**-nay / **poh**-loh
fish / seafood	pesce / frutti di mare **peh**-shay / **froo**-tee dee **mah**-ray
fruit / vegetables	frutta / verdure **froo**-tah / vehr-**doo**-ray
dessert	dolce **dohl**-chay
tap water	acqua del rubinetto **ah**-kwah dehl roo-bee-**neh**-toh
mineral water	acqua minerale **ah**-kwah mee-neh-**rah**-lay
still / sparkling	naturale / frizzante nah-too-**rah**-lay / freet-**zahn**-tay
(orange) juice	succo (d'arancia) **soo**-koh (dah-**rahn**-chah)
coffee / tea / milk	caffè / tè / latte kah-**feh** / teh / **lah**-tay
wine / beer	vino / birra **vee**-noh / **bee**-rah
red / white	rosso / bianco **roh**-soh / bee-**ahn**-koh
glass / bottle	bicchiere / bottiglia bee-kee-**eh**-ray / boh-**teel**-yah
Cheers!	Salute! / Cin cin! sah-**loo**-tay / cheen cheen
The bill, please.	Il conto, per favore. eel **kohn**-toh pehr fah-**voh**-ray
Do you accept credit cards?	Accettate carte di credito? ah-cheh-**tah**-tay **kar**-tay dee **kreh**-dee-toh
Delicious!	Delizioso! day-leet-see-**oh**-zoh

For more user-friendly Italian phrases, check out *Rick Steves Italian Phrase Book* or *Rick Steves French, Italian, & German Phrase Book*.

INDEX

INDEX

MAP INDEX

Our website enhances this book and turns

Explore Europe

At ricksteves.com you can browse through thousands of articles, videos, photos and radio interviews, plus find a wealth of money-saving travel tips for planning your dream trip. And with our mobile-friendly website, you can easily access all this great travel information anywhere you go.

TV Shows

Preview the places you'll visit by watching entire half-hour episodes of *Rick Steves' Europe* (choose from all 100 shows) on-demand, for free.

your travel dreams into affordable reality

Radio Interviews

Enjoy ready access to Rick's vast library of radio interviews covering travel tips and cultural insights that relate specifically to your Europe travel plans.

Travel Forums

Learn, ask, share! Our online community of savvy travelers is a great resource for first-time travelers to Europe, as well as seasoned pros.

Travel News

Subscribe to our free Travel News e-newsletter, and get monthly updates from Rick on what's happening in Europe.

Classroom Europe®

Check out our free resource for educators with 500 short video clips from the *Rick Steves' Europe* TV show.

Gear up for your next adventure at ricksteves.com

Light Luggage

Pack light and right with Rick Steves' affordable, custom-designed rolling carry-on bags, backpacks, day packs and shoulder bags.

Accessories

From packing cubes to moneybelts and beyond, Rick has personally selected the travel goodies that will help your trip go smoother.

Save time and energy

This guidebook is your independent-travel toolkit. But for all it delivers, it's still up to you to devote the time and energy it takes to manage the preparation and logistics that are essential for a happy trip. If that's a hassle, there's a solution.

Rick Steves Tours

A Rick Steves tour takes you to Europe's most interesting places with great

guides and small groups. We follow Rick's favorite itineraries, ride in comfy buses, stay in family-run hotels, and bring you intimately close to the Europe you've traveled so far to see. Most importantly, we take away the logistical headaches so you can focus on the fun.

Join the fun

This year we'll take thousands of free-spirited travelers—nearly half of them repeat customers—along with us on 50 different itineraries, from Athens to Istanbul. Is a Rick Steves tour the right fit for your travel dreams?

Find out at ricksteves.com, where you can also check seat availability and sign up. Europe is best experienced with happy travel partners. We hope you can join us.

BEST OF GUIDES

Full-color guides in an easy-to-scan format. Focused on top sights and experiences in the most popular European destinations

Best of England
Best of Europe
Best of France
Best of Germany
Best of Ireland
Best of Italy
Best of Scotland
Best of Spain

COMPREHENSIVE GUIDES

City, country, and regional guides printed on Bible-thin paper. Packe with detailed coverage for a multi-week trip exploring iconic sights and venturing off the beaten path

Amsterdam & the Netherlands
Barcelona
Belgium: Bruges, Brussels,
  Antwerp & Ghent
Berlin
Budapest
Croatia & Slovenia
Eastern Europe
England
Florence & Tuscany
France
Germany
Great Britain
Greece: Athens & the Peloponnese
Iceland
Ireland
Istanbul
Italy
London
Paris
Portugal
Prague & the Czech Republic
Provence & the French Riviera
Rome
Scandinavia
Scotland
Sicily
Spain
Switzerland
Venice
Vienna, Salzburg & Tirol

HE BEST OF ROME

ne, Italy's capital, is studded with an remnants and floodlit-fountain es. From the Vatican to the Colos-, with crazy traffic in between, Rome derful, huge, and exhausting. The s, the heat, and the weighty history

of the Eternal City where Caesars walked can make tourists wilt. Recharge by taking siestas, gelato breaks, and after-dark walks, strolling from one atmospheric square to another in the refreshing evening air.

*l Pantheon—which
st dome until the
y 2,000 years old
r over 1,500).*

*f Athens in the Vat-
ties the humanistic
e.*

*adiators fought
nother, entertaining*

Rick Steves books are available from your favorite bookseller Many guides are available as ebooks.

POCKET GUIDES
Compact color guides for shorter trips

Amsterdam
Athens
Barcelona
Florence
Italy's Cinque Terre
London
Munich & Salzburg

Paris
Prague
Rome
Venice
Vienna

SNAPSHOT GUIDES
Focused single-destination coverage

Basque Country: Spain & France
Copenhagen & the Best of Denmark
Dublin
Dubrovnik
Edinburgh
Hill Towns of Central Italy
Krakow, Warsaw & Gdansk
Lisbon
Loire Valley
Madrid & Toledo
Milan & the Italian Lakes District
Naples & the Amalfi Coast
Nice & the French Riviera
Normandy
Northern Ireland
Norway
Reykjavík
Rothenburg & the Rhine
Sevilla, Granada & Southern Spain
St. Petersburg, Helsinki & Tallinn
Stockholm

CRUISE PORTS GUIDES
Reference for cruise ports of call

Mediterranean Cruise Ports
Scandinavian & Northern European
  Cruise Ports

Complete your library with...

TRAVEL SKILLS & CULTURE
Study up on travel skills and gain insight on history and culture

Europe 101
Europe Through the Back Door
Europe's Top 100 Masterpieces
European Christmas
European Easter
European Festivals
For the Love of Europe
Italy for Food Lovers
Travel as a Political Act

PHRASE BOOKS & DICTIONARIES
French
French, Italian & German
German
Italian
Portuguese
Spanish

PLANNING MAPS
Britain, Ireland & London
Europe
France & Paris
Germany, Austria & Switzerland
Iceland
Ireland
Italy
Scotland
Spain & Portugal

Credits

RESEARCHERS
For help with this edition, Rick relied on...

Glenn Eriksen

A solo backpacking trip across Europe and Scandinavia back in the '70s turned out to be Glenn's first step on the road to Rick Steves' Europe. Today, as a guidebook editor and researcher, he indulges his love for the Old Country while helping Rick's readers "keep on travelin'." When not on the road, Glenn lives in Seattle with his wife, Kathy, and enjoys hiking, photography, and staying in touch with his Norwegian roots.

Cameron Hewitt

Cameron Hewitt was born in Denver, grew up in Central Ohio, and moved to Seattle in 2000 to work for Rick Steves' Europe. Since then, he has spent about 100 days each year in Europe—researching and writing guidebooks, blogging, tour guiding, and making travel TV (described in his memoir, *The Temporary European*). Cameron married his high school sweetheart, Shawna, and enjoys taking pictures, trying new restaurants, and planning his next trip.

Ian Watson

Ian has worked with Rick Steves on his guidebooks since 1993, after starting out with Let's Go and Frommer's guides. Originally from western New York, Ian has lived in Europe for many years now, first in Iceland and more recently in southern Germany.

CONTRIBUTOR
Gene Openshaw

Gene has co-authored more than a dozen books with Rick, specializing in Europe's art, history, and culture. In particular, their *Europe 101: History and Art for the Traveler* and *Europe's Top 100 Masterpieces* have helped bring European art to life. Gene also writes for Rick's television shows, produces the audio tours, and is a regular guest on Rick's radio show. For public TV, Gene has co-authored *Rick Steves Fascism in Europe* and the ambitious six-hour series *Rick Steves Art of Europe.* Outside of the travel world, Gene has composed an opera called *Matter,* a violin sonata, and dozens of songs. His latest book is *Michelangelo at Midlife.* Gene lives near Seattle, where he roots for the Mariners in good times and bad.

ACKNOWLEDGMENTS

Thanks to Susana Minich for writing the original version of the Zürich, Central Switzerland, Lugano, Upper Engadine, and Scenic Rail Journeys chapters; and to Cameron Hewitt for writing the original versions of the Luzern and Zermatt chapters.

Thank you to Risa Laib for her 25-plus years of dedication to the Rick Steves guidebook series.

Photo Credits

Avalon Travel
Hachette Book Group
1700 Fourth Street
Berkeley, CA 94710

Printed in Canada by Friesens.
11th Edition. First printing May 2023.

ISBN 978-1-64171-519-5

For the latest on Rick's talks, guidebooks, tours, public television series, and public radio show, contact Rick Steves' Europe, 130 Fourth Avenue North, Edmonds, WA 98020, +1 425 771 8303, RickSteves.com, rick@ricksteves.com.

Rick Steves' Europe
Managing Editor: Jennifer Madison Davis
Assistant Managing Editor: Cathy Lu
Editors: Glenn Eriksen, Julie Fanselow, Suzanne Kotz, Rosie Leutzinger, Matthew Lombardi, Teresa Nemeth, Jessica Shaw, Carrie Shepherd, Chelsea Wing
Researchers: Glenn Eriksen, Cameron Hewitt, Ian Watson
Contributor: Gene Openshaw
Graphic Content Director: Sandra Hundacker
Maps & Graphics: Orin Dubrow, David C. Hoerlein, Lauren Mills, Mary Rostad, Amanda Sharpe

Avalon Travel
Senior Editor and Series Manager: Madhu Prasher
Associate Managing Editors: Jamie Andrade, Sierra Machado
Copy Editor: Kelly Lydick
Proofreader: Maggie Ryan
Indexer: Stephen Callahan
Cover Design: Kimberly Glyder Design
Production and Typesetting: Lisi Baldwin, Rue Flaherty, Jane Musser, Ravina Schneider
Maps & Graphics: Kat Bennett

COLOR MAP

Switzerland

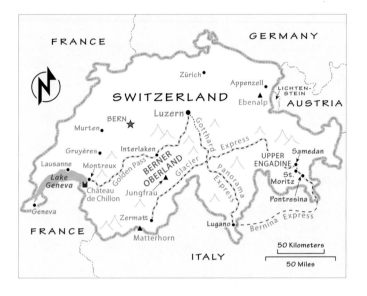

More for your trip!
Maximize the experience with Rick Steves as your guide

Guidebooks
Make side trips smooth and affordable with Rick's France, Italy, and Germany guides

Phrase Books
Rely on Rick's French, Italian & German Phrase Book & Dictionary

Rick's TV Shows
Preview your destinations with a variety of shows covering Switzerland

Rick's Audio Europe™ App
Get free travel information for Switzerland

Small Group Tours
Take a lively, low-stress Rick Steves tour through Switzerland

For all the details, visit rmarksteves.com